PERSON TO PERSON

Positive Relationships Don't Just Happen

FIFTH EDITION

SHARON L. HANNA
Southeast Community College

ROSE SUGGETT
Southeast Community College

DOUG RADTKE

PEARSON
Prentice
Hall

Upper Saddle River, New Jersey 07458

Library of Congress Cataloging-in-Publication Data

Hanna, Sharon L.
    Person to person : positive relationships don't just happen / Sharon L.
    Hanna, Rose Suggett, Doug Radtke. — 5th ed.
       p. cm.
    Includes bibliographical references and index.
    ISBN-978-0-13-228814-9
    ISBN 0-13-228814-1
    1. Interpersonal communication. 2. Self-actualization (Psychology)
    3. Interpersonal relations. I. Suggett, Rose. II. Radtke, Doug. III. Title.
    BF637.C45H32 2007
    158.2—dc22   2006102297

Editorial Director: Leah Jewell
Executive Editor: Jeff Marshall
Editorial Assistant: Jennifer Puma
Project Manager: LeeAnn Doherty
PH HE Director of Operations/Associate Director of Production: Barbara Kittle
Assistant Managing Editor: Maureen Richardson
Production Liaison: Louise Rothman
Prepress and Manufacturing Manager: Nick Sklitsis
Prepress and Manufacturing Buyer: Sherry Lewis
Director of Marketing: Brandy Dawson
Senior Marketing Manager: Jeanette Moyer
Director, Image Resource Center: Melinda Reo
Manager, Visual Research: Beth Brenzel
Photo Researcher: Kathy Ringrose
Image Coordinator: Nancy Seise
Manager, Cover and Visual Research & Permissions: Karen Sanatar
Composition and Full Service Project Management: Techbooks/Vijay Kataria
Printer/Binder: RR Donnelley/Harrisonburg
Cover Printer: RR Donnelley/Harrisonburg

Credits and acknowledgments borrowed from other sources and reproduced, with permission, in this textbook appear on appropriate page within text.

Pearson Education LTD.   Pearson Education Australia PTY, Limited
Pearson Education Singapore, Pte. Ltd   Pearson Education North Asia Ltd
Pearson Education, Canada, Ltd   Pearson Educación de Mexico, S.A. de C.V.
Pearson Education–Japan   Pearson Education Malaysia, Pte. Ltd

PEARSON
Prentice
Hall

10 9 8 7 6 5 4 3 2 1
ISBN–13: 978-0-13-228814-9
ISBN–10: 0-13-228814-1

The Fifth Edition of *Person to Person: Positive Relationships Don't Just Happen* is dedicated to Sharon Hanna. Sharon's vision was to write a textbook that would not only educate readers about themselves and their lives but also teach them skills to assist in continued growth and achievement throughout life.

We greatly appreciate the opportunity to continue Sharon's vision and want to express special thanks to the following people:

- Sharon's husband, Bob Dinkel, and daughters, Lisa and Lyn Patterson, for their invaluable support, encouragement, and contributions to this edition
- To all who contributed to previous editions of *Person to Person*
- To the special people who have touched and enriched our lives

CONTENTS

PREFACE

Person to Person: Positive Relationships Don't Just Happen, Fifth Edition is intended to encourage and guide you on a journey, first within yourself and then into the world of positive interactions and relationships. Ann Landers once wrote: "Life is peculiar. It waits until we flunk the course and then it teaches us the lesson." All of us will make mistakes during our lives; however, the fewer "courses we flunk," the better. This book, whether you read it as part of your formal education or just for personal reasons, can help you make wise choices and live a happier, more fulfilling life.

Building a positive relationship is not an accident; each one requires understanding and effort. Relating with people is an art to be learned and practiced. Because the self is the foundation of all relationships, the goals of the first part of the book are self-discovery and self-satisfaction, with an emphasis on heightened self-esteem, ability to make wise choices regarding emotional and physical health. Because through interpersonal communication human beings interact and relate to one another, it is essential to learn how to communicate in a positive way which is the objective of the second part of this book. Learning about yourself and developing effective communication skills will assist you in building positive relationships. The last part of this book teaches about various interactions and all kinds of relationships. Career, love, couple relationships, marriage, and family are given special emphasis. Today the workplace demands interpersonal and communication skills. This book can assist its readers in all walks of life and can help us live positively in a world of diversity.

Features of this book include: "Looking Ahead" objectives so that you know what is important; "Reflect and Apply" mini-sections to stimulate thoughts and actions that will make the learning more personal; "Looking Back" summaries and listings of resources for your use; suggested readings marked in the References to encourage further exploration; Reflections and Applications, a separate section at the back of the book that you are encouraged to complete. Please read and reflect! The more you "get into it," the more you will gain.

At the end of the book you can be satisfied that you have become better educated about yourself and life. Hopefully, you will have a clear vision of what you want, a realistic idea of how to satisfy your goals, and the positive attitude and high self-esteem needed to achieve harmony and happiness. The realization that life has an ebb and flow can enable you to live life to its fullest with purpose and meaning and to reflect on your past while looking forward optimistically to continued growth and achievement.

If the book does for you what it has for others, we will be delighted. Several people have credited the book for making their lives much more positive. A student commented: "Thanks so much for my first real lessons about life. I will never forget it. Now to put it all into practice . . . I cannot wait!" We hope that you, too, will learn, grow, and benefit, and then put all you have gained into practice. Do experience joy along the way!

Acknowledgments

Appreciation and praise are vital to positive human relationships. Although acknowledging by name everyone who has contributed to this book is not possible, we want to express special thanks to the following people:

- A special thanks to Bob Dinkel, Lisa, and Lyn Paterson for their support and encouragement in the completion of this edition.
- The thousands of students, colleagues, and friends who have contributed to our personal growth as well as to this book by sharing their lives with us.
- A special thanks to Laura Mann and Jeff Marshall for their support and guidance with this project.
- We would like to thank the Prentice Hall reviewers and all the Prentice Hall staff who provided help in numerous ways.

Reviewers:

Daniel Anger, Erie Community College
Margaret Baier, Baylor University
Patricia Berton, The University of Findlay
Roxana Carlo, Southeast Community College
Carol Cofer, Texas State University
Donald Collins, The University of Findlay
Mary Doyle, Arizona State University
Cheri Dragoo, Southeast Community College
Cheryl Edley-Worford, Central Virginia Community College
Kathy Faircloth, Chemeketa Community College
Ed Gardiner, Weber State University
Stephanie Johnson, Southeast Community College
Luann Larsen, Southeast Community College
Jason Lyons, Tarleton State University
James Potterton, San Jose City College
Doug Price, Tulsa Community College
Joan Stahly-Rouse, Southeast Community College

Reviewers of previous editions:

Fay Gentle, Chemeketa Community College
Nancy Koschmann, Elmira College
Joan Rollins, Rhode Island College
Candace Widmer, Elmira College

About the Authors

Sharon L. Hanna was a lifelong educator having taught in Nebraska, New Jersey, and Illinois. She received both faculty achievement and outstanding teacher awards during her career. Her research on the strengths of stepfamilies was published in academic journals, and she served as national president of the Stepfamily Association of America. She authored both the first and second editions of *Career by Design* published by Prentice Hall.

Dr. Doug Radtke has been an educator for the past 37 years. Currently he is a high school administrator. He has taught secondary students, undergraduate students, and graduate-level students. He has published several articles in professional journals on a variety of topics and has been a speaker at several regional and national conventions. He is co-author of *Career by Design*, Third Edition.

Dr. Rose Suggett is chair of Social Sciences, Academic Education, at Southeast Community College. She has received awards for teaching and research. Her research on the impact of divorce in children has been presented nationally and internationally. She is co-author of *Career by Design*, Third Edition.

Section One
Relating: Beginning with the Self

LOOKING AHEAD

After completing this section, you will be able to

- Describe a positive relationship, define interpersonal relations, and understand how they are related to each other.
- Explain how people learn interpersonal skills.
- Contrast personal and professional lives with past generations and explain why interpersonal skills may be needed even more in today's world.
- Describe personal and professional benefits of interpersonal skills.

The journey to the development of positive relationships begins within.
—Sharon Hanna

Do you want to relate positively to others? Hopefully your answer is "yes" because human contact and connections enhance development. Personal growth and happiness are by-products of positive relationships.

What are positive relationships? A **positive relationship** is one in which individuals experience the following reactions:

- Significantly more emotional pleasure than pain
- General feelings of satisfaction and happiness
- Personal growth grounded in a genuine regard for self and others

In order to develop positive relationships, we engage in **interpersonal relations,** an ongoing interactive process that includes initiating, building, and enriching relationships with different people in a variety of situations. If the process goes well, we are likely to live happier lives. Interpersonal skills must be learned. This book can help you develop a deeper understanding of human interactions and relationships. The beginning of this understanding is knowing and loving yourself. The foundation of respect for others is self-respect (Branden, 1992). In turn you can reach out positively to others.

Be gentle with yourself.
Learn to love yourself, forgive yourself.
For only as we have the right attitude toward ourselves,
can we have the right attitude toward others.
—Author unknown

Individuals do not always understand the importance of communication in developing positive relationships. Because relationships are so important and

1

usually complex and unpredictable, specialized training in interpersonal relations can make a significant difference in the quality of our lives. In a national study (Packard, 1992), 66 percent of family relation teachers identified interpersonal relationships and communication skills as essential. Adjustment and relating skills are even more necessary today than they were in the past because life today is more populated, mobile, diverse, complicated, fast changing, and full of choices. Can you think of more examples?

Gender and family roles are also different from the past. In the past, roles were clearly established and people were limited in their number of relationships. Today individuals experience many more interactions and relationships. Interpersonal and communication skills are needed but are frequently overlooked or avoided. Although a logical learning environment for relationship skills is the educational system, how many of your classes have taught you specifically about yourself? Leo Buscaglia (1982), who taught college classes about love and relationships, questioned an educational system that has a worthy goal of self-realization but does not teach it. If interpersonal relations courses are not required, people will continue to learn from experience and untrained teachers.

The home is the first learning environment. Our skills begin in the cradle. The sad truth is that families may teach negative interactions. Examples that can influence children are:

- Direct instruction ("Do not hit your sister")
- Modeling (watching a parent hit your sister, which is confusing if you have been told not to hit!)
- Experience (hitting someone and receiving encouragement or discouragement for doing so)

We also learn from friends, school experiences, the media, and other worldly sources. What have you learned about love? For many, information about relationships comes from television soap operas, which is neither helpful nor adequate. Additional benefits of learning good communication skills include taking charge of your own life, being motivated to change, gaining insight into how to adjust, and learning coping strategies. Although some changes may be impossible, you can always improve yourself. Limitations exist only in your mind. You can improve your interpersonal relations with training.

> I believe that wherever you are in life, and however you learned it, that if you want to learn it differently, anything that can be learned can be unlearned and relearned. (Buscaglia, 1982, p. 66)

People can develop healthy relationships as easily as unhealthy ones. The quality of our relationships influences our productivity and our lives both personally and professionally. If people learn positive interpersonal relationships, problems can be solved or avoided. One approach to interpersonal relationships starts with developing your own voice first, and then you can inspire others and create a workplace where people feel engaged (Covey, 2004).

Positive interpersonal skills can benefit your career by helping you:

- Know yourself well enough to choose a satisfying career and rewarding jobs.
- Have a high level of self-esteem, which will increase your chance of getting the job you want.
- Use people skills to enhance your value as an employee or employer.

This book will help you gain insight into yourself and others, learn to communicate in a positive way, and discover how to develop healthy relationships. Take the time to complete the self-appraisal at the beginning of Reflections and Applications (p. 371). Even if you already interact with others in a positive way and enjoy fulfilling relationships, new interpersonal challenges will arise as you grow and change. Your present level of interpersonal skills can be improved. You can appreciate the goodness of life as you learn, grow, and relish the joys and rewards of positive relationships. The interpersonal journey can be interesting and highly rewarding. It begins with you!

> *I am convinced that much human misery is rooted in ignorance of self and relationships.*
>
> —Teresa Adams

KNOWING AND VALUING YOURSELF

LOOKING AHEAD

After completing this chapter, you will be able to:

- Explain the concept of self and discuss the benefits of self-knowledge and understanding.
- Name and describe the four developmental areas of the self and how they relate to each other.
- Define attitude, optimism, and pessimism.
- Explain self-concept, self-esteem, and ideal self.
- Give reasons why high self-esteem is important and identify its sources.
- Use cognitive restructuring.
- Define self-fulfilling prophecy and recognize its existence in your own thinking.
- Define self-efficacy expectations and discuss their importance.

The unexamined life is not worth living.

—Socrates

How would you answer the question, "Who are you?" Each of us is a unique whole self, an integrated human being.

What is the self and why is it important in the development of positive relationships? Think of the **self** as a separate being within an environment. Early in life each human being distinguishes himself or herself from others. Self-knowledge continues throughout life.

> The greatest joy in life is to know oneself from the inside out. Such knowledge enables us to know another and be known. (Adams, 1987, p. 1)

An early pioneer in understanding the self was sociologist George Herbert Mead. Mead (1934) believed that social experience shapes the self and that, in fact, selves only exist in relationships to other selves. Psychologists, too, have a keen interest in the self. The humanistic approach, which is emphasized in this book, features a complete, or holistic, view of the self. The focus is not on selfishness but rather on the goals of self-discovery, self-awareness, and self-fulfillment.

Humanistic psychology seeks to help people become fully functioning and achieve their full potential so they have more to give to others.

Although learning about the self can be fascinating, the reluctance to seek insight is common. It may be painful. If you are hesitant, push yourself to learn more. The rewards are many, and as the process continues, the discomfort lessens. Maturity comes from self-discovery, a slow and never-ending study. The *self* is a "vast continent whose exploration we can never complete" (Branden, 1983, p. 173).

Exploring Developmental Areas of the Self

Recognizing that the self is a whole person, human development researchers pay attention to four developmental areas: physical, mental or intellectual, emotional, and social. First, we will study each area to gain an understanding of how each part contributes to the whole person. Then we will explore how the four areas come together to interact with each other to define who we are. As we explore the four areas, try and relate the following quote to your personal life in relation to the four areas of self.

> *God grant me the serenity to accept the things I cannot change,*
> *Courage to change the things I can, and*
> *Wisdom to know the difference.*
>
> —Author unknown

Just as this quote is used in some "self-help" programs, readers can also use the quote as a guide when applying the textbook reading to their personal situations.

Physical Self

Condition of the body and appearance are included in the physical self. Certain characteristics are either determined or greatly influenced by heredity. Examples are but not limited to race, hair texture, the natural color of hair and eyes, bone structure, and height. We have more control over other physical aspects such as weight, hairstyle, and muscle tone. Accepting what cannot be changed, such as your age, is a wise decision. Each of us will age as long as we are alive! Viewing the aging process as depressing is setting yourself up for despair.

Appearance.   Americans often pay too much attention to one part of the physical self, the outer shell. **Body image,** defined as a perception of one's appearance, is strongly correlated with regard for the self. Females are significantly less satisfied with their appearance than males (Stowers and Durm, 1996). Many people, seemingly obsessed with appearance, work hard to achieve high standards of beauty. Women may not consider comfort important in their attempts to look attractive. For example, they squeeze their feet into pointed-toe spiked heels that may be stylish, yet quite uncomfortable!

Can a desire for attractiveness interfere with good health? Achieving the "thin look," so prevalent in the media, can become an obsession. Unhealthy ways to lose weight, such as using laxatives, taking diet pills, inducing vomiting, and restricting caloric intake to under 1,200 calories a day, are commonly used by high school female students, especially those who are frequent readers of beauty and fashion magazines (Gorrell, 2001). Putting such a high premium on the "thin look," especially if it endangers health, is alarming. **Anorexia nervosa** is a life-threatening disorder that includes a distorted body image, refusal to maintain a healthy weight, and an intense fear of being overweight. An attempt to achieve close to an ideal weight and a fit body is highly recommended. How to lose weight in a healthy way is covered later in this chapter.

Men experience similar pressures to achieve the perceived perfect look. They may use steroids to build muscle mass. Although men may achieve the desired look, anabolic steroid abuse has been associated with a wide range of adverse side effects ranging from some that are physically unattractive, such as acne and breast development in men, to others that are life threatening, such as heart attacks and liver cancer. Most are reversible if the abuser stops taking the drugs; others are permanent such as infertility and the shrinking of the testicles (National Institute on Drug Abuse, 2006). A survey conducted by the *Lincoln Journal Star* (1998a) found that 2.7 percent of 965 middle school athletes, some as young as 10 years old, used steroids and that girls' involvement was about the same as boys, involvement. The desire to be muscular is not worth the price, especially since other ways to achieve that look are available.

Individuals continue to take health risks in other ways when, for example, they believe that a "good" tan is desirable in spite of conclusive research on skin cancer. Across cultures, young people who are highly concerned about physical appearance are more likely to sunbathe and not take proper precautions (Prentice-Dunn, Jones, and Floyd, 1997). Excessive sun exposure puts a person at risk for melanoma, a serious type of skin cancer that claimed an estimated 9,600 lives in the United States in 2006 (National Center for Chronic Disease Prevention and Health Promotion, 2006). According to the National Cancer Institute, the annual number of new cases has more than doubled since 1973. This could partly be due to the introduction and use of tanning beds. Exposure to sun-lamps, tanning beds, and all types of solar radiation are identified as known human **carcinogens,** substances that tend to cause cancer (U.S. Department of Health and Human Services, 2001). A survey sponsored by the Centers for Disease Control and Prevention (CDC, 1999) found that approximately 43 percent of white children under age 12 had at least one sunburn during the past year. Ironically, sun exposure leads to skin wrinkling, which is not a standard for attractiveness. Proper use of sunscreens can prevent the effects of long exposure to the sun.

Judging others only on their looks can limit possibilities and lead to unhealthy relationships. People often miss opportunities to meet wonderful individuals. Those who evaluate themselves only on the basis of appearance put their self-esteem at risk. Trying to look as attractive as possible can be an enjoyable expression of how we feel about ourselves as long as appearance is not the yardstick by which we measure our self-worth.

Mental Self

The mental self is fascinating. Learning abilities, thought-processing patterns, as well as attitude and motivation are facets of this important area of the self. Cognitive development, as it relates to the thought process, occurs throughout life.

Mental abilities.   What intelligence means and how to assess it are controversial issues. For years **intelligence** was considered to be an intellectual capacity or potential. Recently, attempts have been made to broaden this definition. Believing that a narrow scholastic definition of intelligence can cause children with various other abilities to think they are stupid, Howard Gardner (1983) introduced the concept of seven **multiple intelligences.** More recently he has expanded the number of possible intelligences and emphasized the abilities to solve problems and to create products that are of value in a culture (Gardner, 1999).

Which of the Multiple Intelligences Do You Possess?

- Musical (related to performance, composition, and appreciation)
- Linguistic (related to language)
- Logical-mathematical (related to problem solving, mathematical operations, and scientific investigation)
- Bodily-kinesthetic (using the body and handling objects skillfully)
- Spatial (related to manipulation of space)
- Interpersonal (related to understanding and working with others)
- Intrapersonal (related to understanding oneself)
- Naturalistic (related to sensing and observing the environment)

Continued research by Gardner (1999) led to the identification of an eighth type of intelligence, naturalistic, as described in the foregoing list. Regardless of definition or number of intelligences, problem solving, display of curiosity, and ability to get along with others are important intelligences to develop.

Intelligence is believed to be a complex result of the interrelationship between heredity and environment (Singh, 1996). The prenatal environment probably plays a significant role (Devlin, Daniels, and Roeder, 1997). An IQ (intelligence quotient) test is typically used to measure intelligence. A score indicates a person's level of ability and potential mainly in the areas of language and mathematics. Other tests such as the ACT and SAT measure academic aptitude and play a major role in college admission and financial aid awards. Caution is advised because low achievement can be caused by other factors such as cultural bias in testing, test anxiety, or **learning disabilities,** a group of related and often overlapping conditions leading to low achievement by people who have the potential to do better (Smith, 1993). Most people with learning disabilities are talented and bright; however, traditional schooling is often challenging. The educational system has found ways to recognize and help those who learn differently. Reading a book such as *ADD and the College Student* (Quinn, 2001) and also seeking help from a specialist can make a great deal of difference. College students with learning disabilities who ask a lot of questions and seek support are more likely to graduate than those who do not seek help. Students with learning disabilities can acquire a better way to learn and realize their potential.

Figure 1-1   Reading is a favorite way to improve mentally.

No matter how an individual learns, achievement and grades in school are usually a reflection of how much effort a person is willing to make. A study of high school valedictorians revealed that they were not always the brightest students; they were, however, the hardest working (Arnold, 1995). Whatever your measured degree of intelligence or your style of learning, you can choose how to use it.

Learning readiness and strategies. Willingness and eagerness to learn are valuable traits, and employers view them as important assets for an employee to have. Curiosity about a number of subjects can result in a well-rounded person who is both interested and interesting. You may be surprised to realize that feeling confused can set the stage for learning. Students confess that they are afraid to ask questions, citing situations in which they were put down or laughed at because they did so. Unfortunately, it is often the case that only the teachers ask questions in the classroom. If you are reluctant to ask or answer questions, try to overcome the hesitancy. You need to regard both asking and answering questions as an indication of having some knowledge and a desire to learn more. How do you learn most easily? Individuals typically learn from their experiences, so actual hands-on or **experiential learning** is effective. For example, you may have been instructed how to set a videocassette recorder. Would it have been better to have actually gone through the motions as well? You have probably learned through traditional instructional methods and have found one or more that work well for you. Learning is most effective when it involves several of our senses and being actively involved in the learning process (Fig. 1-1).

Critical and creative thinking.   Where did you learn how to think? Were you ever taught actual thinking skills? **Thinking** is the ability to activate and then pursue mental activity. For years our educational system presumed that if students were reasonably intelligent, they were able to think and did not need training. Educators only gave information and told students about ideas. These types of practices do not encourage thinking. Only memorization skills are needed, and those who have difficulty memorizing do not do well. Ability to think is rarely assessed. Years ago, von Oech (1983) criticized our educational system. Unfortunately, what he wrote still applies in some classrooms.

Much of our educational system is geared toward teaching people the one right answer. By the time the average person finishes college, he or she will have taken over 2,600 tests, quizzes, and exams. Thus, the "right answer" approach becomes deeply ingrained. This may be fine for some mathematical problems where there is only one right answer. The difficulty is that most of life does not present itself in this way. Life is ambiguous; there are many right answers—all depending on what you are looking for. But if you think there is only one right answer, then you will stop looking as soon as you find one. (p. 21)

Being "right" or certain can stop us from being curious, and curiosity is the basis of learning. As you read this book, you will see how important thought-processing is. The ability to think is the foundation of human accomplishments. Each person develops methods of processing information and acquires a number of beliefs. These ideas are beneficial only if they are not so rigid that they limit a person's ability to discover, think, and learn.

Taking nothing for granted is one aspect of **critical thinking.** Do you believe everything you read or hear? If so, you are not using critical thinking. Do you dig deeper, challenge assumptions, and examine the logic of differing points? If so, you are thinking! Try to develop a "working knowledge" of material by thinking, talking, and actually using what has been read or presented.

You employ **creative thinking** when you think about ideas in different ways and generate a variety of solutions to problems. The basis of creativity is mental flexibility. Try thinking creatively and come up with different uses for common objects such as bricks. A problem that is not too difficult (although you may be surprised how many times individuals do not seem to be able to solve it) is that it is 7:30 in the morning, and your car will not start. You have a class in an hour. What can you do? Creative thinking is liberating and can solve many problems in your life!

Why are different types of thinking so important? The amount of new information doubles every four years (Shenk, 2004), and we are faced with numerous decisions based on new information. With information production not only increasing but also accelerating, there is no sign that processing will ever catch up. We have quite suddenly mutated into a radically different culture, a civilization that trades in and survives on stylized communication (Shenk, 1998). Too often, people depend on so-called experts and accept all that they see and hear. Using our thought processes in critical and creative ways is important when faced with new information. A student commented at the end of a sociology course, "I do not know for sure how much I have learned, but the course really taught me to think." Learning how to think was the most valuable concept for this student to learn.

Limiting yourself by lack of curiosity, fear of questioning, and lack of confidence is a waste of your human potential. As you read this book and participate in discussions, use your wonderful mind to ask questions, present alternative ideas, and generate thoughts! Be like the students, who wrote: "My mind has been resting on a shelf for too long, and now it is ready to apply its power!" "Thank you for making me do this challenging assignment—it made the textbook come alive!"

Attitude.   An extremely influential aspect of the mental self is **attitude,** a state of mind that is reflected in how a person approaches life. In referring to the future, **optimists** have positive thoughts, whereas **pessimists** view life negatively. Optimists think that they will never die or, if they do, they will wake up to the glory of heaven, whereas pessimists are certain that they will not live much longer and that if they wake up in heaven, they will not like it (Chapman, 1993). In a study of college students, high optimists enjoyed the highest overall quality of life satisfaction whereas low optimists were dissatisfied and used more alcohol in an attempt to cope (Harju and Bolen, 1998). Optimists and pessimists interpret the same experiences very differently and, therefore, live much different lives. Think of your own attitude about how your life is progressing and determine if you have an optimistic or pessimistic outlook.

Quite a Contrast

Optimists

- Protect their personal health (Greenberg, 1997)
- Cope with extremely difficult situations through activity (Greenberg, 1997)
- Have fewer serious disease and health problems (Goleman, 1997)

Pessimists

- Discontinue their medicine and report poorer health (Aversa and Kimberlin, 1996)
- Have a higher risk of death from cancer (Schulz et al., 1996)

Some people have been "attituded" excessively, with such common statements as "Your attitude stinks," "If you would only improve your attitude," or "You have an attitude." The effects of our attitude on ourselves and others are so powerful that they cannot be disregarded.

> If you can create and keep a positive attitude toward your job, your company, and life in general, you increase your chance of success. If you are unable to do this, you may find many doors closed to you on the job, and your personal life less than exciting. (Chapman, 1993, p. 20)

Attitude is described as positive or negative; it usually varies between these two extremes. A positive attitude is not the same as a "Pollyanna" way of looking at life. That is, you can have a positive attitude and realize that life is not absolutely wonderful all the time. Being positive means that you look on the brighter side of events, that you are more "up" than "down," and that you usually feel responsible and in control of yourself. Positive people are generally more energetic, motivated, and alert. With a negative attitude the world almost always appears bleak, a "down" feeling is apparent, and blaming and excuse making are common. Think of someone you know whose attitude is negative. Any of these descriptions may come to your mind: fault-finding, irresponsible, lazy, apathetic, complaining, or gloomy. An individual who fits this description is likely to be avoided by others. "Misery may love company, but company does not love misery" (Myers, 1992, p. 20).

> Attitudes are acquired more than they are taught. Both negative and positive attitudes are transmitted on the job. A persistently negative attitude, like the rotten apple in the barrel, can spoil the positive attitudes of others. (Chapman, 1993, p. 23)

Think about those who influence you and those who look to you for guidance. The tone of the day can be set by one person. Having a positive attitude can be contagious!

In specific situations, employees can especially benefit from positive attitudes. Pretend you are a supervisor. You have two employees who have a disagreement, and they come to talk to you. Carlos is a positive person, and he rarely complains.

Sean's attitude is generally negative, and this is not the first gripe he has brought to you. The two tell different versions of the same event. Which one will you believe? Even if Sean's version is accurate, the odds are that you will believe Carlos.

Having a positive attitude is also highly desirable outside the workplace. Ask athletic coaches, teachers, and others who work with people about the advantages of a positive attitude. Positive athletes are better competitors and give up less easily; they try harder in the classroom and use their mistakes to improve. Those with positive outlooks are enjoyable people and interactions with them are more productive. Think about individuals you know. Do you prefer to be around those who have a positive attitude or a negative attitude? An outstanding example of a positive attitude maintained against all odds was Mike, a student who wrote as a description of himself: "I have a slight health problem, cystic fibrosis, but I will not let it get me down." Cystic fibrosis is much more than a *slight* health problem. Mike has never let it change his marvelous attitude.

Examine your way of approaching life. You have an opportunity to rate your attitude in Reflections and Applications and compare it with what others think about you. Remember that attitude is always a choice; the key is to change both thoughts and behaviors. The book *Learned Optimism* (Seligman, 1998) is an excellent guide with ideas on how to become more positive. Coursework can also help. Reading and putting into practice the ideas and methods presented in this book can empower you to develop an even more positive attitude.

You have probably heard about the power of positive thinking. Norman Cousins (1979, 1983, 1989) told remarkable stories of his recoveries from a serious illness and a heart attack and of research showing how intense determination and hope influence the course of disease. Others believe that pain can be caused by belief or attitude and that a person's way of thinking can decrease or eliminate pain (Benson, 1987). In this book you will learn more about the power of belief and how to change your thoughts.

Emotional Self

A third part of the self is emotional; it is composed of feelings and ways of expressing them. Human beings are often unaware of their emotions. For example, when asked, "What are you feeling right now?" a person commonly answers, "I do not know," "Fine," or "Okay." Rarely are emotions identified. Personal expressions of emotions vary considerably. Because of its importance, Chapter 5 is devoted to the subject of the emotional self.

Social Self

The social self is defined as "the idea that the self is produced through interaction with two or more people" (Glossary, Social Science Department, University of Colorado, 2005). For example, a mother is a social self because a mother cannot be without a child. Important aspects of the self are **statuses,** defined as what we are or our social positions, and **roles,** the behaviors that are a part of those statuses. A father's statuses may be son, father, husband, employee, and friend. Within each status, he performs certain roles such as provider and nurturer. Consider your own

Figure 1-2 Interacting with people is an important part of the social self.
Source: www.indexopen.com

statuses and roles. Other parts of the social self are relationships and social behaviors. How do you get along with other people? Humans require social exchanges with others in order to be loved and to learn to love. Nobody can survive in a vacuum, and social relationships are vital to our well-being (Fig. 1-2)!

A primary objective of this book is to guide you in the development of relationships. A beginning step is to understand how you have developed socially. Personality, addressed in Chapter 2, plays a major role in the social aspects of life.

Integrating Your Whole Self

Fortunately, you are not like Humpty-Dumpty, who could not be put back together again! The parts make up a whole, and examining your integrated self is fascinating. "Every baby born into this world is a living question mark. The first question is about the self: 'Who am I?'" (Powell, 1976, p. 47). Humans continue to search for the answer. By discovering and valuing your own self-identity, you can have a positive relationship with yourself (Fig. 1-3).

Coming together, or integration of the self, is illustrated in Figure 1-3. The arrows indicate that the parts are interrelated, and they influence each other both negatively and positively. Recall a time when you were not feeling well physically. What were you like mentally, emotionally, socially? Even if you did not realize it, you were probably diminished in these other areas, too. The good news, which has already been mentioned, is that a positive spillover also occurs. For example, attitude can make a positive difference in the physical, emotional, and social parts of life. Studies indicate how important it is to pay attention to a person's emotional distress and offer social support along with the physical. From his work with support groups for breast cancer patients, David Spiegel (1996) of Stanford University School of Medicine found that social contact not only had positive emotional effects but also reduced the death risk. He also discovered that a reduction in depression and anxiety seemed to increase the activity of natural killer cells in the body. A positive emotional state was related to improved physical health.

Improving yourself physically, mentally, emotionally, or socially will create benefits in other developmental areas. Pat was unhappy and shy. She started on an exercise program and had her hair cut and styled. She reported how much better she felt physically, mentally, and emotionally and described a definite improvement in her social relationships. An activity in Reflections and Applications gives you an opportunity to describe yourself in all areas. Checking to see that you are balanced in the four areas is also important. Some people devote a great deal of time and energy to their

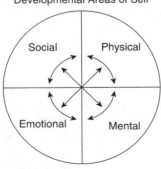

Figure 1-3 Developmental areas of self.

mental self and exclude their social development. Others build their bodies but are strangers to their feelings. For example, although Jack had been happy-go-lucky and sociable, after he left home to attend college he became depressed and sought counseling. He had been concentrating too much on social activities and found himself failing in school and feeling ill. He didn't get enough sleep, his diet was poor, and he drank excessive amounts of alcohol. Jack learned the hard way how the various aspects of the self are integrated and how important it is to maintain a healthy balance among them.

Discovering Your Self-Concept

When you consider who you are, what do you perceive? Whether we realize it or not, each of us carries with us a mental blueprint or image of ourselves. How this self develops is of interest to both sociologists and psychologists. Influential is the **generalized other,** which Mead (1934) described as the organized community or social group. Thinking of a whole community's attitude gives you a concept of the generalized other. Have you ever thought, "I cannot do that. What would *they* think?" If by "they," you do not mean specific people and are describing a collective attitude, you are tapping into the generalized other. How does this guide our behaviors and development of self?

What are your ideas, mental representations, and understanding of your own self? The **self-concept** is the totality of your thoughts and feelings with reference to yourself and is the foundation on which almost all your actions are based (Rosenberg, 1979). When does self-concept form? During infancy, emotional experiences form the basis for its development (Eder and Mangelsdorf, 1997). Carl Rogers (1961) wrote about self-concept and how it develops. As a psychotherapist, he believed that a search for the self was at the heart of most of his clients' problems. Fulfillment of self means that one is basically positive, open to experience, trustful of one's own thoughts and feelings, self-evaluative rather than at the mercy of others' approval, and willing to be a process rather than a product. Rogers, a humanistic psychologist, was optimistic about human potential.

The self-concept consists of self-descriptions, ideal self, and self-esteem or self-worth. Use the key word *like* to help conceptualize self-concept. Think of it as (1) what I am like, (2) what I would like to be like, and (3) how much I like what I am like. Your current self-descriptions and your **ideal self** may be similar or quite different. Because of external standards, you may have an unrealistic ideal. If so, that image is more hurtful than helpful. Amy described herself as overweight, short, of average intelligence, shy, and unhappy much of the time. Her ideal self was slim, at least 4 inches taller, brilliant, friendly, and always happy. Which descriptors of her ideal self can help her improve and which would just be hurtful? As was mentioned earlier, knowing what you can change and what you cannot is valuable. Amy has formulated an ideal self that is not possible and is likely to lead to dissatisfaction and frustration.

People can be absorbed with their ideal selves to such an extent that their self-esteem could be at risk. Do you realize that it is possible to compare yourself to a person who does not exist: your ideal self? If your self-description and ideal self are very different, your self-esteem will be low. You may be underestimating

Figure 1-4   What are your areas of self?
Source: www.indexopen.com

your actual self or harboring an unattainable self-fantasy. **Perfectionism** is having an inflated and impossible ideal self. Perfectionists believe that they must set the highest performance standards or be considered second-rate. No matter what, they are not good enough. In a study of college students, a high level of perfectionism was associated with a low level of self-esteem(Flett, Hewitt, and DeRosa, 1996). A step in increasing self-esteem is to create a realistic ideal or possible self and then use it as a friendly guide, not as an enemy.

A study of college students found that preoccupation with the ideal self was correlated with anxiety, self-consciousness, and vulnerability (Bybee et al., 1997). Rather than an ideal, try thinking of this image as your **desired self.** Then use it to discover how to improve in realistic ways. Realize that if you want the best possible relationships, you will want to create the best possible "you." Striving for improvement makes life interesting as well as challenging. Regardless of your level of self-satisfaction, positive changes can be made. Awareness of self followed by a sincere desire to change are the forerunners of personal growth. Throughout this book, you will be encouraged to improve in each of the developmental areas (Fig. 1-4).

Valuing Yourself

Another critical part of self-concept is **self-esteem,** or the value that we place on ourselves. It is indicative of a positive or negative orientation toward the self (Rosenberg, 1979), an overall self-evaluation or degree of self-worth. Whether you perceive yourself to be competent to cope with life's challenges and to be deserving of happiness is a reflection of your self-esteem (Branden, 1992). Think of it as a point on a scale ranging from very low to very high; this self-respect goes beyond acceptance of self and is virtually self-love. You may be thinking, "Love myself? That is selfish!" However, such a notion was disputed by Fromm (1956), who asserted that a selfish person does not possess true self-love. Fromm's belief that self-love is necessary in order to love others is now widely accepted. If you are a loving individual and care about yourself, then you can be of value to others.

Can you think too highly of yourself? What is the difference between self-love and vanity or conceit? Vain individuals do not truly love themselves. Self-inflation is typically a sign of self-doubt. A person whose self-esteem is low may try to mask inadequate feelings with a false show of pride (May, 1953). Genuine love for self is a feeling of worth and dignity. Branden (1983) makes a sensible point: "No one would ask, 'Is it possible to enjoy too high a level of physical health?' Health is an unqualified desirable and so is positive self-esteem" (p. 15).

An important note is that esteem for the self that is unwarranted (Seligman, 1998) or what could be described as a false sense of self-worth is not conducive to living a productive, worthy life. Self-esteem that is earned by one's own efforts is, however, of utmost significance. One of our primary needs as humans is to feel worthwhile (Glasser, 1965; Maslow, 1968).

Effects of Self-Esteem

What specific areas of life are affected by self-esteem? A quick and wise response would be, "All areas." Specifically, note the following.

Academic success. Studies have found a significant positive correlation between self-esteem, grade-point average, and positive classroom behavior (Baker, Beer, and Beer, 1991), as well as academic achievement and intrinsic motivation (Skaalvik, 1997). In terms of potential academic performance, a student's IQ score may not be as important as the self-esteem rating. "Self-confidence permits a student to perform well academically; whereas brilliance may be trapped in low self-esteem" (Briggs, 1970, p. 270). Although individuals with low self-esteem can achieve, the path is usually more difficult.

Emotions and behaviors. Low self-esteem, loneliness, and depression are often connected (Bothwell and Scott, 1997). After controlling for depression, a study showed that self-esteem was associated with thinking about, threatening, and attempting suicide (Vella, Persic, and Lester, 1996). Low self-esteem was found to be a factor in abnormal eating behaviors (Button, Loan, and Davies, 1997) and children's use of tobacco and alcohol (jackson et al., 1997). "Self-esteem is the armor that protects kids from the dragons of life: drugs, alcohol, delinquency, and unhealthy relationships" (McKay and Fanning, 2000, p. 279). A search for markers of happiness found that self-esteem definitely mattered. "When the going gets tough, those with strong feelings of self-worth keep going" (Myers, 1992, p. 108).

Relationships. Friendships and love relationships thrive in the presence of high self-esteem. Feeling liked and loved by others is not possible until you believe

you deserve it. A study revealed that socially uncertain college students had lower levels of self-esteem as well as higher levels of depression, stress, and loneliness (Salmela-Aro and Nurmi, 1996). How you treat others is related to self-worth. "You will do unto others as you do unto yourself" (Briggs, 1977, p. 4). High self-esteem encourages us to seek out others and to develop healthy relationships enhanced by caring, democratic behaviors. According to Maslow (1968), the best helpers of others are those who feel positive about themselves. "So often the sick or inadequate person, trying to help, does harm instead" (p. iii) (Fig. 1-5).

Figure 1-5 A healthy relationship.
Source: www.indexopen.com

Long-term relationships are more likely to succeed if both people feel self-love. Falling in love is easy; sustaining love over time requires high self-esteem. Parenting is one of the most critical responsibilities in life. A classic study found that parents with high levels of self-esteem have a better chance of raising children with high levels of self-worth (Coopersmith, 1967). Relationships built on high levels of self-esteem are more likely to be nourishing. When you love yourself, you are not going to deliberately hurt yourself or anyone else (Hay, 1991).

Career success. Job seekers with high self-esteem will almost always achieve better interview ratings and receive more job offers than those with low self-esteem. Because employees' work will reflect the degree of their own self-worth, employers seek applicants who value themselves. Managers with high self-esteem have less trouble giving up control and delegating. Qualities such as innovation, personal responsibility, self-management, and self-direction are all by-products of high self-esteem (Branden, 1992). "In the workplace self-esteem is a survival requirement" (p. 77). In addition, a higher level of self-esteem helps in assessing ourselves realistically and making desirable changes. When faced with choices and decisions, a feeling of self-worth is a powerful ally.

A benefit to those with high self-esteem is the ability to recognize self-improvement possibilities and the tendency to view criticism as constructive. They do not interpret a *"no"* as an assault or a rejection; instead, they usually learn from mistakes and have more energy to begin anew. Both Lisa and Jessica were criticized by their track coach for not pacing themselves over a long race. Lisa accepted the criticism and changed her pattern. Jessica, whose self-esteem was below average at the time, became disheartened and quit the team. Self-worth allows people to view a problem as a challenge, choose a solution wisely, and engage in positive personal growth.

In its influence on all aspects of life, self-esteem is the foundation on which happiness and well-being are built. Nathaniel Branden (1983), who has studied and written extensively about self-esteem, expressed it well: "Of all the judgments that we pass in life, none is as important as the one we pass on ourselves, for that judgment touches the very center of our existence" (p. 1).

Sources of Self-Esteem

Human beings are not born with self-esteem. You have learned who you are and how worthy you feel from internalized messages and a variety of experiences. Four broad contributors can be identified (Baron, 1990): (1) social interaction, (2) social information, (3) social comparison, and (4) self-observation. The first two categories have to do with relationships. How people reacted and treated you in social interactions and their value comments about you have had much influence, and they still do. An early study found that the quality of the relationships between children and significant adults in their lives laid the foundation for self-love (Coopersmith, 1967).

Babies and young children are especially vulnerable in terms of the actions of others; parents usually serve as the most significant influences.

Children learn they are lovable by being treated as if they are special. A tragic price of low self-worth or worse is paid if there is a lack of warmth, love, care, and attention. Parenting effects remain influential throughout a child's life. A detrimental parental message is that a child is not good enough. Sometimes the messages are blatantly negative such as "You will never amount to anything," or "What did I do wrong to deserve you?" Without a doubt, these remarks do damage to the child's self-esteem. Others are more subtle or underlying but are still injurious. In a January 2, 2006, article in the *Lincoln Journal Star,* an 18-year-old girl was interviewed about running away from home. She reported that her mother's name-calling, nagging, and verbal abuse made their relationship difficult. Comments that the girl was too fat, lazy, and worthless led to her stuffing her belongings into a garbage bag and going on the run for over a year.

> "Can you do something different with your hair?"
> "When I was your age, I had a full-time job and still got good grades in school."
> "You could do a lot better if you would just try."

Several students have identified the last message as common. "No matter what grade I brought home, short of 100 percent or A+, my dad told me I could have done better," a troubled young woman shared. Can you think of similar messages you received? The underlying theme is that something is missing or wrong. Parents' opinions usually continue to have an impact after a young adult leaves home. A 25-year-old confessed:

> I do not know why I care what my parents think of me anymore. Most of what they did was criticize me, and that is what they still do. But I care so much, it hurts. I am still trying to be the way they want me to be.

Opinions of other family members can also diminish self-worth. Students often mention siblings who teased and ridiculed them. "I am convinced that there are no genes to carry the feeling of worth. It is learned. And the family is where it is learned" (Satir, 1972, p. 24).

Joyce remembered her childhood and a negative family environment. She wrote of feeling clumsy, skinny, and not as smart as her siblings. Those feelings came from her parents. "My dad said until the day he died that I was the clumsiest kid he had. When Mom made clothes for me, she said I was so straight that nothing fit me. They both told me I should do better in school because the other kids did." Sadly, she could not recall any positive messages. In fact, she said that any pride in accomplishment was frowned upon. Her parents thought that pride was the same as bragging. When Joyce was 40, she finally came to grips with her feelings of low self-esteem. The pain resurfaced when she prepared a childhood analysis for extra credit. She wrote: "I did not want to do this paper, and I did want to. I knew I did not have to. But something kept pulling me to do it. I realize now I needed to unload some more, and I felt better afterwards." Her postscript was: "This has been a painful experience for me. Lots of feelings that I did not want to deal with came back. Not one of us kids came out of that family with anything but low self-esteem" (Fig. 1-6).

Figure 1-6

Another student, Linda, optimistically wrote: "A self-esteem tip that hit home with me was not to belittle or label your children negatively, which is what happened to me. Unfortunately, my own parents' self-esteem was negative, and it was passed on to me. *But cycles can be broken, and this one is already beginning to crumble.*"

Self-esteem can also be damaged when a person is ignored and neglected. "I just felt it did not matter whether I was alive or dead, there or not there," said a young man. "I still have a hard time thinking that I matter to anyone."

In addition to family contributions, interactions with and information from others continue to be influential. Various groups impact our self-descriptions whether we are aware of what these are or not. Children often learn to tease others because of physical appearance. Another source of ridicule is perceived or actual knowledge of a gay male's or lesbian's sexual orientation. A review of studies indicated difficulty for gay adolescents in achieving healthy levels of self-esteem as a result of stigmatization (Radkowsky and Siegel, 1997).

Think back to school experiences and relationships with teachers and peers. For some, school is a nightmare. Hanna (2004) recalls a junior high teacher who delivered a daily assault of put-downs to a timid boy. "Can you write any neater than that?" "Hurry up. You are so slow!" "That is a dumb question." One day he announced that the lowest grade in the class was Gary's as usual! Several students followed the teacher's lead, and Gary became the object of many cruel tricks and insults. That Gary survived is remarkable; the damage to his self-esteem is hard to imagine (Hanna, 2004). As a warning, Ellen Rosenberg, author of *Growing Up Feeling Good* (1983), told an audience of teachers, "Self-esteem may not be a separate subject in school curriculums, but children's self-esteem is being chipped away or built up at every minute at school or elsewhere." If educators understand this, fewer children like Gary will suffer.

Once self-esteem is high, input from other people is less influential. Nevertheless, students remind teachers how rewarding it is when instructors praise their work (Hanna, 2004). One way to assess whether a relationship is healthy is to ask if it enhances feelings of self-worth. We may be secure, yet replenishment is invaluable!

How often do you compare yourself to others? Social comparison is a powerful source of ideas about the self. People tend to measure themselves against other individuals often on the basis of physical appearance, talent, and popularity. Comparisons within the family are common. When students were asked how many of them had been compared to their siblings, almost all students responded that they had been compared to their brothers and sisters. They acknowledged that the comparisons were not motivating or helpful and could even be harmful. One young man realized why he harbored negative feelings about his older brother: "I was never as good as Scott. He was better looking, smarter, and more athletic. I was nicer, but that did not seem to matter to Dad." Any comparison can diminish your uniqueness if you try to be someone you are not. Keep in mind that someone who is better looking, smarter, friendlier, or more popular likely exists somewhere so what difference does it make? Individual comparisons are helpful only if you learn constructively from them.

Broader comparisons can also be damaging. Members of a **minority,** a disadvantaged group that lacks power within a society, are frequently and unfairly perceived as inferior. People who differ from the majority group in race, ethnicity, or sexual orientation often face self-esteem challenges. For example, gays and lesbians are raised in a society oriented toward **heterosexism,** the belief that anything other than a heterosexual orientation is wrong. Do you think the following observation that was written years ago is still true today? "Homophobia, a fear or hatred of lesbian women and gay men, is so interwoven in society that lesbian and gay youth face especially difficult struggles for self-esteem, emotional security, and a sense of a caring community" (Whitlock, 1989, p. 1). Even though racism and heterosexism are rooted in ignorance and untruths, individuals can be immeasurably damaged.

Culture, which consists of behaviors, values, beliefs, and lifestyles that are characteristic of a particular social group as distinguished from other groups, is a key factor in self-esteem. Any group or individual difference can be either ridiculed or looked at positively. Aspects of self, when affirmed rather than condemned, will bolster self-esteem. **Multiculturalism,** a movement that recognizes cultural diversity, appreciates everyone's "roots," and promotes equality of all cultures, can yield high rewards for everyone.

Another source of self-esteem, self-observation, comes from one's own actions, interpretations, and feelings. Picture two young children on a playground.

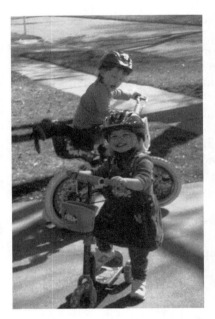

Figure 1-7   Kids having fun playing builds self-esteem.

Haley successfully climbs the ladder of the slide and glides down. Melissa stands at the bottom, fearful of the ascent. After working up the courage to mount the steps, she sits frozen at the top and begins to cry. Haley comes to her rescue by sitting behind her and helping her down. Can you see how Haley's and Melissa's self-observations were quite different?

Adults continue to be self-observant. Mike and Angela are newly hired firefighters. Angela has been involved in two heroic rescues. Mike has spent most of his on-duty time cleaning the station, playing cards, and keeping in shape. He has participated in a few minor fire calls and is feeling frustrated. In the two situations Haley and Melissa as children and Mike and Lisa as adults have different self-observations that increase or decrease their self-esteem. Self-observation becomes increasingly important as you mature. What are you doing with what you observe about yourself? At this point in your life, you have a great deal of control over your level of self-esteem.

Part of self-observation that is of utmost significance are your thoughts. Consider two young men who are insulted by a coworker. On one hand, Tim thinks, "I must be a hard person to work with if that's what he thinks of me." On the other hand, Greg thinks, "I do not know what his problem is. He must be having a bad day." How will the two different thoughts affect each person's self-esteem? Do you see how powerful your thoughts are? In essence, your thoughts create your reality (Fig. 1-7).

Self-Esteem Building and Strengthening

What is your current level of self-esteem? You can use the rating scale in the self-concept inventory in Reflections and Applications (p. 371) to measure it. For those with healthy levels, self-esteem strengthening is a wise investment. Even if yours is low, you can do much to change it! Beginning to realize your sense of worth is a vitalizing experience. "You literally uncover the hidden jewel of your own value" (Mckay and Fanning, 2000, p. 89). Use the following suggestions in your building or strengthening process.

Heal psychological pain.   Another major stumbling block in terms of self-esteem is extreme depression. Anyone suffering from untreated clinical depression lacks the energy and willpower to build self-esteem. Depression must be alleviated before the self can be elevated. Ways to do this are covered in Chapter 5.

Perhaps, it is a matter of **self-verification,** an intriguing theory that maintains that individuals have a strong desire to preserve their self-concept even if it is a negative one (Andrews, 1989). Jenni wrote in her journal, "I think sometimes I am afraid to feel good about myself, to not be insecure. It sounds so odd, but it is almost like letting go of something you know so well and for so long for something you have never known." Paul expressed it as "just too afraid to feel good." Self-verification by confirming what a person already believes may make the world seem safe and predictable. Yet another possibility is **self-handicapping,** which refers to actions taken to sabotage performance and increase the opportunity to excuse failure (Berglas and Jones, 1978). Self-handicappers appear to have a valid reason for not succeeding other than their lack of ability. When self-sabotaging was discussed in the classroom, a young man said, "That sounds like me. What can be done?" Awareness is the first step. The enlightening book *Making Peace with Your Past* (Bloomfield, 2000) focuses on identifying and healing a painful past by coming to grips with shame, guilt, regret, blame, and unresolved grief.

If you think you are beset by self-handicaps or might be in need of healing, explore the avenues for healing that have been discussed in this section and then take steps to change your life. You deserve it! As Debra, a vibrant student, expressed it, "I found that a decision that you are *for* yourself is the beginning of an entirely different life."

Choose healthy, conscious living.   Increasing your level of wellness, as discussed earlier, is basic to self-esteem development. Existing in a mental fog, even partially, limits potential for self-love. Think about how often you choose the level of consciousness at which you function. The choice may be between habitual drug use and alertness or between fatigue and getting enough sleep. Lack of alertness is not conducive to creating a positive self-image. The visibly alive, bright-eyed students we see each day have made a wise choice and are completing the first step toward building high self-esteem. Others are severely limiting themselves.

Set priorities.   Think about where you rank yourself in comparison to others. Generally, those with low self-esteem place others ahead of themselves. Although being self-centered or selfish is not recommended, making yourself a priority is. You will then have more to offer the world. After a relationship in which she described herself as totally dependent, Faith, a young woman, said, "I finally learned how to put my love into myself rather than in someone else. Since I did this, my relationships have been much better, and a love relationship will just add more beauty to the life I already have."

Concentrate on your strengths.   What do you like about yourself? Even the simplest positive quality is significant. Do you listen well? Are you considerate? What are your talents? You can make a list of strengths and post it where you will notice it. Positive statements about self are called **affirmations.** Statements such as "I am worthy" and "I deserve happiness" are powerful tools. More specific ones reflect unique positive aspects, such as "I am kind." Easy to repeat frequently, they empower the self. A woman working on self-esteem started each day by repeating to herself three affirmations and ended the day with three others. She reported a positive outcome: "I have become a much better friend to myself." In addition to writing, reading, and thinking affirmatively, you can visualize yourself in a positive light.

Beware of a tendency to focus on weaknesses and become bogged down. All of us have drawbacks. The key is to be aware of positive characteristics and appreciate yourself as you are. Concentrating on your potential, not on limitations, is a way to build self-confidence and self-esteem.

Demonstrate your strengths.   Acting on your strengths is even more affirming. **Self-enhancement** is the process of finding and interpreting situations that result in a positive view of self. College students experienced enhanced self-esteem after receiving high grades; they believed that this reflected their abilities (Woo and Mix, 1997). If you have musical talent, join a performing group. If you are a whiz in the kitchen, cook a meal for someone. Accept positively any compliments. Contributing to worthwhile causes can also be a tremendous boost. Tina volunteered to accompany elderly people on shopping trips. Brad became involved in an environmental cleanup project. Each reported heightened feelings of self-worth. One of the surest ways to sustain a change in self is by helping someone else. Giving to others is a gift to yourself!

Make positive changes.   Constructive changes improve your present self and ensure future well-being. Create an attainable, yet challenging, ideal self. Then choose an improvement area and set up an action plan. Chapter 3 suggests ways to achieve a goal. Express the change in a positive way. Say, "I will become assertive" rather than, "I do not want to be passive." Emphasize self-directed action. Instead of saying, "I hope I improve my grades," think and say, "I am studying so I can improve my grades." Think, "When I lose weight, I will feel better," not "If I lose weight . . ." (Canfield and Siccone, 1993).

Allowing yourself to make mistakes along the way is healthy. High self-esteem does not mean that you never make errors. Feel good about yourself in spite of mistakes; do not wait until all has been corrected (McKay and Fanning, 2000). Use mistakes as helpful information and change your course of action.

Seek positive relationships.   Building self-esteem is easier with the help of positive, supportive people. Cassie, who had low self-esteem, said she was bothered by a friend who was critical. She was advised to seek new relationships with individuals who feel positive about themselves. These people do not need to put others down, and modeling yourself after them is beneficial.

Evaluate sources.   Analyzing how your self-esteem developed can be helpful. All of us have been criticized or put down at times. Instead of accepting negative assessments from others at face value, you might ask, "For what reason did they say or do that? Could it have been because they felt inferior or lacked self-esteem? Were they taking their frustrations out on me? Were they just being hateful? Did they just not know better and even think they were helping me?"

Parents raise children with the resources they possess, and they almost never intend to harm their offspring. If you understand that your parents probably did the best they could do within their limitations, you can free yourself to repair self-esteem. Extreme cases of psychological or physical abuse can be helped with therapy. The helpful book mentioned earlier, *Making Peace with Your Parents*

(Bloomfield, 1996), gives reasons and methods for releasing resentments. When we hold on to past resentments toward parents, current peace of mind and the ability to experience satisfaction in our here-and-now relationships are in jeopardy. Take responsibility for your own self-esteem. Consider the simple but true statement: "You make up your adulthood" (Spezzano, 1992, p. 17).

Perhaps you were not criticized by others, yet your self-esteem has suffered because you think you have disappointed someone. Troy berated himself about his career choice. "My folks want me to go to law school, and they think I am crazy for deciding to be a teacher. Dad said I am afraid to use all my abilities, and he is disappointed. I am at the point of believing him." Children often feel forced to live according to their parents' expectations and to reach for unrealistic standards of excellence.

Can you think of some areas in which you did not measure up? A frequent one is tidiness. Some parents demand perfection in bed-making, cleaning, and organization of belongings. "No matter how hard I tried, I could not make my bed to please my mother," said Ashley, "so I finally quit trying. It is only been recently that I can challenge the importance of being perfect at bed-making!" Breaking away from others' expectations is liberating. "If your life is a continual assessment of whether or not you please others, you are having your buttons pushed from behind" (Satir, 1978, p. 90). Caring what others think about us can be beneficial; however, we may pay a price in decreased self-esteem for trying to satisfy someone else. Similarly, taking responsibility for ourselves is affirming.

Change your thoughts.   Let's continue the esteem-building process by taking a close look at **cognitive restructuring,** or thought-changing. The first step is to tune in to **self-talk,** your thoughts. "The practice of self-love begins in your mind. You must learn to control your thinking" (Dyer, 1976, p. 54). What do you think about yourself, your appearance, your behavior, and impact on others? Self-talk can be pictured as drops of water that become either a clear, unpolluted body of water or a toxic one. Do you hear critical remarks? To decrease the criticisms, follow a valuable suggestion: "I live by a helpful little motto, I will not criticize myself, and there are more than enough people willing to do this for me" (Glasser, 1984, p. 165).

Most of us find it virtually impossible to eliminate all negative thoughts. Yet restructuring an unrealistic self-thought is useful. **Irrational beliefs,** unreasonable and exaggerated thoughts, are at the heart of negative feelings about the self, and people who persist in such thinking make themselves miserable, according to Albert Ellis (1977), a well-known cognitive therapist. You can debate irrational thinking in regard to yourself just as you probably would do with a loved one. Try using these four steps:

1. Identify an irrational thought, exaggeration, or belittlement about yourself.
2. Determine the truth and the facts by asking: "What is the reason for the original thought? What is the truth?"
3. Then use this way of restructuring: "Just because (*the truth as identified in Step 2*) doesn't mean (*the irrational thought in Step 1*)."
4. End with an affirmation related to the specific situation or use a general one.

Pretend you have been told that you are no longer loved by someone. Following are the four steps:

1. "Nobody will ever love me." *This is an irrational thought (Step 1).*
2. A significant other has told you he or she doesn't love you. *This is the truth (Step 2).*
3. "Just because this person does not love me does not mean that I will never be loved." *This is the actual cognitive restructuring (Step 3).*
4. "I am a loving person and deserve someone special." *This is the affirmation (Step 4).*

If you do not succeed in switching to positive self-talk using these steps, try a cognitive technique called **thought-stopping.** Mentally, you can say any of the following loudly, clearly, and angrily: "Stop thinking this way!" "This is unrealistic." "I will not think it!" or just "STOP!" (Chapter 5 addresses in more detail changing what you feel and the power of your thoughts.)

Drawing on all the self-esteem recommendations, individuals can overcome the past and build and strengthen self-worth in the present. One basic question has to do with whether you are as kind and supportive to yourself as you are to a good friend. If you are not, why not become your own best friend?

Creating a Friend or Foe: Self-Fulfilling Prophecy

Predicting the future is usually the work of astrologers or those who claim to be prophets. In reality, each of us predicts what will be, and we also make it come true. A **self-fulfilling prophecy** is a thought or expectation that helps bring about a predicted event or behavior, which then strengthens the original thought. The concept was introduced by Merton (1948), who used it to refer to situations in which false beliefs become true. A classic study by Rosenthal and Jacobson (1968) demonstrated that teacher expectations could influence student achievement.

Examples of the self-fulfilling prophecy are easily found. A youngster who is labeled a brat is likely to believe and, thus, become one. I remember my first year of teaching. Jimmy, a sixth grader, suffered from an eye disease. I had been told that he could not be expected to do what other students did, neither in quantity nor in quality. Being new to teaching and optimistic, I asked Jimmy how he felt. He said he wanted to be treated like the others and expected to handle it. We spent hours after school; his determination made the difference. He left sixth grade with average grades; the next fall he strutted into my classroom with a beautiful smile on his face. "Guess what?" he said. "I made the honor roll in junior high!" Jimmy provided a wonderful lesson. What others believe can become internalized and then actually create one's reality. An expansion on this concept is a self-created prophecy.

Relationship Between Thoughts and Behaviors

Behaviors are usually the demonstration of thoughts. Let's say that you think of yourself as shy. **Shyness** involves a feeling of discomfort and usually apprehension in a social setting. Listen to your self-talk:

Self-fulfilling Prophecy
Thought
or
Belief

Confirming
Thought   Behavior

Figure 1-8   Self-fulfilling prophecy.

I am a shy person. I have always been that way. I was born shy. And because I am, I do not like to be around people. I cannot talk to them, and I am always uncomfortable. I will go through the rest of my life being shy, and that's it.

Powerful thinking, right? A friend invites you to a party. What is your reaction? "I do not want to go. I never have a good time at parties. I am shy, so I cannot look at people or talk to them. I would just have a terrible time because I am the way I am."

In this case your friend persuades you to attend the party. "I know I will not have any fun because I am shy," you tell yourself. How will you act at the party? You stand next to the wall away from the others and you look up, down, at the wall. You appear unapproachable and do not smile because shy people act this way! After a miserable evening, a strong confirming thought surfaces:

See, I knew I would not have any fun. Nobody talked to me, and I could not talk to them. I never enjoy myself at parties because I am shy.

As illustrated in Figure 1-8, this type of self-fulfilling prophecy becomes a vicious circle. A thought about the self is carried out in behavior, which then brings about an even stronger confirming thought. You, the shy person, have fulfilled your own prophecy. If the descriptor is a positive one and increases your self-esteem, the self-fulfilling prophecy is a friend. Too often, though, thoughts are limiting or berating and serve as our enemies.

Self-fulfilling prophecies are powerful. A story is told of two brothers, one who was alcoholic and one who hardly drank liquor. A psychologist wondered why they differed. One brother said that because his father was an alcoholic, he had become one, too. The other explained that because his father was an alcoholic, he learned the horrors of the habit and decided to abstain (Branden, 1983). Clearly, two people with the same background are capable of forming opposite prophecies with different outcomes and, thus, create their own unique realities.

Changes in a Self-Fulfilling Prophecy

Examination of self-fulfilling prophecies is valuable. If you want to change any of yours, two avenues are possible. Psychologists who emphasize cognitive techniques would tell you to change your thoughts. Learning theorists would have you alter your behavior. I recommend, as do many in the cognitive-behavioral area, changing both (Fig. 1-8).

Go back to the example of shyness. An unrealistic thought would be, "I am no longer shy." However, you could use cognitive restructuring and think, "Just because I have been shy in the past does not mean I have to continue. I do not like it, and I am going to change." One authority on shyness says that you are shy if you think you are (Zimbardo, 1977). Empowered with a different belief, you can attend another party and change your behavior. As difficult as it may be, you

For Better or For Worse®   **by Lynn Johnston**

Figure 1-9

position yourself near people. A next step is to look at others with an open expression. You may even smile! If you are not approached, you can muster your courage and go up to someone and say hello. In almost all cases, the person you approach will respond positively. At that point you have broken out of the vicious circle (Fig. 1-9).

With success, new ways of behaving become easier. For a class self-improvement project, an overweight female student decided to change. In the process, she learned an invaluable lesson as she recalled the pain of her self-fulfilling prophecy.

I felt so insecure as a teenager. I felt I was being judged because I was fat so I would not give people the chance to reject me; I rejected them first. It was a perfect example of a self-fulfilling prophecy. I mourn all the friendships I missed out on. With the help of this course I see that when most people look at me, they see *me*, not an overweight person, and when I look at them, I see them as they are and not just as individuals who could hurt my feelings.

Examining all of your self-fulfilling prophecies is wise. As a way to strengthen self-esteem, keep the ones that are friends; work on the foes!

> *The greatest discovery in our generation is that human beings, by changing the inner attitudes of their minds, can change the outer aspects of their lives.*
>
> —William James

Increasing Your Capabilities: Self-Efficacy

Whether you have the confidence to improve yourself will depend on what was defined by Bandura (1977) as **self-efficacy,** "the conviction that one can successfully execute the behavior required to produce the outcomes" (p. 79). Self-efficacy expectations are beliefs regarding capability or competence related to a particular task or activity (Bandura, 1986). Notice the difference between thinking, "I can handle this task," rather than, "I cannot do it." You may remember the story of the little engine who succeeded in ascending a mountain by saying, "I think I can, I think I can." People who have self-efficacy expectations think they can handle the task.

How positively you assess your capability in a specific situation influences success in several ways. First, you are more likely to attempt a particular task if you think you can do it. Second, if you expect a positive outcome, you will exert more effort. Finally, you will persist much longer.

Extensive studies have shown that self-efficacy is a primary factor in behavioral change (Cervone, 2000) and can improve outcomes in a number of important areas. Self-efficacy is related to the following:

- Prevention of and adaptation to cancer (Lev, 1997)
- Better outcomes for smoking cessation (Etter et al., 2000) and for alcohol dependence treatment (Allsop, Saunders, and Phillips, 2000)
- Continuation in exercise programs (Sullum and Clark, 2000)
- Higher grades (jinks and Morgan, 1999)

Even though perceptions of self-efficacy are likely to be generalized across situations (Cervone, 2000), believing that you can handle any and all tasks is unwise because this is not possible. And, if you are perceived as being capable of everything, others may not think you need any help.

Think of times in your life when your own self-efficacy has motivated you. Has a lack of self-efficacy ever hindered you? By take the opportunity to describe self-efficacy and one of your self-fulfilling prophecies in Reflections and Applications. Building and strengthening self-esteem, creating empowering prophecies, and increasing self-efficacy expectations are wise investments in yourself. By taking all these concepts in consideration and applying them to your everyday life, you will have the serenity to accept the things you cannot change, the courage to change the things you can, and the wisdom to know the difference (Reflect and Apply).

REFLECT AND APPLY

Reflect

- *Identify a negative self-fulfilling prophecy from your past or present. Then determine how it could have been or can be changed.*
- *Think of a recent task in which your self-efficacy expectations were high. Then think of a skill you lack or a task in which your self-efficacy expectations are low.*
- *Recall a time your "I can" belief was beneficial.*

Apply

- *Behave differently from a past or present self-fulfilling prophecy.*
- *Act on a skill or expertise in order to demonstrate high self-efficacy expectations.*
- *Try something new!*

LOOKING BACK

Awareness of self is at the heart of interpersonal relations, and self-understanding is an ongoing process.

- Each of the four developmental areas (physical, mental, emotional, and social) influences the others, and together all four form an integrated, whole self.
- Self-concept is a collective view of self including self-description, ideal self, and self-esteem. Ideal self is an image of what one wants to be and is most helpful when it is realistic and attainable. Self-esteem is the value placed on self.
- Improving one's physical and psychological health requires wise choices in the areas of physical activity, nutrition, weight, rest, and stress management.
- Because high self-esteem has numerous advantages, learning to value yourself is highly recommended.
- Self-esteem develops through feedback and interactions with others and through one's own observations and judgments.
- In order to build self-esteem, it may be necessary to first heal psychological pain.
- Self-esteem can be built and strengthened by conscious living, prioritizing, concentrating on and demonstrating of strong points, positive changes, healthy relationships, cognitive restructuring, and evaluation of self-esteem sources.
- Self-fulfilling prophecies can be helpful or damaging. A way to improve one's life is to examine, evaluate, and change negative prophecies.
- Self-efficacy is the sense of competence in the face of a particular task. Many studies have shown that self-efficacy expectations are related to well-being and success in life.

I am convinced that the crucial factor in what happens both inside people and between people is the picture of individual worth that each person carries around.

—Virginia Satir

RESOURCES

Overeaters Anonymous. (505) 891–2664. http://www.overeatersanonymous.org

Learning Disabilities Association of America (LDA), 4156 Library Road, Pittsburgh, PA 15234. Toll free: (888) 300-6710. http://www.ldanatl.org

Parents and Friends of Lesbians and Gays (PFLAG), 1101 14th Street NW, Suite 1030, Washington, DC 20005. (202) 638-4200. http://www.pflag.org

Counselors in educational institutions can help with learning disabilities as well as personal problems.

Self-esteem classes are often offered through wellness centers at hospitals, social service agencies, colleges, and organizations.

2 UNDERSTANDING YOURSELF THROUGHOUT THE LIFE SPAN

LOOKING AHEAD

After completing this chapter, you will be able to

- Discuss what is meant by and known about personality.
- Describe psychological theories of personality development and explain how socialization influences behavior.
- Explain Erikson's psychosocial theory of personality development and relate it to your life.
- Discuss transactional analysis and use your understanding of ego states, life positions, scripts, and strokes.
- Understand personality typing and describe eight preferences.
- Distinguish between extraversion and introversion and note advantages and disadvantages of each.
- Define gender role, summarize how it is learned, and discuss its influences.
- Define androgyny and describe its potential benefits.
- Contrast assertiveness with aggression and nonassertiveness.

> *When one is a stranger to oneself, then one is estranged from others, too.*
> —Anne Morrow Lindbergh

How well do you truly know yourself? Because self-understanding is the foundation of healthy relationships, it deserves attention throughout life. In Chapter 1 you were asked to think about yourself and your sense of self-worth. From this chapter you will gain deeper self-understanding.

Begin to describe yourself. If you are like many people, you start with physical descriptors. Some people have difficulty going further. **Personality** is the "unique you." It consists of characteristics or traits related to how one thinks, feels, and acts. The combination of these qualities that only you possess is the cornerstone of your separate identity. You have probably heard someone say, "She has no personality." This usually means that the person is extremely reserved or dull. The personality may not be projected, but one surely does exist!

How Does Personality Develop?

With a perfect memory, you could describe the numerous experiences that have influenced your personality. However, even that would not tell the entire story. Identical twin and adoptive studies seek to discover how heritable personality is. The findings vary although most agree that heredity and environment both contribute to your personality. This means that within a group of individuals, genetic differences account for about half of the variation in personality traits. Parents may wonder about their children's personalities and ask, "How can they be so different? We raised them the same." They are forgetting about other important factors such as genetics, sex, physical and mental abilities, birth order, and, most importantly, other people's influences and the unique experiences of each individual. You may have heard this referred to as the interaction between **nature and nurture.**

Influences on Personality

An early pioneer in personality development was Sigmund Freud. His theories dealt with early childhood influences, the role of the unconscious, psychosexual stages of development from birth through adolescence, and a structure of the personality made up of three parts (id, superego, and ego). Later in this chapter you will learn about ego states based on Freud's concept. The **psychodynamic** perspective and its theorists continue to contribute to the ongoing study of personality, emphasizing the influence of the unconscious on personality development and human behaviors.

Another perspective is **learning.** Divided into behaviorism and social-cognitive theory, it focuses on environmental influences, observational learning, and cognitive processes in the development of personality. B. F. Skinner (1953, 1987) showed that personality develops in response to stimuli in the environment. Rewards and punishments strengthen and weaken behavior. Any characteristic that has been **reinforced** or made stronger is probably recognizable in your personality. Social-cognitive theorist Albert Bandura (1977, 1986) credits **modeling** as a strong influence on personality. If your personality is similar to a family member's, observational learning undoubtedly played a part.

Social-cognitive theorists point out how a person's mental processes affect behavior as well as the contribution of variables within each person. **Expectancies,** one of these variables, are predictions about the outcome of behaviors. They, along with the perceived value of behavioral choices and outcomes, have an influence on personality (Rotter, 1972, 1975). For example, Binh, a recent Vietnamese immigrant to the United States and a college student, is deciding how to spend his weekend. He has an important exam on Monday. He wants to do well because of self-pride and future career opportunities along with the realization that his parents have high expectations for him. He also wants to go out with friends. He thinks, "I will feel great if I do well and terrible if I do not do well. My parents will be so disappointed if I get a low grade, and I am happiest when I please them."

Can you see that the way he is thinking about his behaviors and what he eventually decides reflect and influence his personality? Learning theory is especially useful in helping to make desired changes using behavior modification and cognitive principles.

Humanism, often combined with existentialism, is a major personality perspective. Emphasis on the development of the self-concept and the use of individual choices in improving personality are central points. Healthy personal growth includes openness to experience, responsibility, and trust in the self. Developing one's full potential is an ideal goal (Rogers, 1961). Because humanism focuses on choices and self-control, its ideas are emphasized throughout this book.

The **trait** perspective identifies key aspects of personality. A trait is a relatively stable quality. When you describe yourself as trusting or suspicious, you are making use of a trait theory. This perspective helps to describe and compare individuals as well as to predict behavior. Personality theorists generally accept the "Big Five" factor model (Wade and Tavris, 2005), which includes (1) extraversion, (2) agreeableness, (3) conscientiousness, (4) openness to experience, and (5) emotional stability. Each dimension has a wide range. For example, in emotional stability a person could be poised and calm at one extreme or anxious and excitable at the other. Cross-cultural research has identified these five dimensions throughout the world (Benet-Martinez and John, 1998).

Cultural psychology looks at how individuals develop as they participate in particular cultural contexts (Markus and Kitayama, 1998). Consider the following:

Elvira, a Mexican American, and Sarah, a Jewish American, were 21-year-old college students who lived with their parents. At 11:30 P.M. Saturday at a party, Elvira was preparing to leave because she had to be home by midnight. Sarah said, "I do not see how you stand having a curfew." Elvira replied, "I do not mind. As long as I am living at home, I do as my parents want. I do not want to worry them." How and why are their personalities different? Think of a person raised in a different society and consider aspects of personality that are different from yours because of cultural influences.

Like psychologists, sociologists are interested in personality development and emphasize **socialization,** a process of learning how to behave according to the requirements of society. Personality is developed gradually as an individual interacts with others (Mead, 1934). Various sources or **agents of socialization** such as family, education, religion, and the media teach the culture and encourage us to form basic personality characteristics. We learn to follow **norms,** those behaviors expected of us as contributing members of society. In Reflections and Applications, you can describe your own personality and compare it to family members.

Stages of Development

Personality develops in a series of stages, according to Erik Erikson, an influential theorist in the fields of psychology and human development. Using Freud's psychoanalytic theory as a basis, he emphasized social interactions and the influence of social development and believed that personality formation continued throughout one's lifetime.

Erikson (1963) described eight psychosocial stages throughout the life span. Each stage has a crisis or challenge to be resolved in order for a personality strength or virtue, as Erikson called it, to be developed. These virtues are the result of a favorable balance between two possible outcomes at each stage. Successful resolution at each stage helps a person meet future developmental challenges and build a healthy personality. According to Erikson (1963, 1968), each item of personality is related to all others, and they all depend on proper development in a particular sequence. Think of a set of blocks and imagine trying to build a tower. Maybe the first block is not on a solid surface. Or maybe the second block is not centrally placed, so the tower teeters a bit. Another poorly placed block will surely cause the blocks to topple. Just as the tower can be rebuilt at any point, a person can later work to develop a favorable balance (Erikson, 1963).

The stages are related to chronological age, yet Erikson (1963) wrote that there could be variations in the timing and intensity of each stage. Order and timing can be affected by historical and cultural conditions. Understanding Erikson's theory can help identify your developmental stage as well as show how you can assist others in resolving the challenges. In the following descriptions, the strength or virtue that emerges is identified after the two possible outcomes. Remember that ages may vary.

I. (Birth–1 year) Trust versus Mistrust [Hope]. A newborn needs to feel secure in the environment in which he or she lives. Trust develops when a baby is loved. What are the behaviors that demonstrate love? Parents or other primary caregivers who respond to the baby's needs and express caring by holding and touching are helping the baby develop trust. A stressful, unpredictable, and unloving environment can lead to a higher degree of mistrust. Holding a newborn during this stage is of utmost importance. "Based on early good-enough holding, children reach out for experience with the expectation that the world will not let them fall" (josselson, 1992, p. 33). If there is not a healthy balance between trust and mistrust, hope is at risk and all stages after this will be more challenging.

Jason cried often, and his parents believed that they would "spoil" him if they responded. When he was only a few months old, a sitter began to spank him for crying and when he did not respond to her requests. Jason became detached and mistrustful of people. In contrast, Kevin received loving attention on a regular basis including when he cried. He was often cuddled and felt secure and loved.

II. (1–3 years) Autonomy versus Shame and Doubt [Willpower]. A typical 2-year-old is learning about independence. The toddler has developed a measure of control over the environment, and a show of defiance is common. The "terrible twos" are normal! Yet parents who do not realize this often respond with force and a suppression of any attempt at autonomy. A constant barrage of "No," "You cannot do that," and "You are naughty" upsets the balance between autonomy and shame and doubt.

Kristen was a clinging toddler. Her mother bragged about how much the little girl depended on her. She was so attached to her mother that she cried whenever she was left with a relative or sitter. An interesting addendum to this story is that when Kristen was 13 years old, her parents divorced, and she chose to live with her father. She had finally achieved independence from her mother! One of her playmates, Lisa, was encouraged to play by herself and praised for certain independent behaviors. She enjoyed the attention of others but did not require it (Fig. 2-1).

Figure 2-1   Life can be fearful as a young child develops autonomy.

III. (3–6 years) Initiative versus Guilt [Purpose]. Initiative is developed when a child undertakes, plans, and proceeds with a task or uses creativity. Children at this stage often have their first experience with a nursery school or day care center. Wise parents will check to see what the facility does to encourage initiative. For example, beware of perfect artwork: it is probably the product of the staff, not the children. Adults who criticize or deprive children of opportunities to engage in appropriate activities are not contributing to a child's healthy development.

Tony was a curious child who wanted to try new things. His mother was a perfectionist who wanted the house to be immaculate. She seldom let him do anything that might make a mess. He also liked to put on his own clothes and button his coat but was rarely allowed to do so. "I am in a hurry. Let me do it for you," his mother would say. Tony struggled in trying to develop self-direction or purpose. Compared to Tony, Luis engaged in a variety of activities both at home and at his preschool. He was praised for his creativity and developed a sense of pride in what he did.

IV. (6–12 years) Industry versus Inferiority [Competence]. During this stage, children want to develop skills and complete tasks. They like to help and may even ask to stay after school to assist the teacher! At this stage, they are ready for household chores, paper routes, and various projects. Think of the eager Girl Scout selling cookies at your front door. Praise at this stage is so important. A young woman wrote, "I did not have any encouragement. I cried for attention at this time, but the only person who heard me was me."

Jodi wanted to help her dad with yard work. She was 8 years old and so enthusiastic. Her dad was in a hurry and thought she would just be in the way. He told her to go inside and watch television. Seven years later Jodi was lying in front of the television when her dad asked her to help him outside. She said she did not want to miss her favorite program. "When you were young, you wanted to help, and now that you are old enough, you will not. I do not understand." No, Dad did not understand!

V. (12–19 years): Identity versus Ego Diffusion [Fidelity]. The critical task of this stage is to determine one's ego identity. Calling this a formidable task, Erikson (1968) conceptualized **optimal identity** as a sense of psychosocial well-being,

Figure 2-2   Peer influence is great at this age.
Source: www.indexopen.com

which includes "a feeling of being at home in one's body, a sense of knowing where one is going, and an inner assuredness of anticipated recognition from those who count" (p. 165). As adolescents seek identity, they will "try on many hats" and probably take risks. Extremely influential is the peer group. Can you think of some crazy things you did during these years? This can be an exasperating time for both teenagers and parents as separation begins to occur. The trauma of this stage is influenced by successful development of earlier strengths (Fig. 2-2).

Chris had been a passive child who seemed to change dramatically after puberty. His parents divorced when he was 14, and he and his mother moved to a different city. Chris started running around with a gang that had a reputation for drug use. He became surly and quiet. When he was home, which was not often, he stayed in his room and played loud music. Inwardly, he struggled with mixed feelings of rebellion versus love for his mother. He felt conflicted and was not sure who he really was. His older sister Jessica's story was quite different. She seemed to handle her teen years without a great deal of turmoil. At each stage she had seemingly developed the strengths required to help her adjust to adolescence.

VI. (20–40 Years) Intimacy versus Isolation [Love]. After a successful resolution between identity and ego diffusion, which may or may not be completed during adolescence, an individual can strike a balance between intimacy and isolation. This means developing a close, meaningful, and stable relationship with another person while continuing to feel inwardly secure. In most societies this type of relationship leads to marriage. Erikson's theory can explain why teenage marriages are much more likely to end in divorce (Strong, DeVault, and Sayad, 1998). Tammy wrote, "I married too young and never developed my own identity. I had children while I was still a child myself. Instead of growing and learning about myself, I became Mommy and nothing else. My divorce has brought me to college. I need to learn professional skills and, most importantly, about myself. Losing a husband is hard, but finding myself is wonderful."

Eric was 19 years old when he entered the U.S. Army. He had been struggling with identity questions for years. He had not successfully completed several of the earlier psychosocial stages, and his adolescence was troubled. The army was helping him find who he really was. He received orders to go overseas, which prompted a threat from his 17-year-old girlfriend. "Marry me so I can go with you, or I will not be here when you return." Against the wishes of family, Eric and Teresa married. They had numerous disagreements and power struggles. Their relationship was a classic example of a union between two people who had not resolved their identity crises and were not ready for intimacy. Within a year they divorced.

Many individuals remain within a marriage for years unable to achieve intimacy; instead, they feel isolated. The importance of finding out who you are is illustrated in Linda's story. She recalled that the identity stage was extremely difficult for her. She had come through the earlier stages feeling inferior for being "the kid with red hair, freckles, buck teeth, and used clothes." She used alcohol and drugs excessively, engaged in promiscuous sex, had a horrible relationship with her mother, and quit school at 16. At 17 she ended up in a disastrous marriage. Several years later she realized that she wanted to grow. Counseling and college helped her discover who she truly was and, as she puts it, "I am rebuilding my block tower, it is going well, and I feel great!"

VII. (40–65 Years) Generativity versus Stagnation [Caring]. Looking beyond one's self rather than remaining inwardly focused is one way to describe what is needed at this stage. Erikson (1963, 1968) viewed it as a desire to guide the next generation and identified parenthood as a common avenue. He did acknowledge that not everybody progressed through this stage by raising children and included the possibilities of productivity and creativity in other realms. For most parents, this time of life includes children leaving home, which can result in what is called the *empty nest syndrome*. Pursuing a purpose beyond self and family would likely diminish any sense of emptiness.

Margaret's marriage was an unhappy one. She tried to compensate by devoting her time and energy to her two children. After her younger daughter was married, Margaret lapsed into a severe depression; she felt worthless. She became preoccupied with her health and was frequently ill. She described herself as "stagnant and bored." Quite different was Susan's generativity stage. Feeling secure in herself, she had a satisfying relationship with her partner. She held a top position with an accounting firm and involved herself in meaningful volunteer activities. She felt she was making a difference in the world.

VIII. (65 years–death) Integrity versus Despair [Wisdom]. The last stage of life is one of acceptance and satisfaction. If all the preceding crises have been successfully resolved, Erikson (1968) believed that in this person "the fruit of the seven stages gradually ripens" (p. 139). Acceptance of one's life and others in it and acknowledgment that no other path would have served one as well are hallmarks of integrity. Contentment and peace are possible if memories are meaningful and fulfilling. Strength at this stage takes the form of wisdom.

Harvey, a 70-year-old man, had periods of irritability and bitter nostalgia. He often spoke of what he wished he had done and of how life had cheated him. He had retired from a long career and had developed no hobbies. He spent many hours alone watching television. In contrast to Harvey and his despair is a dear friend, Marilyn. A wonderful parent and grandparent who does so much for others in her work as a therapist and volunteer, Marilyn believes that it is vitally important that she contributes something of value to the world. Describing herself as somewhere between generatively and integrity, she says:

I love stumbling upon new insights. If I am lucky, I will be looking and learning until my last breath. I think beauty is innate, that somewhere within each of us lays the ability to discover beauty, and that truth is what we search for all our lives. My world is made up of many truths and each one holds a special beauty of its own. I feel more connected with life each time I share what I have discovered.

Think about your life up to this point. Answer the questions about your developmental stages in Reflections and Applications. You can concentrate on working through unresolved stages, keeping in mind that neither of the extremes (e.g., trust versus mistrust) is ever totally developed and that the conflicts are present throughout life. For example, what could happen that would cause a weakened sense of identity? Any dramatic change may necessitate a new struggle. Familiarity with the psychosocial stages is like a road map for your life as long as you realize there may be detours. This book can help you discover what is missing and give you the tools to develop the virtues Erikson deemed important.

Challenges to Personality Development

At any stage of life, dysfunctional family experiences and psychological trauma will likely hinder positive growth. Low self-esteem and depression can block substantial progress at any stage.

Challenges can also stem from issues related to adoption and minority status. For example, an adopted child often feels a need to locate biological parents or at least learn about them. Racial and ethnic minorities can go through a period of questioning their "roots." Kaili, a biracial student, said, "I have struggled with the difficult identity question of being a part of two racial groups. I would be happy with a biracial identity if society would be more accepting."

Sexual orientation also poses a challenge. U.S. society is predominantly heterosexual. The popular press assumes a homosexuality rate of 10 percent of the U.S. population. A 2002 Gallup survey estimated that 21 percent of men are gay and 22 percent of women are lesbian (Meyers, 2006). The U.S. census for 2004 included approximately 295 million people. On the basis of 2004 census data, if only 10 percent of the population is homosexual that would total 29.5 million gays and lesbians in the United States. What causes sexual orientation has not been determined for either heterosexuals or homosexuals. Most scientists believe that there is no single cause for sexual orientation and these causes may vary among individuals. Biology, cultural influences, and experiences are just a few of the factors identified (Wade and Tavris, 2002; Yeoman, 1999). Professionals including members of the American Psychological Association do not consider same-sex orientation to be a deviance, illness, or psychological disorder.

Most lesbians and gay males begin to realize their sexual orientation during or shortly after puberty, although hints of it may appear earlier. When gay males and lesbians discover this uniqueness, choices have to be made. Most feel forced to hide an important part of themselves out of fear. They feel "different" and in a heterosexist society are condemned solely on the basis of sexual orientation. Self-esteem can be a major help. Even though the researchers acknowledged that gay and lesbian young people often experience isolation and emotional stressors related to harassment and abuse, self-esteem was strengthening, especially for females (Grossman and Kerner, 1998).

Gays and lesbians who are hiding their identity may feel unauthentic. They live a lie, fearing that they will not be accepted if people know the truth (Herek, 1996). Risk of negative reactions by parents is a major concern. Mike, a young male student, talked candidly about his pain at keeping his sexual orientation hidden from his parents. "I think they suspect because they make remarks. Dad said once, 'If I ever found out you were queer, I would kill you.' It really hurts to not be able to be who I am with people I love." Hopefully, Mike and others can be helped by the book *Mom, Dad, I'm Gay: How Families Negotiate Coming Out* (Savin-Williams, 2001), designed to help bridge the gap between gay and lesbian youth and their parents.

Gay male or lesbian sexual orientation, like a heterosexual orientation, is not a matter of wanting only a sexual relationship. Just like heterosexuals, gays and lesbians are also attracted to a special person with whom they can spend time, have fun, and share deepest thoughts and feelings. Close relationships between two gays or two lesbians are as loving, close, healthy, and nourishing as those developed by heterosexuals (Peplau, Cochran, and Mays, 1997).

One young man explained that sexual orientation is not a choice any more than race or sex is and added, "Think about it folks, with homophobia, AIDS, discrimination, hate crimes, what sensible teenager would make a choice like that?" (Minton, 1993). During a discussion of sexual orientation, one student suggested that being gay or lesbian may not be a choice, but acting on it was. She thought a gay male or a lesbian *should not* act like one. A simple question is an effective response: "Would you want to be told you could not act on your sexual orientation?"

According to Jim, a gay adult, the decision to "come out" or stay closeted is an extremely difficult one for most because of the risks involved with family, other relationships, and career. Extreme courage is required if gay individuals want to live open and truthful lives. One such person is Amy, who wrote a wonderful and motivating note at the end of an interpersonal relations course concerning the first edition of this book.

> I think this book is wonderful. As I read it, I noticed that it is very heterosexually focused as are most textbooks. I have to switch things around to make them apply to me. Can you imagine how it feels to read and read and never see yourself in words? I had such a hard time dealing with my sexuality when I was younger. I thought I was the only one who was having these feelings, and I found nothing to validate that what I was feeling even existed. I remember my feelings the first time I read a book that dealt with a homosexual relationship. It was only a brief mention, but my feelings were so intense, I almost cried. I know that human relationships are all basically the same, yet I think there are enough differences to at least warrant a mention. I think if non-gay people had to read chapter after chapter about relationships from a gay point of view, they would have a hard time relating. I do not want to sound as if I am jumping on my soapbox, but I get so frustrated at never being validated or placed first. I know some people are very open-minded and understanding, but I would like people to at least give thought to what I have said. Maybe sometime in the future you can make a difference to someone like me who wanted to kill myself because I never had any positive reinforcement or situations I could relate to about the way I was feeling.

Acknowledging that misunderstanding, prejudice, and social stigma regarding sexual orientation create major developmental challenges for most gay and lesbian adolescents; researchers offer a heartening note that most sexual minority youth lead healthy, productive lives (Tharinger and Wells, 2000).

Predictions about Personality

What will you be like in 20 or 30 years? Those who believe that there is consistency of personality over a lifetime point out that even though there is likely to be some change, especially in those traits identified in the "Big Five" factor model, personality is stable in most people (Costa and McCrae, 1997). Changes in single traits are more likely; after age 30, women's personalities seem to change more than men's (Ardelt, 2000). Benefits of having a good idea of what you will be like in the future are predictability and reassurance in who you are.

Understanding Through Transactional Analysis

Transactional analysis (TA) is helping people comprehend why they would feel compelled to hide their true personalities. Described as a system for understanding human behavior and as a personality theory, it provides insight into self-awareness and personal growth (Clarkson, 1992).

Eric Berne, a psychiatrist who developed TA, used it to help his clients. The general public learned about the theory and methods when the book *I'm OK, You're OK* (Harris, 1969) became a best-seller. Other books, seminars, and classes teach practical applications. This section will describe the basics of TA and show how to use them in your own life.

Ego States

Basic to TA are **ego states,** which are facets of personality and related patterns of behavior. Serving as the model for ego states was Freud's personality structure of id, ego, and superego. Berne's names for them are related to actual life figures, and personality consists of all three.

Impulsive, spontaneous, emotional, and creative are words that describe the **child ego state.** It was so named because this part is childlike (like a child between the ages of 2 and 5, according to Berne) and acts on feelings. In the "child" are "the countless, grand 'a-ha' experiences and feelings of delight" (Harris, 1969, p. 27). People of all ages have a child ego state, although it varies in how noticeable and freely expressive it is. Your "child" is the part of you that loves and hates, feels exhilarated or completely miserable, relishes ice cream and pizza, laughs and cries, and can enjoy life (Fig. 2-3).

The child ego state did not develop freely. As soon as you were able to understand parental figures in the environment, another ego state began to develop. This part consists of verbal and nonverbal messages you received. Think of it as a collection of recordings in the brain that functions as a conscience. This ego state contains rights and wrongs, "shoulds," "oughts," and strong ideas of what to do and not to do.

The messages poured in during your early years and were largely unedited; that is, you did not question or reject them (Harris, 1969). And no matter how old you are, you continue to receive directive messages that can sound like commands. These opinions, judgments, values, and attitudes are recorded and automatically play back in your mind. Or you have a visual image of a nonverbal message. A good example came from Lisa: "When my mother was watching television, she usually ignored me when I would ask her a question. As a kid, I would always feel as if I had done something wrong. And when I am ignored today, I tend to feel that way, too." Even though these messages can come from a variety of sources, because so many come from actual parents, this is called the **parent ego state.**

Remember that the messages originally came from an external source and are now internalized. A partial list of some ridiculous messages contributed by students follows. Can you think of any of your own that strike you as silly?

- Benjamin Franklin took a bath every day of his life, and he was never sick. So be sure to bathe daily.
- Lift your feet off the floor of the car when you cross over railroad tracks.
- Swallowed gum will stick to your spine, and you will not be able to stand up straight.
- Nice girls do not wear red fingernail polish or pierce their ears.
- Masturbation will cause blindness.
- Clean the house before you leave in case of a fire.

Incidentally, wise and useful "parent" messages such as, "Look both ways before you cross the street" and "Do not drive if you have been drinking" also exist and are worthy of attention!

Often, when you are in your parent ego state, you feel, think, and act like one of your own parents. If this has not yet happened, you will probably have the experience of saying something to one of your own children that has a familiar ring to it. Even though "parent" messages affect your parenting behavior, ideally you will parent from all ego states.

Before we discuss the third ego state, imagine this scenario. It is 7:00 on a cool, rainy morning. The alarm clock rings, and you hit the snooze button. You feel warm and happy lying in bed and your child ego state is enjoying it immensely. "Oh, to just stay here and sleep, skip class. This feels so good." Then another voice penetrates your relaxed state. "Get up! You should not miss school! Do not be so lazy!" It sounds like Mom or Dad, but it is not because you do not live at home anymore. You are hearing your own parent ego state. What a dilemma—the struggle between "child" and "parent" continues in your mind.

Figure 2-3   The child ego state can be alive and well at any age!

How fortunate that you have another ego state that can enter the picture at this point. "Let me think— I have not missed that class yet, and I remember the instructor saying there was going to be a film. I could watch that at another time. I have not been getting enough rest lately. I think I will sleep this morning." This is one possible resolution. A second one is, "I have missed that class several times, and I do not think it is wise to be absent that much. Besides, the lecture is always full of important material! I think I will go to class." This part of the personality thinks and is able to logically and objectively analyze. It sees alternatives and acts as a decision maker using facts in a cool, calm way. The name **adult ego state** is quite appropriate. Like a computer, the "adult" gathers information from the three sources of "parent," "child," and stored "adult" data as well as new evidence in the present (Harris, 1969). The "adult" can find either the "child" feelings or the "parent" messages appropriate and allow them to prevail. Also possible is to strike a balance between the two or gather additional information and make an original decision. The "adult" begins to develop at about 10 months of age (Harris, 1969) as an infant assumes some control over the environment; choices are then possible!

Each ego state has its positive and negative qualities. The "child" is exuberant, enjoys life, and readily expresses affection; yet, it also can be depressed, fearful, wounded, and defeated. The "parent" has useful knowledge and reacts quickly. How fortunate we are that our parent ego state tells us to be on time for work. Unfortunately, the "parent" contains some outdated and negative information, can be close-minded, and passes on potentially damaging messages. The "adult" is a necessity in most situations; however, it can be programmed with detrimental or inaccurate information and be a stranger to emotionality.

A well-adjusted individual uses all three ego states. In some cases, an ego state is more powerful and overwhelms or contaminates the others. An overpowering "child" is what Kushner (1986) cautioned against: "Fun can be the dessert of our lives but never its main course. It can be a very welcome change of pace from the things we do every day, but should it ever become what we do every day, we will find it too frivolous a base to build a life on" (pp. 69–70).

Which of the three ego states is dominant in the following examples?

- Joan is aloof and reserved. She does well at her accounting job and finds it easy to analyze data. She is a calm person who rarely shows emotions.
- Kim is a 12-year-old who has strong convictions about many issues. She tends to be domineering and judgmental.
- Paul is a twinkle-eyed 80-year-old. He is witty, enthusiastic, and readily shows his feelings. However, he often acts on impulse and can be moody.

If you named "adult" for Joan, "parent" for Kim, and "child" for Paul, you are correct. An imbalance can occur regardless of age. Even a 4-year-old can exhibit an expanded "parent" ego state.

Adults are wise to ask themselves if they have a healthy child ego state. Do you ever act on impulse? When were you last spontaneous? Can you wonder and dream? Do you truly feel your emotions, and do you express them? When did you last really laugh? Are you a hugger; do you enjoy being hugged?

Leo Buscaglia, who was widely known as a big hugger, encouraged people to "let down their hair" and be a little crazy once in a while. He told of coming home from Wisconsin on a late-night flight. He carried gifts he could not check in as luggage: a large pumpkin, leaves (which he loved), cheese, and homemade bread. When airborne, he impulsively spread the gifts across several seats and pushed the call button. The tired flight attendant was quite surprised and, amazingly, reenergized by the craziness. She called the other attendants; they brought wine and had a party! A potentially boring flight was special because of someone's "child." Some do not notice that they are not using their child ego state until it is too late. In a live presentation, Leo Buscaglia described an 85-year-old reflecting on life.

> If I had my life to live over again, I would dare to make more mistakes next time. I would relax. I would limber up. I would be sillier than I have been this trip. I would take more chances. I would take more trips. I would climb more mountains and swim more rivers. I would eat more ice cream and fewer beans. I would perhaps have more actual troubles, but I would have fewer imaginary ones. You see, I am one of those people who lived seriously and sanely hour after hour, day after day. Oh, I have had my moments, and if I had to do it over again, I would have more of them. In fact, I would try to have nothing else, just moments, one after another, instead of living so many years ahead of each day. I have been one of those people who never went anywhere without a thermometer, a hot water bottle, a raincoat, and a parachute. If I had to do it again, I would travel lighter. If I had my life to live over, I would start barefoot earlier in the spring and stay that way later in the fall. I would go to more dances. I would ride more merry-go-rounds. I would pick more daisies. If I had my life to live over again, but I do not.

Think of all the "parent" messages that restricted her "child." Can you think of any "child" wants and wishes you are denying yourself? If you were 85 years old, what would you wish for yourself? What can you do about it now? Remember, an 85-year-old does not have life to live over, and neither will you.

A problem lies with receiving inconsistent messages. Did you have a parental figure who said one thing and did just the opposite? Did anyone say, "Do not drink and drive," and then proceed to do exactly that, or say, "Religion is important, so go to Sunday School," yet who rarely went to church, or a significant person who maintained, "All people are equal," but then said, "I do not welcome one of those people in this house"? A sad "parent" message is, "Do as I say, not as I do."

"Parent" messages can be retrieved by thinking about why you do what you do, why you have certain beliefs and ideas, and where they came from originally. A major task of healthy adulthood is to process "parent" messages through the adult ego state. Getting rid of extremely harmful and hateful messages is highly recommended. Buscaglia (1982) revealed that he has been more involved in unlearning than in learning during various stages of his life. "I have to unlearn all the garbage that people have laid upon me" (p. 147). That "garbage" consists of "parent" messages. With each discarded piece he became freer. As you process messages through your "adult," you become more your own person. Use Reflections and Applications to describe your ego states. Recognizing your own ego states can be beneficial in making decisions.

Ryan is a 36-year-old factory worker who quit high school to marry and get a job. He realizes he is going nowhere with a career and is considering quitting and going back to school. Of value to Ryan would be awareness of the role of each ego state. His "parent" has such messages as, "A man is supposed to support his family," "You are too old to go back to school," "Everyone will think you are dodging responsibility." The "child" in him is frightened by risk yet somewhat excited at the prospect of a new experience. Ryan will benefit from "plugging into" his adult ego state. This ego state will gather more information about costs, management of the family's financial situation, and benefits compared to losses.

A goal of TA is to encourage freedom of choice—the freedom to change (Harris, 1969). This can happen if you, like Ryan, become aware of each ego state and use your "adult" in the decision process.

Life Positions

The book title *I'm OK, You're OK* (Harris, 1969) came from the preferred life position in the TA framework. A **life position** is a perspective on the world based on feelings about self and others. Berne (1962) identified four positions. The preferred, or healthy, position, **I'm OK, you're OK,** is based on equality and positiveness. In one's initial approach to people and situations, hope and optimism are present. "Persons in this position are winners. They reflect an optimistic and healthy outlook on life and freely relate with others" (Woollams and Brown, 1979, p. 107). This position requires self-love and esteem. The "I'm OK" belief is followed by tolerance, equality, and acceptance of others.

The **I'm not OK, you're OK** position is not unusual. In fact, some consider it to be the most common one (Woollams and Brown, 1979). Self-esteem is low; the individual feels inferior. "I am unworthy, and everyone else has it together" would be a typical thought. These people appear defeated; they usually have difficulty accepting compliments or communicating positive self-talk.

Several years ago a man by the name of Patrick Sherrill committed a violent crime; he killed several coworkers and then himself. The headline read, "Gunman Hated the World and Himself." This is an extreme example of the position **I'm not OK, you're not OK.** The position reflects an extremely negative, pessimistic attitude. These people seem to hate themselves and the world. They can behave in various ways, and most are not criminals. Some retreat from the world and become loners, and others simply give up and just manage to survive. The frightening ones are those, like Pat Sherrill, who take out their self-hatred on others.

An annoying and potentially damaging position is **I'm OK, you're not OK.** People in this position feel superior to others. They show it in annoying ways by maintaining that they are always right, judging or patronizing others, and telling others what to do.

What position are you occupying? The question is frequently asked, "Can you be in more than one?" You may have characteristics that fit more than one position; however, view yourself in a general way. What orientation do you usually take toward others and the world? If it is not **I'm OK, you're OK,** decide to work toward it!

Life Script

A **script** is an ongoing program, first developed in early childhood, that directs behavior (Berne, 1972). The TA framework does not suggest that your life is predetermined or that you simply read lines and play a role. Unless you become aware of your life script, you may be playing it out without realizing it. Self-fulfilling prophecies serve as powerful directions within your script. Julie could be counted on to be late to class. She explained, "I am late to everything, including work. I have always been this way. Mom told me I was not organized, and Dad said I had no concept of time. My friends just expect me to be late and would not believe it if I were ever on time. I am just a 'flake.'" Julie played the part of the always-late, disorganized "flake," and she played it well.

Does Julie have to continue playing this part? The TA framework provides a technique called **script analysis,** a way of becoming aware of how your script developed. You then can decide to take different courses of action. Julie did not have to continue in her role, but the decision to change had to be hers. After college she landed a job. A few months later she was fired for chronic tardiness. She rationalized that it was not her dream job anyway. Within a short period of time she was hired as a fashion buyer—an ideal position for her! When she was warned about lateness during her first evaluation session, she made an attempt to be on time, yet it was short-lived. Losing that job was depressing for Julie, yet it proved to be the jolt she needed. She resolved to change her script and, with the help of a counselor, set up a behavior modification program. She rewarded herself for each on-time experience and relished the praise of others. The always-late, disorganized Julie is different, and part of her new script is, "I can make positive changes if I really want to!" She proved what Nathaniel Branden (1992) wrote, "We need never be the prisoner of yesterday's choices" (p. 73).

Scripts are based on the past. Even though you cannot change your past, learning from past experiences is invaluable. Ask yourself, "Is my past illuminating my present or contaminating it?" (Satir, 1976). The present is where change is possible, and you can rewrite your future script if you choose to do so. Can you think of some changes you would like to make in your script? Taking charge of your own life and destiny is not necessarily easy, but being your own scriptwriter is very rewarding!

> *We are not prisoners of the past. We are pioneers of an exciting future.*
>
> —John Powell

Strokes

"I enjoy having you in class." "I like you." "You did a great job." These phrases, along with a smile, a hug, and a friendly wave, are special verbal or nonverbal behaviors called **strokes.** The strokes that feel good to the receiver are positive strokes. Negative strokes do not feel good and are generally meant to be hurtful. Think of some negative verbal and nonverbal strokes. See Table 2-1 for examples of each type. Human beings need recognition, and positive stroking is effective in letting people know that they count. Strokes can be *conditional* (based on certain behaviors or conditions) or *unconditional* (given simply because the receiver is alive). A mother commented, "I realize that I have been giving positive strokes but only under set conditions. I decided to tell my son that I appreciated him simply for being here—to stroke his person." She had realized the beauty of unconditional strokes! Can you add others to the lists in Table 2-1?

TABLE 2-1	Strokes	
Verbal Positive	**Verbal Negative**
"I love you."	"I don't like you."
"I like your smile."	"Get lost!"
"You're a great employee."	"You're so lazy."
"Hello, how are you?"	"You look awful!"
Nonverbal Positive	**Nonverbal Negative**
A pat on the back	A shake of the fist
A wink (if it feels good!)	A hit or a slap
A back rub	A frown
A special card or gift	Inattention
A hug or kiss	Laughter at someone

Young children definitely can learn about the nature of strokes. A director of an early childhood center used the program "TA for Tots." Positive strokes were called "warm fuzzies," whereas negative ones were "cold prickles." The children soon recognized how much more comfortable the atmosphere was when "warm fuzzies" were being given and received. In the "warm fuzzy" circle, the children gave and received positive strokes. In the beginning, several were hesitant—an indication that "warm fuzzies" were not too familiar to them. Gradually, verbal strokes seemed easier. Two boys interacted during this time. Danny was a spontaneous and expressive boy with a healthy child ego state. Tim was reserved and unexpressive. On this particular day, when it was Danny's turn, he did something out of the ordinary. He gave Tim a big hug and kiss on the cheek. The others seemed embarrassed, and the director quickly said, "I really like that warm fuzzy. I would like to have more of those!" Because young children regard teachers as the final authority, they reacted in a positive way—all except Tim. The director was saddened that this boy, at the age of only 4, recoiled from his friend's gesture. For whatever reason his script included, "I do not want to be touched." During the course of the year he became more open to expressiveness.

Strokes, or lack of them, influence scripts and life positions. An all too common scenario goes like this: A child makes the bed and completes assigned tasks each day but receives no recognition, no positive stroke. One day the bed is not made! What happens? A negative stroke is delivered immediately: "You are irresponsible and lazy!" This scenario is played out frequently in the home, at school, and even at work. Even though evidence shows that positive strokes are powerful motivators, negatives are more common (Fig. 2-4).

When people do not receive positive strokes, they tend to settle for negative ones. "Taking negative strokes is like drinking polluted water; extreme need will cause us to overlook the harmful qualities of what we require to survive" (Steiner, 1974, p. 127). A child who is misbehaving or an adolescent who "acts out" may be deprived of positive strokes and willing to settle for any kind. One student remarked that we give pets more pats than we do human beings. Positive strokes can also be lacking in marriages. A young married female wrote:

For Better or For Worse   by Lynn Johnston

Figure 2-4

Sometimes I feel as if I am dying of lack of attention. We have been married only five years, and the only time he touches me is in bed. I have not heard a positive word from him in a long time. I feel dried up and starved for affection, and I do not know what to do.

In your life, monitor the strokes you receive and record them in the personality activity in Reflections and Applications. Ask, "Whom do I receive them from? What kind are they? Under what conditions do I receive them? What do I want?" Also become aware of the strokes you give by asking the same questions. The TA framework has much to offer. Only the basics have been presented here. If you want to learn more, read any of the books cited in this section. Transactional analysis can be used to enrich your life.

What is Your Personality Like?

Carlos is miserable at work. He enjoys being around people, yet his job demands that he analyze data in a back office. Connie is frustrated in a certain classroom situation. The instructor does not seem to be organized, and the class discussions focus more on possibilities than on realities. Rich and Jamie were so happy when they first married. Three years later, they both feel dissatisfied. Rich does not like the way Jamie seems to make irrational decisions, and she finds him too analytical and inconsiderate of others' feelings.

An understanding of personality types can help each of these individuals. Psychological typing categorizes several related personality traits. Carl Jung (1921), an early psychologist, believed that behavioral differences are based on the ways people prefer to approach life (jung, 1968). Based on Jung's typology with some of their own refinements, Isabel Myers and her mother, Katharine C. Briggs, developed the Myers-Briggs Type Indicator (MBTI). It achieved widespread acceptance in the 1970s and has remained a popular instrument useful in career selection and satisfaction, education and learning preferences, and interpersonal relationships. A study confirmed that the MBTI reliably measures personality characteristics associated with Jungian theory (Wheeler, 2001). Intended for use with "well" people, the indicator focuses on positive aspects. You can use it to make life decisions, gain personal insight, understand differences, and learn how to work well with others.

Originally published in 1980s, the book *Gifts Differing* (Myers and Myers, 1995) describes personality preferences as well as ways in which people can use their own strengths and understand the differences of others. The author explains:

> All too often, others with whom we come in contact do not reason as we reason, or do not value the things we value, or are not interested in what interests us. The merit of the theory is that it enables us to expect specific personality differences in particular people and to cope with the people and the differences in a constructive way. (p. 1)

Personality Preferences

Following is a brief summary of the four pairs of personality preferences. The MBTI will show your inclination for one or the other.

- **Extraversion-Introversion (type E or I).** Relates to an inward or outward orientation and to life energy sources. (*Note:* The spelling *extraversion* is used in this book to correspond to the MBTI. The spelling *extroversion* is also common.)
- **Sensing-Intuition (type S or N).** Pertains to the preferred ways of taking in information as well as what is of interest.
- **Thinking-Feeling (type T or F).** Indicates whether one prefers to use thought or personal values in decision making and judgments.
- **Judgment-Perception (type J or P).** Shows how one deals with the outer world and the type of environment that is preferred.

Understanding their meanings and knowing that we do not have absolute preferences are important. A common misconception is that an extraversion preference means being totally extraverted. Instead, individuals are both extraverted and introverted, yet in differing degrees.

The meanings of extraversion and introversion are typically misunderstood. This confusion has led to an assumption that a person needs to be extraverted in order to be successful and happy. Western culture seems to more strongly reward the outgoing, sociable person (Keirsey and Bates, 1978). Although introversion is often associated with such descriptors as shy, lonely, and snobbish, these do not define introversion. This inaccuracy is unfair, and a true understanding can correct these misconceptions.

Let's look at what these preferences really are. Think in terms of life energy or force. What charges your battery? If your preference is **extraversion,** you get much of this force from external sources, including other people, and you probably project energy outward. Extraverted behavior is outgoing, showing an outward orientation and a preference to operate in the outer world of people and things. **Introversion** means an inner orientation and having an interest in the inner world of concepts and ideas. If there were such a word as "ingoing," it would describe an introverted preference well. The source of energy is within and comes from solitary experiences. Those with a preference for introversion can reenergize themselves and do not rely on external stimuli. In fact, interaction drains their energy, and they need to spend time recharging themselves.

People who prefer extraversion will usually behave in a friendly fashion, and they appear to be open to interaction with others. They are not necessarily any more emotional, caring, or loving than those who prefer introversion. Those with an introversion preference will generally be more reserved in a social setting, and they do not usually seek out others. This does not mean that they are uncaring, snobbish, lonely, or shy. They are often skilled in working with people but their preference is for smaller numbers and an opportunity to know people well. People who are described as shy, lonely, and uncaring are lacking in social skills and may be either introverted or extraverted.

Another difference is that extraverts will usually respond more quickly than introverts. Introverts think about what they are going to say; extraverts tend to think out loud. In fact, extraverts commonly talk their thoughts! If you often "put your foot in your mouth," extraversion could be partially to blame. Talkativeness is not necessarily an exclusive characteristic of either extraversion or introversion. Because introverts prefer smaller groups, you could be sitting next to a person on a bus or airplane who talks and talks in a one-on-one situation and be surprised to know he or she has an introverted preference. In classrooms introverts may participate often and surprise their classmates when their personality preference is identified.

Both preferences have advantages. Extraverts frequently report greater happiness and satisfaction with life. Reasons could be the experience of more potentially positive interactions, ease with affectionate behaviors, greater acceptance by society, and greater social support (Myers and Diener, 1995). Extraverts are usually eager to interact. Does it surprise you to know that extraverts can behave in a shy manner? **Shyness** is timidity and a feeling of unease in a social situation. As an extravert, you may have felt and acted shyly at some social activities because you did not feel at ease or were not in the mood to talk. The dissatisfaction you felt after the event came from not using your extraverted preference. If you were an introvert, you probably would not have been bothered. That leads to one distinct advantage for introverts. They do not require social exchange and can get along just fine alone for long periods of time. In addition, introverts are often thought of as sincere people and good listeners even though they may be neither. Can you think of other advantages for each preference?

What about disadvantages? Extraverts can be overwhelming in social settings and be perceived as obnoxious loudmouths. If extreme in their extraversion, others may see them as superficial or phony. Another potential problem for an extraverted person was expressed by Jodi.

> I am quite extraverted, but there are still times when I am quiet. If that happens around friends, they act upset with me and ask, "What is wrong with you anyway?" I find it hard to have any quiet time when I am around others. They expect me to be the life of the party.

Introverts are frequently criticized for their lack of conversation and what is often interpreted as aloofness. They may be perceived as uncaring or uninterested. If an extreme introvert does go to a party, the stay will likely be short.

The accusation of "party pooper" is inaccurate; in actuality, the party "pooped" the introvert (Keirsey and Bates, 1978). How might a person with an extraverted preference (E) and one with an introverted preference (I) seem to each other? Without understanding their differences, an E can seem shallow to an I, and a I may seem withdrawn to an E. After a program I gave on preferences, a woman in her sixties approached me and laughingly asked, "Where were you three years ago when I got divorced? I thought I was married to a dud, someone who just did not know how to have fun. Now I realize he was just introverted, which to me seemed terrible. This could have saved my marriage!"

Carl Jung looked at extraversion and introversion as valuable opposites. He believed that most individuals use both preferences but not with equal ease (Myers, 1980). The most important points are that both extraversion and introversion include positive behaviors and advantages, and we have preferences in varying degrees for both.

All categories and preferences are important, and if their meanings are not clarified, confusion and misunderstanding are probable. The other three pairs of preferences can be understood as follows:

- **Sensing and Intuition:** When you want to find out something, your preference may be **sensing** (S), which means a preference for gathering facts through the senses. "You tend to be realistic, practical, observant, and good at remembering a great number of facts and working with them" (Myers, 1980, p. 2). If you prefer **intuition** (N), "you tend to value imagination and inspirations, and to be good at new ideas, projects, and problem solving" (Myers, 1980, p. 2). In perceiving reality differently, sensors are concrete and attuned to details, and intuitives are visionary and ablaze with possibilities and ideas. Any successful business needs people with both preferences. When working on a task, sensors prefer a systematic step-by-step procedure and do not seem to be bothered by repetition. Intuitivists often devise their own methods, will work on several steps or projects at once, and prefer variety. An intuitive preference gets restless with "sameness," has an appreciation of new and different experiences, and wants to modify life.

Can you see how these preferences can affect job satisfaction? Think of jobs that a intuitive would dislike. What would bother a sensor in a work situation?

- **Thinking and Feeling:** Once you have found what you want to know, you may have a decision to make. If your preference is for **thinking** (T), you will predict the logical results of your actions and decide impersonally. The other way to decide is through **feeling** (F). You will consider anything that matters or is important to you or to other people (logic is not required) and decide according to personal values (Myers, 1980). Those who have a clear thinking preference view emotions as more of a problem than as part of a solution (Keating, 1984). This person can be oblivious to other people's feelings, whereas the opposite (a strong feeling person) can bend over backward to avoid hurting anyone. Either can become a problem. In one study (Shermis and Lombard, 1998), thinkers had lower test anxiety scores than feelers. Can you see why? Both preferences can care a great deal about people and believe that their decisions are based on the "right" motives. Caring from a thinker is more apt to be sympathy and from the feeler empathy (Jeffries, 1991). The two preferences can clash or complement each other. Clashing is probably more common.

A crucial difference between a thinker and a feeler that isn't easily bridged is how issues are perceived. A thinker prefers to deal with them in a detached manner outside of the self, whereas a feeler takes them to heart and thinks in terms of everyone involved.

- **Judgment and Perception:** The descriptors judgment (J) and perception (P) reflect one's orientation toward the outer world. **Judgment** means that you prefer living in a "planned, decided, orderly way, wanting to regulate life and control it" (Myers, 1980, p. 6). Planning and preparation are typical behaviors. A judging person seeks closure and prefers to reach a decision or judgment quickly. If instead you like living in a "flexible, spontaneous way, wanting to understand life and adapt to it," (Myers, 1980, p. 6), your preference is **perception.** You often "go with the flow" and prefer to delay closure and continue perceiving. Key words are *organization* and *order* for the judging preference and *flexibility* and *adaptability* for perceivers. Paul is a strong judger and stated, "I like the idea of someone throwing me a surprise party, but I want to be prepared for it." He also wrote, "I live by my planner. I take it everywhere, even parties." In contrast to Paul, a perceiver probably would not have a planner or would be like Kari, who said, "I bought a calendar diary but just do not bother to use it!" In the workplace, colleagues of these two extremes can have difficulty getting along. The judging person would probably view the perceptive individual as disorganized or flighty, whereas the perceptive one could become frustrated with a perception of an overly organized and inflexible coworker. An appreciation of both in the classroom can be made. Judgers give reminders of due dates, times, and schedules, and perceivers readily adjust to any deviation!

Think about which of the preferences in each of the four categories sound most like you and then elaborate on these in Reflections and Applications. Combining two or more preferences provides even more insight. For example, you can come up with your temperament type (Keirsey and Bates, 1978) by doing the following.

1. Determine your preference in the second category (either S for sensing or N for intuition.)
2. If it is S, pair it with your preference in the fourth category (either J for judgment or P for perception). Your temperament type is either SJ or SP.
3. If it is N, pair it with your preference in the third category (either T for thinking or F for feeling). Your temperament type is either NT or NF.

See if the following description of your temperament type is accurate.

- SJ is orderly, dependable, and realistic; expects others to be realistic; strives to belong and contribute; is conservative, well-organized, and can easily be critical of mistakes.
- SP is flexible, open-minded, willing to take risks, highly negotiable, hungers for freedom and action, can be indecisive, lives for the moment, and does not like to plan or be hemmed into a definite plan.
- NF is empathic, highly responsive to interpersonal relations, keeps in close contact with others, sees possibilities, searches for meaning and authenticity, gives and needs praise, and may be overly swayed by feeling.
- NT is responsive to new ideas, hungers for competency and knowledge, works well with ideas and concepts, is not always aware of others' feelings, and likes to start projects but may not follow through.

Learning styles can also be examined using other combinations (McClanaghan, 2000). Which style seems most like you?

- ST wants specific information, knowledge of what's right and wrong; does better in a structured environment and learns best from repetition, drill, memorization, and actual experience.
- NT wants solid evidence and reason; does better when challenged and allowed to be creative; is skeptical, analytical, and logical and learns best when allowed to be independent.
- SF wants material to have personal relevance; does better in a harmonious setting where there is cooperative learning; learns best by talking and being involved in group activities.
- NF wants to see the "big picture" as well as possibilities, patterns, and connections; does better in a flexible, innovative setting; is bored by routine and established learning procedures.

How strong your preference is will affect how closely you match any of the preceding descriptions. For example, if you have a strong preference for both sensing and thinking, the ST learning style will likely sound just like you.

Interesting research is conducted with the MBTI. A study revealed that even though women in the general population tend to be feelers, women in executive-level positions often have a thinking preference usually combined with intuition; however, NFs made up 31 percent of the group (Daugherty, Randall, and Globetti, 1997). Can you think of reasons why an N preference would be useful?

A college library or counseling service may have a version of the MBTI you can take, or you may have an opportunity in a class or workshop. The book *Please Understand Me* (Keirsey and Bates, 1978) offers a questionnaire that yields scores in the four categories. Remember that with any measurement the results may vary for a number of reasons. Taking the test more than once and being honest in answering the questions will give you a more reliable profile. The four preferences together become a **psychological type.** Remember that being an ENFP does not mean you do not have and will not use the other preferences of ISTJ. For example, you may have a strong preference for using your right hand, yet you can also use your left.

Personality typing indicates your strengths and comfort zones; in certain situations, you are wise to use the lesser preference. For example, in the world of work, you will likely use more thinking and judgment, and in your personal life, the feeling and perceiving preferences lend themselves to warmth and enjoyment. The extent of the difference between the two will influence your degree of ease in various personal and professional situations. If the two preferences are close, you probably are comfortable using either one. In some cases, all four preferences will be extremely strong as in the case of Chad, a definite ISTJ. He agreed to share the following.

> All clothes in my closet hang in a particular order on white plastic hangers. Dress pants, because they are worn the least, hang together followed by sweat pants, then jeans. In the center of the bar are empty hangers separating the pants from the shirts. I have exactly as many hangers as I do articles of clothing. There would be no point in having extra hangers in my closet. Next to the empty hangers are white T-shirts, then casual shirts and dress shirts. At the bottom of the closet are two laundry baskets; one is for colors, and the other is for whites. I also have a system for clothes that are not in my closet. All my boxer shorts are numbered on the inside tag. I wear them in the right order so they will wear out evenly and can be replaced at the same time.

Even if this sounds unlike you, what thoughts and behaviors are indicative of strong sensing, thinking, and judging preferences? Chad also said that he cannot believe many of the "stupid" things people do and then added, "It is a good thing I am so introverted because I just think this and do not say it!"

Remember that the MBTI is not intended to pigeonhole people or arm them with excuses for certain behaviors (e.g., "I cannot help that I am disorganized. I am a P" to which I would respond, "You also have a J preference into which you can shift"). Reading books on the subject will give further ideas for using this understanding in career, marriage, parenting, and leadership situations. Can you recognize how personality was creating hardships for the individuals in the examples at the beginning of this section? Carlos is extraverted, and his job does not allow him to be in contact with people. Connie is more sensing, whereas her instructor appears to be intuitive. The marriage is in trouble because Rich, who has a thinking preference, and Jamie, who prefers feeling, do not understand each other. Knowing more about your personality can help you make wiser choices and maximize your potential. By understanding your own personality type and that of others, you can draw on your strengths and appreciate and grow from the differing gifts of others. Remaining open to and understanding differences will lead to enrichment.

How Does Gender Influence Your Life?

How would your life be different if you had been born the opposite sex? This may be difficult to imagine and possibly even distasteful. Years ago when I asked students to react to this, I received a quick, loud response from a 37-year-old man: "It makes me sick to think about it!" His reply demonstrated an attitude I was planning to discuss later with the class and made a salient point more dramatically

---

REFLECT AND APPLY

Reflect

♦ *How is your personality similar and/or different from five years ago?*

♦ *Recall two "parent" messages, a time when you acted from your "child," and a decision you made through your "adult."*

♦ *Think of an acquaintance, friend, or family member who has a personality different from yours. Does it bother you? If so, can you relate it to the personality preferences identified in this chapter?*

Apply

♦ *Ask a friend or family member to describe your personality. See how it compares to your description of yourself.*

♦ *Give two positive strokes to someone within the next 24 hours.*

♦ *Shake hands with your less preferred hand. How does it feel? The feeling is somewhat like you probably feel when behaving according to a weaker personality preference.*

♦ *Try to think or act in an opposite way from one of your personality preferences.*

---

than I could have otherwise that a perception exists that being male is preferable to being female (Reflect and Apply).

Gender Differences

Over several years, more than 3,000 students have been asked the question, "How would your life be different if you had been born the opposite sex?" (Hanna, 2003). Following are the categories most often mentioned with a general explanation of the differences imagined by the men and women.

Career choice.   This area was by far the most commonly mentioned. When considering being raised male, women would have made a different career choice, had an earlier pursuit of career, put more emphasis on career, and realized a definite increase in financial assets. Some felt they would be more restricted: "I would have been forced to take over the family farm or business." Men indicated that, as women, they would either have a different, stereotypic female career, slow advancement, or no career at all! "I would be more sheltered and let others take care of me" and "I would just go out and trap a rich guy!" were two male observations. One man said, "Maybe I would really do something different and be a doctor!"

Education.   Women said they would have gone to college earlier, finished earlier, attended a more prestigious college, and planned their education on the basis of future earning power. One woman said, "I would have been forced to achieve more from my education all the way through because I would need it to earn a living." Men mentioned the option of not going to college, and a few said that, if female, they could not have afforded further education.

Sports and other activities. Although opportunities in women's athletics have increased since legislation passed in the 1970s, women still maintained that they would have been involved in a wider variety of sports. Men, conversely, would have been less involved. One outstanding female basketball player remarked, "I may have taken a shot at playing professionally. As a female, there was not much of an opportunity for that." Another woman said that, as a boy, she would not have been a cheerleader. She added, "But I would have had to really be into sports." A distinct difference was mechanical. Women were sure that they would know more about automobiles and other machines. And a young man said, "As a female I would not know anything about a car. I would just expect a man to handle it!"

Household tasks. A definite difference was clear in this category. Males, if raised female, would do more housework and cooking and no outside chores. Women would move out of the kitchen and into the garage and yard. Most females said that they would be paid more for allowances. One man stated, "I got more money for mowing the yard than my sister did for doing dishes."

Marriage and child raising. Several women said that they would have married later or not at all if they had been men. The men envisioned being married, having the role of housewife, and being the primary parent. One male reply was, "I would probably have married young, been married two or three times, have lots of kids, and be looking again for someone to support us!" "If male, I would not have custody of my children," said a divorced woman.

Self-esteem and self-efficacy. Both sexes viewed women as placing a lower value on themselves and having less confidence. An older female student said that she would have had higher self-esteem earlier in life and would not have wasted her talent. Another woman reported that her family favors boys: "Boys are very special, and they know it." However, a disadvantage to men was also noted. A woman said, "I would be under a lot more pressure and have more stress. I would probably die younger thinking I had to handle everything."

Independence and assertiveness. Both sexes perceived men as more independent, self-sufficient, assertive, and in control of their lives. One woman said, "I would have more guts." Two other comments from women were, "I would not be taken advantage of" and "My needs would come first." A female with disabilities said, "I would have a harder time being handicapped because as a female, it is easier to ask for help." More evidence of the stereotype of the nonassertive female is found in a book first published in 1975, *The Assertive Woman* (Phelps and Austin, 2000). Can you imagine a similar book written for men? As you will learn later, both sexes can benefit from assertiveness; yet, the attention is usually on women.

Emotions. The stereotype of men as unemotional, unfeeling, and in control came through repeatedly. Both sexes mentioned that being female meant being more sensitive, aware of feelings, and expressive. One man said, "I would not have gotten spanked for crying when I was young." Women were seen as more fearful by both sexes.

Gender-Role Stereotypes and Development

If a woman has difficulty imagining any difference in her life, I ask, "Do you plan to marry?" Most say they do. "Will he take your name?" I have yet to hear a "yes." Most individuals have not given the question much thought; after they do, this difference is apparent. Because of a desire to keep a family name alive, for professional reasons, or simply because of personal preference, women may want to keep their birth name, yet few do. In a national sample of married persons and of their married offspring, only 1.4 percent in the main group and 4.6 percent of the offspring made a nonconventional last name choice. Those who did were ones who married later in life, were better educated, were more career oriented, and held more liberal gender-role values. Additionally, the marital naming choice of the mother had a strong effect on her daughter's choice of names (Johnson and Scheuble, 1995). Whether female or male, if you were the opposite sex; would name changing make your life different?

Name changing came up in a sociology class. Impatiently, a young man asked, "What is the big deal anyway? It is just a name." Yet, when asked, "Then would you take your wife's name?" he quickly shook his head and said a definite, "NO." Another student interjected, "Then it *is* a big deal, isn't it?" Calling the name problem for married women a clumsy mess, Lance Morrow (1993) noted that if men were to wake up one morning and find themselves transformed into married women, most would insist on continuation of their name. Hyphenation maintains both names; however, men do not usually use a hyphenated name. Gloria Steinem (1992) comments on the path from "Mrs. John Smith" to "Mary Smith" to perhaps "Mary Jones" as becoming independent much like slaves became free and gradually assumed different names from their masters. The practice of women taking the husband's name does come from a **patriarchal** (male-dominated) marital history. The tradition is still strongly supported in actuality, although attitudes are more flexible. One can question whether the sexes are equal until couples at least seriously consider this issue.

Other differences are in the areas of finding an intimate partner and physical attractiveness. Women pay far more attention to both. Romance novel readers are predominantly women. Magazines for teenage girls have almost no articles on career success and financial independence; instead, the themes are beauty and dating. In a study, half of the fourth-grade girls said they were dieting. One girl said, "We do not expect boys to be that handsome. We take them as they are." Another added, "But boys expect girls to be perfect and beautiful. And skinny" (Kilbourne, 1995, p. 395). An observational question regarding a difference: "Have you ever seen two heterosexual females dancing together? What about heterosexual males?" We do tend to make distinctions in appropriate behavior on the basis of biology alone. A logical "why" remains a mystery.

Avenues to Prestige—Does Biological Sex Matter?

What are the leading avenues for prestige? Significant gender differences emerged for 14 out of 15 respondents (Suitor and Carter, 1999). The main findings were:

- **Males:** Sports, grades, intelligence
- **Females:** Physical attractiveness, grades, intelligence

Turn to the personality activity in Reflections and Applications and answer the questions related to gender role. You may be surprised that your life, too, would have been different.

Thinking about how one's life would be different reveals a great deal about perceptions and the limitations created by stereotypes. A **stereotype** is a preconceived idea or belief, often a generalization, about an identifiable group. Stereotypical expectations and behaviors related to being female or male have influenced your life and continue to do so. Some of these are so subtle that they go unnoticed and yet have an impact.

Studies of male–female differences have been numerous in the last 30 years. A classic study (Maccoby and Jacklin, 1974) addressed both actual and perceived differences and encouraged researchers to explore gender, an aspect of self that had been virtually ignored. Gender-role development is covered in most introductory psychology and sociology courses and is frequently offered as a separate course in colleges and universities. **Gender** refers to the meanings that societies and individuals attach to being female and male. Even though popular and research-based usage suggests that *gender* and *sex* are synonyms, social scientists separate the two and define **sex** as the biological division of humanity. **Gender identity** is an individual's emotional and intellectual awareness of being either male or female, whereas **gender role** consists of personality characteristics, attitudes, behaviors, and expectations about femininity and masculinity. Even though our images of feminine and masculine typically are physical ones, when thinking about gender, femininity and masculinity refer to personality traits and behaviors that are culturally determined. Gender is best thought of as independent of a person's biological sex (Doyle and Paludi, 1998). This is makes sense because both feminine and masculine traits make up a well-adjusted personality.

Explanations of gender differences focus on learning. Sociologists believe that **socialization,** the process by which individuals learn their culture, is instrumental. See the following "Socialization and Sex Differences" discussion, regarding two recent versions of the socialization explanation. Psychologists also credit the environment as a source of learning through observation and conditioning. Sandra Bem (1993), in explaining gender-schema theory, says that we view the world through "the lenses of gender" and develop cultural female or male scripts. As an example, in a study of professional men, Hispanics had significantly higher masculinity scores than non-Hispanics, which coincide with the Mexican and Latin American value on self-confidence, courage, and masculinity or what it means to be macho. Interestingly, the Hispanic males had self-acceptance scores that were significantly lower than other males (Long and Martinez, 1997).

Encouragement and discouragement regarding emotional behaviors and the tasks/activities of children play an important role in gender-role development. One student said her brother's only household task was to take out garbage. "My mother even cleaned his room, and now his wife does it!" Humorous or pathetic? Clearly, parental influence is of utmost importance. A recent study found that girls devote more time to household tasks while high school males spend more time on extracurricular and leisure activities. Girls work longer hours in both unpaid and paid labor (Gager, Cooney, and Call, 1999). The field of cognitive psychology emphasizes thoughts and processing of information. Young children begin to make distinctions between what is masculine and feminine and then act on these distinctions. Years ago, I taught in a preschool language-development program and knew little about gender roles. One of the activities involved categorizing toys into a boys' pile and a girls' pile. Almost every child by the age of 3 could do so without hesitation. This grouping carried over into their actual activities. Seldom did a little boy venture into the play kitchen, and then it was usually to ask what was for dinner! Have things changed? Certainly, children are being exposed to a wider variety of toys and activities today. Yet notice how toys are categorized and even how greeting cards are displayed in stores. Gender stereotypes are reinforced in a variety of ways.

Socialization and Sex Differences . . . Two Newer Versions

Why is he less emotionally supportive than she is? Could it be?

- *Different cultures account:* Because of socialization, women and men end up in two different emotional worlds or cultures. A man may not offer emotional support in the same way; however, he and his male friends are satisfied and feel "comforted."
- *Skill specialization account:* Women and men share one culture. Because of differences in socialization, females develop emotional support skills. Males are lacking in skills that lead to emotional support (Kunkel and Burleson, 1999).

Any difference between females and males is more pronounced if children are raised stereotypically. For example, consider two young children with skinned knees. Both begin to cry. Terri is hugged and consoled, while Terry is scolded for not being brave. Learning theory emphasizes the rewards, punishments, encouragements, and discouragements that humans receive.

The Way It Was

Which of these norms described by a 50-year-old still exist?

- For school dances, the girls made the decorations while the boys got on the ladders to put them up.
- At the dance, the boys were expected to risk rejection when they requested a dance while the girls waited and tried to look appealing but uninterested.
- At church events, only women worked in the kitchen.

Controversy exists as to the influence of biology on gender. Studies of cognitive skills yield certain "on average" differences between females and males that do not point to a smarter sex or to the fact that such contrasts are permanent (Halpern and Crothers, 1997). As in all of human behavior, biology has a role. Gender behaviors are undoubtedly the result of an interplay between nature and nurture. Important to keep in mind is that studies indicate only generalities and do not take into account the variations within large groups of males and females. Differences resulting from social and cultural expectations tend to fade if individuals are not bound by stereotypic gender roles and, in fact, there are more similarities between men and women than there are differences. No matter how gender role developed, your personality, behavior, and aspirations have been influenced by it. Of value now is to become aware of your thoughts about your own gender role and that of the opposite sex. How have perceptions influenced expectations of yourself and your behaviors? How do they affect your relationships? Are you stereotypic or not?

Disadvantages of Stereotypic Gender Roles

Conforming to gender-role stereotypes has several disadvantages. Both men and women suffer from a rigid perception of roles. As evidenced by the earlier student responses, men are generally regarded in a more positive light by both sexes. Thus, many women may behave like the weaker sex and feel inferior. When asked what sex they would prefer if they could have only one child, 42 percent of Americans said a boy compared to 27 percent who indicated a girl. This preference for boys has not changed much over a 60-year period and is even stronger than it was in 1997 (Simmons, 2000). Surveys taken by students include reasons for a sex preference that follow stereotypic thinking. "I want a girl because they are so cute and cuddly" compared to a boy preference because "He would carry on the family name and be a protector to his siblings." The book *Reviving Ophelia* (Pipher, 1994) is an excellent wake-up call regarding adolescent females and our "girl-poisoning culture."

> Girls today are much more oppressed. They face incredible pressures to be beautiful and sophisticated, which in junior high means using chemicals and being sexual. America today limits girls' development, truncates their wholeness and leaves many of them traumatized. (Pipher, 1994, p. 12)

Cases of wasted female talents are evident at all ages. Skills are not used because of lack of confidence or reluctance to move beyond the stereotype. A bright young female student disclosed that she had always wanted to become a physician. She was settling for a career as a medical assistant, she said, because her fiancé was in school too, and she needed to work to help pay his tuition. "He doesn't really want me to go to medical school," she reported. This reluctance to develop a self-supporting career puts women at risk during at each stage of life. Only 50 percent of working women have retirement plans, and more than 80 percent of retired women are not eligible for pensions. Is it any wonder that 75 percent of the elderly poor are women? (*Women in Business*, 2000). The **feminization of poverty,** the increase in the number of women and often their children who are poor, is a tragic result of relying on someone else to take care of them, as women have traditionally done. A woman may not end up among the poor; however, hundreds of thousands of divorced women in their sixties are forced to stay in the workforce because they cannot afford to retire, according to the *New York Times* (*Omaha World-Herald*, 2001).

- Women earn less than men—76 cents to the dollar.
- Women spend 11.5 years out of the workforce caring for children.
- Only 30 percent of women are in jobs that earn pensions.
- Women live longer.
- Women comprise most of the low-income or no-income population (Goodman, 2001).

Even when women excel, they have found it difficult to achieve top positions. In 2000, women made up only 12.5 percent of top positions in *Fortune* 500 companies. Ironically, bosses rated female managers more highly than male managers in 16 of the 20 skills areas (Choi, 2001). A male author (Farrell, 1986) warned women: "The beauty-focused woman who depends on men to 'tow my car,' 'pick up my packages,' and 'pay for the dates' pays a high price for her dependence on men and becomes less happy the older she gets" (p. 76).

Men, too, have suffered. Pressures to achieve and to be the primary bread-winner have caused undue stress. In a tragic situation in Lincoln, Nebraska, a middle-aged man killed his family and himself. He had been depressed because of his financial difficulties and what he perceived as his inability to support his family. "Men pay dearly for the privilege of dominating" (Keen, 1991, p. 42). Depression in men often is ignored because it is perceived as unmanly; then, without treatment, it leads to extreme individual and relationship pain (Real, 1997).

Although the exact cause is unclear, men have shorter life expectancies. In the United States, a woman can expect to live about 5.7 years longer than a man (National Center for Health Statistics, 2001). Two enlightening books, *Why Women Live Longer Than Men . . . and What Men Can Learn from Them* (Crose, 1997) and *How Men Can Live as Long as Women* (Goldberg, 1993), explain reasons for this, ranging from biological theories to stereotypic behaviors. Do you know men who resist help until their symptoms or pain is acute? Women visit doctors 30 percent more often than men (Swartzlander, 1998). Stereotypic men if they view health-giving behaviors as feminine, would seemingly be at higher risk. Women tend to be more in tune with their bodies, seek more professional help, engage in more preventive health measures, have less destructive health behaviors, and take less risk (Crose, 1997). More men than women get cancer; they also more often die from cancer and adapt less favorably to a cancer diagnosis (Nicholas, 2000).

Another reason for an earlier death stems from aggression. Male violence is destructive and clearly poses a threat to physical and emotional health. The common message for "real" men is to be tough, physically aggressive, and violent when necessary damages psychological health (Brooks, 2001). "The blueprint for masculinity is a blueprint for self-destruction" (Farrell, 1986, p. 17).

Aside from health and mortality, men, like women, can be restricted and limited. In certain situations, they feel forced to behave not as they want to but to satisfy the stereotype. They go into unsatisfying careers and are deprived of certain activities for fear of ridicule. One man said that he was an excellent volleyball player and would have liked to have been on the high school team. "It never went beyond a secret desire. Volleyball was considered a girl's sport, and I would have been the laughingstock of the school." A good point to consider is that women who increasingly take on additional roles in their personal and professional lives have an advantage over a stereotypic male who lives only a provider role. Multiple roles allow us to be productive throughout our lives, which is conducive to sound health (Crose, 1997). In contrast, a stereotypic man is ill prepared for retirement because it denotes the end of productivity.

In addition, men generally are not raised to be nurturing and expressive, which can lead to physical and psychological problems and deprive them of close relationships with others. A stereotypic man is much less likely to be comforting, to value comforting skills, or to be emotionally supportive (Kunkel and Burleson, 1999). Men generally do not create adequate emotional intimacy when they are not in partnership with a significant other; because of this, they can suffer from lack of social support (Vandervoort, 2000). One woman shared her greatest wish as wanting to be close to her dad and to have him verbalize and show his love. "He keeps saying that he just can't show it. He does not know how because men aren't like that." The belief that "men aren't like that" plays itself out in repressive behaviors that can be destructive. Anger and despair that build up in men can result in both homicide and suicide. Men who cling to macho images of invulnerability, power, violence, and dominance are at risk (Crose, 1997). The typical male way of coping with stressful events appears to increase men's risk for coronary heart disease (Weidner, 2000).

Because men have long been dominant, what is considered masculine is viewed as worthy. In higher-prestige occupations, masculine personality attributes were found to be necessary (Cejka and Eagly, 1999). By contrast, feminine traits are devalued. For example, women who develop stereotypic masculine personality traits such as independence are praised; not so for men who reflect the softer feminine side of nurturance and warmth. This leads to a devaluation of what is considered female. Wendy wrote in a paper on gender: "As a girl, at times it was "cool" to be a tomboy; other times we learned it was better to dress up. We could show both sides and be accepted; that was not the case for boys."

Her point that males have fewer socially approved gender-role choices is well taken. In addition, as times have changed, men have become targets of negative stereotyping and "male bashing." One young man commented, "It is considered out-of-line to put women down but really funny to degrade men." Although "turning the tables" may please some, such behavior only polarizes the sexes and will not bring about gender equity. William Pollack, author and faculty member of Harvard Medical School, stated, "The stereotype of men as bad without any virtuous pieces is not right. It is time to stop arguing about which is the better half and to look for what is good in both" (Rios, 1993, p. 6).

Does it seem reasonable to continue gender stereotyping? The answer would seem to be a resounding "no." Assigning people to roles because of their sex makes no more sense than assigning them to play positions on a football team based on their shoe size (Worchel and Shebilske, 1989). Because bipolarity and stereotyping ultimately hurt everyone, what is fair and reasonable is to recognize that, psychologically, we are much more similar than dissimilar and to proclaim and live out our full human potential.

Benefits of Androgyny

Androgyny, a blend of positive masculine and feminine personality traits, will result in a better balanced individual. Sandra Bem (1974) challenged the idea that a person has to be either masculine or feminine in personality traits and behaviors and suggested that strongly sex-typed individuals might be seriously limited. Her research indicated that stereotypically feminine women were limited by being less independent and assertive, whereas masculine men were less playful, warm, and responsive. Even though stereotypic individuals would have benefited from different behaviors, they resisted. In contrast, androgynous men and women coped more effectively with diverse situations (Bem, 1975). Androgynous (from *andro,* "male," and *gyne,* "female") behavior allows for flexibility. Responding to the demands of a situation is more practical than adhering to the restrictive behaviors of a stereotype, and valuing all positive behaviors regardless of their appropriateness for one sex or the other is advantageous to society (Doyle and Paludi, 1998).

Androgyny in early research was found to be related to a number of positive qualities and outcomes. For example, in love relationships, androgynous individuals scored higher on verbal expressions of love and nonmaterial evidence of love and were more tolerant of their loved ones' faults and more likely to express their feelings than feminine or masculine individuals (Coleman and Ganong, 1985). "It is not macho men and feminine women who make the best lovers, at least not as love is measured in this study" (p. 174). Families with one or more androgynous parents scored highest in parental warmth and support, and the researcher (Witt, 1997) maintained that parents who wish to be gender-fair and encourage the best in both their sons and daughters would benefit from an androgynous personality.

In recent years, androgyny and how it is measured have been challenged, mainly because naming polar opposites as masculine and feminine may defeat androgyny's original purpose, which was to promote a blend of characteristics (Hoffman and Borders, 2001). Instead, researchers are now focusing on concepts of **instrumentality**—traits related to competence, accomplishment and self-sufficiency—and **expressiveness**—traits associated with warmth, nurturance, and communication. A cross-cultural study conducted in Singapore supported the value of both instrumentality and expressiveness in human beings (Ward, 2000). Another study demonstrated that the use of qualities associated with both reported more positive outcomes (Stake, 2000).

A female student described her own path to androgyny.

> Self-doubt came from years of my mother's coaching: "Stephanie, get a job in a hospital so you can marry a doctor" or "Stephanie, become a stewardess so you can find a pilot to marry," or "Stephanie, put on your makeup because your looks are all that count." My response today: Well, Mom, I am going to be the doctor or the pilot. I'm not going to watch others achieve while I sit on the sidelines and put on makeup!

Good news for androgyny is a study in which 60 percent of the males and 63 percent of the females identified with nontraditional gender roles (Dawson-Threat, and Huba, 1996). To make positive changes, a person needs to realize how stereotypic or androgynous she or he is. Check yourself by responding to the personality questions in Reflections and Applications. "We are all pioneers in this era of loosening and changing gender definitions to fit human needs rather than to reinforce masculine and feminine stereotypes. It is both an exciting and a threatening time" (Goldberg, 1979, p. 275).

Becoming Assertive

Because nobody is born assertive, we all share the challenge of developing a learned set of behaviors. **Assertiveness** includes maintaining one's legitimate rights, choosing for self, and expressing genuine thoughts and feelings in nonthreatening ways. Assertive behavior promotes equality, and people can exercise their personal rights without denying the rights of others (Alberti and Emmons, 1995). In contrast, **nonassertive** or **passive behaviors** allow others to be in control and always choose. Essentially one denies the self. Also opposite of assertive are **aggressive behaviors** when a person tries to control and choose for others. An aggressor enhances the self at another's expense.

How does one develop assertiveness? You can begin with attention to body language. Do you sit, stand, and walk with assurance? The way that you listen and speak indicates a great deal about your level of assertiveness. You will learn communication skills in later chapters of this book. Deciding that saying no is healthy is a primary step. Other cognitive techniques are also helpful. Ask yourself, "What is the worst thing that will happen if I say no? How does that compare to what happens to me when I say yes and resent it?" Then continue to think, "What if the person is angry with me because I say no? How bad will that be?" Keep telling yourself that you have the right to say no. Once you have decided to learn to say no, behavioral techniques are useful. Practice how you will say it. Of course, you can just say the two-letter word, but most people feel more comfortable with other kinds of statements, such as these.

- I have decided not to take on any more obligations.
- I would like to say yes; however, this time I am not going to.
- I want to spend more time with my family, so I'm not going to get involved with any more outside activities right now.
- I have been doing some time management work and prioritizing, and right now other things are more important to me.
- Thanks for asking; however, I am not going to participate now.
- Believe it or not, I am really going to say no.

Note that you are not using the word "cannot," which is usually inaccurate. Making up an excuse is generally not as convincing as the truth. It is your choice as to how much to explain. You do not owe anyone a reason, although offering a statement of fact can make saying no easier. "I have not felt well lately, and I am not taking on any additional responsibilities" is brief and clear. By speaking the truth and saying that you do not want to or you will not, you are being assertive. A primary key to assertiveness is the use of "I" statements. Do you see how each way of saying no clearly speaks for itself and is not hostile or aggressive? Effective assertiveness is usually courteous, kind, and gentle. At times saying no can be the greatest act of love (Buscaglia, 1992).

You can decide to give an indefinite or a limited no by saying no now and indicating that you might reconsider in the future. "I do not want to have any responsibility in the fall fund-raiser; however, I may help out next spring." If possible, anticipate the other person's response. You probably know some people who will accept your reason without argument. On the other hand, you may have relationships with people who have a hard time accepting no for an answer. With this latter group, you are wise to fortify yourself. One idea is to acknowledge their persuasive abilities and still be firm. "I know you are a hard person to say no to, yet I am going to do it this time."

Check your own assertive behavior by responding on the personality activity in Reflections and Applications. Assertiveness may not be one of your needed changes, although professionals agree that because no one is born assertive, almost everyone can benefit from skills training. Whatever you desire, within

REFLECT AND APPLY

Reflect

◆ *How would your life be different if you had been born a person of the opposite sex?*

◆ *What is the first stereotype that comes to your mind for females? Males? Come up with an example of a female and a male who do not fit these stereotypes.*

◆ *Do you posses any androgynous behaviors? If yes, what are these?*

◆ *Are you generally aggressive, nonassertive, or assertive? In what ways?*

Apply

◆ *Observe examples of stereotypic and nonstereotypic gender-role behaviors.*

◆ *Ask some engaged couples if they have discussed name changing after marriage. Whether they have or have not, ask what they plan to do in this regard.*

◆ *Behave assertively in a personal or professional situation.*

reasonable parameters, can be accomplished. Understanding what you are all about, how you developed to this point, and what you can do to improve can turn a desire into reality. The choice is yours! (Reflect and Apply).

LOOKING BACK

- The core of self is your personality, the unique combination of qualities and behaviors that only you possess.
- Personality is influenced by both heredity and environment.
- Major theories in both psychology and sociology explain personality development.
- Erik Erikson linked personality to social development and identified eight psychosocial stages.
- Challenges to personality development are possible for a number of reasons that include being a racial/ethnic minority or an adopted child. Especially challenging because of heterosexism is forging one's identity as a gay male or lesbian.
- Personality over a life span is marked by both consistency and variation.
- The TA framework can help to understand yourself, others, and your interactions. Three ego states compose the personality. The four life positions are perspectives on life, with the preferred I'm OK, you're OK seen as a healthy orientation. A script is a personal design of life. Strokes are positive or negative, verbal or nonverbal behaviors. Types of strokes influence one's script and life position.
- The MBTI can be used to understand personality by identifying preferences in four areas. One deals with extraversion and introversion, which are important in social interaction. The other areas are related

to gathering information, making decisions, and dealing with the world. The four combine to form a personality type.

- A perception of your gender role and how you view the opposite sex are valuable. Masculinity and femininity are learned as part of one's culture. One's gender role influences personality, behavior, and expectations. Stereotypic behaviors are disadvantageous for both sexes.
- Androgyny, a blend of positive feminine and masculine traits and behaviors, has positive effects. Instrumentality and expressiveness are especially useful to well-adjusted human beings.
- Assertiveness is a set of learned behaviors that helps people maintain their legitimate rights and express thoughts and feelings in nonthreatening ways. Being assertive can improve self and relationships.

EXPLORING VALUES AND MAKING WISE CHOICES

LOOKING AHEAD

After completing this chapter, you will be able to

- Define and evaluate values and list sources.
- Identify and give examples of the methods and influences in receiving and learning values as described in values programming analysis.
- Explain the decade theory of values development and relate it to at least two decades.
- Describe and give examples of reasons for a change in adult values.
- Define morals and discuss Kohlberg's theory of moral development.
- Discuss reasons for ridding oneself of poor health habits and engaging in safe, sound practices.
- Define goals, explain their importance, and relate the three ego states to goals.

> *All values, when pushed too far, become demonic and destructive. Beliefs not examined, as the life not examined, are hardly worth having. Values held thoughtlessly are without substance.*
>
> —Charles Stephen

Following is a series of questions designed to help you examine your thoughts and feelings about various aspects of your beliefs. Indicate your degree of agreement or disagreement with the following statements by placing the number that most closely indicates your value next to each statement.

1. Strongly Agree   2. Agree   3. Ambivalent   4. Disagree   5. Strongly Disagree

_____ I would lie to another person.

_____ I would withhold hurtful information from a loved one.

_____ Spending time with family members is important to me.

_____ High grades are important to me.

_____ If a cashier gave me too much change, I would give the money back.

_____ I often do favors for friends.

_____ I would break a law.

_____ I have exceeded the speed limit while driving my car.

_____ I would drink alcohol even though I was under the legal age limit to drink. (Note that the last two are lawbreaking behaviors!)

Your answers to these questions reflect your **values,** which are qualities, conditions, and standards that are desirable, worthy, and important. Values are directly related to the kind of person you are and will be, as well as to your goals and aspirations, beliefs, behaviors, and the quality of your relationships. Even though choices, decisions, and courses of action are based on them, rarely are values examined. You may know your values. Do you also know how they came to be and how they may change? Are your behaviors in harmony with what you value? Do you realize the impact that values and relationships have on each other? This chapter will offer insight and suggest ways to clarify your values and to achieve wellness and success.

Values

Values determine behaviors or modes of conduct. Once a value is internalized it becomes, either consciously or unconsciously, a standard for guiding actions and making choices. Because values are at the basis of choice, the choices people make reflect their perception of what is right, just, or cherished at a particular time.

We all have a number of personal and professional values. In certain situations, it may become apparent that some of these values are in conflict. For example, a health care provider may value life. He or she may also value the alleviation of pain. As a rule, these are not conflicting values. When working with a terminally ill patient a conflict may arise. By providing intravenous fluids, the patient's life is sustained but pain is prolonged rather than alleviated. When individuals are challenged and their values conflict, they may find it necessary to reexamine their values. Through this reassessment process people may acknowledge that, under certain circumstances, it is possible to hold values that are inconsistent with one another. For example, health care providers are unlikely to come to the conclusion that they should stop valuing life or the relief of pain based on their interactions with a terminally ill patient.

Challenging situations may arise that will lead people to conclude that their values have changed. Early in their careers, health care providers who value life may do everything humanly possible to prolong a person's life. Over time, however, their experiences may lead to a subtle shift in their values. If they begin to value the quality of life, rather than life as mere existence, there may be a change in their interactions with and feelings toward terminally ill patients. They may no longer experience the emotional struggle they once did when the decision is made not to resuscitate a patient.

This change in values over time often is a result of changing life experiences. Recognizing these changes and understanding how they affect one's actions and behaviors is the goal of the values clarification process. Values clarification will not tell you what your values should be; it simply provides the means to discover what your values are.

For the purpose of values clarification, Roths, Harmin, and Simon (1966) identified seven criteria that must be met if a value is to be considered a full value. These criteria can be divided into three categories: choosing, prizing and acting. To be a full value, the value must be chosen freely from a list of alternatives, only after thoughtful consideration has been given to the consequences of each alternative. The value must be cherished and made known to other people. The value must also be translated into behaviors that are consistent with the chosen value and integrated into the lifestyle.

Criteria for a Full Value

- *Choosing:* choosing freely from alternatives after thoughtful consideration of the consequences of each alternative
- *Prizing:* cherishing, being happy with the choice and willing to affirm the choice publicly
- *Acting:* doing something with the choice, doing something repeatedly in a consistent manner

Where do Values Originate?

You and I were not born with a set of values. An individual cannot be understood apart from the context in which he or she grows up. Family, friends, classmates, and our own desires all affect the choices we make. Remember parent messages from transactional analysis (TA)? Most values originate as verbal or nonverbal messages from others. We learn the values of our culture through socialization. Parents' values determine both the outcomes they want for their children and their parenting behaviors. Your values will affect your parenting behaviors just as your parents' values influenced how you were raised and what kind of person you are today. Parental expectations are important for young people. Growing up in your family you become aware of what your parents and other family members expect from you. You may not always be consciously aware of these expectations because they become so much a part of your own value system. For example, many parents value education and assume that their children will continue their schooling after they graduate from high school. Their children make plans for college but may never have independently made the decision to attend. Family expectations often have a positive influence on children and choices they make, but if parental expectations are too strict or inflexible, young people may rebel.

Institutions within a society are other sources of values. Although some people oppose formal instruction regarding values in the classroom, everything a school does is value laden. The written rules, the rules that are enforced, the dress code, the rules of conduct, and the manner in which people treat each other will all relay a set of values to the students. Even if no values development programs exist, teachers, counselors, and coaches do convey values. Peer pressure, the need

TA Revisited

"Parent" messages tell you what is of value. For example, "A dollar saved is a dollar earned," "Take your vitamins," "Get good grades," and "Work hard and play later" are value-laden messages. Nonverbal messages also continue to be influential. Did your parents always buckle their seat belts? Did they attend church? Were your friends accepting of others who were different? What messages regarding values do you receive from the media?

The "child" ego state can motivate you to act according to your values. For example, the value you place on friendship is usually expressed emotionally from your "child." It can also tempt you to act against your values. The passionate "child" in each person can put sexual morals to the test. The "child" also feels guilt when values are not acted upon and feels pride when they are.

The "adult" plays an essential role by questioning values embedded in the "parent," looking at alternatives, and making choices on the basis of your own thinking process. The "adult" can choose to retain, modify, or reject a value.

to be accepted by people in your age group, is significant. Peer pressure can lead students to do things they might otherwise not do in order to gain acceptance and approval from others, even if their actions are contrary to the values in the home. If you were brought up in a home where religion was valued, your beliefs and values were modeled by its tenets. A societal function of religion is to convey values. Another powerful source of values is the media. Messages from television programs and advertisements are geared to appeal to our self-image. An example is the value portrayed in the media on looking younger. Your experiences have influenced your values and will continue to do so. For example, if you frequently seek and receive the support of friends, you likely place a high premium on friendship. If you have been hurt by dishonesty, you probably value honesty.

After looking at "TA Revisited" think of times in your life when your behavior did not reflect the values in your "parent" ego state. For Julio, religion was an important value as it had been for his parents and other influential people in his life. One week he was exhausted from a full schedule of work and classes; he overslept and missed the worship service. He could hear an inner voice admonishing him for sinning. The "parent" essentially serves as a conscience; as such, it is capable of creating guilt or in directing us in positive ways. Can you think of times when your "child" helped you act on your values? How about situations when you were greatly tempted by the wants of the "child"?

Have you used your "adult" to question and evaluate the values you have? You may be wondering why that is important. Let's assume that many of your values reflect those of your parents. Their values were possibly acquired from questionable sources and definitely developed during an earlier time in different environments and situations. Conflicting ideas can come from "parent" messages. "Our family values human equality and goodwill toward all people," you may have been told. Then you came home with a new friend of a different race and received a different message. Because personal values direct your life and could possibly influence the next generation, taking a critical look at them is advisable.

One of the best things we can do for ourselves is to take a look at our values and ask ourselves if they really fit who we are, or are there some values we practice just because we are expected to follow them. Is it a carryover from the past that we have accepted without any critical investigation? (Satir, 1978, p. 113)

Another critical answer to this question that values only become your own after "adult" evaluation and processing. How do you know when this occurs? A way to check is to ask yourself, "Why do I believe or value this?" Henry, at age 75, attends mass every week without fail. One of his grandchildren asked him why he went to church even when he wasn't feeling well. He replied, "You are supposed to, so I do." Henry's value on religion and church attendance is based in his "parent." His wife, Helen, goes to church regularly, and she explains, "I value my religion and enjoy going to mass because I feel spiritually fulfilled afterward. I can miss and feel fine, too; however, I prefer to attend." Do you see the difference? Helen's value is an "adult" value. When values become yours, they feel comfortable and are easier to act upon.

Any evaluative process can be challenging, and people typically experience discomfort when confronted with possible change. If your values came from someone whose support is important, any deviation is difficult. Processing, however, is in your best interest. "Neither pride nor self-esteem can be supported by the pursuit of second-hand values that do not reflect who we really are" (Branden, 1992, p. 41). New thoughts and beliefs expand your horizons and encourage you to become your own person.

How Do Values Develop?

After recognizing the source of values, the next step is to look at the ways values are acquired and transmitted. Think of your life as you read this section.

Developing Values

In the videotape "What You Are Is What You Were When," Dr. Morris E. Massey points out methods and influences at different age periods. He calls this **values programming analysis.** Think about your own life as you look at Table 3-1 and read about his ideas.

TABLE 3-1	Receiving and Learning Values	
Chronological Age (approximate)	*Method*	*Influence (who/what is most influential)*
1–6	Imprinting	Family, especially parents and significant caregivers
7–12	Modeling	"Heroes" and "stars," usually those in the media
13–19	Socialization	Peers

Early years.   The first stage reveals the importance of early childhood. The earliest method of receiving values is **imprinting.** Think of making an imprint of your foot in wet sand or imprinting a design on a shirt. Imprinting of values means that young children do almost no editing and receive values as absolutes. You may be thinking of a 2-year-old who balks at what you say. "Eat your vegetables. They are good for you," a parent says. "No," is the typical reply. "I hate vegetables." Is the child rejecting the idea? Follow that same child to the day care center and listen as he or she tells others, "You're supposed to eat your vegetables. They are good for you. My daddy says so." The message registered. Do you know people who eat everything on their plate even if they aren't hungry? Ask them why, and the response may be, "I was told to do it. I have done it all my life. You are supposed to." They are hanging onto a powerful early idea.

Little children are open to the values of people they trust and love. Think about this when you choose caregivers outside your family. Of all considerations, one of the most significant is the values these caregivers can instill. Preschool children regard their teachers as "supreme beings." "Teacher says that is why" is a frequent comment. Try to recall early messages related to values. "Our first map is usually made up of the one right way" (Satir, 1978, p. 112).

Middle years.   The second stage is **modeling.** The family remains influential; however, the child is looking outward, away from home. The role models could be older children, teachers, and local sports leaders; however, the primary influence comes through the media. Because of the popularity of television, this stage may begin earlier than age 7 and overlap with the first. The principal role models are those in the entertainment industries (movie and television) and the sports world.

In 1982, columnist Sydney J. Harris wrote about these models. He described a study in which 2,000 eighth-grade American students were asked to name their top 30 heroes, the people they most admired and would want to be like when they grew up. Their leading role model was the screen actor Burt Reynolds, followed by entertainers and actors Richard Pryor, Alan Alda, Steve Martin, Robert Redford, and the late John Belushi, who died from complications of a drug overdose. All 30 were entertainers or sports figures. Harris wrote the column because he was concerned that not one of the 30 individuals listed had made a humanitarian contribution to the world (although some had been involved in worthy causes). He said, "Our heroes and heroines are not people who have done big things, but people who have MADE IT BIG" (p. 6).

In a survey replicating Harris's work, 114 Nebraska elementary school students in 2001 were asked to name their heroes (Hanna, 2003). Even though they most often named athletes (32) and entertainers (15) for a total of 47, family members were listed by 41 children. Parents led the family list. Of the "stars," Sammy Sosa was named most often. The obvious and most common reason was his ability to play baseball. However, one child added: "He seems nice and respectful." Other answers given for admiring an individual are worth savoring.

- "I admire my mom because she doesn't smoke or get drunk so I hope I do not when I grow up." "I admire my dad because he wants to keep our family safe and cares about us."

- "Jesus because he is nice and does not sin. He is a very good person who didn't like killing or violence. I am kind of like that. I hope I will be nice and go to heaven like him."
- "I would want to be myself because I do not want to act like someone else. I want to be my own person."

The survey reveals that children admire family members and others, yet continue to be enamored with "stars." Parents' understanding of star power can be used in positive ways. "It is a good idea to use important people to deliver messages. Parents tell us this all the time, and we do not listen," said one young girl. Can you remember some of your own idols from the preteen years? What did they represent, and how much influence did they have?

Teen years.   "Everyone else is doing it, so I want to do it too" typifies the next step in values programming analysis. The stock answer from generations of parents is, "If everyone else jumped off a cliff (or bridge), would you do it too?" Frankly, a teenager might! Encouragement, discouragement, and modeling are included in this method called **socialization,** the same term sociologists use for the lifelong process of learning the culture.

The adolescent period is a time of searching for an identity. Feeling a part of the group is critical. A **peer group,** composed of people of similar age with whom one identifies, has great influence. In a review of research about antisocial behavior and social failure, peer affiliations during childhood appeared to be related to choices during adolescence (Henry, 2000). This period of life can be a frightening, stressful time for both teenagers and parents. The young person will likely experiment with "in-vogue" behaviors and attitudes. Cigarette and alcohol use is strongly related to peer norms, substantially more so than with parental involvement (Olds and Thombs, 2001). Not surprising, 89 percent of adult smokers began in their teens (*Health,* 1997). Perceptions of whether their peers are sexually active appears to be related to teenagers' engagement in sexual intercourse. Adolescents have a strong preference to either act like their peers or believe that their friends are like themselves (Nahom et al., 2001).

If the peer group reflects most of the parents' values, this period can be relatively easy. This is a time when teenagers challenge parental values. Parents can make this an easier time by being understanding and flexible. Expecting a teenager to uphold all parental values and ideas if they are opposite those of a normal peer group is asking for supreme sacrifices and potential damage to self-esteem and the sense of belonging. According to at least two experts (Steinberg and Levine, 1997), adolescents generally choose friends whose values, attitudes, tastes, and families are similar to their own. A study of adolescents showed that academic success and intelligence are their most important life concerns (Tiggemann, 2001). Also helpful is to be aware of the findings from "The State of Our Nation's Youth" (2001) survey. A majority of teenagers said that there is no pressure to look a certain way, have sex, use drugs, or drink alcohol. Instead the pressure was to get good grades. Future success was defined by 84 percent as having close family relationships, and nearly all said they could confide in a family member. The report concluded that today's youth seem to be grounded and striving.

TABLE 3-2	Decade Theory of Values Development		
Birth Decade	**10-Year-Old Decade**	**Significant Events**	**Influence on Values**
1920s	1930s	The Great Depression	Conservation of money and resources
			Strong work ethic
			Government seen as an aid to the citizens

Parents who remember the issues and problems in their own teenage years are more apt to be understanding and supportive as their children seek their own identity. Teenagers can help by trying to understand themselves and their parents and by being reasonable. Parental values are not necessarily wrong just because of their ownership, and rebelling just for the sake of being a rebel is neither mature nor healthy. Open communication and democratic discipline techniques (covered in later chapters) can make a major difference during this challenging time. Adolescents are more likely to make wise choices if they have parents who practice the values development techniques described later in this chapter.

Societal influences. According to values programming analysis, children at about the age of 10 become more aware of events, issues, and trends in the world and begin to incorporate these into their value systems; these continue to influence values throughout life. Because the model is divided into 10-year periods, think of it as a **decade theory.** Table 3-2 outlines one decade and one event. Think about issues during and since your 10-year-old decade. Do you recognize how they have affected you? Looking at various decades will also help you understand why people of other ages have dissimilar viewpoints. "Now I know why my grandmother does some of the crazy things she does!" exclaimed one student. Her grandmother might say the same about her granddaughter if she knew about the decade theory.

Comparing specific decades is interesting. For example, the major event of the 1940s was World War II. People who were 10 years old and older then are usually patriotic and, in many cases, fairly definite about right and wrong. The war demanded a united national effort, and almost all U.S. citizens had no question about the justness of their cause. Quite the opposite is true of the 1960s and 1970s, when the Vietnam conflict and the civil rights movement split the nation, followed by a sense of disillusionment resulting from the Watergate scandal and the resignation of President Richard Nixon. Thinking more in "gray" than in "black and white" and doubting the absolute rightness of a country or philosophy are more characteristic of individuals influenced by those decades.

What about 10-year-olds today? How might current issues influence their values? Because the world is figuratively at their fingertips due to mobility and the media, few happenings escape the minds of young people today. Unexplainable violence in schools and elsewhere, AIDS, controversy regarding abortion, concerns of minority groups, and equal rights are issues that will probably have effects.

Undoubtedly, the most influential event will be the horrific terrorist attacks on the World Trade Center and the Pentagon and the incomprehensible loss of lives that occurred on September 11, 2001. The graphic displays of this international tragedy impacted all of us. Truly, our lives are forever changed. Pause and reflect on the different possibilities in regard to values. We can be pessimistic or view this and other challenges as opportunities.

Young people have several alternatives. They can "cop out" and value only their self-interests, or they can decide to take action and do what they can to solve widespread problems. Being actively involved in society is as important today as it ever was. However, a 1998 national survey of first-year college students by the University of California, Los Angles (UCLA) found that just 27 percent believe that keeping up with political affairs is important, a decrease from 58 percent in 1968. One speculation is that students have a feeling of powerlessness. In comparing the 1960s to the 1990s, another possibility is that people get involved in politics when things are bad, not during times of relative contentment (Greene, 1998). Interestingly, an Internet Google search of college students and apathy came up with 179,983 "hits." Perhaps the threats posed by terrorism will activate many people. Regardless, a wise course for each of us is to value the moment because the future is uncertain and then to take action to make the future better.

Altering Your Values

After adolescence, values are established from imprinting, modeling, socialization, and societal influences. Other general influences explained in this section could also be involved. Although values could remain similar throughout the rest of life, most people will change. Let's explore the general influences on values that are most likely to occur from young adulthood through old age.

Major life change.   Just as stress is related to a major life event and change, so are an analysis and a possible alteration of values. At age 23, Joe valued health, sports, and bodybuilding. One summer day he was riding his motorcycle and had a terrible accident. He was left paralyzed from the waist down and confined to a wheelchair. After soul-searching and values analysis, he revised his emphasis on sports and bodybuilding so that he could participate, yet in a different way. Other values became important, and he began to help individuals with special needs.

An accident or injury is one type of major change. Others are birth of a child, loss of a job, divorce, or death of a loved one—any of the crises that will be discussed in later chapters. A change can motivate you to develop worthier values. Melanie was an adolescent, unmarried mother. She candidly talked about her values.

> At 16, I valued friends and good times. I partied a lot and did not care much about school or working; I just wanted to have fun. After Jason was born, I changed my whole way of thinking. Because of him, I realized how important it is to take care of my health, get some education, and learn to support us. I am a new person, and I like who I am.

Figure 3-1   Having a baby is likely to change one's values.

Mental unrest. Exposure to new ideas can cause you to think more deeply about your beliefs. You may question them and experience mental unrest. This can happen within a formal learning experience. Tony took a sociology class and became aware of different ideas regarding equal rights. Kelly began to question her strict religious upbringing after studying philosophy and religion in college. In informal ways such as reading a book, talking with people who have different beliefs, traveling, and watching television you glean new information. Having a closed mind to new ideas will make learning less likely; however, most people are open enough to at least wonder.

Changes in wants. Values will probably be altered as you and what you desire change. If you just want to have fun during a particular phase of life, your values will be different from those you will need to succeed in a career. Values can vary as statuses and roles change. A business owner is apt to adjust values and think differently than he or she did as an employee. New parents almost always alter some values. Mike told his classmates, "If you believe that having kids will not change your values, just wait. Their presence just forces you to change." Commonly, one value will take precedence over another. Sara had always valued her social life but then she was diagnosed with an autoimmune disease that required long-term rest. She put her own health ahead of her desire to go out with friends. A change in priority does not mean a rejection of a value; the emphasis just shifts (Fig. 3-1).

Evaluating Your Values

The likelihood that you will experience a major change, mental unrest, and different wants during a lifetime is extremely high. For this reason, flexibility is necessary. Having a strong value system does not necessarily mean upholding the same values throughout a lifetime. Instead, it includes the ability to process and evaluate. Well-adjusted people understand that they may discard, modify, add, and change values or their relative importance.

Sherri, who had valued marriage, traditional suburban life, and a lovely home, found her life dramatically changed when her husband divorced her. She was no longer married, was no longer a part of traditional, couple-oriented suburban life, and was unable to make house payments. Flexibility allowed her to change her priorities and to develop new values in order to survive. Independence, education, and career emerged as high values. Lack of flexibility has definite drawbacks. Inflexible values tend to make individuals judgmental.

The more we adhere to any system, the more this belonging will be limited to others who believe as we do. We even see our children as "bad" if they don't follow "our" way. (Glasser, 1984, p. 85)

Close relationships have been threatened and even destroyed by people's unwillingness to adjust their thinking. Inflexibility and certainty can also stifle learning.

> When we think we are absolutely right, we stop seeking new information. To be right is to be certain, and to be certain stops us from being curious. Curiosity and wonder are at the heart of all learning. The feeling of absolute certainty and righteousness causes us to stop seeking and to stop learning. (Bradshaw, 1998, p. 8)

Practicing flexibility rather than rigidity seems justified.

If you were asked to assess a value, what criteria would you use? Even though values are not necessarily positive or negative, it's helpful to evaluate yours as healthy or unhealthy (McKay and Fanning, 2000). What's the difference?

Healthy Values Are . . .

- Owned
- Realistic
- Behaviors that promote positive outcomes
- Life-enhancing

After you have read through the words that describe healthy values, think deeply about each one. Do you own your own values or are you living by the values of someone else? Ask yourself why you chose the career field you did. Why did you marry, or why will you marry? Until a careful analysis is done, people are unaware of how their behavior might be based on someone else's "should." This is the reason that processing values through your "adult" is so essential.

Are your values in touch with reality and apt to foster positive outcomes? One student wrote on an assignment, "I do not believe in divorce, no matter what." I posed some questions to her such as, "Even if you were being abused? Even if your children were being abused? Even if the person became a despicable individual who was involved in all kinds of unethical behavior?" She thought and then replied, "I had not even considered those possibilities, and in those cases, I certainly would not hold fast to that value." She was able to realistically look at situations and understand that her value could result in negative outcomes. Then flexibility allowed her to change her mind.

If a value does not enhance life, it likely restricts it. An example would be to value another person in such a way that you allow him or her to rule your life. "I will not go back to school because he wants me to stay home" is life-restricting. Conversely, life-enhancing values encourage you to do what is nourishing.

Freedom is destroyed by restrictive, rigid values. Adopting a broad-based approach to values is advisable. This means that instead of having set answers to all moral dilemmas, using an evaluative process when confronted with a conflict is recommended. Ask questions such as, "Are the behaviors I choose likely to harm others or myself? What are the probable consequences? If pain is a possible side effect, does the outcome warrant it?" Critical thinking about values is healthy.

Values are personal, and you may be more comfortable with absolutes. If so, at least consider options and the healthy values criteria that have been recommended. Being flexible allows you to accept different ways of thinking and to develop respectful relationships with people who are different from you. How different individuals respond to specific circumstances underline both the differences in our values and the difficulty of establishing or maintaining some degree of ethical commonality among all citizens.

How Do Morals Develop?

Morals are related to rightness or wrongness and are more specific than values. Because values and morals essentially guide your life, you can benefit from knowing how they evolved. **Moral judgment,** or a sense of right and wrong, was traced by Kohlberg (1963), who presented short stories with moral dilemmas to individuals and then asked them what they thought the characters should do. Kohlberg was more interested in discerning the reasoning behind the answers than the actual answers.

Kohlberg identified three levels of moral development that were each composed of two stages. An ability to process, evaluate, and possibly modify values is related to the level at which individuals make moral judgments. First is the *preconventional* level of moral development when rewards and punishments are most impressive. This is obvious in ideas expressed by young children: "I will not take her toy because the teacher will send me to the time-out area." *Conventional* is the second level; individuals at this level conform because of social disapproval from peers or authorities. "I will take her book because the other kids think it's funny to tease her." Many adults are still at the conventional level. "I laughed at the racist joke because I wanted to be a part of the group" is an example of this kind of thinking. Authority is respected, and a law is a law and should be obeyed. Research shows that many people never progress beyond the conventional level (Conger and Peterson, 1984). Using the healthy values criteria discussed in the last section requires a person to move beyond this level.

The *postconventional* level is the highest level of moral development. Those at the first stage of this level follow democratic laws. They generally behave according to societal rules, yet see the arbitrary nature of laws. If they see a law as unfair, they usually work to change it. Few people reach the later stage in which individual principles take precedence; universal ethical ideas can supersede a law. Examples of such individuals are Mahatma Gandhi, Rosa Parks, and Martin Luther King, Jr., who followed their own consciences and defied laws that they considered unjust.

Consider the following example and apply Kohlberg's three levels of moral development.

The fundamental ethical issue regarding assisted suicide is whether acts by physicians that help others kill themselves (or let others die) can be morally justified, not whether these acts should be legalized. Those who believe assisted suicide is morally prohibited maintain that it is impermissible for a doctor to kill a patient and that a defensible distinction exists between killing a person and letting a person die who may exist is actually irrelevant to the question of whether assisted suicide can be justified. Advocates of assisted suicide note that it is generally agreed that killing is justified under some conditions—for example, in cases of self-defense. Therefore, they argue, correctly applying the label "killing" or the label "letting die" to a set of events does not, by itself, indicate whether an action is acceptable or unacceptable. Instead, supporters argue, rightness and wrongness depend on the justification underlying the action.

Medical ethicists agree that physicians may forgo treatment when a patient or the patient's authorized representative refuses treatment. Valid refusals justify a physician's decision to "allow" a patient to die when the patient could be kept alive with treatment. Supporters of assisted suicide believe that some acts of assisting in bringing about death can be framed similarly to refusals of treatment. Such actions could then be justified by a request of the patient. They contend that a patient's request for a fatal medication is analogous to a patient's refusal of life-sustaining medication. However, the traditional view in professional medical ethics is that a request for assistance in dying by a competent patient does not have the same authority and obligatory force in law and morality that a valid refusal of treatment has. Therefore, such a request does not justify an action of physician-assisted suicide.

Major medical professional organizations—including the American Medical Association (AMA) and the Canadian Medical Association (CMA)—maintain that physician-assisted suicide is not justified by a patient's request under any circumstance. However, this conclusion is controversial. Others believe that whether physicians are either morally permitted or morally required to honor requests for direct assistance that will lead to death depends on the nature of the request and the nature of the patient–physician relationship.

One of the most critical issues underlying the question of justified killing in medicine is whether the act of assisting persons in bringing about their deaths causes them a loss or a benefit. If a person chooses death and sees that event as a personal benefit, then helping that person bring about death may neither harm nor wrong the person and may provide a benefit. On the one hand, avoidance of intentionally causing the death of patients is a deep and primitive restraint encouraged by many reservations that society has long had about killing innocent persons. To change this perspective would seem to be sweeping and dangerous. Opponents of assisted suicide fear that doctors will become less committed to saving lives, that families may respond to financial pressures by subtly encouraging suicide, and limitations in the resources of the health care system might dictate decisions of life and death. On the other hand, some people question whether physicians should be restricted by law and morality if they may benefit patients in ways other than just by healing and providing noncurative pain relief (Beauchamp, 2004).

Another aspect of this topic is the participation of doctors or anesthesiologists in executions. "Doctors should not help put inmates to death by lethal injection or work with the legal system to ensure condemned inmates feel no pain at execution," the president of the American Society of Anesthesiologists told his colleagues (*Lincoln Journal Star*, 2006d).

Even though Kohlberg's theory is widely accepted, it has critics. Noting that his study participants were all men, Gilligan (1982) broadened the concept of morality to include meeting the needs of others and caring—behaviors that are more often associated with females. Another limitation to Kohlberg's study is that the participants only represented one culture (Baron, 1998). A strong value in other cultures is obedience to authority. Moving beyond this way of thinking is extremely challenging and Kohlberg's theory would not necessarily be a fair way to assess moral development in those cases. Nevertheless, think about yourself in relation to these levels and, especially, ponder the "why" of your moral decisions.

How are Values Developed?

While it is interesting to examine how values and morals are received, it is just as valuable to examine transmission of values. As you read this section, ask yourself:

- How did your family convey its values?
- If you are or become a parent, how will your values impact value development of your child(ren)?

Traditionally, adults have used two distinctly different ways of imparting values, neither of which is recommended. **Moralizing** is the direct, although sometimes subtle, transmission of the adult's values to young people (Simon, Howe, and Kirschenbaum, 1991). Assuming that the adult has experienced life and knows best, moralizing is telling others to believe and value what the moralizer believes and values. Delivery of values comes from the parent ego state. The controlling "parent" states definitely what is of value and how life should be lived. "A well-paying job is essential, so go out and find one" is the command. The nurturing "parent" delivers essentially the same message in a different manner: "Now, honey, you know how nice it is to live comfortably, so you really need to find a well-paying job." Indirect messages are also possible: "I will bet John's parents are really proud of him. He got a well-paying job last week."

Moralizing is common. Parents, teachers, members of the clergy, and administrators are among those who use direct, commanding statements to tell others what is important. Even friends can moralize: "Jessica, you should break up with Jacob. He is not going to amount to anything." As common as it is, moralizing is often ineffective and can generate resentment on the part of the recipient. Why? One reason is that each of us is unique, and moralizing takes away our individuality. What is good for one person may not be for another. As the decade theory shows, people are influenced by events that occurred at different times in history. What might have been a worthy value for a grandparent or parent may not fit in today's world. Another problem is that a moralizer may have questionable values. Can you think of someone who loudly champions some questionable viewpoints? A child becomes confused when parents say one thing, teachers say another, and the media offers a third. Furthermore, the words and behaviors of a single moralizer may not mesh, so that a young person is left hearing and seeing two different things. "Do as I say and not as I do" is a common refrain of moralizers because they often have a hard time living up to their words.

Reactions to moralizing provide added reasons why it is not recommended. People exposed to moralizing can rebel, or they might passively and obediently follow strong leaders. They also are handicapped by an inability to think for themselves. "I think that's been my problem for years," said a 30-year-old student. "My mother always told me what to do; I did not make decisions for myself. My mother is dead, and I have a hard time trying to decide what to do about most things." In contrast, I enjoyed what a newly divorced student wrote, "I think that some people believe I need to rely on my family because they are all I have now. I have news for them, I have ME, and that sounds good!" (Fig. 3-2).

Figure 3-2

The opposite means of transmitting values is by a **laissez-faire method,** which means "hands off" (Simon, Howe, and Krischenbaum, 1991). The young person is left to discover values without leadership or guidance. "Go out and find your own way" is the message. This approach is not recommended because, quite simply, children need guidance. Young people do not want adults to run their lives; what most youth seek is help. Children who suffer from a values vacuum float at the mercy of circumstances and situations (Eyre and Eyre, 1993).

Recommendations for Values Development

What does work? Most agree that a warm, stable, and loving family setting is most conducive to values development and controls (Megargee, 1997). The following suggestions are likely to lead to worthy values and specific behaviors that enable an individual to make life-enhancing decisions.

Set a positive example.   The message of "Do as I say, not as I do" is not likely to produce desired results. People are more influenced by behavior than words. Modeling the values you want to see in others is extremely important. This means that if you want someone to value health, first examine your own health habits. If education is of value, make sure you are broadening your own level of knowledge. Parents who are pursuing college degrees are sending powerful messages to their children of the values of education, hard work, and pursuit of worthy goals. Be aware that modeling can work in a negative way. A study of children showed that children's tobacco and alcohol use was associated with parental use (jackson et al., 1997). What you do as a parent definitely makes a difference.

Encourage the values you think are important.   Offer praise when someone demonstrates one of your values. **Positive reinforcement,** presenting a pleasant stimulus that strengthens a response or behavior, is not used nearly as much as it could be. Instead of waiting to criticize when others don't measure up, give credit or praise when they do. "I am proud of you for telling your teacher the truth," "I like it when you share your possessions," and, in the workplace, "I appreciate your loyalty to the company" are powerful motivators. Give rewards to show your approval. Even though you may simply expect others to behave morally, showing appreciation doesn't hurt and is usually reinforcing.

Teach and guide.   Instead of teaching and guiding, moralizers tell individuals what to value, which is a much less effective technique. Teaching opportunities regularly present themselves. For example, watch a television show with children and then discuss situations that require moral reasoning and judgments. Ask questions and encourage them to express their opinions. "The lyrics of that song are immoral, and I won't let you listen to it," says a moralizer. A teacher or guide would ask, "What do you think about those lyrics? Do you see any potential harm from listening to them? What do they say to you? What do they say to younger children?" You can eventually express your own opinions *after* encouraging an open, free discussion. Chapter 8 presents a positive way to do so.

Giving options to younger ones and explaining why other choices are not allowed is instructive. With adolescents, rather then telling them what to do, first discuss the situation and then guide them toward understanding the values you think are important. They may persist in different ideas, yet your chances as a teacher and guide are better than as a moralizer. At times you may feel compelled to try to prevent certain behaviors by children; however, do so only *after* you have been open to their opinions.

> Children need limits. They need guidelines. They need them for their security, and they need them for their survival. One can teach with respect, or one can teach with intimidation. One can speak to a child's intelligence or to his or her fear of punishment. One can offer a child reasonable choices within sane and comprehensible ground rules, or one can lay down the law (Branden, 1983, p. 136).

Allow a person's own experiences to teach.   Do you remember learning from your mistakes? Consequences of behavior are among the best teachers in the world. Michelle was slow and nonchalant about getting ready for school. After weeks of begging and nagging Michelle to be ready on time, her parents, who took turns driving her to school, left the house one morning at 8:00 A.M. Michelle walked to school in a rainstorm, was late, and suffered the consequences. The problem was solved because she discovered firsthand the value of punctuality. If she had not gone to school, other consequences would have taught the lesson. Most individuals are influenced by consequences.

Instill a value of self.   Of all the values a parent can inspire in a child, a most important one is the value placed on self. Parents do not help children by doling out false messages and treating them in ways so that unwarranted self-worth develops.

Instead, motivating children so that they develop healthy self-esteem is a precious gift. Already covered in Chapter 1, the value of this type of self-esteem cannot be overemphasized. Although most students acknowledge this, "self" rarely appears when they are asked to identify their five top values, whereas friends, family, and others are listed by almost everyone. You may need to remind yourself how important it is to value yourself so you can show genuine and healthy regard for others. "Self-esteem is one of the most powerful forces in the universe. Self-esteem leads to joy, to productivity, to intimacy. That is why I advocate a value system that promotes self-esteem. Self-esteem is like faith: it can move mountains!" (Burns, 1989, p. 115).

Emphasize universally acceptable values.   Throughout history and in almost every society, humane values such as honesty, integrity, kindness, generosity, and love have proven their worth. Today's world cries for values of freedom, peace, and diversity. Children and adults can learn to assess their values in terms of outcomes. Does a value spawn behaviors that are beneficial both to the practitioner and to those on whom they are practiced?

Encourage thinking for oneself.   Critical and creative thinking requires a questioning mind. Parents too often stifle children's questions either because they do not want to answer or because they just don't like being questioned. Children who are fearful about questioning a parent grow into adulthood afraid to ask, which interferes with learning and the ability to make wise decisions. Often parents react negatively when a child disagrees with their opinions. Rather than rigidity in thinking, a realization that life is full of many rights and

---

REFLECT AND APPLY

Reflect

♦ *Think of some "parent" messages you have received that are related to values.*

♦ *Give an example of how you were influenced and by whom in each of the three values programming analysis stages.*

♦ *What are some recent events, issues, and trends that will probably influence the values of young people?*

♦ *Recall a moralizing statement you have received or given.*

Apply

♦ *Look through a newspaper or newsmagazine and find an example of a story that can influence values.*

♦ *In Reflections and Applications for Chapter 3, answer questions about your own values development.*

♦ *Use one or more of the recommendations for values development with a friend or family member.*

♦ *List two or more of your values. Then check each in terms of the criteria discussed in this chapter: ownership, realism, promotion of positive outcomes, and life enhancement.*

numerous ways of thinking, not of absolute sets of right or wrong options, is beneficial. "Things are not usually all good or all bad, all right or all wrong. Life is just not that simple. The answers and solutions we seek usually lie somewhere between the opposites" (Buscaglia, 1992, p. 9; Fig. 3-3).

Learning to Choose Wisely

Choices set the stage for decisions. **Decision making** means to select one alternative from various possible courses of thought or action. Because change is involved, decision making is usually stressful, and some people resist or have difficulty making decisions. Keep in mind that indecision, or not making a decision, is a decision. Seeking closure too early may be problematic; however, at some point, decisiveness is in order. Knowing how to make any decision has value in reducing stress and putting you in charge of your life.

Figure 3-3   Learning to value differences is highly desirable in a diverse society.

Understanding your MBTI personality preferences, as covered in Chapter 2, helps to know your strengths and weaknesses in making decisions. Combining two preferences can be used to describe decision making as follows.

- Sensing-thinking (ST) focuses on verifiable facts and then makes judgments by impersonally evaluating the facts. Decisions are usually practical and matter-of-fact.
- Sensing-feeling (SF) focuses on verifiable facts and then makes decisions by weighing values and considering others. Decisions tend to be sympathetic and friendly.
- Intuition-thinking (NT) prefers a variety of possible solutions and then selects by impersonal analysis. Decisions are likely to be logical and ingenious.
- Intuition-feeling (NF) recognizes a wide range of possible solutions and decides by weighing values and considering others. Decisions are generally enthusiastic and insightful.

You may want to call on others who are strong in your weak area. For example, because Jessica's personality preference was "feeling," she had difficulty keeping her personal values detached from business decisions. A colleague with "thinking" strength provided logic. The preferences may annoy one another. Those with a judging preference are apt to experience stress until a decision is made; therefore, they often decide or press for a decision fairly quickly, whereas perceivers enjoy keeping options open and will change their minds more easily. Those who are both intuitive and perceiving will have numerous ideas and will delay making a final choice. This can be interpreted by others as stalling or being wishy-washy.

Taking Control of Your Health and Well-Being

Choosing wellness is the first step in getting rid of unhealthy behaviors and preventing disease. Motivation comes from being informed on health issues. If you truly value yourself, you can make wise choices. Ask yourself how healthy you want to be. In Chapter 6 you will learn about many health risks and how to make healthy choices.

Regardless of personality preferences, we can all benefit from learning the process of decision making. Six steps can be spelled out with the acronym CHANGE (Olson, DeFrain, and Olson, 1999).

The Change Model

- **C**ommit yourself to a specific goal
- **H**abits—break old and start new
- **A**ction—take one step at a time
- **N**ever give up—lapses may occur
- **G**oal oriented—focus on the positive
- **E**valuate and reward yourself

Achieving Goals

In order to have a successful life, the first question is how you define success. If you describe yourself in the future as "a success," what will you be like and what will you have done? Then it is time for decisions and choices regarding what you want and how you become successful. A **goal** is a specific and measurable accomplishment to be achieved (Rouillard, 1993). Nobody doubts that in order to do much of anything, a person has to be motivated. **Motivation** is the energy or force that activates and propels an individual in the direction of an activity or a particular goal.

Decades ago, three social motives were identified (Murray, 1938). **Achievement** is accomplishment or carrying through to a successful end. Achievement motivation is highly correlated with grades and grade-point averages (Chiu, 1997). Even though

---

TA Revisited

"Parent" is full of shoulds, shouldn'ts, do's, and don'ts and often tries to push for quick decisions.

"Child" has its wants that influence decisions and will be swayed by emotions.

"Adult" analyzes the issue, sees and considers alternatives, and decides on the basis of reason and logic.

Decision making deserves attention and study. As with other life skills, you have probably received little formal training in how to evaluate choices and make decisions. Because we must make so many decisions in life, an essential choice is basic: Do you want to take charge of life or let life be in charge of you?

achievement is typically related to education and career, in all endeavors, individuals vary considerably in their motivation to achieve. A coach described a female basketball player as "the most determined person I have ever worked with" and "an individual who with less ability than many has achieved more than most." Who or what has been influential in terms of your achievement motivation? The other two social motives are **affiliation,** associating or connecting with others, and **aggression,** defined as behavior designed to intimidate or harm. Obviously, connecting with others in a positive way is a motivation that is strongly encouraged and emphasized in this book. Similarly, learning to channel your aggressive tendencies into constructive actions and more desirable behaviors is a worthy goal of interpersonal relations.

An employer speaking to a career development class said, "Human beings will if they want to and will not if they do not. I want employees who are motivated to work and will be enthusiastic about it." Thinking about what motivates you is worthwhile, and you might be asked about this in a job interview. If you are someone who is self-motivated by the thrill of accomplishment or the pride of achievement, you're ahead of the rest. Once a person is motivated, a major decision is in order: How do I get what I want?

Jason stifled a yawn in the career planning class. "We are going to discuss and set goals," the instructor announced. Several other students looked bored. Jason thought, "If I have heard this once, I have heard it a thousand times. I am only 20, and I am already sick of goals. Is there a new way to approach this?" Jason would be pleased to know that there is by using the transactional analysis ego states. Did you receive messages about goals from your parents, teachers, and counselors? The idea of even having goals was originally a "parent" message: "You should have goals." "You will never amount to anything without goals." A student put it so well: "When I got out of high school, all I knew was that I had to get 'there,' wherever 'there' was, and it did not sound like fun." Although their importance is realized, goals may seem tedious.

Even the language underlying most goals is "parent" language. How many of these sound familiar? "I should lose weight." "I ought to be on time." "I must get a job." Is it surprising that so many goals are not achieved or even acted upon? Restricting them to the parent ego state makes them boring and dreadfully task laden. Harris and Harris (1985) wisely recommend that getting the child ego state involved makes a positive difference. A first step is to allow yourself to dream; let the "child" out without restrictions from "parent" or "adult." Get rid of the "parent" language and let the wants flow! A want is fun and spontaneous. The emotion within the "child" is motivating and energizing. The "icing on the cake" is enthusiasm.

> *Enthusiasm is one of the most powerful engines of success. When you do a thing, do it with all your might. Put your whole soul into it. Stamp it with your own personality. Be active, be energetic, be enthusiastic and faithful, and you will accomplish your objective. Nothing great was ever achieved without enthusiasm.*
>
> —Ralph Waldo Emerson

How does the adult ego state get involved in goal achievement? Remember that the "adult" is the thinker that processes information and makes decisions. Your "adult" can look at your wants, determine how realistic they are, put them into order of importance, and then direct you in the process of achieving them.

It also helps in evaluating your goals and in changing them, if necessary. A goal may not be achievable, so the "adult" adapts and selects an alternative. It can also make sure that your goals enhance personal growth and well-being. What you become as you work toward a goal is of utmost importance.

Assess the goal.   Through your "adult" ego state, you can ask specific questions based on goal criteria (Walker and Brokaw, 1998).

- *Is the goal mine and not someone else's?* Can you think of some examples of trying to live another person's goal? Do you know anyone who is in college pursuing a degree only because a parent wants it? A characteristic of self-actualization, the pinnacle of human achievement, is to make growth choices rather than fear choices. Values based on what someone else wants are usually based on fear.
- *Is the goal in accord with my values?* Because values are powerful motivators, you will find the path difficult if you do not feel in harmony with what you believe.
- *Is the goal a priority of mine?* Goal overload is suffered by people who do not recognize honest human limitations. Can you achieve high grades, work full time in order to advance in your career, be an outstanding parent, build a successful marriage, develop close friendships, and serve as an organization's leader at the same time? A study showed that compared to students who worked 10 or fewer hours a week, those who worked 10 to 20 hours had lower grade-point averages (GPAs) and attendance, and those who put in over 20 hours a week were lower in GPA, attendance, and test accuracy (Lenarduzzi and McLaughlin, 1996). Human beings do have limits. The key is to concentrate on what you specifically want at any given time.
- *Is the goal realistic?* Sometimes the answers are obvious. Trying to lose 25 pounds in one week is not realistic. You could want too much or be shortchanging yourself. Look for challenges that you can manage.
- *Is the goal specific?* A common problem is to have a vague goal such as, "I want to be rich," "I want to travel," or "I want to be thin." Identify how rich you want to be, where you want to travel, and how thin you want to be. Then add a "by when" date to each (Fig. 3-4).

Figure 3-4
Source: ADAM @ HOME © 2006 by Universal Press Syndicate. Reprinted with permission.

Success in life is achieved by focusing on what you believe is important and acting in ways that move you closer to your goals. Once you have identified goals you would like to achieve, the CHANGE model developed by Olson, DeFrain, and Olson (1999) is a useful tool to help make the goals a reality.

Commit yourself to a specific goal. Put your goal in writing and post it where you will look at it daily. Goals that are floating around in your head stand little chance of being acted upon. Example: John set a goal to improve his grades by spending 45 minutes each evening on coursework.

> A goal shapes the plan.
> The plan sets the action.
> Action achieves the result.

People often do not get what they want because even a realistic goal can seem overwhelming. The first way to change this is to pinpoint, or set goals with realistic numbers attached (Schmidt, 1976).

Habits—break old habits and start new. Prior to setting his new goal, John attempted to study while watching a television program or movie. John decided that his new study routine would be to spend 45 minutes each evening at his desk, with the television turned off, working on coursework. John is taking specific action steps to create a study environment where he will be more successful in attaining his goal.

Action—take action one step at a time. John will commit to this study plan for one month. Doing something every day in the direction of a goal is important. John might consider keeping a journal or a log of time spent on each subject or assignment. By doing this he will be able to determine whether he has accomplished what he intended. The good feeling of accomplishment every time the goal is achieved will be a motivator to continue.

Never give up—lapses may occur. There may be days when studying for 45 minutes at one time is not possible for John. A temporary problem with one step in the plan will not defeat him unless he lets it. John could schedule two shorter periods of homework time one day and return to the original plan the next day.

Goal Oriented—focus on the positive. Acknowledging his successes and abilities to overcome temporary obstacles will keep John from reverting back to his previous study habits.

Evaluate and reward yourself. At the end of one month John will review his progress. John may notice that he is not only completing homework on time but also that he is participating more in class or taking the initiative to begin homework assignments early. With satisfaction that his goal has been achieved John has taken a step toward adopting a new pattern of academic behavior.

A worthwhile goal now is to do the activities related to getting what you want in Reflections and Applications. Consider a goal related to interpersonal skills and meaningful relationships. Happiness is created and esteem is built by striving toward worthwhile, reasonable goals with first-rate efforts. Any decision has a risk factor. Most people worry about making a wrong choice. Should I take this job or wait for a better offer? Would going to a community college be better than attending a university? Consider that for most decisions there is no absolute right and wrong. Whatever you decide will merely be a different course of action. When a mistake is made, you are wise to accept it and realize that this is necessary in any learning process. If you are not failing occasionally, you may not be taking any risks or charting new territory. View mistakes as information about what worked and what did not and as errors that can be corrected. You will not want to make mistakes on purpose; however, do regard mistakes you make as offering valuable insight.

> *Either you let your life slip away by not doing the things you want to do, or you get up and do them.*
>
> —Roger von Oech

Managing Your Time

Too much to do in too little time is a common challenge for almost everyone. The benefit of effective time management was evident in a study of college students as it had a greater positive effect on academic stress than did leisure time activities (Misra and McKean, 2000). A fallacy in our thinking is that we either do not have time or we will accomplish our tasks and goals when we have more time. The reality is that we will never have more time available than we have right now, which is 86,400 seconds each day. The key to achievement is time management.

How to Find Time

A constructive action is to keep track of exactly how you spend your time over a week. Angela's reaction was: "I was amazed at how much time I spent on the telephone with unimportant calls!" You will probably find small segments of time that can be saved and used differently. At work, can you spend a few less minutes at lunch or on break? Can you consolidate trips from one part of the building to another? Is it possible to shorten your telephone conversations? At home, can you give up a television program? How much time are you actually using for pleasure? Even though enjoyment is necessary, you may be indulging yourself more than you realize. Consider that just 30 minutes of time a day gains you about 183 hours a year, and by the time you are 70, cutting out those wasted minutes gains you over a year's time!

Even consciously increasing your rate of speed can save precious time. Rick walked to different parts of a college campus. "I doubled my walking speed, saved time, and in the process probably did something good for my health." In other activities, without realizing it, you may be taking longer than necessary. Becoming aware of this and then deciding that you can easily increase your speed are precious time-savers.

How to Eliminate Time Wasters

Do you spend a lot of time looking for misplaced items such as papers? Over a lifetime, the average person spends an entire year searching for misplaced objects (*Lincoln Journal Star,* 1998b). We benefit by being more careful where we place things. Taking precious time to organize a desk and file cabinet and then making sure to put items away can increase the amount of time you have later. Your own personality may be responsible for wasting time. Each of the preferences identified on the Myers-Briggs Type Indicator (Myers, 1980) has its own potential drawback, as follows:

- *E (extraversion):* Because energy is drawn from human interactions, those with a strong extraverted preferences may spend far too much time connecting with others. Also, the individual may be easily distracted by the activities of others.
- *I (introversion):* Living in an inner world and relishing introspective activities may result in time passing with no observable accomplishments.
- *S (sensing):* The strong sensor can become immersed in details and needless facts and figures and let a great deal of time go by.
- *N (intuitive):* Endless possibilities are usually in the mind of a person with a definite intuitive preference. Mulling over endless ideas can become overly time-consuming.
- *T (thinking):* Deep analysis is not usually done quickly. Strong thinkers weigh facts objectively and then apply reason to their decisions. These behaviors take time.
- *F (feeling):* Because they want to make everyone happy, people with strong feeling preferences agonize over any choice that might upset another person. Also, individuals with definite feeling preferences have a hard time saying no to requests, and doing for others does take time.
- *J (judging):* Although these people are usually well organized and skilled in scheduling, they may spend more time than necessary figuring out how to accomplish a task and not enough time actually doing it.
- *P (perceiving):* "Going with the flow" has its advantages; yet a strong perceiver is typically a procrastinator. Being laid back can mean that time passes, and when a deadline is on the horizon, these people are in trouble.

Being aware of potential pitfalls that stem from personality preferences allows you to use your weaker preference when that's in your best interest. A perfectionist is an expert time waster and is bound to be frustrated because no matter how hard he or she tries and regardless of the amount of time spent, perfection is impossible.

How to Use Time Wisely

What else can be helpful? You can find practical ideas in the book *Take Back Your Time* (jasper, 1999). Experts in time management offer the following tips.

Make use of self-knowledge.   Are you more energetic in the morning, afternoon, evening, or late at night? Unless you are getting adequate rest, this answer may not be obvious. "I am just not a morning person. Of course my going to bed at 1:00 or 2:00 A.M. may explain that!" said Jennifer laughingly. With enough rest, you will feel more energetic at all hours yet still have more productive times of day. Tackling the most difficult tasks during this time makes sense. Self-knowledge will tell you whether or not you work better according to a fairly rigid time schedule or if you favor flexibility (Knaus, 1998). If you have several tasks, which one do you undertake first? If you are energized by doing the easiest ones, that's the best choice. Conversely, you might opt to begin with the least pleasant or difficult ones in order to get them out of the way.

What physical environment works best? You may require a quiet atmosphere with few distractions or be more productive in the middle of noise and activity. What skills can you utilize to increase your productivity? For example, can you save time by typing a memo rather than handwriting it? What tasks are time-consuming for you? If you are slow at some tasks and speedier at others, you may be able to do some trading. For example, in their shared apartment, Chris cooked and Nate cleaned. Why? Each was more efficient at his designated task, and this saved them both time.

Use planning and scheduling to your advantage.   You may be well organized and an excellent planner. If so, you have probably already discovered what method works best, and if it is effective, you may skim this part! If you are lacking in this area, read on.

- *Decide whether to develop a schedule that is macro (bigger picture and longer span of time) or micro (more focused over a shorter time frame).* You can also create a schedule for both. For example, you may want to look at what to accomplish during a month (macro) or decide to focus on one day at a time (micro). Often people opt to maintain a weekly schedule. You can use a planner, a simple calendar, or just make a list.
- *Categorize what you want to do.* You may have "must-do" activities such as meeting with your supervisor or paying a bill. Other activities could be classified as either moderately important or unnecessary but nice to accomplish. Once you have the lists, you can select appropriate days and times. Other ways to categorize are by type of activity, goal, or subject, such as school, work, or household.
- *Plan efficiently.* If you take time to plan, you can often save both energy and time. Either the night before or early in the day, spending time looking ahead can reap benefits.
- *Be realistic and flexible.* A major problem stems from planning to accomplish too much. Having a reasonable perspective on task completion alleviates frustration and stress.
- *Reward yourself.* We typically forget to give ourselves a pat on the back for completing tasks. Instead, we fret about what we did not get done. Emphasizing our lack of accomplishment creates the illusion that our time management efforts didn't work.

People who are effective time managers avoid a great deal of stress. In order to succeed and enjoy the process, what is most useful is to manage time in a way that works for you.

LOOKING BACK

- Values are top priorities in life—qualities, conditions, and standards that are desirable, worthy, and important. They motivate behavior and affect all aspects of life.
- Assessing what you value and why you do is important in self-understanding and achieving your own identity; this is a lifelong process.
- Values originate from external sources. The three ego states play principal roles in values development and implementation.
- The ways in which values are received can be traced by values programming analysis. Imprinting, modeling, and socialization are three methods of receiving values from different influences. Societal events and issues in various decades also affect values.
- During adulthood, values may alter because of a major life change, mental unrest, or a change in wants.
- Flexibility and ability to adjust are encouraged. Other characteristics of healthy values are ownership, realism, and life enhancement. Restrictive and absolute values can destroy individual freedom of choice.
- Morals are standards reflecting right and wrong. Your morals and values develop in stages.
- Values are transmitted by parents and other authority figures. Moralizing and laissez-faire (or hands-off) methods are not recommended because of their ineffectiveness and potential problematic results. Several other methods are more likely to produce well-adjusted individuals capable of making healthy decisions.
- Choices are a part of a free society. Making responsible decisions is a learned process, and decision-making models are useful.
- Goals help us to act on our decisions and get what we want in life.
- All ego states are involved in goal achievement. Our "adult" can check a goal for the possibility of success and help determine how to accomplish it.
- Effective time management improves many aspects of life.

RESOURCES

AIDS Hotline. Toll-free: (800) 342-AIDS (2437).
Project Inform: http://www.projinf.org
Al-Anon Family Group Headquarters, Inc. (for friends and relatives of someone with an alcohol problem), 200 Park Avenue South, Room 814, New York, NY 10003. Toll free: (800) 344-2666. http://www.al-anon.org

Alcoholics Anonymous. http://www.alcoholics-anonymous.org
American Cancer Society. Toll free: (800) 227-2345. http://www.cancer.org.
American Society of Addiction Medicine. http://www.asam.org
Center for Substance Abuse Treatment Hot Line. Toll free: (800) 662-4357. http://www.samhsa.gov

Centers for Disease Control and Prevention. http://www.cdc.gov
Mothers Against Drunk Driving. http://www.madd.org
National Council on Alcoholism and Drug Dependence Hope Line. Toll free: (800) 622-2255. http://www.ncadd.org
National Institute on Alcohol Abuse and Alcoholism. http://www.niaaa.nih.gov

4

ACHIEVING HAPPINESS AND SATISFACTION

LOOKING AHEAD

After completing this chapter, you will be able to

- Describe a general concept of happiness.
- Discuss factors that contribute to happiness and recognize the role of needs satisfaction and the influence of culture.
- Explain how expectations can be obstacles to happiness and ensure your expectations are realistic.
- Tell why dependency on external sources of happiness is inadvisable.
- Be positive, use alternative thinking, and act on desired changes.
- Concentrate on the present and enjoy life's pleasures fully.
- Identify what is worthwhile in your life.

> *Happiness is having a sense of self, not a feeling of being perfect, but of being good enough and knowing that you are in the process of growth, of being, of achieving levels of joy. It's a wonderful contentment and acceptance of who and what you are and a knowledge that the world and life are full of wondrous adventures and possibilities.*
>
> —Leo Buscaglia

What do human beings desire and seek? You may think the answers are health, wealth, relationships, success, and love. Each is a probable avenue to what is sought by nearly everyone and crucial to psychological well-being and happiness. Numerous studies show that happy individuals are successful across multiple life domains, including marriage, friendship, income, work performance, and health (Lyubomirsky, King, and Diener, 2005). In developing healthy, nourishing relationships, a happy person has definite advantages.

As valuable as happiness is, not much is done to help people learn how to be happy. Don, a troubled 19-year-old student, wrote in a paper:

> I have spent a large part of my life in mental health facilities. The personnel there taught us that we have problems but do not direct us the right way. They prevent suicides, but do not give reasons to live. I think I am finally finding it here.

Sadly, his therapy sessions and the class discussions on happiness were not enough. Don's body was found in his apartment a few weeks after the term ended. What appeared to be a suicide is another tragic reminder that we are not doing enough to help people live happy, satisfying lives.

What is happiness? How does one become and stay happy? These important questions are easy to ask; the more significant answers are difficult to find. This entire book provides insight. Specifically, this chapter provides a basic overview of the concepts of happiness and satisfaction and suggests ways to achieve them.

What Is Happiness?

A starting point in any search is to know what you are looking for; however, defining happiness is difficult. Happiness, like trust and love, is intangible. It cannot be seen, heard, or touched. Abstract words are not easy to define. Another challenge comes from our own uniqueness; what is happiness for one person may not be so for another. Mary found satisfaction in creating beautiful paintings in art class. Beth was unhappy trying to achieve even average work in the same class. Each has a slightly different path to follow. For the purpose of clarity, think of **happiness** as a general sense of well-being that can range from contentment to ecstasy. Happiness is a state of mind that is not determined by one's circumstances. Adult happiness stems more from honor and integrity of the self than from simply an experience of pleasure (Pittman, 1998). Even when you are not excited about anything special, happiness means that you will like yourself and appreciate life.

Satisfying Your Needs

Related to happiness is satisfaction. Satisfaction can precede or follow happiness and almost always accompanies it. One way of looking at both is to equate them with the fulfillment of needs.

Hierarchy of Needs

Abraham Maslow's (1968) **hierarchy of needs** has become a standard in outlining human motivation. He identified five levels of needs. The first four are *survival*, *safety*, *love* and *belonging*, and *self-esteem*. Before you can begin to satisfy higher needs, you must first satisfy your basic or survival needs. For example, "If you spent a long time without water in the desert, you would feel that you were the happiest person in the world if you found an oasis. Even the word *ecstasy* might not adequately describe your feelings as you took your first sip of water" (Williams and Long, 1983, p. 339). After your thirst has been quenched, extreme happiness will probably not persist; then a higher need will take precedence, and you will be motivated to strive for something more (Fig. 4-1).

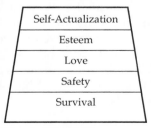

Figure 4-1   Self-actualization chart.

Even though the order of the levels is not exactly the same for everyone and for all conditions, individuals achieve satisfaction by fulfilling needs at each stage. The highest and most difficult level to attain is self-actualization. Individuals do not even begin to work at this level until the previous four stages are completed. To Maslow, self-actualization meant achieving one's full potential, fulfilling a mission, possessing fuller knowledge of and accepting one's self, and feeling unified or integrated. Self-actualizers want to become all they are capable of becoming. Maslow described self-actualization as full humanness. After satisfying their needs in the previous four levels, people who are unhappy and dissatisfied with life would each benefit from asking, "What can I do to become a self-actualizer?" Self-actualizing individuals are striving to achieve the following characteristics.

- Fully experiencing life in the present
- Searching for self-knowledge on an ongoing basis
- Assertively expressing feelings and thoughts
- Making growth choices instead of fear choices
- Being honest and genuine in interpersonal relationships
- Setting and achieving goals of excellence
- Becoming involved in meaningful life activities
- Remaining open and flexible about ideas and beliefs

If you believe that you are working toward self-actualization, which of the characteristics do you possess? Which still need to be more fully developed? Because happiness and satisfaction are closely related, a recommendation is to use Maslow's hierarchy and focus on achieving at the level of your needs.

Associated with Maslow is transpersonal psychology, which focuses on health and human potential. As did Maslow in his hierarchy, this approach looks to models of full human development and the growth-oriented nature of humankind. In addition to the four developmental areas of self, transpersonal psychology addresses the spiritual realm as well. A balanced development of the all parts of the self is conducive to happiness.

Basic Human Needs

Glasser (1965) also discussed needs when he introduced **reality therapy.** Glasser contended that individuals who need psychiatric treatment suffer from one basic inadequacy: an inability to fulfill their needs. Being involved with other people is essential in satisfying two basic needs: the need to love and be loved, plus the need to feel that we are worthwhile to ourselves and to others. As a psychiatrist, Glasser felt that people had to learn how to fulfill their own needs without depriving others of the ability to fulfill their needs—what he called *responsibility*. He identified the following additional needs.

- Surviving and reproducing
- Belonging, loving, sharing, and cooperating

- Having power, which includes having recognition and influence
- Being free
- Having fun

Fun, Glasser believed, is an integral part of life and needs to be incorporated into our learning experiences and work. People can be happy if they spend their time and energy working on fulfilling their needs instead of choosing to be miserable. Think of your own needs. Working toward fulfilling your needs could lead to satisfaction and the quest for one often leads to the other.

Removing Obstacles to Happiness

Several obstacles can hinder you in the pursuit of happiness. Before you can create happiness and become satisfied, eliminating these barriers is essential.

Unrealistic Expectations

Expectations often set up a roadblock. Far too many people expect happiness to just happen. "They do not see it as something they have to do. People will go to a lot of trouble to learn French or physics or how to operate a car, but they will not be bothered learning how to operate themselves" (Newman and Berkowitz, 1974, p. 21). Those who view happiness as a given are seldom happy because rarely does the emotion just happen.

Others have opposite expectations and believe that they cannot ever be happy or do not deserve to be. To them, happiness is not possible. Dan had suffered many disappointments and he believed that he never had any luck. Good things just did not happen to him and happiness was for others. What would you predict for him? Dan succeeded in fulfilling his own prophecy, as discussed in Chapter 1. Happiness is neither automatic and easy nor impossible and too difficult to achieve. Expectations at either extreme are an obstacle.

Another unrealistic expectation is that we will be, or even need to be, happy all the time. Life is just not like that. All around are possibilities for happiness and satisfaction, yet life is not just a "bowl of cherries." It seems sensible to accept what is called the **10-80-10 spectrum of happiness** (Bloomfield, 1996a). For 10 percent of the time, life is spontaneously wonderful and deliriously happy, and another 10 percent is extremely difficult, tragic, and miserable. The remaining 80 percent of life is what you make it. Regardless of the weather, you have a wonderful time, or even when somebody else is in a bad mood, you enjoy a pleasant experience. Check your own "happiness pulse" in the activity "Happiness, It Is Up to Me!" in Reflections and Applications.

The realization that all people go through unhappy times can help us accept trials and tribulations and appreciate the many positives in life. In fact, unhappiness can be a forerunner to happiness. Buscaglia (1982) was a firm believer in the value of unhappiness: "Joy is a great teacher, but so is despair" (p. 74). A widow in a workshop on coping with crisis shared her personal experience with the participants. "My husband died 18 months ago. I loved him, and I miss him. It was painful. However, a few months ago I realized that I felt reborn. While married, I did not take classes or use talents outside the home. I have been doing so lately; from my loss has come happiness." Accepting pain and allowing the reality of unhappiness to contribute to learning and growth translate into long-term happiness.

Searching Outside of Self

Where is happiness found? How can satisfaction be achieved? Too often people engage in a frantic, fruitless search for these elusive feelings. Looking outside of ourselves is common. What are some external sources? A partial list includes material possessions, money, a certain person, a job, marriage, a baby, drugs, the weather, activities, and even a day of the week (maybe Friday?). How often do you think that a particular person or a specific thing can make you happy? This belief carries grave risks such as dependency. Relying on an external source for happiness puts control of your life outside yourself. If externals make you happy, they can also make you unhappy. Expecting happiness from things or others often means that we do little about our own happiness except depend on others for it.

We further risk losing happiness by putting all our "eggs in one basket." Relying on only one source is dangerous, and being dependent on another person is a mistake. Julie believed that her fiancé made her happy. She was devastated when he broke their engagement, and she believed she could never be happy again. She became severely depressed because she did not recognize other potential sources of happiness. Her situation illustrates the importance of being responsible for your own happiness. People may equate a certain achievement with happiness. Although satisfaction and temporary happiness accompany a successful experience, the achievement is not the answer.

We constantly tell ourselves such things as, "If I could just go back to school and acquire more knowledge—perhaps get a master's degree—then I will be happy." But are people with master's degrees or Ph.D.'s any happier than the rest of us? It is beautiful to acquire knowledge, but it is misleading to expect it to bring us peace, love, and happiness (Keyes, 1975, p. 5). Another misleading thought is that money will bring happiness. "People grossly exaggerate the impact that higher incomes would have on their subjective well-being," said Alan Krueger, a professor of economics and public affairs at Princeton University. (*Lincoln Journal Star*, 2006d). A wealth of data in recent decades has shown that once personal wealth exceeds about $12,000 a year, more money produces virtually no increase in life satisfaction. From 1958 to 1987, for example, income in Japan grew fivefold, but researchers could find no corresponding increase in happiness.

Another problem is that this "mad search" is unending. Happiness is always at the next turn or over the hill ahead. For example, once one plateau is reached, those who seek money to make them happy will simply want more and continue the endless quest. We all are so busy chasing after external objects of one kind or another that we have no time left for enjoying our lives (Dyer, 1990). Even though finding satisfaction outside ourselves is impossible, unhappy people persist in trying to do so.

Because advertisers realize that people desire happiness and have a tendency to look for it externally, they use it to sell products. Look through any magazine or watch television commercials; an ad may show the merits of a product, but what entices us is the subtle message that the product will bring happiness. Alcoholic beverages are sold almost exclusively with this theme. Picture the scene: A group of young people are playing volleyball on the beach with a cooler of ice-cold beer near at hand. The play is often interrupted for one guzzle after another. Each beer seems to increase their skill level. They seem ecstatic. What is the message? Drink beer and be happy. The tragic side of alcohol abuse will never be shown in the product's advertisement, and usually the taste is not the point. The sales pitch is concentrated on consumer happiness.

The same could be said for clothes, cars, and other material goods. Research shows that the relationship between consumption of products and personal happiness is weak. Happiness is also not correlated with age, being female or male, or money. Once people can afford the necessities of life, increasing levels of wealth matter little, and having money is no guarantee of happiness (Myers and Diener, 1995). Think about your ancestors. You may have or will have more spending power, yet are you happier just because of it?

Advertisements also persuade parents to buy products to make their children happy. This is potentially damaging. Because children learn from their parents, the message that happiness comes from their things is perpetuated. "We are raising the next generation of frustrated consumers on a steady diet of television ads. Most children have fantasies of desire long before they have fantasies of achievement" (Spezzano, 1992, p. 170). By relying on a happiness-producing product to entertain, parents may deprive their children of valuable personal attention and meaningful parent–child interaction.

It is always a by-product, never a primary goal. Happiness is a butterfly—the more you chase it, the more it flies away from you and hides. (Kushner, 1986, p. 23)

Although the media and general public have many ways of creating the illusion that happiness is out there "somewhere" and can be sought and bought, the belief is a fallacy. If you do not become happy by pursuing happiness, what does make a difference? Factors include culture, specific aspects of the self, and individual actions. Agreeing that national and cultural factors are involved, Myers and Diener (1995) named four traits common to most happy people: self-esteem, a sense of personal control, optimism, and extraversion. In terms of the latter, one can speculate that extraversion helps people make social contacts that increase happiness or that being happy encourages outgoing behaviors. Happy people also are able to filter out ideas that others are better; they pay more attention to their own internal standards of performance and do not use how well others do as a measure of success (*Health*, 1998). Without a doubt, what people do is critical. Individuals of all ages who continue to use their brains to think and their bodies to move are happier. Older people who keep mentally active are most likely to maintain their intellectual abilities and to be generally happier and better adjusted than those who do not. Importantly, the source is not outside waiting to be discovered. *Potential happiness is inside waiting to be created* (Reflect and Apply).

REFLECT AND APPLY

Reflect

♦ *What do you need? Relate this to your degree of happiness in the past and present.*
♦ *Where would you place yourself on Maslow's hierarchy of needs?*
♦ *Think of examples of unrealistic expectations or searching outside of yourself for happiness.*

Apply

♦ *Ask other people what they consider to be their greatest needs. Note how similar these are to your needs.*
♦ *Check with friends and family members. What factors do they relate to their personal happiness?*
♦ *Identify some advertisements that try to sell happiness.*

Creating Happiness and Well-Being

Developing an inner reservoir or base of happiness is something only you can do: from that, you can derive even more happiness from externals. Without this solid foundation, positive feelings are fleeting. Think of this reservoir as an "inner joy," which is a power source, not something that happens to you but something you create (Bloomfield, 1980).

A fine-line difference exists between someone or something making you happy and using externals to increase a personal store of internal happiness. For example, with self-satisfaction and a general sense of well-being, becoming happier because of another person, material possessions, and the like is possible. However, *they do not make you happy.* Happy people become happier from outside sources; unhappy people continue to seek in vain. How can a person create this reservoir and add to it? No magic formula exists, and no one way is right for everyone. Consider the suggestions in this chapter and the rest of the book as building blocks and action steps that can empower you to create your own happiness.

Cultivate Self-Knowledge, Self-Esteem, and an Optimistic Attitude

A basic recommendation is to know yourself well. This will enable you to determine what happiness and unhappiness mean to you. Nothing is more destructive to the human spirit and to personal happiness than never quite knowing who you really are, what you really want, and what you were put here on earth to accomplish (Bloomfield, 1980). Developing self-esteem is essential. People with low self-esteem put themselves into situations that perpetuate unhappiness. "If we care little for ourselves, we are likely to end up as someone's doormat" (Buscaglia, 1992, p. 285). Years ago, "women who love too much" were described as not believing that they deserved to be happy, tending to depend on others for their sense of self-worth, and believing that they must earn the right to enjoy life. At the crux of their unhappiness was critical low self-esteem (Norwood, 1985).

Mary Hollins, an insightful young woman whose self-esteem had been low, shared some of her writing.

> You cannot live for or be another person. The joy and the happiness is to know, accept, and grow, becoming uniquely you.

Mary made a conscious effort to build her self-esteem, as can each of us. Closely related to self-esteem is an optimistic attitude and both are characteristic of happy individuals (Myers and Diener, 1995). Unhappy feelings follow a pessimistic way of thinking. Optimism lends itself to endless choices and opportunities to make the most of and enjoy all of life.

Have Realistic Expectations

People who create happiness have a realistic self-appraisal and accept their true potential. They do not live their lives at one extreme, where they require perfection, or at the other extreme, where they allow themselves to "just get by." A student, for example, would be unrealistic to expect all top grades if she or he were not capable of them. Yet thinking "just so I pass" is self-defeating if you can do better. In the first case, failure and unhappiness could result; in the latter, not giving yourself the opportunity to feel pride and satisfaction will not produce happiness. "It is well to challenge ourselves with dreams of what we would like to be, but it is wiser to stay within the realistic realm of who we are" (Buscaglia, 1992, p. 285) (Fig. 4-2).

The deadly "perfectionist trap" is not conducive to happiness. Wanting to do well is one thing; thinking that one must be perfect is another. A perfectionist is someone who thinks that anything short of perfection in performance is unacceptable (Hendlin, 1992). Often the obsession with perfection stops people from trying and robs them of potentially rewarding activities. Hannah believed that she had to be a perfect golfer. She took lessons and became quite skilled. Then one day she "whiffed." Having missed the ball completely, she knew she was not going to play a flawless game. She left the course and decided that she was through with golf! She gave up hours of potential pleasure because she could not be perfect. Her case is an exaggerated one, yet many persons who participate in sports do not truly enjoy themselves unless they are performing almost perfectly. The happiness comes not from playing but only from superb performance. Perfectionist people frequently avoid challenges and do not comprehend the value of failure.

Baseball and Perfection

A perfect batting average is 1.000, which means that a hitter always gets on base. Nobody expects this out of baseball players. In fact, an average of .400 (4 hits out of 10 times at bat) is outstanding and rare. As in baseball, it is neither possible nor wise to expect perfection in life.

Figure 4-2

Perfectionists do not welcome mistakes as sources of learning, and this deprives them of helpful information. "The dream of perfection turns mistakes from warnings into sins" (McKay and Fanning, 2000, p. 135).

More common is hearing the message, "Whatever you choose to do, do your very best." Does that sound familiar? Most of us have heard it from parents, school personnel, coaches, and friends who had well-meaning intentions. Allow yourself to challenge this belief. Think of at least five of your statuses, such as student, employee, parent, son or daughter, and friend. In order to do your very best, what is required of you in any one status? Time, energy, effort, commitment, and determination certainly are necessary. Is it possible to do the very best you can in all statuses at the same time? Buying into the belief of having to be the best in all you do and then kicking yourself when you do not succeed leads to unhappiness. Fully enjoying what you are achieving is impossible if you are carrying around the guilt from not always performing the best in everything. Nobody has or can have unlimited power.

Ann was a full-time student, mother, wife, friend, member of her original family, and church member. She did not seem to be satisfied with anything in her life as she kept thinking, "I must be the best student I can be, the best mother, wife, friend, family member, and church member." One day she came to an important realization. "It is not realistic for me to expect to be the best in each of these. Right now being a student is primary, and I think I can still do a better than average job as mother and wife. I will just put the others on the 'back burner' and learn to feel okay about that." She freed herself to be happy. This liberation is difficult for those of us who have been led to believe that we must excel in all endeavors.

As long as this "be-the-best" belief persists, happiness is not possible. Instead, happiness can be created, as Ann did, by prioritizing your statuses and deciding that you will do the best you can in each one—under your present circumstances. Creating happiness means looking for challenges that are reasonable.

At the extreme opposite of those with overly high self-expectations are those who are apathetic about life and their accomplishments. They seem to lack self-pride and any hint of motivation. For whatever reason, they have little direction and seldom try to achieve. They pretend that they are happy just getting by, and perhaps they feel as happy as they want to be. They may be depriving themselves of the potential for much greater life satisfaction.

> *Do not be timid and squeamish about your actions. All life is an experiment. The more experiments that you make the better. What if you are a little coarse, and get your coat soiled or torn? What if you do fall, and get fairly rolled in the dirt once or twice? Up again. Never be afraid of a tumble.*
>
> —Ralph Waldo Emerson

Initiate Activity and Pleasure

Satisfaction eludes many people because they do not take the initiative in bringing about pleasure. They play a waiting game. It is as if they believe that there is a "happiness godmother" who will invite them to participate in life. Conversely, those who create happiness realize that there is much they can do for their own well-being. Happy people are active in life. They know what can add pleasure to their lives, and they go for it. They are willing to take risks. Carolyn, who was just starting college, wrote, "I have been taught to take a 'better safe than sorry' approach to life. I am now throwing that safety role out the window and taking chances. It is really invigorating!" The fully alive person asks, "How can I enjoy this person, place, situation, or challenge?" This requires a positive, creative mental attitude.

How alive do you feel? How often do you seize the moment and create delight? "Mentally healthy people keep a vital forward thrust through life until death" (Adams, 1987, p. 198). In contrast, noninitiators are inactive and wait for a "bolt of happiness" to strike them. They put someone else in charge.

> Most of us do not "sculpt" our lives. We accept what comes our way, and then we gripe about it. Many of us spend our lives waiting for the perfect mate, waiting for the perfect job, waiting for perfect friends to come along. (Jeffers, 1987, p. 63)

Julie, who was divorced, talked about her desire for a social life. On Monday mornings she would usually say, "I had a boring weekend. I wanted to go out, but nobody called. After you are divorced, couples do not want you around, you know, so I sat home. I could not call them." Laura, a widow, said, "I get so tired of sitting home, and I wish my family would visit more often and take me places." Julie and Laura are not incapacitated; they just do not initiate. You may want to look at how much pleasure there is in your life and ask what you are doing to bring it about.

> *For those of you wondering what to do while waiting for your prince to come, I say, "Enjoy the frog!"*
>
> —Ric Masten

Take Responsibility

Excuse making, a common way of not taking responsibility for one's happiness, can create dissatisfaction and misery. In order to avoid the harmful excuse-making habit, it helps to recognize the difference between an excuse and a reason. A reason is a statement of fact usually offered with acceptance of responsibility and control. An excuse can consist of facts; however, responsibility for behavior is lacking. Instead, an excuse usually includes a "that-should-get-me-off-the-hook" presumption. Contrasting excuses with reasons is helpful in distinguishing between the two. For example:

I could not go visit him.	versus	I did not go visit him.
I did not have time to study.	versus	I did not take the time to study.

Lack of time is a common excuse. When I remind students that they really did have time to complete a paper or study for an exam, I can get indignant protests. There was not *any* time, I hear. How much time do we literally have? The answer is that each of us has 24 hours a day, 8,760 hours each year. In reality, we do have time; we just may not have time left over. "We always have time, if we but use it aright (sic)," said the German poet and dramatist Johann Wolfgang Goethe, who died in 1832. This is still true today.

When we persist in thinking that we do not have time, it really does seem to be nonexistent. Potentially satisfying experiences can be delayed or never accomplished. Melissa insisted that she wanted to "work out" regularly, but she just did not have time. So she did not exercise. One day she decided to awaken earlier and exercise. She found time that had actually always been there!

Another common excuse and a definite obstacle to happiness is age. "I am too old" is a phrase that, if recognized as an excuse, can be eliminated. When exercising, I sometimes feel winded. It is tempting to think, "It is my age." My preferred thought is, "I am just not in shape yet!" Do you see the beauty of thinking the latter? In doing so, I can change my physical condition and stamina; my age is unchangeable. Certain obstacles exist if you have some type of disability. Having an artificial eye has been challenging for me, and using it as an excuse is occasionally tempting. I recall trying to do so once when discussing a tennis match with my daughter Lisa. She showed up with a patch over her eye and proceeded to win the set and remind me of the senselessness of excuse making! A more dramatic example is an amazing man who calls himself Mitchell. He describes himself as someone who could be called the unluckiest man alive because of two devastating accidents that left him badly scarred and disabled from severe burns and paralyzed from the waist down.

> With my scarred face, my fingerless paws, my wheelchair and real, genuine happiness in my heart—I want to be your mental image of the power of the human mind to transcend circumstances. (Mitchell, 1997)

Having read his book and heard him speak, it is obvious that because he refused to make excuses, Mitchell has overcome immense obstacles and has taken responsibility for his own life.

Sources for excuses are bountiful. Passage of time, people, the weather, a car, and even the dog can be at fault. Another convenient scapegoat is an emotion. Have you ever thought or said something like, "I was so angry that I just had to honk my horn," "I was so frustrated that I couldn't help screaming"? Ask yourself what part of that statement is true. You were angry (even *so* angry) and frustrated; the rest is inaccurate. You did not *have* to honk the horn or scream. A young woman said, "I was so depressed, I could not go to work." Have you ever gone to work or to classes when you were depressed? She could have gone to work, but she did not. Taking control of her life would mean thinking, "I was depressed, and I chose (or decided) not to go to work." Then she is free in the future to be depressed and go to work if she chooses. Emotions are important influences in our lives; however, they do not have to control or justify behavior. "I could not help it" usually means "I did not help it."

Excuses limit choices. Blaming outside forces takes away freedom and power. "This class is boring," someone might say, and then the class or the instructor is at fault. This blaming could prevent a person from ever enjoying the class because the responsibility is elsewhere. Don complained that he was unable to study for a test because his roommate was talking on the phone. He blamed his roommate for his poor test score. Who was actually responsible for his score? As long as Don continues to blame others, he will be at their mercy and will be unable to change his life. Responsibility gives us the power to make changes and to create the kind of life we want.

Excuses are like antacids; they can bring temporary relief but do not contribute to long-term happiness. Excuses decrease self-control and dim feelings of success. For example, how can you feel proud about a high grade if you do not take responsibility for the low ones? Even though it may be temporarily upsetting to realize that you have created pain for yourself, this realization is your biggest blessing. When you take responsibility for your own misery, you discover you have the power to find pleasure and create happiness.

People who take responsibility have or develop an **internal locus of control,** the belief that they are in control of their own lives. A perception that outside-self factors control one's life is **external locus of control.** Over the years there has been increasing interest in whether individuals believe that outcomes of their behaviors are due to their own actions or personal characteristics or due to chance, luck, fate, or under others' control (Rotter, 1972, 1990). People recognized as being psychologically hardy (Kobasa, 1979) have an internal locus of control, and one of the traits of happy people is a sense of personal control (Myers and Diener, 1995). Think about your own locus of control and strive to empower yourself by taking responsibility. Happy individuals welcome control over their lives. Excuses prevent present happiness and block potential well-being.

Change Can't and Couldn't Thinking

Excuses frequently include the words *can't* or *couldn't*. People think and verbalize in these terms. Have you ever said or heard this common expression: "I *could not* get up this morning"? Really? Picture what would be necessary for this to be true. Perhaps you were lying there in a full-body cast? Usually the person means "I had a hard time getting up," or "I did not want to get up." A person does not mean *cannot* or *could not* in actuality, yet without realizing it, potential happiness can be jeopardized. Analyze *cannot* and *could not* messages and then challenge them. Read the following thoughts and then reflect on what a person will likely miss by thinking and then behaving accordingly.

I just *cannot* ski.
I *cannot* talk to people.
I *could not* ask her to go to the party with me.

Do you see how limiting such thinking is? Think of as many literal uses of the words as you can, and you will discover that the words are correctly used in only a few instances such as, "I *cannot* live forever." Even if you cannot do something now, in most cases, you could eventually! A wise decision would be to stop using the negative words unless they are entirely accurate. "Adulthood is the time for doing what you can and not talking about what you can not" (Spezzano, 1992, p. 20). Life has circumstances or external forces that cannot be changed. You cannot control the weather, many tragedies, and other people's behavior. You do control your reactions and future actions regarding these uncontrollable events. Learn to recognize your own internal power and avoid thinking *cannot* when you actually have control.

Cannot may be a cover-up for fear. Other times use of such words is just wishful thinking. A student wrote on an evaluation form, "I liked this class. I wish

I could have put more into it." She *could* have put more into it. Replacing the word *could* with *would* means she can be more involved in future classes and have a happier experience. How frequently do you say, "I cannot," or "I could not"? To create happiness, eliminate as many as possible and think, "Yes, I can."

Rethink Should and Should Not

Closely related to *cannot* and *could not* are *should* and *should not*. Perhaps you are not feeling happy or satisfied about what you do because you think in these ways.

I should study more.	I should lose weight.
I should visit my grandparents more often.	I should not waste time.
I should work harder at my job.	I should not ever be late.
I should exercise more.	I should not get angry.

What emotions are likely to follow a thought of should when it is not acted upon? What feelings do you have when you believe you *should not* and then do it anyway? Guilt, frustration, and anger are common responses, and these emotions go hand in hand with unhappiness. "Shoulditis" is what Briggs (1977) calls this. She points out that "should-ought-must-have-to" messages lower self-esteem and lead to unhappiness. Also, an expression of *should* does not sound like fun. When someone says, "We should go to lunch" or "We should get together," does it sound inviting? Would not it be more positive to hear, "I would like to go out to lunch with you" or "I want us to get together"? Part of being fully alive is enjoying activities and wanting to participate rather than thinking you have to. Other forcing words similar to *should* that are best to avoid include *must*, *have to*, *need to*, and *ought* (Fig. 4-3).

So what is better to think and say? Happiness is more likely if, whenever possible, you replace forcing words with *want* or *do not want*. Consider first the activity or task. You probably do want to spend more time with friends so instead of "I should spend more time," you can think, "I want to spend more time." Wanting to do something may not be the case. Then you can focus on the outcome. For

Figure 4-3

example, you may not want to study, yet you do want better grades. You can think, "I want better grades so I will study more." If you honestly do not relish doing the task and you do not want the outcome, either finish it anyway or get rid of the thought and move on with enjoyable living! Reword the other forcing words as well. When a student says, "I have to leave class early to visit a friend in the hospital." I reply, "Remember that you do not *have* to. You want to and have decided to leave, and it is fine."

These forcing words are used in **irrational beliefs,** unreasonable and exaggerated thoughts identified by Albert Ellis (1977), a well-known cognitive therapist. Some of these include "I cannot help it," "I cannot stand it when things do not go well," "I should be liked by everyone," and "I must be perfect." Ellis explained that people who carry around such overgeneralizations end up making themselves miserable. Challenging irrational beliefs is necessary for mental health. You can begin by changing the forcing words and, thus, chalk up another step in creating happiness!

Concentrate on Positives

Personal put-downs are also obstacles to happiness. "I am no good." "I cannot do anything right." "I cannot make friends." "I am not attractive." A most devastating example of negative self-talk is, "I cannot change."

Consider the following damaging thoughts.

> We do not like the way we look. We can not stand our bodies. We think we are stupid, incompetent, untalented, and in many cases, unlovable. We think our thoughts are wrong and inappropriate and our feelings are wrong and inappropriate. We believe we are not important, and even if our feelings are not wrong, we think they don't matter. We have never come to grips with ourselves, and we look at ourselves not through rose-colored glasses but through a dirty, brownish-gray film. (Beattie, 1987, p. 109)

Other thoughts are less blatant. "She is smarter than I am," "My brother was more popular," "I wish I were prettier," or "I could have done better." Because they are subtle, you may not even recognize their damage. Any time you use a qualifier and think or say, "I am *only* a kid," "I did not do *much* in high school," or "I have *just* had work experience on a farm," you are taking away from your sense of self-worth and well-being. During job interviews, many applicants who make the mistake of emphasizing what they lack lower their chances of getting the job.

People who engage in negative self-talk and see the worst in everyone and everything seem addicted to negativity and can be called *negaholics.* Those who suffer from negaholism limit their own abilities, convince themselves that they cannot have what they want, and sabotage their wishes, desires, and dreams (Carter-Scott, 1989). They also dampen the spirits of others. Qualifying thoughts and comments can emerge even under positive circumstances. A clerk said, "Even when I feel proud, I qualify it by thinking that we were so busy at work that anyone could have made as many sales as I did." After recognizing this, she began to challenge such thoughts by telling herself, "Even though we were busy, I do not know that anyone else could have done as well as I did. I made the sales, and that's great!" Whenever you hear yourself saying something like, "I received a good grade, but it was an easy test," rephrase the thought. Why would anyone use negative self-talk instead of positive? Such a person might have had well-meaning parents who did not want their children to seem conceited or vain. They might have encouraged them, instead, to be modest and not to think too highly of themselves. For an unfortunate few, it is the result of direct put-downs that they have internalized. Negaholism is frequently handed down from generation to generation (Carter-Scott, 1989). Julie spoke of her mother's emphasis on negatives. "I was excited about a piece of pottery I had finished and told my mom to come see it. She walked in, and the first thing she said was that the table where I had placed it needed dusting!"

Thinking and speaking negatively about yourself lowers self-esteem and leads to unhappiness. What about other negativism? The use of what are called "bummer" words (Buscaglia, 1982) can depress your spirits. Try saying these words aloud slowly.

no	never	gloomy	bored	hate
not	ugly	dumb	bleak	wrong
negative	sick	bad	worthless	awful

Did you notice any change in your feelings? Most people become aware of how depressing both the sounds and the images of the words are. *Depressing*, by the way, is a "bummer" word. Now say the following words aloud.

yes	laugh	fun	able	love
cheerful	right	smart	great	excited
super	well	good	wow	alive

A fascinating study showed that higher use of positive emotion words relative to negative ones was associated with better health (Pennebaker, Mayne, and Francis, 1997) and that people who used more positive emotion words and fewer negations were perceived more favorably by others (Berry et al., 1997). Just by using different words you have more control over your mood, health, and interactions. Imagine going through life thinking and verbalizing in "bummer" language. Instead, think differently and increase the number of positive words you use.

After you rid yourself of negatives, remarkable things can happen. When you employ positive self-talk, your mental image will focus more often on what is good about yourself, what you can do, and what you have done well. Most important, you will know that you can change if you want to change. You will no longer put yourself second or third in all aspects of life. If someone is truly better looking or more talented, you can acknowledge this as a reality yet understand that it is only as important as you make it. Concentrating on positives in yourself and others creates a happier reality.

Be not afraid of life. Believe that life is worth living and your belief will help create the fact.

—William James

Seek Alternatives

An important part of the thinking process, and essential for achieving happiness and satisfaction, is the ability to recognize alternatives. "Locked-in" thinking can be depressing because it limits you to only one way of viewing life; it can also be tragic. The story is told of a woman who is waiting for a phone call from her boyfriend, Buster. The call does not come and, in despair, she kills herself (Buscaglia, 1982). This tragic and desperate behavior, as in most suicides, is the result of an inability to think of any possible alternative. In contrast, my students can suggest several other scenarios. First, they let Buster off the hook by giving reasons for his not calling. A unique one is that he had not paid his phone bill and found that his line was dead. If, in fact, Buster no longer loves the woman, alternatives are still possible. "Find a better Buster!" is a common recommendation. "Maybe the truly mentally healthy individual is the one who has the most alternatives, the most viable alternatives" (Buscaglia, 1982, p. 108). Remember that any problem has more than one solution.

The happiest people are those who do not limit their choices. Being confident that you can solve your problems by thinking of several options is a sign of maturity and strength. Critical and creative thinking skills, discussed in Chapter 1, emphasize unlocking people's minds, seeing a multitude of possibilities, and then exploring alternatives.

Deciding on choices is difficult for some people. Because of our original socioeconomic status and upbringing, the concept of alternatives may not be easily grasped, or effective decision-making skills may be lacking. In addition, life delivers some devastating blows, and we may feel trapped by circumstances. Education about choices is a necessity, and society can be instrumental in providing encouragement, training, and resources related to bettering one's life. This book encourages individuals to learn how to make wise choices.

Take Positive Action

Seeing alternatives is not beneficial if you do not act. In fact, understanding what to do and then not doing anything can be stressful. A frustrated student came to me one day after reading several self-help books. She said, "I am so upset because now I know what to do, but I am not doing it!" I reminded her that human beings are not perfect, helped her plan some action steps, and encouraged her to continue to work on desired changes. Taking action and taking responsibility for outcomes are signs of a mentally adjusted person. Lack of action often leads to unhappiness.

> It costs far more not to change than to change. The alternative to change is stagnation. To stagnate is to die while still breathing. (Adams, 1987, p. 206)

Looking for what can be done in any circumstance is happiness producing, and you can be proud of any positive action. Cheri is unhappy about her sloppy roommate. What can she do about it? If she does nothing, is she pursuing happiness? Cheri can start with the easiest possible solution and act on it. If it does not work, she can go to the next one. If she exhausts all the alternatives, she still has a choice. She can accept what she has not been able to change, or she can remove herself from the depressing situation. A story is told of a man who prayed every day that he would win the lottery. One day he heard the thunderous voice of God: "If you want to win the lottery, at least buy a ticket!" Wasting precious time and energy bemoaning your plight in life is draining and not conducive to happiness. Instead, do something constructive, learn from mistakes, and avoid negative situations in the future. Then pat yourself on the back for taking action and enjoy the energizing feelings from taking even a small step!

> *Life is in your hands. You can select joy if you want or you can find despair everywhere you look. Kanzantazkis says, "You have your brush and colors. You paint paradise, and then in you go."*
>
> —Leo Buscaglia

Avoid Chronic Procrastination

Putting off activities, which is known as **procrastination,** can deprive you of a more positive future. Procrastination can be used in a creative ways. You can, for example, choose to postpone a tedious task in order to engage in a pleasurable activity. You may decide to put something off because it is low on your priority list or because you want to allow time to make a thoughtful decision. In that case, delay can work in your favor.

Chronic procrastination is the habit of postponing and it blocks happiness. If you want and plan to complete a task, putting it off delays the happiness of achievement and creates stress in the meantime. It becomes a major obstacle to happiness. "The demands and responsibilities of adult life are much greater, and procrastination begins to feel more like a prison than a game" (Burka and Yuen, 1983, p. 15). Despite the difficulty, when the consequences of procrastination are faced, most people want to change. Consider the costs (LeBoeuf, 1979).

- *Waste of the present:* I will do it tomorrow, but tomorrow may not come.
- *An unfulfilled life:* Today will not count for anything if nothing is accomplished.
- *Boredom:* Life can become dull and flat when filled with things undone.
- *Anxiety:* Working under pressure at the last minute is a stressor.
- *Impotent goals:* Goals not acted upon are like hot air, one "I am gonna" after another with no results.
- *Unsolved problems:* A constant plague of these is like vermin, one breeding another and another.
- *Continuous frustration:* Not getting any "wants" becomes disheartening.
- *Poor health:* Putting off taking care of self or maintaining safety can be harmful.
- *A mediocre career:* Delay and inaction lead to nonproductivity, and even though most procrastinators claim that they will be different at work, the habit lingers.

A study of college students showed that procrastinators reported higher stress and more illness late in the term; overall, they were ill more often. They also received lower grades on all assignments. Procrastination of this type was a self-defeating behavior marked by long-term costs (Tice and Baumeister, 1997). Anyone who wants to live a happy life would adopt the worthy goal of defeating procrastination.

Discovering why you procrastinate can help you find another way to satisfy your need or to decide whether the reason is worth the costs.

1. *Do you procrastinate because the task seems overwhelming or unpleasant?* In Chapter 3 you learned how to break a goal into smaller action steps. This puts an end to initial procrastination and motivates you to take the second step. Unpleasant tasks can be evaluated. (1) How important is this? (2) How bad will it be if I don't do it? (3) What are the rewards? For example, cleaning toilet bowls is not high on most people's lists of desirable tasks. Next time you are faced with the chore, apply the three questions. If you honestly decide that cleaning the toilet is unimportant, that it won't be so bad left undone, and that the rewards are not worth the effort at the time, then you are not procrastinating!

2. *Is an procrastination excuse for a poor performance?* This is like trying to make two wrongs into a right. Most students who leave major projects to the last minute do poorly.

3. *Are you waiting for more time?* Ironically, people will say, "I did not do well because I ran out of time," and they will expect to be excused because of lack of time. Another procrastinating message about time is, "I will do it when I have more time." We will never have more time and allowing too many demands on our time leads to pressure. Procrastinators are often time-wasters who do not use small time segments. Even though enjoyable activities are important, people who say they do not have time are often using a great deal of it for enjoyment. If you are not an effective time manager, review the time management section in this book.

4. *Do you use procrastination to gain sympathy?* Donna played the "poor-me" game to explain why things did not get done. "I wanted to be a good mother and take the kids to the zoo, but too many other things came up" and "I have more things to do than most, and I cannot afford to take time for myself" were some of her pleas for sympathy. When a friend told her that she was tired of hearing all her tales of woe, Donna maturely took a look at herself and decided to end the game.

5. *Are you defending against blows to self-esteem by putting things off?* "I did not get it done" may be a cover-up for "I was afraid it wouldn't be good enough." Perfectionists tend to procrastinate for this reason. Check your behavior. If you have a pattern of procrastination, do something about it now!

Live in the Present

When are you living your life? This may sound like a senseless question, yet asking it *is* sensible! Do you harbor thoughts such as "I will be happy when I graduate" or "I cannot wait until I get to move away from home and be on my own"? Describing this type of thinking as "futurizing," Dyer (1990) calls it a most destructive habit.

Your life is not a dress rehearsal for the future. It is right here and now. (Carlson, 1999)

In the book *Making Peace with Yourself* (Bloomfield, 1996a), a chapter is devoted to "I will be happy when." It is interesting that many of the events are opposites (when I get married, when I get divorced, when I have children, when the children leave home). All are excellent examples of "The grass is always greener on the other side of the fence." Many of us live the first half of our lives postponing satisfaction and the last half with regrets. Fulfillment is just over the hill (Bloomfield, 1996a). When I hear people say, "I cannot wait until the weekend," I often reply, "I hope you can, and I certainly hope you enjoy each minute from now until then!" Too many people seem to be focused on endings—the end of the week, the end of the day, the end of the school term—and then want time to go even faster. Happy, satisfied people create happiness by an ongoing process of living *now*.

Another habit is one I somewhat jokingly call "pasturizing," or mentally living in the past. "If only I had married John instead of Jim" and "I wish I had started college right out of high school instead of later" are examples of wishful thinking that destroys opportunities for present happiness. People who converse only about accomplishments or problems from the past are not living in the here and now.

Well-adjusted people accept and appreciate the past and can enjoy nostalgia. Wise individuals use the past as a series of vast learning experiences to make the present more rewarding. Happy people plan for their future and anticipate to a certain extent, yet they keep focused in the present. What is happening now can be unpleasant, and you will, at times, hope tomorrow comes quickly. If you make a habit of living elsewhere, you will realize too late that you have not really lived. Focusing on life as a journey, not a destination, is helpful.

Recognize that "now" is the only time you ever really have. For example, when Lynn graduated from college, she began her career full of excitement and hope. That same month a malignant brain tumor was discovered and removed. Lynn survived the delicate surgery and the cancer treatment and spent several months in a rehabilitation center. Lynn was very positive and hopeful for the future. Nine months after the tumor was found, Lynn was buried in the local cemetery, leaving behind many who loved her. Nobody is guaranteed a future. It is a depressing thought but one that can keep us focused. Happiness must be practiced in the present. A consolation is that Lynn created and experienced happiness in the "now" of a short life before her illness.

> The only reality is the now. Yesterday is gone, and there is nothing you can do about it. It is good because it brought you to where you are right now. Tomorrow is a wonderful thing to dream about, but it is not real. And if you spend your time dreaming about yesterday and tomorrow, you are going to miss what is happening to you and me right now. (Buscaglia, 1982, p. 75)

Enjoy Life's Pleasures

"Stop and smell the roses." What a delightful idea! How often do you do it? "Roses" can be anything as long as pleasure is felt. Sensory delights are everywhere. Do you see sunsets? Do you feel awe when viewing nature's treasures? Do you smell the scents of the seasons? Do you marvel at a snowflake? Do you hear

Figure 4-4   Take time to enjoy the beauty of nature.

the delightful songs of birds? Positive feelings are generated by pleasurable sensory stimulation. **Peak experiences** are brief moments of extreme pleasure (Maslow, 1968). Often these come from the simpler pleasures of life. Being open to new experiences allows us to create happiness. "Fully alive people are aware of the thorns but concentrate on the roses" (Powell, 1976, p. 57).

Why would people not take the time to marvel at life? "I am too busy. I do not have time" is a common excuse. Ask yourself when will you have time and when will you not be busy? "If we wait for everything we want accomplished to be completed before we celebrate, we will miss the party of life" (Pearsall, 1988, p. 61). "But I have to clean the house" and "I cannot stand it if the yard is not in good shape" are detriments to enjoyment (unless you enjoy cleaning the house and doing yard work). Joys are missed when we are rushing through life. Be sure to slow down and experience joy—over and over (Fig. 4-4).

Count Your Blessings

One day a student remarked, "Sometimes it helps when I stop and think of what is not wrong with me and then I feel grateful." Too often we forget how fortunate we are. Think right now of how many blessings you have. Are you healthy? Do you have loving relationships? Can you see and hear? Consider what life would be like without one or more of your senses. Peggy, a remarkable blind woman, told of overhearing a person complain about having to take a bus. Peggy's thought was: "I wonder how she would feel if she always had to walk 10 blocks to a bus stop even on the coldest day, and she was also blind." In the process of creating happiness, it can help to experience an occasional reminder of how bad things could be and be reminded of our blessings. Equally affirming is to keep in mind that for every act of unkindness, there are a million kind acts, a network of good (Dyer, 1992).

Give to Life

Happy people not only take in the wonder and beauty of life, but they also give back to life and pursue a meaningful existence. Self-centered people tend to be unhappy, whereas those who contribute develop a positive legacy that will remain after they have died. Self-actualization, the pinnacle of the hierarchy of needs, is more likely for those who are reaching beyond self and contributing to the greater good of humankind. Joy comes from giving, not getting; from contributing, not acquiring (Dyer, 1992).

Giving to life does not necessarily mean great works. You can create satisfaction by doing worthwhile and purposeful deeds. Possibilities are all around. When was the last time you visited someone in a hospital or a nursing home? Have you recently volunteered to help in a worthy cause? Have you taken the

---

REFLECT AND APPLY

Reflect

♦ *Think of a "cannot" statement you have used or heard. Then reword it.*
♦ *If you have a "should" in your life, change the thought to a "want" in one of the suggested ways.*
♦ *Select one of the ways to create happiness and use it.*

Apply

♦ *Practice saying both "bummer" and "positive" words and then compare your emotional reactions.*
♦ *Make a list of your blessings.*
♦ *Do something positive for another human being.*

---

time to do a favor for anyone? When did you last send a "just thinking about you" card or note? Have you even smiled at someone recently? Buscaglia (1982) underscored this point, "Every day you take from the ground, you take from the air, you take from the beauty, what are you giving back?" (p. 82). Even the smallest gesture can do wonders for another and, in return, for you. In the depths of the tragedy of the terrorist attacks on the World Trade Center and Pentagon in 2001 came countless expressions of generosity and giving that shed some light on the anguish. A major reason for enhancing self-esteem is to have something to offer. We can only give what we possess, and the more we have, the greater our capacity to give.

> Each of us can make a difference. We can choose to live a life in which we can say, when we die, that the world is a better place for our having been here. (Jampolsky and Cirincione, 1990, p. 5)

Develop Nourishing, Rewarding Relationships

A primary objective of this book is to help you learn to develop positive relationships. Their value in the creation of happiness is unquestionable. Love and belongingness are human needs. Enjoying a supportive network of close relationships is associated with happiness (Myers and Diener, 1995). In Chapter 12 we will explore these concepts of relationship building further (Reflect and Apply).

LOOKING BACK

- Having realistic expectations about happiness is wise. Realizing that unhappiness is a part of life is realistic and can help you appreciate your happiness even more.
- Happy people learn from their misfortunes and grow from adversity. They know that happiness does not magically come from external sources. One must be happy inside; if not, all the outside sources in the world will bring only temporary happiness at best.

- Happiness is within reach, yet it does not automatically fall into anyone's lap. Initiative and effort are necessary. A reservoir of internal happiness must be created. Externals then can add to what is already there.
- Creating happiness means developing a high degree of self-worth, a positive attitude, and an internal locus of control.
- Happy people rarely use excuses and negative words. They look for possibilities, not limitations.
- Happy people see alternatives. Avoid negative self-talk and chronic procrastination.
- Individuals who create their own happiness are active and do what is best for them. They do not "futurize" or "pasturize." They make good use of the past and strive for a happy future, yet they live in the present.
- Happy people are seekers in life who enjoy discoveries and simple pleasures. They stop to "smell the roses" and count their blessings. Because they are truly happy within, they tend to reach out and provide happiness for others.

Alas for those who never sing but die with all their music in them.

—Oliver Wendell Holmes

EXPERIENCING AND EXPRESSING EMOTION

LOOKING AHEAD

After completing this chapter, you will be able to

- Realize that emotions are a complex and important part of the self and of relationships.
- Give a general description of emotion and explain three components.
- Describe ways in which emotion can be expressed.
- Name and describe influences on emotional expression.
- Relate the transactional analysis ego states to emotional expression.
- List benefits of expression in each of the four development areas.
- Use rational emotive behavior therapy and control theory to change what you feel.
- Differentiate between mild feelings of sadness and major depression; name symptoms of and explain treatment options for major depression.

> *Emotions can be viewed as the spice of life; they give our lives character and pizazz.*
>
> —Stephen Worchel and Wayne Shebilske

A letter arrives congratulating you on a scholarship that will pay a full year's college expenses. Your supervisor refuses to give you a day off to attend a wedding. You and a family member disagree, and your reasonable suggestions are being misinterpreted. An automobile coming toward you seems to be out of control. What do these situations have in common? All usually bring about an emotional response.

Were you able to predict what feelings would probably be present in the examples? The emotions of joy, disappointment, frustration, and fear come readily to mind and, in most cases, would be accurate predictions. As you will discover, these particular feelings do not have to occur; you may respond with different emotions, depending on several factors.

Emotions make up a most interesting and important developmental area of self. Human beings are emotional, and our feelings both enrich and disturb our lives. Feelings bring texture, color, and sensitivity to life. Without them, we would

112

be robots (Satir, 1988). If you stop to consider how drab life would be without emotions, you will begin to grasp their value and importance.

Emotion is a feeling state that involves certain components. The complexity of emotions frequently creates problems in individual lives and within relationships. Check yourself to see how puzzling the elements of your emotional self can be.

1. Are you in touch with your feelings? It can be difficult to decide if a state of being is an emotion or some other aspect of self. For example, confusion indicates a mental lack of understanding, not an emotion. "I feel tired" is a physical description.
2. Can you identify which emotion you are experiencing at any given time? Most people will typically reply that they feel fine, good, or bad rather than naming a specific emotion.
3. Can you pinpoint the reason for your feelings? Several emotions are situational, which means they are preceded by an event. Others seemingly come from "out of the blue," and the cause is not apparent.
4. How accurate are your predictions of emotions? Do you know how you will feel under certain circumstances? Nisha was shocked to discover on her wedding day that she felt sad. She loved Matt and wanted to marry him. What would cause this?
5. Can you tell by behavior what emotion is being experienced? Picture this scene. Three individuals are waiting in line to go on a thriller ride at an amusement park. All three are smiling, laughing, and pacing. What are their emotions? Possibly one person could be excited, another mildly anxious, and the third terrified!

In recent years **emotional intelligence** has been conceptualized (Goleman, 1995, 1998). The cornerstones are having a vocabulary sufficient to accurately express emotions, accepting responsibility for one's own actions, and using emotions in thinking and problem solving (Mayer, Caruso, and Salovey, 1999). Benefits include being attuned to the feelings of others and being able to handle disagreements. This chapter will clarify the mysterious emotional self. Developing emotional well-being and emotional intelligence can lead to meaningful interactions and positive relationships.

Identifying and Categorizing Emotions

How do you understand your feelings? Three components of emotion—physiological changes, subjective cognitive states, and expressive behaviors (Tangney et al., 1996)—can provide insight.

The component called **physiological arousal** refers to biological reactions and activities of the nervous system, various glands, and organs within the body. If frightened, your glands secrete hormones into your bloodstream, causing your heart rate to quicken and your pupils to enlarge. You may or may not be aware of the arousal. In some cases, the reactions are observable. Have you ever blushed? The redness was caused by what was going on inside your body. Many of these responses can be measured by medical monitoring devices and biofeedback equipment.

A second component is **subjective cognitive state;** this can be thought of as awareness and appraisal. For example, how do you know you are happy? You may identify an experience with happiness because of your thoughts. Cognitive appraisal, according to one theory (Schachter and Singer, 1962), is largely responsible for the label we give to emotion. Any physiological arousal could be labeled anger, fear, jealousy, or even love, depending on the circumstances.

The third component is **expressive behavior**—observable verbal or nonverbal actions. How do you show happiness? Sadness? Anger? Sometimes expression is confused with the feeling state itself. For example, crying is an expression, not an emotion. You have probably heard someone say, "I was so angry I just had to scream!" In reality, the person did not have to scream. Expressive behavior is the one component over which we have the most control. In the following, see if you can identify the three components.

> Joan continued to cry. She had received a letter telling about the death of a close friend. She was shocked and extremely sad. She felt numb. "Why did this happen?" she asked her husband. He reassuringly took her hand in his and noticed how cold it felt. Joan gulped and said, "I feel almost dead, inside, too."

Physiologically, Joan's hand temperature reflects a reaction to the shock. Her numbness is probably also due to physiological changes. The realization that her friend had died and her description of "feeling almost dead inside" make up her subjective cognitive state. Her expressive behaviors are crying, talking, and gulping.

Researchers, in an attempt to clarify the emotional self, have identified and categorized possible feelings. One model identified six major clusters or group: love, joy, surprise, anger, sadness, and fear (Shaver et al., 1987). Although several emotions may fit within one cluster (e.g., anxiety is a type of fear), the researchers pointed out that some emotions are blends or combinations of feelings. Sympathy, for example, can be a mixture of sadness and love. Even categorizing an emotion is a challenge (Fig. 5-1).

Emotions can vary in intensity. For example, you may be mildly annoyed if a friend is 5 minutes late meeting you for lunch, upset after a half hour, and outraged when you discover that she or he has deliberately avoided you because of a preference to have lunch with someone else. The underlying emotion is anger. Regardless of how emotions are described and categorized, the realization that they are an integral part of you is basic to self-understanding. Because the components of expressive behaviors influence relationships to such an extent, they deserve special attention.

Expressing Feelings

Abby dramatically explained, "I am an emotional person. I cry at weddings, funerals, movies—you name it. I let people know when I am mad or happy. But that is just the way I am." In contrast, Shamiso said, "I am a controlled person. I do not let others know my feelings. But that's just the way I am." Is it just the way Abby and Shamiso are? Opinions and theories vary. Expressiveness likely does have a genetic base (Ekman,

Emotion Clusters

Figure 5-1

TA Revisited

"Child" is the home of all emotions, the feeling part of personality.
"Parent" contains messages that tells you to express feelings and how to do so; it can also tell you not to express.
"Adult" is unemotional yet is involved as it can decide to permit or deny emotional expressions; it also can help you change what you feel.

1994), yet because our emotional socialization and experiences are different, much of "if, what, how, and to whom" we express has been learned and strongly influenced by other factors that will be covered later (TA Revisited).

Expression occurs verbally and nonverbally. For what reason would you suspect that another person is upset? She or he may tell you, "I am upset because you borrowed my book and didn't return it right away." Or the words could be less direct and might even deny the feeling: "I just do not understand why some people do things like that, but I guess it is really nothing." Other possibilities are profanity or hostile insults. One of the problems with verbal expressions is that people may not accurately state what they are feeling. Perhaps the person does not really know, feels embarrassed, or simply does not want to share his or her feelings. Individuals may worry about hurting someone's feelings. Generally, we have not been trained to express our emotions assertively and, obviously, this can easily create relationship challenges.

More commonly, individuals reveal feelings through their body language. Facial expressions, changes in voice, behaviors such as laughing and crying, and posture offer glimpses into the emotional self. It is best to be cautious when you try to interpret others' nonverbal expressions. For example, why does a person cry? An obvious answer is because of sadness. Can you think of other emotions that may result in crying? Even at a wedding, interpretations can be inaccurate. Mark shed a tear at his daughter's wedding. Monica, the mother of the bride, sniffled into a handkerchief. Another young woman sobbed. Mark's tears were the result of pride and happiness. Monica was sad and somewhat regretful that her daughter was old enough to be married. What about the young woman? She had once been engaged to the groom and was feeling resentful and jealous!

Feelings can often be gleaned from facial expressions, and this ability is found in different cultures (Jolley, Zhi, and Thomas, 1998). However, emotion can be disguised. You may have heard the expression "It is written all over your face"; but true feelings can be masked. "Facial expressions are imperfect communicators of emotional states" (Plutchik, 1980, p. 268).

Influences on Emotional Expression

Remember the ways that we learn? Whether and how to express ourselves are acquired through direct instruction, modeling, and experiences. Think of some messages about emotions. A partial list follows:

Keep a stiff upper lip.   Do not wear your heart on your sleeve.
Do not be a crybaby.   Do not be a fraidy cat.
She is too emotional.   You will get over it in time.

Cheer up.   Cool it.
Others have it worse than you.   Shut up or I will give you something
                                           to cry about!

Do you see a common theme among them? "Keep your feelings to yourself" is the underlying message. Using the transactional analysis (TA) framework, you can see that there is often a conflict between "parent" messages and the expressive desires of our "child."

Emotional expression is greatly influenced by one's culture. The North American message has generally been one of control. The strong, silent type is heralded as a hero. Even in extremely sad situations, you may hear someone being praised for being "strong," which means that grief isn't being shown. Other societies also can be restrictive. A student from Kenya described how horrified her mother was when she came to the United States for a visit. "Those people were actually hugging each other in public. Shameful!" she said. Emotional crippling is being afraid to feel, afraid to express, and afraid to have others feel (Rubin, 1998). Other cultures encourage expressiveness. A Chinese student, Ann, told the class: "At Chinese funerals everyone is encouraged to cry and cry because it shows you really care and will miss the person; it reveals the extent of your love."

Expressiveness is also related to gender role. In general, men are given the "don't express" message more than women. As pointed out in Chapter 2, boys and girls are often socialized differently, and the skill specialization account (Kunkel and Burleson, 1999) can explain how they develop different ways of handling emotions. Even though male infants are as emotionally expressive as females, a crossover at later ages occurs because male emotionality is suppressed by parents and peer groups. Boys experience sharp limitations especially when it comes to the expression of caring/connection emotion (Levant, and Brooks, 1997).

Many societies are in a transitional stage, and gender differences are far less extreme than they once were. Yet, as long as males and females are given opposite messages, differences in actual expression are inevitable. Can you name emotions that men are allowed or encouraged to feel more than others? Over the years the typical first response in my classes has been anger, a feeling of strong displeasure because of an actual or perceived wrong. On the other hand, fear, an emotional response to a perceived threat or danger, is customarily off limits for men. Women are allowed to be afraid of spiders, mice, the dark, and strange noises. Can you picture the reactions if a man demonstrated the same fears? Some examples of stereotypic differences in the emotions that men and women are encouraged and allowed to express are shown in Table 5-1.

A list of discouraged or not allowed emotions could be made just by switching the male and female columns. For example, women traditionally have been discouraged from awareness and expression of anger. In fact, a fairly recent study, which found no significant variations between boys and girls in total anger level, did reveal significant differences in expression of anger. Boys had higher levels of aggressive responses (Buntaine and Costenbader, 1997).

These differences are not "cast in stone." A Central American student expressed amazement during the discussion of gender-role differences. "In my culture the men are usually the expressive ones, and women are expected to be more controlled," she said. Within the world of athletics, changes in expressiveness

TABLE 5-1	Emotional Expression and Gender Role
Encouragement and Allowance	
Men	**Women**
Anger	Sadness, depression
Bravery	Fear
	Hurt
	Love, affection
	Worry, anxiety
	Disappointment

have definitely occurred. Males are given permission to show more emotion and even engage in behaviors commonly off limits, such as hugging and shedding a few tears. Female athletes are encouraged to display anger and aggression.

Changes are desirable because stereotypic masculine nonexpressiveness can create problems. Expressive behavior has its benefits, as the next section will show. Does it make sense to restrict these benefits to one sex? And is it fair when innocent people pay a price for stereotypic toughness? An account of an airline crash in Washington, D.C., during a blizzard illustrates this. Judging from the tape-recorded conversations of the crew, the pilots' attitude about the buildup of ice on the wings of the airplane was casual. They decided to just "go for it." The jet slammed into a bridge and plunged into the Potomac River, killing 72 passengers, four passing motorists, and the pilots (*Time*, 1982). How tragic that those individuals not wanting to display even legitimate fear frequently take unnecessary risks with their own and others' lives. After being asked about bravado, David Spiegel, M.D., pointed out another potentially dangerous unemotional reaction: "Some men, when they start having chest pains with a heart attack, get down on the floor and do push-ups to prove to themselves that it's not happening" (Moyers, 1993 p. 167). Obviously, this could have serious effects.

Are you aware that lack of expressiveness causes male–female relationships to suffer? Ironically, when women are asked to identify characteristics they would like in a man, they mention the ability to express emotions such as fear and sadness. "I wish he would just cry sometimes," one young woman said. On the other hand, men can be confused about women's expressiveness and feel frustrated when they are accused of not understanding. Heterosexuals might benefit from understanding and adopting certain dynamics of gay and lesbian relationships, which tend to be more emotionally revealing (Huston and Schwartz, 1996).

Another powerful influence in emotional development is the family. Which sounds most like a description of your family?

- Almost no emotions are expressed. Parents are controlled. They rarely touch others or express warm, loving feelings. Neither do they display anger or frustration. Relationships are rather businesslike.
- Some emotions are encouraged. Occasionally, the parents show love and warmth. They express anger at times; however, the children are scolded if they behave angrily. A common command is, "Go to your room and

don't come out until you're over it." Children are not supposed to cry often or loudly, and praise is given for being brave and strong.

- Several unpleasant emotions are acted upon. Parents let the children know when they are angry, frustrated, disappointed, depressed, and hurt. The children react with displays of negative feelings. However, almost no expressions of warmth and affection are present.
- All emotions are present. Parents express feelings and let the children do so. The household is emotionally charged, and many hurtful behaviors can be observed. A verbal or physical assault almost always follows anger.
- Emotional expression is encouraged. Parents try to model constructive ways of dealing with feelings. Open communication allows for discussion of emotions. When a person hurts others with emotional expression, an apology is given.

Variations of the five models are possible. If your family sounds like the last one, you are fortunate. Most families either suppress emotional expression or allow hurtful behaviors. Few make the attempt to model and teach constructive emotional expression.

Other agents of socialization play a prominent role in expressiveness. From childhood through adolescence, the influence of the **peer group** (those of similar age and interests) is strong. Peers may demonstrate warmth and affection, or they may be more reserved. Young people may openly cry and hug each other in support, or they can be uncomfortable with displays of sorrow. Additionally, the media and religion present standards of emotionality. From all of the external sources, if your models of expressiveness encouraged constructive behaviors and if you were generally accepted and praised for showing feelings, your emotional self is likely to be healthy (Fig. 5-2).

Internal reasons and experiences also influence emotional. Difficulty could come from perception of your social role or a fear of disclosing your true feelings. Certain people believe that they must be controlled in their professional positions, and they become almost emotionally sterile. Protection may be a reason. If you have been hurt as a result of expressing your feelings, you may have built a wall around your emotions. Jeff told another firefighter how apprehensive he felt at an accident scene. The fire captain heard about it and cautioned Jeff about his fear. Jeff resolved to keep future emotions hidden. Dave expressed his love for Kelli; in return, she said that she preferred just being friends. His hurt feelings led to a layer of defensive inexpressiveness.

A major barrier lies in what expression means. Many people equate emotional suppression with self-control. If you are one who believes that any show of feeling means you are weak and not in control, you will probably suppress rather than express your emotions. With pride, a woman said, "I never get angry." What she meant and eventually said was that she did not show her anger, and to her, this was a virtue. Did her anger disappear? As Rubin (1998) describes it, her anger probably went into a slush fund only to surface in other ways.

Of benefit would be a change to a different belief: *Showing feelings requires strength, and expressing doesn't mean lack of control.* In fact, control could be defined as deciding whether, when, and how to express your feelings. Andrew, a man not

Figure 5-2

used to expressing his feelings, heard a rumor at work that he had been passed over for promotion. He seethed all morning, then stormed into his supervisor's office, announced loudly that he was quitting, and walked out. He stopped to pick up his mail and found a memo congratulating him on his promotion. His display of emotion was not only inappropriate but also disastrous. Sometimes you are wise to wait before venting a feeling. A well-adjusted person can choose to express emotion, can select from any number of responses depending on the situation, or can decide not to show a particular feeling. Use "Emotional Monitoring and Learning" in Reflections and Applications to gain personal insight.

Constructive behaviors can be developed at an early age or learned later. Healthy messages would be:

- Experiencing all feelings is acceptable.
- Any way of expressing feelings that are not intended to hurt would be allowed.

Is lack of expressiveness related to health problems? Research has focused on this question. The calm that can come from suppression is bought at a price of a higher risk for asthma, high blood pressure, colds, and overall ill health. Female suppressors with breast cancer may be more likely to have future tumors

(Goleman, 1997) and could be at greater risk for early death (Pennebaker, 1997). Are you aware of times when your suppressed emotions seemed to play havoc with your physical condition? Anxiety often leads to headaches and stomach distress. John Powell (1969) said it well: "When I repress my emotions, my stomach keeps score" (p. 155).

Emotion and biology appear to be closely connected. Years ago, a type of personality was identified as cancer prone; it combined two major features: an inability to express emotions such as anger, fear, and anxiety and an inability to cope with stress with a tendency to feel hopelessness, helplessness, and depression (Eysenck, 1988). On a positive note, a fighting spirit and emotional expressiveness are associated with better adjustment to breast cancer (Classen et al., 1996). The message seems to be that constructive outlets are preferable to lack of expressiveness.

Benefits of Constructive Expression

Constructive emotional expression is a way of behaving that provides a healthy, nonhurtful outlet for feelings. A person can learn, model, and teach positive expressive behaviors and reap many benefits. Let's look at benefits in the four developmental areas.

Physical self.   Does it seem possible that emotions in early life might have an effect on a person's life span? A study of Catholic nuns revealed an association between positive emotions in their early life stories and longevity 60 years later (Danner, Snowdon, and Friesen, 2001). Emotional expression and health are also related. Allowing patients to express their feelings seemed to improve their health (Spiegel, 1999). On the positive side, the following expressive behaviors are health producing.

Touching   Both hugging and therapeutic touch can relieve aches and pains and alleviate muscle tension. For most people, a hug is both soothing and energizing. In babies it appears to ease pain (Motte, 2000). Therapeutic touch is recognized as a valuable medical tool, as it can relieve pain, speed healing, and clear energy blockages that may be interfering with healing (Weil, 1995b). Studies have shown that therapeutic touch and massage therapy relieve pain (Moore, 1999) and decrease levels of anxiety and depression (Diego and Field, 2001). Premature infants who were massaged gained significantly more weight than that of a control group and showed far fewer stress behaviors (Field, 1996). Massage has even proven to enhance immune function (Diego and Field, 2001) (Fig. 5-3).

A hug is a great gift—one size fits all, and it is easy to exchange.

—Anonymous

Figure 5-3   A hug is healthful and feels so good!

Laughing   When people laugh, muscle tension is relieved. Body movements related to laughter are physical exercise. More importantly, laughter is

Amazing Story of Laughter and Healing

Believing that laughter contributed to his miraculous recovery from what was thought to be an irreversible, crippling disease, Norman Cousins (1979) described laughter as a form of inner jogging and a behavior that creates a mood in which other positive emotions can more easily function. "Laughter helps make it possible for good things to happen" (p. 146). Infection in Cousins's body was measured before and after a few minutes of robust laughing. The amazing results showed a decrease in inflammation that held up over time. Years later when much more had been learned about the biology of the brain, Cousins (1989) speculated that laughter had helped to activate the release of endorphins, neurotransmitters in the body that act as painkillers. He cautioned not to substitute laughter for medical care but to use it to bring forth love, hope, festivity, determination, will to live, and purpose. "The positive emotions can be no less effective in bolstering the immune system than the negative emotions are in weakening it" (p. 91).

Figure 5-4

associated with stimulation of the immune system, reduction in stress hormones, pain reduction, decrease in blood pressure, and improved respiration (Berk, 1996). Researchers conclude that humor therapy and related laughter may have both preventive and healing effects (Berk et al., 2001). A study revealed that people with heart disease were 40 percent less likely to laugh than healthy individuals (Hickling, 2000). This could be a result of laughter's ability to reduce stress. When did you last really laugh? (Fig. 5-4).

The most wasted of days is that during which one has not laughed.
—Sebastian Chamfort

Crying   Most people feel psychologically and physically better after crying, and it has long been recognized as a way of releasing feelings. How is crying related to physical health? Interestingly, a laboratory test revealed that the chemical composition of emotional tears differs from that of irritant ones (induced with freshly cut onions). Thus, shedding tears may be a way of ridding the body of substances that build up in response to stress (Levoy, 1988). Making a strong case for emotional release is a cardiologist who believes that crying also opens the chest and enhances healthy breathing. He advocates crying as protection against heart disease and contends that next to love, crying is perhaps the most healing activity for the heart (Sinatra, 1999).

Stereotypic gender-role behaviors can negate the physical benefits of emotional expression. In most societies, boys are typically ridiculed for crying and discouraged from doing so. Males may actually have to give themselves permission to cry.

A good healthy cry can be a sign of maturity. We have got it all wrong if we still believe that crying is a sign of weakness. Real weakness is in not allowing ourselves access to the emotions expressed through tears. (Buscaglia, 1992, p. 280)

Restrictions on expressing emotion can be prevented from the beginning. If you have input into a child's life, avoid the common message "Do not cry" or "Boys do not cry."

Men are also given less freedom to hug than women are. Watch men interacting with others. Typically, they will just shake hands. Only in recent years have genuine hugs been exchanged between men. Perhaps as we learn more about the benefits of behaviors such as hugging, laughing, and crying, all human beings will become freer in their expressions of positive emotion.

Mental self.   Not recognizing or experiencing what you are feeling can cloud your thinking. Greg was considering a job change and a move to another city when his fiancée ended their engagement. Even though he showed little emotional reaction, his thinking abilities seemed impaired; he was confused and indecisive. He talked to a friend who was a counselor. With a great deal of encouragement, he began to talk about feelings of shock, hurt, and anger. The breakthrough in his seemingly blocked mental state came after an intense session of physically working out his feelings. After beating on a stack of large pillows with a tennis racket, he felt absolutely cleansed of negative feelings. "It was a cathartic experience, and I felt as if a weight was lifted from my body. It is hard to really describe." His reward was renewed ability to think about himself and his life. "As feelings are experienced, the mind clears" (Branden, 1983, p. 155).

Being overly concerned and anxious can affect mental performance. Emotional expression can lead the way to resolving a mental block. Test anxiety is a good example. Britt found that if she expressed her feelings before an examination, she could think in a calmer, more organized manner. In a similar vein, relaxation therapy and intensive physical exercise are used to reduce test anxiety (Burke, 1999). An interesting study suggests that emotional suppression can impair memory. The researchers conclude that "keeping a stiff upper lip" decreases recall of the details of an emotional situation (Richards and Gross, 2000). As more is learned about cognitive processes, a clearer link between emotion and cognition is forged.

Social self.   Communicating emotions forms a bridge between two people. If you want to develop close relationships, being able to express feelings is a necessity. Two robotic persons may not notice how colorless their relationship is. When one robotic person interacts with a functioning emotional being, neither one feels fulfilled, or the emotional individual is apt to be frustrated. The closest, healthiest, and most meaningful relationships are between two emotionally expressive individuals.

Expression has long-lasting effects. A study showed those adults who had experienced expressions of warmth and demonstrated affection as children enjoyed happier and better-adjusted lives as adults (Franz, McClelland, and Weinberger, 1991). Even expressing unpleasant feelings can lead to loving feelings. Think of emotional expression in relationships as a positive circular effect. As you feel and express genuine feelings, you learn about yourself. Others will get to know who you truly are and will appreciate knowing you as a whole person. Then it is likely that they will feel free to share their feelings with you, which will lead to close relationships.

The price of not expressing emotions can be high. A letter to Ann Landers from No Name, No City, No State is quite moving.

A few weeks ago I kissed my son for the first time and told him I loved him. Unfortunately he did not know it because he was dead. He had shot himself. The greatest regret of my life is that I kept my son at arm's length. I believed it was unmanly for males to show affection for one another. I treated my son the way my father treated me and I realize now what a terrible mistake it was. Please tell your male readers who were raised by Omaha dads that it is cruel to withhold affection from their sons. I will never recover from my ignorance and stupidity.

On a positive note, a study of fathers and preadolescent sons showed that intimate and nurturing types of touch were a frequent and important part of their relationships (Salt, 1991). Expressing your feelings gives nourishment to relationships.

Emotional self.   Does it make sense that the expression of feelings enhances the emotional self? Kimberly felt resentful because she thought her mother favored her sister Kris. She bottled up this feeling for years and found herself becoming angry and even hostile. One day she told Kris a lie about their mother and then suffered from guilt. She became depressed and went for counseling. After a period of time, she realized that the initial resentful feeling had led to several others. She decided to express in writing her true feelings to her mother and sister and acknowledge the lie she had told. The three of them came together and honestly expressed their emotions; relief followed. "I felt as if the clouds had lifted, and my only regret is that I didn't do it sooner," said Kimberly.

Emotional relief is stymied by suppressed feelings. Expressing one emotion often reveals the presence of another. During a cancer-coping session, Marian went through a process that stripped away one emotion after another. She began by expressing depression, which was covering fear. Underneath all this was intense anger. She had felt emotionally drained; after the expressive experience, she was energized. People risk the experience of joy when they have too much control over their emotions (Pearsall, 1988). Suppression inhibits all feelings. As Marlon, a young student from Jamaica, expressed: "Having feelings and not showing them is like having a bird that does not sing!"

Honest emotional expressions help people feel authentic. Individuals who do not express their feelings can feel phony, frustrated, and depressed. Especially damaging is not expressing resentful feelings, which are like tiny pockets of venom that never disappear (Bloomfield, 1996b). Even when aware of having resentment, expressing it is difficult. "It is easier to keep quiet," said one woman. After she was encouraged to let her resentment be known in a nonthreatening way, she admitted, "I feel so relieved now. Keeping a lid on resentment was causing me frustration and unhappiness. Being assertive has made all the difference in how I feel about myself."

In all developmental areas, positive growth is a benefit of genuine emotional expression. True sharing of feelings usually leads to heightened self-esteem and a healthier lifestyle.

Steps to Expressiveness

"I realize that I could benefit from becoming more expressive, but how do I go about it?" is a common question. As with any change, the primary step is the desire to change. Telling yourself, "I want to express my feelings more, and I am going to try," begins the process. Being determined, yet patient is good advice. Just as you could not expect to lose 30 pounds in a short period, you will not become expressive overnight. We can, however, act ourselves into a new way of thinking and think ourselves into a new way of acting. "We may be products of the past but are also architects of our future" (Myers, 1992, p. 122). Concentrated effort and practice are required, and you can expect to feel uncomfortable at first as you face challenges involved in expression. As with other behaviors, repeated expressiveness becomes a part of whom you are.

If you are not a naturally warm, demonstrative person, use your adult ego state to the "child" to act. Stephanie had a life-threatening accident from which she recovered. She decided that she wanted to become more affectionate and demonstrative. She told her husband, children, and friends, "I want to give and receive more hugs and pats on the back." She actually had to tell herself in the beginning, "Go give Michael a hug," and she kept track of how many she gave and received. Anyone in the family could request a hug. They treated it as somewhat of a game until they found that hugging had become second nature. Because we are unique, you may prefer to express affection in other ways such as words, writing, gifts, favors, helpful behaviors, and just listening.

Anger

Few people have received constructive modeling or advice on expressing anger. Most people describe anger as unpleasant, although it can be a positive motivating force. Anger itself is neither good nor bad. How you express it is what counts. Becoming aware of how anger affects people and why anger is experienced can lead you into making wise choices about expressing anger (Reflect and Apply).

REFLECT AND APPLY

Reflect

- *Think of a time when you were aware of physiological arousal due to an emotion.*
- *On a scale of 1 to 5 (5 being almost always): How often do you recognize your feelings? How often do you express emotion?*
- *Identify an emotion you usually express as well as one you often do not express.*
- *Considering each developmental area of the self, how have you benefited (or not) from emotional expression?*

Apply

- *Keep a one-day log of your emotions. Include all three components that you recognize.*
- *Observe facial expressions and guess how the person feels. If you feel comfortable doing so, verify your guess.*
- *Engage in any or all expressive behaviors. Hug or touch someone in a loving way. Laugh! Have a good cry.*

Effects of anger.   Although being angry doesn't have to cause problems, not constructively expressing the anger can damage individuals and relationships. Anger appears to be related to risk for heart attack and death because the emotion is likely to raise blood pressure, speed up the heart, and narrow blood vessels (*Consumer Reports on Health,* 2001). Researchers at Harvard Medical School found that the most common emotion experienced in the two hours before a heart attack was anger (Goleman, 1997). Another study showed that an increased risk of heart disease is related to proneness to anger (Ahmad, 2000). In fact, coronary heart disease risk is related to both heightened expression and inhibition of anger (Stoney and Engebretson, 2000).

In *The Angry Book,* Rubin (1998) points out many "assorted poisons" related to repressed anger: anxiety, guilt, depression, overeating, high blood pressure, self-imposed starvation, sleep problems, psychosomatic illnesses, obsessions, and compulsions. He also identifies a serious side effect of what he calls the "freezing" of anger, which is the stifling of all emotions, including love. Just as a person cannot feel with a frozen finger, a person cannot feel with frozen emotions. Is it any wonder that anger management is needed?

Understandably, anger and love occur in the same relationships. Expressing your anger can be a sign that you care and want a change for the better. However, too much anger in a relationship is unhealthy, and negative ways of handling it will definitely erode loving feelings. Teresa Adams (1987), a therapist and author, writes: "In every divorce, the mishandling of anger is a major cause of the failure of a marriage" (p. 151). Continually suppressing your anger is a way of mishandling it.

A dangerous type of anger mismanagement is the use of aggression and violence. Obviously, too many individuals vent their anger in violent, abusive ways. Random assaults and killings have become far too common. Since 1990 what have been termed *road rage* cases have increased by 51 percent (Stephen, 1999). Certainly, it is difficult to drive today without feeling frustrated and even angry at times. Yet, to allow such feelings to escalate into violent acts is alarming and demands concerned attention and intervention.

Reasons for anger.   Recognizing the sources of anger can be instrumental in bringing it under control. Annoyance and hostility can result from an inability to accurately make **attributions,** deductions about the causes of behavior or events; in other words, you may have difficulty determining the correct reason for a behavior. Biases in attribution generally lead to problems. For example, if individuals in an automobile wrongly believe that another driver with bright headlights is just trying to make them mad, hostility is highly probable. In relationships, attributions play a significant role. Consider the following incident.

At a class reunion Katrina danced with a former boyfriend. Her husband Ryan thought, "I know that she's doing that just to make me jealous." He became angry.

Could Ryan's attribution be incorrect? What effect would this likely have on their relationship, at least for this period of time? Can you come up with a different attribution?

Believing that others make you angry and that you are not in control of your feelings makes you a victim. If anger is appropriate, use it as a "call to action" and make the situation better. If the anger doesn't make sense, decide to release it in a constructive way and use cognitive restructuring to "talk yourself out of" the anger. Taking pride in yourself means that you don't just respond without thinking; instead, you decide how to respond. Responding to hate with hate, or anger with anger, is not because of an outside event; it's because of what's inside of you (Dyer, 1992). Ask yourself, "Why am I angry and what can I do to change that?" Use anger in a productive way to make your life better, not worse! In Chapter 6 you will learn techniques for anger management.

Changing What You Feel

Being an expressive person does not mean that you are at the mercy of your feelings. A significant way of taking charge of your life is to be able to change what you feel. Being more in control of emotions can also improve your health. Negative feelings of anger, anxiety, and depression, if strong and prolonged, can make us more vulnerable to disease, worsen the symptoms, and get in the way of recovery (Goleman, 1997). Doesn't it make sense to know how to eliminate or at least diminish the intensity of these emotions?

The Power of Your Thoughts

Cognition is thought. Often a person's thoughts about an event determine the particular emotion. If your interpretation of the event is accurate, any emotion will be normal and appropriate (Burns, 1980). Thoughts can create pleasant or unpleasant emotions and can also relieve unpleasant ones. For example, pretend that you are driving a car and have stopped at a red light. The instant the light turns green you hear a horn honking behind you. Do you feel surprised, concerned, angry, annoyed, or calm? Whether you realize it or not, how you feel depends on your thoughts about the honking, not the event itself. "Oh, I wonder who is honking at me. Maybe it's someone I know" would elicit surprise and possibly even delight. "The person must have an emergency to be in such a hurry" is a thought that could result in concern. "How dare anyone honk at me! I know what a green light means" would spark anger or annoyance. "Somebody likes to use their horn. I am glad I am not that stressed," you think and then feel nothing but calmness. We actually can create our own emotional reality.

What you think and feel then guides your behavior. You may turn around, scowl, and shake your fist, or worse. Or you may turn around, smile, and wave, or choose to do nothing. You have the choice. Cognitive therapy trains people to change the way they interpret and look at things so that they can experience different emotions, feel better, and act in a positive, productive way.

Rational emotive behavior therapy. One of the best known and applicable cognitive systems, rational emotive behavior therapy, or REBT, was developed by Albert Ellis (1977, 1984). The central theory of REBT is that events or situations do not upset you; instead, it is your belief about what has happened that does.

Irrational beliefs, discussed in Chapter 4, are responsible for unpleasant or negative consequences. The approach uses the letters "ABC."

A stands for *activating* event, situation, or experience.
B represents *beliefs* or thoughts about the activating event.
C means *consequences* (emotions, further thoughts, and behaviors).

Ellis (1993) points out that cognitions, emotions, and behaviors are interactive in that each influences the other. According to Ellis, REBT is opposed to rigidity, thoughts, and one-sidedness and strongly favors openness, alternative seeking, and flexibility. REBT helps people challenge irrational beliefs and change their lives.

Let's put REBT into practice: You receive a failing grade on your first college examination.

This is the activating event:

(A) Your initial belief or thought
(B) "That is it. This proves I cannot handle college-level coursework. I might as well quit right now." Can you see that your initial belief is irrational?
(C) These thoughts would probably lead to emotions of disappointment, depression, and hopelessness followed by actions to quit school.

Instead REBT changes the belief and alters the consequences. Remember the cognitive restructuring formula from Chapter 1? Consider this alternative:

Just because I received a failing grade on the first exam does not mean I can't handle college-level work. I didn't perform as well as I wanted to; however, one bad grade does not mean I will fail this course.

You have now eliminated the irrational thought. How would the consequences be different? Your initial emotion may still be disappointment, yet you would then feel hopeful; your thoughts and behaviors would be more positive and directed to doing what you could to improve. You would not quit school on the basis of one examination grade!

Cognitive techniques work best for those who have the ability to reflect on their own thoughts. Individuals with a thinking preference in decision making as shown on the MBTI (Chapter 2) may have an advantage over feeling types. However, if you are inclined to "think with your heart," you can especially benefit from the use of REBT.

REBT is not useful when your thoughts are rational and suitable to the occasion. You do not want to create unpleasant emotions by thought-changing. For example, Mike had been invited to go out of town for the weekend with friends. His original thought was, "It was neat that they asked me, and it sounds like a good time." His feelings were anticipation and happiness. Later he found himself thinking, "I wonder why they asked me. I bet they needed another car, and I have a nice one." Do you see how quickly his feelings would then change? Be careful that you do not replace pleasant, realistic thoughts with unpleasant, irrational ones.

The Power of Your Behavior

Closely related to REBT is **reality therapy** developed by William Glasser (1965). According to Mlasser, rational thought and behavior are both necessary as is the ability to think of several possibilities. Glasser (1984) has also taught and written about **control theory.** In the earlier example of failing your first examination, control theory would say you are depressing yourself. If you want to feel different, first change your behaviors. Instead of moping around, you can choose to socialize with friends, go to a movie, or do whatever is pleasurable. You can alter your thinking, too, as suggested before; however, more emphasis is placed on changing the behavior. When people who are miserable do something different, they invariably change their feelings. Have you ever whistled or hummed cheerily and then recognized a slight mood elevation? If so, you were using basic control theory.

A fascinating idea is that facial expressions can change feelings, at least to a modest degree (Averill, 1997). People have been able to feel fear and disgust by creating the related expression on their faces. Studies have shown that a particular type of smile, one in which the eye muscles are active, is associated with enjoyment and reports of positive emotions (Ekman, Davidson, and Friesen, 1990). Simple experiments in my classes indicate that happy facial expressions and positive behaviors can pleasantly affect feelings. Try putting on a happy face and see what happens!

Cognitive and behavioral techniques can be used effectively to change most emotions, including minor depression or a "down" feeling. Experiencing a "blue mood" once in awhile is common, and to feel better, you can use any of the ideas for creating happiness covered in Chapter 4, plus thought and behavior changing. Exercise, which has been already highly recommended in this book, has definite mood-lifting benefits (Jaret, 1999). Other ideas include engaging in enjoyable activities such as reading, shopping, going to a movie, or watching television. We really do have control over those brief occasional bouts with the "blues." Another option is simply to allow yourself to feel mildly unhappy for a brief time! An underlying theme of this book is that human beings have numerous choices, one of which is deciding to change what you are feeling.

When Should You Seek Professional Help?

Certain emotional states do not lend themselves exclusively to self-help. A common psychological disorder that affects thoughts, feelings, physical health, and behaviors is **major** or **clinical depression.** Far different from just a "down" feeling, it is characterized by a depressed mood or loss of interest or pleasure in most activities for a period of at least two weeks. Other symptoms are diminished ability to think, concentrate, or make decisions; feelings of worthlessness; recurrent thoughts of death or suicide; increase or decrease in appetite or weight; insomnia or sleeping too much; fatigue; and loss of energy. "Passive negativity—being stuck—is the hallmark of depression" (Baumel, 1995, p. 5).

Often called the "common cold" of mental illness, major depression along with other types of mood disorders is suffered by one out of every seven people. Many do little or nothing to alleviate their pain. Nearly 60 percent of people who score positive for depression have never been treated (Screening for Mental

Health, Inc., 2001). Yet of those who seek help, approximately 80 percent respond well to treatment and go on to lead productive lives, according to the National Depressive and Manic-Depressive Association (2001).

Not only is clinical depression a dreadful feeling that impinges on quality of life, but it also is related to physical health. A study showed that chronically depressed older people had an 88 percent increased risk of developing cancer when compared to those who weren't depressed (Penninx et al., 1998). Because treatment of depression in cancer patients leads to better patient adjustment and reduced symptoms, it appears to influence the course of disease (Spiegel, 1996). People with depression also have an increased risk for coronary heart disease (Henderson, 2000). The *British Medical Journal* (2001) called depression the largest determinant of disability in the world. In addition to decreasing the potential for disease, successful treatment usually helps a person resolve additional psychological and relationship problems.

Why is help not sought? Often a person may be aware of the symptoms but not suspect depression as a cause. Other factors are the continuing stigma attached to any type of psychological problem and gender role socialization. The revealing book *I Don't Want to Talk About It* (Real, 1997) focuses on depression in males and maintains that men, more easily than women, "get depressed about being depressed and allow their pain to burrow deeper and further from view" (p. 35). Depression in men is often hidden, which may be one of the reasons that depression appears to affect nearly twice as many females as males. Females are more likely to seek help. Three to four million men in the United States have major depression (National Institute of Mental Health, 2001), and they usually pay a high price: an inability to develop and maintain intimate relationships (Real, 1997). A medical doctor who suffered from depression expressed a reason for seeking help. "With the right guidance and the right support, a breakdown can become a breakthrough" (Ornish, 1998, p.76).

What causes major depression? The general consensus is that genetic, biochemical, and environmental factors can all be involved (National Depressive and Manic-Depressive Association, 2001). According to the National Institute of Mental Health (2001), major depression presents itself in generation after generation in some families; yet, it also occurs when there is no family history. One type of depression, **seasonal affective disorder (SAD),** stems from lack of sunlight and is usually experienced only in the fall and winter. In many cases, light therapy is effective, which involves the use of a special light box consisting of a bank of white fluorescent lights on a metal reflector and shield with a plastic screen. For mild symptoms, spending time outdoors during the day or arranging homes and workplaces to receive more sunlight may be helpful (Society for Light Treatment and Biological Rhythm, 2004).

Proper diagnosis is extremely important in determining treatment. If the cause is biologically based, antidepressant drugs are usually prescribed and work for about 70 percent of people (*Harvard Health Letter*, 2000). "But I do not want to use drugs" is a common protest. It can help to realize that the proper prescription of an antidepressant merely restores the functioning of the brain. The medications "fix" what is in need of repair and do not create something artificial or unnatural (Podell, 1992). Antidepressant medicines are not addictive or habit forming according to the National Institute of Mental Health, although there can be side effects (*Harvard Health Letter*, 2000).

Taking the best drug in the correct dosage is essential. A person is advised to carefully select an experienced psychiatrist or, ideally, a psychopharmacologist whose specialty is drug therapy. Then being carefully monitored and following the treatment plan in its entirety will make the difference in the degree of success (Preboth, 2000). The results of successful drug therapy seem like miracles. "I feel like a completely new person," said Mark, as he walked confidently into the classroom.

> When medication can ameliorate the symptoms of a chemical imbalance, why should we be made to feel that taking it is somehow irresponsible? Do we condemn those with hypertension for their dependence on medications that lower blood pressure? (Dowling, 1991, p. 25)

A depressed person typically needs more than just drugs to eliminate depression (Trickett, 1997). Combining drug and psychological therapy has significant advantages over just one or the other (Keller et al., 2000). Even therapy alone can be successful. A program of cognitive-behavioral therapy significantly reduced depressive symptoms and negative thinking while it increased self-esteem (Peden et al., 2001). Cognitive-behavioral therapy seems to be especially helpful in preventing future depression (Fava et al., 1998). Physical activity is again beneficial. Among clinically depressed older people, regular physical activity was associated with fewer depressive symptoms (Moore et al., 1999).

Suicide and Depression

A most compelling reason for seeking professional help is that suicide is often a way out for a severely depressed person. More than 90 percent of people who kill themselves have a mental disorder, which is commonly one of depression, according to the National Institute of Mental Health (2001). Regardless of the cause, suicide is a tragedy that affects many. In the United States, 31,484 deaths—more than 80 deaths per day—are because of suicide (National Center for Health Statistics, 2004). In a 17-year period, the rate of suicide among 10- to 14-year-olds has increased by 109 percent; and 11 percent for 15- to 19-year-olds. Tragically suicide is the *leading* cause of death in the older adolescent group (Stanard, 2000). Because of social stigma, gay and lesbian young people are at a higher risk than heterosexuals (Hartstein, 1996). The U.S. Department of Health and Human Services has estimated that "as many as 30% of completed youth suicides each year" are performed by gays and lesbians (National Center for Health Statistics, 2004).

An excellent book for anyone even remotely considering suicide is *A Reason to Live* (Beattie, 1991). The book gives many ways to feel in control of life again, suggestions of options to suicide, and numerous resources. One strategy is to imagine how devastating your death would be to someone with whom you are not angry and for whom you care deeply, such as a grandparent. "Anytime

Figure 5-5 Severe depression can be difficult and dangerous.

the idea came into my mind, I saw my grandma's face and knew I would never do that to her," said one young man. Remember if you ever consider suicide: "Keep it a question. It is not really an answer" (Colgrove, Bloomfield, and McWilliams, 1991, p. 69) (Fig. 5-5).

Ideally, a depressed person will seek help. However, because lack of motivation or energy is usually present, this may not happen. An estimated 70 percent who commit suicide tell others of their intentions (Baron, 1998), yet 79 percent of youth who kill themselves never see a mental health counselor (Stanard, 2000). If you know someone who has any of the symptoms of depression, displays drastic changes in behavior, or talks about death or suicide, do all you can to get that person to a professional and don't promise to keep it a secret. Selecting a professional can begin with a licensed or certified counselor or therapist or a physician who knows enough about depression to refer the person to a specialist in mood disorders. References are also available from hospitals, universities, or professional associations (see Resources at the end of this chapter).

Hopefully, the stigma attached to depression and all types of therapies will be eliminated and the future will be brighter for those who suffer from major depression as well as for their families and friends. Having the proper diagnosis, using drug therapy if needed, enhancing one's physical health, and then working with an effective therapist can make the difference between living in the depths of despair and enjoying the beauty of life.

Coping with Emotional Crises

My sister-in-law sounded numb when she called at 3:30 in the morning. "Steven was killed in an automobile accident about midnight. A drunk driver going over 80 miles an hour on the wrong side of the highway hit his car head-on." I managed to gasp, "Oh, no," as a jolt of disbelief and horror hit. Steve, my beloved 22-year-old nephew, was dead. The grieving began at that moment, and years later the sorrow remains, diminished somewhat by time, coping strategies, and beautiful memories. Emotions run rampant when a crisis occurs (Hanna, 2003).

The death of a loved one is a profound tragedy. Losing a child is the ultimate crisis. Not only is there a loss of a precious life, but also a young person's death seems so unthinkable and unfair. It was supposedly Albert Camus who explained: "The order of nature is reversed. Children are supposed to bury their parents" (Stearns, 1984, p. 15). A child's death is not only the pain of losing a beloved person, but also it means a loss of the parents' dreams, a part of themselves, and a part of their future (Davis, 1991). "A child's death is like having part of ourselves sliced away" (Sanders, 1992, p. 120). One study had hopeful findings in that bereaved parents reported slightly higher levels of marital satisfaction and expressed different sources of life satisfaction and sources of worry (deVries et al., 1997). A bereaved father said, "I truly do not 'sweat the small stuff' anymore, and I am satisfied with a lot of little stuff." In a book designed to help cope with the loss of a child, the author (Donnelly, 2001) assures parents that recovering doesn't mean forgetting.

Steven's tragic death began a series of crises for my family. Within a little over a year I underwent cancer surgery and was fitted with an artificial eye, my

16-year-old daughter experienced a prolonged illness and surgery as a result of an autoimmune disease, and my father died unexpectedly. I was beginning to believe what I had read on a greeting card: "Into every life some rain must fall," and on the inside, "followed by large hail and damaging winds." On a positive note, these crises led to personal learning and can now provide hope, encouragement, and suggested coping strategies to you (Hanna, 2003).

The Path of Life

Life isn't easy. "The farther one travels on the journey of life, the more births one will experience, and therefore the more deaths, the more joy and the more pain" (Peck, 1978, p. 75). An introduction activity to an interpersonal relations course, the instructor draws, on the chalkboard, a line depicting life. What do you think it looks like? It is not a straight line, nor is it vertical or horizontal, and neither does it go up for a period of years (maybe 40?) and then head downhill. The "dip 'n do" line goes up and down like a series of peaks and valleys. The drawing reveals the certainty of change. Life has both positive and negative experiences from which we cannot escape.

What can the line teach? The word *choice* comes to mind. All of us will spend time in the valleys. What are your choices? One is to make the situation worse. Tragedy can become more tragic because of one's thoughts or actions, or both. Kurt was badly injured in an accident. He had not used alcohol much before; now its effects seemed to lessen the hurt. He became frequently verbally abusive to his family. Another possibility is to remain stagnant, do little, and maybe wallow in self-pity. The thought "There's nothing I can do about this" is common. The best choice is to gather your resources and strength and begin to ascend from the valley. Recognizing the pattern of the life line reminds you that dips eventually curve upward.

Another relevant point has to do with learning. Joyful and peaceful times are too often unappreciated. "I look back on those days before I was ill and kick myself for not enjoying them more," reported a cancer patient. "Now I am grateful for each minute of life." Because we often take the peaks for granted, generally, less learning is experienced there. Valuable lessons are learned in the trenches, the dips of life. Also, the variety of life's experiences adds depth and meaning to existence.

> A full life will be full of pain. But the only alternative is not to live fully. (Peck, 1978, p. 133)

Without a doubt, the terrorist attack on the World Trade Center and the Pentagon on September 11, 2001, was the greatest collective crisis in recent history. The tragic loss of so many lives and the damage to property and the economy were devastating. The following is both poignant and meaningful.

> Grief and love, rage and vengefulness, pride and defiance—a volatile set of emotions was let loose in America. They can be dangerous, but they can also be constructive. It hardly seems possible or even fitting, to imagine that some good could come out of such horror. But the best memorial to those who perished would be the achievement of a safer, saner world. And it is not out of reach. (Auchincloss, 2001, pp. 18–24)

As a result of Hurricane Katrina, which struck the Gulf Coast on August 28, 2005, over 1,100 lives were lost. The flood waters left a million people without homes, jobs, and schools. The shock wave to the U.S. and world economies will have a long-term impact. Crises of this magnitude as well as all others are traumatic, yet the possibility of positive change offers a beacon of hope.

> *Sometimes when the bottom falls out of our lives, we are set free. Loss can make artists of us all as we weave new patterns into the fabric of our lives.*
> —Charles Stephen

Any unexpected negative or positive event that dramatically changes your life is a **crisis**. Loss is commonly experienced directly, such as losing a job, a loved one, a personal possession, or a dream, and indirectly in cases of rape, chronic illness, or the birth of a child with disabilities. Answers to how long is the path to recovery and how much time it will take are only speculative.

> When a significant loss has us in its grip, a minimum of six months to a year is usually required for healing. Some aspects of the process continue into the second year. Resolution may not come until even later. (Stearns, 1984, p. 19)

When a crisis of loss isn't resolved or healed, problems can emerge later. "Unresolved grief haunts us" (Kennedy, 1991, p. 12).

How to Cope

The coping mechanisms that will be most effective in a situation depend on the nature of the crisis. Often we are wise to do what the title of a helpful book suggests: *Hoping, Coping, and Moping* (Jevne, 2000). Whenever a loss is involved, the following coping behaviors make the going easier, perhaps faster, and increase the possibility for growth.

Feel your feelings. An emotional response is inevitable in any crisis. Keep in mind that suppressed feelings can cause unwanted problems and almost never help the situation. You may be reluctant to express emotion, especially if the feeling is an uncomfortable one for you. Depression is one of my least favorites.

> Any emotion that is repressed will eventually seek manifestation at a later date. What you resist emotionally persists. And by experiencing the emotion I don't mean you need to act out the emotion. Simply feel the emotion fully. (Ellsworth, 1988, p. 77).

Feeling the emotion goes beyond naming it or talking about it. During my first cancer-center session, I eagerly volunteered to be the first to tell my story. The leader stopped me after a few minutes and asked, "How did you *feel* about losing your eye?" I glibly put names to the feelings: anxious, sad. When she pressed me to actually feel what I felt, I found myself resisting. She said, "I don't think you have really dealt with that loss." To my surprise, I felt the tears coming. She asked me why losing an eye was so sad. Without thinking, I blurted out, "Because I have always been complimented on my blue eyes. My husband said it was one of the first things he noticed about me, and now one is gone." Both my husband and I cried then, a welcome release and a sure sign that until then we hadn't truly experienced the pain of the loss (Hanna, 2003).

> Lean gently into your pain. You will not find it bottomless. Let yourself be with the pain. When it is at its worst and you feel it all, you're already starting to heal. (Bloomfield, 1980, p. 268)

Release feelings.   In any crisis, emotional expression can be extremely therapeutic. Crying, deep breathing, and hugging are appropriate behaviors intended to relieve tension. Being touched is reassuring. I remember the horrible night I was told that there was a 98 percent probability that my eye tumor was cancerous. Crying was a welcome release; being held by my husband got me through the night (Hanna, 2003). Relaxation techniques described in Chapter 3 can be quite soothing. Some audiotapes are designed to help people release feelings and then move on with their lives. Another possibility is to keep a journal. I remember feeling a release during several crises as the feelings seemed to move from inside me onto the paper. Often, when thoughts are put on paper, a person can begin to see "form in the chaos" (Kennedy, 1991, p. 29).

Research supports the benefits of writing (Smyth, 1998). Writing about emotional upheavals improved the physical and mental health of grade-school children, nursing home residents, asthma and arthritis sufferers, college students, maximum security prisoners, new mothers, and rape victims (Pennebaker, 1997; Suedfeld and Pennebaker, 1997). Recommendations are to focus on current issues and explore both the objective experience and your deepest feelings about it. Talking into a tape recorder can be substituted for writing.

Take charge of your thoughts.   Thoughts can help or hurt. The cognitive techniques, explained earlier, are especially beneficial. Be aware of what you are thinking during a crisis. Is it realistic? If not, remember that you can change it using a method such as rational emotive behavioral therapy. Cognitive restructuring, discussed in Chapter 1, helped breast cancer patients shift to problem-focused coping that resulted in positive life changes (Spiegel, 1996). The doctor who led support groups for these patients offers recommendations in an inspiring book *Living Beyond Limits: New Hope and Help for Facing Life-Threatening Illness* (Spiegel, 1993). Sustaining positive thoughts is critical.

Acceptance of reality and realization of what you cannot change are healthy. "My husband no longer loves me and wants a divorce," "My child is addicted to drugs," "I have a serious disease," "My mother is dead" are difficult realities to think about; yet, as facts, they need to be acknowledged so they can be dealt with. Denial is usually a first reaction, and it helps to absorb the shock. After a time, denial is unhealthy. A challenging question may be advisable: "What are you going to do now?" The question will force you to take action, and the answer will free you to move on with your life. Recognizing what you can do and then acting upon it make any crisis easier to bear.

Become educated.   Educating yourself about any topic related to the crisis can make a positive difference. Libraries and bookstores contain many resources on coping and offer positive examples of those who "have gone before you." For example, the book *Just Get Me Through This!* (Cohen and Gelfand, 2000) is highly recommended as an excellent tool to help deal with breast cancer. Decide how much you want to know, ask questions, and reframe your thinking in a positive direction. It's important to note, though, that too much obsession isn't advisable. Thinking and talking only about your crisis is not only unhealthy, but also it is likely to "turn off" others.

Seek support.   Isolating yourself for a long period of time during any crisis is not a good idea because, more than ever, support is necessary. Social networks and support have been shown to reduce mortality rates, to improve recovery from serious illness, and to increase the use of preventive health practices (Hurdle, 2001). Who can provide support? Family and friends can be comforting and helpful; in some cases, they are not. A life crisis can overwhelm loved ones and erode their abilities to be supportive. Typically, other people need to know what you need and want as well as what you don't want. A woman in a cancer support session reported that her family had descended upon her when they learned of her diagnosis. They were overly helpful and refused to let her do anything, even though she could. She decided to tell them to stop doing certain things for her because feeling helpless and out of control could make her condition worse. *The Healing Family* (Simonton, 1984) is an excellent resource for families. The author writes: "So often family members, even those with the best intentions, give the wrong kind of support, which sometimes hurts more than it helps" (p. 2). Likewise, the book mentioned earlier, *Just Get Me Through This!* (Cohen and Gelfand, 2000), enlightens potential supporters. Friends and family can be asked to carry out tasks, talk, listen, touch, or just be there. Tell them what you want.

Support groups made up of others who have had similar crises can be invaluable. If you have any reservations about seeking support, you are probably equating it with being weak. Instead, believe that you *deserve* help and that you are showing internal strength by seeking and responding to external support. An immediate benefit is the realization that you are not "different" and weren't singled out for this particular hardship. Education and a safe place to vent feelings are necessary ingredients of worthwhile groups. What is not helpful is a group that dwells only on problems and offers little that is positive. A partial listing of resources is given at the end of this and other chapters. Most telephone directories list support groups in a special section. You may need courage to pick up the phone or attend a meeting, yet the benefits almost always outweigh any initial discomfort. "Buried feelings fester. Shared feelings enrich and lead to growth and healing" (Smolin and Guinan, 1993, p. 164).

Professional help is frequently needed, and you do not have to be feeling desperate to seek it. Any one of several reasons could motivate you. You may not be receiving needed support from family, friends, and groups. Therapy could move you along faster in a healing process and can certainly enhance the quality of life. In cases of sudden, traumatic death of a spouse or a child, grief is never "normal," and mental health treatment is almost always warranted (Wortman, Battle, and Lemkau, 1997). Words of caution about selecting a counselor are in order. Be as careful as you would in choosing any medical specialist. Do not just pick a name out of the yellow pages. Use suggestions given in the earlier discussion about depression. Ask people for recommendations. Feel free to interview a few counselors and find out their level of expertise, their degree of familiarity with your particular crisis, and, most important, how much rapport you have with them. Then, if you are not satisfied with the counselor, find another one.

Be extra kind to yourself.   Taking good care of yourself is good advice at any time; during a crisis, it is of utmost importance. Because ordinary stress affects us physically, it stands to reason that during periods of unusual strain, our bodies will suffer. Eating well even if you do not feel like it, exercising, and getting plenty of rest become even more important. You can also pamper yourself without feeling guilty.

Stay active and set goals.   Even though a crisis generally saps motivation, activity is a reassuring measure. Even simple tasks such as showering, brushing your teeth, and making coffee can be energizing. Staying involved with your work, if possible, is highly recommended. Pleasurable activities divert your thinking temporarily and convince you that life can still be enjoyed. A change of scene is especially refreshing. Sometimes a crisis opens doors. Widowed at 54, Bernice decided to attend college and acquire career skills. She discovered a new person within herself and thoroughly enjoyed her learning experiences. Others do volunteer work, refresh their talents, learn skills, and acquire new hobbies and interests. Setting goals says that you can move beyond the crisis, your thinking becomes more directed, you are acting upon life rather than being acted upon, and you are sending positive messages to your body. Goals stimulate feelings of hope and anticipation and are a reinvestment in life. Delaying major decisions, however, is wise, as your judgment will probably be clouded for awhile.

Death: A Universal Crisis

Any crisis is challenging; however, the death of a loved one is most stressful. This could be because death is often so unexplainable. Judy Mize, whose husband died unexpectedly, expressed it so well. "It is so hard. Relationships do not die with death. I still have a relationship with Paul; yet Paul is not here to have a relationship with me." Rita, a widowed student, reflected on additional reasons for pain:

> I have come to realize there are many more losses tied to John's death. I lost my husband, my lifetime partner, my best friend, and my son's father. Resulting losses from his death included leaving my job and moving from Virginia. I felt I had lost myself along with John. The "me" that was, was no more. She was gone forever.

Rita's words remind us that death usually precipitates another crisis, one of identity. Death is a universal crisis because all of us, unless we die before every other person we care about, will face a loss. "One out of one dies. Nothing, no one, lives forever. All things end at some point (Sims, 1985, p. 1). Death is especially painful because each loss is connected to all loss, and every death reminds us of our own death. Because dying is considered such a taboo subject, most people try to avoid it in their thinking and talking. Unfortunately, this avoidance means that coping strategies are not being developed.

Americans tend to have a negative attitude about grieving, feeling that it is something we should get over with as soon as possible. Grief, whether our own or that of
someone in our social or business life, is an inconvenience, an interruption in our
hectic schedules. We harbor many misconceptions about the grief process and
scarcely comprehend or appreciate its value and purpose. (Vail, 1982, p. 52)

Grief is an emotional, physical, spiritual, and intellectual response to loss
(Edwards, 1989). In addition to sorrow, a person can experience anger, relief, frustration, guilt, and self-pity (DeSpelder and Strickland, 1999). Even though grief is
the hardest work we will ever have to do, it's a way to heal from pain, and we
must "go through to get through" (Edwards, 1989, p. 16).

Stages of death and grieving.   Five stages associated with acceptance of
death were identified by Elisabeth Kübler-Ross (1969). The five stages are denial,
anger, bargaining, depression, and acceptance. Her theory has led to a closer look
at the grieving process and, like other stage theories, suggests that acceptance of
death is a series of somewhat predictable thoughts, feelings, and behaviors that
are subject to individual differences.

Each stage has its challenges and its usefulness. Denial, the instant shock
and disbelief in the face of tragedy, is initially a protector. Judy, after the sudden,
unexpected death of her husband, Paul, said, "I am so grateful for denial." The
next stage of anger, even if incomprehensible at the time, may allow a bereaved
person to vent deep feelings. If the death was untimely and/or perceived as preventable, anger will likely be the dominant feeling (Wortman, Battle, and Lemkau,
1997). Bargaining is an attempt to change the circumstances. Often the attempted
"deal" to not let this happen is proposed to a supreme being, and disappointment
is a definite possibility. The next stage of depression, which is so unpleasant, can
indicate that one is approaching the acceptance stage. A survivor experiences sadness throughout every stage; the throes of agony are more apparent during this
stage. The final stage of acceptance does not mean that the pain is over; however,
it is not as acute, and one can move on.

Understanding the basic stages can help you see where you are in the process
and why you feel as you do. A student read a book about dealing with death for a
class project. Her comment was, "Until now I didn't understand what I went
through when my mother died. It was over a year ago, and the book still helped me
see that what I feel is normal." A college classmate of mine hinted at the stage process
in a lovely book she wrote for her two children before her untimely death in 1976.

When you are very close to someone who dies, there will be sadness. You won't be
sharing your life with that person anymore. Sadness hurts. You may feel as though a
big hole has been torn in your life. And there will probably be feelings of loneliness as
you remember the good times you had with the person you loved. Sometimes it takes a
very long time for the sadness to melt away, but slowly you will begin to remember important shared times without the hurt tugging at your memories. (Potter, 1979, p. 12)

Thinking only in terms of stages has some disadvantages. People can get discouraged if they believe they should progress in a certain order and time frame.
More helpful is to think of the process as a "fluid experience of a variety of emotions with one underlying theme: coming to terms with the loss" (Davis, 1991,

p. 13). Do you ever get over the death of a loved one? Most experts say that you don't. Most people will never reach a time when they completely stop grieving; however, the feeling is less intense and not as frequent. As one bereaved mother expressed, "You don't get over it; you get used to it" (Wortman, Battle, and Lemkau, 1997). Recovering doesn't mean forgetting, but a sense of acceptance can be reached.

> The rainbow hues of your grief—the red-yellow anguish, the blue-green questions, the purple confidence—are woven permanently into the tapestry of your life. Grief invariably leads to new strengths. When you allow yourself to experience fully the subtle gradations of its colors and textures, grief adds to your personal richness and depth. (Tubesing, 1981, p. 57)

Behaviors of grief.   Someone may say to you, "Do not grieve when I am gone. I don't want you to mourn my death." Although the remark was well meant, the person is not doing you a favor. Grieving serves as a natural and necessary path to healing. A young mother tried hard to block the process: "Crying would be good for me, but my children have lost a father, and I have to be strong for them." She and her children would be better served by getting rid of the equation between strength and suppression of feeling. Her children could benefit from her sharing her sorrow and modeling grieving behaviors.

Grief is invariably unsettling. Many times death is irrational, illogical, and crazy, so a reaction that can feel like the "crazies" is normal (Donnelley, 1987). "Significant emotional loss is an abnormal event in a person's life, and there is no normal way to react to an abnormal event" (James and Cherry, 1988, p. 11). Even though grief is painful, like death, it is a part of life. Experiencing all of life means that you and I will grieve.

> I do not like being hurt. I don't really enjoy experiencing pain. But I believe that I become less of a human being if I learn the art of detachment so well that I can experience the death of a friend or relative and not be emotionally affected by it. To be alive is to feel pain, and to hide from pain is to make yourself less alive. (Kushner, 1986, p. 89)

Grieving behaviors vary from one person to another. Stereotypic gender differences may emerge. Men and women share equal feelings of pain and grief, yet women seem to use a social support system whereas many men either do not have one or do not use it. During times when partners need each other's support, the differences can cause relationship problems. Honest communication can bridge the gap and lessen the pain.

Other differences have to do with cause of death. Suicides appear to be the most difficult. In addition to depression, guilt is the most intense emotion for parents. They first blame themselves (Smolin and Guinan, 1993). In a study of adult next-of-kin who were mourning a suicide, the participants either did not ask for support or encountered barriers when they sought it. Professional help was identified as the most pressing need as well as what was most wanted (Provini and Everett, 2000). Because so little had been written for survivors, two authors wrote a book in which they point out that for every suicide about seven to ten others are intimately affected. Immediately finding a therapist who is an excellent listener is

---

Grieving and Healing

- Let feelings loose.
- Do not isolate yourself. Stay engaged in activities and involved with people.
- Tell people what you want and do not want.
- Ask for help and also insist on doing things for yourself, if that is what you feel.
- Create a sanctuary for grief, a place where you can be alone with your feelings.
- Spend focused, yet brief, times in this sanctuary and concentrate on memories and personal grief.
- Give yourself a "vacation" from pain whenever possible. Focus on diversions.
- Set up or donate to a worthy cause in the person's memory.
- Create a new nonphysical relationship with the deceased.
- Write to the person and/or about the person.
- Stay involved with family and friends.
- Engage in something that has a meaningful purpose.
- On a regular basis, manage your personal stress.

Figure 5-6

strongly recommended. It can also help parents to keep in mind that they can do a thousand things for a child but perhaps not a thousand and one (Lukas and Seiden, 1997) (Fig. 5-6).

Recommendations for grieving.   When you are in the throes of deep despair, realize that "grief is the price we pay for love. Though death comes, love will never go away" (Sims, 1985, p. 6).

Writing about the deceased is therapeutic. Writing a tribute to the person who has died can serve more than one purpose.

Lisa Patterson wrote the following memorial to her mother.

One student commented, "Thanks so much for my first real lessons about life. I will never forget it. Now to put it all into practice . . . I cannot wait!" There are scrapbooks filled with similar evaluations of Sharon Hanna's impact on the lives of her students.

A lifelong educator, Sharon had a passion for teaching students, not only about information they needed to know, but about how to live positively in the world by mastering the art of interpersonal communication. With her trademark warmth and humor, she taught self-awareness and self-esteem as a prelude to the development of positive and effective communication skills and healthy relationships. Her aim was nothing short of empowering her students to take responsibility for their lives, make wiser choices, improve their relationships, appreciate diversity, and live happier, more productive lives.

It was Sharon's expressed desire to continue to be of service to the students whom she cared about so deeply. To honor her 24-year career as a college instructor an endowed memorial scholarship was established in her memory with the Southeast Community College Foundation to be awarded to an SCC student each year. The outpouring of love for Sharon and her memory made it possible.

Sharon's legacy is embodied in her heartfelt advice to her students, "We come to college not only to make a living, but to learn to live a life!" Sharon will always be remembered as an extraordinary teacher who significantly enriched and inspired the lives of her students, colleagues, friends and family.

Sharon encouraged Bob, Lisa, Lyn, Jeff, Greg and all who have grieved to remember:

We never lose the people we love, even to death. They continue to participate in every act, thought, and decision we make. Their love leaves an indelible imprint in our memories. Memories make us immortal. (Buscaglia, 1992, p. 230)

Other creative talents such as composing a song or just singing one in memory or tribute, painting, sculpting, or drawing are all ways of releasing (Reflect and Apply). A tragedy can lead to worthwhile actions, and becoming involved in a cause related to the death is an excellent idea. Mothers Against Drunk Driving (MADD), an organization that has made a significant difference, was started by a woman whose daughter was killed by a drunk driver. A student's death launched a campaign at Bowling Green State University called "Never Again" to combat drunk driving. Grief can be channeled into positive energy. To gain insight into crisis and coping, use the activity in Reflection and Applications.

At some point—and only the grieving person can decide when that point has been reached—moving on with life is essential. You then may be able to see that death can be a teacher helping us appreciate each other, ourselves, and life itself. You may become closer to loved ones, share feelings more fully, tell people that you care, take extra safety precautions, become healthier, and contribute to a worthwhile cause. "An awareness of death increases my appreciation of the preciousness of life. The glory of life is inseparable from the fact that it is finite" (Branden, 1983, p. 200).

Life, a lovely, lively flame dancing inside us. At death, the dancing stops. But the special feeling for the person we loved never stops.

—Linda Lytle Potter

REFLECT AND APPLY

Reflect

♦ *Recall an activating event, your beliefs about the event, and the consequences the ABCs of rational emotive behavior therapy.*
♦ *What do you do when you're in a "blue" mood?*
♦ *Think of what you would say or do if someone you know talks of suicide.*

Apply

♦ *In the Reflections and Applications section for Chapter 5, fill in the boxes showing that you can use rational emotive behavior therapy.*
♦ *When you experience an unpleasant emotion, use control theory and change the "doing" part of your behavior. Be aware of what happens.*
♦ *If you feel comfortable doing so, tell a friend how you have effectively coped with a crisis.*

LOOKING BACK

- The emotional self is interesting, complicated, and challenging; confusion about emotions is common.
- Researchers identify and categorize emotions. Combinations of the basic emotions make up other feeling states.
- An emotion has three components: physiological arousal, subjective cognitive state, and expressive behavior. The behavioral component is the most controllable.
- Expression is learned from a variety of sources. Men, especially, receive restrictive messages.
- All four developmental areas are strengthened by constructive emotional expression; self-esteem is also bolstered. Relationships thrive on open, honest, and constructive expression. For many, demonstration of feelings is not easy but can be developed.
- Anger will occur, and the key is to learn to manage the emotion so that interactions and relationships are not damaged.
- Emotions can be changed by altering thoughts and behaviors through rational behavioral emotive therapy and control therapy. This is beneficial when emotions are unpleasant and causing harm.
- Clinical depression, different from minor mood changes, is serious, and therapy is highly recommended. Suicide is the tragic outcome of many cases of deep depression.
- Crises of any kind create stress and can wreak havoc on the emotional self. Specific strategies can lessen the impact and help resolve the crisis faster, reduce the harmful effects, and use the situation for positive growth.
- Death, which affects everyone, is the ultimate crisis. Grief, although not welcome, is necessary. You can cope and, in some cases, use the tragic event to improve your own life and make needed changes in society.

The full and free experience and expression of all our feelings are necessary for personal peace and meaningful relationships.

—John Powell

RESOURCES

American Psychiatric Association, 1000. Wilson Blvd. Suite 1825, Arlington VA: 22209-3901. (703) 907–7300. http://www.psych.org

American Psychological Association, 750 First Street NE, Washington, DC 20002-4242. Toll-free: (800) 374-2721. http://www.apa.org

Center for Healing & Wellness, 2235 Grant Road, Suite 6, Los Altos, CA 94024. (650) 625-1987. Support children who have a parent with a serious illness http://www.healingandwellness.org

Compassionate Friends (support for bereaved parents), P.O. Box 3696, Oak Brook, IL 60522-3696. Toll-free: (877) 969-0010. http://www.compassionatefriends.org

Emotions Anonymous International (for anyone wanting to learn to deal with emotions), P.O. Box 4245, St. Paul, MN 55104. (651) 647-9712. http://www.mtn.org/EA

Heartbeat (support for survivors of suicide victims), 2015 Devon Street, Colorado Springs, CO 80909. (719) 596-2575. http://www.heartbeatsurvivorsaftersuicide.org

Heartbeat Suicide Hotline: (719) 596-5433.

Menninger Clinic (mental health), P.O. Box 829, Topeka, KS 66601-0829. Toll free: (800) 351-9058. http://www.menninger.edu

National Association of Social Workers, 750 First Street NE,

Suite 700, Washington, DC 20002. Toll free: (800) 638-8799. http://www.socialworkers.org

Depression and Bipolar Support Alliance, 730 North Franklin Street, Suite 501, Chicago, IL 60610. Toll free: (800) 826-3632. http://dbsalliance.org

National Institute of Mental Health, 6001 Executive Blvd., Room 8184, MSC 9663, Bethesda, MD 20892-9663. (301) 443-4513. http://www.nimh.nih.gov

Rainbows for All God's Children (support for children and adults who have experienced death, divorce, separation, or abandonment), 2100 Golf Road, #370, Rolling Meadows, IL 60008. Toll free: (800) 266-3206. http://www.rainbows.org

Human Service Directories (included in most telephone directories) list agencies and support groups dealing with almost all situations.

IMPROVING YOUR HEALTH

LOOKING AHEAD

After completing this chapter, you will be able to

- Understand a variety of health issues as they relate to wellness.
- Distinguish between good nutrition and poor eating habits.
- Define the use of stress relief in terms of your health.
- Define meditation and relaxation.
- Understand the use of anger management.

Health

How do you define health? For many, being healthy means being free of disease, yet is that all there is to it? Think of **health** as a general feeling of physical and mental well-being. A realistic picture places health on a continuum from being very ill to very healthy.

Very healthy is synonymous with **wellness,** a high level of physical and mental well-being. Total wellness includes being the following (Bloomfield, 1978).

- Trim and physically fit
- Full of energy, vigorous, rarely tired
- Free of minor complaints (such as indigestion, constipation, headaches, insomnia)
- Alert, able to concentrate, clearheaded
- Radiant, with clear skin, glossy hair, and sparkling eyes
- Active and creative
- Able to relax easily, free of worry and anxiety
- Self-assured, confident, optimistic
- Satisfied with work and the direction of your life
- Able to assert yourself, stand up for your rights
- Satisfied with your sexual relationships
- Free of destructive health habits, particularly smoking, overeating, and excessive drinking
- Fulfilled and at peace with yourself

Even though few people possess every characteristic, wellness is possible; the closer you come to it, the greater your chance for a fulfilling life. Try thinking of the body as a machine. How well are you taking care of it? Machinery can be replaced; whole bodies cannot. Unfortunately, most people treat machinery better than they do their own bodies.

An important beginning for you is an understanding of your degree of wellness. This section will emphasize ways you can become an active participant in maintaining good health. The following "Tips to Wellness" are a few of the possible health-enhancing suggestions.

Tips to Wellness

- *Increase physical activity.* For most, the easiest way to increase physical activity is to walk more. The key is to find activities that you enjoy and will do on a regular basis—then move your body!
- *Improve your nutrition.* Learn what is healthy and then put that knowledge into practice. Realizing that you will have only one body, care for it better than you do a vehicle or other material object.
- *Maintain a healthy body weight.* Set a realistic goal. People feel and look better when their weight is "right" for them. If you are obese, aim for 5 percent to 15 percent weight reduction and notice a dramatic difference.
- *Get adequate sleep.* Being well rested improves all areas of the self.
- *Effectively cope with stress.* You can't escape stress; however, you can manage it and make it beneficial in your life.

Even though most people consider their health to be a high priority, a large number admit that they do not practice health-enhancing behaviors, and several even pursue unhealthy lifestyles, especially during high school and college years. Do you take your health for granted? Any disregard of your health in the present has ramifications for the future. Former governor of Colorado Richard D. Lamm stated:

> The single most important factor determining our quality of life is our health and the single most important factor affecting our health is the degree to which we as individuals are willing to take responsibility for our own diets and exercise, no matter what age we are at the present time. (Carlson and Seiden, 1988)

In thinking about your health, which of the following three categories best describes you (Crose, 1997)?

Health gamblers: They take their health for granted and assume that there is little they can do about changing the way they are. "My dad died at a young age of lung cancer so I'm expecting that will happen to me, too," said a 30-year-old man as he smoked another cigarette.

Health mechanics: They are willing to tend to their health when illness strikes, yet do little to promote wellness. "I figure if it isn't broken, why do anything?" was how one woman described her attitude.

Health gardeners: They are mindful of their physical and mental health, take steps to prevent illness, and are active in promoting wellness. "I eat sensibly most of the time, use supplements to elevate my health and protect my body, exercise regularly, and get sufficient rest. I feel absolutely great most of the time!" commented a woman.

Are you satisfied with your category? Later in this chapter you will read about several ways to become a "health gardener."

Taking Control of Your Health and Well-Being

Choosing wellness is the first step in getting rid of unhealthy behaviors and in preventing disease. Motivation comes from being informed on health issues. Then, if you truly value yourself, you can make wise choices. Ask yourself how healthy you want to be and then educate yourself about making healthy choices.

Eliminate unhealthy behaviors and habits. Choices that add to or detract from the quality of life are yours to make.

Let us explore why putting the wellness tips into practice will enhance your life and learn ways to accomplish each one.

Physical Activity

Physical activity is positively related to:

- Living longer (Fozard, 1999)
- Lower risk of heart disease (Lee et al., 2001)
- Decreased risk of both colon cancer (Batty, 2000) and breast cancer (Verloop et al., 2000)
- Prevention and better management of diabetes (Folsom and Kushit, 2000)
- Lowered blood pressure (*Harvard Health Letter*, 1999)
- Relief of stress (Bartolomeo, 2000) and of depression (Mangum, 2000)
- Increased cognitive skills especially in older adults (Larkins, 1999)
- Protection against and better management of Alzheimer's disease (Friedland, 1998)
- Fewer chronic medical problems, higher levels of functioning, and greater strength in older adults (Fozard, 1999)
- Lowered risk of osteoporosis (Adler and Raymond, 2001)
- Healthy weight maintenance (Anderson and Wadden, 1999)
- Smoking cessation (Aschwanden and Cederborg, 1999)

Becoming more active seems to benefit all areas of the self. How much activity is healthy? A U.S. study showed that the risk of death can be reduced 19 percent by adding just one mile to an ordinary daily walk (Hakim et al., 1998). Also the "10,000 Steps Program" is an easy-to-use, interactive way to get physically active. Taking 10,000 steps each day will help you:

- Boost your energy
- Reduce stress
- Manage your weight
- Feel great

Figure 6-1 Enjoyable physical activity contributes to wellness.

An important point is to be sensible about exercise, as intense, long-duration exercise can actually depress the immune system (Pedersen, Rohde, and Zacho, 1996).

Reasons for not becoming more physically active are often heard. "I cannot afford to join a health club right now" or "I do not have time" are among the most common. In Chapter 4 you read how excuses can block happiness. Be honest with yourself. If you sincerely want to add physical activity to your life, you can. Simple ways are to just walk farther and to climb stairs instead of using an elevator or escalator, walk during break time, park further away or walk with a friend on a regular basis. To motivate you, read what a well-known authority on wellness says:

Human beings are meant to walk. We are bipedal, upright organisms with bodies designed for locomotion. Walking exercises our brains as well as our muscular skeletal systems. When you walk, the movement of your limbs is cross-patterned. This type of movement generates electrical activity in the brain that has a harmonizing influence on the whole central nervous system a special benefit of walking that you do not necessarily get from other kinds of exercise. (Weil, 1995b, p. 188)

Enthusiastic walkers enjoy the psychological benefits as much as they do the physical gains. Another benefit is a more pleasing appearance. When asked to identify the everyday hassles in life, middle-aged people listed weight as their main concern (Lazarus, 1981). Does it seem likely that exercise would do much to alleviate this problem, thus reducing stress? A medical examination before you begin any strenuous program is suggested. Realize that you can feel better, have more energy, and save money on medical bills. The time spent in physical activity could be the wisest investment you will ever make (Fig. 6-1).

Nutrition

Would it surprise you to learn that many people know little about this subject? Do you know what foods contain certain vitamins and minerals and how much of each is healthy? What about the foods that are definitely unhealthy and that make up a large portion of the typical American diet? Are you aware that:

- Food and supplements can be used to maximize brain power, boost memory, elevate mood, improve IQ and creativity, and prevent and reverse mental aging (Carper, 2000).
- Diet is related to the most common chronic diseases including coronary heart disease, hypertension, cancer, and osteoporosis (Shikany and White, 2000).
- Calcium deficiencies lead to osteoporosis (Cromer and Harel, 2000). Calcium saves bones, relieves premenstrual symptoms, helps prevent colon cancer, and fights fat (Carper, 2000). Yet, of those over 50, only

60 percent of men and less than 50 percent of women consumed the recommended daily allowance; for teens it was far worse with only 25 percent of boys and 10 percent of girls getting enough calcium. (Raloff,
2000). Do you consume enough calcium?

- Antioxidants in several foods are associated with a decreased risk of cardiovascular disease and cancer (Agarwall and Venketeshwer Rao, 2000).

These facts will come as no surprise if you consider that your body uses
what you put into it to build cells and strengthen your immune system. Unless
you are certain that you are taking in the amount of nutrients not only to stay relatively healthy but also to serve as a potential preventive force, you will not
achieve a high level of wellness. Even a small increase in fruit and vegetable intake has the potential to prevent disease (Khaw et al., 2001). Unfortunately, half of
us do not get the minimum of three vegetable servings a day; three-fourths do not
eat the suggested two servings of fruit. In fact, no fruit whatsoever passes the lips
of half of American adults on any given day (Jaret, 1998).

Even government experts say that a good diet may not be enough. Scientists
at the Institute of Medicine recommend supplements to get enough B vitamins,
which appear to play an important role in the prevention of heart disease and
birth defects (*Health*, 1998). Other recommended supplements are calcium and vitamins such as vitamin E if you are not getting enough from your diet. Even
though a person can overdo with supplements, this is rare. Rather than being
overly concerned about getting too much, you would benefit by getting the
proper amounts of nutrients.

By learning about nutrition from reliable sources and then by practicing better eating habits most of the time, you can fuel your body in healthy ways. One reliable source is *Your Miracle Brain* (Carper, 2000). The author, a noted health
journalist, recommends how to optimize your health with nutrition as well as
what not to do. For example, she offers compelling evidence that eating breakfast
can boost brain functioning whereas while starting the day on an empty stomach
leaves the body short on fuel and more vulnerable to failure. Citing research at
Harvard Medical School, elementary school students who ate breakfast had
40 percent higher math grades and were less likely to be absent or tardy from
school than those who rarely ate breakfast. Much can be learned about the fascinating field of nutrition. Challenge yourself to be among those who are "in the
know" and use the power of nutrition to enhance your health. Not only are
healthy foods important, but also water is essential to balanced health (Fig. 6-2).

Weight Maintenance

Practicing healthier eating habits and being physically active lead to the
added bonus of weight maintenance, which is a health issue as well as one of attractiveness. What is a healthy weight? A simple answer is a weight at which a
person's health is not at risk and at a level that feels good. A measure that more accurately reflects healthy weight is body mass index (BMI). Values of 19.0 to 24.9
fall in the desirable range (Anderson and Wadden, 1999). A calculator comes in
handy as you figure BMI. Multiply your weight in pounds by 703 and then divide
by your height in inches squared.

Fats, oils and sweets
(use sparingly)

Dairy
(2-3 servings)

Meat and other proteins
(2-3 servings)

Fruit
(2-4 servings)

Vegetables
(3-5 servings)

Bread and grain
(6-11 servings)

Figure 6-2   Healthy eating habits are important for life.
Source: EMG Education Management Group

Obesity, defined as a BMI of 30 or greater, kills 300,000 Americans prematurely each year by contributing to heart attacks, high blood pressure, strokes, diabetes, and many other serious diseases. "The fatter you are, the sicker you will be and the earlier you will die" (Fumento, 1998, p. 36). Evidence suggests that obesity can increase the risk of dying from certain cancers by up to 50 percent (American Cancer Society, 2001). Of all behaviors leading to illness, only smoking takes more lives than obesity (Fumento, 1998). On the positive side, being at a healthy weight contributes to overall good health and lessens the risk of disease (Reflect and Apply).

How are we doing? Not well, at least not in the United States, according to many experts. In fact, U.S. society has the dubious honor of being the second fattest society in the world with first place going to a tribe in the South Pacific (Butler, 2001). A recent national survey found that 59 percent of adults are overweight, and 23 percent of those are obese (Sturm, 2000). Children are three times as likely to be overweight today as they were 30 years ago (Wingert, 2000). Eating too much high-calorie, fat-laden junk food and drinking sugar-filled beverages while sitting in front of a television screen or computer monitor have contributed to children being overweight. That is the bad news. The good news is that even modest weight losses (5 to 10 percent of initial weight) can result in substantial improvements.

How do you achieve and maintain a healthy weight? Wise choices regarding nutrition and physical activity are necessary. Going on a diet isn't the answer. People who do this often end up in repeated cycles of weight loss and gain. Called **yo-yo dieting,** it is unhealthy and does not work. Yo-yo dieting is being on a weight loss roller coaster. A dieter may successfully lose 10, 50, or more pounds only to gain them back and begin another period of dieting. In addition to being

---

REFLECT AND APPLY

Reflect

♦ *What physical improvements would you like to make?*
♦ *Do you wear a seat belt when riding in a vehicle? If not, use critical thinking and find comparison figures regarding fatalities and serious injuries.*
♦ *In what ways has self-esteem affected your life?*
♦ *Recall one "message" that you have received about yourself.*

Apply

♦ *In the next week or so, improve your physical self.*
♦ *Demonstrate a positive attitude the next time you face an adverse situation.*
♦ *Use one word or phrase to describe yourself in each of the four developmental areas.*

---

frustrating, repeated cycles of weight loss and weight gain may also be harmful to health. Permanent weight loss is a lifetime commitment to lifestyle changes in diet and exercise. Instead, the key is to eat sensibly and healthfully most of the time and increase physical activity so that you increase metabolic rate and decrease body fat. Remember a simple bit of mathematics: Weight loss comes from burning off more calories than you take in. Walking, which is easy for most people, burns calories. Most experts recommend 45 minutes a day in order to lose and keep weight off (Bilyeau, 1998). The top fat-burning exercises are bicycling, jogging, and swimming (Napier, 1998). Enjoyable physical activity, along with better nutrition, does away with the idea of dieting and becomes a way of life.

Because most people will consider weight loss at some time in their lives, education is a practical idea. A misconception is that not eating is the way to lose weight. When the body is deprived of food, energy level is low and metabolism slows down so you don't burn off fat nearly as efficiently. Breakfast wakes up your metabolism. According to a Mayo Clinic study, people who chronically skip breakfast burn an average of 150 fewer calories a day than those who eat breakfast even when both groups consume the same amount of daily calories (Thornton, 2000). Eliminating most junk foods and those high in fat (remembering that we need some fat in our diets) and, instead, eating fruits, vegetables, and foods that contain fiber, controlling portion sizes, and eating at regular intervals are highly recommended. Because extreme overweight is likely related to genetics as well as environment and is such a serious health challenge, obese people are advised to seek the help of a professional in developing a successful weight management plan. Being realistic about your weight, learning all you can about weight loss, and making it part of a total wellness program are the answers to a challenge faced by many Americans.

Adequate Rest

How much rest do you get? Seven to eight hours of sleep in a 24-hour period is recommended. Teenagers require approximately $9\frac{1}{4}$ hours of sleep to maintain optimal alertness, and most are sleep deprived (Black, 2000). Sleep serves many functions so it seems obvious that not getting enough would affect health. Think of how you feel when you are very tired. Even more serious are the other consequences of sleep deprivation.

- Impaired cognitive and motor performance equivalent to alcohol intoxication (Williamson and Feyer, 2001)
- Decrease in learning abilities (Segall, 2001)
- Heightened risk of accidents (Libbon, 2000)
- Reduced memory abilities (Butcher, 2000)
- Negative effects on health especially metabolism and hormone production (*Current Health* 2, 2000)

College students were studied to see what accounted for grade-point average differences. Sleep habits headed the list (Trockel, Barnes, and Eggert, 2000). As is obvious, sleep rejuvenates the body. Making a choice to get enough sleep is undoubtedly in your best interest.

Smoking Cigarettes

If you smoke, you inhale several potentially dangerous substances, including the most potent cancer-causing substances known as **carcinogens.** A number of substances in tobacco smoke cause cancer in human beings (Centers for Disease Control and Prevention, 2001a). The high risks have been apparent for years, and the future for a smoker is bleak. Nearly 5 million children living today will die prematurely because of a decision they will eventually make-to smoke cigarettes (Centers for Disease Control and Prevention, 2001a). Tobacco use worldwide, which causes nearly 4 million people to die each year, is the leading preventable cause of death (Satcher, 2001) (Fig. 6-3).

Overall Mortality

Tobacco use is the leading preventable cause of death in the United States. Cigarette smoking causes an estimated 440,000 deaths, or about one of every five deaths, each year.

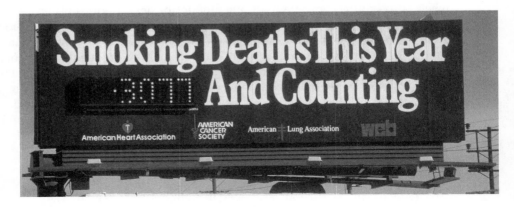

Figure 6-3
Source: Bill Aron

- This estimate includes 35,000 deaths from secondhand smoke exposure.
- Cigarette smoking is related to erectile dysfunction in men and general sexual fitness (Wuh and Fox, 2001).
- Cigarette smoking kills an estimated 264,000 men and 178,000 women in the United States each year.
- More deaths are caused each year by tobacco use than by all deaths from human immunodeficiency virus (HIV), illegal drug use, alcohol use, motor vehicle injuries, suicides, and murders combined.
- On average, adults who smoke cigarettes die 13 to 14 years earlier than nonsmokers.
- Based on current cigarette smoking patterns, an estimated 25 million Americans who are alive today will die prematurely from smoking-related illnesses, including 5 million people younger than 18.

Mortality from Specific Diseases

Lung cancer (124,000), heart disease (111,000), and the chronic lung diseases of emphysema, bronchitis, and chronic airway obstruction (82,000) are responsible for the largest number of smoking-related deaths. The risk of dying from lung cancer is more than 22 times higher among men who smoke cigarettes and about 12 times higher among women who smoke cigarettes compared with those who have never smoked. Since 1950, lung cancer deaths among women have increased by more than 600 percent. Since 1987, lung cancer has been the leading cause of cancer-related deaths in women. Cigarette smoking results in a two- to threefold increased risk of dying from chronic obstructive lung disease. About 90 percent of all deaths from chronic obstructive lung diseases are attributable to cigarette smoking.

Pipe smoking and cigar smoking increase the risk of dying from cancers of the lung, esophagus, larynx, and oral cavity. Smokeless tobacco use increases the risk for developing oral cancer. If health is not that important to smokers, other reasons may be. As employers become more aware of the relationship between health and cigarette smoking, smokers may find it difficult to get jobs. Typically, smokers average more sick days. Another reason is skin ageing. A student said, "I have heard it all, and nothing has jolted me to quit smoking until I heard about wrinkling. That did it!" She was referring to research that found that those who smoke have much more prominent wrinkling (Lauerman, 2001). Or perhaps a smoker will consider money. Jon figured how many dollars he would save in a year by not smoking and was motivated to quit. And cigarettes are not the total cost. Smokers spend more on cold remedies, health care, and life insurance. Tobacco addiction is a major economic handicap.

Knowing all this, the obvious question is "Why do people take up smoking?" Again, look at research-based facts.

- Approximately 80 percent of adult smokers started smoking before age 18 (Centers for Disease Control and Prevention, 2001a). Individuals at young ages are more suggestible and tend to conform.
- Many start because their peers and family members smoke (Williams and Covington, 1997).
- Smokers are significantly less knowledgeable about smoke-related diseases than ex-smokers or nonsmokers (Najem et al., 1997).

After a habit is established, nicotine, the stimulant in cigarettes, creates an **addiction,** a physiological dependence (Kessler, 1995). If you have not started smoking, the obvious wise choice is to never start. If you have, are you willing to risk years of life or experience a low-quality existence? Having emphysema and depending on an external breathing device that you may have to drag around is a difficult way to live. Hopefully, you will place more value on health and quality of life and want to quit. The two current strategies are just quitting immediately or gradually or using pharmacologic agents (Mocharnuk, 2001). Medications can double your chances of quitting (Centers for Disease Control and Prevention, 2001a). Help is readily available. One easy source is the Web site of the Centers for Disease Control and Prevention (see Resources at end of chapter). The following guidelines are offered.

You Can Quit!

The following tips come from the Centers for Disease Control and Prevention (2001):

- Prepare by setting a quit date. Get rid of all cigarettes and ashtrays. Stay away from others who smoke in your presence.
- Announce your intentions and get support.
- Replace smoking with other activities such as taking a walk. Refrain from environments and activities associated with smoking.
- Get medication and use it correctly.
- Be prepared for a relapse usually within the first three months. If you smoke again, set a new goal and be even more determined. Keep your "eye on the prize."

Because environmental tobacco smoke (ETS) is a critical factor in health, a person might decide to quit out of love. Passive smoking, as ETS is called, kills more Americans than either auto accidents or AIDS (*The Futurist*, 1999). An alarming study concluded that environmental smoke has all the cancer-causing substances contained in tobacco smoke (Anderson et al., 2001). ETS, which is completely preventable, is a significant predictor of increased disease and ill health among children, including sudden infant death syndrome (SIDS), asthma attacks, chronic ear infections, and lower respiratory tract infections (Centers for Disease Control and Prevention, 2001a).

> Environmental tobacco smoke is a serious health risk to children. (Ferrence and Ashley, 2000)

Children are not the only potential victims. Research reveals higher risks in nonsmoking spouses and fellow employees for lung cancer (World Health Organization, 1998), heart disease (Wells, 1998), and atherosclerosis (Howard et al., 1998).

Nonsmokers have choices. Opting not to breathe someone else's smoke may require assertiveness; however, if you value health, the choice is clear. If you are a smoker, you can show consideration by checking with nonsmokers about smoking and then understanding and accepting their wishes. Your choice to quit smoking may well be the best health decision you will ever make. Thousands have quit; you can, too!

Drinking Alcohol

Alcohol, the most widely used and abused drug in many societies, has wreaked havoc on health and personal lives. About 14 million people in the United States are alcoholics or abuse alcohol (Brink, 2001). Alcohol abuse is frequently at the root of domestic violence, child abuse and neglect, crime, lost productivity, chemical dependency, and fatal accidents and injuries. In excess, alcohol and other drugs are "truly the crutch that cripples" (Eliot and Breo, 1984, p. 200). Alcohol is linked to violence and aggression (White, 1997) and to risky sexual behavior (Poulson et al., 1998). The innocent suffer, too. Centers for Disease Control and Prevention studies show rates of fetal alcohol syndrome at 1.5 per 1,000 live births in different areas of the United States. Other prenatal alcohol-related conditions, such as alcohol-related neurodevelopment disorder (ARND), and alcohol-related birth defects (ARBD), are believed to occur approximately three times as often (Centers for Disease Control and Prevention, 2005).

Without a doubt, alcohol affects all developmental areas of the self and overall health. Heavy drinking and alcoholism can seriously affect the functioning of the entire nervous system, especially the brain. Impairments in perception, learning, and memory are likely. Studies have found alcohol use to be associated with a heightened risk of large-bowel cancer (Baron et al., 1998), cirrhosis of the liver, and cancers of the mouth, esophagus, pharynx, larynx, and liver (Thun et al., 1997). Studies in four countries involving over 300,000 women associated alcohol consumption with breast cancer in women (Smith-Warner et al., 1998). Intensity of drinking is a higher risk factor than the number of years a woman consumes alcohol (Bowlin et al., 1997).

Underage drinking is described as epidemic (Fig. 6-4). At least once a month, over 5 million high school students engage in **binge drinking,** defined as four consecutive drinks for a female and five for a male. Consider that those who begin to drink before age 15 are four times more likely to become alcohol dependent than those who begin after 21, and a tragic road to addiction becomes apparent. Besides the damage to health, alcohol is the major factor in the three leading causes of teen death—accidents, homicide, and suicide (Center on Addiction and Substance Abuse, 2002). Wiser choices are definitely needed.

Although health definitely suffers from heavy consumption, a few benefits are associated with light to moderate use, and panels of experts even advocate moderate alcohol consumption at meals (de Gaetano and Simini, 2001). A study found that moderate wine consumption was associated with decreased odds of developing age-related macular degeneration, a serious threat to vision (Obisesan et al.,

Figure 6-4   Young people are often unaware of the consequences of their behavior.
Source: www.indexopen.com

1998). Because alcohol is a depressant, it can also relieve stress. It is important to know how much alcohol changes the balance from benefits to risks. Based on results from the Physicians Health Study, that amount is quite small—one drink a day for men and a little less for women (Brink, 2000).

Myths and Facts about Drinking Alcohol

(Kowalksi, 2001)

Myth: I can think clearly when drinking.

Fact: Alcohol targets the brain and interferes with judgment and motor functions.

Myth: I can handle alcohol.

Fact: When drinking heavily, a person can't judge the effects of alcohol.

Myth: Drinking will make me popular.

Fact: Alcohol use often causes problems in social interactions and relationships.

Myth: I'm not an alcoholic so I do not have a problem.

Fact: Any kind of alcohol use that leads to problems is a problem.

Myth: Underage drinking is "cool."

Fact: The earlier a person starts drinking, the greater the chance of becoming an alcoholic.

Myth: Everybody drinks.

Fact: Many people do not drink at all, and most do not drink excessively.

Most researchers agree that both environmental and genetic factors are involved in susceptibility to alcoholism (Anyanwu and Watson, 1997). Regardless of the cause, wise choices are more likely to be made by those who are informed and do not try to fool themselves into thinking that no harm can come from drinking alcohol. All of us know that irresponsible drinking has disquieting effects. A person may not be an actual alcoholic yet still have a problem. A definition of a "problem drinker" is anyone who causes problems because of drinking. If an individual becomes extremely obnoxious, abusive, or hurtful, it's time to modify habits.

The potentially devastating effects of drinking and driving are unquestionable. Every 30 minutes, someone in the United States dies in an alcohol-related crash. Even though alcohol-related fatalities have decreased by 3 percent in recent years, 40 percent of 18-, 19-, and 20-year-old crash fatalities are still tied to alcohol use (National Highway Traffic Safety Administration, 2003). If you have not been affected by someone's death from a drunk-driving incident, you are lucky. Keep in mind that you or someone you love could be.

Your personal support for and involvement in organizations such as Mothers Against Drunk Driving (MADD) and Students Against Drunk Driving (SADD) can show that you act on your values and will help decrease the number of tragedies. Candy Lightner started MADD in 1980 after her daughter was killed by a drunk driver. By 1985, that same driver had been arrested six times for drunk driving, and in one accident injured another young girl. Lightner says, "We have kicked a few pebbles, we will turn a few stones, and eventually we'll start an avalanche" (Lee, 1985, p. 77). Most of the strides against drunk driving are the results of efforts by MADD and other activist groups.

For those who are addicted to alcohol or even have problems with its use, support groups such as Alcoholics Anonymous and treatment programs are available in most communities. Because individuals are unique, no one program works for all. People are advised to try a different one if there is no improvement. For many, personal counseling is necessary. The focus on alcohol is not intended to lessen the tremendous amount of damage suffered from other drugs. Learning about the long-term effects of all of them is the first step in taking control of your own use. Then, if you continue to have a problem, seek help for yourself and for all those who care about you.

Drugs

What is a Drug?

A drug is any chemical that produces a therapeutic or nontherapeutic effect in the body. Chemicals, in contrast, are a broad class of substances—including drugs—that may or may not produce noticeable effects in the body. Many chemicals (such as tin, lead, and gold) have harmful effects on the body, especially in high doses. Most foods are not drugs. Alcohol is a drug—not a food—in spite of the calories it provides. Nicotine is a chemical that is also a drug. The group of "illegal" drugs includes dangerous chemicals that have only toxic actions (e.g., inhalants) (Addiction Science Research and Education, 2004).

Teenagers may be involved with legal or illegal drugs in various ways. Experimentation with drugs during adolescence is common. Unfortunately, teenagers often do not see the link between their actions today and the consequences tomorrow. They also have a tendency to feel indestructible and immune to the problems that others experience.

Adolescence is a time for trying new things. Teens use drugs for many reasons, including curiosity, because it feels good, to reduce stress, to feel grown up, or to fit in. Using alcohol and tobacco at a young age increases the risk of using other drugs later. Some teens will experiment and stop or continue to use occasionally without significant problems. Others will develop a dependency, moving on to more dangerous drugs and causing significant harm to themselves and possibly others. It is difficult to know which teens will experiment and stop and which teens will develop serious problems.

Based on Substance Abuse and Mental Health Statistics Association's (SAMHSA, 2005) National Survey on Drug Use and Health, 14.6 million persons aged 12 or older used marijuana daily. Daily marijuana users (63.3%) were more likely than less-than-daily users or nonusers to use other illicit drugs. Daily marijuana users were also more likely to be current cigarette smokers and heavy drinkers. Results of the National Survey on Drug Use and Health (SAMHSA, 2003) indicate that as many as 19.5 million Americans aged 12 and older currently use an illicit drug. According to SAMSHA, emergency treatments related to drug abuse involving narcotic analgesics increased 153 percent in the nation between 1995 and 2002. The great increase during this period occurred for oxycodone (512%), methadone (176%), hydrocodone (159%), and morphine (116%). Amphetamines, including methamphetamine, were the primary substance of abuse reported in more that 98,000 substance abuse treatment admissions. The most common route of administration was smoking, (44%), injection (26%), and inhalation (19%). More than 2.6 million youths aged 12 to 17 reported using inhalants at least once in their lifetime.

The health risks involved in using drugs include rapid or irregular heartbeat, increase in blood pressure, cardiovascular problems, elevated body temperatures, convulsions, hallucinations, delusions, and paranoia. Of particular concern is the increase in the use of methamphetamines. Physical dependence occurs because meth changes the ways cells in the brain function. A single dose can damage nerve terminals in the brain and prolonged used can cause irreversible stroke-producing damage to blood vessels in the brain. Addicts are depressed, unable to concentrate, and anxious; relationships are damaged and death may occur.

For additional information go to http://www.drugabuse.gov/infofax/HSYouthtrends.html. This site has all the current data on teenage use of drugs, alcohol, and tobacco.

Engaging in Risky Sexual Activities

Sexual behavior in today's society can pose a dire health risk. **Acquired immune deficiency syndrome (AIDS),** is a fatal condition resulting from an extremely weakened immune system. First identified in 1981, it is caused by human immunodeficiency virus (HIV) that is transmitted by exposure to infected blood, semen, and vaginal secretions usually through sexual activities or the sharing of hypodermic needles and other drug paraphernalia by injection-drug users. Transmission from mother to her newborn is also possible (Jemmott and Jemmott, 1996). In 1981, fewer than 100 people in the United States had died from AIDS. Between then and the end of 2003, 524,060 deaths had been reported. Worldwide AIDS has killed more than 25 million people, infected 40 million others, and left a legacy of "unspeakable loss, hardhip, fear and despair (*Omaha World Herald*, 2006, p. 1). The Centers for Disease Control and Prevention reports that 518,568 adults and adolescents and 5,492 children under 13 suffer from new HIV infections occurring in the United States ever year (Centers for Disease Control and Prevention, 2005).

AIDS should be a household word; the good news is that 90.6 percent of students nationwide have been informed about AIDS and HIV infection (Centers for Disease Control and Prevention, 1999). This is fortunate because HIV-positive symptoms usually do not materialize for years, and teenagers would not otherwise know that they can be infected (Kassin, 1998). "It's the worst feeling to be 26 years old and hear a doctor say you have AIDS. Then I thought about all my sexual partners during the past 10 years," lamented a young man.

Accurate information is available, and anyone who values health will seek it. AIDS is not curable, but it is preventable. Recommendations are to become well informed, either abstain or practice only safe sex, and avoid multiple sexual partners. Continue to ask yourself about the value of your own life and use your mind to protect your life.

Other than abstinence, the best way to avoid getting HIV and other sexually transmitted diseases is to use a latex condom whenever you have sexual intercourse. Remember: Whenever you have sex with someone, you're also having sex with everyone your partner has ever been sexually active with (Altshul, 2001).

Education about AIDS can also help to change people's attitudes and feelings about victims of the disease. Fear of HIV victims and homophobia among college students lessened over an eight-year period; those with the least knowledge had the greatest fear of victims (McCormack, 1997). Blaming a certain group of people for a disease is ridiculous. For example, decades ago polio was a serious, often fatal disease. Polio, like AIDS, was caused by a virus. Who were its victims? For the most part, they were children. It would have been ridiculous to harbor and voice such thoughts as, "Those children caused polio," "We should get rid of all those kids, and that would take care of polio," and "They deserve what they're getting." Yet uneducated people blame the victims of AIDS who, initially, were at one time mostly gay males and intravenous drug users. Today, AIDS is every group's potential disease.

Risks related to sexual behavior are of special concern because of the activities of increasing numbers of younger people. Generally, teenagers lack complete, accurate information and following a developmental norm, believe that nothing bad will ever happen to them. Results from the Add Health survey show that teens' reports of ever having had sexual intercourse increase dramatically with grade level, from 16 percent among seventh and eighth graders to 60 percent among eleventh and twelfth graders. Additionally, the Add Health survey reaffirms the findings of a large body of existing research that teenagers who are black or from low-income or single-parent families are more likely to have had sexual intercourse than their peers.

The societal messages in the United States are confusing to young people. At the same time that they are being told to abstain, they are also being bombarded with thousands of sexual encounters from television alone. This has resulted in an attitude that is described as **nonchalance** and the presumption that relationships will inevitably lead to sexual intercourse. Some even see sex as an entitlement; this attitude breaks down respect for self and other (Stodghill, 1998). "I do not think it is as special for many of us as it was for our parents. Too much exposure takes away any sense of mystery and most anticipation," was how an 18-year-old expressed it.

Being sexually active and not using birth control often leads to teenage pregnancy. The United States has the highest teenage pregnancy rate of all developed countries. About 1 million teenagers become pregnant each year, and 95 percent of those pregnancies are unintended (Centers for Disease Control and Prevention, 2004). The costs in terms of health and well-being are high. Hardships for young mothers include dropping out of school and reduced employment opportunities leading to social service dependence, repeated childbirths, increased health and developmental risks to the children, and a greater likelihood that these "children of children" will repeat the cycle. In a comparison of teen mothers who kept their babies compared to those who placed them for adoption, giving up the baby resulted in more favorable outcomes (Namerow, Kalmuss, & Cushman, 1997).

On a positive note, birthrates among American teenagers have reached a 60-year low due mainly to a decline in sexual activity and improved contraceptive use (Davis-Packard, 2000). As many as two-thirds of sexually active teenagers now use condoms, three times as many as in the 1970s (Stodghill, 1998). Parents can make a difference. Warm, supportive parent–adolescent relationships are essential for the sexual well-being of teenagers (Meschke, Bartholomae, and Zentall, 2000). Could it also help to teach young people how to make responsible decisions based on healthy values? All through life, decisions about sexual behavior will be required. Choosing wisely is essential to well-being and, perhaps, a matter of life or death.

Growing Older

Even though you cannot escape growing older, you may have an unhealthy attitude about aging. Essential to your well-being is to recognize you also have many choices. Many have bought into the media messages that extol the virtues of staying young. Old age is not considered of value and, in fact, is actually looked down on and thought of as a dreary wasteland. Attacking what she calls the mystique of age, Betty Friedan (1993) contends that almost all images of older people are bleak. Consider the absurdity of such an attitude. As long as you live, you age. If you do not want to grow old, you will have to die young. If aging continues to be viewed as negative, anyone who remains alive is heading for depression and despair.

Getting rid of inaccurate stereotypes about old people would be beneficial to everyone. Common beliefs are that memory will be lost and that elderly people will become seriously impaired both physically and cognitively. One-half of Americans incorrectly believe that forgetfulness is by itself Alzheimer's disease (*Geriatrics*, 2000) when, in fact, there can be many reasons. Interestingly, when young people are asked, "Do you ever forget things?" the answer is almost always yes. Yet, it carries no meaning of losing mental capacities. Even though, unfortunately, 4 million Americans suffer from Alzheimer's, only half of people over the age of 85 are affected, according to the Alzheimer's Association (2001).

A review of "normal" changes reveals a great deal of diversity among older adults with many individuals maintaining high levels of functioning into very advanced age (Carman, 1997). A final blow to the "woe-is-me" stereotype comes from a survey of 1,200 individuals 100 years of age and older. Reporting themselves to be in good to excellent health were 82 percent, 75 percent were fully mobile, and 30 percent were still doing some work. After we have broken the stereotypes of what older people cannot do, a floodgate of opportunity opens (Bortz, 1991). Having examples of positive aging helps. Can you think of any? I'm fortunate to have several, including both my parents whose mental states and physical levels of agility and energy were high until right before their deaths.

In addition to changing our picture of old age, we can realize that there are advantages to aging besides the obvious one of continuing to be alive! For most people, stress declines because of fewer daily hassles and upheavals, short-term illnesses are not common, and frustrations are less because of added realism. Many report newfound sources of pleasure. Leisure time is usually more plentiful. The successful completion of Erikson's seven preceding stages leads to an old age of fulfillment and the achievement of integrity.

Do not think about how old you are; think of how you are old (Bortz, 1991).

Wise choices help to bring about a high quality of life throughout the life span, so taking care of yourself while still young is important. Analysis of a 60-year-long study showed that men younger than 50 who developed good health habits fared much better physically and mentally than those who did not (Bower, 2001). It is truly a case of use it or lose it, and this is a choice we can all make. Most of what contributes to healthy, positive aging is within a person's control. Experts identify the following as significant (Hensrud, 2001).

- Physical activity and fitness
- Mental activity such as reading, doing crossword puzzles, and playing cards
- Healthy nutrition
- Nonsmoking and no more than small amounts of alcohol
- Proper weight maintenance
- Active lifestyle with involvement in activities
- Optimistic attitude

Other identified factors in living a higher-quality life as an older person are engagement in activities with a meaningful purpose, continued curiosity and a desire to learn, a sense of humor, and close social ties. Love and intimacy tend to protect us from disease (Ornish, 1998). What is tragic is to stagnate, to pull away from activities, and to allow negative thoughts to prevail. If you continue to value yourself throughout life, you will value aging, because to age is to live.

Choices reflect how much you care about yourself and affect your present and future health. We will never be perfect; nonetheless, improvement in health and well-being is worth pursuing.

Stress Management

How well do you handle stress? Stress management deserves special attention. **Stress** is what the body experiences when there is a perceived demand to adjust. Stress cannot be avoided; it is a by-product of life. **Stressors,** the conditions that cause stress, are numerous and never ending. Instead of life being a bowl of cherries, one could say that life is a bowl of stressors! You have an opportunity to rate your level of stress in Reflections and Applications.

Effects of stress. The "father of stress research" Hans Selye (1976) described the body's stress response as a sequence of three stages called the **general adaptation syndrome.** In the *alarm stage,* the body mobilizes itself for defense; if stress continues, the body draws on its resources during the *resistance stage.* If there is no relief, during the *exhaustion stage,* a person is susceptible to illness. Stress that is either not handled or mishandled is related to numerous problems, including poor health conditions. This has been recognized for several years.

"Stress may be the greatest single contributor to illness in the industrialized world" (Eliot and Breo, 1984, p. 14). Approximately 60 to 90 percent of doctor visits are for conditions related to stress (Benson, 2001).

Stress appears to be involved in cardiovascular disease and cancer (Senior, 2001) along with high blood pressure, pain, insomnia, allergies, and infertility (Benson, 2001). After being exposed to viruses, 47 percent of individuals under high stress came down with a cold compared to only 27 percent under little stress (Goleman, 1997). How can stress be involved in such diverse physical conditions? The common thread appears to be the immune response, which can be lowered by chronic stress (Senior, 2001).

Other areas of the self can also suffer. Mismanaged stress contributes to relationship or social problems, emotional distress, and severe mental challenges. When you consider how unmanaged stress affects your life, it is no surprise to know that stress is connected to mental concentration (Vernarec and Phllips, 2001), depression (Evans, 2000), and anger in the workplace (Calabrese, 2000).

Even with its potentially high cost, stress is not necessarily negative. Certain types and degrees of stress can be motivating and healthful. Equate stress to the strings on a violin. If they are stretched tightly, the tone of the violin is sharp, too loose and the sound is flat and lifeless. Either way beautiful music is not possible. The key is to adjust the strings to a desirable degree of tightness. Similarly, individuals can benefit from knowing how much and what type of stress is good for them. Each person is different. For example, you may be one who feels quite relaxed sitting in a boat all day fishing. Another person would be bored and actually experience stress while engaging in the same activity.

Stress that is good for you is called **eustress.** In its positive form, stress is motivating and contributes to an interesting life. "Stress is the spice of life. Who would enjoy a life of no runs, no hits, no errors?" (Selye, 1974, p. 85). How do you know when your level of stress is unhealthy? There will be clues. Are you experiencing frequent headaches, stomach distress, minor aches and pains, muscle tension, or fatigue for no apparent reason? Do you feel uneasy, tense, or irritable? Are you having difficulty sleeping or concentrating? Even apathy may be a sign. Learning what is an optimal level of stress for you and how to handle it in a positive way is a "must" in terms of self and relationships.

Sources of stress.   What are the stressors in your life? Most of us have long lists. Researchers have uncovered many sources of stress. In one of the first studies, participants identified major changes in their lives. Each event was then given a value based on its magnitude or effect. The top five stress-producing events then were (1) death of spouse, (2) divorce, (3) marital separation, (4) jail term, and (5) death of close family member (Holmes and Rahe, 1967). Both positive and negative events, if they prompted some type of coping or adaptive behavior, were stressful. The study indicated that when too many events happen in succession, the strain can produce unhealthy effects. Because change results in stress, you are advised to regulate your stress by not attempting too many changes at one time.

Another study (Lazarus, 1981) dealt with minor irritants, or the hassles of everyday life. Viewed as ongoing stressors, these are often left unattended because they occur so often and are seemingly routine. Lindsey was annoyed by a tiny squeak every day as she drove to work. She kept telling herself that some day she would get it fixed. That day never seemed to come until she realized that her irritation at work and at home might be related to the annoyance she experienced each day. "The petty annoyances, frustrations, and unpleasant surprises that plague us every day may add up to more grief than life's major stressful events" (Lazarus, 1981, p. 58). College students were asked to identify stress sources. Overall, 81.1 percent of these were daily hassles. The top five stressors were a change in sleeping habits, vacations/breaks, change in eating habits, new responsibilities, and increased class workload (Ross, Niebling, and Heckert, 1999). Adult female community college students identified child care concerns as their greatest stressor (Johnson, Schwartz, and Bower, 2000). What everyday hassles bother you? What are you doing about them? If your answer is "nothing," the accumulative effects of stress may be harmful.

Stressors are either external or internal. **External stressors** are demands from outside of the self. Other people, events beyond our control, and the environment deliver daily doses of stress. Can you name some others? **Internal stressors** are those we create or magnify. One of the more common ones is worry, a process involving negative thoughts and uneasy feelings. How is worry different from concern? Concern stems from actual events whereas worry is rooted in relatively uncontrollable images and thoughts that are usually about future negative possibilities. Certain unrealistic myths such as "If I worry, the negative event will not happen," "Events and people make me worry," and "Worrying shows that I care" perpetuate worry (Goulding and Goulding, 1989). Worriers usually do nothing about their feelings, which contributes to a feeling, of powerlessness.

The reality is that if you are a worrier, you manufacture stress and waste a great deal of time. Compared to nonworriers, chronic worriers spend up to 8 hours a day fretting, which significantly disrupts their lives (Kelly and Miller, 1999). A worrier also increases the risk of illness (Michaud, 2000). Sorting out real concerns from the mass of imaginative and insignificant worries is a worthy challenge. Ninety percent of what we worry about never happens. "Worry never robs tomorrow of its sorrow: it only saps today of its joy" (Buscaglia, 1992, p. 182).

The book *Worry: Controlling It and Using It Wisely* (Hallowell, 1997) suggests several ways to avoid turning minor problems into potential disasters. Other tips are to change "what if" to "so what if," set aside a short period each day to really worry and refuse to do so at other times, keep a worry journal so that the thoughts are put on paper and then check to see how many worries even materialized, use deep breathing, and definitely *act* on your worry. Exercise and a technique discussed later called *thought-stopping* can also help.

Also falling into the category of internal stressors are irrational thoughts, unrealistic expectations, an inability to express emotions in a healthy way, task overload, neglect of physical health, negative self-talk, and boredom. An awareness of the sources can enable you to analyze, possibly decrease the numbers, and reduce the impact of stressors.

Coping with stress.   The subject of handling stress is well covered in a variety of books and articles, and the number of suggestions is mind-boggling. Yet many people still do nothing about stress. You may be one who already copes well because of **psychological hardiness** (Kobasa, 1979). In a classic study of executives who experienced high stress, those who didn't get sick had personality characteristics of hardiness: strong commitment to self and various areas of life, a sense of meaningfulness or purpose, the attitude that change is challenging, and an internal locus of control. If these descriptors don't sound like you, consider what you can do to become hardier!

When faced with a stressor, you can either face the problem directly or avoid it. Withdrawing may involve getting out of a stressful relationship or getting rid of other people's problems and returning them to their rightful owners. Even if a stressor is not apparent, you are wise to employ regular stress management strategies that protect you from the effects of daily stressors. All of the wellness tips offered earlier are excellent strategies. Several other practical stress-reducing suggestions follow. The challenge is to put them into regular practice.

- Reduce or prioritize major life events. For example, don't begin college, start a job, get married, quit college, and get divorced all in the same year!
- Learn techniques to eliminate unnecessary worry and anxiety.
- Use cognitive techniques to change stress-producing thoughts.
- Develop a decision-making process.
- If you feel frustrated or worried, ask yourself what you can do about it. Be realistic about what is possible and realize that some things are beyond your control.
- If you truly don't want to do something, say no and stick with it.
- Learn to manage time and to schedule events so you aren't rushing through life.
- Express your feelings and begin to communicate more openly with others.
- Find a reliable support system.
- Write in a journal or diary. Studies confirm the value of expressing stressful thoughts to others or getting them down on paper (Stone et al., 2000).
- Have a relaxing massage.
- Laugh and enjoy life.
- Breathe deeply. Deep breathing is a full, deep expansion of the lungs followed by complete expiration. The rhythm of the breath is slow and quiet (Weil, 1995a). Proper breathing involves the diaphragm, the thin muscle that separates the lung and abdominal cavities. Breathing properly is not only relaxing; but also it facilitates health by increasing the amount of oxygen in the blood (Williams and Harris, 1998). See directions for deep breathing in Reflections and Applications (page 371).
- Use a deep relaxation technique and meditation. Consider the use of biofeedback.

Deep relaxation is a profoundly restful condition in which one feels physically relaxed, somewhat detached from the immediate environment and usually to some extent even from body sensations. It involves a feeling of voluntary and comfortable abandonment of one's conscious control and

Figure 6-5   Exercising with friends.

stewardship over major body functions—a distinctly passive attitude in which one simply turns over control of the body to its own built-in "autopilot" (Albrecht, 1979, p. 191).

Besides a wonderful feeling, deep relaxation allows the body to become balanced, or homeostatic, and, thus, work as it is intended to. One of the first to enlighten society about protection from "overstress" was Herbert Benson (1975), a physician and associate professor of medicine at Harvard Medical School, who taught and wrote about the relaxation response (Fig. 6-5).

Meditation can be thought of as a physical act of remaining quiet and focusing on one's breath, a word, or a phrase. The actions quiet "inner chatter" and reduce stress (Barbor, 2001). Meditation and other relaxation techniques helped elementary school students score higher on standard achievement tests (Benson, 1987) and college students attain significantly higher grade-point averages (Hall, 1999). Other dramatic results from ongoing meditation programs include a 40 to 45 percent reduction in medical symptoms and psychological distress (Salzberg and Kabat-Zinn, 1997).

In addition to deep relaxation and meditation, methods that produce similar results are self-hypnosis, yoga, guided imagery, and autogenic training. Individuals remain awake and alert and remember all that occurs; the person is in control of himself of herself (Miller, 1978). Employing a technique for only 15 to 20 minutes on a regular basis can produce astonishing results, including increased energy, optimism, contentment, and reduction in pain. The effects of stress on the body seem remarkably diminished.

Relaxation exercises are used in **biofeedback training,** a series of steps by which a person learns to regulate physiological responses such as muscle tension, skin temperature, and heart rate. Through the use of monitoring equipment, an individual becomes aware of changes within the body and then discovers how to control them using relaxation. In addition to lowering stress reactions, there are biofeedback treatments for a variety of problems including anxiety disorders, depression, alcoholism and addiction, attention deficit hyperactivity disorder, migraines, hypertension, asthma, chronic pain, and rheumatoid arthritis (*Patient Education Management,* 2001). If an organic basis for an ailment has been ruled out, a strong recommendation is to see a stress management specialist.

Technology has ushered in EEG (electroencephalogram) biofeedback also known as **neurofeedback** or brainwave training. Neurofeedback is a specialized kind of biofeedback that involves operant conditioning of the brain's electrical activity in order to improve brain function. This, in turn, impacts emotions and behavior (Othmer, Phillips, and Roost, 2001). According to Andrea Sime, a specialist in biofeedback training, "Research in neurofeedback has demonstrated positive results especially with epilepsy and attention deficit hyperactivity disorder. Neurofeedback has also been used successfully with anxiety and panic disorders, sleep disorders, chronic pain, posttraumatic stress disorder, alcoholism, and numerous other conditions. Many athletes, performers, executives, and others are using neurofeedback to promote peak performance."

Both biofeedback and neurofeedback are based on the mind–body connection that is so important in healing. Based on the idea that stress that leads to depression and despair can set the stage for cancer growth, a research team (Simonton, Matthews-Simonton, and Creighton, 1978) used psychological interventions with medically incurable patients and noted that a number of them improved and were living longer and better lives. Psychological intervention (relaxation, visualization techniques, and perception changing) reduced stress, decreased feelings of depression, and helped patients feel more hopeful. This made cancer regression possible.

Yoga is wonderful for nurturing a state of mental and physical well-being. It promotes a balanced and healthy lifestyle. Yoga techniques can also be applied to removing excess weight, thus bringing you an extra benefit, that is, if being overweight is a problem to you. Practicing yoga will increase your metabolism. An increased metabolism leads to an increase in the calorie-burning process, so combining yoga with a calorie-burning program may bring you excellent results. Of course, the use of yoga is no rapid weight-loss method. Used over a period of time, though, it can bring good results. If you keep to the rigors imposed by yoga discipline, you should gain a holistic, long-term solution to balance your lifestyle and help you reduce and prevent any surplus weight. In addition to losing weight, you will also experience an increased ability to concentrate and focus, higher resistance to stress factors, and overall a healthier way of life. (See again Figure 6-5.)

Several recommendations in this book are related to the mind–body connection and to stress reduction. Stress will be a part of your life; by learning about it and taking charge, you can make a positive difference in your health and well-being. Wellness choices reflect how much you care about yourself and affect your present and future health. We will never be perfect; nonetheless, improvement in physical and psychological well-being is worth pursuing.

Anger Management

Remember the three components of emotion? Physiological arousal is usually a clear sign of anger. Typically, blood pressure rises, and the heart may seem to beat harder or faster. Cognitively, angry people believe that they are being mistreated and can experience frustration. Behaviorally, they have a tendency to lash out at others. A person can also cry, become very quiet, and even act in constructive ways.

Too often, anger leads to negative behaviors. In relationships, the emotion can erupt in violence. One of the risk factors for alcohol, tobacco, and other unhealthy drug use is **trait anger,** defined as a state of general hostility (Thomas, 1997). Rather than accept the idea that very little can be done about your angry expressions, decide to become an effective anger manager.

Choices in expressing anger.   Beyond understanding the effects and determining the reasons for anger, what can help? The issue becomes one of discovering constructive ways to express anger. Following is a partial list of possibilities.

Walk, jog, swim, and engage in any type of physical exercise.
Hit a pillow, punch a punching bag or stuffed object.
Talk to someone you trust.
Scream (in a private place), write angry thoughts, cry.
Clean house, pull weeds.

A physical act seems to be especially relieving. However, if you find that your actions serve to escalate anger, another method is advisable.

An excellent technique is to look at anger-provoking events from different perspectives and not personalize everything that happens. If you are angry with an individual, try to let him or her know. The key is to use assertiveness and positive communication techniques covered in this book rather than to engage in unbridled expressions of anger.

After awareness of the problems of suppression and the benefits of expressiveness, the next steps become obvious. Select behaviors that seem to fit you and even experiment with some that at first seem uncomfortable. Continue to practice your new expressive actions and monitor yourself to see how you are doing. Have you hugged anyone recently? When was the last time you really laughed? What did you do or not do the last time you felt angry? What could you have done? Are you allowing any tears? Keep in mind what most people do not realize: Suppressing any emotion will affect total expressiveness. Negate anger and you also negate love (Rubin, 1998). In an emotionally healthy

REFLECT AND APPLY

Reflect

- *Think of examples of people whose wellness level is lower because of a poor health habit.*
- *Pretend you are a parent of a young teenager. What information related to smoking, alcohol use, and sexuality would you give?*
- *Using a past or present decision, check yourself using the action steps in Figure 3-4.*
- *Think of recent situations in which better time management would have really helped. Which tips would have been useful?*

Apply

- *If you can "see" yourself in terms of some unwise health choices, make at least one positive change.*
- *Look for examples of positive aging in the media or as demonstrated in people you know.*
- *Set a goal to become healthier. Ask the questions based on the criteria given in this book. Then use action steps and pinpointing.*

climate, feelings are not labeled good or bad, and all are given ample play and freedom.

It is all right to feel love, and it is all right to feel anger. It is all right to express love, and it is all right to express anger. Your feelings are welcome here, and we would like to know what they are. You are loved and accepted and safe with all your feelings. You need not stifle any of them to please us (Rubin, 1988, pp. 21–22) (Reflect and Apply).

LOOKING BACK

- Health
- Tips to Wellness
- Categories (health gamblers, mechanics, gardeners)
- Mortality (diseases)
- Growing older

Section Two
Communication: The Key to Relationships

LOOKING AHEAD

After completing this section, you will be able to

- Define communication and describe its process.
- Discuss the importance of communication.
- Explain how and where people learn to communicate.
- List ways in which family communication could be improved.
- Give reasons for formal training in interpersonal communication.
- Describe characteristics helpful in being a positive communicator.

I see communication as a huge umbrella that covers and affects all that goes on between human beings—the largest single factor determining kinds of relationships and individual happenings in the world.

—Virginia Satir

When asked in an informal survey to list the three most important factors necessary for a good marriage, 81 percent of respondents named communication and placed it ahead of love and friendship. Couples who desire satisfying long-term relationships need to invest time and energy into improving their communication skill. "We do not communicate," was the couple's agreed-upon answer when asked why they wanted a divorce. "Oh, but you do," came the surprising reply from the counselor. The couple did not realize that whenever two people occupy the same environment, communication is taking place. Although people can stop talking, they continue to communicate with body language. An accurate reason for wanting to end a relationship is "We do not communicate well" or "The way we communicate has caused problems and damage to our relationship."

Whether intentional or not, communication influences all relationships. Without communication, interaction would not occur. **Interpersonal communication** is a complex process of mutually exchanging messages between two or more individuals. Models of communication are not simple diagrams. When verbal exchange is taking place, what exactly is happening? Speaking and listening are two necessary parts of the process. Nonverbal behaviors accompany both. A communication interaction is an encompassing process in which:

- A message is sent verbally and nonverbally.
- The message is received and interpreted.
- Verbal and nonverbal feedback is usually given.
- Feedback is offered by the sender.

167

As you can see, the individuals in the exchange are simultaneously sending and receiving messages.

A major purpose of interpersonal communication is to share a common meaning. Both the sender and receiver are responsible for clarity. When different meanings come from messages, the outcome can be negative. "But that's not what I meant" is far too common. What is worse is not being aware that you have been misunderstood. What was true years ago is probably still accurate today: As much as 70 percent of our communication efforts are probably misinterpreted, misunderstood, rejected, disliked, or distorted (Donaldson and Scannell, 1986).

Communication is the foundation for all relationships and the primary cause of their success or failure. Ineffective or faulty communication is at the root of most interpersonal difficulties. Effective communication is necessary to develop and maintain any positive interpersonal relationship.

> *Human communication is the most awesome force in the world. It can be directly responsible for peace or war, love or hate. Communication is unavoidable, and our communication skills are directly related to the quality of life we experience.*
>
> —Jacquelyn Carr

Most of the research on communication has focused on couples. Leo Buscaglia (1984) conducted a study in which he asked couples about problems and strengthening factors in their relationships. The same factor was identified as being both the most problematic and the most strengthening. Not surprisingly, it was communication. More than 85 percent of the hundreds of respondents said that the most essential quality for a lasting relationship was the ability to communicate (Buscaglia, 1992).

Studies have indicated that positive communication contributed to the strength of the stepfamily (Hanna and Knaub, 1981; Knaub, Hanna, and Stinnett, 1984). When stepchildren were asked to identify areas of concern, communication was frequently mentioned (Knaub and Hanna, 1984). One girl offered this response: "The worst thing about my stepfamily is that my stepfather thinks he is always right and we are always wrong; what he says goes" (p. 87). She suggested that he should listen and show a willingness to compromise, two important ingredients in positive communication.

Being able to communicate effectively benefits you in everyday situations, in a job search, in the advancement of your career, and in all types of relationships. When you think about your friendships, is communication an essential component? It is highly unlikely that you will remain friends with someone with whom you have difficulty communicating. Between patient and physician, full communication is indispensable because communication can be as important to healing as medicine (Cousins, 1989). Strong communication skills were listed as one of the top three aptitudes that employers want (Fisher, 2001). How well we communicate affects how others perceive us and all aspects of interpersonal relationships.

All communication is learned. Every baby who comes into this world comes only with raw materials—no self-concept, no experience of interacting with others, and no

Figure II-1   Copyright King Features Syndicate. Reprinted with permission.

experience in dealing with the world. Babies learn all these things through communication with the people who are in charge of them from birth on. (Satir, 1988, p. 52)

Realizing how important communication skills are, one could assume that they would be taught as systematically as other valuable behaviors. How did you learn to communicate? Were you taught by trained professionals? Almost everyone learned by observation, modeling, and feedback; teaching came from untrained individuals. Communication is part of the socialization process. Most high schools have some type of communication classes to offer students. They can and should be taught right along with the three R's (McKay, Davis, and Fanning, 1983, p. 8).

A survey of psychology students at Southeast Community College assessed family communication on a 5-point scale ranging from excellent to poor, first within the family as a whole and then separately with their fathers and mothers. The results were interesting (Fig. II-1).

- Almost 50 percent rated overall family communication as good or excellent. About 20 percent placed it below satisfactory, and 30 percent rated it as satisfactory.
- A definite difference between fathers and mothers was noted. Thirty-five percent said their fathers needed improvement compared with 14 percent for mothers. Excellent were 28 percent of the mothers and only 8 percent of the fathers. If males are not raised to be communicative, they will be less capable as parents, another unfortunate outcome of gender-role stereotypic training.

Several suggestions for improvement were offered.

- Set aside time to talk and listen. Be sure that communication takes place daily. Statistics revealed that mothers on a typical workday spent only 11 minutes in focused conversation with their children, and fathers spent just 8 minutes (Cutler, 1989).
- Talk about everything, not just gripes and problems. Include as many or more positive subjects than negative ones.

- Allow and encourage everyone to talk. Consider all points of view and do not judge.
- Be sincerely interested and show this by actively listening.
- Ask questions, especially those that require more than a one-word answer: not, "How was school today?" but, "What class did you like (or not like) today and for what reason?"
- Be open, honest, and flexible when you communicate. Open communication is covered in Chapter 7.

Do you see how much is involved in communication? If you have followed the suggestions offered in this book, you have a head start in becoming an excellent communicator. Several attitudes and behaviors are important in the communication process.

- A life position of I'm OK, you're OK is at the heart of positive communication. Participants have high self-esteem, and they treat each other with respect.
- Honesty in communication means authenticity. Communicators do not play games, mislead, and try to manipulate each other. Knowing that another person will be up-front with you creates a positive atmosphere.
- Openness is a necessity. A closed person who is not interested in learning and growing is a poor interpersonal communication candidate. You are likely to be enjoyed as a conversationalist if you are open.
- Willingness to share means that you are able and willing to disclose about yourself and to express your ideas. Listening is a valuable skill; however, if you only listen, you are not completely participating in an exchange.
- Expressiveness has been praised in terms of health and well-being. Willingness and ability to show your feelings also help you to be a better communicator.
- Appropriateness relates to the content of a message. An effective speaker knows what is suitable to say and what is not.
- Flexibility is needed in positive communication. Being closed-minded is detrimental to a give-and-take communication process.
- A sense of humor, although not a necessity, separates good communicators from excellent ones. Having a sense of humor does not mean telling one joke after another. Instead, you see humor in life, add a witty spark to conversations, do not take yourself too seriously, and appreciate others' humor.
- Understanding and the ability to interpret are needed in order to achieve a shared meaning. Being a critical thinker with the ability to process and see alternatives can solve communication problems caused by locked-in thinking.
- Patience, often referred to as a virtue, is extremely helpful. Impatient communicators are typically poor listeners.

Positive communication is gratifying to the participants. During an exchange, each may experience frustration; however, gratification often comes with the outcome. The outcome *could* be a realization that you misunderstood the other. If you learn from mistakes, you can still feel satisfied. Rewards of affirmation, understanding, and intimacy are viable products of healthy communication (Fig. II-2).

> *If you and I can honestly tell each other who we are, what we think, judge, feel, value, love, honor and esteem, hate, fear, desire, hope for, believe in and are committed to, then and then only can each of us grow.*
>
> —John Powell

Figure II-2   Communication can be a joyous experience!

BECOMING A POSITIVE LISTENER

LOOKING AHEAD

After completing this chapter, you will be able to

- Differentiate between hearing and listening.
- Give reasons why listening is important.
- Identify barriers to positive listening.
- Understand the importance of body language and verbal responses.
- Describe negative listening behaviors.
- Name and give examples of the types of listening.
- Become a better listener!

> *Listening is the most profound ingredient of communication. Listening is a hallmark of loving another.*
>
> —Teresa Adams

The day care director spoke to an excited group: "Children, you need to listen to your teachers and me." The bright-eyed children nodded. They had heard about listening at home and knew that it was expected. If we could follow each child from that time until adulthood, we would find that a few had somehow learned to listen well, several had an average skill level, and others were poor listeners. They were told to listen yet not instructed in how. What is often not realized is that good listeners are made, not born.

Understanding the Art of Listening

Positive listening is made up of skills that are learned and can be improved. **Listening** is an active process of paying attention, hearing, interpreting, and then acknowledging. **Hearing,** using the auditory sense to take in a message, is the first step in the process. Understanding, which comes next, depends on an accurate interpretation of both the content and nonverbal clues. Acknowledgment requires activity. If you are a good listener, you are not passive. When you listen positively, you are attentive, involved, stimulated, and animated. The next time you are in the listener's role, ask yourself, "Am I truly listening? Do I give the impression that I am?" (Fig. 7-1).

The Why of Listening

Listening has purpose. You may listen for any of these reasons.

Enjoyment: Of particular pleasure are the times spent in enjoyable listening. Examples are daily conversations at work and home, the radio, television, and movies.

Information: People seek information from the media and in conversations. Students in the classroom listen primarily to become informed. Enjoyment and listening for information can coincide; often the best listening situations are those that include both. Isn't a classroom more interesting when you are engaged in listening for both information and enjoyment?

Help: You will receive and provide help by listening. Relationships thrive on a positive listening environment.

"I really look forward to your visits."

Figure 7-1 Copyright © Jim Unger/Dist. by Laughingstock Licensing Inc. Herman® is reprinted with permission by Laughingstock Licensing Inc., Ottawa, Canada. All rights reserved.

Whatever the purpose, positive listening in relationships will help you understand another person's thoughts, feelings, and actions.

The Importance of Listening

Listening is basic to learning, and people who cannot hear must employ other means to receive messages. Because listening is the first language skill developed by those who hear, all other skills depend on it. Yet listening is often the most neglected subject taught in school. Consider the amount of time students spend listening in classrooms alone and how essential it is that they have good listening skills. If you want to succeed academically, good listening is essential.

The workplace, too, demands good listening skills. Initially, you will receive information and directions during a job interview. Demonstrating good listening skills to get a job is only the beginning. Besides helping employees learn required technical skills, positive listening builds satisfactory customer relations and enriches work relationships. Inefficient or poor listening becomes costly to both businesses and consumers.

Listening creates and improves personal relationships. Being a good listener is a frequently mentioned characteristic of a cherished friend. A person who has difficulty listening may be avoided by others. Satisfying communication in love relationships requires excellent listening skills.

True listening is love in action. Yet most couples never truly listen to each other. Consequently, when couples come for counseling or therapy, a major task is to teach them how to listen. (Peck, 1978, p. 128)

In creating and preserving intimacy, listening is the most important of all the communication skills (McKay, Fanning, and Paleg, 1994). Listening has significance throughout the world. In Turkey, a person shows respect by not interrupting; in fact, the longer he or she listens, the more respect is shown. In Japan listening is a sign of authority (Axtell et al., 1997).

Good listeners stand out in a crowd.
They are cherished by family, friends, teachers, and employers.
Good listeners get hired, they get promoted, and they are more informed. (Petress, 1999)

Removing Barriers in the Listening Process

If you are planning a trip by automobile, you can make it more pleasant by knowing about any road construction, poor weather conditions, or detours along the way. Then you can avoid them or at least be prepared to face the delays. Recognizing barriers in the listening process will definitely help you to avoid or decrease their negative effects.

Preoccupation or Lack of Interest

A major obstacle is preoccupation or lack of interest. If you are not interested, you will not want to listen. You have at least three choices. You may listen anyway and attempt to develop an interest. You might pretend to listen, or you can be honest and tell the person you aren't interested. The decision would be based on the situation and your feelings at the time.

Besides disinterest, preoccupation can be caused by other factors. You may have said or heard someone say, "I can listen to you while I am reading the newspaper (or watching television)." People can do more than one thing at a time; however, they are not doing any with complete concentration. Full attention is required if you are going to do your best listening. Carefully listening to someone is a precious gift that communicates care and concern (Miller, Nunnally, and Wackman, 1979). Chronic preoccupation is sure to deaden a relationship. A study designed to predict marital success identified a pattern of listening called stonewalling, a behavior in which the listener presented a "stone wall" to the speaker—not moving the face very much, avoiding eye contact, holding the neck rigid, and not using any listening response. Husbands used this more than wives, and over time it led to marital dissatisfaction (Gottman, 1991).

Environmental Factors

Think about barriers in the environment. Noise detracts, and even with the best intentions, listening is difficult in the middle of an explosion of sounds. Have you ever tried to communicate when a television set is turned on somewhere in the room? Even if nobody is actively watching, or even if the sound is turned off, the set attracts attention. Visual distractions, temperature, and lack of airflow can be just as bothersome as auditory distractions. The extent of listening I can expect from students is directly related to the climate of the classroom. Important listening situations deserve an environment free of distractions.

Psychological Filter

Of prime importance in the listening process is the listener's psychological filter, which is composed of preconceived ideas, moods, assumptions, labels, stereotypes, past experiences, hopes, memories, and his or her own self-concept. We form impressions of a speaker quickly, and our filters influence what those impressions are. Attitudes predispose us to respond positively or negatively. For example, if you know that you do not agree with a speaker and there will be no opportunity to respond, you will probably not listen well. A negative self-fulfilling prophecy may keep you from even trying to listen. John commented that he has been told often by teachers and parents that he is a poor listener; he believes it and continues the inactive listening behaviors he developed early in life.

As selective listeners, we are capable of filtering out anything we consider unimportant. Obviously, we can miss important and interesting information. Just as a homeowner checks a furnace filter periodically, examining your psychological filter is a good idea. You may not be able to eliminate it entirely, yet being aware of clogging elements and discarding whatever you can will help you become a better listener.

Emotions

A challenging obstacle arises from the listener's emotional state. Think of a heated discussion between you and another person. Any frustration and anger undoubtedly interfered with positive listening. Immediately after Holly saw the low grade she received on an examination, she became extremely depressed. "I totally tuned out everything the professor said about the test and had no idea why I had done so poorly. I did not learn anything that could help me next time." Listening and, thus, our perceptions in general are altered by emotion.

Rate Differences

A person talks at a slower rate than the listener thinks. The average rate of speech is about 125 to 175 words a minute, whereas the brain can think at the rate of 500 to 1,000 words a minute. This means that you, as a listener, are ahead of the speaker! You might think of the speed of an automobile compared to that of a jet airplane. The span of time can hinder your continued concentration, and the mind can wander. Positive listeners remain focused.

Negative Intentions

Although they may not realize it, listeners can have negative intentions. Do you know people who almost always want to lead the conversation? They listen briefly and then jump to conclusions, interrupt to disagree, and attempt to impose their perspective or solution on the speaker. They do not truly listen; instead, they are thinking about and rehearsing what they will say. Because of this, they frequently interrupt. A similar style of nonlistening comes from wanting always to be right, which can result in lying, shouting, changing the subject, justifying, quibbling, making excuses, and accusing (McKay, Fanning, and Paleg, 1994)—everything except positive listening.

Other negative intentions are listening only enough to gain an advantage or to win, to devise a way to manipulate another, to use the information in a harmful way (as in the case of gossip), or to feign an interest that does not exist. Just as insincere or phony talkers eventually reveal their true colors, listeners with negative intentions generally end up losers in interpersonal relationships.

Improving Listening Behaviors

Eliminating any of the barriers sets up a positive listening atmosphere. Being aware of your own behaviors, improving your skills, and becoming active will lead to positive listening.

Open and Attentive Body Position

Do you appear to be listening? The way you position yourself in relation to the speaker makes a difference. Establishing a comfortable distance apart is basic. Physical space zones are covered in Chapter 8. Being on the same level sets the tone for the interchange, because if one stands and the other sits, the person seated can feel at a disadvantage. Facing the speaker is essential. Turning your body away carries a message of disinterest and lessens your involvement, whereas facing the speaker squarely and leaning slightly forward demonstrates attentiveness.

Adopting an open, attentive posture indicates interest, openness, and involvement. Sitting with legs and arms crossed, slouching, or leaning away from the speaker is likely to give negative impressions. Instead, you can sit with your hands at your sides or on your lap. In situations such as a job interview, you appear more professional if you keep your feet together on the floor. A slumped posture may be comfortable, yet if you are truly interested, your body reflects it by an upright position. Having attentive posture does not mean being rigid and tense. A relaxed position of openness and attentiveness is ideal.

Positive Eye Contact

Maintaining eye contact in U.S. society is expected. In fact, conversation usually does not even start until eye contact is made. A person who does not look at you or who often avoids eye contact can cause discomfort. Employers will likely have negative impressions of applicants who don't keep their eyes on the interviewer. Poor eye contact may be interpreted as a lack of confidence or as indicative of dishonesty or lying. Knowledge of various cultures is important. For example, a student from the Middle East commented that direct eye contact is discouraged in his society. In other societies looking down rather than at the speaker is considered respectful.

Knowing how important eye contact can be and being able to actually maintain it may be altogether different. A student said, "Sharon, I hope in your book you will do more than just say, 'Have good eye contact.' I already know that, but how?" First, realize that eye contact is almost never a direct meeting between pairs of eyes. You do not have to look squarely into a speaker's eyes; you can focus anywhere on the face, including the nose, mouth, or ear. As long as you are at least 18 inches away from the speaker, the person usually cannot tell that you are not maintaining exact eye contact.

A recommendation is to look at the speaker's face for roughly three quarters of the time, in glances lasting from 1 to 7 seconds. A speaker will look at a listener for less than half the time, and these intermittent glances rarely last for more than a second (Marsh, 1988). Staring is definitely not recommended. Knowing that you can look elsewhere and keeping a relaxed frame of mind make it easier to maintain eye contact.

Facial Expression

To a great extent, feedback is delivered by changes in facial expression. A "poker face" is helpful in a card game; it is generally useless, and often demeaning, in the listening process. A positive listener reacts to what is being said by registering thinking and feeling responses. Avoiding inappropriate facial expressions is also very important. A smile, a frown, and a look of bewilderment or surprise are just a few of the expressions your face can make. Actually, about 20,000 different facial expressions are possible (Carl, 1980). Changing your facial expression is not that difficult! Look into a mirror and actually practice changing your expressions. Joel said, "I know it is important to smile, but I hate the way my teeth look." He finally decided that getting his teeth fixed was worth the price he had been paying in decreased relationship skills.

Head and Body Movements

One of my favorite listening behaviors is nodding the head. An affirmative nod shows the speaker not only that you have heard but also that you agree. A nod can motivate and energize a speaker. "Nodders" are worth their weight in gold! Even a side-to-side nod indicating confusion or disagreement can be helpful in arriving at a shared meaning. Nodding can be developed. You may want to tell yourself to do so until the behavior becomes natural. Since it is possible to nod too much, be sure to use the movement moderately and when appropriate. Other body movements such as tilting the head to one side or shrugging the shoulders also provide feedback to the speaker. Certain listening gestures and sounds can bother the speaker and create a negative communication climate. Several are identified by Ernst (1973):

- Cheek puffing and corners of mouth going down
- Eye rolling
- Shoulder shrugging to indicate an I-do not-care attitude
- Foot or leg bouncing up and down at high speed
- Drumming the fingers or thumping the hand or arm
- A "tishing" sound made by the tongue, or sighing

Students in role-playing activities have added a few of their own, such as loud gum chewing, yawning, and knuckle-cracking. Can you identify the negative messages these behaviors might communicate? If you recognize any of the behaviors in yourself, try to eliminate or at least decrease them.

Touching

Depending on your relationship with the speaker, listening can be improved by an appropriate touch. One day a student came in to talk about a personal conflict and was having difficulty expressing herself. I reached over and touched her hand, and the words poured out. The touch had evidently reassured her that she could speak freely. Even though touching can serve as a positive listening behavior, be sure that it is appropriate and acceptable to the other person.

Verbal Responses

Listening is usually a nonverbal activity; however, verbal responses are also included in positive listening. These can vary from a simple "Oh" or "Hmm" to "I see" or "That sounds interesting." You can, however, use too many responses and literally interrupt the speaker's flow. "Really," "I know," or "I understand" stated after each comment is distracting and annoying. A question that encourages the speaker to continue is an excellent response. Some possibilities are: "How do you feel about that?" "What are your alternatives?" "What happened next?" If you are an attentive listener, your question will not move the conversation away from the point. Note the difference in these two examples.

1. SPEAKER: I am upset with my supervisor. She scheduled me to work this weekend after I told her I wanted the time off.

   LISTENER: Did she just get mixed up?

2. SPEAKER: I am upset with my supervisor. She scheduled me to work this weekend after I told her I wanted the time off.

   LISTENER: Well, did you hear that she fired Joe?

Open questions requiring more than a simple yes or no answer are preferred because they are encouraging and move the conversation forward. You are telling the speaker, "What you are saying is of interest, and I want to hear more."

Verbal responses can involve more than short reactions or questions. **Paraphrasing** is restating in your own words what you think the speaker said. Here is an example of paraphrasing.

SPEAKER: My kids have been driving me crazy.

LISTENER: It sounds like you are really bothered by them.

When you paraphrase, you do not add to the message; instead, you repeat the meaning you received. This shows that you received the message and want to be sure the meaning is shared. You can use such lead-ins as, "It sounds like," "You mean that," or "Let me make sure I understand what you mean." Paraphrasing may seem clumsy at first; yet once you find and practice a few phrases that sound natural, using them will become easier.

The benefits of paraphrasing are worth the initial discomfort. They include:

- People appreciate that they were heard.
- The possibility of misinterpretation is greatly reduced because errors can be corrected immediately.
- Anger and other emotions can be defused.
- What was said is more likely to be remembered.

Paraphrasing can work beautifully with children, who often just want to know that their message was received. For example, picture a 4-year-old girl who tearfully tells you that an older brother has yelled at her. "It sounds like you didn't like him to yell at you" is the parent's paraphrase. In most cases, the child will nod and return to whatever she was doing.

Gaining a clear understanding of the speaker's emotions is also helpful. Jason tells Anja that he is "down in the dumps." She says, "It sounds as if you are really depressed." Jason can then think about her impression. He may respond, "I'm not really that unhappy," or he can say, "Yes, I am really down." When the listener provides an idea of the feeling that is sensed, the speaker receives valuable information. The speaker may also feel free to elaborate further about the feeling and even express other emotions. A listener who echoes a feeling is essentially saying, "I'm here for you."

Clarifying goes just a little further than paraphrasing. You not only restate, but you also ask questions to get more information and background. Your questions are genuine attempts to ensure that the two of you are sharing the same meaning. In doing so, both the exchange and the relationship are enriched. Even if you don't agree with the speaker, positive listening means that you first do everything possible to understand the other's perception.

Feedback, the last step in the listening process, comes after other listening behaviors. **Feedback** is responding with what you, as the listener, think, feel, or sense. You may still clarify with questions such as, "Is this what you meant?" or "Is this the way you feel?" Then you respond with your perspective or point of view. A few tips for engaging in feedback are:

- Provide input in a timely way.
- Be honest, yet react in a nonhurtful way. Avoid beginning your response with the word "you." Instead of "You would be crazy to take a job for that kind of pay," say "I think you would be wise to consider how satisfied you will be with that pay."
- Support the speaker. Do not put the speaker down. If you are entrusted with thoughts and feelings, handle them with care.

Feedback is more accurate if you have paid attention to the speaker's nonverbal behavior, voice, and words. For example, a friend's son responded to a question of where he was going with, "Over to my friend's house for a while." The mother noticed his facial expression, which appeared hostile. Her thought was that he really did not like her, and she was glad that she asked him if she had done something to offend him. He looked genuinely surprised and said, "No. What makes you think that?" She gave him feedback by describing what she thought his face was saying and how she felt. He laughed and said, "I probably looked mad because I was thinking about my car's empty gas tank!"

Tone of voice can be confusing to a listener, and again, feedback is appropriate. Judy said to her friend, "I am just fine. I do not need any help." The words said one thing, and her weak, quivering voice revealed another meaning. Her friend responded with concern. Usually, the quality of voice is more honest; however, a good listener will check to make sure. Are you surprised by the number and complexity of listening behaviors? Can you see why listening is considered active and animated?

Elimination of Negative Listening Behaviors

Knowing what to do is essential; knowing *what not to do* is equally important. The opposites or extremes of the behaviors just described are obvious negatives. For example, have you ever tried to describe a serious incident to a listener who is slightly grinning?

Interrupting is common and is one of the surest signs that a person is not truly listening. Individuals who enjoy talking have more difficulty with this bothersome behavior. Families composed of outgoing, talkative members can have frustrating scenes. A conversation starts. Instead of remaining attentive, the listener begins to speak about a different topic. The speaker can either stop, continue with the original topic, or switch to accommodate the interrupter. If the speaker stays with the first topic, a two-way conversation results and shared meaning is completely lost.

Using Different Types of Listening

All listening is not the same, even though the active listening behaviors described earlier are essential ingredients in all positive communication exchanges. Different types of listening are most effective in certain situations.

Empathic Listening

Empathy—being able to put yourself in another's place and see and hear from that person's perspective—is a quality to be treasured. **Empathic listening** means that you first become aware of the speaker's experiences and feelings. Then you communicate this. A comment such as, "I can see why you feel (or think) that way" makes an exchange more pleasant and positive.

Because emotional expression is beneficial, an empathic listener has a worthwhile role. As was pointed out in Chapter 5, people can have difficulty verbalizing feelings. A safe, comfortable climate for communication encourages expression, and an empathic listener sets the tone. Instead of just reacting to the words you hear, listen with concern and caring. For example, when a mother says, "I wish you just were not so busy," she may sound critical and angry; however, she could be feeling disappointed, hurt, and sad. An empathic listener is likely to recognize the difference or probe to discover the underlying emotions. Listening in depth and with empathy makes it easier to effectively help others and is an appreciated skill.

A communication empathy scale, proposed by Messina (1982), is a good way to check your empathic listening. Pretend that a friend has just told you that he has lost his job. Following are descriptions of four levels and examples of responses.

Level 1: Listener misses the facts and the feeling—"Let's go get a bite to eat."

Level 2: Listener grasps facts but misses the feeling—"It's too bad you lost your job, but something else will come along."

Level 3: Listener understands the facts and realizes that the speaker has a feeling but isn't empathic enough to be correct about which one—"It's too bad you lost your job. I'll bet you're really mad."

Level 4: Listener correctly understands both—"I realize that losing a job is a bad deal. It sounds like you're upset and depressed, and I can see why."

The fourth level is a worthy goal. Notice that the use of the word "but" in Level 2 seems to negate the speaker's situation.

Empathic listeners express empathy by tone of voice and body language. In addition, they can use short verbal responses. Some listeners are quick to say, "I know just how you feel." Such a response is not recommended. Even though people can empathize, they do not know just how another feels. A better response would be, "I have a strong sense of how you feel." Can you detect the use of empathic listening in the following?

> SPEAKER: I was trying to lead the group discussion, and she kept interrupting. I felt like she thought that I was not handling it right.
>
> LISTENER: It sounds like you were in a difficult spot.
>
> SPEAKER: I tried to politely tell her to quit distracting us, but she kept doing it.
>
> LISTENER: I would have been frustrated.
>
> SPEAKER: I was really frustrated, and by the time the evening was over, I was ready to scream.
>
> LISTENER: I can almost feel what you were going through. It sounds like it kept building up until you were really angry.
>
> SPEAKER: That is right. I am glad you understand.

Note that the listener expressed a personal sense of frustration and then picked up on the escalation to anger. The "I can almost feel" phrase is much more honest than "I know exactly how you feel."

Empathic listening is desirable in most exchanges. Once in a while you can better serve the speaker by being objective and honest. If the person is in a rut or is demonstrating inappropriate feelings, first express your understanding. Then, because empathizing would validate the person's inappropriate emotional reaction, use feedback to express your true reaction in a nonthreatening way.

Receptive Listening

All listening is receptive; however, **receptive listening** is a specific type with certain restrictions placed on responses. In some cases, silence is best if accompanied by appropriate nonverbal behaviors. Perhaps it is no coincidence that "silent" and "listen" contain the same letters (Wolvin and Coakley, 1988). When using receptive listening, you will do the following.

Listen without interrupting.   Except for preventing an injury, nothing justifies interrupting, and it is extremely annoying in a conversation. Keep silent, and if you do interrupt, apologize and let the speaker continue.

Listen without judging or "putting down."   People seem to have great difficulty keeping critical, judgmental, and admonishing reactions to themselves.

> SPEAKER: I charged over $1,000 on my credit card bill this month.
>
> LISTENER: Oh, no! (in a horrified tone of voice)
>
> SPEAKER: I have a budget, but I just could not pass up buying stuff and going away for a weekend.
>
> LISTENER: That is crazy. You know better than that.

What do you think the speaker's reaction would be? Most people would react defensively and, usually, the interaction would end on a negative note. Note the following improvement.

> SPEAKER: I charged over $1,000 on my credit card bill this month.
>
> LISTENER: Oh. (In a neutral, somewhat concerned tone.)
>
> SPEAKER: I have a budget, but I just could not pass up buying stuff and going away for a weekend.
>
> LISTENER: That is too bad. Are you going to be able to pay for all of it?

Listening openly is not easy and requires patience. Later, in the feedback stage, the listener can express any concerns. Being judgmental will only cut off further communication.

One reason that individuals do not express their feelings is that judgments are frequently leveled at emotions. "How could you be angry about that?" "That is stupid," "I would not have let that bother me," or one of the worst, "You have no right to feel that way," are almost sure to prevent further disclosures of emotion. Ironically, judging can be so ingrained that we tend to use it even in simple exchanges. For example, you may have told someone you enjoyed a movie and then been told, "Oh, I don't see how anyone could like something like that." In Chapter 8 you will learn ways to voice an opinion that does not sound like a judgment.

Listen without one-upping.   When I present this in class, the reactions clearly indicate how common this response is. "One-uppers" have a definite intent, which is to tell their own story because it is more dramatic, more interesting, better, or worse than yours. In some cases, one-uppers just react from habit or because they want to relate to the speaker's experiences. Whatever the reason, to be one-upped is annoying.

> SPEAKER: I went fishing yesterday and caught two bass. I—
>
> LISTENER: (interrupting) That is nothing! I caught six last week.
>
> SPEAKER: I have been really depressed because my favorite aunt died a few days ago.
>
> LISTENER: I know just how you feel. My grandmother died a few months ago, and I'm still trying to get over it. She was such a wonderful person, and we all loved her. Why, just before she died, she was helping my cousins settle an argument . . . (Story would continue!)
>
> SPEAKER: I'm really excited. We are leaving for Mexico next week.
>
> LISTENER: You are going to Mexico? I am going to Europe. I will be in England a few days, then on to Scotland, then to France. I will be gone for at least four weeks, then I am going to . . .

When role playing the last conversation, after the listener stopped, the speaker said loudly, "And I hope your plane goes down!" The laughter indicated that any of us would probably harbor similar thoughts! Notice the lead-in of "That's nothing!" in the first example. Besides preceding a one-upping comment, the phrase is negating and is one to avoid.

Do you recognize anyone, even yourself, as a "one-upper"? Awareness can eliminate or decrease most of its use. Remember not to jump in too quickly and sound as if your story is better. If you slip, acknowledge that you took over the conversation and lead the speaker back to the original story.

Listen without advice giving and problem solving.   Caring individuals have difficulty with this one. They want to be helpful, so they are quick with advice, not realizing that it can stop the exchange prematurely. Either feeling or thinking MBTI personality preferences can respond too quickly. Thinkers do so because they enjoy problem solving, and it's logical to do so as quickly as possible. Feelers can experience so much empathy; they just feel compelled to help.

> (*Advice giving*)
>
> SPEAKER: I'm having trouble communicating with my parents.
>
> LISTENER: I can suggest several good books for you to read.

> (*Problem solving*)
>
> SPEAKER: I am upset about my relationship with him.
>
> LISTENER: I think you should just call it quits.

Can you see how the quick response can end the exchange or steer it in another direction? A better response would be to paraphrase or express understanding of the feeling when appropriate or show that you are receptive just by body language. In most cases, the speaker has more to express verbally, nonverbally, or both.

I was reminded of the importance of listening without attempting to problem-solve when one of my students stayed after class. She looked sad, and I asked her how she was. She replied, "Just terrible. I've been sick, and now my husband has started drinking again." I stifled a strong urge to tell her about support groups for families of alcoholics and books she could read. Instead, my facial expression was one of concern. I said, "Oh," and because she looked so forlorn, I put my arms around her. She started to cry, and we stood there for about two minutes while she sobbed. Afterwards, we talked, and I eventually made some suggestions. If I had responded immediately with my well-meaning advice, the opportunity for her to release stress and genuine emotion would have been lost.

Receptive listening means that you remain in the listening role longer and don't jump in too soon. Think of it as keeping an invisible piece of tape over your mouth for awhile. Show encouragement nonverbally or with short responses.

Directive Listening

This type of listening is more controlling than either empathic or receptive listening, and the listener is more verbal. Asking questions is the key technique. Five different types of questions can be used; they are listed here in the order of most to least effective (Miller et al., 1988).

Open questions: These usually begin with who, what, where, when, or how, but not why. Open questions allow the speaker choices and encourage longer responses.
Multiple questions: These ask for more than one answer at a time. They flood the speaker, and the questioner often does not get the desired information. For example, a job interviewer who asks, "What are your strengths and weaknesses and how might you improve?" is unlikely to get complete responses in each area.
Closed questions: These are questions that can be answered with just one or a few words.
Leading questions: These are designed to get a certain response. For example, "Don't you think you'd be wise to check the benefits they are offering?" is a disguised way of telling the other person what to do.
"Why" questions: "Why" questions often cause reactions of defensiveness and tension. Instead of using "why," try "How did you go about making that decision?" or "What reasons did you have for that choice?"

Directive listening is appropriate when you want to resolve issues efficiently or make decisions quickly. Job interviews, other business exchanges, and consultations employ directive listening. And, at times, parents feel a need to use it as well! Knowing how to direct conversations with effective questions is a practical skill.

Listening is of great significance in the communication process. Take the opportunity to check your own listening on a scale in Reflections and Applications. Then use positive listening to create an open communication climate that leads to healthy relationships (Reflect and Apply).

REFLECT AND APPLY

Reflect

♦ *Think of examples of when you listen for enjoyment, for information, or for help, plus situations in which you listen for more than one reason.*

♦ *Select a particular barrier and think of the last time it hindered the listening process.*

♦ *Recall a situation in which empathic listening was used. Do the same for directive listening.*

Apply

♦ *With a partner, practice both negative and positive listening behaviors.*

♦ *Use receptive listening when someone shares an experience with you.*

LOOKING BACK

- Listening is an active process of attending, receiving, and interpreting auditory stimuli and then providing feedback. Listening well includes observing and interpreting nonverbal behaviors and reacting to a speaker. Listening goes beyond hearing because it involves interpretation and responding. Listening skills can be learned and improved.

- Individuals listen for various reasons. Three purposes are to enjoy, to become informed, and to help. A goal of listening is to share a common meaning with another person.

- Positive listening cannot be overemphasized. In work situations, friendships, and family relationships, listening is the key to healthy interactions. Poor listening creates problems.

- As important as listening is, almost everyone learned to do it informally. Little, if any, formal instruction is offered in school curriculums. Becoming a positive listener is an individual's responsibility.

- General barriers to listening are preoccupation, environmental factors, psychological filters, emotions, different rates of speaking and thinking, and negative intentions.

- Improvement comes from eliminating barriers and demonstrating positive nonverbal and verbal behaviors.

- Paraphrasing, clarifying, and delivering feedback are important skills. Negative listening behaviors can be identified and eliminated.

- All listening is active. Specific types include empathic, receptive, and directive forms of listening.

IMPROVING COMMUNICATION: HOW TO SEND MESSAGES

LOOKING AHEAD

After completing this chapter, you will be able to

- Explain the importance of how messages are delivered.
- Describe and give examples of open and closed communication.
- Recognize dogmatic, commando, and grandiose wording.
- Use "I" statements, tentative words and phrases, and qualifiers to change the closed style of communication to an open one.
- List and describe dimensions of effective expression.
- Recognize metamessages.
- Define and realize the importance of both paralanguage and body language.

The "how" of communication is as meaningful as the "what."

—Sharon Hanna

In all interactions, information and meaning are communicated. Often overlooked are the manner and method of delivery, yet they are equally critical in the communication process. This chapter will focus on improving how messages are delivered both verbally and nonverbally. Specifically covered will be openness, effectiveness, paralanguage, and body language.

Improving Your Verbalizing Style

Have you ever thought about the way you deliver your thoughts, feelings, and needs? **Style** refers to how a person verbalizes. A particular style influences how the speaker comes across and usually elicits a certain response. Communication styles can be identified and changed.

Pretend you are the listener in the following conversations and assess each one in terms of your reactions:

1. The supervisor does not care how well I do my job. The only thing she thinks about is how much money the company makes. She puts so much pressure on

everyone and never says we are doing good work. You are crazy to ask to be transferred over here.

2. I get the impression that the supervisor is not very interested in how well I do my job. It seems to me that her major concern is how much money the company makes. We feel a lot of pressure from her, and I hardly ever hear her tell us we are doing good work. I do not think you would like to work here.

Essentially, the same message was delivered. Yet, if you are like most people, your reaction to each would have been different. In the first one, the speaker is using the **closed style of verbalizing.** This means that the comments are definite and, if the listener disagrees, leave little opportunity for a reasonable response. The closed style, because of its absoluteness, finality, forcefulness, and all-inclusive/exclusive language, stifles positive exchange. The closed style fosters a negative communication climate. Opinions stated as inflexible truths invariably close the door to open communication.

In the second example the **open style of verbalizing** is used, and discussion is encouraged. A point of view is stated in a flexible manner. Because the expressed ideas sound open, they invite a reasonable, positive response. Open communicators are refreshing! Rather than offending or turning others off, open communicators attract people and are more likely to develop and maintain positive relationships. The old adage "It's not what you say, but how you say it" has a great deal of merit.

Closed and Open Communication

Awareness of the closed style and recognition of its use is the first step toward becoming an open communicator. Following are descriptions of three types of closed communication and ways to change to the open style.

1. *Dogmatic*—"definitely definite," rigid, absolute, and inflexible. When verbalizing, a dogmatic communicator sounds like the final authority. A key measure of dogmatism is closed-mindedness (Vogt, 1997), and in verbalization this comes across as *expression of opinion as fact or truth.* Here are some dogmatic statements:

"The weather is lousy" or "It is a beautiful day today."
"Valentino's has the best pizza in the world" or "Valentino's has the worst pizza in the world."
"He has been a very ineffective president" or "He has been an excellent president."
"Religion is necessary for a happy life" or "It is not necessary to be religious to be happy."

TABLE 8-1	Actual "I" Statements		
I think		I like	I want
I believe		I consider	I feel
I feel that		I prefer	I am or was

Note: An opposite could be made of each by inserting don't or another appropriate word.

TABLE 8-2	Phrases Conveying "I" Meaning
In my opinion	In my way of thinking
As far as I am concerned	My thoughts are
It seems to me	To me it appears

How a comment is stated, not its content, makes it dogmatic. Each example expresses an opinion; yet it comes across as the "way it is" (Table 8-1).

Using "I" statements. The basic technique of open-style communication is to rid yourself of dogmatic comments by the use of "I" statements. Because you are speaking for yourself, "I" statements are also regarded as assertive language and are self-empowering. "I" statements are less inflammatory, put responsibility on the speaker, and are much more likely to be heard (McKay, Fanning, and Paleg, 1994).

"I" statements can be divided into two categories. The first group consists of phrases known as actual "I" statements. The word "I" is said first or begins a phrase used elsewhere in the sentence (see Table 8-1). The second category is made up of phrases that give an "I" meaning. These, too, demonstrate that the speaker's opinions do not necessarily take precedence over others (see Table 8-2).

A common error is to use "I know" for "I think" such as "I know students do better in smaller classes." The speaker does not *know* this. Only when a fact is being stated would "I know" be correct.

Following are rewordings of the dogmatic statements made earlier.

"I like (or do not like) the weather."
"As far as I am concerned, Valentino's has the best (or worst) pizza in the world."
"In my opinion, religion is necessary (or not necessary) for a happy life."

Remember that "I" statements are not necessary in all verbalizations. When you express facts, they certainly are not. My dad expressed many of his opinions in a dogmatic way. I suggested that others would react much more positively to him if he used "I" statements. He "leaped" into this in his usual enthusiastic fashion, and it was as if the three words "in my opinion" gave him freedom to say anything. In his zeal, he used the phrase frequently. One day he came into the house and said, "It is raining outside," and then, looking directly at me, added, "in my opinion." I hurriedly explained that when expressing a fact, "I" statements are not necessary! Also, simple dogmatic observations such as "That is interesting" are seldom considered offensive.

To become an open communicator, listen for your dogmatic statements and concentrate on using "I" statements. A world of difference exists, *in my opinion*, between saying, "College does not prepare you for the real world" and "I think that college experiences rarely prepare you for what goes on in the world." Remember that you affirm yourself when you express opinions in an open style.

2. *Commando*—forcing, pressuring. This category includes words and phrases such as "should," "have to," "must," "ought," and "need to" that leave little, if any, opportunity for alternatives. Note the authoritarian, commanding nature of these statements:

"You must get a job."
"She should listen better."
"You had better take my advice."

Consider how you react to forcing words, especially when they are preceded by the word "you." Defensively? In a study, adolescents described accusatory "you" statements as likely to evoke stronger antagonistic responses than assertive "I" statements. The teenagers reported that the use of "you" with angry messages increased their hostile responses and provoked resistance and rebellion (Kubany et al., 1992). When people speak in a "commando" way, reactions of defiance, resentment, or passivity are possible; none would appear to be healthy and positive. The "commando" type is usually expressed dogmatically as well, which obviously makes such statements sound even more closed. This style may remind you of moralizing, which was discussed in Chapter 3. Moralizers make use of commando-type words.

Being tentative and flexible. When the "commando" type has been used, first check to see whether the statement is also dogmatic. If so, create an "I" statement and then replace the forcing part with a flexible and tentative phrase. See Table 8-3 for examples.

Following are changes in the "commando" statements given previously.

"I think it would be a good idea for you to get a job."
"I believe she would benefit from listening better."
"It seems to me that my advice could be helpful to you."

The forcing words "should," "must," "has to," and "had better" were replaced with tentative phrases, and "I" statements were used. The same point is made in a less demanding way.

3. *Grandiose*—exaggerated, all-inclusive or all-exclusive, and often dramatic. The use of this type can lead to inaccuracy or a distortion of the facts. Following are examples of grandiose words and statements in which they are expressed:

everyone—no one
everybody—nobody
all—none
always—never
everything—nothing—anything
only
every

TABLE 8-3	Some Tentative Phrases
It would be a good idea if	
He or she, they, or you could benefit from	
It could be helpful if	
It seems important that	
He or she, they, or you might be wise to	

"All kids today are disrespectful."
"She is always late."
"The only way to become skilled in word processing is to take a class."
"I do not have anything to wear."

Consider a statement such as: "Everybody's having kids." My quick reaction is, "I am not!" Note that grandiose statements are almost always (not always) dogmatic.

A statement that contains grandiose words is usually inaccurate. How often is "always" correct? Be careful you do not answer that with "never."

At times, "always" is accurate. Years ago I suggested the possible elimination of the words "always" and "never" from the language until Ed, a good friend, reminded me of their accuracy in certain statements. He noted that the Pope is always Catholic and never Jewish! In most cases, grandiose words are used only for their dramatic effect. Yet, because they usually create an inaccurate statement, the point can be lost. Parents are advised not to say to a child, "Your room is always a mess" or "You never clean your room." Why? The child can clean once in a five-year period and prove that you are wrong!

Listening for examples of the grandiose style from others as well as yourself can actually be fun. Keeping a sense of humor, you can challenge the obvious inaccuracy of such comments. Try inwardly responding to the suggestions in parentheses when you hear these types of statements:

"All men are that way." (All? Really?)
"You never do anything right." (Surely once in a while the person does!)
"All he does is eat." (That's all he does? Amazing!)
"I'm always late." (Not even once are you on time?)

Depending on your relationship with the grandiose speaker, you may be able to verbalize these questions. When students say, "There was *no* way I could have come to class," I try to humorously challenge them! Awareness is the first step toward improvement.

Adding or replacing with qualifiers. To correct the "grandiose" type, an "I" statement may be needed to get rid of dogmatism. Then replace or modify the grandiose word with a qualifier (see Table 8-4). For example, if "always" or "never" has been used, ask "Is the word correct?" If not, select a qualifier that does not change the meaning to any extent. In the statement "She is always late," what word could be used to qualify "always"? Some possibilities are "often" or "hardly ever" as replacements or adding "almost" in front of "always" as a modifier. Be

TABLE 8-4	Words Useful as Qualifiers		
almost	quite a few	frequently	infrequently
nearly	probably	often	rarely
many	possibly	usually	seldom
most	some	generally	sometimes
several	few	in general	hardly ever

Can You Find All Three Closed Types?

"Politicians should tell the truth, and they never do."

"You ought to save part of your paycheck."

"Students need to study hard to get good grades."

How well did you do? All are dogmatic because they express opinion as fact. Did you find the forcing words (*should, ought,* and *need to*)? In addition, politicians and students with an implied "all," and the word "only" are grandiose. Don't the following reworded statements sound open and positive?

Figure 8-1

careful that you do not change the meaning to any great extent. For example, if you are rewording "Everyone is so rude," the meaning would be significantly changed if you replaced "everyone" (the grandiose word) with "someone." Instead, use "many people" or add "almost" to "everyone." Some possible open statements are "I have noticed that she is rarely on time" and "It seems to me that most people are rude."

Using qualifiers makes statements accurate and less hurtful. A young man said that his father repeatedly told him, "You will never amount to anything." "Never" and "anything" felt like arrows accentuating the attack on his self-esteem (Fig. 8-1.) Qualifiers decrease the sting of a critical remark. Again, compare the statements that follow with the ones given in the description of the grandiose type.

"In my opinion, many kids today are disrespectful."

"It seems to me that she is often late."

"I found that taking a class in word processing really improved my skill, and I would recommend it."

"I do not have many things to wear."

These reworded statements are accurate, less dramatic, and open. Note that each is an "I" statement. All three types of the closed style set up obstacles to communicating effectively. Either they stop communication or, if exchange does take place, disagreement or combativeness is apt to occur. Statements that contain all three types are not unusual. In a book written for teenagers in stepfamilies (Getzoff and McClenahan, 1984), closed communication, called aggressive language, is associated with responses of defensiveness, attack, or resentment. None solves a problem (Fig. 8-2).

Can You Create Open Communication?

"In my opinion, most politicians hardly ever tell the truth, and I think it would be much better if they did."

"I believe that it's a good idea to save part of your paycheck."

"I think that most students who study hard can get good grades."

Figure 8-2

Open communication is worth the time and effort spent in developing the techniques. The first step in becoming an open communicator is a desire. The second requires listening to your usual style. Then rewording mentally and restating aloud will complete the process. Accomplishment comes from practice and more practice! To help, **Reflections and Applications** asks you to identify and rewrite closed statements. Eventually, open communication will become easy and natural.

Becoming an Effective Communicator

In addition to using an open style, you can improve communication by expressing yourself effectively. This can be accomplished by paying attention to certain guidelines (McKay, Davis, and Fanning, 1983).

Directness

Being direct means stating what you want to say. You do not assume that others know what you are thinking or feeling. People, often those with a feeling personality preference, may not say what they mean because they do not want to offend others. Yet indirectness can cause deeper hurt. For example, since her parents' divorce, Tiffany had spent two months each summer visiting her dad. One summer she did not want to stay the full time, yet she was concerned about hurting his feelings. Because she was not direct with her dad, she stayed and felt resentful, causing their relationship to become distant. This hurt both of them. Other reasons for indirectness are indecisiveness, shyness, and nonassertiveness. "We cannot hear what the other is not saying; and, sometimes, when we finally do, it is too late" (Buscaglia, 1992, p. 152). A message worth sending deserves to be delivered directly.

Straightforwardness

Related to directness is straightforwardness, which means being honest and not disguising information or intention. A **metamessage** is one in which the true meaning is not openly expressed. Instead, an underlying message is transmitted by accenting a word, changing the tone of voice, or making suggestive comments. For example, if a person says, "*Obviously*, you're right," the real meaning probably is, "You act like you are always right." A metamessage is often sarcastic. Note the following metamessages and the possible intended meanings.

"She must have really been an interesting person to talk with."
(Meaning: I was hurt that you spent so much time talking to her.)
"Do not worry about being out of town when we have the graduation party. We
    will manage without you."
(Meaning: I am unhappy that you will not be here.)

Instead of using a metamessage, either be straightforward, say what you mean, or just keep silent. In the next chapter you will learn how to respond to metamessages effectively; you undoubtedly know someone who uses them!

Clarity

Effectiveness calls for the delivery of a clear message. Individuals who say "I feel funny" or "There is something wrong" are not being clear. Another example is the practice of asking a question when a statement would be more effective. For example, "Why don't you try harder?" would be much clearer as: "I have noticed you have not been turning in as many projects of high quality lately, and I would like you to try harder." Simple requests may be harmless. Lack of clarity and confusion can lead to serious relationship problems. For example, what does "I will call you later" mean? It could be 15 minutes in one person's mind and a week in another's. Abstract words such as *love, trust, loyalty,* and *honesty* often have different meanings for people. What does respect mean to you? Ask a few others and see if meanings are the same. A couple was having an argument. She said, "I just wanted you to be honest with me." He replied, "I was honest. I did not lie to you." Her comment was, "You may not have lied; however, you did not tell me all about it, and that's dishonest!" Do you see how their meaning of honesty was different? To avoid this, effective communicators do more than use a word; they describe, behaviorally if possible, exactly what they mean.

Another problem with clarity comes when someone says one thing and indicates another with body language. "I am listening!" she says as she continues to write a letter. How do you know which to believe? Effective communicators strive for clarity. "A message clearly given that is clearly received is a rare and beautiful phenomenon" (Adams, 1987, p. 135).

Supportiveness

Effectiveness is not enhanced by hurting someone or trying to appear superior. Nonsupportive communication includes using sarcasm, calling attention to past errors and problems, comparing others unfavorably, attacking in a judgmental way, and delivering threats. Effective communicators are not out to prove points or win; instead they want to be supportive and promote understanding and goodwill.

Efficiency and Sharing

Effective communication is damaged by using fillers, adding unnecessary details, meandering, and monopolizing the conversation. What creates a barrier in the following?

"Well, you know, I go to college, you know, and it has been a good experience, you know. I have really, you know, learned a lot, you know, and I think you oughta well basically, you know, try it!"

Is there any doubt? The filler "you know" is heard in all walks of life from the playground to the corporation boardroom. A **filler** is a word, phrase, or sound used for no reason except to replace silence. Other common ones are "basically," and saying "right?" after every statement such as "I went to the movies last night, right? There was this guy there, right? And he struck up a conversation with me, right?" How many other types of filler can you identify? Overuse of any word or expression gives people a reason not to listen. An effective communicator eliminates fillers. A speech class can do wonders in this regard. Another idea is to ask someone else to catch you using the filler.

An efficient speaker reaches the point with only interesting details so that listeners are not frustrated or bored. For example, let's listen to two people tell about their vacation.

> SPEAKER 1: We left last Monday morning.
>
> SPEAKER 2: No, it was after lunch.
>
> SPEAKER 1: No, it was morning because it was before the mail came.
>
> SPEAKER 2: I know we left in the afternoon. Don't you remember that we got an invitation to a wedding reception and knew we could not go because we'd be on vacation?
>
> SPEAKER 1: No, we got that invitation the day before. We stopped for lunch in Platte City, or was it North Platte? I think it was North Platte. Do you remember?
>
> SPEAKER 2: No, I just know we left after lunch!

If you are smiling, this probably reminds you of someone. The disagreement is annoying, as is the length of the story with the unnecessary details!

Have you ever been engaged in a conversation with a person who did almost all the talking? People who monopolize conversations by either telling one story after another, repeating stories, or giving you endless accounts of themselves and others they know are ineffective and annoying. In fact, such an individual could rightly be described as a poor communicator. Efficiency and give- and-take in conversation are most appreciated.

Effective communication takes practice. To achieve your purpose, follow the guidelines of effective expression and use open communication.

Recognizing the Importance of Paralanguage and Body Language

The "how" of communicating is greatly influenced by other factors. In fact, about 93 percent of an expression is conveyed by vocal changes and nonverbal behaviors and not by the words alone (Mehrabian, 1968, 1981). Becoming aware of paralanguage and body language and learning how to use yours effectively are valuable tools in communication.

What Is Paralanguage?

A vital part of meaning is conveyed by **paralanguage,** the vocal changes or variations in the human voice. Paralanguage has several components.

Rhythm.   When emphasis or accent is placed on different words, rhythm varies. In the phrase "It seems to me," if you accent *seems,* you are giving the impression of openness; if you emphasize *me,* you have defeated that purpose.

Rhythm can be used in a negative way to convey sarcasm and criticism. For example, "Oh, no. You did not say *that!*" can sound critical.

Inflection and pitch. Inflection is a change in pitch or in tone of voice. Pitch ranges from low to high, and people have varying degrees of natural voice tone. In normal conversation, positive communicators will vary their pitch purposefully; for example, when asking a question, pitch usually rises. Depression or physical fatigue can create a lower voice. Altering rhythm, inflection, and pitch can make a major difference. Note the variations that change the meaning of the same series of words.

You received an award.
You received an *award*!
You received an award?

Robert Frost, the famous poet, said, "There are tones of voice that mean more than words." Listening to the variations in your own voice and, at times, recording yourself can be very helpful. You may be expressing more than you realize!

Volume. Loudness or softness of speech changes the meaning and can create a dramatic effect. A professor told a group of aspiring teachers that in order to get the attention of noisy students, they should whisper; this, she contended, would quiet them faster than a loud voice. I can honestly report that whispering has worked for me, and then again, it has not! It depended on the group of students and the specific situation. Regardless of its effectiveness in quieting others, varying the volume of expression can add interest and meaning to your speech.

Speed. The rate at which one speaks makes a difference in the degree of understanding as well as the interest level of the receiver. People who talk very fast are often misunderstood, or they tend to overwhelm the listener. In contrast, a slow speaker can easily put others to sleep or create a great deal of frustration! Again, variety and appropriateness are important.

Articulation. "What did you say?" The question is often asked because of poor articulation. A speaker mumbled and was not understood. Enunciation, or distinct pronunciation, is a necessary element in delivering a clear message; however, you can overenunciate and give an unfavorable impression. If problems exist in this area, awareness and practice can be beneficial.

Effects of Paralanguage

Paralanguage adds meaning to what you say and makes you a more interesting speaker. Because of paralanguage, you can seem insensitive or be hurtful. You can also sound warm and caring. If you want to realize the profound effects of paralanguage, try expressing a few thoughts or feelings without any variation in your voice.

At times, certain paralanguage usages are demeaning. You probably will, or already do, engage in conversation with elderly people in a work or personal setting. Speaking softly and slowly and articulating dramatically, as if the receiver were incapable of understanding, is unnecessary in many cases and can diminish the self-esteem of the elderly person. I was delighted one day when an older friend of mine told a young receptionist, "I am quite capable of understanding you if you speak to me exactly as you did to the last patient!" You may not be made aware of this habit as the receptionist was; it is up to you to become more aware of how you sound to others.

Components of Body Language

Body language consists of nonverbal communication and, by itself, may make up as much as 55 percent of the meaning of a message (Mehrabian, 1968, 1981). Think of times when what was expressed by body language carried more impact than the person's words. Misinterpretation is common. For example, Steve was surprised and dismayed when Melissa frowned, tossed her head, and turned away. "Why are you mad?" he asked. Her reply was, "Mad? I just remembered a phone call I was going to make." Three areas of body language can be monitored and analyzed.

Body movements. Facial expressions, eye contact, gestures, and other body parts can vary immensely while verbalizing. Animated is a positive way to describe a face. I received a wonderful compliment when I asked my class how they could tell that I enjoyed teaching. One student quickly replied, "It shows all over your face during class."

How often have you "read" someone's eyes? They, too, are capable of expression. The eyes have been called "the mirror of the soul." According to one expert on body language, it is not the eye itself that creates expression but the length of the glance, the extent of the opening of the eyelids, and the manipulations of the skin around the eyes (Fast, 1970).

Even less expressive eyes can be a positive factor if the person maintains direct eye contact, at least in U.S. society. Not doing so can cause others to doubt the words or to feel uncomfortable. In other societies, direct eye contact is not necessarily viewed as positive. In most Asian cultures, eye contact is limited. Incidentally, in all cultures, direct eye contact is generally more difficult when speaking than it is when listening.

Gestures are movements of the hands and arms. As an accompaniment to speech, they help to convey meaning and, even with no verbalization, can send a message. Gestures are symbols; their meanings vary across cultures, and the differences are worth learning. For example (Axtell et al., 1997):

- The OK sign (index finger forming a circle with the thumb with the other three fingers extended) is a rude gesture in Germany and Greece.
- The "hook 'em horns" gesture (index and little fingers extended from an upheld fist commonly used at the University of Texas) means in Italy: "Your spouse is having an affair.

- In Italy, if a man twists his index finger into his cheek, it is a compliment meaning, "That woman is beautiful."

The meanings of gestures can also vary from time to time so you are wise to stay informed especially if you travel to other countries.

As helpful as they can be, gestures can be overdone, as in the case of people who "talk with their hands." Cultural differences are apparent in this regard, too. For example, Italians are generally quite animated and active in their use of hand movements.

An ordinary gesture can express negativism. Think about how you react to a finger pointed at you to emphasize a statement. Defensive or resentful? These are common reactions even though the "pointer" may just be doing so from habit. Clearly, these behaviors are learned. In your gestures, aim for the "happy medium" between enough movement to add interest and emphasis and too much motion, which detracts. Do avoid potentially annoying gestures.

Body position.   Another element of body language has to do with how you sit or stand because you create an impression. Expressions of agreement, disagreement, interest, boredom, respect, affection, dominance, and harmony are possible. Degree of self-confidence is often indicated. Positioning yourself at a different eye level than another is not recommended. Try sitting and carrying on a serious conversation with another person who is standing. "I do not like it at all!" is a common comment. Closed positions include crossed arms and legs, the head turned slightly away, and a slouched posture. Open positions are achieved by just the opposite. A relaxed position, as opposed to a rigid, tense one, generally creates a positive atmosphere. The situation will influence body position. Your position when conversing with a friend in a home setting will usually differ from your posture during a job interview. In the classroom, others, including the professor, assess students' body position. How would you describe yours? In all situations, appearing open and interested is positive.

Spatial relationships.   Where you position yourself in terms of distance from another reflects spatial relationships. Four distinct zones have been identified (Hall, 1969).

Intimate—actually touching to 18 inches apart
Personal—1½ feet to 4 feet apart
Social—4 feet to 12 feet apart
Public—12 feet or more apart

Individuals vary in their personal-space preferences. Generally, the closer the proximity, the more intimate the relationship. For most people, conversations within the personal zone are comfortable. The social zone is used more in business or other formal interactions. Again, cultural differences are important to note. For example, in most Latin cultures, people stand closer when engaged in interactions.

Often an attitude or emotion is communicated simply by the amount of personal space. Standing close to someone could imply invasion or domination or

Figure 8-3   What nonverbal message is being communicated?

could signify dependence. Keeping your distance may indicate disinterest, discomfort, or dislike. Being aware of the appropriate physical space distances and placing yourself accordingly are advantageous behaviors (Fig. 8-3).

Importance and Interpretation of Body Language

Nonverbal behaviors can express emotions, communicate messages, and control human beings; both individual preferences and cultural influences are involved (Scheflen, 1972). Because body language transmits more than half the meaning in most messages, its influence is immense. Body language is also used in what is called presentation of self, the attempt to present ourselves to others so they will see us as we wish to be seen (Goffman, 1959). Think of appearing capable your first day of work or sociable at a party. How many ways can you communicate these traits through body language? Joshua came to an interview in a nice-looking dark gray suit, white shirt, and a fashionable necktie. From his polished shoes to his neatly combed hair, he looked the part. He smiled confidently, looked directly into the interviewer's eyes, and responded to the outstretched hand with a firm handshake (Fig. 8-4). He was off to an excellent start!

Nonverbal behaviors also indicate aspects of personality. "He is so rude," was the comment. Why? "Because he just stared fixedly at me when I talked to him." One could also be considered rude for not looking directly at a speaker. Aggressive, shy, and confident are just a few of the personality traits that may be assigned to individuals because of their body language. Those skilled in sign language certainly understand the power of body language. The impression you make and the ones you receive, as well as the health of your relationships, are greatly influenced by nonverbal behaviors.

Entire textbooks have been written on the subject of body language. The science of body language is called **kinesics** (Fast, 1970). After learning about body language, one student said, "I never thought about it like that. I have become much more aware of how I may appear to others." If you are in the presence of others now, ask yourself, "What impression am I giving right now with my body language?" Throughout your personal and professional life, this question is a crucial one.

Figure 8-4   People usually feel comfortable conversing within the personal spatial zone.

How your body language is interpreted will make a marked difference in how you are perceived by others.

Some caution regarding body language is recommended because a few simplistic interpretations have emerged. One seminar leader tried to convince participants that all behaviors carry deep psychological meanings. When he said that stirring an iced drink with the tip of one's finger always has a sexual meaning, I reacted with nonverbal behavior—a shake of my head, which meant "I do not agree!" He seemed to be using imagination in his interpretation. Experts in the field say that most body language is learned and then develops into habits (Scheflen, 1972). Stirring with a finger usually comes from convenience or habit rather than from deep sexual longings.

Videotape can be used to see how you appear to others. As students in a career development class watch themselves during a mock interview, the amazed reactions are predictable: "I did not know I did that," "I am going to have to sit on my hands," "I sure looked a lot more confident than I felt." If you have an opportunity to see yourself as others do, take advantage of a unique learning experience. Even though it may be a jolting experience, it will undoubtedly be well worth it if you make necessary changes. An activity in Reflections and Applications lets you work with both paralanguage and body language.

Are you recognizing that communication is complicated? Its many dimensions can be somewhat overwhelming, yet awareness of all aspects is needed to understand and improve interactions and relationships. Be patient. Positive communication techniques, in the beginning, can be awkward and difficult. Start

---

REFLECT AND APPLY

Reflect

- *How often do you use forcing words? Grandiose words? Start paying attention to your style of verbalizing and reword when necessary.*
- *Think of some words that have different meanings for various people.*
- *Think of a recent conversation. About what percentage of the time were you talking? About what percentage of the time were you listening? If the two percentages aren't about the same (50–50, 60–40, 40–60), evaluate the interaction closely. If you were doing far more talking than listening, change this in future conversations. Or you may want to increase how much you contribute verbally.*
- *Give a negative example and then a positive example from each of the three areas of body language.*

Apply

- *Listen for the three types of closed communication and then inwardly reword them.*
- *Tune into any words or phrases you use as fillers, and then eliminate them.*
- *Answer the question under the photo (Fig. 8-3) using an "I" statement.*
- *Using the following statement, see how many different ways you can change the meaning using paralanguage: "That is really funny."*

listening to yourself and others and, if necessary, reword, add, subtract, and modify in an attempt to improve. Clear, effective, and open verbalizations, combined with positive uses of paralanguage and body language, are rewarding interpersonal skills. Remember that you learned how to communicate, and you can unlearn and relearn (Reflect and Apply).

LOOKING BACK

- How people communicate is an area not often analyzed and is as important as the information and message that are given.
- Open communication and closed communication are two verbalizing styles; they usually result in quite different reactions and responses.
- People commonly express their ideas and feelings in a closed style using dogmatic, commando, or grandiose expressions instead of being open, flexible, and accurate.
- Open communication consists of "I" statements and tentative words and phrases and qualifiers. Because this style is likely to result in positive relationships, developing the skills is a worthy goal.
- Effective verbal communication is a worthy goal. Being direct, straightforward, clear, timely, supportive, and efficient are beneficial.
- Paralanguage, the variations in voice, adds depth and meaning to expressions.
- Body language, the nonverbal behaviors related to movement, position, and spatial relationships, is of utmost importance in communication.

Positive communicators lift us by their warmth; their eyes light up in response to us, showing their openness. They refresh our spirit, making us glad to be around them. Negative communicators repel us and arouse feelings of uneasiness within us. We feel lonely, shut out, or attacked around them. Even if they are in our families, we want to avoid negative persons because they zap our energy.

—Teresa Adams

IMPROVING COMMUNICATION: WHAT TO SAY

LOOKING AHEAD

After completing this chapter, you will be able to

- Discuss how people verbalize on different levels.
- Name and give examples of the four levels of self-disclosure.
- Recognize appropriateness of and benefits of healthy self-disclosure.
- Give and receive compliments in a positive way.
- Explain perception and use perception checking and dimensions of awareness in order to express thoughts clearly.
- Respond positively to criticism, metamessages, and bothersome language patterns.

> *Only if we honestly reveal ourselves can we truly know and appreciate each other.*
>
> —Sharon Hanna

"Yackity-yack, yackity-yack" is a recurring phrase in a light, popular song of years ago. **Content** consists of the words and sentences uttered during the communication process. "Yackity-yack," composed of idle comments, makes up the content of many conversations. However, content also includes words that go down in history such as President John F. Kennedy's famous line, "Ask not what your country can do for you, ask what you can do for your country." Examining what you say and finding positive ways of expressing yourself will help you become a better communicator, which leads to positive relationships.

Understanding Content

Think of all the topics of conversation you cover during the day. "What time is it?" "How are you?" "Nice day, isn't it?" "I got a speeding ticket on the way to work!" "I do not like greasy food." "I am feeling depressed." "I think that employees deserve more input into company policy." These are just a few pieces of possible conversations. Although some comments lack depth and may even be trivial, talking with others is nonetheless important.

Levels of Content

Categorization of content is useful. Five levels identified by Powell (1969) are related to an individual's willingness to share parts of the self. The levels are listed here in order of least revealing to deepest sharing.

Cliché conversation. This is made up of superficial and conventional comments such as "How are you?" and the predictable response of "Fine," "What do you think of the weather today?" "Nice party," and "Have a nice day." Sometimes called cocktail-party talk, such comments are usually safe, with no sharing of self. This type serves its purpose, however, and life would be dreary without it.

Facts about others. Just a step above a clich{eacute} is a comment about a neighbor, friend, coworker, or family member. Whether positive or negative, nothing is revealed about the speaker except that she or he can talk about other people. "Our new neighbor works for the school system."

Ideas and judgments. This is riskier because the speaker reveals thoughts and opinions. Fearing rejection, the usual pattern is to say only so much and retreat if any adverse reaction is noted. "I do not think Joe was a good choice for the neighborhood association position."

Feelings (emotions) or "gut level." Because of emotional suppression, this level is difficult for most speakers. Improving verbal expression of emotions is an important life skill.

Peak communication. Openness, honesty, and complete willingness to share occur at this level. For most, this level is achieved only with close friends and loved ones. Sadly, too often what would seem to be a close relationship lacks this level of communication. "Your friendship is important to me."

Excellent communicators use all of the levels in appropriate situations and in reasonable amounts.

Awareness of Content

The words we use reveal a great deal about our attitudes and personalities and directly influence the effect we have on others. Based on the premise that we create and shape our relationships through talk, the book *I Only Say This Because I Love You* (Tannen, 2001) is a useful guide in helping people become more aware of content. A positive communicator wants to avoid potential pitfalls in the communication process. Specific areas of possible difficulty follow.

Semantics.   A major common problem is a difference in **semantics,** the meaning of words. A Vietnamese man in a career development class heard the instructor talk about the need to sell oneself in order to get a job. He responded that "Selling myself is bad." Understandably, he had literally interpreted the word "sell." After it was explained to him there was another meaning, he was reassured and said, "Yes, that is good." Even if people share the same native language, misunderstanding can occur. Using clear expressions, stating your own meaning, and then using examples that are concrete or describing behaviors will decrease the opportunities for semantic problems. Feedback by listeners is helpful in this regard. "If verbal communication is to be reasonably clear, both the sender of a message and the receiver have the responsibility to make it so" (Satir, 1983, p. 88).

Dialect.   Related to semantics is **dialect,** a variety of a language that differs from other varieties of the same language, including distinct pronunciations, unique meanings, and different words altogether. Dialect often reflects differences in region and culture. Differences in dialect can be interesting and fun and only disconcerting when some people insist that their way of speaking is the only way.

Bias-free language.   Awareness is necessary in order to avoid the use of **biased language,** words and statements that are insensitive and demeaning. Sensitive people do not want to offend, and in the workplace, using biased language will keep you from being hired or could get you fired. Certain examples related to race, religion, gender, disabilities, and ethnic background are obvious. Derogatory labels such as "broad," "retard," "nigger," "honky," "spick," or "fag" and words that historically are demeaning such as "boy," "colored people," "little woman," "deaf and dumb," "poor white trash," or "illegitimate child" are degrading and are to be avoided.

People may use biased words because they forget or are unaware of the meanings. A challenge in using bias-free language is that meanings change. Sex-equality consciousness has challenged language that denotes male dominance. For years the use of male pronouns and other words did both openly and in subtle ways deliver messages of superiority and exclusion. Fortunately sexist language is being used less frequently today. Subtle examples of undermining females that in many cases have no overt sexist intention are references to a woman as "honey" or "sweetie" and to women as "girls" or "gals." Have you ever heard of a group of men referred to as "boys" or "guys?" What one is called is significant.

Nonsexist language is now taught and its use encouraged in classrooms, the work environment, and within the mainstream of society. For example, the word "chairman" is more appropriately "chairperson" or "chair," and because women have established nontraditional careers, firemen and policemen are now firefighters and police officers. Fair-minded men recognize that they would not like it if things were reversed and are positive about elimination of outdated sexist speech. Because anyone can suffer from biased language, its elimination is definitely necessary.

One difficulty in sensitivity is that individuals have various preferences and attach personal meanings to words. You may not know, for example, whether to refer to a person as Hispanic or Latino; white, Caucasian, or European American; black or African American. Students in a diversity class were enlightened when they were told by a female panel member: "My family and I live in the United States. I prefer to be called Mexican because I was born in Mexico. My children are Mexican Americans because they were born in the United States." If you want to know a racial or ethnic designation for someone, a wise solution is to ask an individual what she or he prefers.

College students sometimes struggle with what to call an instructor or professor and wonder whether one title is better than another. For example, some women professors prefer Dr. Smith; others want to be called "Mrs. Smith," whereas others are irritated with the "Mrs." title and prefer "Ms.," even if married.

Still others solve the problem by telling students to address them by a first name. Your best course of action is to let others know your preferences and to ask about theirs. A person who is skilled in interpersonal relations will keep abreast of new developments and be sensitive to all human beings.

English language learners (ELL).   As a result of significant increases in immigration among people who speak other languages, many are in the process of learning English. Rather than criticize or ridicule anyone, consider that English is a difficult language filled with as many exceptions as rules. Then admire those who are working hard to master it. How many languages do you speak? Learning a second one is a definite asset.

Emotion-packed phrases.   Inadvertently, you may use **emotion-packed phrases** (Walker and Brokaw, 1998), groups of words usually said as lead-ins to statements that carry an emotional punch. Some of these are:

After all I have done for you
When I was your age
You should know better
After you have worked here as long as I have

Note that many emotion-packed phrases begin with "you" and can easily be reworded. Listen to yourself and to others. How many such phrases do you hear? They can turn off the listener or sidetrack a positive exchange, so try to eliminate as many as you can.

Disclaimers.   An expression that denies or shrinks from responsibility is a **disclaimer.** A common one is "Not to change the subject, but." The speaker has said that the intention is not to change the subject; however, he or she will do so anyway! Confusing? Instead, why not say, "I am going to change the subject," or "I would like to change the subject for the moment." Disclaimers may seem easier and less offensive; however, others can become annoyed or resentful of the indirectness. The key word in disclaimers is "but," which is a way of saying yes and no in the same sentence (Satir, 1976). Here are some examples:

I love you, but I wish you would take better care of yourself.
I am sick, but don't worry about me.

These statements often leave the listener feeling uneasy and confused. A definite improvement is to substitute the word "and" for "but."

Another example of a disclaimer is the "just in jest" remark. If there is negative reaction to a comment such as, "You are so slow, a turtle could get there faster," the disclaimer is, "Just kidding." Yet the person probably was not kidding. Disclaimers are ineffective ways of verbalizing.

Slang, colloquialisms, and vulgarity.   **Slang** consists of terms that are popular at a given time. They are usually interesting and fun to use yet can become a problem if they are misinterpreted or overused. A job interviewer wrote on an evaluation form: "I do not like the company referred to as 'you guys' as in, "What kind of products do 'you guys' sell?" Incidentally, the applicant did not get the job. Monitor your use of slang and be aware that it can cause problems. Informal folksy words and phrase are **colloquialisms.** They can add color to expressions yet can also be overused and misunderstood. An added problem is that they can create an unfavorable impression. For example, in the Midwest, the word "yes" is commonly replaced with "yeah." In formal situations such as a job interview "yeah" sounds unprofessional. Others include "nope," "ya don't say," "no kiddin'?" and "how ya doing?"

Vulgarity and the use of profanity have become commonplace. Relying too heavily on substandard expressions can leave others wondering about the extent of the speaker's vocabulary. Also, swearing and crudeness do affect people's sensitivities and can be offensive, so limit or eliminate vulgar and profane expressions. Keep in mind that patterns of expression are difficult to change from one situation to another. An applicant was embarrassed during an interview when he said, "People who do not give a damn annoy me." He later said, "I swear a lot, but I was sure I could control it during a job interview." He learned the hard way that positive language patterns, like all skills, require daily use.

Vocabulary and Grammar.   People who are limited in vocabulary and accepted grammar are likely to express themselves poorly. In certain situations, their self-esteem will suffer as a result. I remember a period of time when my daughters and stepsons were in school and proper grammar was not "cool." As a parent and a teacher, I managed to endure "ain't" and "he don't" and even "it do not make no difference" coming from the mouths of intelligent human beings! We purists were competing against the lyrics of music and words uttered by role models of the time.

Although perfection in language skills is not necessary, effective communication goes hand in hand with the ability to speak a language acceptably. If your vocabulary or grammar skills are poor, you can take advantage of courses or use self-study resources to improve. You might consider a refresher course in writing skills as well. When you use the best of the language, you are a better communicator.

Revealing Yourself: Self-Disclosure

Self-disclosure is defined as making the self known by revealing personal information. In doing so, people can know and understand each other. Individuals disclose verbally and nonverbally. The earliest research on self-disclosure revealed that women disclosed more than men. Unmarried participants revealed more to their mothers than to fathers, male friends, or female friends and married individuals shared more with their partners (Jourard, 1971).

Self-disclosure continues to be a focus of interest. Generally, women enjoy more personal levels of disclosure than do men; this holds true in both opposite-sex and same-sex relationships (Wood, 2001), although personality differences are extremely influential. After learning more about levels of self-disclosure, we will examine the benefits, obstacles, and steps that are involved (Fig. 9-1).

A word (or more) about E-Mail

Because face-to-face paralanguage and body language are nonexistent in e-mail communication, both clarity and effectiveness are at risk. These tips can help.

- Choose your words carefully. Try reading your message aloud if possible. Does it sound like what you want to say?
- Be specific—especially about names, places, dates, and times.
- If this is a business message, be brief. Realize that the receiver probably has many messages to read.
- Do not send a message unless you are relatively sure that the receiver will appreciate it or unless it is absolutely necessary. There are far too many forwarded messages circulating.
- Learn e-mail etiquette. For example, using capital letters often comes across as if you are yelling.

A recommended guide is *E-Writing: 21st Century Tools for Effective Communication* (Booher, 2001).

Figure 9-1

Degrees of Self-Disclosure

Just as all kinds of content can be organized into levels, self-disclosure also has its degrees. Identified by Glaser (1986), the following reveals what can be disclosed.

Basic data refer to biographical and demographic information: I am 22 years old. I was born in Denver, Colorado. I am attending college in Columbus, Ohio. I live in an apartment.

Preferences are likes and dislikes, pleasures and displeasures, what one would rather do or not do: I like pizza. I enjoyed going back to Colorado this summer. I would rather attend a small college. I do not like having two roommates. I love summer.

Beliefs consist of thoughts, opinions, and attitudes: I believe that young adulthood is a challenging time of life. I think that small colleges offer more individualized attention. In my opinion, educators are not paid enough.

Feelings are disclosures about emotions: I am proud to be in college. I feel sad when I think about moving to a new city. I was scared when I heard about the accident.

These degrees are arranged in order of least to most difficult to disclose, in general (see Fig. 9-2).

In most cases, basic data are risk free and relatively easy to reveal. Even though preferences can usually be disclosed with little risk, some people will challenge you. For example, have you ever told someone that you liked a certain kind of food and heard the reply, "That stuff? How could you like it?" Arguing over preferences seems trivial and unnecessary, yet you will find some people who seem to have difficulty accepting differences even about preferences.

Degrees of
Self-Disclosure

Basic Data
Preference
Belief
Feeling

Figure 9-2

For a number of people, or in certain situations, beliefs may be more difficult to disclose than feelings. Both include a degree of risk and indicate a deeper level of disclosure. Thoughts and opinions, as pointed out in Chapter 7, are often verbalized in the closed style of communication. If the open style were used, beliefs would likely be more acceptable and, consequently, easier to reveal. Emotions can be hidden from others for a variety of reasons. Even if you are in touch with your feelings, they may be difficult to explain.

All relationships benefit from self-disclosure. The levels can be useful in checking out how open you are. Do others reveal all degrees to you? If they do not, do you know the reason? The depth of self-disclosure is generally an accurate reflection of the closeness of two people.

Benefits of Self-Disclosure

Matt frowns at Sue when she says, "I wish you would share more of yourself with me." "Why?" he asks. If Sue is well informed, she will be able to explain the benefits of self-disclosure. One reward has to do with knowing and understanding oneself. Each self-disclosing statement brightens the light of self-understanding. As you reveal your true self, you feel more honest, authentic, and validated. "This is who I am" can be an exhilarating feeling. Self-disclosure is usually a self-esteem builder.

Other benefits are related to the developmental areas of the self. In terms of health, a self-discloser seems to benefit. Inhibiting one's thoughts and feelings gradually undermines the immune function, the action of the heart and vascular system, and even the biochemical workings of the brain and nervous system. Not disclosing has been linked to the severity of asthma, diabetes, anorexia nervosa, and even pain thresholds. In an experiment, high self-disclosers showed significant drops in blood pressure compared to low self-disclosers (Pennbaker, 1997). Talking to others about disturbing aspects of life is relieving.

Sharing can be relieving. Stress and certain emotions can be managed positively by self-disclosure. Erin described a change.

> I was negative, and now I am positive. I think it is because I am being more open and honest. I am willing to share my "real" self now. I am glad because people now are starting to look at me from the inside to the outside.

Specific benefits of self-disclosure were identified in a study of lesbians. Degree of disclosure was related to overall levels of social support (Jordan and Deluty, 1998). Building close relationships is also an outcome of self-revelation. In fact, achieving intimacy is impossible without disclosure of self. **Social penetration theory** (Altman and Taylor, 1973) explains that close relationships develop in terms of increasing self-disclosure. Among dating couples, self-disclosure is a significant predictor of relationship satisfaction (Meeks, Hendrick, and Hendrick, 1998). As discussed in Chapter 5, expression of feeling is beneficial. "None of us who value our relationships can afford to retreat from communication on an emotional level" (Branden and Branden, 1982, p. 66). Self-disclosure has been related to positive outcomes for supervisors in a work setting (Ladany, Walker, and Melincoff, 2001) and perceived understanding in stepchild–stepparent relationships (Martin, Anderson, and Mottet, 1999).

A major plus is that self-disclosure makes relationships interesting. Think how boring life would be if people conversed only on basic data and preference levels. Disclosure affirms the other by saying, "I care enough about you to share my personal self."

Finally, when people self-disclose, the communication process is improved. Individuals can understand and provide feedback to each other and create an open, accepting environment. Self-disclosure is usually reciprocated. There is a relationship between what persons are willing to disclose and what others reveal to them. The openness of one person can begin a sharing process that creates a close relationship.

Obstacles to Self-Disclosure

Even if Sue convinces Matt that the benefits are well worth his consideration, he still may resist self-disclosure or find it difficult. He has a great deal of company in this regard. Why? The most common reason is fear: "I am afraid that others will laugh at what I believe." "I was hurt before when I revealed how I felt, and I'm not going to let that happen again." "I told her how proud I was of my final grade, and she put me down for bragging." The threat of rejection is frightening. "But, if I tell you who I am, you may not like who I am, and it is all I have" (Powell, 1969, p. 20). Fear of intimacy could be involved.

Most people receive "parent" messages telling them to not self-disclose. "Do not let others know about your financial situation," "Your sex life should be private," and "What would the neighbors think if they knew?" are common "parent" messages. Knowing what type of communication sharing is for "family" only and what type is appropriate outside of the family is important. Culture has an effect on self-disclosure. A study found that Asian Indians tend to suppress rather than express feelings. Being exposed to American culture somewhat modified their perceptions and expressive patterns (Hastings, 2000). Gender roles are a part of the culture. As mentioned earlier, the stereotypic masculine role is "at odds" with self-disclosure. Men tend to be less self-disclosing especially about their emotions and weaknesses (Dolgin, 2001), which is unfortunate for both them and their partners (Fig. 9-3).

For Better or For Worse   **by Lynn Johnston**

Lynn Johnston Productions Inc./Dist. By United Features Syndicate, Inc. Reprinted with permission.

Figure 9-3

Before You Self-Disclose

- Is my level of disclosure appropriate in this situation?
- Do I trust the person to whom I am self-disclosing?
- For what reason am I self-disclosing? Is it a positive one, or am I being manipulative, petty, or cruel?
- Are the risks worth my self-disclosure? What can be gained versus lost? Will my self-disclosure unreasonably burden another person?
- Is this the most opportune time and place to self-disclose? Is the atmosphere conducive to a positive interchange?

Positive answers give you a "green light" to self-disclose.

Figure 9-4

Personal circumstances and attitudes can be barriers. A study revealed that lonely individuals negatively evaluated deeper levels of disclosure and viewed them as risky and undesirable (Rotenberg, 1997). People with low levels of **interpersonal trust,** defined as the expectancy that another's word or promise can be relied upon, would likely have more difficulty in self-disclosing. Obviously, after trust is developed, people are more likely to disclose.

How to Self-Disclose

After a consideration of the benefits and a removal of obstacles, people who want to feel more authentic and to develop healthy relationships will elect to self-disclose. The critical question for many is how to do so. Before disclosing, honestly answer the questions in "Before You Self-Disclose" (Fig. 9-4).

After deciding to self-disclose, the question becomes how to do so. The use of "I" statements is highly recommended. The open style lends itself to being more positive. Body language in harmony with the verbal message is important. Stating that you think open communication is important while maintaining a closed body position is confusing. Being clear, specific, and descriptive are invaluable. Vague disclosures may be worse than none at all. Importantly, telling too much and monopolizing the conversation are very likely to turn off any listener. After disclosing, be ready to accept feedback and keep the exchange open.

Giving and Receiving Compliments

Like breaths of fresh air, **compliments** are comments of admiration and praise; in the TA framework, they are verbal positive strokes. Compliments can initiate a relationship. On his first day at work, Bill was complimented by Rick, a coworker. The expression of praise started a conversation. After a few weeks, the two were socializing with each other. Compliments definitely enhance relationships and build a bond between individuals.

Recommendations for Giving Compliments

Do you give compliments? Although opportunities for expressions of admiration and praise are plentiful; too often such opportunities are overlooked. Stinginess in compliment giving may come from a tendency to take others for granted or an inability to recognize a situation in which a compliment would be appropriate. Hesitation can come from shyness, embarrassment, or concern about how the compliment will be received. If you have any difficulty, consider how valuable a compliment can be. Jennifer was depressed and had decided to quit school. Then she was complimented about her class participation by an instructor and praised by another student for her note-taking abilities. "Those compliments were like a tonic to me," she said. "I had lost faith in myself, and all at once it was restored. I changed my mind about quitting school."

Compliment-giving guidelines.   Raise your awareness level to the point that you notice praiseworthy situations. Everyone has a positive quality. Do not confine your compliments to people you know. A clerk in the department store, a taxicab driver, a waiter or waitress, a person behind the voice on the phone—all are candidates for compliments. Being sincere is important. Phoniness and insincere flattery are likely to be detected and will be disturbing. If you do not truly admire something, you are better off saying nothing.

Vary the reasons for your compliments. People usually compliment others on the basis of appearance. Certainly, people appreciate this type of praise. However, you can also compliment people on other qualities and behaviors. "I enjoyed your comments in class," "I thought your work on the project was terrific," "I admire your positive attitude," and "I love your laugh" are generally appreciated by recipients.

When you compliment someone, check to see that your words, paralanguage, and body language are all saying the same thing. Without meaning to do so, you can express a genuine compliment in a tone of voice that sounds negating. Beware of giving "backhanded" compliments. These are comments that start out sounding positive and end with a stinging remark, a question, or a qualifier that implies they aren't wholly true. Some examples are: "You drew a beautiful picture *for a change*," "I *cannot believe* your room is clean," and "*How did you manage* to throw such a great party?" Can you see why these need to be reworded or are better left unsaid?

A positive behavior is to be a third-party compliment giver. What can you do if you hear a positive comment about someone? Passing it on to that individual is almost as good as giving it originally. You can also add to it. For example, "Craig said that you are a great golfer. I can see why he thinks so. Shooting par on that hole was not easy."

Thinking about yourself as a compliment giver and realizing the benefits of these positive comments can encourage you to increase both their number and their variety. You might want to set a goal of doing so. Your acquaintances, friends, and family members will benefit as will you.

Responding to Compliments

"I enjoy giving compliments, but I feel funny getting them," was Jordan's honest comment. How do you react to a compliment? The comment is, "I really like your suit." Do any of these responses sound like you?

"This old thing? I have had it for years."
"I hate it. I just pulled it out because everything else was dirty."
"Your taste in clothes is slipping."
"Really?" (while wrinkling your nose)

Rejecting or denying compliments is common, and the potential for damage is extensive. A compliment rejection is essentially an insult. It is as if the positive comment is hurled back into the face of the giver. Once rejected, a giver will be reluctant to deliver more compliments. A relationship can be harmed because one individual did not graciously receive what was offered. People with low self-esteem are often guilty of this practice and so do not benefit from a sincere comment of praise. Finally, the communication climate can become negative. Imagine a black cloud settling in because the compliment giver feels diminished.

How to receive compliments.   Receiving a compliment in a positive way is simple. A "thank you" is enough. If you want to add more, some possibilities are "Thank you, I really appreciate that," "Thank you, I have been feeling a little down, and you helped," and "Thank you, I did spend a lot of time on the project."

If you honestly do not agree with the comment, you can choose to keep quiet or you can mention it without a rejection. For example, you really do not like the suit you are wearing, and you receive a compliment. A possible honest response is, "Thank you. I had my doubts about it, and it's nice to know that you think it looks good." You may wonder about returning a compliment with a compliment. In response to "I like your suit," someone could say, "I like your outfit, too." If the response is sincere, no harm will result from a mutual admiration exchange.

Checking Your Perception

Picture a person standing on the roof of a house with arms waving over the head. Three people from across the street look at the scene. Later, each tells about the incident.

> Mary to her husband: "This guy was acting really crazy. He was on top of the house and waving his arms like he was trying to scare someone."
> Tom to his children: "A man was trying to get my attention by waving his arms at me. I thought he was in trouble, so I came into the house and called 911. I have not found out yet what was going on."
> Ed to a friend: "I did not have my glasses on, but it looked like a woman up on the roof who was ready to jump. She was yelling really loudly, too."

Each person offered a different perception of the situation.

What is perception and how does it affect the communication process? **Perception** is a mental process of creating meaning from **sensory data** that we receive through stimulation of our senses. A message is carried to the brain, which then organizes and interprets the data. In perceiving, our brains are like computers. Once "turned on," we take in data through the senses of sight, sound, smell, taste, and touch. The perception process begins when sensations are received (like raw data being fed into a computer) and continues as the brain quickly interprets. It tries to make sense out of the sensory data (as a computer computes) and attaches meaning to the input.

In differentiating between sensory data and interpretation, think of a courtroom scene. On the witness stand, a person is allowed to give only the facts, or sensory data: "I *saw* the suspect drive away in a red car." If a witness begins to add interpretation such as, "I *thought* that he had come out of the bank and was probably fleeing from a robbery," a good attorney will object. Interpretation is not allowed as evidence.

In interpersonal relationships we receive most information from seeing and hearing, although touching and smelling can also be involved. Perception affects communication and all other aspects of human relationships. If perception were always accurate, several interpersonal difficulties could be avoided. But is perception correct in all situations? At the beginning of this section, three people described the same experience differently. Because of uniqueness, no two people's perceptions are ever exactly the same, and our perception in any given situation can be inaccurate.

Effects on Perception

For what reasons could perception be faulty? What we perceive is affected by such factors as background, self-esteem, personality, values, age, sex, physical condition, mental health, and expectations.

Expectations do influence what you actually see and hear. If you expect to see or hear a certain thing, that may well be your sensory data. A custodian, who was cleaning an office, was facing a window. An office manager came in, sat at her desk, and said, "You are really working late. I will bet your girlfriend or wife does not like that very much." To her surprise, a female voice replied, "Actually it is my husband who minds!" Expecting custodians to be male led to incorrect sensory input.

In addition, the senses and their abilities to gather accurate information differ from person to person. Limitations can lead to errors. Even though well-adjusted people are generally capable of receiving accurate sensory data, there are no guarantees. Ask a police officer about an investigation of an accident scene! Usually, more than one account is heard. Even if the sensory data are correct, what about comprehension? Have you ever been misinterpreted? Have you ever misunderstood another person? The potential for errors is enormous. In fact, misperception causes much of the conflict and difficulties in relationships. You may often have heard or said, "That is not what I meant!"

As an example, imagine the following scenario.

You are in the cafeteria at school or work, and a friend who is usually outgoing walks past your table. She glances at you and then turns away.

You saw what she did, so the sensory data are correct. Recognize, however, that another person might have "seen" it differently. Next is your interpretation. Think of as many possibilities as you can.

Perception Checking

1. **Give sensory data**: Exactly what did you see, hear, or smell? Include who, when, and where if possible. Use behavioral terms in your description. Paint a picture in words. Use any of these: "I noticed," "I saw," "I observed," "I was told," "I heard," "I overheard," "I smelled," "I touched."
2. **Give interpretation**: What did the sensory data mean to you? Interpretation is delivered tentatively, not as if it is the truth or factual. Don't say, "I wonder if." State in a positive way what you think. Use any of these: "I thought," "it seemed to me," "to me it appeared," "I took that to mean," "I believe," "that led me to believe or think."
3. **Check both sensory data and interpretation**: The question checks the accuracy of your sensory data and perception. At this point you are not asking whether the person wants to talk, needs help, or the like; nor do you offer to give help yet. Use any of these: "Is that right?" "Am I correct?" "Is that how it is or was?"

Figure 9-5

She is mad at me.
She did not really see me or recognize me.
She just does not want to talk right now.
She is stuck up.

Which is correct? One cannot know at this point, and a person skilled in communication and interpersonal relations will want to clarify it. A first step is to be aware that you do not *know* for sure. Even though evidence may point to one interpretation more than to another, the human experience is full of inconsistencies.

Perception Checking as a Communication Technique

When you have doubts about either the accuracy of sensory data or your interpretation, a communication technique called **perception checking** can be helpful. This process involves describing the specific sensory data you have received and the interpretations you are making about those data (Glaser, 1986). In cases in which you have no doubts as to accuracy, the technique would be senseless. For example, if someone says, "I do not like you," and punches you in the face, you are receiving a clear message (Fig. 9-5).

Perception checking includes three steps. First, describe your sensory data—what you have actually seen and heard or, in some cases, smelled, tasted, or touched. It is important to be specific and descriptive. Second, give an interpretation of the sensory data. What did they mean to you? Third, ask a question to check the accuracy of the sensory data and interpretation. Ideally, "I" statements are used in the first two steps, whereas the third step is framed as a question.

In using perception checking, certain phrases or ways of asking the question will probably sound more natural to you than others. If the language seems awkward at first, with use you will become comfortable with it.

In the situation in which your outgoing female friend has glanced at you and then looked away, you can use perception checking as follows:

1. "In the cafeteria this afternoon when you walked past my table, I saw you glance at me and then look away." (sensory data)
2. "It appears that you were upset for some reason." (interpretation)
3. "Am I right?" (question that checks both)

The friend can then confirm, modify, or deny either your sensory data or your interpretation or both.

You may be wondering why going through all three steps is important. Let's consider other possibilities such as a "why" question. "Why are you mad at me?" This is an assumption that your interpretation is accurate, and it may not be. How do you react to most "why" questions? Generally, people are put on the spot and feel defensive. Many "why" questions are not asked to find out the real answer. As one man commented, "Whenever my folks asked 'why,' I knew they did not approve of what I had done, and I was going to hear about it."

Another poor way to begin a discussion with your friend is what many people do: "You are mad at me, aren't you?" or "You do not like me any more, I guess." An even worse approach would be to say, "I *know* you are mad at me." These leave out all sensory data and leap directly to conclusions. Instead of checking, you have already made an interpretation, concluded that you are correct, and now your friend is being told the reason for her behavior. In many cases, people just assume that their interpretation is true, become upset, and do not say anything. "I will treat her just like she treated me" is their way of handling the situation. Too often, relationships suffer because people do not openly share their sensory data and interpretation. Perception checking is direct and honest. Unless you are speaking to a troubled person, perception checking will be nonthreatening. The goal is to clarify a situation and, in most cases, the person will respond in such a way that this is possible.

Using Dimensions of Awareness

Perception checking is used to clarify your sensory data (sensations) and interpretation (thoughts): You and your relationships can benefit from sharing even more. Although you may be unaware of them, five key pieces of information are present in a given situation (Miller et al., 1988). Let's examine each of them.

- **Sensations:** Verbal and nonverbal input from people's actions, as well as subtleties of what you see, hear, smell, taste, and touch.
- **Thoughts:** The meanings, interpretations, or conclusions from the sensations. Interpretations are not "the way things are." They are the way you put your world together—the way you make sense out of data.
- **Feelings:** Emotional responses, which are important to share in most interpersonal relationships. Review the information about expressing feelings in the section on degrees of self-disclosure.
- **Wants:** Intentions, desires, and wishes for yourself, for others, and for your relationship together.

- **Actions:** Behaviors consisting of past, present, and future actions. These are, or will be, observable, and they indicate commitment.

Confusion between wants and future actions is common. The difference is that intentions do not carry a definite commitment to act and are only desires. You may share what you have done, are presently doing, or will do.

Becoming aware of the five dimensions in any interaction and then expressing these to another person indicate a willingness to reveal what you know. Using "I" statements is important. Following is a way to use dimensions of awareness in the situation of the friend in the cafeteria.

(Sensing) "This afternoon as you walked by my table in the cafeteria, I saw you glance at me and then look away."
(Thinking) "It seemed to me that you were upset."
(Feeling) "I am concerned about this."
(Wanting) "I would like to straighten this out."
(Acting) "In fact, I asked Michele whether she knew if something was wrong. She did not, so I am checking it out with you."

You may not want to express each dimension in exactly the same way or order presented here. You can begin with any dimension and use wording that is comfortable for you. For example,

I am concerned because I noticed that you looked away from me when you walked by my table in the cafeteria this afternoon. I was sure you had seen me, and it led me to think that you are upset with me. In fact, I even asked Michele whether she knew if you were upset and she did not. I would like to straighten this out, and I have time to talk about it right now if you do.

If you are thinking that this is too involved and will be time-consuming, ask yourself how worthwhile clarity is. Being partly aware is a major problem in the communication process. You owe it to yourself and to your relationships to become as fully aware as possible.

Thinking about these dimensions can help you discover areas of self-*un*awareness. For example, you may be able to communicate four dimensions and recognize that your feelings are not clear—even to you. Learning the skills initially is the easiest part; putting them into practice is the most difficult. Usually, it helps to announce that you want to share your dimensions of awareness and would like the other person to do so too.

Delivering Criticism

A life in which criticism is unnecessary may sound wonderful; however, such an ideal world does not exist. Because you will undoubtedly deliver criticism, learning how to do so in a constructive, positive way is advisable. A first step is to ask yourself the reason for criticizing. Is it justifiable? Is it potentially beneficial? Think about whether the criticism is destructive or constructive, and speak only if you believe you can help.

Preparing yourself by thinking about what you will say, and even rehearsing it, is highly recommended. Picking a suitable time and place, if possible, is also a good idea. Be aware of body language and paralanguage. When you deliver a critical remark, use "I" statements. "You" statements will most likely elicit a defensive, combative response. Directing attention specifically and descriptively to behavior or a situation you do not like is more acceptable than being critical of the person. You can choose to use perception checking or, more completely, the dimensions of awareness to increase the chances of a receptive response. Another suggestion has been called the "Mary Poppins rule" (Levine, 1988). Based on the idea that "a spoonful of sugar helps the medicine go down," the aim is to make the criticism more acceptable by prefacing it with a sincere compliment. For example, "Professor Martin, I enjoy your lectures a lot; however, I do not think that the examination policies are as fair as they could be." Using the person's name, also, can be affirming. Check the following steps in criticizing a sloppy roommate.

1. Begin with a sincere positive comment.
    "Rhonda, I really like you and have a lot of fun living with you."
2. Specifically describe the situation and behaviors. Again, draw a picture with your words.
    "We had agreed to keep our apartment clean and neat, yet your clothes are in the living room, and I have cleaned up the mess in the kitchen for the last four days."
3. Acknowledge the other's thoughts, feelings, and personal situation.
    "I realize that you have been so busy and maybe just forgot."
4. Give reasons for your criticism and tell exactly what you want and expect.
    "I am frustrated, and I do not want this to become a bigger problem. I do expect you to keep our agreement."

Unless Rhonda is an extremely defensive person, this criticism will not offend her and should get the results you desire. If it does not, you can at least be satisfied that you have expressed your criticism in an open, nonthreatening way.

Responding Effectively

Criticism is almost impossible to avoid and can be difficult to receive. If constructive and delivered in a nonthreatening manner, it is easier to handle; however, sizable numbers of critical statements are made negatively and for reasons that are not evident. Whether the criticism is deserved or not, a response determines, to a great extent, the course of the exchange and possibly the relationship itself.

Inappropriate Responses to Criticism

Eliminating ineffective or negative responses can clear the way for responses that work in your behalf. In general, individuals respond either aggressively or passively or with a combination of the two. An aggressive method is one of counterattack. A person feels wronged, justifiably or not, and then lashes out at the perceived attacker. The criticism may be stopped for the moment; however, the aggression is resented, and the situation is only worsened. In the workplace, an aggressive response will probably get you fired.

Passive responses are ones that apologize and acquiesce; they can be delivered verbally or nonverbally. Silence is often a form of surrendering to criticism. If you are a "peace-at-any-price" person, passivity may seem inviting. Nevertheless, the potential damages to your psychological well-being and to the relationship are seldom worth the price. Meek receivers of criticism also invite further attacks.

A combination of the two occurs when an individual responds passively and then acts aggressively at a later time: "Yes, dear, I know I have neglected paying the bills, and I will make sure it does not happen again," is the agreeable response. The bills get paid, and two checks are returned from the bank for insufficient funds. The person who was criticized either purposefully or unconsciously has found a way to get back at the critic. Because this behavior is essentially manipulative and indirect, a relationship can be badly damaged.

Other possibilities are denial and defense. Excuse making is a far too common response. Usually, the criticized person recognizes that the criticism is appropriate yet still finds it difficult to accept. "Yes, *but*" is an irritating response. Blaming other people or external situations is part of excuse making and makes an individual appear immature and irresponsible.

Positive Responses to Criticism

If your goals are to maintain or increase your level of self-esteem, preserve or improve the relationship, and make the situation better for yourself, positive responses to criticism are the key. "The effective way to respond to criticism is to use an assertive style. It does not attack, surrender to, or sabotage the critic. It disarms the critic" (McKay and Fanning, 2000, p. 162). The key is to not overreact and make matters worse (Fig. 9-6).

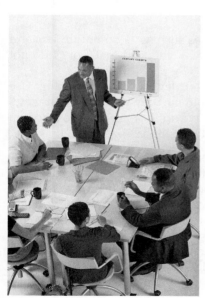

Figure 9-6   During a performance evaluation, constructive criticism is given in a positive way.
Source: Photos.com.

Agreement with Criticism. Even if you realize that the criticism is justified, you can still feel somewhat defensive and hurt. Hence, you may respond in a way that will make the situation worse for you. Instead, follow these steps using "I" statements.

1. Agree with the criticism, using such phrases as "I realize," "I agree," "I know," and "I understand."
2. Optional: State the reason briefly and be sure your reason is fact, not excuse. (This step is optional because you may not want to tell the "why.")
3. State what you plan to do to prevent future occurrences or to solve the problem.

Pretend you have been late for work for the past few days, and your supervisor has criticized you. A common reaction is to make an excuse or place blame elsewhere. Refrain from both! Instead, use a response that is refreshing and much more likely to bring about positive results, such as one of the following.

1. I know I have been late, and I can understand your concern.
2. I have had several frustrating problems with my car (optional).
3. I am taking it in to be fixed tonight, and I plan to be careful about my punctuality in the future.

Or, if you do not want to mention your car, skip step 2, and in the third step just say, "I will correct this problem in the future." Dramatically promising that you will *never* be late again is unwise because it happen again.

You can also agree with part of the criticism. You might understand the person's interpretation and want to clarify. For example, if your supervisor said, "You seem to have lost interest in doing a good job," you can respond, "I can see why you would think that because I have been late the past few days. I have not lost interest. My being late is due to other factors that I plan to correct."

In certain instances, humor can be used to defuse the situation. When former Nebraska Senator Bob Kerrey was running for Congress, a loud critical voice from the audience said, "I do not know why I should vote for you. During one whole year when you were governor, I do not remember anything you did except entertain that actress, Debra Winger." Kerrey smiled, rubbed the side of his head, and replied, "I know what you mean. Sometimes I do not remember much else about that year either." The crowd broke into laughter, including the critic, and what could have become a negative situation, became a positive one for Senator Kerrey.

Not understanding the criticism. Frequently, criticism is vague, and you honestly do not understand what the person means. Emotionally, this is difficult to handle. You are probably inclined to defend yourself even if you do not know the reason for the criticism. Resist the temptation! The following response technique, using "I" statements, is particularly helpful.

1. State your lack of understanding. Use phrases such as "I do not understand why you think that," "I am confused as to why you said that," or "I do not know why you have that impression."
2. Tell the person what you need to increase your level of understanding. Use phrases such as" I would like you to explain to me why you think that way," "I would appreciate your telling me what I have done or not done to lead you to think that," or "I would like to know what you are basing that on."

Now the critic is in the responding position. You have been honest and politely requested what you want while giving yourself time to calm down if needed. You wait for the explanation, which usually gives you enough information to respond specifically. Interestingly, if the critic had used either perception checking or dimensions of awareness, you likely would not need more information. Vague criticism usually does not include sensory data.

To illustrate this response, pretend a coworker has said to you, "You do not like to work with me anymore." You have no idea why she believes this because she has not given you her sensory input. You can use a two-step response and say:

1. "I do not know why you think I do not like to work with you."
2. "I would appreciate your telling me what has caused you to think that."

You now wait to hear what led to her interpretation, which she has poorly stated as fact. Then you can deal with a concrete description of her sensory data.

Surprisingly, the person may not be able to provide what you have requested. The response may be, "Well, I do not really know. I just do not think you like to work with me." This is frustrating; however, you are wise to continue to behave positively. You can ask key questions such as: "Can you give me some examples?" "Can you specifically describe what I did?" In some cases, you may have an idea of the reason for someone's criticism and can guess. Be careful about this, however. For example, you may respond, "Is it because I told the supervisor that you had not finished your share of the project before you left yesterday?" If you are not certain that this is known by the coworker, you will be in for a surprise when she says, "No, I did not know you did that, and now I am really upset!" If you have probed and still have not received any useful sensory data, you can conclude by saying, "I do not feel that way; however, until you can give me some specifics, I am not able to offer more than that."

Not agreeing with the criticism.   Emotionally, the most difficult situation to deal with is one in which you disagree with the criticism. The person has given you sensory data either initially or after you have requested clarification, and you do not agree. A positive response is still the best one.

1. State your disagreement: "I do not agree," "I guess we do not agree on this," or "I do not see it the way you do." Be sure that you are expressing this in a nonthreatening way and keeping your voice calm. Usually, a quick "I disagree" sounds aggressive and is not recommended.
2. Either use your own sensory data to give reasons for your disagreement or simply end the conversation. Your choice will depend on what is at stake, what chances you think you have of coming to some sort of an agreement, and other extenuating factors such as fatigue levels and time constraints. You can suggest a future discussion as well as an acknowledgment that disagreement is not always negative.

Other tactics may be helpful. You may opt to neither agree nor disagree. Instead, you simply acknowledge criticism and let it go. For example, a parent says to you, "Your apartment (or house) is such a mess, I do not know how you stand to live here." You can reply, "Yes, it is a mess," or "It *is* amazing how I stand it." Other useful phrases are: "You *may* be right" and "That could be true." If you feel strongly about the criticism, acknowledgment isn't advisable. However, in many situations, criticism can be like "water off a duck's back" if you allow it to be.

Another choice is to delay. If you are completely surprised by the criticism and, especially, if your reaction is anger, you can express your confusion or surprise and state that you want to think about it for awhile. A good response is, "I am not sure how to reply. I am going to think about it, and then I will get back to you."

> By backing up for a moment to examine our feelings, rather than simply reacting from panic, we can most effectively sort out and respond to the realities of the critical message. (Butler, 1992, p. 165)

Positive responses to criticism are not difficult to learn. They lead to a feeling of enhanced self-esteem and of being in control and serve to move relationships in a positive direction. Checking your skills in the communication exercise in Reflections and Applications will help.

Effective Responses to Metamessages

Metamessages, comments with a double-level meaning, were discussed in Chapter 8. Metamessages are usually hidden criticisms, yet they may not be. Recipients of such messages cannot be sure until they check. First figure out what you think the message means. The second step is to state what you think the person is saying and ask whether you are correct. Imagine that your mother says, "You are *so* busy these days." The emphasis on "so" creates a metamessage. The statement means more than just that you are busy. Is concern about your welfare being expressed, or does your mother mean that you do not spend enough time with her? Whichever you decide, state clearly and tentatively, "I wonder if you are worried about me" or "It seems to me that you do not think I am spending enough time with you." You can phrase it as a question such as, "Do you mean that I am not spending enough time with you?" Or you can choose to ignore it; however, realize that a relationship based on openness and positiveness is then in jeopardy.

Ways of Responding to Offensive Language Patterns

Being able to respond assertively to offensive language patterns is a worthwhile skill. "I hate it when people make bigoted remarks. I just do not know what to say," said one individual. Because a response is usually preferable to silence, knowing what to say makes a major difference.

- Assertively state your opinion; in doing so, you set limits.

  "I do not appreciate profanity."
  "I do not approve of those kinds of jokes."
  "I do not like to hear others being put down."

- Tell how you feel.

  "I feel resentful when you start your sentence with 'Let me tell you.'"
  "I get frustrated when you make frequent references to 'when I was your age.'"
  "I am hurt by those kinds of comments."

- Politely challenge with a question.

  "Can you clarify that?"
  "Is that your opinion or is it based on research?"
  "What do you mean?"

- Suggest another alternative.

  "As far as I'm concerned, talking positively about people is much better than being so negative."
  "I would prefer that you did not say, 'You have no right to feel that way.' I do have a right to my feelings."
  "I would like to talk about something else."

Too often, individuals simply react and respond with whatever happens to come to mind, not realizing what impact their response has on both the communication climate and the interaction. Being prepared with positive responses is an important part of communicating and deserves attention.

Verbal Abuse: What to Do

When a person is told over time that his or her perceptions and feelings are wrong, the challenge is learning to respond to verbal abuse. This type of abuse does not leave physical evidence; however, it is just as painful, and recovery takes much longer (Evans, 1996). Prolonged verbal abuse damages the spirit and reduces joy and vitality.

The first step is awareness of verbal abuse. The book *The Verbally Abusive Relationship: How to Recognize It and How to Respond* (Evans, 1996) describes possible characteristics and different types of abusers, some of which may surprise you. One not often recognized is verbal abuse disguised as a joke. This kind of abuse "cuts to the quick, touches the most sensitive areas, and leaves the abuser with a look of triumph" (Evans, 1996, p. 93). Some examples are "You could not find your way out of a paper sack," "You would lose your head if it was not attached," "What can I expect from a blonde?" The abuser makes a disparaging remark and, if challenged, will often accuse the "victim" of having no sense of humor. Common is the rebuke or "Can't you take a joke?" "I was just kidding."

Any verbal abuse tactic requires assertive responses. Allowing yourself to be verbally abused is belittling and will lead to more unhappiness in the future. After

REFLECT AND APPLY

Reflect

- *See if you can think of your own examples for each of the five levels of content given at the beginning of the chapter.*
- *Think of different examples of dialect variations.*
- *What are three benefits of self-disclosure?*
- *For what reason(s) would you think a significant other no longer cares about you? Be sure you are coming up with sensory data to support your thoughts.*
- *How many interpretations can you come up with for this situation? You receive a low evaluation on a project at work.*

Apply

- *Give two sincere compliments to two different people.*
- *Look and listen. Then provide three examples of sensory data beginning with "I saw," "I noticed," "I heard."*
- *Ask other people how they would interpret the situation of receiving a low evaluation at work and see how many interpretations agree with yours.*
- *Pretend you have heard something that is offensive. Select a type of response given in the book that you are comfortable using. What exactly would you say?*

recognizing a pattern of verbal abuse, you can start to set limits: "I will not accept jokes that put me down or belittle me." The abuser may not honor your limits, but you have other choices. Finding a supportive counselor and asking the abuser to go with you is one possibility. If you decide that the abuse is not going to end, you are well advised to end the relationship. Handling the abuse with positive, assertive responses may not be the only step you take; however, it is the beginning of finding the respect you deserve.

Whether you are responding to or initiating an exchange, learning about content and then practicing can greatly improve what you say. Many people, after gaining awareness of content, say, "I did not realize so much was involved. I used to just open my mouth and talk. Now I think about it first!" Awkwardness is to be expected initially. Do you recall learning to ride a bicycle, to water ski, or to type? Your first attempts probably felt clumsy, and you may have thought that you would never learn. If you persisted, it was likely you wondered how it could have seemed so difficult at first. Learning communication skills is similar. After exposure and practice, less intense thinking is needed, the skills become natural, and you will wonder at your initial lack of ability.

You are now ready to complete the communication exercises in Reflections and Applications. If you do well on the ones in Chapters 7 and 8, you deserve a pat on the back. Keep in mind that content does make a definite difference in all interactions and especially in close relationships, and you influence the course of a relationship by what you say.

LOOKING BACK

- Communication pitfalls can be avoided by awareness of semantics, dialect, bias-free language, second-language challenges, emotion-packed phrases, disclaimers, slang, colloquialisms, vulgarity, vocabulary, and grammar.
- Self-disclosure can be organized into degrees or levels that move from basic data through preferences to beliefs and feelings.
- Compliments are comments of admiration and praise given to a person. Increasing the number of sincere compliments you give, doing so in positive ways, and receiving compliments graciously improve relationships.
- Sensation and perception include taking in sensory data and making interpretations. Individuals can err in the accuracy of either the initial input or the meaning they attach to it.
- Techniques such as perception checking and verbalizing dimensions of awareness aid in understanding and clarifying situations.
- Effective responses are usually as important as initial comments. Learning positive responses to criticism, metamessages, and offensive language patterns is a beneficial interpersonal relations skill.

It is certain that a relationship will be only as good as its communication.

—John Powell

Section Three
Positive Relationships:
The Ultimate Achievement

LOOKING AHEAD

After reading this section, you will be able to

- Explain why your own relationships are important.
- Describe loneliness and what the research shows.
- Give examples of how relationships can be beneficial.

Relationships with others lie at the very core of human existence.
—Ellen Berscheid and Letitia Anne Peplau

Understanding and love of self along with interpersonal communication skills are the foundation of positive relationships. Our exploration of interpersonal relations continues with a look at the benefits of relationships.

For what reasons do people relate to others? "I do not think hermits have much fun, and loners look sad," a student said when asked this question in class. Another man mentioned that people need others to avoid loneliness, which he described as a "bummer." His description was accurate. "Acute loneliness is a terrorizing pain" (Rokach, 1990, p. 41). **Loneliness,** as defined in one study, is "a feeling of being alone and disconnected or alienated from positive persons, places, or things" (Woodward, 1988, p.4). Besides a dreadful feeling, are there other reasons to be concerned about loneliness? The answer is a definite yes. The book *A Cry Unheard: New Insights into the Medical Consequences of Loneliness* (Lynch, 2000) describes numerous studies linking loneliness to premature death. The author describes loneliness as one of the most lethal risk factors in matters of life and death.

Who is lonely and why? An interesting study looked at both these questions. Loneliness was found in all age groups; however, young adults (19–30 years old) had the highest scores on each of the categories of perceived causes of loneliness. Women scored higher in loneliness than did men (Rokach, 2000). Young children are also lonely, and the causes stem from early family experiences and subsequent peer interactions (Solomon, 2000). The first year of college is a particularly vulnerable time, especially for those who live away from home. Coining a new term, *friendsickness*, which means preoccupation with and concern for the loss of or change in precollege friendships, researchers found that it was related to loneliness (Paul and Brier, 2001).

Can people be lonely in the presence of others? The answer is a resounding yes, and the feeling can be dreadful. Julie commented, "You can be in the center of a crowd and be dreadfully lonely." Rita, whose husband had left her, said, "I have periods of loneliness now, but it is nothing compared to how lonely I felt when he was sitting in the same room with me." In fact, **living together loneliness (LTL),** the result of a perceived discrepancy between expected and achieved contact, has been identified. Dan Kiley first noted this phenomenon among his female patients in 1970. He began to realize that loneliness comes in two varieties. The first is the loneliness felt by single, shy people who have no friends. The second is more elusive because it involves the person in a relationship who nevertheless feels isolated and very much alone (Kiley, 1989).

The baby boom generation is headed for a crisis of loneliness. The reasons are simple: demographics and social isolation. More boomers are living alone than in previous generations, and those living with another person will still feel the nagging pangs of loneliness (Anderson, 2003). Compared with their parents, boomers are marrying less often, marrying later, and staying married for shorter periods of time. The most dramatic growth in single-person households is expected to occur among those aged 45 to 64, as baby boomers become middle-aged.

If you experience loneliness on a regular basis, do something about it. One suggestion is to strengthen your level of self-esteem. Finding someone to love is not the solution. Instead, learn to love yourself (Burns, 1985). Cognitive restructuring is useful because thoughts create reality. Behavior techniques also help. Engaging in enjoyable activities is one way of coping. Ways to create happiness, suggested in Chapter 4, can alleviate loneliness. Some suggestions that help prevent or end loneliness are to volunteer your time in the community, increase your personal interests, and join a support group. If getting involved does not interest you or if you lack the willpower to take the first step, seeking counseling may be a good next step. Lonely high school and college students may believe that they just need to get out and do things with large numbers of people. Instead, the time could be better spent deepening and enriching their relationships.

> There is no complete escape from loneliness. It is part of being born, of being human, of living, of loving, of dying. Perhaps there should not be a complete escape. Why would anyone want to be deprived completely of an emotion? To experience the emotions of passion, happiness, grief, love, and loneliness is part of living, part of being human. (Woodward, 1988, p. 85)

Other reasons for having relationships are apparent. Pleasure is a prominent one: "We have fun together," and "We just like to be with each other." Jointly participating in activities and just being together are major benefits. Even brief encounters with people can be interesting and stimulating. We look to friends for favors, help, advice, and support. "My car did not start, so my neighbor gave me a ride to work," "My buddy loaned me money until payday," and "When I moved, I called everyone I knew to help" are some examples of how people rely on friends for help and support.

Support is a major benefit of relationships. Being able to share stress, emotional challenges, and problems with someone else decreases their impact. When interviewees were asked to describe their most important relationships, the word *there* was often used: "She is always *there* for me," "I can count on him to be *there*." Consistently, "being there" seemed to be the key element in the "why" of their relationships (Josselson, 1992).

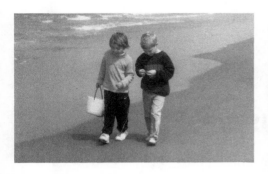

Figure III-1 Positive relationships are important at an early age.

Just like a song says, "We all need somebody to lean on." Do you remember a time when you had to call a friend for help? Having a **confidant,** a significantly close personal friend with whom you can safely share your deepest concerns and joys, is related to higher levels of well-being, health, satisfaction, and lowered distress (Ornish, 1998). One of the earliest studies on confidants found that older people who had a confidant lived longer than those who did not (Belsky, 1988). "Close relationships help people weather life's slings and arrows and may even reduce our chances of getting physically ill" (p. 73). Several studies show an increased rate of disease, alcoholism, and premature death that is associated with a lack of social support. Both receiving and giving love and intimacy are healing (Ornish, 1998).

Your self-concept benefits from healthy relationships. When you feel affirmed, your self-esteem level increases. Even a friendly hello can lift your spirits and spark a feeling of "I matter." Growth can occur as you interact with others. "I learned a lot from that relationship" and "I am a better person because of her" are statements of growth. "I may not have gone to college if it had not been for my friends' influence" shows how relationships can motivate.

> They also energize. Human contact has the power to increase your energy. Human beings need contact with other human beings the way a lamp needs electricity. Contact energizes people and can relieve stress. (Tubesing, 1981, p. 85)

We need human contact in both our personal and professional life lives. Being able to interact and get along with others are valuable skills for everyone. Learning everything possible about relationships is essential if you are to achieve success in your own life. The rest of this book focuses on positive relationships (Fig. III-1).

Joy comes to those who succeed in their human relationships.
—Sharon Hanna

BUILDING POSITIVE RELATIONSHIPS

LOOKING AHEAD

After completing this chapter, you will be able to

- Define codependency and recognize that it is not healthy.
- Discuss positive behaviors in relationships and interactions.
- Discuss different types of relationships, including friendships.
- Trace a path from tolerance to appreciation of diversity.
- Define stereotyping, prejudice, and discrimination and explain ways to rid yourself of each.
- Know what is required to approach others, tell how to look for approachability cues, and discuss ways to initiate and maintain a conversation.

> *Humans are conceived within relationships, born into relationships, and live their lives within relationships with others. All human society has a stake in the nature of people's close relationships. We all benefit from the existence of successful relationships and share, at least indirectly, the costs of relationship deficiencies.*
>
> —Ellen Berscheid and Letitia Anne Peplau

There is a science to our words. Learning how to apply that science is the key to effective communication skills: accurate and respectful ways of communicating that prevent costly miscommunication and time-consuming misunderstanding (York, 2006). Without self-knowledge, self-love, and positive communication skills, you will encounter difficulty and disappointment in interpersonal relations; with them, you are ready to become even more skilled in building positive relationships.

Creating Healthy Relationships

Review the description of a positive relationship in Section One of this book. The ability to recognize the difference between what are sometimes called healthy and unhealthy relationships is the first step in reducing the chance of becoming involved in those that are not positive.

Features of a Healthy Relationship

Have you ever been a part of what can be called an unhealthy relationship? Most unhealthy relationships are sources of frustration and pain. Inevitably, one or both of the participants are hurt. Building a positive relationship is in everyone's best interest.

High self-esteem. In order for a relationship to be satisfying and nourishing, the people involved must exhibit certain traits. Love for self is a primary one. Genuine self-esteem, as described in Chapter 1, is healthy and allows an individual to reach out positively to others. Both people in a relationship are committed to achieving an "I'm OK, you're OK" life position, and they accept and affirm each other.

Freedom from enabling behaviors and absence of codependency. When two people care about themselves and each other, the relationship tends to be balanced. **Enabling** occurs when someone's actions directly, yet unintentionally, allow irresponsible, dysfunctional, or destructive actions of another person to continue. Enabling behaviors often lead to *codependence,* a term that originally was related to substance abuse and is now used in describing various types of relationships. **Codependency** is often the result of an enabler focusing too much on the needs and behaviors of the other, and both suffer as a result. Codependents feel compelled to help others, they do for others what others could be doing for themselves, and they never think they have done enough. People often do not recognize the condition because it is second nature to them. Because nurturing and caring are typically the bedrocks of codependency, the person usually feels affirmed and justified for his or her sacrifices. In sum, codependents are responsive to the needs of the people around them to the exclusion of their own needs.

Joanna is one of the kindest individuals in the world. She remembers friends' and clients' birthdays and anniversaries, she is the first to visit someone in the hospital, and she does favors for people regularly. She used to dote on her two grown sons and grandchildren to the exclusion of her own best interests. She was always there for them as well as everyone else she knew. Stress-related symptoms led her to a therapist, who identified her as a codependent. After several therapy sessions, extensive reading, and soul-searching, she is psychologically healthy again.

> Holly expressed codependency so well: "I am afraid to leave him because he is so dependent on me. I also think that I am dependent on his being dependent on me."

Codependency can be related to self-concept. Individuals with low self-esteem are more likely to take extra steps to please others. The stereotypic feminine gender role is often at fault. A nonassertive, appeasing person is more likely to become codependent.

What can be done about codependency? Identifying it and increasing one's level of self-esteem, if necessary, are key elements. One of the first to write about codependency was Melody Beattie (1987). In a later book (Beattie, 1989), she points out that because society provides many invitations to be codependent, maintaining a firm personal boundary is necessary. She also reminds a recovered codependent that relapse is possible and describes how to get back on track. In many cases, individual or group counseling is extremely beneficial. It helps to remind yourself that you are not only making these changes for yourself; other people will also benefit. Then you can arrive at a place in which you can say, as did Jean: "I have been so many things to so many people. It is time to be someone for me."

Genuineness.   Besides love for self and assertiveness, which help to eliminate codependency, Carl Rogers (1980) identified four features of a healthy therapist–client relationship, applicable for all types of relationships. One is **genuineness,** which means revealing your true self and striving to be honest. This creates trust in the relationship. Honesty between people is more than the absence of lying; openness and authenticity are significant facets. Participants in the relationship feel comfortable showing their true selves. Game playing is unnecessary, and individuals can express what they think and feel. This means that hurt is likely; however, healthy relationships can tolerate some pain.

Warmth.   Another feature that Rogers (1980) calls **unconditional positive regard** is a warm acceptance of each other's personhood. Conditional regard means that conditions are attached to the relationship: "I like you when you do me favors" and "I expect you to be there every time I call" are examples. Unconditional positive regard means that two people appreciate each others' unique personalities.

Empathy.   A key element in healthy relationships is **empathy,** or the ability to experience another person's perspective. This is the third ingredient identified by Rogers (1980). You are able to participate in another's feelings and ideas. Empathy is related to a high feeling preference on the Myers-Briggs Type Indicator, although those with a thinking preference can also empathize, as can both sexes.

Understanding others and being empathic are challenging. What can help is to accept differences in how people think and feel and not categorize them as right or wrong. Even though you may not have experienced a similar situation, you can still empathize.

Being empathic requires a person to comprehend underlying meanings. Bob talked incessantly to his coworkers about his hospital stay and the results of his laboratory tests. Dave realized that down deep Bob was scared that there was something seriously wrong. He recognized that the nervous chatter was a cover-up for some anxious feelings. He empathized and encouraged Bob to talk about his fear. After the feeling was released, Bob's discussions about his health occurred less frequently.

Self-disclosure.   In order to build and enliven a relationship, individuals share information about themselves. Self-disclosure, according to Rogers (1980), is essential. As discussed in Chapter 9, all relationships require some level of disclosure. In order to develop closer ties, people express their emotion on deeper levels. As they reveal more of their hidden selves, a powerful basis for trust can be formed. In there may also be some cases in which self-disclosure will indicate that a relationship is not one you want to pursue.

Social exchange.   One way to check the health of a relationship is to ask yourself, "Is it good for me?" If you believe that you are receiving a benefit that outweighs costs, then yes is the likely answer. **Social exchange theory** maintains that relationships can be assessed by their outcomes, or what the participants are receiving compared to what they are giving. A study suggested that friendships are more likely to be reciprocal, a give-and-take, and that those who felt either deprived or advantaged in their relationship reported much more loneliness (Buunk and Prins, 1998).

Think about your friendships. What do you receive and give? Did you once experience a friendship that you no longer have? Relationships can end because one or both people are no longer receiving enough from the other. Elizabeth and Courtney shared an apartment. Both were single and pursuing careers. Courtney received a job transfer to a nearby city. "We will still be close friends," said Courtney. "Oh, yes, it is not that far," agreed Elizabeth. Contact gradually decreased, and within two years, the relationship had essentially ended. Their relationship was based on enjoyable daily contact, so when this was no longer possible, neither received enough. The costs exceeded the benefits.

One of the basic principles of the behavior approach to psychology is that most people seek pleasure and avoid pain. Although relationships will have elements of displeasure, in those that are positive, rewards either outnumber or are more powerful than punishments. Evaluating a relationship on its rewards is practical and healthful.

Enjoyment.   "I love movies," said one woman, "and I will go to one alone. But it is so much more enjoyable to go with someone." A healthy relationship will have times of unhappiness, yet the overall vibrations will be those of joy. People enjoy relationships that are encouraging, supportive, and affirming.

Dependability.   In a positive relationship you can count on the other person to treat you with respect, and this is reciprocated. Dependability also means that each of you will do what you say unless circumstances prevent it. Trust develops between individuals who can rely on each other to be fair and dependable.

Energizing feelings.   Being energized means that an interaction with another person makes you feel good. Do you have some relationships that drain your energy? In positive relationships, individuals feel fulfilled because each provides sparks of energy. "The most important thing you can ever do for other people is to leave them feeling better emotionally after being in your presence" (Ellsworth, 1988, p. 115). Be cautious if energy flows out of you and is not restored by the relationship.

Demonstrated mutual interest.   Why do people sever certain relationships? One woman replied, "She just did not ever seem interested in me. I asked about her life; mine never seemed important to her." You show interest by asking questions such as "What is new in your life?" "What plans do you have for the holidays?" "How are your children doing?" People who show little or no interest in others seem self-absorbed, whereas positive individuals enjoy

Figure 10-1   An ordinary interaction is more pleasant when individuals are friendly and positive.

sharing with others, and they love to be asked about their lives!

Positive Interactions

Think of those with whom you interact. What distinguishes one interaction from another? College students identified several characteristics of positive interactions (Fig. 10-1).

- Acknowledgment (e.g., calling me by my name when greeting)
- Active interest and concern for my "feelings"
- Willingness to offer help; often before being asked
- Good sense of humor
- Willingness to admit mistakes
- Interesting conversation
- Giving, but not overdoing it
- Willingness to make decisions; doesn't always depend on me to choose activities
- Sharing; will pay his or her share and contribute in other ways
- Listening skills; will listen openly
- Positive attitude
- Trust; the other person will not put me down or embarrass me
- Ability to keep confidences and secrets
- Willingness to stand up for me, if necessary

How many of these do you demonstrate in your relationships? How about the other people involved? Can you add to the list?

As human beings rush through busy days, small positive actions can mean so much. Because these are not time-consuming favors or dramatic gestures, their impact may be overlooked. Check the list of "Little Acts of Kindness" in Figure 10-2. How many have you done or experienced? Did any brighten the day for you?

Making the world a better place by giving of yourself is a rewarding experience. Volunteers are greatly needed. Nursing homes are full of opportunities to reach out and help someone. Rewarding feelings and meaningful relationships are the likely results. Being a person who asks for and graciously receives kind deeds and favors helps a relationship. Because our society has come to regard dependency as negative, people often find it difficult to take from others; yet, by the act of taking, we solidify relationships. Understanding about healthy relationships and positive interactions can reveal what you have to offer and what you might want to develop. Unless people are aware, they may ruin potentially positive relationships or accept less than nourishing ones (TA Revisited).

Little Acts of Kindness

- When driving, if possible, stop and wait for another car to pull out onto a busy street ahead of you.
- In a checkout line, when you have several purchases, allow a person behind you with just a few items to go ahead.
- Offer to help someone who is having difficulty carrying a package or crossing the street; hold a door for another person.
- Send a note or card to someone who is not well. Send more than one if the illness is prolonged.
- Congratulate people either verbally or in writing.
- Use the words "thank you" and "please" with clerks, cashiers, cafeteria servers, and others.
- If you smoke, show courtesy to others around you.
- Offer your seat on a bus or in a waiting room to someone who looks as if he or she needs to sit more than you do.
- Smile and greet people, even those you do not know.

Figure 10-2

Examining Various Types of Relationships

Relationships vary from casual or informal to close and intimate. They also differ in their **interactions,** those exchanges that occur in face-to-face situations. You may pass a person on the street, exchange smiles and greetings, and continue on your way, possibly not realizing that you have just interacted. You may see someone on a daily basis for a period of time and then not again for months. Because of these variances, several types of relationships emerge.

Acquaintances

Social interactions give people a psychological sense of belonging. "Familiar strangers" are people whom you may not know by name but who have a regular place in your life, a waitress in a restaurant, the postal carrier, a cashier at the grocery store, or a neighbor you occasionally see. You and the other person may just

TA Revisited

The "child" ego state is the driving force within relationships. What would a relationship be without emotion? How could relationships continue without motivation?
The "parent" ego state is full of "do's and don'ts" regarding relationships. Some are wise messages whereas others are in need of processing.
The "adult" ego state helps us assess relationships and can logically guide us through the building and enriching processes.

smile or chat briefly. Even though such interactions seem inconsequential, their contributions to positive feelings and self-esteem levels are measurable (Montgomery and Trower, 1988).

Friendships

What does friendship mean to you? You may be surprised to discover that the meaning of friendship varies from person to person. Obviously, some common themes exist. How many of these are part of your image of friendship?

- Fondness and liking
- Continuity over time
- Perceived support and dependability
- Compatibility and help
- Similarities in enjoyable activities, beliefs, and values
- Self-disclosure and sharing of information and stories
- Personal growth
- Understanding, acceptance, and unconditional positive regard

Friendship is almost always high on a person's list of values (Fig. 10-3). "I do not know what I would do if it were not for my friends. I would be lost," said a woman. This is probably because to live without friends is a lonely journey (Kasl, 1997). Good friendships provide depth and meaning to life. Friendships, in contrast to acquaintanceships, take time and effort to develop and maintain; yet, in most cases, the benefits far outweigh the costs. Take advantage of a chance to enrich a friendship by doing the activity in Reflections and Applications.

Steps in developing a friendship. You were born into a family, not into a friendship. How does one move a relationship with an acquaintance to a friendship? Following a first meeting, further encounters are positive and affirming. You enjoy each other's company as you plan and engage in mutually satisfying activities. Self-disclosure at deeper levels occurs, and trust is developed. "Progressive stages of increased openness can peel off layers of our outer selves, like the skins of an onion" (McCarthy, 1988, p. 169). As in all relationships, you may experience

Figure 10-3   Friendship has rewards throughout a lifetime.

conflict and have moments of doubt in the friendship; however, if the social exchange factors are strong enough, differences get resolved. As the relationship progresses, it is easily distinguishable from an acquaintanceship.

Cycles of importance.   Friends are important during all stages of life, yet the extent of significance varies. Friendships become meaningful when an individual enters school and participates in activities outside the family. During junior high and high school, friends typically dominate most aspects of life. Parents are not far from wrong when they say, "Your friends are your whole world."

As intimate love relationships are formed, individuals usually drift away from reliance on friendships. A common complaint is, "She does not have anything to do with me or her other friends any more since she is involved with him." Significant other relationships and parenthood take precedence over friendships in most people's lives, yet friends often remain important as social companions and confidants. If divorced or widowed, friends usually, again, take center stage.

Types and dilemmas.   The word *friendship* indicates a wide range of closeness. A friend can be a best friend, a close friend, a friend, or just a buddy. How do you differentiate? Usually, this is based on an important gauge of friendship, closeness. A very good friend is often a **confidant,** a person with whom you can be totally open and self-disclose on all levels. Most people reserve this label for only a few.

Long-distance friends can be as close emotionally as ones whom you see regularly. When you connect, there is a feeling of comfort. "The cadence of friendship is measured in decade-long rhythms" (Keen, 1991, p. 174). It is a wonderful feeling to know that you can telephone or e-mail a number of precious, long-distance friends right now and feel connected and supported.

A dilemma related to friendship is enrichment. Even good friends can take each other for granted and not nourish the relationship. Most friendships can survive some neglect; however, investment of time and energy is wise. If you are thinking of a friend with whom you have not been in contact for some time, why not do something to change that? Another dilemma of suitable recognition is probable. At special events, best friends, "just friends," and casual acquaintances are usually not distinguished from one another. A researcher recalled the death of a dear friend. At the funeral she sat in the back of a filled church. In the middle of her grief, she realized that even though she was one of the deceased's closest friends, even closer than one of the siblings, she was being treated the same as a casual acquaintance (Rubin, 1985). The English language provides specific distinctions for family relationships, yet not for friendships.

Sex differences.   Are same-sex friendships different for females than for males? The answer is not clear-cut. Men do tend to have more "active" friendships. They tend to talk about and engage in more mutually enjoyable activities, many of which are related to sports and outdoor activities, whereas women seem to want to talk more about relationships. Women's friendships tend to be deeper. Although men may care as much for their male friends, they are less likely than women to verbally express or demonstrate their feelings (Wood, 2001). In a study, gender differences were found to be relatively small; both sexes rated equal-power friendships significantly higher than unequal-power ones (Veniegas and Peplau, 1997).

Stereotypic males are less likely to self-disclose and become close to other males. Sue and Marc had been married for 13 years and had several couple friends. When they decided to divorce, both were depressed. Sue suggested that Marc talk with a male friend. He replied. "I do not feel comfortable talking about my personal life with the guys I know." As gender roles become less stereotypic, the likelihood of being deprived of a same-sex confidant may no longer be a problem. We all share a need for connection. Because friendships offer connection and other significant benefits, both men and women are wise to cultivate them.

> *A friend is one*
> *to whom one can pour*
> *out all the contents of one's heart,*
> *chaff and grain together*
> *knowing that the gentlest of hands*
> *will take and sift it,*
> *keep what is worth keeping*
> *and with a breath of kindness*
> *blow the rest away.*
>
> —Arabian Proverb

Support Groups

Your primary support group is made up of "people in your life who help you realize the meaning of your existence. They know the 'real' you; they understand where we have been; and they help us grow" (Johnson, 1986, p. 68). They are your primary support system and contribute immeasurably to self-esteem.

A secondary support system is composed of groups at work, school, church, and within neighborhoods and organizations. Self-help groups are recommended as a way of dealing with challenges. During crises and tragedies, a self-help group can be invaluable as long as the focus is on resolving issues and the emphasis is positive. Being aware of your support systems and how each group affects your self-esteem is important. Any type of relationship that genuinely affirms you is precious.

Caregiving

The special support provided by a person in a caregiving role is of particular value. When individuals are unable to care for themselves, they are either placed in nursing homes or rehabilitation centers for long-term care or someone voluntarily assumes the responsibility. Often that someone is a significant other. Another common caregiving group consists of adult children who care for aging parents. The term *sandwich generation* applies to those who find themselves caring for both their parents and their own children. The average age of such a person is 46 (Emerson, 2000). The caregiver role is both challenging and rewarding. How to ease stress and maintain a positive relationship between a caregiver and the person for whom care is given deserves attention. One way is to make plans before circumstances demand absolute decisions. Another is to learn and use open communication and other techniques covered in Chapters 6, 7, and 8.

Without a doubt, caregivers need help themselves. Those who tend toward codependency are particularly at risk. A study of caregivers found that those who had more tasks, spent greater amounts of time in their caregiving role, and had lower self-efficacy about self-care and care of a spouse had a greater number of depressive symptoms and negative health behaviors (Gallant and Connell, 1997).

Solid recommendations are to try to maintain a balance, use stress-coping methods on a regular basis, and develop a broad plan with the help of professionals who specialize in caregiving issues. In recent years a number of resources have become available. Caregivers are not alone (see Resources at end of this chapter).

Initiating Interactions

Initiating interactions is a valuable interpersonal skill in which your personality will make a difference. If you have an extraverted preference, you are motivated to reach out to a new person. People who are introverts can be just as skillful but it may be more difficult. Whatever your preference, particular attitudes and behaviors are necessary skills for an individual to succeed at initiating interactions.

Open-Mindedness

First impressions, those immediate judgments that people make, cannot be avoided. Think of the aspects of a person you might consider when you first meet. Perhaps it has happened that you have been turned off immediately. If an individual appears too different from you, negative assumptions are often made. A way to overcome this effectively is to be open when you first meet someone and challenge any negative first impressions that form.

Ideas expressed by others also can influence your impression. In a classic experiment on expectations and first impressions (Kelley, 1950), students received short differing descriptions about a substitute instructor. Some sketches described the new instructor as "rather cold" whereas others used the words "very warm." The substitute led the class, and someone else recorded the frequency of participation for each student. After class, the students were asked to write descriptions and ratings of the instructor. A clear difference was evident. Those who had read that the man was "very warm" participated more freely and gave him a higher rating than those who had been given the "rather cold" description.

Any time you form a first impression, analyze it. Whatever the judgment, allow time and involvement to determine how realistic the impression was. Expectations are powerful. Your expectations can influence your thoughts and attitudes about a person or situation. What you expect frequently becomes a reality.

Tolerance, Acceptance, and Appreciation

Tolerance of people who are different is a worthy, basic goal of interpersonal relations. **Tolerance** can be defined as putting up with something you do not like and not acting against people about whom you feel negatively (Vogt, 1997). Ideally, tolerance will evolve into acceptance, which is more positive. Then the development of appreciation, which requires thought and action, is possible. The following brief coverage can help you examine your attitudes and commit to any necessary positive change. Try to approach this discussion with an open mind and be ready to challenge any preconceived ideas.

Classifying people into groups is a normal mental process called **social categorization.** Unfortunately, it is quite possible to overcategorize and then form a **stereotype**—a fixed belief about the entire category. Stereotyping is thinking in generalities. When you meet a person of a different race, do you have a generalized thought? Even though we may not like to admit that we have such automatic thoughts, awareness of their existence is the first step in eliminating stereotypes.

Stereotyping typically focuses on negative characteristics that are applied to an entire group when, in fact, all people within a group are not the same. Stereotyping of groups then leads to labeling of individuals. A loving individual, according to Leo Buscaglia (1982), does not label others. As a child, Buscaglia himself was bothered by the distancing effect of a label applied to him regarding his Italian ancestry.

> They did not know who I was by calling me a "dago" and a "wop." If you want to know me, you've got to get into my head, and if I want to know about you, I can't say, "She is fat. She is thin. She is a Jew. She is a Catholic." She is more than that. (p. 25)

When negative labels stick, they can damage self-esteem (Hyatt, 1991). Reducing an individual to a category is offensive and misleading (Tannen, 1990).

Actor and comedian Eddie Murphy, appearing on a television show, described a stereotyping experience.

> I was walking out of a grocery store, and I had my head down. Some kids went by and said "Nigger!" They did not see it was me. That tripped me out because if my head had been up, they would have screamed, "Hey, Eddie!"

Labeling based on what the eye can see limits perceptions. The eye can be the "most inaccurate, most inconsistent, and the most prejudicial organ we have in the body. What is truly essential is invisible to the eye" (Buscaglia, 1982, p. 94). Assigning labels to family members is common: "That is my good-for-nothing brother." "I have an old-fashioned dad." "He is my lazy kid." These ideas put human beings into boxes; then they usually act out the label.

Even positive stereotypes can be a problem when they are limiting or force unrealistic expectations on individuals. The field of sports psychology is well aware of stereotypes that label individuals and then become self-fulfilling prophecies (Horn, Lox, and Labrador, 1998).

Negative stereotyping and labeling usually lead to **prejudice,** an attitude that others are inferior or less than you in some way. What results is a feeling of dislike or hatred. Prejudice is learned either from others or by generalizing from experiences. Jodi discovered that prejudice has many targets as she acknowledged: "Prejudice is not limited to just race and sex. I have been judging people negatively on looks, clothing, body size, and age. I have now learned that what is inside a person is what's important."

Historically, American society has experienced myriad problems caused by prejudice. Countless numbers of individuals have suffered. A hope that prejudice would soon become a thing of the past abounded for some time after the civil rights movement in the 1960s. That hope has not become a reality, although there are some promising signs. Even though more than half of both white and black youth in a *Time*/CNN poll still consider racism "a big problem," more than a third classified it as "a small problem." A surprising 89 percent of black teens called it "a small problem" or "not a problem at all." Most said that both on a personal level and as a socially divisive issue, race is less important to them than it is for adults (Farley, 1997). When Americans were asked in a Gallup poll to identify the most important problem facing the country today, only 4 percent named race relations (Newport, 2001). That does not mean that racial prejudice has disappeared; instead, it is merely more disguised.

Probably more extreme prejudice in recent years has been directed toward gay males and lesbians (Vogt, 1997). A significant number have been targets of verbal abuse, discrimination, and physical assault because of their sexual orientation (Herek, 1996). On a positive note, there has been a gradual improvement in attitudes. From 1992 to 2001 acceptance of homosexuality as an alternative lifestyle has risen from 38 percent to 52 percent with 54 percent saying that homosexual relations between consenting adults should be legal. Although over 80 percent of Americans believe that homosexuals should have equal opportunity protection in the workplace (Newport, 2001), many states do not have laws prohibiting sexual orientation discrimination. Although federal government workers are currently protected from such discrimination, there is no federal law that specifically outlaws workplace discrimination on the basis of sexual orientation in the private sector. Currently 15 states and the District of Columbia have laws that prohibit sexual orientation discrimination in both public and private jobs. In addition, seven states have laws prohibiting sexual orientation discrimination in public workplaces only (NOLO, 2006).

To continue to harbor prejudices against those who are different is insensitive and illogical. In some cases, the stereotypes have a factual basis because a majority of a group exhibits a particular behavior. You can accept a fact and still not apply it to all members of a group. People who feel and act upon prejudice are limiting themselves in terms of relationships. Ira, an African American, volunteered her personal feelings about prejudice in a psychology class. She said, "Prejudice causes people to miss out on the spice of life. To be influenced by prejudice is hogwash. It keeps you from being free within." I would add a challenging question: *Can anyone offer one good reason for the continuation of prejudice and hatred?* Everyone is eventually harmed. Each generation is more diverse than the one before, and by the year 2060 no one racial group will be numerically dominant in the United States (Fonow, 1998). Because of the continual increases in diversity, getting along harmoniously can be considered a necessity.

Discrimination is treating people unfairly. Because discrimination is usually observable behavior, a society can adopt laws against it; this has been the case in recent years. Covert discrimination, which is hidden or subtle, is still widespread and is commonly based on prejudice. Perceiving others to be evil or inferior often leads to treating them as such. Both prejudice and discrimination cause personal and societal problems (Fig. 10-4).

Figure 10-4

We can never achieve peace of mind as long as we attack others (Jampolsky and Cirincione, 1990).

Prejudice is learned or develops during one's life. Self-esteem seems to play a part. People with low self-esteem tend to be more critical of themselves and of others (Baumeister, 1997). Tolerance is related to high self-esteem and self-actualization (Vogt, 1997). This does not mean that self-esteem leads to or keeps one from prejudice; however, it can be a factor. Having an **authoritarian personality,** a belief that one's ideas are right and others are wrong, is related to prejudice and lack of tolerance (Vogt, 1997).

Authoritarians resist new ideas, tend to think in absolutes, and are dogmatic in their beliefs. **Heterosexism,** the belief that only heterosexuality is right, is a type of authoritarian thinking. A lack of education and experiences with those who are different are also important factors. Ignorance often leads to fear and fear to hatred.

Because prejudice is learned, it can be unlearned, and education is a strong foe of prejudice. Studies show that education increases tolerance and reduces prejudice and stereotyping by giving people new information, changing ways of thinking, altering personalities, and providing new social experiences (Vogt, 1997).

What can be done about prejudice? First, a person must decide to challenge the rigid thinking. Believing that your sex, race, and sexual orientation are the only way to be is a barrier to tolerance. Being open-minded is imperative.

Knowledge is the anecdote of fear.

—Ralph Waldo Emerson

Becoming more educated, building self-esteem, and ridding yourself of anger and an "always right" attitude are major contributors. Deciding that differences are not frightening or wrong is necessary and leads to feeling enlightened as you learn about multiculturalism and **minority groups,** defined as categories of people who lack power and who are disadvantaged in a society. You can challenge prejudice cognitively, emotionally, and socially by asking the questions in "How to Combat Prejudice"(Fig. 10-5).

How to Combat Prejudice

Honestly ask yourself these questions and then reflect on the recommendations that follow.

- *Is my thinking reasonable and rational?* If you take pride in your mental abilities, you will want to reject inaccurate and unreasonable stereotypes. Refuse to accept the idea that blacks and whites, Catholics and Protestants, old people and young people, and heterosexuals, gay males, and lesbians are all one way. "People who think and like to think are more likely to be tolerant" (Vogt, 1997, p. 137). In a compounding of the September 11, 2001, terrorist attacks, a news program reported that a man yelled, "I hate all Arabs, and I always will!" Not only is this type of thinking unreasonable and irrational, but it also is counterproductive because hatred will never create a better world. Even if you have an initial negative opinion, you can change it.

- *Am I being fair? How would I feel if I were the victim of prejudice?* Most people are concerned with justice and fairness. Discrimination is unfair, and even the thinking that leads to it can be challenged as unjust. Empathy is a powerful enemy of prejudice and discrimination. A study revealed that feeling empathy for a member of a stigmatized group was found to improve attitudes toward the group as a whole (Batson et al., 1997).

- *Am I basing my impressions on a knowledge of an individual as a person or only as a representative of a group?* Labeling often keeps us from getting to know the real person. Moving from a collective analysis, which is a stereotype, to an individual assessment is the key. Being free of prejudice means that you may like or dislike, but your feelings will not be based on an external factor or label. I was delighted when Jennifer, a white student, said, "I have never been around African Americans before because I grew up in a small rural community. Glenn [another student in the class] is the first I've gotten to know. I'm so glad the experience was such a positive one!"

Figure 10-5

Research supports the value of getting to know individuals and to have pride in one's own group. Close friendships with whites seemed to change negative images and stereotypes held by blacks (Powers and Ellison, 1995). Increased ethnic identity among adolescents contributed to better feelings about their own group and to those who were members of different groups (Phinney, Ferguson, and Tate, 1997).

Besides ridding yourself of prejudices, you can help the victims of prejudice and society by asserting yourself in the face of demeaning words and behaviors. A study showed that hearing someone else express strong opinions against prejudice led students to have similar thoughts. The researchers concluded that a few outspoken people who are vigorously antiracist can establish a positive social climate that discourages prejudice (Goleman, 1991). As with any subject, silence is usually interpreted as agreement. Suggestions for responding to prejudicial comments were given in Chapter 9.

> When anyone of us is demeaned, we are all diminished. (Blumenfeld, 1992, p. 13)

Lack of prejudice does not mean blindness to differences; you simply do not let differences stop you from relating. A positive practice is to view differences as opportunities. Getting to know people who are different broadens your perspectives and enriches your life. This growth then allows you to appreciate human diversity. Sameness can be boring. Diversity provides opportunities for expansion of the self. Multiculturalism benefits individuals as well as societies.

> Embrace the many-splendid colors; revel in the wisdom and the power of a different race and culture. Invite it to spill over us and know that, if our invitation is accepted, it is we who are recipients of an honor. (Schulz, 1988, p. 2)

How to Approach and Converse with Others

After a person gets beyond obstacles created by negative first impressions or intolerance, individual traits can block attempts to interact. Shyness is a significant disadvantage when it comes to interacting. People who demonstrate shy behaviors have difficulty initiating or inviting encounters. A book designed to help people defeat shyness, *Shyness: A Bold New Approach* (Carducci, 1999), lets shy people know that they are not alone. Shy people make up almost half the population, and between 75 and 95 percent of people have been shy at some time. What can you do? Stating that inaction is the most common feature of shyness, Zimbardo (1977), who conducted classic studies on the subject, suggests taking specific steps. Being realistic about what is possible to achieve is critical, and dividing a goal into smaller, manageable parts, as recommended in Chapter 3, is part of any sensible behavioral plan. Saying hello to a certain number of new people in a week's time might be a practical goal. Support groups are beneficial, and for severe cases of shyness, therapy is suggested.

> *"I overcame shyness by telling myself that I have so much to offer to others."*
> —Wanda, a college student

Even if you are not shy, you may, in some situations, hesitate to approach someone near because of fear of rejection or embarrassment. Realize that embarrassment is not the worst thing in the world; letting fears stop you from what could be a satisfying interaction is certainly worse! When you do initiate an exchange, you do not want to do so at an inappropriate time or in an undesirable manner. **Approachability** is a combination of circumstances when the initiation of contact is likely to be positively received.

Approachability cues.   Being observant and looking for cues are helpful in initiating conversation. Can you think of times and situations when people would not be at all approachable or when approachability would probably be diminished? Consider individual moods, physical states, and activities. If you want to initiate contact and realize that the other person is in a hurry, involved, or preoccupied, simply wait for a more opportune time and circumstance. Approachable situations exist when a person is not preoccupied or absorbed. Such situations are usually indicated by a person's body language. Sitting alone and looking open are good indicators. When people are in waiting situations, such as waiting for a bus, for a class to start, or in a line, they are likely to be approachable. Social occasions are opportunities for approachable situations.

Conversation.   If you know a person, beginning a conversation is usually not difficult. But what about people whom you do not know and would like to meet? You may have no trouble thinking of just the right thing to say. For a number of people, however, thinking of that "something" can be mind-boggling. "I was tongue-tied," is how one young man described it. "I had wanted to meet her for months, and here she was sitting next to me the first day of class. I could not think of one intelligent thing to say, so I kept quiet." Either keeping quiet or saying something "off the wall" puts a damper on interactions.

To initiate conversation in difficult situations, you can use a technique called **search the situation for topics** (Glaser, 1986). Based on the idea that you and the other person share a common environment, you make a comment based on an awareness of what is going on around you. What could the young man in the preceding paragraph have said? The two students had in common the fact that they were sitting next to each other in a class on the first day. Here are some possibilities:

"Have you heard anything about this class?"
"I heard this instructor was a lot of fun."
"Have you ever taken a psychology class before?"
"What year of school are you in?"
"What are your career plans?"

Searching the situation is quite simple; in fact, you probably have already used this technique without realizing it.

Questions.   Questioning is an excellent way to keep conversations going, to learn more about the people you meet, and to make people feel that you are truly interested in what they are saying as well as in them. Failing to ask questions could indicate self-centeredness or lack of interest. Ann recounts a lunch date.

> We did not know each other well, and I was looking forward to an opportunity for us to get to know each other and then see if this might develop into a deeper relationship. We were together for two hours. Afterwards I thought, "I know almost everything about him, and he knows nothing about me except that I ask questions and am an excellent listener! I do not know if he is stuck on himself or just not interested in me, or both. I do not want to spend another two hours with him.

Self-absorption is a major obstacle in communication. Successful conversations are two-way, which means that both participants ask questions and provide information (Reflect and Apply). Different types of questions can be asked.

- Open-ended questions are ones that cannot be answered with one word. Instead of, "What is your major?" ask, "What are your career plans?"

| REFLECT AND APPLY |

Reflect

♦ *Think of a friendship and the theory of social exchange. What do you receive from the relationship? Compare benefits to costs.*
♦ *Suppose you are trying to convince a family member to reject prejudice. What reasons would you give?*
♦ *Having just been introduced to a new person at a conference, think of two comments or questions you could use.*

Apply

♦ *Tell a friend the benefits you receive from your relationship.*
♦ *Make an effort to get to know a person who represents diversity to you.*
♦ *Use approachability checking the next time you telephone someone. Do not forget to use it in person when appropriate.*

- Focused questions are those that are not too broad to be answered. Instead of, "Tell me all about yourself," ask, "How did you decide to go into teaching?"
- Specific questions are those that ask for additional details, specific examples, or particular impressions. Examples are: "What did you think of the psychology course?" or "When did you leave Denver?"

If you think about people you enjoy, chances are that their interest in you and what is going on in your life is a major factor. Very few people resent questions, and most appreciate them. As long as your questions are not too probing or inappropriately personal, your relationships can be enhanced by developing and using this skill.

Internet Dating

According to the Pew Research Center (2006), an estimated 16 million Americans have used a dating site or other sites to meet people. Pew found that 79 percent say online dating is a "good way to meet people" and 52 percent say the experience was mostly positive. But 29 percent say it was mostly negative.

Dating websites are just one of many online avenues that can facilitate a romantic connection. Three out of four Internet users who are single and looking for a romantic partner have done at least one dating-related activity online ranging from using dating websites, to searching for information about prospective dates, to flirting via e-mail and instant messaging, to browsing for information about the local singles scene. Although online dating is becoming more commonplace, there are still concerns in the wider public about the dangers of posting personal information on dating sites and about the honesty of those who pursue online dating.

Connecting with Others

After an interaction takes place, people can choose to build a closer relationship. Why does this happen in some cases and not in others?

Attraction and Liking

If you grow to like another person, you will feel affection or respect or both. These feelings are two fundamental dimensions of liking. **Affection** is based on the way another person relates to you personally and is a feeling of warmth and closeness. **Respect** is liking based on the person's admirable characteristics or actions and is cooler and more distant. (Rubin, 1973)

Why do you like some people and not others? **Attraction,** a force that draws people together or a positive attitude toward another, has been the focus of psychological research. Obviously, physical attractiveness plays a primary part in our impressions. As we get better acquainted, the individual becomes attractive for other reasons. Social psychologists have found that attraction and liking are closely linked to certain other factors. As you read about each, relate it to your relationships.

Proximity.   How many friends are from your hometown? Do most of your friends live near you? **Proximity** is physical occupation of the same geographic area. Obviously, in order to meet face-to-face, two people must share proximity. In terms of attraction, physical sharing of space is the means by which you get to know a person. Becoming more familiar with someone could also lead to a dislike of the person. More often, though, getting to know someone leads to deeper understanding and liking. In recent years, as a result of the Internet, individuals have established relationships without proximity. Getting to know each other through e-mail communications has established itself as a way to meet new and interesting people. Obviously, safeguards are important if an actual meeting is arranged. Getting together in a public place is a common recommendation along with waiting until you know someone personally before you share addresses and other private information. If the relationship seems promising, eventually, there will be proximity!

Similarities.   "Birds of a feather flock together" is an axiom with merit. Differences can be interesting and positive. For years, social psychologists have realized that similarities are strong predictors of attraction (Byrne, 1971) and that people with little in common can repel each other (Rosenbaum, 1986). **Similarities** or being alike in attitudes, interests, degree of intelligence, religion, age, and personality are generally bonding and promote liking. We feel attracted to those who by their attitudes and behaviors confirm our values and beliefs. For example, if equal rights are important, seeing a person actively participate in a rally increases positive feelings. People wanting to meet potential significant others should participate in causes and activities near and dear to their hearts. Agreement is a powerful force.

Complementarity.   A characteristic that is lacking in you can be attractive in another person. This is **complementarity** and, for practical reasons, it can benefit a relationship. Kent was outgoing and loved to tell jokes. His friend Pat was quiet, except when he was laughing loudly at Kent's stories. Complementing each other was a major factor in their relationship.

Reciprocity.   Imagine that you have just met Sarah. You feel neutral toward her; you do not necessarily like or dislike her. As times goes by, Sarah demonstrates a genuine interest in and liking for you. The chances are that you will reciprocate; your feelings will become positive. **Reciprocity** is a tendency to like people who like you. As Rathus (1999) puts it, "If you like me, you must have excellent judgment." This may sound conceited; however, if you genuinely like yourself, you are likely to be attracted to others who share your feelings. When we are liked and admired, we are inclined to return those feelings and behaviors. Conversely, have you ever experienced the realization that another person does not like you? You probably tended to reciprocate and found yourself disliking that person.

The factors of attraction and liking contribute to the onset of a relationship and continue to enhance its growth. Wanting to approach someone and then beginning to like that person are not caused by a mysterious force. Rather, it is fairly easy to predict who will relate to whom and why.

Improving Relationships

You have a choice in the types and number of relationships you develop and maintain, and you influence their quality as well. Certain attitudes and behaviors deserve special attention.

Realistic Expectations of Relationships

Expecting a relationship to be 100 percent harmonious and believing that individuals will always act in certain ways are unrealistic.

> Just as no human being is perfect, neither are relationships. None of us will ever be perfect husbands, wives, children, professionals, teachers, students, employees, employers, fathers, mothers, or friends. We are humanly limited in all these social human roles. (Rubin, 1975, p. 239)

Having unrealistic ideas leads to frustration and disappointment and usually ends a relationship. Even with acquaintances, having realistic expectations is helpful. If you are a renter, what is realistic to expect from the property owner? If you own property, are you expecting too much from your tenants?

In all types of relationships, open communication is helpful; in certain cases, written agreements about expectations are appropriate. A common tale of woe concerns roommates. Hannah describes her roommate as a slob, one who does not do her share and leaves the apartment a mess. Unfortunately, they had no agreement about task management before they became roommates. Discussing expectations and agreeing to policies, preferably in writing, are more likely to achieve desired objectives than simply expecting things to work out.

Sensitivity and Cooperation

Sensitivity is having an awareness or sense about the perceptions and per-spectives of others. In a classroom setting, sensitivity is conducive to learning. When instructors and students understand each other's perspectives, and students are sensitive to one another, the atmosphere is positive. Two older students said that figuring out how to fit in was their biggest challenge. Younger students' sensitivity to their different perspectives was greatly appreciated.

Cooperation means working with others in a positive way toward a common goal. For example, a printing company had to deliver a large order within a week. The owner called the employees together to discuss how the objective could be accomplished. Because one employee's child was in the hospital awaiting surgery, others offered to work longer hours to compensate for the employee's time away from the job. The job was accomplished. Wise parents, teachers, and employers emphasize cooperation in the successful completion of tasks.

Assertiveness

Relationships thrive on **assertiveness**—maintaining one's legitimate rights and expressing thoughts and feelings in nonthreatening ways. The "you win and I lose" approach is a passive solution in which one individual gives up his or her rights to another. The "you lose and I win" approach is an aggressive solution in which one individual ignores the rights of another in order to get his or her way. The "you lose and I lose" approach is a totally passive solution in which both individuals give up their rights. A healthy resolution is impossi-ble. The "you win and I win" approach is an assertive solution in which the rights of both parties are recognized, respected, and utilized in reaching a healthy compromise. Review the material on becoming assertive in Chapter 2 and realize the benefits extend not only to you but also to all those with whom you interact.

Negotiation Skills

Positive negotiation skills are well worth cultivating because conflict can occur in all relationships. **Conflict** means that disagreement or a difference in thinking ex-ists. Most people have been taught that being right is essential. However, individu-als who rate high in interpersonal relations skills are well aware that the need to be right can damage relationships. "You can insist on being right or have a relationship that works, but you cannot have both, and the addiction to being right about inac-curate beliefs will destroy any relationship" (Ellsworth, 1988, p. 19).

Once you realize that conflict is not a matter of who is right and who is wrong and that it is caused simply by differences of opinion, you are setting the stage for negotiation. Conflict management is an art like other interpersonal rela-tions skills. Handling conflict in intimate relationships will be covered in Chapter 13; the negotiation skills described in this section are useful as well.

Not recommended in any relationship is a behavior described as **gunny-sacking.** When you "gunnysack," you keep your grievances suppressed or bottled up (Bach and Wyden, 1968). People who hide their grievances do so because of

Figure 10-6

nonassertiveness, fear, and a desire to preserve peace at any cost. Because gunnysacking is often the result of a fear of criticizing anyone, the methods for delivering criticism suggested in Chapter 8 are worth learning and using. A gunnysack stuffed to its limits is potentially harmful for several reasons. Suppressing annoyances is stressful and can be damaging to health. Keeping quiet about grievances can diminish self-esteem, and relationships suffer terribly. "When complaints are toted along quietly in a gunnysack for any length of time they make a dreadful mess when the sack finally bursts" (Bach and Wyden, 1968, p. 19) (Fig. 10-6).

An aggressive style of conflict management is as damaging as gunnysacking. Closed communication is the norm. An aggressive person tries to dominate and control all issues and will use any steamrolling method available. He or she will turn conflicts into a competition and may win on the surface, but the relationship loses. In long-term relationships this is particularly dangerous.

Understanding Conflict

What is conflict?

Conflict is a normal, inevitable part of life. As long as we are alive and feeling, thinking, questioning, and making decisions, we will encounter conflict. (Office of Dispute Resolution) Conflict is a natural disagreement resulting from individuals or groups that differ in attitudes, beliefs, values, or needs. It can originate from past rivalries and personality differences.

The conflicts we face each day may be small and passing or long and drawn out. We are just as likely to have conflicts with people we like as with those we do not like, and we probably have as many conflicts with people who are like us as we do with those who are not like us. Some conflicts we can see coming; other conflicts come up seemingly without warning. Our ability to deal effectively with conflict is tested constantly throughout our lives, and the effects of conflict on our lives can be enormous.

The Ingredients of Conflict

Needs—Needs are physical or psychological requirements that are essential to our well-being. Conflict arises when we ignore others' needs, our own needs, or the group's needs. Be careful not to confuse needs with desires or "wants" (things we would like that are not essential).

Perceptions—People interpret reality differently. They perceive differences in the severity, causes, and consequences of problems. Misperceptions or differing perceptions may come from self-perceptions, others' perceptions, differing perceptions of situation, and perceptions of threat.

Power—How people define and use power is an important influence on the number and types of conflicts that occur. This influences how conflict is managed. Conflict can arise when people try to make others change their actions or try to gain an unfair advantage.

Values—Values are beliefs or principles we consider to be very important. Serious conflicts arise when people hold incompatible values or when values are not clear. Conflicts also arise when one party refuses to accept the fact that the other party holds something as a value rather than as a preference.

Feelings and Emotions—Many people let their feelings and emotions become a major influence over how they deal with conflict. Conflicts can also occur because people ignore their own or others' feelings and emotions. Other conflicts occur when feelings and emotions differ over a particular issue.

Why Learn Conflict Resolution Skills?

It makes sense that we would want to maximize our ability to resolve conflicts in a satisfying way. Yet few of us receive formal preparation for or education in resolving conflict effectively. The way we approach conflict or behave in a conflict is based on a lifetime of individual experiences, including what we have been taught; our environment; our (perceived) strengths, power, and vulnerability; the behavior of those around us and/or those we admire; and the successes and failures of different strategies we have seen or tried.

The way we deal with conflict is often an automatic reflex, an unconscious choice, a strategy based on fear (what will happen if I do not do the right thing?), confusion (what did she mean by that?), mistrust (I better look out for my interests because he is only looking out for himself), or survival (if I challenge the way things are, I would have to suffer the consequences). When conflict evokes strong feelings in us, we act in response to those feelings and may not apply the same thoughtfulness and skills to resolving a conflict as we would when listening to a close friend. (ODR)

Conflict is not always negative. In fact, it can be healthy when effectively managed. Healthy conflict can lead to:

- Growth and innovation
- News ways of thinking
- Additional management options

If the conflict is understood, it can be effectively managed by reaching a conclusion that meets both the individual's needs and society's needs. This results in mutual benefits and strengthens the relationship. The goal is for all to "win" by having at least some of their needs met.

Positive Steps to Conflict Resolution

When conflict is approached in a thoughtful, constructive way, the result hopefully will be satisfying and positive, not only for ourselves but also for those around us. This approach is effective, collaborative, and constructive conflict resolution. The following model can be used for personal, workplace and even community conflict resolution:

Step 1: Deal Effectively with Anger
- You cannot negotiate a good agreement if you and/or the other person are too angry to think straight or if you do not acknowledge your feelings.

Step 2: Do Your Homework (think before you approach)
- How does this conflict affect each of us?
- What interests or values are at stake here for each of us?
- What prejudices or assumptions do we have about the each other?

Step 3: Set a Positive Tone
- Invite the other person to negotiate. ("Could we talk?")
- State positive intentions. ("I would like to make things better between us.")
- Acknowledge and validate the other person. ("I can see this is difficult for you, too." "Thank you for working with me on this.")

Step 4: Use Ground Rules
- Talk one at a time.
- Work to improve the situation.
- Stay calm.

Step 5: Discuss and Define the Problem
- Share issues and feelings one at a time.
- Use effective listening and speaking techniques.
- Identify interests and needs.
- Discuss assumptions, suspicions, and values if necessary.
- Summarize new understandings.

Step 6: Brainstorm Possible Solutions
- Contribute ideas to satisfy interests and needs one at a time.
- Don't criticize or evaluate ideas at this time.
- Be creative while working toward collaboration ("I can" or "We should").

Step 7: Evaluate and Choose Solutions
- Consider solutions that are:
  - Mutually agreeable
  - Realistic
  - Specific

Step 8: Follow Up
- Check back with each other at an agreed-on time.
- If the agreement is not working, use the same process to revise it.

Categories of Difficult People

1. *Hostile-aggressives:* People who try to bully and overwhelm others.
2. *Complainers:* Individuals who gripe incessantly but do not act to improve the situation.
3. *Silent and unresponsive:* Those who respond very little and, therefore, are not helpful.
4. *Super-agreeables:* Reasonable people who either do not produce or who act differently when not in your presence.
5. *Negativists:* Pessimists whose favorite reaction is, "No, that won't work."
6. *Know-it-all experts:* Those who think that they know much more than anyone else.
7. *Indecisives:* People who do not seem to be able to make up their minds as well as perfectionists who do not complete tasks.

Figure 10-7

Difficult People

"No matter what I do or say, nothing makes any difference," "I work for the most difficult person in the world," and "Nobody can get along with her" are descriptions of difficult people. They may be hostile customers, irritable coworkers, passive-aggressive supervisors, or nitpicky neighbors. They could even be family members. Because he could not find another book on the subject, Bramson (1988) wrote *Coping with Difficult People*. After reading the list of patterns of difficult behavior (Fig. 10-7), do you recognize anyone? If you see yourself in any of the descriptions, realize that you are probably damaging your relationships.

Before you decide that someone's behaviors are difficult, be sure your expectations are realistic. A person with an introverted preference will probably be reserved. Labeling that person as difficult is unrealistic and unfair. However, if the problem is definitely because of a difficult individual, certain strategies outlined previously can help. Keep in mind that although your personality type may *explain* certain aspects of your behaviors, it does not *excuse* them. In other words, do not fall into a trap of thinking that your personality type locks you into certain behaviors.

When dealing with a difficult person, cognitive techniques can also be beneficial. Keeping in mind that other people do not control you and are not able to make you feel, think, or do anything, you can adjust your thinking in various ways. The thought that "just because she was short-tempered (and often is) does not mean it is going to ruin my day" changes your reality. Use your newfound knowledge of personality type to recognize and respect the differences among people. Learn to communicate effectively with them to better understand their needs.

Having an understanding of attribution theory (Heider, 1958) is quite helpful. Discussed in Chapter 5 regarding anger, you use attributions whenever you seek the "why" of behavior. Errors most definitely occur. Social psychologists are quite interested in the common biases we make. For example, if Tim tells a crude joke that demeans women, we might think, "Tim is sexist and rude." The tendency to believe that others' behavior is caused by internal factors such as personality traits, attitude, mood, abilities, or effort is called the **fundamental attribution error** (Ross, 1977). We could have thought, "Tim is a new person who is possibly trying to make an impression on us, and he evidently does not understand that this is not the way to do it." In this case, we are recognizing the situation or circumstances as the major factor. But more often, we are apt to attribute behavior to a facet of the other's self. In our minds, the difficult person is simply difficult.

Why not try to see a situation from the other's perspective? Most people have a reason for being nasty, and if you can figure out accurate underlying causes, your reaction will be less negative. Also be careful not to jump to a conclusion about another's motivation. People are usually more complicated than what is apparent. Being patient, giving people more than one chance, and being empathic are recommended.

Sometimes changing your behavior and reactions toward a difficult person is most effective. Invariably, the interactions and relationship also change. Anna's supervisor was, in her opinion, a difficult person. She began to compliment her supervisor and to thank her for advice. Within a few weeks, Anna said to a friend, "What a difference my behaviors have made! At least I can tolerate her now." What Anna did is good medicine for a difficult person. She provided something that was needed by the supervisor. If you can figure out what a person wants and what may be a cause of his or her difficult behavior, you are helping both yourself and the other person.

Assertiveness, on your part, is most advisable. Difficult people honestly often do not realize how they are affecting others. A simple statement, such as "I did not like being blamed for missing the deadline when it was your part that came in late, and I would like to talk about how we can work together more effectively," can help. A book designed to help you deal with people who make your life miserable is *Toxic People* (Glass, 1995). Several ways of identifying these individuals, plus ways to deal with them, are included. To help you assess your involvement with difficult people, as well as unload your "gunnysack," use the Chapter 10 activity in Reflections and Applications. When confronted with a difficult person, use ideas suggested in this book.

Supportiveness

Picture a roomful of people. One individual is carrying a large, weighty pack on her back, so big and burdensome that it is difficult not to notice. Yet the others mingle about as if they do not see the pack. "How are you?" "Fine." "What do you think of the weather?" Cliché conversation fills the room. People talk about their families and work. They speak of many things but not of the pack on the person's back. Everyone knows that it is there, and it is on each person's mind. Nobody says a thing. Even though the woman sags from the weight and looks as if she could fall, they ignore the heavy pack. We will not discuss it, they think. The woman thinks to herself.

Oh, please talk. Why will you not say his name? I want you to say "Paul." I want for us to talk about his death and his life. Can I say "Paul" and not have you look away and ignore it? For if we do not talk, you are leaving me alone with this dreadfully heavy pack on my back.

People we know will experience crises and tragedies, and they will carry a figurative pack on their backs. If you care, you will want to know how to react at these times. Consider these possibilities.

Marni, a coworker, is diagnosed with cancer.
Todd, a next-door neighbor, dies suddenly. His wife and children are the survivors.
Kari and Jason, a couple you know, are in an accident. She is badly injured.

Are you inclined to do nothing? Do you ignore the pack on the back? A strong recommendation is to show your concern. Completely ignoring another's tragedy sends the message that you do not care. On a rational level, this may be unfounded. "Of course I care," said one man, "I just do not know what to do." On an emotional level, saying and doing nothing is hurtful.

People seem to be afraid of a griever's feelings, so they try to ignore or change the subject, or they intellectualize and try to explain away the grief. Some just may not want to be bothered. The most commonly given reason for not being supportive: "I just do not know what to do." Closely related is the fear that what is done or said will be wrong. Giving support is another area in which little training is offered. Yet enough has been written on the subject that "I do not know what to say or do" can be seen as an excuse. Being effective in interpersonal relations means that you do respond to people and their needs. It is helpful to be aware of what research has identified as *not* helpful.

- Implied total awareness: "I understand exactly what you are going through." "I know just how you feel," or "I know" used over and over.
- Supplied solutions and reasons for acceptance: "It is better this way." "You will recover faster than you think." "It will be just fine." "Just give it time." "He lived a long life; he was ready to go." "Be grateful for . . . " "It was meant to be." "It was God's will."
- One-upping comments: "I know what it's like because my grandmother died last year." "You think you have got problems? Wait until you hear mine." "Not only did my sister's husband divorce her, but then. . . ."

Surprisingly, in one study, slightly more than half of all unhelpful comments were made by relatives or friends (Wortman, Battle, and Lemkau, 1997).

Ideally in any situation, we can express caring feelings. Simplicity and sincerity are the key ingredients. Comments such as "I care" and "I am concerned" are fine. Other possibilities are "I want to do something" and "I remember . . . ," recalling a fond memory of the deceased. If people would realize that they are not expected to explain the "why," solve the problem, take away the pain, or other such dramatic behaviors, they might be more inclined to express concern. Research indicates that the most helpful comments are expressions of personal willingness to help or listen; any behaviors that suppress grief or force too much disclosure are not recommended (Range, Walston, and Pollard, 1992). Verbal expression can open a door of relief for a suffering person. Comfort can be found in just talking. You do not have to have the answers; just listening will help. Usually, people don't remain silent long enough for the griever to fully express his or her thoughts and feelings (James and Cherry, 1988). "I just needed someone to talk to and especially a person I believed was truly listening," said a bereaved parent. Empathic and receptive listening skills are especially advisable. A wise suggestion is to let the grieving person be the only one to make evaluative comments such as "It was a blessing."

Sometimes an honest expression of your perception of the situation is best. A comforting comment given to the writer Max Wylie after his daughter had been savagely murdered was, "This did not happen for the best; it happened for the worst."

One argument you may hear against talking about the "pack on the person's back" is "Maybe they are trying to forget the tragedy or not think about their situation. If I say something, it will just remind them of it." Ask yourself whether you believe that people in anguish have forgotten. If you are thinking about their tragedy or problem, they probably are too. In situations of anxiety, studies show that conversations do not create new fears. In fact, not talking about a fear makes it more pronounced (Buckman, 1988).

As was indicated in the scenario at the beginning of this section, usually one of the greatest gifts you can possibly give to a grieving person is to mention the name of the person's loved one and add some memory you have of him or her.

> People who are grieving are likely to fluctuate between wanting some time to themselves and wanting time with others. They may want someone to talk to about their feelings. Showing concern and thoughtfulness shows that you care. It is better to feel nervous and awkward sitting with a grieving friend than to not sit there at all. (Sherer, 2002)

Writing a note or sending a card can replace verbal expression. Supportive acts are also greatly appreciated. Do not just say, "If you need anything, call." Often a person will not seek help; in many cases, you can either say what you want to do or just take action. Check the list of specific helping behaviors in Fig. 10-8. ("Support: What You Can Do"). Promising to help and then not following through is frustrating, so refrain from idle offers. Do not overlook the supportive impact of your presence.

Support: What You Can Do

- In the case of a death, address sympathy acknowledgement cards.
- In any crisis, do errands, such as shopping.
- Clean the person's house.
- Do laundry.
- Mow the person's yard or shovel snow.
- Take the person out for dinner or to a movie.
- Take care of the children, if any.
- Just come by for a visit.

Figure 10-8

"People do not have to say a word. If they are here, I know they care," commented a widow. "Of course, I would love a little hug or squeeze on my arm if they could," she added with a tear in her eye. Sharing your sad feelings can also be a comfort. Tears are a by-product of our love and compassion (Edwards, 1989).

When you show support, you help another human being. Acts of listening, talking, touching, and doing are what a grieving person probably needs (Donnelley, 1987). Genuine supportiveness strengthens relationships. A poem by Mary Bailey, described by Vail (1982) as "a lovely lady whose cherished teenage daughter was killed in an accident," eloquently expresses what a person in pain wants.

A Plea from Someone Who Has Been There

Please dear friend
Do not say to me the old clichés
Time heals all wounds
God only gives you as much as you can bear
Life is for the living
Just say the thoughts of your heart
I am sorry, I love you, I am here, I care
Hug me and squeeze my hand
I need your warmth and strength
Please do not drop your eyes when I am near
I feel so rejected now by God and man
Just look in my eyes and let me know that you are with me
Do not think you must always be strong for me
It is okay to cry
It tells me how much you care
Let me cry, too
It is so lonely to always cry alone
Please keep coming by even after many weeks have passed
When the numbness wears off, the pain of grief is unbearable
Don't ever expect me to be quite the same
How can I be when part of my being is here no more?
But please know, dear friend, with your love, support and understanding
I will live and love again and be grateful every day that I have you; dear friend.

—Mary Bailey

Sincere Expression

Willingness to express all sincere emotions can greatly improve your relationships. Besides sorrow, other feelings can be hard to express.

Forgiveness.   Are you one who has difficulty forgiving? Do you know people who bear grudges? Forgiveness, especially when you were truly wronged, is among the most difficult undertakings for a person, and most of us have no idea how or even if to forgive (Flanigan, 1992). The benefits of forgiving are worth the difficulties. Harboring grudges and other bitter feelings can be damaging to psychological and physical health.

Thinking about forgiveness as simply *letting go of the past* may make it more acceptable. To "forgive and forget" is not necessary; you can forgive without forgetting. Erasing a wrongdoing from memory is unrealistic and usually impossible. Neither is forgiving the same as condoning or pardoning. Instead, forgiveness means letting go and moving on. You may not resume the relationship at all, or perhaps it will not be as it was before. However, you are free from the bitterness and pain of negativity.

Forgiveness is easier if you are able to forgive yourself. In considering that someone else has wronged you, ask, "Am I perfect? Have I ever hurt somebody else?" The answer to the latter question will likely be that you have. The next question is, "Have I forgiven myself?" If you forgive yourself and learn from the mistake, you will probably find yourself willing to extend your forgiveness to another.

To help you forgive, *Forgiveness Is a Choice* (Enright, 2001) and *Forgiving Yourself* (Flanigan, 1996) are excellent resources. Never to forgive means living a life of unending resentment. When you forgive, you decide to move forward with your life. The alternative is not desirable. "The deeply wounded can either change or slowly drown in a deep pool of hatred" (Flanigan, 1992, p. 68). The choice is yours.

Warmth and demonstrated affection.   These particular feelings and behaviors deserve special attention. Touch is the first sense to develop; in order to develop normally, a baby needs to be warmly and lovingly touched. Adults deprived of physical stroking in childhood often develop compulsive, destructive habits such as nail biting, overeating, or smoking. Some speculate that violent behavior may be a result of touch deprivation (Karr, Morse, and Wiley, 1997). Unfortunately, as people age, touching generally declines. Yet the warmth of body contact and the sensation of strong arms holding us are fundamental. "From the first moments of our life to the last, we need to be held—or we fall" (Josselson, 1992, p. 29). Because touch is so critical, if you do not receive it regularly, self-massage or professional massage is recommended.

Reluctance to behave warmly and affectionately is apparent even in close relationships. Individuals who withhold affection can be filled with regret as evidenced by Matt who said:

> A good friend called me one night and said he needed to talk. I lied and told him I was too busy and said I would get back to him later. The next day I "spaced" it. That night he shot himself. I feel so guilty.

A letter to Ann Landers told of a 13-year-old girl who wanted desperately to "belong" but had few friends. She tried to reach out and was rejected. She committed suicide, and the students from her school turned out in droves for her funeral. The letter ended: "Sally left this world believing she did not have a single friend. If just one of those kids who passed her casket had taken the time and trouble to show her a little kindness, that dear girl might be alive today." Ann Landers' response was to tell people to reach out. Do you know someone you could befriend? Don't put off expressing affection and warmth to a friend or loved one. Because life is tenuous, you can be too late to tell or show someone that you care. Awareness of this can provide the motivation you need. Consider calling or writing to someone for no other reason than just to say, "I love you."

Appropriateness is a key element in demonstrating any emotion. Within close relationships you have more leeway, and warmth and affection can be shown by hugging, kissing, and other physical acts. Among acquaintances, societal guidelines usually direct behaviors. Touch can be a gesture of warmth and concern; however, it may also be perceived as seductive, impertinent, annoying, or degrading. As in other behaviors, being sensitive to individual differences is important. Touching is influenced by culture and gender-role socialization. In some situations, touching is even risky. Teachers are concerned that touching a student might be misinterpreted. Following court action against a male elementary school teacher, a parent in one of my classes expressed this thoughtful opinion.

> I hope that we do not get to the point where people are afraid to touch each other. I have taught my son and daughter to express genuine affection with appropriate touches, pats on the shoulder or back, and hugs. I hate to think that they will go to school and model after human robots fearful of physical contact. Besides, a lot of kids need affirming touches.

Regardless of culture and gender, a study found that people who were comfortable with touching were more talkative, cheerful, socially dominant, and nonconforming; those discomforted by touch tended to be more emotionally unstable and socially withdrawn (Thayer, 1988). As people become more aware of the benefits of demonstrating feelings as described in Chapter 5, they may touch others more freely. "Without the social vocabulary of touch, life would be cold, mechanical, distant, rational, verbal. Deprived of those gestures and their meanings, the world would be far more frightening, hostile, and chilly" (Thayer, 1988, p. 36). Examining the ways in which you express warmth and affection and making an effort to show your feelings appropriately and genuinely will improve your relationships.

Answering the Challenge of Relationships

Are you willing to risk? All relationships involve risks. Besides the pleasures derived from connecting and interacting, you can expect disappointment and pain. When you exist only to avoid these displeasures, you forfeit all opportunities for the joys of relationships.

Are you committed to spending time, energy, and effort in building positive relationships? Wanting to relate means sacrificing time alone as well as solitary pursuit of your own pleasures. Giving up the extremes of independence and dependence for the nurturance of interdependence is healthy in all close relationships. **Interdependence** means that two people can stand alone, yet prefer to have a relationship with each other and strive to do what is best for both. Education in relationship skills can show people how to be interdependent.

> Young people start out without the foggiest notion of how to live in human, personal interaction. I wonder if our educational system would be willing not only to believe, but to prove by their actions that one goal of education is to assist the young person to live as a person with other persons. (Rogers, 1972)

Those words are challenging. Although some strides have been made since they were written, most of us are left to seek out relationship training for ourselves. Learning from this book is a major step. Another good resource is the "Future Intentions" list in Reflections and Applications. You have the opportunity to learn and then act so that you can be enriched by interactions and relationships (Reflect and Apply).

REFLECT AND APPLY

Reflect

◆ *Give an example of a relationship that illustrates one of the attraction factors.*
◆ *Recall the last time you behaved assertively.*
◆ *Think of a difficult person. Which tactic could you try in order to deal with that person more positively?*

Apply

◆ *Perform a little act of kindness.*
◆ *Use the five negotiation steps to resolve a current or future issue.*
◆ *The next time you have a chance to provide support, please do so.*

LOOKING BACK

- Because we are human, we relate to other humans. Social relationships are needed for self-development.
- Positive relationships are characterized by social exchange. Participants remain in relationships because they receive as well as give, and the benefits outweigh the costs.
- Features of a positive relationship include love for self, absence of codependency, genuineness, warmth with unconditional positive regard, empathy, self-disclosure, enjoyment, encouragement, fairness, dependability, energizing feelings, and mutual interests.
- Various types of relationships contribute to life satisfaction.
- Friendships can have both dilemmas and benefits. Although women and men generally differ in the nature of their friendships, the future holds the promise of deep, nourishing relationships for both. Besides friendships, a variety of support systems are available.
- Open-mindedness and tolerance promote a healthy beginning to interactions. Ideally, acceptance and appreciation of diversity will follow.
- Stereotyping, prejudice, and discrimination are not beneficial to individuals or to societies. Because we learn intolerance, we can unlearn and relearn and live productively in a multicultural world.
- In order to connect with others, shyness needs to be overcome.
- When initiating an interaction, approachability is an important consideration. You can learn to check approachability and then in a positive way initiate and continue conversation.
- Factors related to attraction and liking are physical attraction, proximity, similarities, complementarity, and reciprocity.
- Relationships benefit when the participants have realistic and agreeable expectations for the relationship, along with sensitivity, a cooperative attitude, and assertiveness.
- Conflict will occur. "Gunnysacking" and aggressiveness are not recommended. Learning how to negotiate will help in all walks of life. Additional techniques may be needed in dealing with difficult people.

- It is often difficult to know the best way to offer your support to someone in pain. Although ignoring another person's crisis or tragedy is commonplace, it is not recommended. Showing that you care in verbal and nonverbal ways is important.
- Sincere expressions of forgiveness, warmth, and affection significantly improve relationships.
- All relationships involve risks and commitment. A major challenge in maintaining healthy relationships is based on the fact that human beings are rarely trained in relationship skills. If you want to have the joys and benefits that come from positive relationships, you must be willing to risk, commit, and learn.

The singular life experience I would wish every human being before they die is to feel love for, and be loved by, another. All human beings biologically need to be healthily attached, connected with others.

—Teresa Adams

RESOURCES

Codependents Anonymous.
(602) 277–7991.
http://www.codependents.org
Administration on Aging (for health and care providers).
http://www.aoa.dhhs.gov
Southern Poverty Law Center.
http://www.splcenter.org
Anti-Defamation League.
http://www.adl.org
Simon Wiesenthal Center.
http://www.wiesenthal.com
Parents, Families and Friends of Lesbians and Gays (PFLAG).
(202) 638–4200.
http://www.pflag.org
Sources of information

You may also find these publications helpful. They should be available through your local bookstore.
Breaking the Impasse: Consensual Approaches to Resolving Public Disputes. Lawrence Susskind and Jeffrey Cruikshank, 1987, New York: Basic Books.
Creating the High Performance Team. Steve Buchholz and Thomas Roth, 1987, New York: Wiley.
The Eight Essential Steps to Conflict Resolution: Preserving Relationships at Work, at Home, and in the Community. Dudley Weeks, 1992, New York: St. Martin's Press.

Getting to Yes: Negotiating Agreement without Giving In. Robert Fisher, William Ury, and Bruce Patton, 1991, New York: Penguin Books.
Managing Public Disputes: A Practical Guide to Handling Conflict and Reaching Agreements. Susan L. Carpenter and W.J.D. Kennedy, 1988, San Francisco: Jossey-Bass Publishers.
The Planner as Dispute Resolver: Concepts and Teaching Materials. A. Bruce Dotson, David Godschalk, and Jerome Kaufman, 1989, Washington, DC: National Institute for Dispute Resolution.

SUCCEEDING IN YOUR CAREER

LOOKING AHEAD

After completing this chapter, you will be able to

- Differentiate between a career and a job.
- Discuss the aspects of the self and work orientations related to career and job satisfaction.
- Recognize the importance of wise choices of career and jobs.
- Name several characteristics of a valued employee.
- Recognize the many choices you have regarding career.
- Identify ways you can improve your job search.
- Describe behaviors that lead to positive work relationships.

> *We are responsible to ourselves for the quality of our own lives. We can be friends or enemies to ourselves by the choices we make, which in turn make up the lives we lead. Real caring about ourselves is the first step in caring for others and in solving global concerns. May your career choice contribute to your dream of the future.*
>
> —Betty Neville Michelozzi

"What do you want to be when you grow up?" is a challenging question to answer when you are 3 years old. At age 18, or sometimes earlier, there comes another one: "Have you decided on a career?" Then be prepared for an inquiry heard over and over before retirement: "What do you do for a living?" Our self-identities are linked to career choices and current jobs, and the workplace is the source of much of life's satisfaction or dissatisfaction. A positive professional experience is of prime importance.

When you consider how much time people spend pursuing their careers and actually on the job, it is not surprising that so much of what we think about ourselves is related to work. Additionally, our careers may affect our relationships. Years ago we were told that with technology our lives in the future would offer considerably more leisure time. That "crystal ball" prediction was extremely inaccurate. According to *U.S. News & World Report* (2000), the 40-hour workweek, or about 10,000 days of one's life, has expanded into an average workweek of 47 hours!

Even more enlightening is the concept of "24/7,"which means that many people find that they are "on call" and are often doing something related to work 24 hours a day, 7 days a week (*U.S. News & World Report*, 2000). According to a study by the National Sleep Foundation, the average American employee works a 46-hour workweek; 38 percent of the respondents in the study worked more than 50 hours per week (National Sleep Foundation, 2005). Additionally, a number of people take work home with them. Because of the time and effort spent, what happens with our careers and at our workplaces is closely related to life's satisfaction and the quality of our relationships. This chapter will focus on careers, jobs, and interactions at work.

Seeking Satisfaction in Careers and Jobs

How do you differentiate between a career and a job? Did you have a job before you selected a career? Most of us did. Maybe you have a job now and either you haven't decided on a career or the job is not related to what you eventually plan to do. Think of a **career** as a broad field of occupational endeavor that includes a series of work experiences over a span of time. A career path includes planning, training, and dedicating your time and talent. Within each career field are numerous job possibilities. A **job** consists of tasks or duties a person does for pay.

Because career and job satisfaction will dramatically affect the quality of your life, learning what makes a difference is time well spent. A Gallup poll showed only 39 percent of workers had complete satisfaction with their jobs. Complete dissatisfaction was voiced by 14 percent. The most satisfied workers were self-employed people in their own business or professional practice. Significantly, two-thirds of those who were completely satisfied in regard to job stress, personal recognition, and salary levels were also completely satisfied with their jobs. Those most dissatisfied were unhappy with coworkers, their boss, job security, and opportunities to learn and grow (Saad, 1999). To avoid being discontented and to be counted among the number of satisfied individuals, look over the list "What Makes a Difference?" and then think about what you want (Fig. 11-1).

What Makes a Difference?
(from a Gallup Poll, 1999)

What Is Most Satisfying?

- Relations with coworkers
- Physical safety of workplace
- Flexibility of work hours
- Amount of vacation time

What Is Most Dissatisfying?

- On-the-job stress
- Salaries and certain benefits
- Lack of recognition for accomplishments

Figure 11-1

Career Choice

When thinking about satisfaction, it's best to consider career and job separately. In the past, many individuals gave little consideration to career choice. For example, Carl farms because his father and grandfather were farmers. Nathan wanted to remain in his hometown, so he took a job in a local bank and made it a career. Tina chose hairdressing because there was a school near her home, and she did not have other aspirations. People today seem to be more concerned with career selection; however, they can still limit themselves. Most people reply to the question, "What do you want to be?" by naming a title or position; this does not tell you what is required in a job. The critical challenge, instead, is, "What do you want to *do*?" Does your choice afford you opportunities to do what you enjoy? Other important questions to ask yourself may be whether there are the opportunities for growth or responsibility changes within the company and whether there are there travel options and other benefits. Personal aptitudes and interests are important factors as people begin to identify career opportunities. Programs such as Career Pathways give flexible identity and structure to the student career choice process as well as to educational programs and services that contribute to career preparation (State of Michigan, 2006).

As pointed out in Chapter 2, women, in general, still sell themselves short and opt for lower-paying, lower-status career fields. Men continue to feel forced to be financially successful and often choose higher-paying fields even if they have little interest in the work. Other men feel pressured to take over a family business. Both sexes can limit themselves by not considering all possibilities. Before you choose a career, it's wise to know yourself. Reading and applying the material in this book will help direct you. Now focus on specific career-related aspects of your-self. The widely read book *What Color Is Your Parachute?* (Bolles, 2001) can lead you through a series of exercises to identify skills you enjoy and those you do best. The key to being able to find pleasure in your work is the sense that you are using your abilities, not wasting them, and that you are being appreciated (Kushner, 1986).

An activity in Reflections and Applications can help you link enjoyment and job duties. No matter how much you might enjoy certain tasks and activities, satisfaction is still unlikely if you are not skilled in what is required of you. Greg said he wanted to be a journalist, and his personality type was well suited to that field. However, his writing was stilted, uninteresting, and prone to errors. Unless he improves his skills, his pursuit of journalism would likely lead to frustration and dissatisfaction.

Your values also play a part in the process of choosing a satisfying career. If you highly value money or what it can buy, you cannot expect career satisfaction in lower-paying fields no matter how much you enjoy the work. Is prestige important to you? Sociologists have studied prestige statuses of various career fields and, if this is of concern, acquaint yourself with the status ranking of your career choice. Maybe you value advancement and upward mobility. There is a difference between managing a child care facility and being CEO of a large corporation.

Personality type plays a vital role. Do you tend to be more extraverted or introverted? Ask yourself how many interactions you will have on a regular basis.

Figure 11-2   Enjoyment of work is priceless.

Do you want to provide ideas and possibilities and have variety and flexibility in your work, or are you more comfortable with established procedures and prefer to work with facts and figures? The Myers-Briggs Type Indicator, described in Chapter 2, provides insight into preferred work situations for each personality type. For an insightful approach to career choice related to personality type, the two books *Do What You Are* (Tieger and Barron-Tieger, 1995) and *What's Your Type of Career?* (Dunning, 2001) are highly recommended.

How well do you cope? Preferences regarding people environments and living and working conditions can be just as important as what a person chooses to do. Work environment can play a large part in how people feel about their jobs. Often a person's comfort level with the work environment can make the difference between a successful and an unsuccessful career choice (University of Washington, 2003). The essence of career planning is finding a match between who you are and an environment that suits you (Fig. 11-2).

Finally, commitment is a key element. Some career fields require more time, energy, and effort than others. A fire department chief caused a few eyes to widen when he said that a fire-fighting career means spending one-third of your life away from your family. It is important to match your career choice with your degree of commitment.

Wise decisions in the beginning can save you years of wasted energy. Even after starting a career, people may realize they have made a poor choice and change directions. Relatively few decisions are as influential in determining the course of your life as the choice of a career path. Occupational choices have an impact on several aspects of life, including standard of living, lifestyle, friendships, intimate relationships, how you dress each day, and where you live. Sharon Hanna (2004) stated that her daughters were pursuing careers in California. Even though she applauded their choices, their decisions meant that they would see each other less often, and their life choices would be quite different than if they had stayed in the Midwest. Career decisions are choices about the way we live.

Selection of a Job

Within a career pathway there are many possible jobs, and anyone looking for the ultimate in satisfaction does not just settle for the basic choices. For example, in England of the over 40,000 students studying psychology each year, it is estimated that around 15 to 20 percent will become chartered psychologists. In 2004, nearly half of psychology graduates had entered full-time work six months after leaving school, moving into a wide range of jobs in a variety of sectors. A significant number of graduates go into occupations related to health and child care (16.2%), clerical and secretarial jobs (14.6%), and other professional and technical occupations (17.4%). Nearly one in ten psychology graduates works as a manager either in the public or private sector six months after graduating (Prospects.ac.uk, 2005). Take advantage of library and online resources (see list at end of this chapter).

Have you ever had a job you did not like? Do you know why it was not desirable so you can avoid a similar situation? What have you enjoyed in previous or present jobs? Being aware of satisfying factors can be helpful. Using more than your own experiences to make decisions is even more advantageous. In terms of both career and job choices, consider your own work orientation (Derr, 1986). Check the following to see which are significant.

- Valuing upward mobility points to a career field and a job position where you can advance and "move up the ladder."
- Seeking security means you want job security in a stable industry with an established firm.
- Valuing job freedom relates to independence and flexibility to "do your own thing" at work.
- Welcoming risks indicates you want excitement and challenge in your career or job.
- Seeking balance and harmony between personal and professional life indicates you want a career and job that allow time for family and other interests.

The last orientation is a significant one for most people. In fact, the primary career concern of most people is the ability to balance family and work demands (Carrig, 1999). Feeling that your life is out of balance is extremely stressful and a factor in poor job performance. Picture yourself in careers and jobs related to the five identified orientations. Where do you feel most comfortable? Which have little appeal? More than one orientation is possible (TA Revisited).

Other ideas can be used to explain satisfaction in the workplace. You may want to apply Maslow's hierarchy of needs discussed in Chapter 4. If you are struggling with survival, money is a critical factor, and you may postpone other ingredients for satisfaction until your basic needs are met. Because many

---

TA Revisited

The "child" ego state may be tempted by glamorous choices or those that seem fun. "I want to be a truck driver so I can just get behind the wheel and travel and be free as the breeze" is an example of the "child" at work. The student who made this statement, by the way, soon realized that truck driving was not that simple!

"The parent" ego state can send messages of "Get a job—any job—just so you are working" or "Get a job that pays well" or "Be a doctor because your father is one."

"The adult" ego state recognizes the wants and feelings of the "child," analyzes the "parent" messages, and then thoughtfully and logically selects both a career and a job.

individuals are on the self-esteem level, a job that enhances feelings of self-worth would be important.

Considering how many other life choices are influenced by career and job selection, the relationship between professional and personal satisfaction, and the actual time spent at work, your attention to these choices is imperative. How much satisfaction you get from your career and job will directly influence all other aspects of your life. Choose wisely!

Identifying Desirable Personal Qualities and Work Habits

Suppose you own a business and you need employees. What qualities would you seek in your employees? Certain jobs demand special qualities or abilities, yet a common thread of desirable traits runs through most positions. If you have achieved the objectives presented in this book, you possess several of the positive qualities in Table 11-1 listed by employers and career experts. Check to see how many honestly describe you. If you lack any, go back through the book and seek to develop them.

Of utmost importance are interpersonal skills. For workplaces of the present and the future, publications in the United States (Carrig, 1999) and Canada (*Canadian Manager*, 1999) rate interpersonal skills and communication abilities as essential. Executives who eventually fail do so most often because of an interpersonal flaw, not lack of a technical ability (Gibbs, 1995). Workers are often fired for negative personal characteristics and poor interpersonal skills. An employer remarked, "I can help them improve technical skills; however, I do not know how to change a negative attitude and lack of 'people' skills."

As expected, employers list education, training, and experience related to the job as part of the profile of an ideal employee. Other characteristics are **transferable assets,** defined as desirable traits and skills valuable in all career fields and useful in almost every job. Owners and managers have identified the following 10 desirable assets.

Enthusiasm is a quick response. "During an interview, if I do not pick up on some interest and enthusiasm, I will not hire the person, no matter what the other

TABLE 11-1	Positive Personal Qualities and Work Habits
High self-esteem	Understanding of self, including personality and thought-processing
Positive attitude	Freedom from stereotypic thinking
Ability to meet deadlines	Interpersonal communication skills
Ethical character	Ability to feel and manage emotions
Spirit of contributing	Goal orientation and desire to improve
Stress-coping abilities	Sense of responsibility and control
Motivation and action	Ability to give and receive criticism
Ability to see alternatives	Realistic expectations about self and others
A zest for life	Willingness to give positive strokes

skills are," said an owner of an automotive service business. Demonstrating enthusiasm about the career field and the job itself is recommended.

Desire to exert effort is another. During an employers' panel discussion, a child-development student mentioned that she had detassled corn on a farm (a tedious task on a hot summer day). A director of a day care center applauded, "Great! When I have applicants who have stuck with that job, I am convinced that they can work hard—which day care requires." Being a hard worker is a winning quality. Even if you initially lack desired skills, your zest for hard work will compensate, and your efforts will be rewarded.

> Work hard, not only because it will bring you rewards and promotions but because it will give you the sense of being a competent person. (Kushner, 1986, p. 147)

Likability or congeniality, the ability to get along with others, is highly desired. Conflicts will occur; however, people who are congenial and who like others will manage them effectively. Having an appropriate sense of humor is a plus. Qualities such as sensitivity, cooperativeness, and fairness contribute to a positive workplace.

Dependability is invariably a necessity. The fundamental responsibility of any employee is getting to work on time on a regular basis. "I have to be able to count on my employees," says a business owner. "My company has a responsibility to the customers, and they cannot be served if people do not show up." If you have a positive record of attendance and punctuality, be sure to maintain it and use it to your advantage. Dependability goes beyond your physical presence. When you are given a job, can your employer count on you to perform? Productivity is the key to success in businesses and organizations, and hard-working employees are almost always productive. Your employer will expect you to do your share, and if you are interested in advancement, you are wise to do even more.

Three additional qualities go hand in hand and are popular with most employers in today's job market: creativity, innovation, and initiative. *Creativity* is the ability to develop good ideas that can be put into action; it is not confined to artistic pursuits. *Innovation* means change and is closely related to creativity. Being imaginative at work could result in a better product or idea, an easier way to perform a task, or a more spontaneous environment. My husband, a business owner, sees a major contrast between employees who can figure out a way to solve a problem and those who seem to have little ingenuity. You may be thinking that creativity and innovation are rare talents. Keep in mind that everyone has a degree of both, that you can employ each in any job, and that many creative, innovative ideas are simple ones. Critical and creative thinking abilities are a definite plus. Individuals who are ambitious and motivated show *initiative*. Instead of standing around waiting to be told what to do next, they seek productive activity. At times, caution in going ahead is advisable; however, chronic lack of initiative is not appreciated. With almost any job, you can usually find more to do if you look!

Flexibility is like a breath of fresh air. In many work situations, adaptation or adjustment is practical. Jo was considered one of the most valuable employees in an accounting firm, and her flexibility was a major strength. She could adjust her demanding schedule when necessary. During busy times she offered to work overtime or come in early. When new ideas were suggested, she exhibited an open attitude, which made others like her. Being able to "go with the flow" creates possibilities!

"It may seem old-fashioned, but I expect my employees to be loyal," stated the president of a large corporation. *Loyalty* does not necessarily mean that you will never leave a company; however, it does imply that while employed, the employer's best interests will be of concern to you. Speaking negatively about a current or past employer, even if it is deserved, is not recommended.

In contrast to the workplace of years ago, when employees were expected to be "seen and not heard," today's employers value *assertiveness*. There is a difference between being assertive and aggressive. Being aggressive means standing up for yourself in ways that violate the rights of others. Aggressive behavior is typically punishing, hostile, blaming, and demanding. It can involve threats, name-calling, and even actual physical contact. It can also involve sarcasm, catty comments, gossip and "slips of the tongue." In *The Wellness Workbook,* Ryan and Travis (2004) advise, "Assertiveness basically means the ability to express your thoughts and feelings in a way that clearly states your needs and keeps the lines of communication open with the other".

At work, you gain little by being overly aggressive or passive. Lori was determined and ambitious. In business meetings she frequently and loudly interrupted. She was intense and hostile whenever she felt challenged. Her aggressive attitude and behavior made her unpopular and, ironically, blocked the advancement she desired so much. On the other hand, Chad was a "yes" person who was meek and humble. His supervisor and coworkers took advantage of him. At his yearly evaluation he was told he was not ready to move to the management level.

Assertiveness training would have helped both Lori and Chad. On the job, being able to say no to unreasonable requests is important. Otherwise, you can feel overloaded, taken advantage of, and frustrated. Being assertive during an interview can enhance your chances of being hired. Employers share the belief that behaviors during an interview indicate actions on the job.

Keeping in mind these characteristics of valued employees, a practical way of preparing for an interview is to note the qualities and work habits you possess and emphasize them in résumés, cover letters, and interviews. If you can also document when you have displayed them, you stand an even better chance of being the top applicant.

The more positive qualities you demonstrate, the more likely you are to achieve career success. Because individuals differ in their perceptions, success is difficult to define. If you are a positive person who wants to realize your potential, who sets realistic goals, who takes responsibility for yourself, who is nonperfectionistic and strives for excellence, you can be successful. Success can be a feeling of having done as well as you could; see it as a process, not as a final destination.

I'M LOOK'N FOR A SOFT DESK JOB...
LIKE YOURS

Figure 11-3

Choosing Wisely: From the Job Search to Retirement

As in all areas of life, you have and will continue to have any number of choices regarding careers and jobs. Specific choices are related to the stage of your career.

The Search Itself

You may not recognize that you have a choice about how you will go about the job search itself. The majority of job hunters simply look. They do not prepare and seemingly give little thought to the process. The first step is to know yourself and what you have to offer. To help you, complete the "Assets and Liabilities" exercise in Reflections and Applications. Does it seem sensible to spend years gaining knowledge in order to get the job you want and then fail to do so because your job-seeking skills are inadequate? Most individuals who are looking for jobs confine their search to the classified ads in a newspaper. Would it surprise you to know that most available jobs on any given day are not advertised? If you only answer ads, you are tapping into a small share of the job market.

According to Pat Sims, a personnel specialist, many job applicants are unprepared. They do not have any idea of what job they want, know nothing about the business, lack the information needed to fill out an application, and do not even bring a pen. "Several bring their babies, and a few even have pets with them!" Their choice, seemingly, has been to approach the job hunt in a lackadaisical way. Employers will be inclined to believe they will handle their jobs similarly.

Being prepared can make the difference between enjoyment and displeasure in your job search and between success and failure in your career. Begin with research into career and job possibilities and expand into the "how to" of finding a position. An increasingly rich source of information is online. You are also wise to use the Internet to actually search for openings and to post your résumé and cover letter. In regard to these important written pieces, impressive ways of presenting yourself are essential and worthy of your attention. (Hanna, 2002). See Resources at the end of this chapter for some online recommendations (Fig. 11-3).

Most never actually *learn* how to interview. Being unprepared for a job interview can lead to a stressful situation in which you give a less than positive impression of yourself. A common problem has to do with responses that negate or qualify the interviewee.

Jamie was nervous. When asked what her work experiences had been, she replied, "Well, uh, I have not done much except work in a restaurant—really

REFLECT AND APPLY

Reflect

♦ *What do you want in a job? Think of at least three things that you are seeking in a job.*

♦ *In what other geographic location would you be satisfied? What type of work would you want to do there?*

♦ *How would you reply to the interview question: "What are your career goals?"*

Apply

♦ *Ask someone who has begun her or his career: "What is most satisfying? What don't you like, if anything?"*

♦ *List five of your transferable assets.*

♦ *Write an employment ad that describes job duties you would want.*

nothing in the secretarial field." The final question was "Why should we hire you over the other applicants?" She blushed and stammered, "Well, I do not think you know I am better than others so I do not really know uh, I feel I could do a good job, I guess."

Contrast this poor performance with a well-prepared job applicant.

Jamie faced the interviewer with a smile and a look of confidence. When asked about work experience, she replied, "I have worked for two years in a busy restaurant. I developed many interpersonal skills as I waited on customers. I think these skills will be valuable in secretarial work. During college I had simulated office experience, which I really enjoyed." In response to the final question, she replied, "I have my secretarial degree and had many hands-on experiences during my training. My work experience has helped me develop many 'people' skills. I am dependable, positive, friendly, enthusiastic about my career, and very interested in this job."

This impressive interview would not have occurred if Jamie had not prepared by anticipating the questions and rehearsing her answers. Going to a job interview with no preparation can be as disastrous as jumping into deep water not knowing how to swim. If you have an opportunity to take a course to help you build confidence, write a better application, prepare a résumé, and learn to interview, take advantage of it. Detailed information is available in books such as *Career by Design: Communicating Your Way to Success* (Hanna, 2002) (Reflect and Apply).

Because rejection is an inevitable part of most job searches, it is wise to decide how you will handle it. Even though you may be offered the first position you want, for most it is realistic to visualize a job search as a series of "no's" finally followed by a "yes." Important to remember is that a "no" is not a rejection of you personally but merely an assessment of a match between you and the position. Thought-changing can do wonders. Do not think, "Something is wrong with me." Instead, say to yourself, "They sure missed an opportunity to have a first-rate employee. It's their loss!" Then choose to move forward to a better job.

Your Career Path

Worth thinking about before you accept a job is where it may lead. Several decisions will be made during your work life that will dramatically influence the direction of your career path.

Career goals.   Just as you could not plan a trip without knowing the destination, you are unwise to begin a career unless you know your objective. This decision does not have to be made immediately; yet thinking about it can be beneficial. Young people may have aspirations of owning a business or being the head of a company, yet they have not seriously considered what is required to get there and whether they would like what they will find upon arriving. Ask yourself whether you enjoy being in charge and making final decisions. Are you willing to give the time and effort required to achieve higher positions? Advancement is rewarding, yet sometimes the status achieved is not worth the price.

Many overlook the need to integrate career and personal plans. Chris started his own business thinking that he would now be his own boss, be in charge of his life, and not have to work so many hours. He soon discovered that he had many bosses—his customers! He found little time to spend with family. Both his business and his personal life began to suffer. He made a difficult decision to sell the business he had recently established and accept a position elsewhere that did not interfere with his family life.

Another sound reason to establish career goals is because this information is frequently asked in a job interview. Having no goals or poorly defined ones is a liability. Also important is to have goals compatible with what the interviewing employer can offer. "I want to travel on the job, have relocation possibilities, and then eventually start my own business" could be the "kiss of death."

Advancement.   If you decide that you want to advance into different positions, planning becomes significant. First, select employment in which promotion possibilities exist. Then do the following:

- Perform as well as you can and do more than what is expected.
- Take advantage of learning and growth opportunities.
- Display professionalism and demonstrate a high degree of ethics.
- Document your accomplishments and keep your résumé updated.
- Research carefully.

The latter is important because promotion just for advancement's sake may lead to job dissatisfaction. Most of us have been convinced that upward mobility is essential; however, this can lead into jobs we either do not like or don't do well. Granted you may be required to take a position with responsibilities that is not satisfying on the way to a position that is. Be sure that your final goal is where you want to be.

The goal-setting techniques outlined in Chapter 3 work well in charting your career path. Action steps are a necessity. Some students write expansive career goals, such as "I plan to make a million dollars and retire within five years." The critical question is, "How are you going to do this?"

Keeping records.   Maintaining a personal career file is one of the most practical and worthwhile things you can do, yet many people neglect this. One day a frantic former student called: "Did you keep our résumés on file?" My negative reply resulted in a plaintive outburst, "I threw all my stuff from the class away, and I need a résumé right now!" Another individual missed an application deadline because he did not have a copy of his transcripts to submit. Poor organization makes the job search more time-consuming and stressful.

Making contacts.   **Networking,** establishing contacts that may be helpful, can help you get a desired job, advance in your career, and change your job or career. Occasionally, a job seeker will balk at the idea of getting a job through contacts. "I do not want to be hired because of whom I know but on the basis of my abilities," a man said. He was assured that even Albert Einstein found a job after graduation only through the father of one of his classmates (Fisher et al., 1977), a classic example of whom you know being, perhaps, as important as what you know. Besides, you probably will not be hired, even with the best contacts, if you are not qualified. Contacts that can be used as references and sources of job leads and influential sponsors are tremendous resources throughout your career. Begin building your network immediately. A good idea is to exchange business cards with people and keep them in a file. Almost everyone likes to help others. Cultivating multiple and diverse relationships in order to build a "personal board of directors" is recommended by Linda Hill, Ph.D., Harvard Business School (1994).

Continued learning.   Some students are surprised to realize that their education is not over when they earn a degree. Take advantage of educational and skills-building opportunities. Lifelong learners are invariably career-success winners. A worthwhile question to ask in an employment interview is what further educational opportunities are encouraged or provided. Even if the employer does not pay for these, show that you are determined to continue to learn and grow and then do so. Also emphasize how important learning is to you.

Leadership.   Training to become a leader will help in several ways. You may then decide that you really don't want to lead, or you may acquire the skills that differentiate effective leaders from poor ones. Being an effective leader is an art that goes beyond successful job performance. Described in a presentation by Brian Tracy, who is a successful business executive, leadership consists of seven qualities: vision, courage, integrity, commitment, responsibility, concentration, and excellence. As ideal as this list sounds, an outstanding leader has even more obvious behaviors: effective communicating, organizing, delegating, seeing that responsibilities are carried out, giving and receiving constructive criticism, praising employees, and promoting teamwork.

As a leader, you will be expected to make tough decisions, including those of hiring and firing. A strong feeling (F) preference on the Myers-Briggs Type Indicator is a hindrance in this regard. Using more of the thinking (T) preference is necessary. Able leadership requires much more than desire. The rewards can certainly be worth the effort it takes to develop the skills.

Challenges at work.   On the job you will periodically face challenges not directly related to the work you do. Prejudice and discrimination based on such factors as age, sex, race, ethnicity, sexual orientation, and disability are possible. **Sexual harassment**—any uninvited and undesired verbal or physical behavior related to sexuality—is of concern in today's work environment

To avoid being a harasser, assume that off-color jokes and sexual advances are not welcomed, recognize that a "no" means just that, and ask how you would feel if you or someone you cared for was harassed. Faulty communication is a factor in perceived harassment (Markert, 1999). You can take responsibility for sending and receiving clear messages. To handle harassment, be assertive and let the person know the behaviors are not acceptable, talk to someone about any incident, document both the harassment and your own job performance, seek witnesses, go through appropriate channels, and use the legal system, if necessary (Bravo and Cassedy, 1992).

Being sensitive to others by refraining from degrading comments and language is the fair and decent way to behave. Challenging your own stereotypes and eliminating personal prejudice will make this easier. Acceptance and equal treatment of others are keystones of positive interpersonal relations.

Concerns such as discrimination, equal pay for equal work, comparable worth, maternity and paternity leave, and quality child care have arisen and will continue to be consequential. Controversial issues such as drug testing, disease screening, and smoking policies will necessitate difficult organizational and personal decisions. Stay abreast of new developments, be objective, remain aware of the concerns, and be open to possible solutions.

Career and job changes.   If you are unhappy at work or if a better opportunity arises, you will probably consider a change. Changing jobs is common, and even switching careers is not unusual. The average person can expect to change careers 5 to 7 times and jobs up to 12 times (Shakoor, 2000). A career change demands more thought and planning than a job change and is usually riskier. Look objectively at your present situation and note the costs of a career move as compared with the benefits. Critical thinking is helpful. As with any change, stress is a by-product, and any resulting satisfaction and pleasure are well deserved.

Retirement.   The end of a career seems far away for most people; however, the most effective and productive planning for retirement is started years before a career ends. Women who have depended on a husband for their financial well-being are especially at risk. More than 80 percent of retired women are not eligible for pension benefits, and only 47 percent of working women participate in a pension plan. It is no wonder that nearly 75 percent of the elderly poor are women (U.S. Department of Labor 2006).

Both sexes often avoid planning for a retirement life style that can bring similar rewards to those gained from work. About 63 percent of adults have never discussed retirement needs with a professional financial advisor (Lach, 2000) and about 17 percent of workers in their 40s say they have not begun to save for retirement (Clifford, 2000). Thoughtful decisions will make the transition from a career orientation to retirement a positive experience. The earlier a person begins to invest, the better. A 22-year-old who saves $50 a week at an 8 percent return will have almost $1 million by age 65. Waiting a year reduces this amount almost $77,000 (Chandler, 2001). Because people are living longer, you are wise to prepare carefully and then continue to be productive throughout your life span.

From the initial career and job selections to retirement, your career path will bring joy and sorrow, elation and disappointment. Each stage requires choices, and you owe it to yourself to consider all possibilities and make thoughtful decisions about this significant part of your life.

Enjoying Relationships at Work

To whom will you relate as you pursue your career? With whom will you interact on the job? Countless possibilities exist. Let's follow Antonio, a surgical technologist, through part of his workday.

> Antonio said hello to three other employees as he entered the building. In the elevator he exchanged small talk with others. He met briefly with his supervisor and a nurse. He offered a reassuring word to a nervous patient. Later in the morning he had coffee with two coworkers. At lunch he complimented a cafeteria worker on the array of fresh fruit. During the afternoon he met with other members of the surgical team. Before the day was over, he had interacted with approximately 40 people. In almost any job you will have numerous relationships that are enhanced by your positive behaviors.

Personality Types at Work

An understanding of personality preferences from the Myers-Briggs Type Indicator, discussed in Chapter 2, can help you relate better to others. There are no good or bad types, only different ones, according to the book *Type Talk at Work* (Kroeger and Thuesen, 1993), which profiles personalities in the workplace. Also helpful is the book *Work Types* (Kummerow, Barger, and Dirby, 1997). Both describe temperament types that were covered in Chapter 2. Understanding personality differences and being able to utilize others' strengths will make enjoyment of work more probable.

Positive Relations

If you possess most of the positive qualities of a valued employee described in this chapter and are practicing the skills outlined in previous chapters, you will be able to cultivate positive relationships with those in your work environment. Some specific behaviors are especially important.

Give appropriate affirmations.   Positive verbal and nonverbal acknowledgments of others can create a warm atmosphere and be rewarding to you in return. People generally react favorably to a sincere positive stroke. Although we miss many opportunities to affirm others, the workplace provides several. In addition to verbal praise, a written or e-mail thank-you, congratulations, or acknowledgment will likely be well received. Praise is a powerful motivator for most people, so if you are in a supervisory position, make it your ally.

Appreciate diversity.   Today's work world is a mosaic composed of various ethnic, racial, religious, and age groups. Review and continue to remind yourself of the recommendations regarding prejudice and appreciation of diversity given in Chapter 10. Except for some educational institutions, the workplace offers the most opportunities for interactions with all types of people. Take advantage of opportunities to meet and get to know those who reflect cultural diversity. Your career will benefit, and your life will be enriched!

Be helpful and supportive.   Opportunities abound to provide help and support to others. Little actions mean a lot. In some cases, more is demanded. If a coworker is ill, handling additional tasks may be in order. Helping new employees learn their duties may take time but will be appreciated. If your job brings you into contact with people in stressful situations, realize that what you say and do not say and how you behave will make the situation better or worse. Knowing when to offer help and when to suggest professional help is important.

Be friendly and considerate.   Congeniality and regard for others create a more positive work environment and usually bring rewards to the employee. The simple act of greeting may have an impact. Calling a person by name is an added positive behavior. If remembering names is difficult, you might want to try mental association. A man named John had a punctuality problem. Associating him with "Johnny Come Lately" was a simple trick! Another technique is to repeat the person's name. When introduced, say, "I am happy to meet you, Bob." During the time you are together, call Bob by name as often as practical and use it again when you say good-bye. When you are new in a job, you will probably meet several people immediately. In addition to repetition and association, you might write the names, check their names on a company list or directory, and rehearse them mentally. Do not be afraid to ask them to say their names for you again (Fig. 11-4).

Several other gestures are possible. Ask questions and express interest in others. Just be sure you do not go beyond what are sensible inquiries. Consideration means you will be careful to avoid irritating others. In a small office area, Jeff had his radio set on a loud rock-and-roll station. Four employees shared one phone extension, and Rhonda spent several minutes at a time making personal calls. Neither worker was considerate. Approachability checking, as recommended in Chapter 10, is appreciated in the work environment. Because time is a valuable commodity, a considerate person does not assume that a coworker or supervisor is available at all times (Fig. 11-5).

Figure 11-4   Positive relationships enhance the workplace.

The Power of Support

See if you can recognize the helpful and unhelpful, supportive and nonsupportive behaviors in each of the following situations.

- The nurse gave me a reassurinFIGg smile and said, "Do not worry. We see many patients with these tumors, and we know what we are doing!" This was such a relief after being told that mine was a rare cancer.
- The world-renowned specialist muttered to himself and to the medical students who were observing the scan of my eye, "Melanoma does not look like it, but I do not know what else it could be." My stress level was at an all-time high. I knew what melanoma cancer was. I kept thinking, "Does he know that I can hear him?"
- The young radiologist greeted me warmly. Before the scans, she calmly explained to me what she was doing and what would happen. I thought that she was wise beyond her years and seemed to be aware of the psychological studies that show that the impact of stress is lessened when people know what to expect.
- The young doctor in residency said a brief hello and then sat behind a desk and looked at what appeared to be my medical records. I was there for a postoperative visit. For 10 long minutes he did not look at me or say anything except an occasional "Hmmm" as he read and cracked his knuckles! This was another stressful situation in which behaviors of a specialist created more tension.

Figure 11-5

Customer relations are considered the "bottom line" by business owners. Employees who turn customers away or even create negative impressions are usually fired. Being a positive salesperson or company representative is not easy and requires determination, patience, and an understanding of human behavior. As an example, do you like to stand in line for service and then have another customer who just arrived be taken care of first? A sensitive employee would note who was there first - or, if necessary, ask. As much as possible, the best employees avoid letting customers wait.

Other tips include treating the customer as if your roles were reversed, greeting individuals with a smile, listening attentively and actively to the customer's request or complaint, handling complaints in an accommodating and cheerful manner, and asking whether your service was satisfactory. All this may sound difficult, and customer relations are definitely a challenge. Remember that you will be rewarded for your efforts. The reward may come not from others but from your own inner self saying, "Great job!"

Interactions with customers or clients are often on the telephone. Modern technology has created some devices that can be helpful yet can also diminish positive impressions. For example, do you recall being put on hold without even being asked whether you wanted to be? Effective telephone skills can be learned and deserve attention. No matter how or when a customer feels slighted or demeaned, the company or organization suffers.

Do your fair share as well as you can.   In most jobs, you are part of a team with a contribution to make. Lazy workers are not wanted, and an inefficient team member is a detriment. While you are at work, your responsibility is to the job at hand. Maria worked in a law office as a word processing specialist. When the attorneys were gone, she used her time to play games on her computer. She was surprised when another employee told her how offensive her behavior was. Be sure not to cheat your employer and yourself in the long run by just getting by.

Be positive and realize the contributions of others.   Employees with positive attitudes are greatly appreciated. Seeing the bright side of a situation helps everyone. In every company or organization, some times are busier and more stressful than others. You may be tempted to think that your job is the most demanding. Picture this scenario: Kent and Roberto are on their break in the cafeteria. Let's listen to their conversation:

KENT: I am so busy I do not know heads from tails. All the quarterly reports I have to do are really getting to me.

ROBERTO: Just be glad you do not have to fill all the orders that are coming in now. I probably will not even have time to take a break later. You think you guys have it rough. If I have to field one more irate phone call, I think I will find an easier job.

As they are busily trying to "one-up" each other, another employee walks by the cafeteria and thinks, "I do not see how those two have time to take a break. They must not have nearly as much work to do as I do!" Did you recognize the "one-upping" comments? Realizing that you aren't the only one with a heavy load and acknowledging others' workloads would be a refreshing change from this scene. Receptive listening is as important at work as it is in other situations.

Manage conflict effectively.   Despite your best attempts to create positive relationships, disagreement will occur. You have choices. In several situations, your best bet is to ignore the irritation. Most work environments have at least one annoying employee, and even those who are not disagreeable will occasionally bother you. Keep in mind that your behavior is not at the mercy of another person. Only you can determine your actions. Using techniques to defuse your frustration and anger can turn potentially hostile situations into harmless ones.

At other times, avoiding an irritant is not advisable, and your time is well spent trying to resolve the conflict. Familiarize yourself with the chain of command. Be honest and address legitimate concerns. Complaining without suggesting alternatives is not advised, although voicing a concern may be advantageous. If perceived mistreatment comes from a supervisor, you are wise to address it; however, do not let your anger control the situation. All that may be needed is an "I" statement describing your annoyance or the perception-checking technique that was explained in Chapter 9. If criticized, using the suggested responses from Chapter 9 can keep the level of conflict manageable. The key is open communication. If more efforts are required, a negotiation strategy, as described in Chapter 10, can create a positive outcome.

Conflict management techniques, discussed elsewhere in Chapters 10 and 12, can be applied to work situations. Understanding is more likely if people recognize personality differences. No type excels at handling conflict; in fact, disagreeable situations can magnify of our preferences. I recall explaining to a strong ESTJ type that what she had said to a coworker whose type was ESFP had indeed been insensitive. "Why would anyone be hurt by that?" she asked. Even after accepting that it could have hurt, she considered it a sign of weakness and illogical for her to apologize. The ESFP, in turn, had difficulty accepting that the lack of apology was not just a sign of dislike and rudeness.

The section in Chapter 10 on dealing with difficult people can also be helpful. What if the difficult person is your boss or supervisor? How to recognize, understand, and cope with a difficult boss is covered in the book *Coping with Difficult Bosses* (Bramson, 1992). Griping with fellow employees is not recommended. Ask yourself what the person does that is bothersome, what your specific goals or objectives are, and what other people might need to be involved. As you decide on an action plan, you are wise to use a cost versus benefits approach. If you determine after a reasonable period of time that your supervisor is intolerable and you have done all you can to improve the relationship, seek other employment possibilities.

Your degree of satisfaction on the job is greatly influenced by the quality of relationships. The time and effort you spend improving them are well worth it!

LOOKING BACK

- Human beings are typically identified by their career and job choices.
- Career and job satisfaction have a tremendous impact, and thoughtful decisions influence the quality of life.
- Try not to limit your choices and then begin your search by knowing yourself well. Identify your interests, likes, abilities, values, personality, coping skills, and work orientations.
- After career and job choices have been made, possessing and using the personal qualities and work habits desired by employers can make success much more likely.
- Throughout your career you will have choices. Whether and how you prepare for the job search is one of the first ones. A well-prepared job seeker has a much better chance of landing a desired position.
- As you proceed along your career path, you will be faced with many decisions. Recognizing options and making wise choices lead to success.
- Building numerous relationships is common during one's career. Several behaviors can promote positive relations.
- As in all walks of life, if you know yourself well, have a high regard for yourself, demonstrate a positive attitude, gather information, use thought-processing, are open and flexible, and can recognize and deal with adversity, you will direct your career path to success.

That which distinguishes the good teachers from the mediocre teachers is primarily not method, style, or personality—but attitude. They consistently project a positive attitude toward each student as an individual and toward the subject being taught. From such teachers, students intuitively receive the message: You are important, and it's important to me that you learn.

—Bob Resz

RESOURCES

Career counseling and placement services at colleges and universities
Service Corps of Retired Executives (SCORE) 800-634-0245. http://www.score.org (local groups provide free business counseling)
Online sources
Bureau of Labor Statistics: http://stats.bls.gov
The Career Interests Game: http://career.missouri.edu
Europages, The European Business Directory: http://www.europages.com
John Holland's Self-Directed Search: http://www.self-directed-search.com
JobHunters Bible: http://www.jobhuntersbible.com
JOBTRAK: http://www.jobtrak.com
Monster Board: http://www.monster.com
Occupational Outlook Handbook: http://www.stats.bl.gov/oco
O*Net Online: http://online.onetcenter.org
The Riley Guide: http://www.rileyguide.com
The Salary Calculator at Homefair: http://www.homefair.com/Find_A_Place/Calculators/SalaryCalc/index.asp
Salary Wizard: http://www.salary.com
Small Business Administration: http://www.sba.gov/starting

12 DEVELOPING AND ENRICHING INTIMATE RELATIONSHIPS

LOOKING AHEAD

After completing this chapter, you will be able to

- Explain love and the various types of love.
- Recognize obstacles to love.
- Explain the relationship growth and needs fulfillment theory.
- Discuss the barriers, benefits, and development of intimacy.
- Identify ideas for sexual fulfillment.
- Explain marriage in terms of definition and images.
- Tell how couples can prepare for marriage.
- Explain several factors related to marital success.
- Realize that relationships end and explain how couples can go their separate ways in a manner that will benefit both parties.

> *From "I' and "me" to "us" and "we." Your relationships will be as vital and alive as you are. Love is life in all of its aspects and if you miss love, you miss life. Please don't.*
>
> —Leo Buscaglia

"I love you" is a statement that is responsible for experiences of joy as well as despair. To love and be loved is desired by all human beings. Two intriguing books, *Love and Survival* (Ornish, 1998) and *A Cry Unheard* (Lynch, 2000), present evidence that love and interpersonal relationships are critical elements in our health and well-being.

To achieve intimacy within a relationship is to realize the deepest meaning of love. How much do you know about love and intimacy? If you have had little education in these areas, you are not alone. Intimacy has been either ignored or assumed to be so natural that thinking or talking about it is unnecessary. Or it has been incorrectly defined as sexual relations. Consequently, people may have difficulty with their intimate relationships. This chapter will delve into love and intimate relationships. You can use it as a springboard to education in what, for most people, are the most important aspects of their lives.

What is Love?

In writing, music, painting, and the performing arts, love is a major theme. In recent years, research has contributed to our understanding of love. Books and courses are available to help people make wise decisions about love and intimacy. Does studying love take away from the spontaneity or uniqueness of a relationship? "This does not seem very romantic to me," grumbled a woman when she was asked to answer questions about her love relationship. Regardless of one's perception of what is romantic, knowledge and understanding of love and intimacy build a strong foundation for a meaningful relationship.

Love is an art (Fromm, 1956). If you want to have a fulfilling love relationship, first acquire information about love. Meeting the right person does not teach us to love. We must learn about love just as we must learn about other skills (Wegscheider-Cruse, 1988). Because love varies from one culture to another, varies in meaning from one era to another, and even shifts within a single relationship as individuals mature, definitive answers may be impossible. However, we can identify obstacles, types, and components of love as well as important elements of intimacy.

Identifying Obstacles to Love and Intimacy

Individuals can want to love and be loved and still fail miserably. At times, they believe that they are in love, and the results are disappointing and painful. You can shift the odds in the favor of success if you know the potential obstacles.

Low Self-Esteem

The foundation for all love relationships is self-love. The eloquent expressions of other writers concerning the relationship between self-esteem and healthy love for another can benefit anyone who desires a love relationship.

> A positive self-image, a sturdy self-esteem, and a love of self set us free to love others. (Viorst, 1986, p. 55)
> The first love affair we must consummate successfully is the love affair with ourselves. Without respect for who I am and enjoyment in what I am, I have very little to give. If I do not feel that I am lovable, it is very difficult to believe that anyone else loves me. (Branden and Branden, 1982, p. 40)
> One who seeks in another the sense of worth one cannot find in oneself is likely to be disappointed. We cannot find salvation in a relationship. (Sternberg, 1987, p. 275)

Why is low self-esteem so detrimental to love relationships? Sandra Murray states that people with low self-esteem are doubly at risk of feeling vulnerable in a relationship (*Psychology Today*, 1999). When a relationship fails, self-worth diminishes even further. Either an individual will be needy and feel helpless in the grips of passionate love or will devalue the other. Two women describe low self-esteem problems:

Luanne: As I grew and changed, he did all he could to knock me down. He was insecure and could not stand the thought of my growing and being able to manage without him. I hate to admit that it worked. I easily slipped back to our old roles. I can see now where my low self-esteem allowed him to continue to rule me. After almost 10 years and 2 children, I decided I could not take it and left.

Elizabeth: My relationship with my ex-husband could easily be described as "walking on eggshells." I analyzed my thoughts before speaking and was not negative about anything (due to his low self-esteem). I felt my self-worth being dragged down to his level. This is ironic considering it was my optimism and strong sense of self that drew him to me. I finally realized I had to get out to save "me."

Low self-esteem sets the stage for unhealthy behaviors, including manipulation, unfair fighting, extreme negative reactions to criticism, and extended periods of silence, temper tantrums, and abuse. People with low self-esteem feel unworthy of love. They believe that sooner or later, they will lose their lover. Because of their fear of rejection, they frequently bring about the very situation they dread. Their lives become self-fulfilling prophecies (Porat, 1988).

In contrast, high self-esteem creates an attitude that you deserve the finest. This belief influences your behavior and the outcome. Mark confided: "I always said I could never live without her, but I have found that I can. This class has helped me a lot because it has taught me that I deserve better than her." Margaret reported a dramatic experience.

> I used to hate myself. I was told that I was not good enough, was stupid, and would never amount to anything. In six years my ex-husband gave me 27 fractures, killed my second baby in uteri, and then started on my daughter when she was less than two years of age. In order for him to feel powerful, he would bring me down to his level or lower. Then a "feeling" came over me. It wasn't me who was all these things; it was him. I finally realized I was a worthwhile person. I loved and trusted myself enough not to need his sick love, and I sneaked out with baby in my arms.

Margaret learned an essential lesson—that she deserved much better. *Being* the right person is what is important—not *finding* the right person (Ornish, 1998). You can eliminate a major barrier to a healthy love relationship by raising your self-esteem level and choosing a partner who values herself or himself.

Extensive Giving and Addiction

"If you love, you give and give and give" is a belief that persists. "Sacrifice is what love is all about" was the resigned explanation of a 56-year-old woman who did not appear to be loved or loving. Women accepted and lived the sacrificial role more often than men. The past influences the present, and in spite of women's quest for equality and independence, the tendency for many women is to give more than men do. These thoughts are reflected in comments from young female students.

Lisa: I found myself constantly building him up and reassuring him of my love at my expense.

Staci: The part of me that attracted him to me in the beginning I unknowingly gave up. That was ME, my personality, my independence, my self-security.

I was, I thought, so much in love, and to show it, I tried to be everything I thought he wanted me to be. In doing so, I was no longer ME, the person he was attracted to.

Jill: I was *so* in love with him that I forgot the things I wanted and focused only on what he wanted.

Addictive and codependent relationships have usually focused on women's loving too much. Men do not necessarily equate this endless giving with love and often grow to resent it. Men don't feel grateful; they feel suffocated (Cowan and Kinder, 1987).

For both sexes, a cultural factor is Americans' preoccupation with obsessive and violent love (White and Bondurant, 1996). Novels, television, movies, and music depict love-crazed individuals who resort to aggression and violent acts in the name of love. Although the obsessed person may call his or her addiction "love," obsessive love has little to do with real love (Forward, 1991). One of the greatest stress producers is the feeling of subservience and lack of control that is characteristic of obsessive love.

Relationships that are based on misconceptions of love take their toll. In addition to psychological costs, a pressing concern in American society is abuse—whether it's physical, sexual, or emotional—that is found in addictive and obsessive relationships. An enlightening book on the subject is *When Men Batter Women: New Insights into Ending Abusive Relationships* (Jacobson and Gottman, 1998a). Those who are highly dependent on their partners seem to tolerate more physical violence. Sharon, who entered college at age 41, expressed it candidly:

Being married to an abusive alcoholic left nothing for "me." There simply was no "me." There was only what he wanted. My basic need was mere survival.

Recent attention has focused on intimate or "common-couple" violence among heterosexuals. This type is engaged in equally by both men and women. The difference is that women are more likely to be injured than men (DeMaris, 2001). Violence is also present in the relationships of same-sex couples, although incidents are rarely reported (Huwig, 2001). Depending on the survey, 17 percent to 46 percent of lesbians and gay men report abuse by a current or former partner (Office for the Prevention of Domestic Violence, 2003). A sobering finding is that battering seldom stops on its own (Jacobson and Gottman, 1998b). Couples who truly care about their relationship do not put it at risk by physically hurting each other.

Verbal aggression is an even more common type of abuse. **Verbal aggression** is verbal or nonverbal communication intended to cause psychological pain to another person or communication perceived as having that intent. Obsessive love and a verbally abusive relationship share characteristics of inequality, manipulation, hostility, and control. For a review of how to handle verbal abuse, see Chapter 10.

Why would anyone remain in an abusive relationship? The answers are not simple. Reasons given by abused persons who stay in an abusive relationship are lack of financial resources, lack of job security, fear of losing their children, lack of support services in the community, and fear of being alone. Immigrants may fear losing immigrant status and being deported. Some experts believe that women can suffer from what is called **battered woman syndrome,** a type of posttraumatic stress disorder. After so much abuse, they are stripped of self-esteem and falsely believe they need their husbands in order to survive (Jacobson and Gottman, 1998a). Violence at the hands of a partner adversely affects the victim's sense of control (Umberson et al., 1998), making it extremely difficult to break the cycle. Debra described her experience as follows:

> I gave, and he took. I became his "mother," someone to take care of him and solve his problems. I thought that was what love truly meant, that I would only be important if I was needed by and doing for someone else. My needs or wants never entered my mind. I just plain did not exist. He did not want me to work, and he "hit on" every female I brought to the house so I stopped associating with my friends. I did not trust him to care for the children for even an hour on his own so I stayed home. He kept me where he wanted me, and I let him. I despised the fact that even when he hurt me to the point I could not see because my eyes were swollen shut or could not talk because my jaw was broken, I still did not have enough courage to move out. It seems now that I never blamed him—only me—which was fine with him. He got fired from one of many jobs, slammed me against a wall, and I packed his bags. He left, and later the hospital called. He had tried to kill himself. I remember going to see him, and the first words I spoke were, "What have *I* done?" I let Debra be destroyed.

Fortunately, Debra became strong enough to leave, return to school, and begin a new life.

Although most people view only women as the victims in an abusive relationship, research indicates that males can be victims of relationship violence. In his 1975 and 1985 National Family Violence Surveys, Straus (*Psychology Today*, 1999) stated that 12.4 percent of women have assaulted their spouses, compared to 12.2 percent of men. When it comes to severe assaults, the numbers were 4.6 percent for women and 5 percent for men. Irene Frieze (*Psychology Today*, 1999) conducted a survey of college students in dating situations. Of the college students she surveyed, 58 percent of women had assaulted their dates compared to 55 percent of men. Men tend not to report spousal abuse at the same rate as women; partly because they diminish the impact themselves and partly because society, media, police, and courts also tend to diminish its impact.

To see if you may be involved in an abusive relationship, honestly answer the following questions (Forward and Torres, 1986):

- Does the person assume the right to control how you live and behave?
- Have you given up important activities or people in your life in order to keep this person happy?
- Does the person devalue your opinions, your feelings, and your accomplishments?
- Does the person yell, threaten, or withdraw into angry silence when you displease him or her?
- Do you "walk on eggs," rehearsing what you will say so as not to set the person off?
- Does the person bewilder you by switching from charm to rage without warning?
- Do you often feel confused, off balance, or inadequate?
- Is the person extremely jealous and possessive?
- Does the person blame you for everything that goes wrong?

If you answered yes to any of these questions, analyze the relationship carefully. If you answered yes to most of the questions, you are in an unhealthy relationship. People often harbor the misguided belief that the other will change, which usually doesn't happen.

Trying to love someone else before you have yourself in tune is as potentially disastrous as beginning a long journey in a poorly equipped, rundown automobile. Positive relationships demand average or better self-esteem and lack of dependency and addiction. Chad's description of a past relationship is an enlightening account of a person's reaction to obsessive love and can serve as a warning to its victims.

> I ended a relationship because she was not independent at all. She could not make decisions without my advice. She would sit home waiting for me to call while I went out with my friends. She just put her friends out of the picture. Then when I called, she tried to make me feel guilty for having fun without her. She also called me at all hours of the night because she said she just wanted to hear my voice. I wanted to get some sleep! If she had not been so obsessive, things might have worked out.

He wrote about his needs in any future relationship: "She must be able to live for herself and not become a person who lives for me. I do not want a person who thinks the world revolves around me." Until obsession and addiction are no longer considered love, people will make tragic mistakes. The challenge is for both women and men to recognize the difference and to resist thoughts and behaviors that spawn these unhealthy relationships.

Love Schemas

What do you expect from a love relationship? A **love schema** is a mental model consisting of expectations and attitudes about love. Six love schemas have been identified by Hatfield and Rapson (1996). See if you can determine which ones represent obstacles to love.

1. *Secure:* is comfortable with both closeness and independence
2. *Clingy:* desires a high level of closeness and togetherness
3. *Skittish:* is uneasy with closeness; will often run away from intimacy
4. *Fickle:* is never satisfied with the present relationship for long
5. *Casual:* enjoys relationships but doesn't want to be committed
6. *Uninterested:* simply is not interested in any relationship

People formulate ideas about love that usually change over time. Jacob's schema fit the casual category. He enjoyed being with Emily, who, at 25 years of age, wanted to be in a committed relationship. They went their separate ways for 3 years, and then resumed dating. This time around Jacob wanted commitment, and within a few years, they were married.

Fear of Risks

Any relationship is risky. Love is even riskier. Deep self-disclosure leaves a person vulnerable. Some pain is inevitable, and accepting this reality is healthy. In positive relationships the benefits of loving and being loved will far outweigh the pain. Without risk, individuals reduce their hurts, yet they also decrease the potential for happiness. I could decide to stay indoors for the rest of my life because there are risks of getting hurt outside. Would not you question this decision? Resisting a potentially happy relationship because of the possibility of hurt is equally debatable.

Risks of pain are less if you keep self-esteem independent of the relationship. "When our sense of worth whether we feel lovable or not depends on the response of some other person to us, we are off balance. We can do nothing but fall" (Kennedy, 1975, p. 94). With self-love, you can separate the end of a relationship from a rejection of self. The idea that you are unlovable because someone no longer wants to continue a love relationship with you is false.

Lack of Knowledge

The assumption that you don't need to know about love, that "it just happens" and then all is well, has pervaded people's thinking. "An individual can get a college degree today without ever having learned anything about how to communicate, how to resolve conflict, and what to do with anger and other negative feelings. Basic, to my mind, is the need for learning to be partners" (Rogers, 1972, p. 216).

Only in recent years have researchers studied love. Difficulty in defining the term was one of the obstacles. There are almost as many definitions of love as people willing to research it (Coleman and Ganong, 1985). When asked to define love, over 60 percent of nearly 400 college students described it strictly in emotional terms. It appears that education about love and intimacy is needed, and if emphasized (which could even mean required training), could provide the necessary understanding of and tools for building satisfying relationships. In the meantime, individuals can seek education on their own and then practice what they learn in developing loving relationships.

Recognizing Different Types of Love

Types of love can be distinguished. Keeping love as simple as possible, we will focus on two general types: passionate love and intimate love. Realize that other researchers and writers may use different words in describing types of love, such as immature and mature love, which are used by Gordon (1996).

Passionate Love

Sensations and unrealistic notions of love are at the heart of **passionate love.** Experts on passionate love describe it as a "hot," intense emotion, sometimes called a crush, infatuation, or being in love; it is an intense longing for union with another (Hatfield and Rapson, 1996). Young people become aware of this type and then define love in terms of sensations: "Love is the feeling of being swept off your feet." "Love is when your heart pounds hard and you just can not take your eyes off the person." "I love him or her so much I think my heart will burst." "I am so in love I could just die." Is this love? The individuals sound slightly paralyzed and almost unable to function (Gordon, 1996).

Do you remember the image of love in fairy tales? Love is an overpowering force between an attractive man and woman. He is bold, fearless, and capable of overcoming any obstacle to win her. She is frail and helpless and, of course, extremely beautiful. He rescues her, and together they go forth to live happily ever after. Most of us grow up believing in the magic of "chemistry" between lovers. Love feels exquisite and beyond our control (Cowan and Kinder, 1987).

Although the media do express more realistic versions of love relationships, myths and unrealistic pictures of love are still portrayed. Product advertisements even use images of love to entice consumers. Obsession and other aspects of passionate love are packaged as perfumes and sexy lingerie. Compared to obsession, all other love seems humdrum and mundane, whereas romanticized versions appear sultry, seductive, and the ultimate in emotionality and sensuality (Forward, 1991).

Descriptors of passionate love. If you were to write an all-consuming romantic novel, what images of love would you present? Hundreds of students have contributed their descriptors of passionate love, or what I call "fluff stuff." Among the cleverest ones: "I thought it was going to be an everlasting tingle." "It happens instantly in a flash like a Certs encounter." "Love feels zingy, and you get dingy." The responses are grouped into categories in Table 12-1.

One way to know that these notions are still popular is to pay attention to music lyrics. Songs from decades ago were full of messages such as "You belong to me" or "Our hearts are on fire." Songs today still express an idealized, unrealistic version of love—for example, "I will do anything for you; I will even sell my soul for you," and "I will die without your love." One song even asked: "How do you know if he loves you so?" The answer? "It is in his kiss!" Amazing that you can tell if a man loves you by the way he kisses! And just listen to expressive individuals in the throes of infatuation: "It is a real high." "I feel like I am on cloud nine."

Dilemmas of passionate love. So what is the matter with passionate love? The body, in fact, is producing chemicals that contribute to the physical sensations. However, intense sensations aren't enough. Sadly, a song from the past tells us, "Love and marriage go together like a horse and carriage," and individuals with mistaken notions of love do get married in the heat of their passion. "Falling in love is like a space launch, full of flame and fire. Getting married in the fire and flame of the blast-off stage of the relationship is extremely dangerous" (Crowther, 1986, p. 123). Typical dilemmas of passionate love are loving the feeling of being in love more than you do the other person and allowing passions to become destructive.

Mostly love just makes people act silly, but sometimes the afflicted turn violent. Lovers have been known to kill those they love, particularly if the object of their affection is not similarly stricken. If it does not work, they either kill themselves or look for another victim (Chance, 1988, p. 22).

When people are in the throes of passionate love, they are convinced that the wild feelings will last forever. In actuality, they do not. Turbulent emotions become less intense (Hatfield and Rapson, 1996). Passionate love may feel wonderful for awhile, yet is not conducive to long-term happiness. Being responsible and

TABLE 12-1	Passionate Love Descriptors

Survival

"I cannot live without you."
"I am nothing without you."
"I just cannot get enough of you."
"If you ever leave me, I will die."

Physical Sensations

Walking on air or clouds
Palpitating heart, shortness of breath
Weak knees, dizziness
Cannot eat, sleep, and think
"I just melt when you look at me."

Perfection

"No one has ever loved like this before."
"It is perfect. You're perfect."
"Nothing will ever go wrong."

Exaggerated Promises

"Love conquers all."
"All I need is you."
"I would do anything for you."
"We will always be happy (and will not have to even work on it)."
"I will never look at another man (or woman)."

Exclusivity and Possessiveness

"You are the only one for me."
"You are mine."
"You belong to me, and I belong to you."
"I am jealous and you are jealous, and that means we are in love."
"Just the two of us. Nothing else matters."

in control of yourself are the hallmarks of well-being. In contrast, passionate love often means giving control to the other person. "Ernie always makes me feel terribly alone," wrote a 53-year-old student. "He wants to get married, so he causes me to feel so guilty when I say not now." Love that puts someone else in control has unhappy prospects. "Head over heels is an uncomfortable position for human beings" (Chance, 1988, p. 22).

Lovers become disillusioned when they finally realize that this type of love does not last. Those in the throes of passionate love also believe that the other is almost perfect (or at least should be). When reality sets in, these lovers are then disappointed.

This may sound depressing, yet it does not have to be. Most experts believe that the end of the "falling-in-love period" signals the start of a realistic stage when true love can develop. "The most that romance can do is to draw two people to-gether initially, but these feelings tend not to last, and they do not guarantee a sat-isfying long-term relationship" (Burns, 1985, p. 182). If the psychological attraction is not there or disappears, the physiological sensations vanish as well. The glue that keeps love intact has a cognitive base.

Do you remember when you bought a new car and the thrill and joy you ex-perienced just looking at it? Later, you still enjoyed the car but in a different way. The newness wore off, so you did not feel the same "high." The car was familiar, and you felt comfortable and secure with it. Your feelings, including pride, were deep and sure. This experience is similar to the evolution of long-term relation-ships. The glow is still there; however, it is a different, deeper glow.

Jealousy: A major challenge.   Common to passionate love is **jealousy,** a feeling related to the threat of or actual experience of loss. Usually a blend of fear, anger, hurt, and sadness, jealousy is fueled by irrational thoughts, absolutist "musts," and demands (Ellis, 1996). Hurtful behavior is a typical outcome. More than 33 percent of dating university students said that jealousy was a significant problem in their present relationship (Buss, 2000).

Possessiveness fans the flames of jealousy. "You are mine, and I am yours," a part of passionate-love thinking, usually leads to: "Because you are mine, you will do what I want you to do." This can mean not even looking at another attrac-tive person. In extreme forms of possessiveness, a lover may insist that the other not pursue any outside interests. Violence and abuse are common outcomes of possessiveness.

> Absolute control over another person is neither possible, desirable, nor loving. Instead it destroys what it sets out to protect. (Buscaglia, 1992, p. 142)

Does love mean ownership of your lover? Hopefully, you can answer that it does not. "A love that inhibits is not love. Love is only love when it liberates" (Buscaglia, 1992, p. 100). Are your expectations unrealistic? It is unrealistic to ex-pect your partner to become blind to others and to react angrily if a "third party" admires your lover. What Buscaglia (1984) writes is healthy: "What a grand feel-ing to have a relationship with someone who is loved not only by you, but by many. That means you made a good choice" (p. 164).

In addition to damaging a relationship, jealousy has the potential to end it. Jocelyn was irrationally jealous of her fiancè, Troy. She could not bear his talking to other women, especially when they were apart. Because Troy's job brought him into contact with both men and women, jealousy became a major problem. Jocelyn nagged and cried and became suspicious and clinging. Troy felt stifled, and the intensity of their conflicts became unbearable. Eventually, he broke their engagement. "All I did was love you so much!" cried Jocelyn, not acknowledging that she had done far more than that. "Love is not expressed by strangulation" (Branden and Branden, 1982, p. 127).

Recognizing the presence of jealousy helps to control it. Some people are chronically jealous. Low self-esteem is usually at fault. Individuals with higher self-esteem and an internal locus of control are generally less jealous and handle it more effectively. Equality is a powerful factor in the prevention of jealousy.

In any relationship, occasional twinges of jealousy can be experienced without damage. These usually occur when, for some reason, the relationship does not feel secure or, perhaps, you are suffering from a feeling of insecurity. What can you do? Recognizing the underlying thoughts is helpful because jealousy is related to cognitive appraisals and the meaning attached to an incident. For example, your partner is dancing with an attractive person. Instead of letting jealousy take over, examine your thoughts. If you are thinking, "She or he prefers that person to me" or "This is a threat to our relationship," use rational emotive behavior therapy to change these irrational thoughts.

If jealousy is based on rational thoughts, it is not recommended that you suppress the feeling; however, avoid behaviors such as pouting, nagging, threatening, and clinging. Although most people do not like to feel jealous, denying it can cause damage. Much like stress, whether or not you acknowledge its presence, jealousy can wreak havoc on you and the relationship. Instead, using the dimensions of awareness described in Chapter 9 can help the other person understand your perspective. If the relationship is healthy, your partner will understand and help eliminate the reasons for the jealousy. Jealousy may lessen as two people become more mature in their relationship. Creating the kind of relationship in which jealousy will have a low survival rate is well worth the effort.

> Everyone who cares and loves feels jealous at one time or another. The essential decision is whether you will allow your jealousy to become an all-consuming monster, capable of destroying you and those you love, or become a challenge for you to grow in self-respect and personal knowledge. (Buscaglia, 1984, p. 129)

Intimate Love

Unlike the "fluff stuff" of passionate love, **intimate love** is a deep, total experience composed of positive thoughts, feelings, and behaviors. Such love is the foundation of a long-term, mutually satisfying relationship. "Love is a process, not just a feeling, of discovery, of development, of growing together" (Solomon, 1988, p. 82). Saying "I love you" and experiencing the sensations are meaningless without actions. Love encompasses attitudes and behaviors such as responsibility, respect, knowledge, giving, and caring. "Love is an activity, not a passive affect; it is a standing in, not a falling for. Love is the active concern for the life and the growth of that which we love" (Fromm, 1956, pp. 22, 26). True love does not just happen; two people make it happen.

A song from years ago is "Love Is a Many-Splendored Thing." Although love may not always be full of splendor, it is a "many-faceted thing," meaning that there is a variety of components and factors that make up intimate love. Let's examine what these are (TA Revisited).

Rubin's components of love.   Believing that social psychologists had neglected the study of love, Rubin (1970) developed a scale to measure liking and loving. The scale featured three components of love: attachment, caring, and intimacy (Rubin, 1973).

TA Revisited

The "child" ego state feels passion and love and encourages playful behaviors and spontaneous delight.

The "parent" ego state gives out both positive and negative messages about love and loving relationships.

The "adult" ego state encourages the positive feelings, rejects unwise "parent" messages, considers all factors related to a satisfying love relationship, and makes decisions.

Attachment has to do with the desire for the physical presence and emotional support of the other person as well as a preference for each other's company. In contrast to the stifling togetherness of passionate love, healthy attachment means enjoyment and involvement in mutually rewarding activities. Enjoying being with each other bonds a couple. Connie, after her divorce, insightfully commented: "A clue I did not recognize was that Dan and I did not enjoy activities apart from others. We always double-dated, and after we were married, our social life included other couples. The two of us did not have fun just being together."

In a marriage-preparation class, a lack of attachment was apparent. A young woman enrolled in the class alone even though she was engaged. Her fiancé bowled on the nights of class. After a discussion of Rubin's components, she said, "I wonder about that. He is not here tonight because of bowling. Last night was Monday night football, on Wednesday nights he shoots pool, and Thursday and Saturday nights he goes out with his friends. We are together on Friday nights and usually on Sunday when he is not at a drag race. Well, that is one reason I want to get married. Either he will change, or at least I will have more leverage to nag him about it." Not facing potential problems is another facet of passionate love.

The second component, **caring,** consists of feelings of concern and responsibility for another's welfare, Tenderness includes awareness of the other's needs and desires (May, 1969) and is related to caring, as is empathy. You will share stressors and experience anxiety and act in extra-thoughtful ways because you love. Often mistaken for caring is irrational possessiveness. Consider these examples:

Jenni was excited when her friend asked her to come to work in a new business. She could finally pursue a career that she had given up four years ago. Eric, her husband, said, "You are not going to work. The kids and I need you at home."

Raoul received word that his scholarship request had been approved. Although it would mean sacrificing, this was his chance to complete his degree. Amy, his fiancé protested, "I will not see you much if you have to study and work. And you will not earn as much, so we will not be able to get married as soon."

How caring were Eric and Amy? For whom did they care? Genuine concern means that you consider another's welfare. Blocking personal growth is uncaring behavior. Warm, caring behavior is unconditional positive regard, not the "I will love you if . . ." ingredient of passionate love.

Intimacy, the third component, is a desire for confidential, close communication. Rubin's concept of intimacy reflects sharing and disclosing on all levels. A love

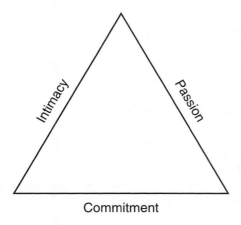

Figure 12-1

relationship resembles a deep friendship. The term *emotionally divorced* is often used to describe relationships that lack intimacy. Vulnerability is necessary for intimacy, and individuals often fear the risk. Teresa Adams (1987), therapist and author, says, "The crowd thins when it comes to intimacy." This component deserves extra attention and is discussed in a later section.

Sternberg's love triangle. Picture a triangle with three equal sides of balanced love. Based on his research, Sternberg (1987) identified ingredients of love: intimacy, passion, and commitment (Fig. 12-1).

Similar to Rubin's component with some additions is **intimacy** that includes closeness, sharing, communication, and support. Intimacy is akin to deep friendship. **Passion** is physiological arousal and an intense desire to be united with the loved one. According to Sternberg (1986), the needs for sex and affiliation give rise to passion. For most people, passion is what distinguishes liking from loving. The glue that holds a relationship together is **commitment** that is expressed in dedication to the relationship and faithfulness to each other.

A deeper aspect of Sternberg's theory is that one, two, or all three of the components can be present. A relationship that just has commitment, called empty love, is composed of two people who have been together for a long time with nothing special about the relationship except its longevity. Intimacy by itself is friendship, and passion is physical attraction.

Consummate love consists of all three components. Two people have a strong attraction and sexual desire for each other; they are close, communicative, and supportive; and because of a strong mutual commitment, the relationship is of high priority. Considering these ingredients, do you recognize any of your relationships? Researchers asked heterosexual couples how they experienced intimacy, passion, and commitment. They found overlap in how the three were demonstrated and concluded that even though these components are extremely relevant, love encompasses even more (Marston et al., 1998).

Ingredients of love. Using a model of a three-legged stool, Carlton Paine, Ph.D., a clinical psychologist, considers three ingredients to be necessary in a viable, ongoing, intimate relationship. In an interview, he stated that **trust,** which means honesty and dependability, is absolutely essential. He said, "A common way people undermine their relationship is by lying. Not knowing whether or what to believe or whether you can depend on the other is devastating." Having a fondness for each other is **affection,** the second ingredient. This can include passion and emotional comfortableness and draws a couple together. Completing the foundation is **respect,** an admiration and high regard for another. Paine recognizes that deeply satisfying relationships typically offer more; yet, as he works with couples, he believes that these are fundamental and must be reciprocal.

Examine any love relationship in terms of the various elements that have been identified. If some dimensions you want are missing, express this to your partner. The more open you can be about love, the greater the possibility of achieving a satisfying relationship. Even with all the components present, love can be strengthened by paying attention to other factors.

Relationship growth and fulfillment of needs.   Healthy individuals grow in a positive direction. So do healthy relationships. Individual growth and relationship growth are associated. If individual growth is stunted, so is the relationship. In order for growth to be positive, individuals have to be free to achieve their potential. When individuals are committed to their own and to each other's positive growth, wonderful things can happen. Each person experiences satisfaction in life and the relationship is vitalized. Conversely, a person who is deprived of growth has little, or nothing, to offer the relationship except frustration.

> Woe be it unto you if you give yourself totally to another. You are lost forever. Maintain yourself as the others maintain themselves. Then you put "They" together and form "Us." Then work on that "Us," and that "Us" gets bigger and bigger while the "You" and the "I" get bigger and bigger and form these enormous concentric circles that grow forever! And if, by chance, you lose that special "Us"—you still have an "I" and loving memories to build with. (Buscaglia, 1982, p. 162)

Intimate love maintains a balance between partners.

A possible area of concern is the course of individual growth. Individuals can grow, contribute to the relationship, and become closer to each other. Or they can grow apart. Couples who do not experience harmonious growth eventually find themselves worlds apart. Being mindful that change will occur and taking care to direct the course of growth are critical. Love flourishes in an environment of positive growth. When you choose to commit to a relationship, be sure your partner is one with whom you can *live* and *grow*.

Based on social exchange theory, which was covered in Chapter 10, love can be examined in terms of **fulfillment of needs.** A major function of any relationship is to satisfy individual needs. In fact, a predictor of happiness is the degree of difference between what you want and what you think you are getting from a relationship (Sternberg and Whitney, 1991). One relationship cannot fulfill all your needs. However, a love relationship, especially a long-term one, is primary and must satisfy a number of important ones. If you know yourself well, then you know what you need from a relationship (Fig. 12-2). A specific one identified by a single parent was the need to have a relationship in which the partner would also be a caring stepparent for her children.

After identifying your needs, you are ready for the next step. Deborah has needs for deep communication, demonstrated affection, and honesty. Can you see what would be likely to happen if Deborah feels a strong attraction for Kurt, who is honest, extremely quiet, and emotionally inexpressive? People who know him describe him as somewhat reclusive and cold. Strange as it may seem, people often fall in love with those who would have difficulty satisfying important needs. "Silent Sam or Sally" will not likely turn into a great communicator overnight. "Boring Bill or Billie" isn't apt to be much fun, and people who are "cold fish" will not find it easy to be affectionate. Some find out in time, as Andrea

What Are Your Needs from a Love Relationship?

- Companionship
- Stimulation and excitement
- Affirmation and caring
- Passion and sexual fulfillment
- Emotional support
- Self-awareness and discovery
- Communication and deep self-disclosure
- Demonstrated affection
- Equality
- Loyalty and fidelity
- Tenderness
- Fun and enjoyment
- Trust and honesty
- Commitment
- Intimacy

Figure 12-2

did: "He showed little caring and did not share with me. I did 95 percent of the caring. He was jealous and showed it in strange ways. I have learned in this class that I am glad I got out of it and that there is still hope for me."

Fulfillment of needs requires that you match your needs with a partner who can satisfy them because it is that person who gives to the relationship what you need (see Fig. 12-3). Relationships have a better chance of remaining romantic if individuals are not frustrated by unfulfilled needs. The needs fulfillment activity at the end of this book can be used for mate selection, premarital assessment, and enrichment of relationships. The key is to communicate personal needs to each other, keeping in mind that the two lists probably will not be exactly the same.

When needs are not satisfied, what happens? Ideally, your dissatisfaction is communicated to your partner, and he or she is willing to change. Such was the case with Rosa and Bill. After 33 years of marriage, Rosa said that she would not remain in the marriage unless her needs for respect and intimacy were met. "Rocking the boat" as much as she did definitely made enough waves to open Bill's eyes. He agreed to marital counseling, which guided them into a mutually satisfying relationship. Their story had a happy ending, but what if no changes are made? A sad possibility is that people will just "settle" and try to be content within relationships that are not nourishing. Unfortunately, this "settling" is quite common and is one cause of what are called empty-shell marriages. Far too many have a dull-but-tolerable coexistence: a kind of death-in-life (Barbach and Geisinger, 1991). The value of a relationship lies in the joy it offers, not in its longevity (Branden and Branden, 1982). Another possibility is infidelity. Many affairs can be traced to an important need not being met in the marriage. A recent

Fulfillment of Needs

Figure 12-3

challenge, according to marriage and family therapist Sue Frahm, is an online affair between two people who meet via the Internet. Unmet needs are probably partially responsible, and a person owes it to a partner to communicate what is lacking. Finally, when needs are not being met, another likelihood is to end the relationship. Most endings to relationships reflect unfulfilled needs.

How do you know that a person can or will satisfy you? Even though no guarantee is possible, you can significantly increase your chances by doing the following:

- Use the activity in Reflections and Applications to identify what you want and try to prioritize as much as possible. What is essential? Be sure that your needs are reasonable. What, if missing, would cause you to be unhappy and possibly end the relationship? Try to specifically describe abstract words such as "honesty." For example, to just say that you want "trust" is not explaining it well. Two partners may have different meanings for the word, and if you are not sure what trust means, you will not know if it is present or not.
- Communicate your needs to your partner. Describe desired *behaviors*.
- Be willing to do what is necessary to satisfy the other person's legitimate needs. This may mean behavior changes on your part.

Do not assume that the other will change after marriage or just because time passes. Behavioral change is possible but requires self-motivation. You can only suggest and encourage. The only one you can be assured of being able to change is yourself.

Two people may not have the same needs, and being compatible in this regard is preferable. For example, if Nicole wants a high degree of togetherness and Kelly prefers personal space, they will have difficulty satisfying each other. This is one reason that similarities are an important attraction factor. In most cases, your needs will not be 100 percent identical; however, equality is of concern. Exchange theory indicates that relationships are more satisfying and stable when outcomes for each partner are more or less equal and when benefits far outweigh costs.

If you find that your needs are unfulfilled and changes in a partner are not likely, you are hurting yourself, and probably the other person as well, by remaining in the relationship. Fortunately, unhappy situations can have happy endings. A student wrote:

> When I thought about needs fulfillment, I talked to my fianc{EACUTE} about our relationship. It was obvious that my needs were not being satisfied, and he really did not seem to care enough to change. I gave back the ring and went through a depressing period. Then I met Matt, and the two relationships are like night and day. We really clicked and are getting married next month. How sad it would have been if I had remained in that earlier relationship.

Behaviors of love.   The actions of lovers deserve attention. "Joe loves me. I know because he beats up on anyone who looks at me." Is this love or is it an uncontrollable temper fired by irrational possessiveness? "She loves me because she will do everything I want." This sounds more like servitude than love. A much more affirming behavior is affection, which couples identified as the most important type of interaction in their relationships (Dainton, 1998).

Be aware of how you are treated by a lover. Is it affectionate and loving behavior? In any love relationship, individuals will occasionally demonstrate some less than loving actions. If hurtful behaviors are frequent or occur for poor reasons, and the aggressor feels no remorse and does not act to rectify the situation, you are not being loved. Ask yourself, "Do I feel loved?" If you can honestly answer in the affirmative most of the time, then the relationship is probably positive. "Do I feel affirmed?" is another essential question. Intimate love enhances self-esteem. Focusing on all behaviors is a good way to assess the quality of the relationship.

Love is complicated and mysterious, as anyone who has loved knows. Being able to differentiate between passionate and intimate love is a first step in understanding love relationships. Taking a close look at intimate love, its components, its potential for contributing to relationship growth and fulfillment of needs, and its behaviors reduces the possibility of mistakes and pain. After you have examined love, you may still wonder whether what you feel is love. Branden and Branden (1982) state: "We suspect that people who ask this question are not in love. In our observation and experience, love reaches a critical point where it tends to generate clarity of its own" (p. 24).

What Is Intimacy?

Intimacy is the pulse of the closest relationships. Intimacy is positively related to individual need fulfillment (Prager and Buhrmester, 1998). Definitions of intimacy, like those of abstract words, vary. To many, intimacy is equated with sexuality. When you consider that retail stores have "intimate departments," which sell lingerie and negligees, it is little wonder that the mind focuses on bedroom scenes. The sexual relationship is only one facet of intimate love. "The most literal meaning of intimate is to really know another" (Rubin, 1973, p. 160). This is an important aspect within intimacy, yet more is involved. Intimacy frees and encourages you to be your own true self and to be accepted and loved because of who you are.

Intimacy has several key elements (Sternberg, 1987).

1. Promoting each other's welfare
2. Experiencing happiness with each other
3. Holding each other in high regard
4. Being able to count on each other in times of need
5. Having mutual understanding
6. Sharing of self and possessions with each other
7. Receiving emotional support from the other
8. Giving emotional support to the other
9. Communicating intimately with each other
10. Valuing each other

Check your own love relationship to see how many of the 10 elements are present.

Development of Intimacy

Building intimacy requires dedication and effort. Individuals have to be willing to rid themselves of personal postures that prohibit intimacy (Malone and Malone, 1987). Check the list "Intimacy Blockers" If you see yourself, realize that you have work to do before intimacy is possible (Fig. 12-4).

Intimacy Blockers

- Withdrawal or isolating the self emotionally; possibly becoming overly involved with interests outside the relationship.
- Personal rigidity leading to an unwillingness to allow differences or to compromise.
- Overt self-righteousness and placing the need to be right higher than love.
- Lack of trustworthiness.

Figure 12-4

The last of the intimacy blockers is of utmost importance. Trust including predictability, dependability, faithfulness, loyalty, and honesty is essential. The essence of trust is emotional safety. "Trust enables you to put your deepest feelings and fears in the palm of your partner's hand, knowing they will be handled with care" (Avery, 1989, p. 27).

In addition to personal characteristics that prevent intimacy is fear. A study of gay men and lesbians revealed that fear of intimacy, as in heterosexuals, was related to feeling uncomfortable with emotional closeness, low levels of self-disclosure, and relationship dissatisfaction (Greenfield and Thelen, 1997). "We can only be intimate to the degree that we are willing to be open and vulnerable" (Ornish, 1998, p. 39).

An obvious deterrent to the development of intimacy is finding a partner to whom one is attracted and who encourages a long-term relationship. This seemed easier years ago when so much attention wasn't being paid to relationship building. "Dating is easy to do, but finding that special someone seems impossible," lamented a young adult. Where does one look? Two obvious locations are where one attends school and at a place of employment. Other possibilities and recommendations follow.

- Get involved with organizations, professional associations, and volunteer activities. If you have values and beliefs that attract you to certain causes, you will probably find people you can admire.
- Become more active. Join a health club and go to movies, plays, and museums. Spend time doing what you enjoy; you will then find others who like what you do.
- Let others know that you desire a serious relationship. Many people find a significant other through networking.
- A study of college students found that over 60 percent were successful in establishing an online friendship. Interestingly, friendship, not romance or sex, was the primary reason for seeking someone (Knox et al., 2001).

Regardless of how you proceed to meet someone, remain open to possibilities and definitely review the features of positive relationships in Chapter 10.

Intimacy can be difficult because of power struggles. Power can be distributed unequally with either the man or the woman having more control, or power can seesaw back and forth in a continuous struggle. The healthiest type of structure is shared power based on perceived equality. Equal attention and seriousness are extended to the emotions, needs, desires, and roles of both. When equality goes out of a relationship, love follows (Solomon, 1988).

A serious obstacle is stereotypic masculine behavior that destroys potential intimacy. Furthermore, intimacy requires expression of emotions and self-disclosure on all levels. The classic male image denies these behaviors and sets up roadblocks to intimacy (Crose, 1997). The willingness to feel vulnerable—to open one's heart—which is difficult for a stereotypic man, is essential to intimacy (Ornish, 1998). Even though many men are changing as they learn the value of intimacy, those who continue in a stereotypic masculine role will face extreme hardships.

Intimacy for all couples is endangered by boredom and the tendency to take each other for granted. Intimacy demands quality interacting time. If, because of relationship longevity or familiarity or both, couples choose to engage in other activities or they simply ignore their relationship, intimacy can be lost for lack of interest. "To have a long-lasting relationship, we must avoid complacency. More love has been lost on the island of contentment than in any sea of torment" (Buscaglia, 1992, p. 166).

What helps the development of intimacy?

- Expression of genuine emotions, even unpleasant ones. During a seminar, Teresa Adams (1987) noted that "frozen anger blocks intimacy; thawed anger enhances intimacy."
- Empathic and nurturing behaviors
- Paying attention to each other
- Mutually enjoyable activities
- Communication, especially deep self-disclosure
- Commitment

Listed last, commitment is one of the most important aids to intimacy. Feelings of security and stability within a relationship create an oasis for vulnerability that, in turn, allows two people to know each other deeply. Although most research has been conducted on white heterosexual couples, commitment and intimacy are not limited by race or sexual orientation. In a study of African American lesbians and gay males, intimacy was a significant factor in relationship satisfaction. A majority of the men and women indicated that they loved their partners and had satisfying relationships. As a salute to commitment, they strongly believed that intimacy would continue (Peplau, Cochran, and Mays, 1997).

Building intimacy is one of the most difficult and challenging tasks within a relationship. The excellent chapter "Pathways to Love and Intimacy" in the book *Love and Survival* (Ornish, 1998) provides insight and guidance. The rewards are significant. If a relationship does not have intimacy, the partners may not realize what they are missing. If two human beings are truly intimate, their potential for joy is infinite.

> *Intimacy demands the highest risk but yields the richest reward. Intimacy is the driving force which makes the painful grit of life worthwhile. Intimacy is the life-giving beam of light, whereby we discover each other from the inside out, never quite fully, never entirely, but enough to find an exquisite inner oasis that replenishes us on our life's journey.*
> —Teresa Adams

Managing Conflict

In order to preserve intimacy, couples have to manage conflict successfully. A "just-kiss-and-make-up" philosophy may carry people through the courtship stage, and they probably will not realize the negative impact of their behavior until later. Years ago, conflict management was not a consideration. The widely held belief was that loving couples did not fight. A disagreement was a sign of weakness in the relationship, so you hurried to patch things up. Important conflict issues were often glossed over for fear that they would spell the end of the relationship. When couples did disagree, they usually did so in an unpleasant, aggressive manner. Then making up was a relief. The crux of the problem was often left untouched.

One of the first and best-known books on the subject of conflict management is *The Intimate Enemy: How to Fight Fair in Love and Marriage* (Bach and Wyden, 1968). The premise is that **verbal conflict,** defined as disagreement, between intimates is not only inevitable and acceptable but also can be constructive and desirable, and the authors provide insight into how to fight. You may inwardly shudder at the word *fight.* Thinking of **fighting** as a way of handling disagreement may make it more acceptable (Fig. 12-5).

Unfair Fighting Styles

Two opposite types of **fighting styles** are identified as unfair. Fight evaders—nonfighters—are "doves." For any number of reasons, these people are fight-phobic and resist fighting. Gunnysacking, described in Chapter 10, is a common behavior. Two "doves" do not level with each other and often pay the price of emotional divorce. Most would not recognize this as a type of fighting; however, remember that fighting is defined as a way of handling conflict. The opposite are "hawks," or aggressive fighters. They are usually loud, observably angry, and hostile. They use unfair, hurtful tactics and damage their relationship.

Both types experience anger, which is inevitable within an intimate relationship. Anger is a signal worth listening to. Anger is potentially constructive when a

---

The Experts and Conflict

Love rarely remains all flowers and sweetness. Disagreements, arguments, and fighting are natural when two people are trying to come together. More important than what you fight about is how you fight (Wegscheider-Cruse, 1988).

The health of a relationship is determined not so much on whether there are conflicts, but whether they are addressed and resolved. Conflict can serve useful purposes (Crowther, 1986).

A fair fight can clear the air and relieve stress. Do not be afraid to fight with ones you love. If you did not care about each other, you wouldn't bother to fight (Tubesing, 1981).

Figure 12-5

Figure 12-6   Fair fighting demands the finest communication skills.

person asks, "What am I angry about, what is the problem, and whose problem is it?" Learning how to fight fairly is essential because the "inability to manage personal conflicts is at the root of the crisis that threatens the structure of the American family" (Bach and Wyden, 1968, p. 31). A key point is that the way in which conflict is resolved determines the health of the relationship.

Fair Fighting

What is recommended in conflict resolution between intimates? **Fair fighting** is a process of resolving conflict without hurting each other or the relationship. What is involved? Most experts suggest that, if possible, couples should carefully choose the best time, place, and conditions for resolving conflict. Too often, individuals fight when they are tired, under inordinate stress, or after drinking alcohol. These conditions set the stage for unfair fighting. When tired, couples can create added problems or, as often happens, one person "gives up" in order to get some rest. The concept of "giving up" and "giving in" places fighting on the level of a wrestling match. Usually, the one who concedes, or "gives in," is left with resentment. Fair fighters can call a time-out, a halt in their discussion, and resume under more positive conditions. Here are a few other criteria by which to determine the extent of fairness (Fig. 12-6).

Winning–losing: If either person "wins," the relationship loses. Getting rid of the win–loss notion is important. The key to win–win is to recognize and satisfy as best as possible each person's highest priorities or most important needs. The health of a relationship takes priority over winning.

Involvement: Have you ever been engaged in a fight that was a monologue? Too often, one person does most, if not all, the talking, and the other simply absorbs or ignores. A behavior that is more often engaged in by men has been described in research as a danger sign (Gottman, 1994b). **Stonewalling** is removing oneself from an interaction and employing a stony silence that conveys disapproval, icy distance, and smugness. As frustrating as it can be, silence is equated with power. The amount of information exchanged is decreased with tactics such as the silent treatment and "I-do-not-want-to-discuss-it" approaches. In a fair fight the two individuals both take turns talking and listening.

Communication: The use of "I," not "you," statements; active, receptive listening; open, honest, and clear messages from both partners without game playing or manipulative techniques are essential.

Injury: Being careful to direct criticism to behaviors, to avoid personal attacks and name-calling, and to maintain consideration for the other is necessary. Unfair fighters attack the other in areas of vulnerability.

Directness: Remaining focused in the present and on the subject at hand is difficult to do yet necessary. If a new topic is presented, the issue can get sidetracked. Agreeing to handle the new topic later is recommended.

Specificity: Clarity and description of behaviors are needed. The use of perception checking and dimensions of awareness helps to clarify meanings. Be sure that you are not arguing simply because you don't understand each other.

Feelings: Frequently, when partners know each other's feelings, they experience empathy and understanding. Be willing to share all emotions.

Responsibility: Both people should take a share of the responsibility for the conflict itself and for the process required to resolve it. "It is your fault" "No, it is your fault," will get you nowhere. Conflict is a two-way street.

Humor: As strange as it may seem, if positive humor creeps into a fight, the mood will probably lighten. Obviously, any use of sarcasm or nasty humor would only hurt. Research supports the benefit of humor to soothe a partner (Gottman et al., 1998).

Another major contribution to conflict management was made by Aaron Beck (1988), a leader in the field of cognitive therapy, with his book *Love Is Never Enough*. Regularly scheduled discussions, what he calls "troubleshooting sessions," give individuals a chance to empty their "gunnysacks." This decreases reasons for nagging. Susan Borkin, a therapist, recommends a 20-minute period for cooling off and digesting the message after one person has expressed anger and displeasure. "Agreement is easier after feelings are vented and allowed to dissipate," she says. Whenever you are not able to manage anger, you are better off calling for a time-out and refusing to continue the fight. An excellent idea is to tape-record or videotape a fight so each person can see what he or she did to escalate the conflict and how to improve. Learn to assess an unfair fight by reading a description of one in Reflections and Applications.

In addition to paying attention to how partners fight, examine the effects or outcome. Has either partner's self-esteem been diminished? If so, the fight was not fair. Do you feel closer, as caring, more intimate? Has the relationship been strengthened or weakened? John Gottman (1994b), a well-known researcher in the field of conflict management, contributes an essential point: No matter how couples fight, they must have at least five times as many positive as negative moments together if their relationship is to be stable.

> Fair fighting is not a sport like boxing. It is an art and a skill like dancing. It takes co-operation and style. In fact, the style of a fight is more important than what you actually fight about. Several days after a fight, you may remember only about 10 percent of the content, but you will probably have almost total recall for the style: whether the fight was fair, how hurt you felt, how strong the emotions were, how satisfied or upset you felt afterward. (McKay, Davis, and Fanning, 1983, p. 136)

Fair fighting leads partners along the path of increased closeness and intimacy. Conflict can be viewed as an opportunity to learn about yourself and your partner. "If you never disagree—never have a conflict of opinion—how can you ever really get to know one another?" was an insightful question by James Parkes, a man from Manchester, England. At that time, he and his wife, Betty, had been happily married for over 60 years!

Despite the best intentions, lovers do lose control at times and angrily erupt. The value of knowing how to manage conflict positively is that you know and can admit when unfair tactics were used. Apologizing and committing to try harder the next time are signs of maturity. When people refuse to attempt positive change, it may be better to end the relationship. Openness and flexibility are key ingredients in positive conflict management.

Enriching a Relationship

Pretend you have planted a garden of vegetables and flowers. You pay little attention to the garden. You never fertilize, rarely water, and you do not weed. What will happen? The garden will have little chance of thriving, and even its survival is in jeopardy. Couples who do not take care of their relationship face the same risks. Compare your relationship to a highway that needs to be upgraded, maintained, and even rebuilt; the process is never finished (Sternberg and Whitney, 1991).

Why don't couples enrich their relationships? The primary reasons are simple unawareness and neglect. An assumption in the past was that if you didn't fight much and life was progressing smoothly, your relationship was in good shape. That is not necessarily true.

> Relationships do not typically unravel because of major conflicts. Most relationships die slowly and without the conscious awareness of either party. There is a fine line between a relationship that moves in a positive direction and one that slips silently into apathy or the slow accumulation of disappointments and resentment. (Cowan and Kinder, 1987, p. 5)

Couples have a tendency to "settle into a life of routine" rather than engage in pleasurable activities such as dining out, attending a movie, dancing, and going on picnics. A couple will often "settle down" in front of the television or computer night after night. Even the sexual relationship can become predictable. "Sameness" becomes a barrier to enrichment (Fig. 12-7).

Why Criticize?

Another destructive habit is chronic criticism of your partner. Criticism invariably leads to contempt, and then the relationship is in jeopardy (Gottman, 1994b). Sadly, lovers often treat each other less kindly than they do their friends. Even in the most loving relationships, there is a minimum amount of criticism (Fig. 12-8).

Picture an intimate love relationship as a large rock. No matter how solid the rock (or the relationship), erosion can take place, and the mass is weakened by a wearing-away process. Resentment from a full "gunnysack" can erode the rock. Criticism, always "being right," and aggressive, hurtful actions chip away at even the most durable relationship.

Figure 12-7

Take a Criticism Quiz—True or False?

- Criticizing is a way of helping another improve, so by delivering critical comments, a person is showing love.
- Love can withstand the onslaught of negativism, so criticism will not hurt.
- Criticism is humorous.

All are inaccurate assumptions and false. How well did you do?

Remember that:

- Criticism, at least the way most people deliver it, is not a sign of love.
- Criticism does hurt, and it takes a toll on love.
- Criticism is not funny. Using sarcasm or ridicule to make a critical point is harmful.

Figure 12-8

If neglect has already led to apathy and boredom, or if chronic criticism and hurtfulness have taken their toll, a couple can revitalize the relationship. Couples benefit when they give enrichment a high priority and then commit themselves to achieving it. Improvements in the vital areas of communication and conflict management are enriching. Use any of the following suggestions on a regular basis.

- Set aside a special time to communicate each day if possible. Ideally, focus on positives and do not use it as a "dumping ground" for negatives. Be sure to self-disclose.
- Verbally and nonverbally express an interest in each other.
- Give positive strokes on a regular basis. Compliment each other.
- Demonstrate affection by physical contact, words, and deeds. Hug and kiss often, yet do not necessarily do it as a routine. Kissing each other good-bye is nice, but do not allow this to replace spontaneous moments.
- Be considerate. Say good-bye when you leave and hello when you come together again. Let each other know where you are and be dependable. Empathize with each other.
- Tell each other "thank you" each day, either for a particular behavior or just to express appreciation for each other and for the relationship.
- Surprise each other with little notes, cards, gifts, and unusual plans. Spontaneity brings delight into a relationship.
- Affirm each other privately and in front of others. Hearing your partner deliver praise about you in the presence of others is like a ray of sunshine on a cloudy day.
- Develop rituals and traditions. Celebrate special days and make everyday events more pleasurable. Provide "pleasers" for each other such as back rubs or a special home-cooked dish.
- Spend time together away from everyday hassles. In spite of best intentions, you may find it difficult to forget the nitty-gritty of daily life. Going away for a weekend or even overnight can be a refreshing and relaxing experience. Even going out for an evening gets you away from the demands of the immediate environment.

- Increase the number and frequency of pleasurable events. Find mutually enjoyable activities and engage in them on a regular basis.
- Express all genuine emotions—the pleasant and unpleasant ones. Sharing true feelings is an enriching experience.
- Laugh with each other at least once a day (more often is even better).
- Talk about your early relationship and what attracted you to each other in the first place. Share other positive memories. Couples who revel in their mutual past are likely to find pleasure in the present.
- Share your hopes and dreams. "Dreams elevate us beyond the mundane. To dream together adds an element of wonder to our relationship and gives us something to look forward to" (Buscaglia, 1984, p. 186).
- Share enrichment ideas with each other. Even if some do not seem feasible, the sharing is enriching.
- Give each other massages and use other types of loving nonsexual touch.

Enrichment revitalizes relationships. The song "Little Things Mean a Lot" delivers an important message.

You and your partner can help each other develop loving behaviors. If you want demonstrated affection, say so. Do not be like Ann, who said, "I know Dave loves me, but he just cannot show it." Yes, he can! Learning new behaviors may be necessary. Knowing that hugging and other forms of touching are healthy for individuals and that they also benefit the relationship is motivating. A loving behavior may be to seek counseling. The process of enrichment may uncover areas where professional help could be beneficial.

Seeking Sexual Fulfillment

"Oh, great, this book has some dirty stuff in it" was the comment of a young student as he looked through a section on human sexuality in his psychology textbook. Accompanying the perception that sex is dirty are other attitudes that can interfere with sexual fulfillment. Many people seemingly have difficulty conversing about sex without resorting to phrases such as "doing it," "humping," "screwing," "getting the groove on," and "getting laid." Discussions about sexuality are frequently filled with jokes (described as "dirty"), innuendos, and insinuating remarks. "There is something wrong with a country that says sex is dirty, save it for someone you love," wrote sex educator and author Sol Gordon (Gibbs, 1993, p. 62). It is ironic that even though most people think that violence is bad and sex is good, parents often do not insist that a child turn off a violent television program. Yet, if that same child were watching sex on Saturday morning, most parents would label it gross or immoral and write a letter to the TV station in protest (Farrell, 1986). The fact that individuals do succeed in their sexual relationships amid such a negative environment is amazing.

Sexuality is a part of being human, and lovemaking has special meaning within an intimate love relationship. Finding ways to enhance one's own sexuality and to maintain a fulfilling relationship is vital. Most of our sexual behaviors are learned, but this section will not offer a quick "how-to" course. Fortunately, in

---

Who's Sexually Active?

College students: 78 percent had experienced a casual sexual encounter.
High school students: 46.7 percent had engaged in sexual intercourse.
Before age 13: 7.4 percent had initiated sexual intercourse.
(Youth Risk Behavior Surveillance—United States, 2003)

Figure 12-9

today's society, anyone who wants to learn about the sexual act can do so. Excellent books on being sensual, handling sexual dysfunctions, and enriching a sexual relationship, as well as sex therapy, are available. Within this limited space, the importance of one's sex life will be emphasized, and general guidelines will be offered.

Sexual Behaviors

If you do not realize that sexual relations are occurring at an all-time high, you have not been paying attention. In today's world, the term *premarital sex* is not even accurate. Why? Individuals who engage in sexual activities may have no intention of marrying, and others who are divorced, widowed, or homosexual are certainly not engaging in *pre*marital sex! A Gallup poll found that only 38 percent of U.S. adults think having sexual relations outside of marriage is wrong (Saad, 2001). This lack of disapproval undoubtedly makes nonmarital sex the norm. In a study of college students, 83 percent reported having had sexual intercourse (Kelley et al., 2001) (Fig. 12-9).

For most people, the best sexual experience occurs within a caring relationship. Sexual fulfillment is a major contributor or deterrent to satisfaction in both heterosexual and homosexual relationships. Marital satisfaction is correlated with sexual satisfaction (Wuh and Fox, 2001), and most of the participants in a study of gay men and lesbians reported satisfying sex lives with their current partner (Peplau, Cochran, and Mays, 1997). In addition to its benefits to the overall relationship, two other interesting findings have emerged. A study reported at the World Stroke Conference showed that men who have three or more orgasms a week are 50 percent less likely to die from coronary heart disease (McCarthy, 2001), and a neurophysiologist who studied 3,500 people for a decade said that regular lovemaking makes people look younger (*Ebony*, 2001). It appears that a healthy sex life benefits us physically and psychologically.

Sexual Enrichment

In order to enjoy the benefits of sexual relations, enrichment is especially helpful. Therapists are quick to point out that sexual dissatisfaction in long-term relationships is common, and usually the underlying cause is not a sexual one. Mark Schwartz, a sex therapist, contends that when clients come to him, he spends 80 percent of the time in relationship therapy and only 20 percent of the

Figure 12-10

time on sexual behaviors. In most cases, he says, each "I" must be fixed before any work can be done on the "we." Incomplete self-disclosure is usually one of the factors; if so, deeper communication is warranted. Sexual problems often stem from other difficulties within a couple is relationship, which then result in sexual frustration. The key is to solve the underlying problems. Even without serious complications, most couples' sexual relationships need attention and nourishment and can be improved. Even though you think you know all there is to know about sex, you can learn more!

Sexual myths. Getting rid of sexual myths is part of the education. Realizing that sex and love are not the same would prevent people, like Kate, from erroneously believing she was loved because "he could not keep his hands off me and wanted to have sex every time we were together." Unfortunately, equating sexual desire with love often leads to being hurt. Young people engaging in sexual relations before they have developed a relationship easily mistake arousal for love. "We thought we were in love because we enjoyed sex. After that wore off, we could see it was not love," admitted Kyle (Fig. 12-10).

Another myth is that passion and sex are most important at the beginning of a relationship. Actually, the longer that individuals are together, the more they are likely to benefit from the relationship. Unfortunately, when people do not understand this, they are apt to let the sexual relationship wane. If you are in a long-term relationship, monitoring affectionate behaviors can be a benefit. If you notice a significant decline from the past, decide to show more affection.

A third myth is that the sexual relationship will always stay the same. For example, the length of a marriage negatively affects the frequency of marital sex (Liu, 2000). That does not mean it becomes less enjoyable. A common myth is that as people age, their sexual interests and activities die. Is this true and inevitable? No, say the experts, unless you choose this course. Look at the following figures from a survey of Americans age 60 and older (National Council on the Aging, 2006). In fact, an active sex life appears to be as normal a part of aging as retiring and having grandchildren. According to the survey, almost half of Americans age 60 and older are still sexually active.

- 61 percent of men and 37 percent of women report being sexually active.
- 39 percent want sex more often.
- 61 percent of men and 62 percent of women find sex equal to or more physically satisfying than it was in their 40s.
- 76 percent of men and 69 percent of women find sex at least as emotionally satisfying as it was in their 40s.

- 72 percent of men and 47 percent of women consider sex important to their relationship with their partner.

An equal number claimed that they're satisfied with how often they have sex. Only 4 percent of all respondents said they wanted less sex. Men were more than twice as likely as women to report wanting sex more frequently. This was true in all age segments, even in men age 80 and older.

Biological changes occur with age and will alter some aspects of lovemaking. Most important are attitudes that can become self-fulfilling prophecies. "It is all over," they say, and it is. "It is not all over," they say, and it is not. Lovemaking can be better with age. Tenderness and love are powerful sexual motivators.

Satisfaction guidelines.   In order to enjoy a satisfying sexual relationship, a cardinal rule is to communicate openly and honestly with each other. "We do not talk about it . . . we just do it," mumbled a husband in a counseling session. Even among university students, complete sexual self-disclosure was the exception, not the rule. The couples were more likely to disclose about sexuality when there was a high level of self-disclosure about other topics and when they perceived their partner to also be sexually self-disclosing (Byers and Demmons, 1999).

When you openly communicate, you learn about each other's likes, dislikes, needs, and wants. A word of caution is in order. Communicating does not mean just complaining about what you do not like. You want to be honest and suggest positive changes but put the emphasis on the positive and use communication as a means of enhancing your wants and desires.

A couple should consider sexual intercourse as just one important aspect of their total relationship and to enjoy more than the physical act. Also deeply involved are the mental and emotional parts of the selves. Lovemaking means literally that—interacting physically and emotionally with someone you care about. Is arousal, intercourse, and orgasm or ejaculations essential or are there other possible lovemaking options? (Williams, 1988, p. 19). The emphasis in lovemaking is often placed on the climax phase. Sex therapist Mark Schwartz caused laughter in his audience when he said, "Even foreplay is sometimes seen as unimportant. The word *foreplay* makes it sound as if all the good stuff is still to come." Lovemaking, in its entirety, is best seen as an ongoing interaction between two loving people.

A barrier to sexual fulfillment may be routine and boredom. It is important to add variety and zest to your sexual relationship. Although sameness in time and place may be determined by family situations, work schedules, and other factors, this does not have to deter the enjoyment of sex. Can you think of reasons for sexual boredom in a relationship?

What typically works best in long-term relationships is to first engage in sensual behaviors because passionate feelings almost always follow. In other words, let actions lead into the feelings. Other ideas are to stay in good health, care about your appearance and hygiene, learn how to discover each other's needs and wants, and dare to be spontaneous and creative! Introducing variety can help. There are lots of ways to add novelty to your sex life—a new location, technique, sexual position, or even some great lingerie could be just the spark a couple needs (Hutcherson, 2006).

The myth that love means a constant sexual "turn-on" damages relationships and it is unfair to think that an occasional lack of interest means lack of love. The belief that only men are interested in lovemaking and should make the first advance decreases spontaneity and freedom within sexual relationships.

Final guidelines deal with misinterpretations and manipulative uses of sexuality. "We will make love if . . ." or "I will not have sex with you if . . ." are manipulative techniques that reduce lovemaking to a game. If the relationship is troubled, you can rightfully refrain from lovemaking. Saying, "I do not want to make love because I do not feel loved (or loving)" is direct and honest. To use sex as leverage is to demean yourself and the relationship. Sexual fulfillment is a choice. To achieve satisfaction requires commitment, time, energy, and a great deal of communication. A goal of lovemaking is to relax and enjoy being in close contact with your lover.

Living Together

If you remember the phrase "shacking up," you have firsthand knowledge of how attitudes have changed over time. When a couple was described as "shacking up," it was not meant to be positive. Today this is called **cohabitation,** meaning two partners living together as if married, and it is no longer viewed in such a negative light.

Who Lives Together and Why?

Research about cohabitation focuses on heterosexual couples. However, gay and lesbian couples also live together in a loving relationship. In fact, the 2000 census counted 601,209 same-sex unmarried partner households in the United States, which is likely an undercount (Smith and Gates, 2001). Such relationships are typically enduring, meaningful, and rewarding. As Ruth describes her committed relationship: "Having spent the past 23 years with Shelly has made me really appreciate what a caring and loving relationship can mean" (Fig. 12-11).

For heterosexuals, living together outside of marriage has dramatically increased as a result of a more permissive societal attitude and liberalization of laws.

Communication Comparisons

Picture a group of recently married couples being videotaped as they discuss and try to resolve a problem. When given a problem to discuss and resolve, do you think there would be communication differences between those who cohabited and those who had not? Which couples do you think were better communicators?

More negative and fewer positive problem-solving and support behaviors were demonstrated by the cohabiters. Both partners tried to coerce and control each other. Wives who had cohabited tended to be more verbally aggressive. Researcher Catherine Cohan, Ph.D., strongly recommends communication-skills training for all couples.

Figure 12-11

In 2000, 3.8 million couples cohabited (Fields and Casper, 2000). Among young adults surveyed in a Gallup poll, 44 percent had at some time lived with an opposite-sex partner (Whitehead and Popenoe, 2001). Even though cohabitation in heterosexual relationships can serve as a replacement for marriage, usually couples cohabit as a testing ground or as preparation for marriage.

Whether cohabitation can enhance chances for marital success is questionable. Several studies paint a negative picture, including cohabiters having more conflict and less relationship satisfaction as well as a higher likelihood of divorce for those who do marry (Terry, 2000). Even though figures show that cohabitation has not improved the success of marriages, the reasons remain elusive. One suggestion is that those who cohabit may be less traditional and more independent in their thinking. Or could it have to do with communication, as discussed in Figure 12-11? What do you think the reasons might be?

Cohabitation may have a favorable aspect that seems to get overlooked and certainly is worthy of more research. About 40 percent of heterosexuals who cohabit do not marry each other (Terry, 2000). Most cohabitations last for about a year or a little longer and then either end in marriage or dissolve (Waite, 2000). It appears that living together does screen out potentially troubled marriages. This, undoubtedly, has lowered the divorce rate. Also beneficial is that living together has led to a postponement of marriage until later ages (Strong, DeVault, and Sayad, 1998). This delay can create better unions.

Few studies look at cohabitation prior to remarriages (Hanna and Knaub, 1981). Of 80 remarried couples in the Lincoln, Nebraska, sample, 40 had lived together for at least a month prior to their remarriages whereas 40 others had not (Hanna and Knaub, 1981). Unlike studies of cohabitation before first marriage, the cohabiting group scored higher on three measures of marital success, including family strength, marital satisfaction, and their own perception of adjustment.

Living Arrangements

If cohabitation has any benefits in terms of testing the strength of a relationship, the attitudes and conditions must be realistic. In addition, giving deliberate thought and action to living together increases the enjoyment of the experience and the likelihood for long-term satisfaction.

Because roles are flexible and responsibilities are shared, the question arises of who does what. A simple answer is: either or both. The couple may use communication and negotiation in the designation of tasks. A number of criteria can be used. For example, who cooks? The two can share responsibilities, either taking turns or working together in the kitchen. Or couples can consider preference, ability, and convenience.

Maintaining a truly shared arrangement can be challenging. An unequal division of labor was evident in a study of unmarried opposite-sex roommates and cohabiters. Even though there was no difference in time availability and contributed resources, women spent more time and effort on the majority of tasks (Mikula, Freudenthaler, and Brennacher-Kroell, 1997). Among same-sex partners, the most common division of labor involves flexibility; tasks are either shared or divided according to personal preference (Peplau and Spalding, 2000). In lesbian relationships, when one is the primary breadwinner and the other the

REFLECT AND APPLY

Reflect

♦ *For each of the obstacles to love, write one problem that would likely occur. In other words, give an example of how each one is an obstacle.*

♦ *Of the various components of love, which are especially important to you?*

♦ *After reading the Teresa Adams quote at the end of the section on intimacy, think of a relationship that the quote brings to mind. Hopefully, it is your own or the relationship of someone who is close to you.*

♦ *Think of a recent disagreement you have had with another person. How was it resolved? Did you fight unfairly or fairly? If unfairly, what can you do better next time?*

Apply

♦ *Listen to a current song about love. Are the lyrics indicative of passionate love, intimate love, or both?*

♦ *Look for examples of both traditional and egalitarian behaviors in your own and others' relationships.*

♦ *If you are in a love relationship, use one of the enrichment ideas. If you are not, ask someone what he or she does in terms of enrichment.*

homemaker, inequities are more common. The researcher noted that the one in the stereotypic woman's role is often negatively affected by economic dependency (Sullivan, 1996). Negotiating roles and responsibilities and then ensuring that you do your fair share can strengthen a living together relationship. Egalitarian men who reject stereotypic gender roles are more likely to intend to have a child and less likely to divorce than traditional men (Kaufman, 2000) (Reflect and Apply).

What else makes a difference in nourishing a living-together relationship? In a study comparing opposite-sex and same-sex couples, intimacy, autonomy, equality, and constructive problem solving contributed to relationship satisfaction for both groups (Kurdek, 1998). For all couples, remembering why you are living together and treating your day-to-day relationship as a precious gift as well as an opportunity for happiness and satisfaction are sound guidelines.

Choosing to Marry

Should everyone marry? Despite a consensus of opinion that marriage is not for everyone, most heterosexual individuals assume that they will marry, and marriage rates remain high. Nearly 9 out of 10 Americans will marry at least once (Belsie, 2002).

Ideally, marriage is truly a choice. Unfortunately, a feeling persists that unless one marries, life will be meaningless. Since the option of remaining single is more appealing than it once was, getting rid of this notion is beneficial in choosing a happy life, married or not. With no pressure driving individuals to marry, they can be either satisfied with single life or free to decide to marry for positive reasons. If the choice is to marry, thoughtful preparation and knowledge can set the stage for a successful union.

Definitions and Images of Marriage

Too often, couples embark on a marital journey with little or no information except what their own images supply. Looking at a committed relationship through a realistic lens can prove to be extremely beneficial.

What is marriage? Agreement on a general definition, as well as on expectations, is a first step in understanding. In its simplest sense, marriage is a legal institution. Sociologically, **marriage** is a socially approved and legally sanctioned mating arrangement, usually involving sexual activity and economic cooperation. In the United States, marriage is based on **monogamy,** having one mate at a time. For many, marriage is also a commitment based on religious beliefs, personal values, or both.

Currently, marriage is considered a heterosexual institution, and gays and lesbians have been deprived in most states of its legal and monetary benefits. In recent years attempts have been made to allow civil unions for same-sex couples. Currently in the United States, the Commonwealth of Massachusetts recognizes same-sex marriage, whereas California, Connecticut, the District of Columbia, Hawaii, Maine, New Jersey, and Vermont grant persons in same-sex unions a similar legal status to those in a civil marriage by domestic partnership, civil union, or reciprocal beneficiary laws (Wikipedia, 2006).

Commitment, obviously a necessary component of marriages and civil unions, is a declaration of loyalty, loving conduct, and honor and includes mutuality of purpose, a willingness to put forth effort, and a pledge of fidelity. Two people who share this idea of commitment are likely to exert effort and succeed in their relationships. Additionally, being in a state of interdependence in which the partners lose neither their identities nor their sense of autonomy is desirable (Lauer and Lauer, 1985).

Images of marriage have undergone changes. In a 2001 Gallup poll, 94 percent of never-married singles agreed that, first and foremost, one's spouse should be a soul mate, a special "someone" who is both lover and friend. In decline were religious, economic, and parental reasons for marriage. The survey indicates that individuals are expecting even more from marriage, yet, overwhelmingly, 86 percent said that marriage is hard work and a full-time job (Whitehead and Popenoe, 2001).

Types of Marriage

Marriages vary in a number of ways, and it is important to know what type satisfies you and your partner. In the past, rules for who did what within a marriage were predetermined and inflexible; this marriage is the **traditional** form. Based on a patriarchal framework, the wife defers to her husband. She makes decisions about home management and the children while he retains final control over family decisions because he is the dominant partner. This "father knows best" type of arrangement was more common and suited to the society of yesteryear (Fig. 12-12). Is this type of marriage arrangement common today?

Are You Willing to Take a Risk?

In the event of divorce:
Rita and Jim were in a traditional marriage for 13 years. He said, "I want you at home taking care of my two boys and not working." She was agreeable, and his business brought them a more than adequate income. Suddenly, Jim left, deserting the family. He left neither a forwarding address nor any money. Rita, who had never worked before, was able to earn only minimum wage. She had to move from her townhouse because she couldn't make the payments. "I never dreamed that this would happen to me," she said.

In the event of a spouse's death:
Colleen, a 56-year-old, was left with no means of supporting herself after her husband's death. To add to her serious misfortune, 6 months before his death, his job had been eliminated and, along with it, the medical benefits and company-paid life insurance. They were uninsured.

Within a marriage:
Dan and Joan were in their late forties, their children were raised, and they were living in a nice condominium when Dan made a job change. Joan had not pursued a full-time career. Soon after the job change, Dan was terminated because of a company downsizing. He sought a professional job with no luck. Without income, they moved in with one of their children for a time. When Dan started work as a security truck driver and Joan took a job at the local hospital, they found a small apartment, similar to one they lived in when they were first married.

Figure 12-12

Another type, the complete opposite of the traditional marriage, is the **egalitarian** or **shared arrangement.** A shared marriage is fair and sensible and fits our current economy and society. Most families today need or want two incomes. Studies on marital success reveal benefits to this arrangement. Marital satisfaction is related to a perception of equity and satisfaction with division of labor (Huppe and Cyr, 1997). Practical benefits have to do with acquiring a variety of skills and being capable of supporting yourself.

With all its advantages, actually practicing a shared marriage is challenging because of past patterns of thinking and behaving. As is true of most categorization methods, the lines can be fuzzy. Couples today may describe themselves as being in an egalitarian marriage and still engage in behaviors based only on their sex. For example, most women correspond with relatives and send greeting cards. Why? The honest answer is just because they are women. Many husbands drive the automobile, and the wives ride. Why? Again, most often, just because they are men. And couples can forget their commitment to a shared relationship on special occasions. At a holiday dinner in most homes, do you see equal distribution of labor? If it exists, the couple is achieving egalitarianism against the odds.

What is today's reality? Even though many couples say they prefer a shared marriage and the majority of women work outside the home, research shows that division of labor is not shared equally in most households. Generally, women continue to carry primary responsibility for household tasks, child care, and care of the elderly even when they work outside the home (Knudsen-Martin and Mahoney, 1998). Taking into account all tasks related to the household, time-diary data from couples showed the following (Bianchi et al., 2000):

- Women have cut their housework hours in half since the 1960s.
- Men are doing more housework than they did in the 1960s.
- Wives perform twice as much household labor than husbands, especially in the areas of cleaning and laundry.

Times are changing, yet roles and responsibilities seem quite resistant to modification.

What makes a difference in division of household labor? Time availability, relative resources of the spouses, and gender-role beliefs are factors accounting for the gap between husbands and wives (Bianchi et al., 2000). Racial diversity corresponds with differences in the participation of males. In off-reservation Navajo Indian families, fathers spent about 75 percent as much time as mothers in household tasks, which is more time than for other cultural groups (Hossain, 2001). Similarly, African American husbands spend more time in household labor than other races (Kamo and Cohen, 1998). Reaching agreement about household tasks before making a commitment and then insisting on adherence to the decision are strong recommendations. A study revealed potential problems. Of the 93 percent of teenagers who said they expected to work as adults, 60 percent of boys and 50 percent of the girls said their spouse would likely stay home to raise the children (Jackson, 1998). So what will the future hold? Obviously, communication about such a vital part of marriage is in order. Problems are inevitable when people marry without forethought or discussion about marriage type.

Another way of defining a marriage is to look at its quality as rated by perceived satisfaction. Several dimensions are possible. Let's look at two basic groups identified in *Coupleship* (Wegscheider-Cruse, 1988).

- The spirited or centered couple expresses their satisfaction. Each feels happy and fulfilled. The relationship not only works—it thrives.
- The spiritually dead or estranged couple expresses dissatisfaction. The partners feel lonely, hurt, and angry. Their relationship is unfulfilled.

Preparation for Marriage

The time to ask serious questions about marriage is before the wedding ceremony. Some of these questions could be:

- Does my partner have habits that I dislike?
- Do we have similar styles of spending and saving?
- Am I satisfied with how we share household responsibilities?
- Do we have similar parenting styles?
- Are our religious beliefs the same?

For a more complete list of possible questions go to http://www.prepare-enrich.com (Olson, 1998).

TA Revisited

"Parent" messages range from "Do not get married. You are not ready" to "You better get married soon, or you may never have another chance."

The "child" ego state experiences love and desires marriage because of perceived future happiness and the prospect of pleasure.

The "adult" ego state is needed to process, prepare, and make a conscious choice based on reason.

The potential for success is increased when careful examination is followed by thoughtful decisions. A lack of any formal preparation is the norm even though research reveals that couples can benefit a great deal from a premarital education program (Stanley et al., 2001). Some religious groups may either require or offer premarital counseling. The value of the counseling lies in the skill of the clergy member to utilize sound, practical advice based on research. Premarital counseling by therapists is available yet not commonly sought. Some high schools offer coursework regarding relationships, and almost every college and university have a course in marriage and family.

Unless all students are required to learn how to succeed in long-term relationships, large numbers will remain uneducated. A marriage license is no certainty that individuals know anything about relating. The emotional and financial damage to adults and children as a result of unhappy marriages is apparent (TA Revisited).

How to prepare. Preparation for marriage begins within the self. Chronological age is definitely a factor. Adolescent marriages are especially likely to end in divorce (Strong, DeVault, and Sayad, 1998). The older a woman's age, the longer the marriage is likely to last (National Center for Health Statistics, 2001). The median age for women is about 25.1 years and for men 26.8 years. A young adult is more likely than a teenager to have achieved independence, identity, maturity, and experience. When individuals marry without having had other close relationships, they may wonder what they have missed and are likely to feel restless and dissatisfied.

Do you recall Erikson's psychosocial stages? Regardless of age, establishing identity is needed before intimacy is likely to be successful. People who are divorced or widowed are wise to think about this because identity is easily "lost" after a major life change. Related to identity is independence. Are you able to live on your own? Any healthy relationship is only as strong as its two individual parts. Partners must have a strong sense of "I" to form a successful "we." The symbolism about "two becoming one" may seem romantic; however, a strong "I" and another strong "I" are more likely than an enamored "we" to sustain the stressors of a long-term relationship.

> Love thrives when two people are quite capable of living without each other but choose to live with each other. (Peck, 1978)

Clearing away personal litter from past relationships and experiences is important. Bonnie, a friend since grade school, became a clinical psychologist.

Reflecting on being raped when she was 16 years old, she said, "Nobody thought of a need for counseling. I was, I guess, just expected to recover over time. I realize now that unresolved issues related to the rape contributed to unhappiness in marriage and then to my subsequent divorce."

Other personal factors related to success are self-esteem and self-created happiness. Desirable behavioral characteristics such as temper control, assertiveness, and open communication lead to better long-term relationships. In a study designed to predict marital success, one factor that emerged was the husband's willingness to accept influence from his wife. For both partners, contempt, belligerence, and defensiveness were destructive patterns (Gottman et al., 1998). Obviously, a well-adjusted person has a much better chance of having a successful marriage than one who is struggling with personal issues. "You want a partner, not a private nurse, caretaker, or entertainer." Finally, maturity and an understanding of commitment are essential. Each person's "self" determines the success of a marriage. "Your relationships travel the same course that you travel" (Dyer, 1992, p. 114).

> Look for a partner who is also happy, so that you are not burdened with the impossible responsibility of trying to fix someone else. (Goulding and Goulding, 1989)

After personal readiness has been achieved, education about long-term relationships is recommended. College courses, personality exploration, marriage-readiness tests, reading, and openly discussing issues with a prospective partner are beneficial. A practical, easy-to-understand book highly recommended for all couples is *Why Love Is Not Enough* (Gordon, 1996). Cohabitation, as discussed earlier, can prepare mature couples for marriage if they live together in a realistic way.

Succeeding in Marriage and Other Committed Relationships

A thorough discussion of identified success factors can increase the probability of happiness and success in marriage and other long-term relationships. A couple is also advised to consider the opinions of others. Remember the romantic tale of Romeo and Juliet? That story leads us to believe that their families were wrong for objecting. Do not be blinded by this belief. If your family and friends do not think you are making a good choice, at least consider their reasons. Then draw upon research and credible information in making a decision.

Success Factors: Questions to Ask

Whether in a preparation program, counseling setting, or by themselves, couples can answer questions and evaluate potential success. If married or already in a committed relationship, many of the questions can be used to assess areas of strength and weakness. Following each question are reasons for their importance as well as recommendations.

- *Have we known each other well for a long enough period?*

Length of acquaintance.   Knowing each other well for at least a year is recommended. This does not guarantee readiness; however, giving yourself that amount of time so that you experience the four seasons and all the holidays is revealing. One student remarked, "You need at least a year just to discuss all of these questions!"

- *Why do we want to make a long-term commitment?*

Reasons for marriage or commitment.   Counselors believe that the answer to "Why do we want to enter into a committed relationship?" is one of the best predictors of success. Think of all the possible reasons for marriage. Among them are a number of poor reasons. Pressure is one. This can come from a lover, family, friends, or society itself. Even age exerts pressure. "I am almost 27 years old, and I feel like I should be thinking about marriage," said a man. If you feel any kind of pressure, force yourself to resist. Janeen, a student, wrote about her experience:

> We did not look at the "marriage" but listened to the pressure of being married. He was a closed person and a loner. They say opposites attract, but we were too opposite. I also was thinking I had to have someone and was not looking at that "someone."

Other reasons come from the child ego state: "Oh, marriage seems like such fun." "It will be like playing house." "The wedding and honeymoon will be so much fun." "I am so in love." Even love is not a sufficient reason to marry because satisfying long-term relationships require even more. A need to have someone to feel fulfilled comes from our "child" and is a deficiency-based reason for marrying.

Looking at the advantages and disadvantages of marriage can help you identify the reasons and evaluate costs versus benefits. Some advantages are companionship, caring, sex, learning from and helping each other, financial sharing, legal benefits, and raising a family. Several of these advantages are possible without getting married; however, in this society, marriage is the recognized and legal way of achieving them. Other advantages are related to psychological and physical health. In an international study, marriage increased degree of happiness in 16 of the 17 nations sampled, with the exception being Northern Ireland (Stack and Eshleman, 1998). Compared to unmarried people, those who are married tend to have lower mortality, less risky behaviors, more monitoring of health, higher sexual frequency, more sexual satisfaction, more financial savings, and higher wages (Bramlett and Mosher, 2001). The percentage of persons surviving at least five years after diagnosis of cancer was found to be greater for married than unmarried persons (Ornish, 1998). Love and intimacy, especially in a socially approved context, apparently contribute to our well-being. Disadvantages include relinquishing personal freedom to a certain extent, added stressors, having to share resources, and the risk of an unhappy relationship as well as possible divorce.

Eliminating all the poor reasons still leaves a question. What is a positive reason for marrying? A couple whose marriage has great potential for success might say, "We are marrying because we are sure that we share an intimate love, we have carefully prepared and considered all known factors, we believe we have an excellent chance of succeeding in marriage, and we want to make a legal and deep commitment to this relationship."

- *What do we expect?*

Expectations about marriage.   This question can yield some intriguing answers. Incompatible or unreasonable expectations by one or both partners should be a warning signal. "I expect you to be there for me always. I expect you to satisfy all my needs. I do not expect that we will fight." Even if the two agree on these expectations, they are being extremely unrealistic. A large gap between what people expect and what actually occurs leads to disappointment and frustration.

Myths about marriage abound. "We will live happily ever after without having to work on the relationship," "Neither we nor our relationship will ever change," "Fighting is bad for a relationship," "What goes on outside of our marriage will not affect us," and "People stay in love forever." Too often, individuals will look at marriage as either "a bed or roses" or "a bed of thorns," and neither extreme is accurate. A couple would benefit from dispelling the myths.

An underlying expectation, usually quite subtle, is that marriage will be fantastic for a brief period and then downhill after that. "The honeymoon is over" is a phrase used to describe a marital relationship after the initial stage. Have you heard people describe marriage in the following ways?

"They have settled down." (Does not this sound inviting?)

"They are an old married couple now." (Probably because they have actually "settled down.")

"You can tell they are married." (This describes a couple that appears bored or uninterested in each other)

"They must not be married." (This describes a couple that is holding hands or showing affection.)

"They tied the knot." (Ouch!)

When discussing his upcoming marriage to a young woman, he replied, "Yeah, I am going to bite the dust this weekend." He evidently did just that and in less than a year was divorced. The "ball and chain" stereotype is apt to lead to unhappy outcomes. Also, if you begin to take each other for granted, either or both partners suffer. Then negative images can become the reality. Checking expectations is essential. If yours are unrealistic, dismal, or incompatible with your partner's, either change your thoughts or postpone marriage.

- *What type of marriage do we want and how will we achieve it?*

Possible types of marriage.   As discussed earlier, types of living-together arrangements are related to roles, responsibilities, and quality in a marriage. A study of Chinese young adults provides a reason for an honest discussion. Females were far more likely than males to believe that household chores and tasks should be equally shared and that women were entitled to careers (Xie and Lin, 1997). When one partner desires an egalitarian marriage and the other favors traditionalism, opportunities for conflict are greatly increased. Differing gender role beliefs and differing perceptions of role equity significantly affect marital stability (Guilbert, Vacc, and Pasley, 2000). Not only do most women want men who will share in household responsibilities (Kaufman, 2000), but also satisfaction with division of labor was a significant predictor of martial satisfaction for both sexes (Stevens, Kiger, and Riley, 2001). Periodically, checking with each other concerning perceptions of fairness will help prevent resentment and contribute to a more satisfying union.

- *Are we both going to pursue careers and, if so, how will we handle such aspects as work schedules, relocation, and conflict between career and relationship?*

Careers and jobs.   If you opt for a shared marriage, you will probably both be contributing income. Men and women work not only for incomes, but also often they prefer having careers and enjoy their work. However, even though employment has benefits, dual-career couples can find that issues of relocation and career advancement cause conflict. If couples believe in equality and comparable levels of power, decisions will be made jointly by weighing costs versus benefits. The best interests of both will be considered, and either may be expected to make a change.

- *What are our career and personal goals and are they compatible?*

Goals.   If compatible, all goals can have positive effects on a relationship. Two people moving in similar directions can share excitement and challenges. Discussing career goals and personal ones such as homeownership, further education, and travel is important, and doing so with a flexible attitude is essential. Total honesty is imperative. Cynthia sadly mentioned how Rob, before marriage, had talked about his desire to travel. "Since we have been married, all he wants to do is stay home." A positive note about goals is that the more education people have the more likely they are to stay married (Armas, 2002).

- *Have we explored our financial situation? Do we know each other's present income and potential debts and past financial history? Will we budget? How will we manage our finances? What are our feelings and attitudes about money?*

Financial issues.   Financial incompatibility and struggles can bring even the strongest relationship to its knees. Even with a more than adequate income, couples can face problems if they disagree on how money is to be used and have different attitudes about money. Karen was a saver and would spend money only for essentials. Luxuries were not important. "The money is better in the bank" was her philosophy. Lee believed in using money and living for today without much thought of tomorrow. "You cannot take it to your grave" was his motto. They argued regularly and bitterly about money. The handling of finances covers many areas. Will you keep your incomes separate? Will one or both of you pay the bills? How will you make financial decisions? These are practical and necessary issues to resolve.

Another valuable exercise is to assess financial independence so that one is not overly dependent on the other. Ask yourselves the following questions (Farrell, 1986).

- Are we committed to sharing all expenses equally? If not, for what reason? (Hopefully, this does not indicate a future of financial dependency.)
- Am I able to support myself in the style I prefer?
- If my partner works less than I do, am I comfortable with that?
- If I work less than my partner, am I comfortable with that?

An excellent resource is *Smart Couples Finish Rich* (Bach, 2001), a book designed to create a financially secure future. A frank discussion of finances reveals a great deal about both people and the quality of the relationship. Part of this discussion should be about any assets or debts that you have that will be brought into the marriage. At times a prenuptial agreement may be necessary to clarify financial rights and responsibilities during marriage. Or couples may want to avoid potential arguments if they ever divorce by specifying in advance how their property will be divided (Nolo, 2006).

- *How similar are our values and religious beliefs? How similar are we in important aspects of life? How will we handle conflicts in these areas?*

Similarities. Differences are interesting and can be positive; however, relationships are strengthened when partners share similar values and attitudes, have some of the same interests, and share a common lifestyle. Couples who have compatible religious and philosophical beliefs find it easier to be intimate. Strong values and attitudes, if unshared, are especially troublesome. For example, if you are opposed to prejudice and committed to human rights and equality, a partner's bigotry would pose a serious threat to a relationship. Minor differences, which lend spark and variety to a relationship, are acceptable. Major differences, especially in sensitive areas, are disruptive.

Homogamy is the tendency to enter into a relationship with someone who is similar to you. Differences in socioeconomic backgrounds and age are good to examine. Do you feel comfortable in each other's worlds? Do you view the differences as positive or potentially negative? A question for many in today's society has to do with interracial and interethnic marriages. In recent years there has been a substantial increase in rates of interracial marriage especially between black men and non-black women (Crowder and Tolnay, 2000). Asian women have the greatest tendency to marry outside their race. In 2000, nearly 32 percent did so (Gardyn and Lach, 2000). Interracial couples are together for love, affection, and shared values, which are no different from same-race couples (Moore, 1999). Understanding the special challenges interracial couples in a world that is still prejudiced and discriminatory is critical. Having several other similarities and a strong intimate love will be instrumental. Realistically, interracial couples will be contending with additional obstacles because of their racial differences. That does not preclude them from being successful and, if so, deservedly, with a deep sense of pride.

- *Do we have common interests? How do we like to spend vacations? How will we use leisure time? How important are our hobbies?*

Interests and leisure time. People want enjoyment within an intimate relationship. Even though it is not necessary to have exactly the same interests and hobbies, sharing several and being open to others lead to mutual pleasure. If both generally agree about vacations and holidays and are open-minded when these are being discussed, the relationship benefits.

- *Are our lifestyles compatible? Do we have some of the same friends? Do we like each other's friends?*

Lifestyles and friends.   "Amber really likes to party, and when we first started going out, I found her wild ways attractive. As time went by, I realized that I did not like the drinking scene, the late hours, and all the running around. We fight about this a lot," said Chris. Compatibility of life styles impacts on long-term happiness, and if neither is willing to change, marriage is not the answer. Lifestyle is also reflected in how you demonstrate your socioeconomic status (i.e., large, showy home versus small, average-looking residence) and time allocation (i.e., work before play or fun comes first).

Even though you do not necessarily have to like all the friends of your partner, not liking *any* or *few* is a red flag. It is important to explore reasons for liking and disliking; in the process, you will learn more about the other person. Although maintaining friendships throughout life is important, putting friends ahead of a significant other is asking for trouble.

- *Are we independent of our families? What role will our families play in our lives?*

Extended family issues.   Overly strong ties to one's biological family can cause conflict. "He spends more time with his parents than he does with me," complained a young woman. "It seems like they always want him to help them, and he just picks up and goes." Families will remain important, and successful couples usually have positive relationships with extended family members, yet these relationships should be secondary to the marriage.

What about not liking or not getting along with each other's families? Again, caution is in order. For what reasons do not you like or get along with your partner's family? Are your feelings similar to your partner's? "I do not really get along with two of my brothers, so I do not expect her to like them," said one man. It is true that you are not marrying a family; however, keep in mind that this person spent many years with family members and has certainly been influenced. Special concerns are families with poor communication, inflexibility, lack of warmth, and unfair fighting patterns. Individuals are wise to assess what they do not like about family members and whether their partner is similar in those areas. Upbringing, although significant, is not necessarily an accurate predictor. What individuals have learned is more important. "People are only victims of the past when they choose to be" (Sternberg and Whitney, 1991, p. 14).

- *Do we want children? If so, have we talked about number, timing, birth control, and child rearing? Do we agree about responsibilities for child care?*

Having children.   If you did not do so before, take a close look at your partner as a potential parent. Angela explained why she had made a painful decision to end a relationship: "I concluded that I did not want him to father my children." Couples are remiss if they do not discuss whether they both want to have children. A bizarre case was related by a miserable woman who had suggested to her husband that she was ready to become pregnant. He looked surprised and said, "I do not want to have kids." Such cases are rare, yet to avoid any surprises, talk about desire for children. Discuss parenting and all aspects of raising children, as covered in Chapter 13, including any stereotypic ideas regarding child care. I enjoyed a comment in a study of dual-earner couples: "If fathers want to romp with their children on the living room carpet, it is important that they be willing to vacuum it regularly" (Hawkins and Roberts, 1992, p. 170). Also, a father would share in caring for the romping children.

- *Have we been open with each other about sexuality? Do we have any attitudes that may cause problems?*

Sexuality. Couples may or may not have sexual experience before they marry. Current statistics indicate that most will. In any event, communication about sexual attitudes and desires is highly recommended. This area is not to be avoided because both expect things to work out fine on their own. Dissatisfaction is likely to result if two people do not share similar attitudes about their sexual relationship. Reading together the earlier section on sexual fulfillment as well as other books on the subject is certainly worthwhile.

- *Do we really know each other, including our habits and faults?*

Knowing each other. Spending time together under all kinds of circumstances gives each partner an opportunity to truly get to know the other. Annoying habits can seem cute at first, yet over a long period of time, they erode the relationship. The use of drugs must be evaluated. "I realized that he drank a lot when we went out, but I never dreamed he depended on it so much. Now his drinking is ruining our marriage." People are not apt to change their habits after marriage. In a lively public address, Jim Kern, a professional speaker, told of a young woman who bemoaned her fiancé's drinking. "I am sure he will change after we get married," she said. Kern asked, "How many of you believe that he will?" No hands were raised. "And how many of you think he will find more reasons to drink and blame them all on her?" was the next question. The laughter demonstrated that people know that automatic postmarital changes for the better are rare.

- *Do we have personality differences that may cause difficulties? Do we like each other's personalities and recognize positive traits?*

Personalities. An extravert and an introvert, as classified on the Myers-Briggs Type Indicator, are likely to report significantly more problems than two who are matched in this category. Creative solutions are in order. One couple decided that they would drive two cars to social events. She, an introvert, wanted to limit her time at such events, whereas he, an extravert, liked to be a part of the action for the duration. Each returned home at a different time, and both were happy.

Personality differences do not necessarily create problems; rather, *un*awareness of the differences causes difficulty. Frequently, a person marries an opposite type and then is annoyed when the partner does not think and act in a similar way.

Couples who are too much alike can also run into difficulty. If neither has strength in the MBTI sensing preference, for example, the couple will be at a disadvantage in matters such as budgeting and tending to details. Two individuals with strong judging preferences are likely to butt heads when personal plans and schedules do not coincide. Deciding how to manage these areas could prevent serious problems.

Certain characteristics such as being caring, warm, understanding, humorous, and unselfish are desirable for individuals and serve to create a positive environment. Liking and appreciating each other's personalities makes a significant difference in both the success of the marriage and the happiness of each person.

- *Are we flexible and do we communicate in open and effective ways?*

Positive communication and flexibility.   Not surprisingly, communication is a significant predictor of relationship satisfaction (Meeks, Hendrick, and Hendrick, 1998). Communication skills were identified as the most helpful in a premarital education program (Stanley et al., 2001). Listening may be considered "love in action, and nowhere is it more appropriate than in marriage" (Peck, 1978, p. 128).

> Communication is the lifeblood of any relationship, and the love relationship demands communication if it is to flourish. (Branden and Branden, 1982, p. 63)

Even though it is simplistic to say that poor communication leads to low-quality marriages, communication is at the heart of maintaining and enriching a relationship. A mistake is to believe that communication will improve after marriage. If communication and trust are not established early in the relationship, they are unlikely to develop. Taking an interpersonal communication course before marriage is one of the best possible action steps.

Flexibility influences communication and all other aspects of a relationship. Two rigid persons will not bend, and the marriage is what will break. Similarly, the need to be right is the greatest cause of difficulties and deterioration in relationships (Dyer, 1992). Inflexibility and a controlling personality go hand in hand. Controllers go to great lengths to make sure they come out on top and generally do not consider others' feelings or wishes. Controlling methods include criticism, moodiness, anger, threats, and even overprotection. The person may also deny your perceptions. For example, if you object to a hurtful remark, he or she is likely to say, "You just cannot take a joke," even though you are sure it was not a joke. Extremely rigid individuals are unlikely to be good partners.

- *How well do we handle conflict?*

Conflict management.   Closely related to communication, the ability to handle disagreement is a pivotal skill in marriage. As discussed earlier in this chapter, two people can "make or break" their chances for a successful long-term relationship by learning about disagreement and fair fighting. John Gottman

(1994a), a well-known researcher in this field, says, "If there is one lesson I have learned from my years of research it is that a lasting marriage results from a couple's ability to resolve the conflicts that are inevitable in any relationship" (p. 28). Before commitment, an assessment of conflict management and a willingness to learn and practice necessary skills are highly recommended.

- *Do we enjoy being together and are we good friends?*

Togetherness and pleasure.   Enjoyment of each other's company is essential. Long-term relationships thrive on mutual pleasures. Can the two of you be alone happily while engaging in a variety of pleasurable activities? Can you be alone "doing nothing" and be content?

Friendship.   Being friends and not just lovers is bound to be increase long-term satisfaction. In a survey entitled "What Keeps a Marriage Going?" (Lauer and Lauer, 1985), both women and men listed "My spouse is my best friend" as their top reason, with "I like my spouse as a person" second. All the ingredients of friendship are necessary in intimate love. "We were friends first and then became sexually attracted to each other. I think that is why our relationship is so successful," said one woman. Friendship is a much better model for what you need in marriage than the media images of romantic love.

Friendship does not have to be present in the beginning. You can be physically attracted and then become friends. The key is that at some time friendship must develop. "Is friendship essential to love? No, but it is essential to love's lasting for it is the foundation of love" (Solomon, 1988, p. 315). Individuals who can honestly say that their partners are their best friends are quite fortunate. Friendship is the glue that holds marriages together and makes them so fulfilling. Without friendship, intimate love can easily die.

- *How will we help each other during periods of crisis?*

Support during crises.   From firsthand experiences I realize how significant this question is. If you have encountered such crises as a death in the family, a personal health problem, or a family disruption, you already know how the two of you will react. If you have not, you are wise to discuss possibilities and make some type of commitment to each other. "Being there" for each other is a reasonable expectation and crucial to success in long-term love relationships.

How does the potential partner show support and will that style be helpful to you? A strong thinking preference on the MBTI will immediately begin to problem-solve in a logical way whereas the feeling type will empathize. Certainly, individuals can offer both types of support, although some offer little. Spending a long time with this person means that you are likely to go through rough times together. A high degree of emotional supportiveness makes all the difference in the world.

- *What else?*

Other questions related to your specific relationship may also be in order. The actual discussion of all questions can reveal potential problems.

After you read this chapter and consider the success factors, remember that no person or relationship is perfect. You can use a cost-versus-benefits approach. If you share intimate love, have experienced other relationships, and are committed to equality, then apply a 90:10 rule. In considering all factors, if the relationship is 90 percent positive, go for it! Additionally, be sure that the factors in the unfavorable 10 percent are not the most potentially destructive ones.

Marital Enrichment

Awareness of a high divorce rate and realization that marriage isn't always bliss indicate that **marriage enrichment,** the process of making marriage better, deserves priority. All of the enrichment suggestions offered earlier in this chapter can be used to make a good marriage better and to revitalize one that has declined in quality. For married and other long-term couples, a few areas deserve even more attention.

The sexual relationship over a long duration can easily become an area of benign neglect. Sex therapist Dagmar O'Connor (1985) contrasts lovemaking attitudes and behaviors. Early in a relationship, people describe themselves as being "swept away" by passion and relate the sex act to an "accident that just happened." These feelings usually add to the allure of lovemaking. Over years of togetherness, couples make sex a conscious act that should happen, and then they blame the lack of excitement on being together so long. "That is how it is. After years of being together, the thrill is gone." The thrill in making love does not have to disappear like a puff of smoke. Maintaining a fulfilling sexual relationship is a vital part of couple enrichment.

Enrichment may require therapy. If you decide to see a counselor, go to one recommended by people you trust. Counselors vary in their abilities. Even after you have made your selection, if one of you feels uncomfortable with the therapist, find another one. It is important that each of you feels respected, acknowledged, and valued by the therapist (Weiner-Davis, 1992). Marriage and family therapist Sue Frahm says that most couples come as a last resort, which makes counseling more challenging. She and her husband, Larry, usually begin by asking individuals on a scale from 0 to 10 how committed they are to the relationship. Then they throw out the most critical question: "On a scale of 1 to 10, how willing are you to work on it?" Often the answers to the two questions are not the same. Sue and Larry favor solution-focused and action-oriented therapy. "We believe that if something is a problem to one person, it's a problem in the relationship. Both then must commit to change."

Think of a marriage or any long-term relationship as an investment. What makes an investment portfolio valuable is having more assets than liabilities. Enrichment adds to the assets. A sad commentary on contemporary life is that people will spend more time maintaining houses, automobiles, and other property than they do caring for their relationships. An attitude that "our relationship is precious, and we want to keep it that way" can bring a dream of an enriched marriage to reality. Together, couples can choose how rewarding and successful their relationship will be.

Ending Relationships

"Till death us do part" is no longer a guarantee. The divorce rate since 1960 has more than doubled; the likelihood of divorce now exceeds 40 percent (Raymond, 2001). Contributing to the numbers are certain sociological factors, such as divorce being easier to obtain and being much more acceptable. No matter how personally disquieting the idea of ending a committed relationship, thousands of people yearly find themselves faced with a legal ending to their relationship. This section will focus on divorce; however, much of it is applicable to the ending of other intimate relationships.

Reasons for Seeking an End

"We loved each other so much. I do not know what happened" is not an unusual statement when a relationship ends. Understanding the "why" can help individuals learn from a painful experience. A prime possibility is an inappropriate or poor choice of a partner. An understanding of the needs fulfillment theory, described earlier, will probably reveal unmet needs. One or both partners may decide that the benefits of the relationship are outweighed by the costs. A third person may be involved. As one who does not believe that anyone else breaks up a couple, a recommendation is to examine the weakness in the relationship. Or, perhaps, one individual is simply not committed and engages in repeated self-indulgent outside relationships. In that case, the other is better off alone.

Couples can have unrealistic expectations, and disappointment is the likely result. Or realistic expectations may not have been met. "He is almost never home. If he is not working, he is involved in some community service or leisure-time activity. It is as if I do not exist" is a description of a relationship that falls far short of meeting either a person's legitimate needs or realistic expectations of a marriage.

Problems such as sexual infidelity, jealousy, drinking, spending money, moodiness, poor communication, and anger increase the odds of divorce (Amato and Rogers, 1997). A particularly hateful behavior is abuse, either verbal or nonverbal. Habitual serious physical abuse gives separation a green light. Staying with an abuser is, in effect, saying that such behavior is acceptable. Leaving a person you have loved and may still have strong feelings for is painful; however, in the long run, an unsatisfying or demoralizing relationship hurts even more.

Counseling as an Alternative

Although ending a relationship can be the best solution, seeking divorce isn't always advisable. Either extreme—"never divorce, no matter what" or "no problem; just divorce when the going gets tough"—is an insult to the dignity and value of nourishing relationships. Before making the serious decision to divorce, be sure that the reasons are sound and that everything possible has been done to revitalize the marriage. Counseling can be great help in making the decision to divorce or stay married. Even if you think that it is too late, you owe it to yourself to try. You could be like Gina who said, "I would have bet anyone a million dollars that counseling would not work. All I can say now is that I am really happy I did not make that bet. Our marriage is wonderful, and we continue to make it more so!" Hopefully, if children are involved, you wouldn't hesitate to use all available resources to repair the damage and develop a stronger marriage. In Chapter 13 there is a section on children and divorce.

Letting Go

When faced with the painful reality of ending a relationship, realize that this is a major stressor. Even if you are the one who initiates the breakup, you can expect to experience unpleasant feelings. If you are the one who does not want the divorce, you will sink into one of the "dips" of life. A full gamut of emotions may be experienced, depending on the circumstances.

Depression is common after divorce. Research revealed a significant increase in stressful events and depressive symptoms soon after a divorce that then diminish over the next three years (Lorenz et al., 1997). Whatever is experienced, remember that you are not alone. In response to the increasing incidence of divorce, books have been written, classes and seminars have been developed, and support groups have been formed. If you divorce, numerous resources are available. One that was especially helpful to me is *How to Survive the Loss of a Love* (Colgrove, Bloomfield, and McWilliams, 1991). Picturing the "healing process as more like a lightning bolt full of ups and downs, progressions and regressions, dramatic leaps and depressing backslides" (p. 36) helped me to remain hopeful in the worst of times. Another book, *Rebuilding: When Your Relationship Ends* (Fischer, 1992), is one that Roz, a student, said "saved my life." Fifteen building blocks are described, and the final one is freedom.

The divorce process, like the grief process, is a series of stages. Six are identified by Gullo and Church (1988):

- Shock, usually ranging in duration from 1 day to 1 month and characterized by numbness, disorientation, and disbelief.
- Grief or a feeling of depression of varying duration.
- Setting blame, generally accompanied by anger.
- Resignation, or the good-bye stage, when you decide to let go, which can be either relieving or draining.
- Rebuilding, when you feel like life is good again.
- Resolution, when peace with the pain is acknowledged and you can look back and see evidence of personal growth.

You can gain strength from seeing where you are in these steps and, after time, how far you have come. Because these stages have been experienced by almost every divorcing person, you can feel assured that you, too, will eventually reach the resolution stage. The "traveling time" for most is about 1 year.

A beneficial step is to change the typical thought that divorce is proof of individual maladjustment and the common feeling of regret that your marriage did not last forever.

The value of a relationship lies in the joy it affords, not in its longevity. (There is nothing admirable about two people remaining together, thoroughly frustrated and miserable, for 50 years.) The ending of a relationship does not mean that someone has failed. It means only that someone has changed, perhaps for the better. (Branden and Branden, 1982, p. 206)

Following are some recommendations for coping with relationship endings.

- Use this book and others to find coping strategies and behaviors to create happiness and raise self-esteem.
- If you are not helping yourself, seek counseling.
- Draw on your support system. You need people. Ideally, talk to people who have gone through the process and feel just fine. Support groups are in almost every community.
- Find a skilled attorney. The legal aspects of divorce require expertise. Learn about current laws so you have input regarding legal decisions. Your future is at stake.
- Be aware of financial consequences. The living standard of the partner who earns more money rises by about 10 percent whereas the one who earns less decreases by about 27 percent (Yip, 2001).
- Pay special attention to your own health and needs.
- Allow yourself all your feelings without getting stuck with any. Prolonged depression and unresolved anger, for example, indicate a need for counseling.
- Resist the temptation to think of yourself as a failure. Instead, realize that the relationship failed. Do, however, examine yourself and make positive changes.
- Let go of any magical quality you assigned to the relationship and recognize that you, as a couple, no longer exist.
- Seek new relationships with both sexes; however, do not try to build an intimate one right away. Keep in mind Erikson's identity stage, which is best to establish again before you are ready for a new relationship. This recommendation is difficult to follow because anyone who has been wounded usually relishes positive attention from the opposite sex. Friendships, at this point, are nourishing. Beyond that, you reduce the potential for success in a future intimate relationship.
- Begin to dream, plan, and live. See the ending as an opportunity, not as a death sentence.

Think of these suggestions as a basic "survival kit." You can add ideas by reading, experiencing, and learning. Self-support and self-respect can be developed by going back to school or taking a course, starting a new project, expanding your network of friends, and becoming involved in a worthwhile organization or cause. Think of each of these new opportunities as: "If I had not divorced or ended the relationship, this probably would not have been a part of my life"

During the initial stages, most find it hard to conceive of the possibility of anything positive; however, almost every divorced person can point out several benefits. One is heightened self-esteem after, and often as a direct result of, the divorce. Expanding one's horizons and becoming independent are boosters to confidence and add to the excitement of life. New opportunities present themselves and, if taken advantage of, can lead to positive results. Advanced academic degrees, exciting careers, new or renewed hobbies and interests, and exciting interpersonal relationships can be treasures along the way. If the marriage was painful, the relief from stress and misery is a reward in itself. After their divorces, three individuals expressed their rewards and joy.

Tammy: Now that I have a chance to go to school, I am learning about myself as well as preparing for a profession. I needed this more than words can say. My grandma used to say, "Every dark cloud has a silver lining." Now I understand. Losing a husband is hard, but finding yourself is wonderful.

Shirley: From divorce I have learned to love myself, to not forget me and to think of myself, to live for today, to be an independent person, to make my own happiness, to accept my mistakes, to make my own choices, and, most importantly, that life is up to me. In my marriage I gave all of me. I did not even know who I was. I am now a happier, wiser person and am still growing. I realize I have so much to learn . . . so many miles to travel before I sleep.

John: It was not easy to have someone I loved leave me, yet the feelings I have today are worth it. I now realize that there was even more pain when we were together.

All relationships end at some time. Divorce is an ending that was precipitated by a decision. Whether one person likes the decision or not, understanding the process and electing to move toward a positive ending are beneficial.

An ending such as a divorce is not a failure of the self; usually, it just indicates unwise choices. Objectively, individuals can accept a share of the responsibility and resolve to be wiser in the future. They can become optimistic about future relationships and willing to risk new experiences. The ability to let go and say good-bye is a sign of a well-adjusted person. A quote from Dale Carnegie is apt here: "When fate hands us a lemon, let's try to make lemonade."

LOOKING BACK

- Love and intimacy are important in most people's lives. Although education would be very beneficial in the areas of loving, marrying, and divorcing, unfortunately, it is not required. Love as an art requires attention, skill, practice, and priority.
- Passionate love is the "fluff stuff" of which dreams may be made yet usually not realized. Several problems materialize in a passionate-love relationship; a major challenge is jealousy.
- In contrast, intimate love is renewing and rewarding and can serve as a strong foundation for a long-term, mutually satisfying relationship. Components of intimate love have been identified.
- Examination of relationship growth and needs fulfillment reveals a great deal. Intimate love expands as the individuals grow in compatible directions and as the relationship fulfills primary needs.
- Intimacy includes the freedom to be one's genuine self within a relationship and the development of psychological closeness with another person.

- Building intimacy is challenging. Removing barriers is the first step. The rewards are well worth all efforts.
- Conflict management deserves special attention because the harm caused by mishandled conflict is a major source of relationship dissatisfaction and dissolution. Conflict or disagreement is inevitable in intimate relationships. The key to couple success lies in how the conflict is managed. Fair fighting is highly recommended.
- Enrichment is the exception, not the rule. Without attention and priority, love and intimacy can gradually erode. Enriching attitudes and behaviors are essential for long-term successful relationships.
- Despite an increase in numbers of sexually active individuals, people can be woefully ignorant about healthy sexual behaviors. Enrichment makes a difference.
- Both heterosexual and gay/lesbian couples choose to live together as partners. Successful long-term relationships pay consideration to living arrangements and all aspects of couple satisfaction. Cohabitation is defined as living together in a committed relationship. Whether cohabitation influences the probability of marital success is questionable.
- If one chooses to marry, an understanding of marriage helps foster a positive commitment. Shared and traditional types of marriage based on roles and responsibilities are possible, and individuals are wise to agree on the type they prefer.
- Couples can benefit from marriage preparation. Self-examination comes first. Success factors, as identified by research, can be the basis of relevant, and important questions. The discussion of the answers may reveal personal characteristics that are damaging to relationships. For partners who are already in long-term relationships, the questions can serve as guideposts for positive changes.
- In spite of the best intentions, love relationships can end. Divorce rates are high. For those who divorce, resources are available, and people can learn how to end relationships in less hurtful ways. Pain is inevitable as one passes through predictable stages, yet divorce can lead to personal growth, happiness, and an extremely satisfying future.

Intimate love is manifested by giving, receiving, sharing, and growing—two vital individuals forming a strong "we."

—Sharon Hanna

RESOURCES

Association for Conflict Resolution. (202) 667–9700. http://www.mediate.com
American Association for Marriage and Family Therapists. (202) 452–0109. http://www.aamft.org

National Board for Certified Counselors. (336) 547–0607. http://www.nbcc.org
Collaborative Divorce. (415) 383–5600. http://www.collaborativedivorce.com
Fisher's Rebuilding Seminar. http://www.fisherseminars.com
Classes and workshops on love, relationships, communication, and conflict management are offered through community colleges and university continuing education programs.

STRENGTHENING FAMILY RELATIONSHIPS

LOOKING AHEAD

After completing this chapter, you will be able to

- Define family.
- Recognize the significance of parenting, as well as realize that there is a lack of formal required training.
- Make thoughtful decisions about parenting and preparation.
- Describe areas in which education is beneficial.
- Discuss parenting responsibilities.
- Define discipline, explain three styles, and give reasons that democratic discipline is recommended.
- Describe positive parenting behaviors.
- Discuss grandparenting and the benefits of its many roles.
- Understand ways to help a child cope with parents' divorce.

> *When "I–other" relationships work, then families work. When families work, societies work; when societies work, nations work; when nations work, nature works; and when nature works, the universe works.*
>
> —Thomas and Patrick Malone

Take a moment and reflect on the momentous influences a family has on a person's life. Your family gave you a name, a geographic home, and a societal position, and most important, family members contributed to your self-concept, learned attitudes, values, behaviors, and personality. The family, for most people, is the greatest determining factor in the quality of an individual's life. In the field of sociology, family is called a **primary group,** one that is small, intimate, and enduring.

Diversity is the best descriptor of families today. This chapter focuses on one of a family's most critical functions, that of raising children. A variety of family types will be discussed with emphasis on the importance that families play. The strengths of diverse families will be evident, and recommendations for building even stronger families will be given.

Exploring Families

What is a family? Responses from college sociology students range from the all-encompassing "a group of people who love each other" to the traditional, biological definition of "a mother, father, and child(ren)." According to the 2000 census, only 24.1 percent of households fit the traditional definition (Fields and Casper, 2000). Check your own idea of family by completing the "Family Picture" in Reflections and Applications. Sociologists have long agreed that a **family** is a relatively small domestic group of kin (related by biology, marriage, or adoption) that functions as a cooperative unit. The concept of family among professionals has broadened to include other groups in a committed relationship. Families are expected to provide financial support, affection, companionship, and the important task of **socialization,** transmitting the culture from one generation to another.

Quality of family life is worthy of attention. Even though children can overcome family patterns, they are better off not having to do so. When one considers the tremendous influence a family has on self-esteem, self-efficacy, self-fulfilling prophecies, personality development, happiness, emotionality, values, goal achievement, and interpersonal communication, there is no doubt that a person's life can be positively or negatively affected by his or her family situation. Family members respect and allow fulfillment of one another's needs and rights; support the mental, emotional, and spiritual growth of each individual; and allow and encourage personal growth. Within such families, the following occurs.

- Individuals are treated with dignity and perceived as equally deserving of respect.
- Personal freedoms are upheld; boundaries are maintained.
- Problems are acknowledged and resolved.
- Flexibility is evident.
- Love and affection are present.
- Communication is open and nonjudgmental.
- Mistakes are forgiven and viewed as learning tools.

Even if this does not sound like your family of origin, know that individuals are not destined to suffer permanent, adverse effects from family backgrounds. One benefit of achieving the objectives of this book is that you will be more aware of the skills necessary to develop a strong family.

Parenting in a Positive Way

"The biggest responsibility in the world." "The hardest job you could imagine." "Stressful, joyful, and challenging . . . I would not trade it for the world." These are a few of the responses I have received to the question "What is parenting?" A consensus of opinion is that parenting is a difficult task. A few erroneously believe that the hardest part is giving birth. After that, they think that raising a child will just come naturally. "I know what to do. I was a kid once," said a

Figure 13-1

young parent. You may be able to "parent"; however, positive parenting does not come naturally. **Positive parenting** means doing everything possible to learn about and raise a child with a goal of **optimum development.** This includes the best possible prenatal and postnatal environments. Love, nurturance, and commitment are required. One point is clear: even though parents are not the only factors in a child's life, they are most significant and, as such, bear a high level of responsibility.

The scope of parenting cannot be covered in one chapter or even in an entire book. In learning how to create happiness, express feelings, manage stress, cope with crises, transmit values, communicate, manage conflict, and give and receive criticism, you have developed strategies for positive parenting. You will learn more through other resources and formal training. This chapter will simply open the door to positive parenting and helpful strategies for success in different types of families. The rest is up to you. Raising children deserves priority and training (Fig. 13-1).

The Decision to Become a Parent

You did not select your parents; however, you can choose whether or not to become a parent. This decision will probably be the most important one you will ever make. If you are already a parent and did not give it a great deal of forethought, you are not alone and certainly it is not wise to berate yourself. Your choice now is to learn how to be a positive parent.

The ego states from transactional analysis (TA) are applicable. The "child" will emotionally want a baby and will, perhaps, see raising a child as pure pleasure. The "child" could also react selfishly and not want to parent responsibly. Your "parent" ego state may contain messages such as, "You better have a baby soon. Your biological clock is ticking" or "You cannot be truly fulfilled if you do not have a child." A 19-year-old student told me that her grandmother wanted her to get married and quickly have a baby so that she could be a great-grandmother before she died. Parenting is a decision for your "adult" ego state to make. One suggestion is to read books about becoming a parent and raising children before you decide.

Factors to consider. Adults who are alcoholic or dependent on other drugs, codependent, abusive, rigid, punitive, overly judgmental, unloving, or extremely needy may be poor role models for children. A primary factor is the psychological health of the two prospective parents.

Before having children, it is best if a couple's relationship is stable and time-tested. Bringing a baby into a new relationship is not advisable, and having a baby to strengthen a weak couple relationship is one of the poorest reasons imaginable. A baby does not deserve the responsibility of saving a relationship; furthermore, this repair attempt invariably does not work. The transition to parenthood usually strains a couple. Keeping the relationship healthy continues to be important. A study showed that parenting satisfaction was significantly higher for adults whose marriages were of high quality (Rogers and White, 1998).

A critical question to answer is "Why do we want to have a child?" A list identifying advantages and disadvantages usually reveals more cons than pros. What comes to your mind when you think of the disadvantages? A typical immediate answer is sacrifice. What types of sacrifice?

Couples are realistic when they acknowledge that time, energy, a great deal of effort, and money are required. The estimated cost of raising a child born in 2003 until he or she is 17 is $172,870 for families under $38,000 annual before-tax income; $235,670 for families under $64,000; and for those above $64,000 income, the amount is $344,250. Expenses include housing, food, transportation, clothing, health care, education, child care, and miscellaneous items (U.S. Department of Agriculture, 2004). A wise financial consideration also has to do with how many children are desired. Besides finances, parents' other resources of time and energy are reduced with each child.

What about the positives? Parenting can be one the most rewarding human experiences. The benefits of having children include adding interest and enjoyment to life, opening additional avenues of pleasure and relating, and making life more meaningful. "Realizing that I have given life to a person who is enjoying life and contributing to this world is the greatest reward possible," said a parent of a young adult.

Having a realistic picture of parenting and family life hopefully will cause you to think and hesitate. You may choose to be someone who does not have children, an option that has become increasingly more common. Because of the importance of the decision, you owe it to yourself and to a child to be careful and deliberate. Unlike other statuses you may choose, this one cannot be undone. After a thoughtful decision has been made, make another one to educate yourself.

Parent Education

In the movie *Parenthood*, a teenage boy talks about the irony of requiring fishing licenses to fish, hunting licenses to hunt, and driving licenses to drive, yet having no licensing requirement to become a parent. Society requires less to become a parent than to take on other statuses. Some states require a blood test for marriage.

The good news is that parent education classes and workshops are offered, organizations and support groups focus on family issues, and books and audiovisual aids are available. Importantly, these resources do work. Even with the number of offerings and the reported successes, the tragedy is that parents often do not take advantage of the educational opportunities available. "Canceled for lack of registrants" is a common frustration of those who offer parent courses. The assumption may be that such classes are canceled for lack of interest. Actually, the reason is more complex. Most parents are interested

---

What Positive Parents Can Learn

- Influences on the very important prenatal environment
- Erikson's stages of development and ways of helping children successfully achieve tasks at each stage
- Cognitive development stage theory as conceptualized by Jean Piaget (Piaget and Inhelder, 1969) including exploration within a child-safe environment and different ways that children learn and think
- Self-esteem and self-efficacy enhancement
- Child-raising techniques and methods

Figure 13-2

but are either unaware of how helpful education can be or do not think that they need training. Most parents-to-be take childbirth classes but not child-raising courses (Fig. 13-2).

What specifically is good for parents to learn? Check the list in "What Positive Parents Can Learn." This knowledge will not only help the child but will also make parenting less burdensome and more enjoyable.

If parents practice open communication and handle conflict positively, they will, by example, teach priceless skills. Children often model their relationships after adults in their lives. Simply stated, as a parent, whatever you learn and live will be evident to a child. Another advantage of parenting education is that the more you know, the more secure you can be as a parent. "The security of the parent about being a parent will eventually become the source of the child's feeling secure about self" (Bettelheim, 1987, p. 13).

Goals of Child Raising

One of the most valuable lessons a person can learn about parenting is from Deanna Eversoll, a University of Nebraska professor. "What do you want your child to be like at the age of 21?" she asked our class. After receiving several answers, such as responsible, honest, loving, happy, confident, and independent, she challenged us: "Do you know what to do, and what not to do, to help bring these about?" Parents are certainly not the only influence, yet they contribute immeasurably to the lives of their offspring.

In thinking about what you want, general ideas are preferable. Think "I want my child to be satisfied in a career," rather than "I want my child to be a doctor." This allows for flexibility and uniqueness. "I always wanted my child to get a 4-year degree," one of my students said. "But he seems perfectly happy learning automotive technology at a community college."

> Whenever we try to push our children to become the people that they may be in our heads, we become less effective as parents. (Glasser, 1984)
> Enabling children to discover who they want to be and then helping them to become people who are satisfied with life is a worthy goal. (Bettelheim, 1987)

In contrast to parents 60 or 70 years ago, modern parents seem to have different goals for their children. They are more likely to want their offspring to think for themselves, accept responsibility, show initiative, and be tolerant of opposing views. These characteristics replace such traits as obedience, conformity, and respect for home and church.

One student, in reply to the question about desired qualities in a child, said, "I want for us to be friends." Because parenting is a lifelong commitment, developing a deep friendship with an adult child is rewarding. Liking a child for the person he or she has become is a wonderful feeling.

Responsibilities of Parenting

If you took a moment to write a job description for parenting, what would you include? One weary-looking mother in a parenting workshop answered, "Drive them here and there and everywhere." Transportation is only one responsibility. The number of parental tasks is almost overwhelming, with some responsibilities being more important than others.

Developing love and trust.   Children deserve to live in loving environments. According to Erikson's (1963) developmental theory, trust precedes the other stages, and the early years are critical. The most valuable parenting behavior during the first year is to demonstrate love by being responsive, warm, and nurturing. A child not touched enough will not develop properly; a child touched in a disturbed way will suffer. Adults who were maltreated as children include Charles Manson and Ted Bundy (Magid and McKelvey, 1989). Other outcomes are less dramatic yet still unfortunate.

Withdrawing from an infant also has repercussions. In comparing styles of mothering, babies of withdrawn mothers showed less optimal interactive behavior and had lower mental scores at 1 year (Jones et al., 1997). A convincing 36-year study, ending when the subjects were 41 years old, showed that those who had been raised with the most parental warmth and affection were more likely to have long and relatively happy marriages and close friendships and report greater happiness and less stress (Franz, McClelland, and Weinberger, 1991). Other studies support the benefits of parental warmth and closeness in the areas of physical and psychological health years later (Ornish, 1998). Demonstrated affection by cuddling, hugging, and other physical contact is meaningful at all ages (Fig. 13-3).

When children are loved, they more easily develop an optimistic attitude. Also helpful is the book *The Optimistic Child* (Seligman, 1995). Love continues to be the foundation of positive parenting. As with intimate love, the focus should be on loving behaviors that foster positive personal growth and promote personal responsibility.

Figure 13-3   Trust develops through loving, supportive experiences.

Encouraging wellness.   Parents are responsible for feeding and overseeing other behaviors related to health. Almost all take care of their children's physical well-being. Important parenting tasks include but are not limited to seeing that children are physically active, that they get adequate rest, and that they are strongly encouraged to develop healthy nutritional habits. Research reveals that children who ate breakfast had 40 percent higher math grades and were less apt to be absent or tardy from school from those who did not. The latter were more likely to be hyperactive and have a variety of psychosocial problems (Carper, 2000). Parents must be firm. "What can I do?" asked one. "I try to get them to eat healthy foods, but they just will not." In such cases, wise parents do not give children a choice. For example, my daughters had only what we called "special juice," a blend of apple and grape juice instead of the extremely popular sugar-laden drinks. The examples parents set in this regard are also significant. A child's degree of wellness is greatly influenced by parental choices.

Building self-esteem and self-efficacy. Two all-important responsibilities are the encouragement of children's high self-esteem and the fostering of self-efficacy. The most important task of parenthood is, as the authors of *Self-Esteem* (McKay and Fanning, 2000) describe, helping a child develop high self-worth. In the course of constructing self-esteem, a child is likely to develop an internal locus of control and other positive behaviors discussed earlier in this book. During the early childhood stages, wise parents help their children develop what Erikson (1963) called autonomy and initiative. Encouraging a child to develop skills and talents and to teach "I can do that" instead of "I cannot" helps foster the beliefs that lead to self-efficacy expectancies.

Adults are teachers of and models for self-esteem, and they cannot teach or model what they do not know. Before parenting, building your own self-esteem, as discussed in Chapter 1, is highly recommended. If you became a parent before your own self-esteem was high, do all you can to create a positive outlook on life. Also important are your parenting behaviors. The language and nonverbal behaviors you use with a child are building blocks of self-image and self-worth. "Every day, in the hundreds of interactions you have with your children, you mirror back to them who they are. Like a sculptor's tools on soft clay, your words and tone of voice shape their sense of self" (McKay and Fanning, 2000, p. 293).

Offering positive comments for being capable and for doing well helps to build self-esteem and strengthens self-efficacy. In the TA framework, giving positive strokes is a primary parenting behavior. The "how" of praising is important and descriptive recognition is recommended. The words tell about a specific event and the parent's specific feelings; a child can then draw a general conclusion about personality and character (Ginott, 1969). Here is an example of descriptive recognition: "I really appreciate your helping clean the house. I especially like the job you did in your own room. I am relieved that such a big job is done." An example of evaluative praise, which is not recommended, is "You are an angel. I could not ask for a sweeter daughter. I do not know what I would do without you." When you allow the child to infer positives from your descriptions, the message is stronger. "Our words should be like a magic canvas upon which a child can not help but paint a positive picture of self" (Ginott, 1965, p. 42).

Praise does not have to be present-oriented. If a child is not doing much now to deserve descriptive recognition, recall past situations. Positive offerings just for being alive are rare and are precious gifts of unconditional positive regard and deep love. Priceless is the assurance that what a child *is* counts more than what he or she does.

As valuable as praise is, it can be detrimental when it's unrealistic or lavish. Overpraising is often uncomfortable for children and may put pressure on them to try to live up to an unrealistic standard (McKay and Fanning, 2000). Telling children over and over that they are perfect, wonderful, and angelic will probably be rejected and may even be behaviorally refuted later. Parents should encourage achievement that builds self-esteem. Children then can prove to themselves that they are worthy. A strong recommendation is to avoid backhanded compliments, ones that mix praise with insult (McKay and Fanning, 2000). Examples are "I like the way you cleaned your room . . . for a change" or "I just cannot believe you did so well on your math test." Like adults, children can be hurt by the implied criticism and are better off without any praise at all.

Positive parents will deliver small quantities of criticism in nonhurtful ways. As discussed earlier, criticism delivered with "I" statements and directed toward undesirable behavior will get a better reception and, more importantly, is unlikely to damage self-esteem. A skillful parent will set boundaries and limits and enforce these in consistent ways. One expert describes it as a delicate balance of casting out a fishing line while still holding the rod and reel (Vinton, 1998).

Avoid destructive language styles. These include generalizations (the grandiose type of closed communication) and vague or violent threats such as, "Try that again and you will find out how mad I can get" or "If you do that one more time, I will spank you so hard you won't be able to sit down." Body language and paralanguage can also be potentially damaging. Facial expressions of disgust and anger and sarcastic tones of voice, among others, are potentially detrimental. Not addressing issues of concern and playing the "silent game" are not recommended (McKay and Fanning, 2000).

Constructive criticism points out possibilities for improvement and omits any negative remarks about the child's personality (Ginott, 1965). Matt inadvertently spilled a glass of milk. His parents' criticisms were not constructive:

"You are old enough to know how to hold a glass! How many times have I told you to be careful?"
"He cannot help it—he is so clumsy. He always was and always will be."

Consider that Matt spilled a few cents' worth of milk, yet the caustic remarks are likely to cost much more in terms of self-regard. When you make a situation personal, you damage the relationship and destroy a child's self-esteem (Fig. 13-4).

Figure 13-4   Copyright Universal Press Syndicate. Reprinted with permission.

Children who are spoken to abusively learn to verbally abuse others. These four steps are recommended when correcting a child (McKay and Fanning, 2000):

1. Describe the situation or behavior in nonjudgmental language. ("I notice that you have not cleaned your room yet.")
2. Give a reason for wanting behavior to change. ("I am frustrated when you procrastinate.")
3. Acknowledge the child's feelings and thoughts. ("I know how busy you have been" or "I realize that schoolwork has been stressful lately.")
4. State a clear expectation. ("I want the room cleaned before you go out tonight.")

Parents who place unrealistic expectations on a child do not contribute to either self-esteem or self-efficacy. "I know you can do better," a parent says looking at a report card with mostly Bs. Maybe a B is the best a child can do. Unrealistic expectations, especially about behavior, are frequently the result of what is called "adultism," which occurs when adults forget what it is like to be a child. They then expect and require a child, who has never been an adult, to think, act, understand, and do things as an adult would (Glenn and Nelsen, 1989). Instead, parents should try to know their children well and then be realistically encouraging.

"What can I do to help my son rid himself of 'cannots'?" asked a parent. As discussed in Chapter 4, a "cannot" is extremely limiting to the development of self-efficacy. First, model and encourage children to resist using the word cannot. Then provide opportunities for them to demonstrate what they can do and praise appropriately. According to Erikson (1963), if young children have developed autonomy and initiative, they will move forward to industry versus inferiority. During all three stages, a parent can encourage self-efficacy in children.

Positive parenting behaviors and interactions contribute to **attachment,** the positive emotional bond that develops between a child and another person. The self-image of adolescents was found to be significantly strengthened by attachment to their parents (O'Koon, 1997). In essence, when children develop high self-esteem and self-efficacy, the other responsibilities of parenting are easier and, most importantly, a parent has served a child well.

Developing emotional well-being. Children are affected by their parents' emotional state. An essential task for parents is to develop positive emotional selves so that they will be able to teach and model healthy emotionality. Children with emotionally competent parents are calmer, less whiney, better able to cope, better able to focus their attention, much less negative when playing with friends, less stressed, and more likely to try new things. In addition to using the material presented earlier, a few specific points can be beneficial.

Parents sometimes use the common emotional weapons of guilt and intimidation with grave psychological consequences (Bloomfield, 1996b). The **martyr parent** seeks to instill guilt in children: "How could you do this to me?" "I do not deserve this kind of treatment." "I have given you everything." "I went without so you could have all the nice things." If you recognize any of these messages, because you once received them or because you now give them, realize that the child translates the message as "Being who I am hurts my parent" and "I am not good or nice enough."

The **dictator parent** has the same motive as the martyr parent: to control the child's life even after the child is an adult. The method is intimidation. Fear-inducing statements and temper outbursts are common: "I am the boss around here, and you do what I say." "Do not talk back to me." "You do that again, and I will smack you hard." "Do it or else. Remember, I am your mother." The child remembers quite well. The reason given for the threats and abuse is that the parent knows what is best and is acting in the child's interest. However, the parent is actually inflicting great harm. Trying to produce fear in order to control is the parent's objective; the result is a fearful child.

Do you know any parents who "overparent?" A potentially damaging behavior is the compulsion to help and direct others and do for them what they could be doing for themselves. Such behavior does not serve the best interests of children. In adulthood, they may find it hard to take care of themselves. Playing either the martyr or dictator role or overparenting are not positive parenting practices.

Worrying can be passed down from generation to generation because it is learned behavior. "I am a worrywart just like my mom." How sad that a parent taught a child to worry. If you worry a lot, let children know that they did not cause it. Messages like "I cannot help worrying. That is what parents do," "I love you so much, and you cause me so much worry" are hard on young people. Children placed in this position almost always grow up to be worriers. The truth is that the adults undoubtedly worried before the child was born and are now using the child as a scapegoat. Instead, a positive parent teaches a child to look critically at worries and to challenge them. He or she teaches the joy of problem solving rather than the anguish of fretting.

As discussed in Chapter 5, one's family is a powerful influence on emotional expression. Cold, unemotional children and young adults frequently come from cold, unemotional parents. If children are raised in a cold emotional climate, they become victims of victims. In such an environment, people frequently feel one way and act another, experience few positive emotional expressions, and are subject to hysterical, manipulative outbursts (Rubin, 1998). A healthy emotional climate is maintained by parents who know that:

> Love does not hurt, it feels good. Loving behavior nourishes your emotional well-being. When someone is being loving to you, you feel accepted, cared for, valued, and respected. Genuine love creates feelings of warmth, pleasure, safety, stability, and inner peace. (Rubin, 1998, p. 324)

Knowing what not to do is important; additionally, learning what to do can result in an emotionally intelligent child. EQ (emotional quotient) was discussed in Chapter 5, and parents can contribute to their own child's abilities. How to do so is explained in the book *The Heart of Parenting* (Gottman, 1997). As emotional coaches, parents should do the following:

1. Be aware of your child's emotions, including the most subtle clues.
2. View emotions as an opportunity for intimacy or teaching.
3. Listen empathically and validate a child's feelings.
4. Assist a child in verbally labeling her or his emotions.
5. Help solve a problem by setting limits. For example, "It is okay to be mad at her for not sharing a toy; it's not acceptable to just take it from her."

Teaching children to manage angry feelings is a vital aspect of discipline. Some suggestions are to instruct them in deep breathing and visualization of peaceful settings, counting to 10, working off tension with physical activity, and communicating verbally or through writing (Ginsburg, Fein, and Johnson, 1998). Parents can be effective teachers and trainers in emotional development, which profoundly influences all aspects of life.

Developing positive social relationships. Social development begins with life. As pointed out, trust is the cornerstone of psychosocial development. In all stages, parents play significant roles; knowing what and how to encourage is beneficial.

The identity stage is one of the most challenging stages for both adults and children. It usually begins and is in "full bloom" during adolescence. The more you know about typical adolescent behavior the better parenting skills you will have and the more you will enjoy your teenager. The book *You and Your Adolescent* (Steinberg and Levine, 1997) is a good resource. The authors assure us that the horror stories about adolescence are false and point out that 9 out of 10 teenagers do not get into trouble. The book is full of accurate information about adolescent development plus enjoyable ways to enhance the relationship. Trusting children by assuming the best and treating them with the same respect parents extend to total strangers are worthy recommendations. Positive parents help an adolescent achieve independence and do not put them in a double bind by steering them toward independence and then objecting to how they do things.

Children of all ages learn from their families how to be social creatures. Even though families are not the only socializing agents, we still develop much of our social selves at home. In terms of relationships, love and intimacy are taught or not taught in the family. Parents have a tremendous responsibility to model intimate adult relationships and to help children feel connected to others.

Showing an active interest. Being actively interested in what your child does shows love and respect. A study of 10,000 high school students revealed another benefit. Parents who were more involved in their adolescents' schooling had children who performed better in school (Bogenschneider, 1997). One might think that interest and involvement would automatically be demonstrated; yet, too often, parents seem indifferent. "My folks never came to school events," said Shelly. "Even when I was a homecoming queen finalist, they were not there." Times may have changed; however, the need for demonstrated interest and support remains as strong as ever. With increasing numbers of career responsibilities and other activities and interests, parents who make the time and effort are to be commended.

A Special Word to Fathers

In the past, a mother was responsible for child raising whereas the dad was often seen either as someone who came and went as a heavy disciplinarian. That scenario has changed for many. Today, fathers are more equal to mothers in caring for children, especially on weekends. They also are involved in a variety of their children's activities beyond play and companionship. One factor that made a

Figure 13-5   Fathers play an invaluable part in their children's development.

difference was the mother's contribution to family income (Yeung et al., 2001). Another was the attitude the father had regarding gender roles. A study showed that egalitarian men not only want children more than traditional males, but they also want to share with their partners and be involved in caring for their children (Kaufman, 2000). Fathers appear to be as important as mothers in the traditionally feminine role of emotionality (Cummings and O'Reilly, 1997). They are important in all other aspects as well. A study of dual-earner couples showed that shared parenting was associated with both closeness to children and marital satisfaction (Ehrenberg et al., 2001).

Common understandings of "to mother" and "to father" are quite different. Whereas the former brings forth an image of nurturing, "to father" means to impregnate. Happily, fathering is enjoying a broader meaning with the benefits of being fathered, as well as mothered, becoming widely recognized. Entire books are devoted to fathering (Hawkins and Dollanite, 1997), and studies on infant temperament and emotionality include the effects of both mothering and fathering (Park et al., 1997). Yet the attitude that a mother is the primary parent is sometimes subtle and resistant to change. This was demonstrated in class when a woman commented that her husband was home baby-sitting. She was asked if her husband was the children's father. He was. "Then why call it baby-sitting?" asked another student. "Do you call it baby-sitting when you stay home with them?" (Fig. 13-5).

Only recently has society acknowledged gay fathers. Contrary to popular stereotypes, children of gay fathers are no more likely to be gay, no more likely to be sexually abused, and not at any significant disadvantage when compared with children of heterosexual fathers (Patterson and Chan, 1997). A study showed that 91 percent of adult sons of gay fathers were heterosexual. Those who were gay had actually lived with their fathers fewer numbers of years than the heterosexual offspring, adding to the belief that environmental conditions are not responsible for one's sexual orientation (Bailey et al., 1995). Eric, in his generous, loving way, adopted a child who had been abandoned by her single mother. "My only concern is any repercussions my daughter might face because I am not accepted by many in society because I am gay," he said during a class panel on parenting. Hopefully, there will be none, and she is lucky to have such a loving father.

Fathers have great impact and are as important as mothers in the overall development of children. Societal attitudes that support the role of men in the lives of children need strengthening whereas fathers who want to be involved in an affirmative way are advised to learn as much about positive parenting as they can. For the most part, fathers today want more involvement and are taking parental responsibilities seriously. Greg, who is a wonderful hands-on dad, said, "Being a dad is the most tremendous feeling in the world. I cannot imagine life without my children."

Beginning at the earliest stages of life, a child's entire being is in the hands of the caregiving adults. Each child deserves and profits from the love, warmth, and support of both parents.

Discipline and Its Multifaceted Dimensions

Discipline is an area in which education is sorely needed. Ask adults to define discipline, and you get such answers as "making a child mind you," "correcting a child," or "teaching a child right from wrong." Ask children and you are likely to hear "getting punished" or "not being allowed to watch TV." Parents often use only punishment to accomplish the task of disciplining their children.

A broader definition of **discipline** is the entire process of teaching and guiding children from infancy to adulthood. The word *discipline* means "to teach," not "to punish" or "to hurt." Loving discipline is an essential ingredient in child rearing (Ginsburg, Fein, and Johnson, 1998). The parent has a role of leader and teacher, and the children are learners. Discipline is multifaceted, and parents use a variety of child-rearing techniques to guide children. What you want your child to be like becomes the goal of discipline.

When people think about discipline, they do not usually picture anything positive. The broader concept of discipline is affirmative rather than negative. Punishment should be used sparingly and as a last resort. Inappropriate punishment, which is harsh, unreasonable, violent, or harmful, is never recommended. Parents use such punishment because (1) it brings about immediate change, (2) they are not sure of what else to do, (3) they fear losing their authority, and (4) they have not been taught other methods. If you picture discipline as a pie, *appropriate* punishment is the smallest possible slice. The rest of the pie is filled with various techniques and methods described later. This concept of discipline has unlimited potential!

Parenting Styles Defined

Parenting is a complex activity that includes many specific behaviors that work individually and together to influence child outcomes. Most researchers who attempt to describe this broad parental milieu rely on Diana Baumrind's concept of parenting style. Parenting style is meant to describe normal variations in parenting. In other words, the parenting style typology Baumrind developed should not be understood to include deviant parenting, such as might be observed in abusive or neglectful homes. Although parents may differ in how they try to control or socialize their children and the extent to which they do so, it is assumed that the primary role of all parents is to influence, teach, and control their children.

Parenting style captures two important elements of parenting: parental responsiveness and parental demandingness (Maccoby and Martin, 1983). Parental responsiveness (also referred to as parental warmth or supportiveness) refers to "the extent to which parents intentionally foster individuality, self-regulation, and self-assertion by being attuned, supportive, and acquiescent to children's special needs and demands" (Baumrind, 1991, p. 62). Parental demandingness (also referred to as behavioral control) refers to "the claims parents make on children to become integrated into the family whole, by their maturity demands, supervision, disciplinary efforts and willingness to confront the child who disobeys" (Baumrind, 1991, pp. 61–62).

Four Parenting Styles

Categorizing parents according to whether they are high or low on parental demandingness and responsiveness creates a typology of four parenting styles: indulgent, authoritarian, authoritative, and uninvolved (Maccoby and Martin, 1983). Each of these parenting styles reflects different naturally occurring patterns of parental values, practices, and behaviors (Baumrind, 1991) and a distinct balance of responsiveness and demandingness.

Indulgent parents (also referred to as "permissive") "are more responsive than they are demanding. They are nontraditional and lenient, do not require mature behavior, allow considerable self-regulation, and avoid confrontation" (Baumrind, 1991, p. 62). When parents are permissive children often feel insecure and do not understand the meaning of cause and effect. Permissiveness is not likely to lead to responsible adult behavior and may encourage selfishness and self-indulgence.

Authoritarian parents are highly demanding and directive but not responsive. "They are obedience- and status-oriented, and expect their orders to be obeyed without explanation" (Baumrind, 1991, p. 62). These parents provide well-ordered and structured environments with clearly stated rules. Punitive disciplinary action is common, which often leads to further disobedience. Few desirable qualities are developed with authoritarian discipline. The chances of being loving with high regard for the self are slim.

Authoritative parents are both demanding and responsive. "They monitor and impart clear standards for their children's conduct. They are assertive, but not intrusive and restrictive. Their disciplinary methods are supportive, rather than punitive. They want their children to be assertive as well as socially responsible, and self-regulated as well as cooperative" (Baumrind, 1991, p. 62). Just as authoritative parents appear to be able to balance their conformity demands with their respect for their children's individuality, so children from authoritative homes appear to be able to balance the claims of external conformity and achievement demands with their need for individuation and autonomy.

Uninvolved parents are low in both responsiveness and demandingness. In extreme cases, this parenting style might encompass both rejecting–neglecting and neglectful parents. These parents are often unaware of who their children's friends are, school or extracurricular activities their children are involved in and in extreme cases the children are left to raise themselves.

Because parenting style is a typology, rather than a linear combination of responsiveness and demandingness, each parenting style is more than the sum of its parts (Baumrind, 1991).

One key difference between authoritarian and authoritative parenting is in the dimension of psychological control. Both authoritarian and authoritative parents place high demands on their children and expect their children to behave appropriately and obey parental rules. Authoritarian parents also expect their children to accept their judgments, values, and goals without questioning. In contrast, authoritative parents are more open to give-and-take with their children and make greater use of explanations. Thus, although authoritative and authoritarian parents are equally high in behavioral control, authoritative parents tend to be low in psychological control, whereas authoritarian parents tend to be high.

Consequences for Children

Parenting style has been found to predict child well-being in the domains of social competence, academic performance, psychosocial development, and problem behavior. Research based on parent interviews, child reports, and parent observations consistently finds:

- Children and adolescents whose parents are authoritative rate themselves and are rated by objective measures as more socially and instrumentally competent than those whose parents are nonauthoritative.
- Children and adolescents whose parents are uninvolved perform most poorly in all domains.

In general, parental responsiveness predicts social competence and psychosocial functioning, whereas parental demandingness is associated with instrumental competence and behavioral control (i.e., academic performance and deviance). These findings indicate:

- Children and adolescents from authoritarian families (high in demandingness, but low in responsiveness) tend to perform moderately well in school and be uninvolved in problem behavior, but they have poorer social skills, lower self-esteem, and higher levels of depression.
- Children and adolescents from indulgent homes (high in responsiveness, low in demandingness) are more likely to be involved in problem behavior and perform less well in school, but they have higher self-esteem, better social skills, and lower levels of depression.

The benefits of authoritative parenting and the detrimental effects of uninvolved parenting are evident as early as the preschool years and continue throughout adolescence and into early adulthood.

Democratic Style of Parenting

Authoritative parenting, sometimes referred to as the "democratic style" of decision making, balances clear, high parental demands with emotional responsiveness and recognition of child autonomy. The parent is a leader, guide, and teacher. As such, he or she is approachable, reasonable, flexible, and affirming. A child is encouraged to think, contribute, and cooperate. Power is not a major issue and is shared as much as possible. Open communication is the norm. Who determines the "rules?" The most powerful aspect of democratic discipline and why it is so effective is that input regarding guidelines and consequences comes from all who are able to contribute. Young people are more likely to adopt family attitudes and norms when their voices are heard (Brody, Moore, and Glei, 1994). If you are an employee, are you not more likely to comply with policies if you have been involved in their formation? Children react similarly in usually cooperative ways. Periodically the family can evaluate the guidelines and the consequences.

Recent studies have focused on **corporal punishment,** the use of physical force with the intention of causing pain but not injury for purposes of coercion or control (Straus and Yodanis, 1996). The common habit of spanking is a form of corporal punishment and used by all types of parents. To spank or not to spank is a dilemma for most parents. About 10 percent spank and see nothing wrong with it, about 20 percent never spank, and about 70 percent do and wish they had not (Severe, 1997). For children younger than 2 years old or for adolescents, social scientists generally agree that spanking should not be used (Gunnoe and Mariner, 1997). Beyond that and confusing to parents is the disagreement among the experts. Some are adamantly opposed to any use of corporal punishment whereas others say that light spanking probably does no harm. Almost all argue against harsh punishments. One study found a direct link between frequency of spanking and slapping during childhood and future problems with anxiety disorder, alcohol abuse, and other problems (MacMillan, 1999). Others recommend that parents be trained in alternative strategies of discipline (Day, Peterson, and McCracken, 1998).

In order to sort it out, parents can read an enlightening chapter in the book *How to Behave So Your Children Will, Too!* (Severe, 1997). Whether one believes that spanking may be harmless, a strong recommendation is that parents realize that there are dozens of alternatives to any use of corporal punishment. Sparing a child by sparing the rod is in everyone's best interests.

Openly communicate.   One of the most powerful tools of discipline for parents is open communication. How strange that some parents forget to use it! Verbalizing openly and listening actively and receptively may be all that is required in changing a child's behavior. The use of "I" messages and active listening will make a major difference. When our children were asked about discipline on a television program, I was heartened to hear them say, "We were hardly ever grounded or punished. Instead we talked things out."

Model the behavior you want.   Realizing that parents will have adult privileges that children do not have, discipline includes the positive examples you set. As in transmitting values, your actions will speak louder than words. Children are quite susceptible to watching and then doing. For example, children's tobacco and alcohol use is associated with parents' use (Jackson et al., 1997). Parents also model how to express feelings. Parents discipline simply by the way they live their lives (Fig. 13-6).

Apply behavior modification techniques.   Learning theory offers a variety of tools. The ones that will be effective depend on the age and personality of a child. With young children, changing the environment by **redirection,** either

---

Time-Out Prescription (Azerrad and Chance, 2001)

Assume that your daughter has hit another child. Follow these steps.

1. Say to her, "We do not hit other people." Say nothing more.
2. Take her by the hand and seat her in a small chair facing a blank wall. If she attempts to leave, immediately return her to it.
3. Make sure she stays there for three minutes. Ignore *all* of her behaviors such as screaming, crying, or hitting the wall. Say nothing.
4. After three minutes, keep her in the chair until she is quiet and well-behaved for five more seconds. Then tell her she has been good and may leave the chair.
5. Say nothing about time-out except that "We do not hit other people."

Figure 13-6

attracting them to an alternate location or by diverting their attention, is often sufficient. For example, a 2-year-old is naturally curious (and stubborn!) and will likely attempt to open a cupboard door against your wishes. You can simply get the child involved elsewhere. If a child is not in danger and not likely to be harmed or hurt others, ignoring misbehavior can be effective because children do misbehave to get attention. In fact, studies show that problem behavior is typically the result of misplaced adult attention. In other words, parents tend to pay too much attention to a child who is misbehaving (Azerrad and Chance, 2001).

Time-out means moving a misbehaving child to a neutral (nonentertaining) location for a brief period of time. A child psychologist (Azerrad and Chance 2001) recommends that an adult first ignore minor misbehavior, pay more attention to children when they behave well, and reserve time-out for particularly immature or potentially injurious behaviors. Highly recommended is Azerrad's "Time-Out Prescription."

Time-out does not work all of the time with all children, and it can be overused. And some children enjoy it. "My nephew loves time-out. He sits with his head down and hums, whistles, and smiles." In this case, the method does not deter misbehavior.

Rewarding desired behavior can work miracles. **Positive reinforcement** is presenting a positive stimulus in an attempt to increase or strengthen behavior. Adults relish rewards; so do children. After reading a book on behavior modification, a mother shared a success story:

> My 4-year-old girl misplaced her shoes daily. When we got ready to go somewhere, we had to look for shoes. I scolded and even spanked occasionally with no luck. From a book, I got a new idea. I put a large box in her room and told her that this was her special shoe box. Each night I counted the number of shoes in the box, and she received stickers for each shoe, which she could later use for treats. She has not misplaced a shoe for a month.

The stickers were powerful positive reinforcers. Unfortunately, parents forget to apply an important principle of learning theory, which is that human beings generally seek pleasure or rewards. Verbal awards may be more beneficial than material ones because material rewards can lead children to become motivated only by external factors. Large doses of verbal praise are preferable.

As children get older, different behavior modification methods are more effective. Positive reinforcement continues to be effective. In addition, parents can use **contracting** in which an agreement about specific behaviors is developed. A negotiation process is effective with adolescents. Involving teenagers in discussions about their behaviors shows respect and acknowledges that they can be responsible.

Use logical consequences.   In order to be prepared for adulthood and responsibility, it is important that a child experience consequences. For a child who is old enough to understand, the use of logical consequences as a method of discipline is amazingly effective. The consequences can be natural ones. If a child carelessly breaks a toy, it is no longer available. As in values development, allowing natural consequences to occur is hard on a loving parent yet invaluable in developing responsibility. Consequences can also be created. A key element is including the child in formulating consequences. Some descriptions of effective and fair consequences follow (McKay and Fanning, 2000).

Reasonable: If a child is 45 minutes late coming home after a movie, an earlier time could be set the next time. Grounding someone for a week is not reasonable. In fact, grounding is a consequence (sometimes a punishment for unrelated misbehavior) that can be overused. And it is often as hard on the parents as it is on the child!

Related: If children are careless in completing a task, they are expected to do it over rather than have television privileges suspended. Making the consequences relate to the misbehavior makes sense.

Timely: If grades are unusually low, and the consequence is imposed study time, the time to start is that day. Waiting too long to impose consequences makes them irrelevant.

Consistent: How many times have you heard a parent say, "If you do that one more time, . . ." and the behavior continues? If the consequence for hitting a sibling is time-out, then a parent imposes the consequence until the behavior is changed. If time-out isn't working, change the consequence.

Understandable in advance: If children have input, they will know the consequences before they misbehave. If a bicycle left outside is stolen, the child will already know that money will have to be earned to replace it. Unforeseen situations may occur; a parent can then impose reasonable consequences or involve the child in the process.

Sharon Hanna recalled a favorite story about consequences and her stepson Greg, who was usually quite even-tempered. A phone conversation with a girl got the best of him. He hit the stairwell wall, making a hole in it. "The wall has to be fixed," was her reaction. He paid for, patched, and even painted the entire stairwell! Greg has not used his fist on a wall since. The use of consequences teaches responsibility and prevents parents from having to nag, scold, and use other punitive measures. A child's self-esteem usually remains intact, and the feeling of responsibility can even give it a boost.

The "Why" of Democratic Discipline

- Decreases the likelihood of developing negative traits and behaviors while establishing a fertile ground for the development of positive ones
- Involves children in such a way that it promotes self-discipline
- Teaches children how to live peacefully and cooperatively
- Enhances loving parent–children relationships

Figure 13-7

Provide structure.   Planning with children how the household will operate is an excellent strategy. Having an established system and designated tasks decreases the number of times a parent feels a need to intervene. A family meeting is a good forum to use. A parent can introduce the idea by saying, "I want to include everyone in deciding how our household is going to function. A family is a team: a home requires care and maintenance. Let's first decide what needs to be done, how often, and then how it will be accomplished." For excellent tips on family meetings, read *Positive Discipline* (Nelsen, 1996), a book written for both parents and teachers. Meetings are best if used for positive reasons rather than for problem ones. For a first meeting, plan a family outing or trip. Regarding tasks, my stepfamily used a system in which the children had daily and weekly duties designated by number. I still smile when I think of the neighbors' reaction to one child's yelling to another, "Come on in. It is time for you to do number 2!" The system was not foolproof, and consequences were a part of it. However, it saved hours of complaining and nagging (Fig. 13-7).

Positive Parenting Behaviors

What a parent does and does not do plays an important role in a child's development; yet parents often forget to focus on their own actions. Positive parents practice the following:

Admitting a mistake.   You may wish to be an ideal parent, yet perfection is not possible. A stress-reducing aspect of positive parenting is that parents are allowed to make mistakes. Those who are able to admit an error and apologize to their children are to be commended, because children then learn a valuable lesson. "I never heard either of my parents apologize to each other or to us kids. I would have respected them so much more if they had. I find that I have difficulty saying 'I am sorry,' but I am working on it," said one man. When you apologize to your children, you teach them to trust their feelings and perceptions. "You are right. I did act unfairly." Then taking responsibility for your mistakes puts the "icing on the cake." A sincere apology is a sign of love.

Spending quality time with children.   I would love to have a dollar for the number of times I have heard people say, "I wish I had spent more time with my children. The years went by so fast." Would not it be wonderful if nobody had those regrets? Modern parents are spending four to six more hours a week with their children than did previous generations. Especially affirming is that working mothers are spending even more time (26.5 hours a week) with their children as stay-at-home moms did in 1981 (26 hours) (Wingert, 2001). Positive parenting means you have fun with children. Laughing together is stress reducing and promotes bonding. "Appreciate the child within you and each other. Especially in families, let the child in each of you romp. Having fun together is positive bonding" (Satir, 1988, p. 330).

Communicating openly.   Most important are communicating with and showing genuine interest in children as individuals. Talking and listening to your child are probably the most positive and rewarding parenting experiences of all. Open communication is preferable. As discussed previously, a poor communication habit is to ask "why" questions, especially those that concern personal feelings and motivations. Interestingly, parents feel justified asking a child, "Why were you late?" and resent the same question asked of them by a child. "Why did you break that dish?" is a poor question unless you honestly believe a child did so deliberately, which usually is not the case. A feeling of discomfort or defensiveness is a typical response to a "why." Open communication is a hallmark of positive parenting!

Demonstrating warmth and affection.   Positive parents are warm and affectionate and express their feelings nonverbally and verbally. The importance of demonstrativeness has been repeatedly pointed out in this book and deserves special emphasis between parents and children. Would you want your children to have high self-esteem, and when they are young adults, be more capable of congenial relationships? A longitudinal study showed that these were the outcomes when parents demonstrated high levels of warmth and affection (Franz, McClelland, and Weinberger, 1991). Children whose parents are physically affectionate and warm have a definite advantage (Fig. 13-8).

Some parents tend to refrain from physical expressions of love, especially with older children. "I knew my dad loved me, but I would have loved to hear him say it just once," said a student. When peers become important, a child shuns demonstrated affection from parents, especially big hugs and kisses. Parents can still hug children in private and find other ways to show their love. If demonstrating warm feelings is personally difficult for you, attack the problem. In order to develop a jogging regimen, an adult may have to say, "I will run five miles each day." The same adult can say, "I will hug my child at least once today."

Figure 13-8   A warm hug is good for both parents and children.

Showing appreciation and consideration. Being polite, saying "thank you," and showing appreciation seem simple, yet many do not practice these within the family. Parents and children take for granted the kind deeds of family members and neglect courtesies they extend to other people. A positive parent makes a point of expressing gratitude on a regular basis. Children then learn from observation and benefit from feeling respected.

Teaching and modeling a core values system.   The foundation of a child's values is built in the family. As discussed in Chapter 3, parents have a powerful influence especially during the early, formative years. Neither moralizing nor permissiveness is recommended, and you are advised to review the chapter and the methods that seem to produce the most positive results. Rather than try to instill several specific values in a child, a wise course of action is to teach and model a broad-based core set. Especially important are beliefs in human dignity and freedom to live in harmony with one another coupled with values on self, health, and continued learning. "My folks never told me exactly what to do or not to do. Instead, they helped me realize that respect for others and peaceful interactions are essential. I weigh many of my values decisions on those basics," a student shared.

Exhibiting fairness and equality.   In most cases, children benefit from settling their own disputes. When a parent intervenes, being fair and explaining the "why" of decisions are desirable. A mother wanted to be fair with her young daughters, Nicole and Cindy. To her, this meant keeping everything equal. When one received anything, so did the other. Their needs were different because Nicole was three years older. Yet she was expected to wait until Cindy was ready for such things as a bicycle. This led to her extreme resentment of Cindy. Understanding children's different developmental levels and explaining to them why they were not being treated exactly the same could have solved the problem. Children also differ in what they perceive as love. One may want more togetherness whereas another wants more privacy. Equal does not necessarily mean "same." Making one child overly responsible for another can lead to resentment. "I had to take my little brother everywhere. It got so I hated him," commented Sara.

As mentioned in Chapter 1, parents frequently compare siblings and set up undesirable competitive feelings. Comments such as, "I wish you would be more like your sister" or "Your brother never gives us any trouble" cultivate rivalry and resentment that can damage both a child and the sibling relationship. "Upon hearing these 'loving' comments, there is a desire to drop-kick a sibling into the next century" (Lang, 1990, p. 116). A positive parent treats children democratically and instills a cooperative, not competitive, attitude.

Emphasizing uniqueness and freedom from stereotypic restrictions.   Each child is unique. Unconditional love means loving children for who they *are*, not for what they do. This does not mean you accept or like all behaviors; it means you love them no matter what.

Do you believe that your children will be exactly like you? You realize that each child will be unique. Knowledge of personality differences in preferences and types, as discussed in Chapter 2, can be helpful. A must-read in this area is *Nurture by Nature; Understanding Your Child's Personality Type and Become a Better*

REFLECT AND APPLY

Reflect

◆ *Which of the characteristics of a high-quality family describe your family of origin?*

◆ *If you were asked, "How were you disciplined as a child?" which style would it most fit? From your past, think of an example of learning from logical consequences.*

Apply

◆ *Ask someone who is a parent to describe their parenting behaviors.*

◆ *Write a brief description of what you would want a child of yours to be like at age 21. Importantly, if you have a child or if you plan to become a parent, make a commitment to raise a child in a way that this is likely to happen.*

◆ *Set up a simple behavior modification program based on rewards to change something about yourself. If you have children, do the same with them.*

Parent (Tieger and Barron-Tieger, 1997). The authors believe that all four preferences are apparent by age 3 or 4 and, with some, by age 2. Kari sounded relieved as she told a class: "My mom is really extraverted. For years she told me I had a depression problem because I wanted to be alone in my room quite often. Now I know and can tell her that it is just because I have a strong preference for introversion. We are complete opposites!" Knowing your child's type will also provide insight into discipline. With my older daughter, who is sensing and thinking, clear and logical communication was a necessity; because my younger one is intuitive and feeling, appealing to her emotional side was effective (Reflect and Apply).

As discussed earlier, stereotypic gender-role restrictions and expectations are limiting and unwise. "I expect the woman to wait on me. My mom always waited on my dad" and "I will get married and have him support me like my dad did my mom" are unrealistic ideas. An interesting study reveals that a mother's gender-role attitudes when children are young and parental division of housework when children are adolescents predict children's ideal allocation of housework at age 18. During all stages of growing up, maternal gender-role attitudes appear to influence adult children's attitudes (Cunningham, 2001).

In a plea to parents, two authors (Levant and Brooks, 1997) make some salient points:

> Child rearing may be a pivotal force in the reshaping of the culture itself. Just as there needs to be continued emphasis on helping young girls become better able to access instrumental and competitive skills, there must be corollary shifts in emphasis for young boys with a greater emphasis on interpersonal connection and the ability to interact cooperatively. Boys' activities will need to become less gender-stereotyped with less devaluation of "feminine" activities. Interpersonal sensitivity, empathy, and compassion can receive greater emphasis as emotional skills for young boys. (Levant and Brooks, 1997, p. 265)

Rather than encouraging stereotypic roles, parents who wish to be gender-fair and encourage the best in their sons and daughters would do well to adopt an androgynous gender-role orientation and encourage the same in their children. Studies have shown that families with one or more androgynous parents generally score higher in parental warmth and support (Witt, 1997). Realizing the numerous benefits of an androgynous personality, one can conclude that parents who model and teach androgyny are helping their children and preparing them for a satisfying life.

Equally important, neither do young people in today's world benefit from the locked-in mentality of bigotry, nor does a society. Even if parents aren't free from prejudice, they do a child and the world a service by keeping these attitudes to themselves. Those who model acceptance of all races and cultures are setting the stage for a child to live harmoniously in today's world.

Applying reality therapy. Behaviors described in reality therapy (Glasser, 1965) can be very useful. One suggestion is to laugh and have fun with a child and avoid any criticism during playtimes. If parent and child are playing tennis for enjoyment, this is not the time for the parent to be a critic. The world does not end if a mistake is made, and helping a child learn this is positive. A positive comment may not be welcomed if it is unrealistic. An example of this would be a child playing golf with her mother and hitting the ball about 2 feet and the mother saying, "Great, honey, it went straight!" Somehow that would not be comforting. Can you think of other examples of unrealistic positive comments?

Reality therapy emphasizes choices and responsibility for one's own actions. A positive parent offers realistic choices, whereas authoritarian discipline offers none, and a permissive attitude allows unlimited choices. Giving young children choices, such as selecting among three different outfits for the day, helps them learn to choose within limits. Wise parents do not give options in all situations. "Do you want to go home now?" is a poor question if you, as the adult, have decided to go. Later, choices become more numerous and frequently more challenging for both child and parent. Courage is in order. Children need practice with decision making, yet parents are apt to be impatient or unwilling to allow the pain of seeing them fall on their face (Spezzano, 1992).

Reality therapy also suggests not accepting excuses. Teaching a child that excuses do not solve problems and are only temporary forms of relief, as discussed in Chapter 4, is important. An excellent book, *Raising a Responsible Child* (Dinkmeyer and McKay, 1996), says that the democratic approach to discipline works best because children have choices and are involved in decisions. A final ban from reality therapy is on hurting others, which includes yelling, hitting, and imposing excessive restrictions. Parents are powerful examples. "Do not yell at me," the mother screams. "But you have been yelling at me," protests the child. The usual response is, "I am the parent, so I can yell." Honestly, does that make sense?

Managing conflict successfully. All families experience conflict. If a child does not disagree with a parent, something is wrong. The child is either fearful or incapable of independent thought. The conflict management recommendations discussed in previous chapters also work well in the parent–child relationship. How disagreement is handled is the key. Conflicts over power and control are especially prevalent during adolescence. A teenager strives for self-identity, independence, and separation from home. A normal adolescent will disagree, sometimes unrealistically. Parents can agree with a child's perception while maintaining their own. Saying "I can see why you think that" or "You have a good point" shows respect and affirmation. Almost all adolescents care about their parents and want to be cared about, so conflict can be managed positively.

In the parent–child relationship, as in any relationship, giving in is not healthy. When children become angry and resentful, a loving parent sometimes caves in to stop these negative feelings or for the sake of peace. Sometimes it is much better to suffer painful emotions if you, as a parent, believe that the chosen course of action is heading in a positive direction. If conflict is managed fairly, emotional outbursts will be minimized in both number and intensity.

Even when children leave home, there is potential for conflict. This could be a carryover from unresolved hurts or newly emerging areas of disagreement. "My mom still thinks that everything I do is wrong, including how I handle my children," said a young woman. "We just do not get along," said a mother of an adult child. Breaking the cycle of negative patterns of behavior, opening up lines of communication, and finding forgiveness are discussed in the book *Making Peace with Your Parents* (Bloomfield, 1996b).

Positive parenting is a challenge and a commitment. Education, love, and dedication are required. A realization that you are not only parenting but also *training the next generation of parents* is sobering. If you are or plan to be a parent, be sure to do the activity on "Parenting Behaviors" in Reflections and Applications. The choice of learning and practicing positive parenting behaviors is among the most significant and potentially rewarding ones you will ever make.

Enjoying the Role of Grandparent

"I enjoy being a parent. I absolutely love being a grandparent!" is a commonly heard remark. Many people progress from parenting into special grandparent–grandchild relationships. Grandparents are different from yesteryear in that they are generally healthier, more educated, and more affluent. Because of a longer life span, the role of grandparent can last for many years. Possible roles of a grandparent are caregiver, educator, living ancestor, family historian, mentor, role model, playmate, and friend.

Grandparenting is increasingly becoming a subject of research. An overwhelming number of participants in an American Association of Retired Persons survey (Baker, 2001) said they are delighted in their role as grandparents with less than 1 percent reporting dissatisfaction. One confided, "All my troubles, aches, and pains go away when I am with them. They fill me with so much love." They most commonly keep in touch by telephone and wish that they were together more. The most difficult part of grandparenting is keeping up with the energetic children. A survey of 11,000 grandparents by AARP (Baker, 2001) revealed the most satisfying aspects (see Fig. 13-9, "What Is Most Satisfying about Being a Grandparent?").

What Is Most Satisfying about Being a Grandparent?

- Unconditional love without the burden of discipline
- Watching children grow and develop
- Seeing their faces light up when we come together
- Passing on family and religious values

Figure 13-9

Another study questioned grandchildren from ages 16 to 37. Emotional closeness was reported by 73.1 percent. The "close" group depicted a loving, nurturing grandparent whose devotion and attachment were evident. These grandparents were also described as a valuable source of family history, as well as good listeners—someone to whom anything could be told. The closeness was related to the grandparent's interest in and appreciation for the grandchild, as well as availability for help and support (Boon and Brussoni, 1998).

Although the phenomenon of grandparents raising grandchildren is hardly new, it is an emerging social issue that is garnering a great deal of media attention due to its impact on the welfare of our nation's most vulnerable members. Today, approximately 4 million children live with their grandparents. Further, the literature on this phenomenon suggests that there are probably many more children in informal care arrangements residing with their grandparents than the data can capture. According to U.S. census data, grandparents raise 6 percent of our nation's children. That is a lot of children—4.5 million to be exact—and the number is growing rapidly.

Between 1990 and 2000, the number of children in the United States under age 18 increased by 14.3 percent; within that same decade, the number of U.S. children in grandparent-headed households increased by 30 percent. The data also indicate that grandparent-headed households are twice as likely to live in poverty as other American families.

Whether because of substance abuse, child abuse or neglect, incarceration, mental illness, or physical illness, biological parents of these children may not be able to care for them. Their grandparents—most of whom subsist on meager incomes—are called on to provide for the basic food, shelter, and clothing needs for millions of our nation's children. Due to advanced age, poor health, poverty, minimal education, and lack of transportation, these grandparents are typically unable to provide the grandchildren in their care with much beyond their basic needs. Thus, the children continue to be at risk because their grandparents often have inadequate resources to raise them.

For the grandparents, the full-time care of their grandchildren is sometimes a surprise and almost always a return to responsibilities that they had thought were long past. Some grandparents are in their thirties or forties, but many are old enough to collect Social Security, and they have their share of aches and pains, as well as plans that usually did not include taking on child-rearing responsibilities again. Anyone with children can tell you that child rearing is a challenge. Grandparents have already met that challenge once with their own children, but in this second time around they face some unique disadvantages. Most of them are between ages 55 and 64, and many are over age 65. Although intergenerational families cross all ethnic and socioeconomic lines, the growing numbers of grand-parents raising grandchildren are far more likely to be persons of color and to live in poverty than those who are not (National Center on Grandparents Raising Grandchildren, 2005).

Understanding the Characteristics of a Strong Family

Strong families are not families without problems. Functional families are not, simply, the flip side of dysfunctional families. All families face challenges, but some families are better at dealing with them than others (Olson and DeFrain, 1994). The most extensive series of studies of family strengths and strong families has been done by Stinnett and his colleagues (DeFrain and Stinnett, 1992; Stinnett and DeFrain, 1985). In 20 years of study, the researchers have collected family strengths data on more than 10,000 families in the United States and in more than 20 countries around the world. Perhaps the most important finding is that families in various ethnic groups and cultures across the United States and around the world seem to be much more alike than different. These researchers proposed that six major qualities are common of strong families in the United States and other countries. These qualities are commitment, appreciation and affection, positive communication, time together, spiritual well-being, the ability to cope with stress and crisis (Stinnett and DeFrain, 1985) (Fig. 13-10).

Dual-Earner Households

A change affecting most families is the reality of dual-earner couples. Depending on the age of a child, the percentage of mothers who work outside the home ranges from 59 percent to 73 percent (U.S. Census Bureau, 2000). In 2000, both parents were em-ployed in 64.2 percent of families with children under age 18 (Bureau of Labor Statistics, 2001). When both parents are employed, the common question is, "How does this affect a child?" As with many questions, studies do not necessarily agree. One showed that pa-ternal employment was not consistently related to child outcomes (Harvey, 1999). Another looked at just maternal employment and noted a negative cognitive effect on white, but not on African American or non–Hispanic white, children (Han, Waldfogel, and Brooks-Gunn, 2001). A major study (National Institute of Child Health and Human Development, 2001) showed mixed results (see Fig. 13-11, "Effects of Early Childhood Care").

One point is clear. Parents will continue to work outside the home, and quality child care does make a positive difference. A study followed children over the first 7 years of their lives. Higher-quality child care was related to better mother–child relationships; lower

Figure 13-10   Families have certainly changed!

Effects of Early Childhood Care

- Of children who were in child care for more than 30 hours per week, 17 percent were regarded as being aggressive toward other children compared with 6 percent regarded as being aggressive when in child care for less than 10 hours per week.
- Children who spent more time in child care centers, as opposed to other types of child care, were more likely to display better language skills and have better short-term memory.

Figure 13-11

probability of insecure attachment; fewer reports of problem behaviors; and higher cognitive performance, language ability, and level of school readiness in the children. The opposite results were found when the care was of low quality. Family characteristics and the quality of the parent's relationship with the child were stronger predictors of children's development than the child care factors (Peth-Pierce, 1998).

Within the family, what will help is a fair division of household labor and child care responsibilities. Of utmost importance is the parent's use of time. A comparison between full-time mothers and ones who worked outside the home found no support for the idea that young children fare best when they have a mother at home full time. They concluded that full-time mothering is not critical to good child outcomes. What did make a significant difference was the time parents spent with the children (Bianchi and Robinson, 1997). Making the reality of dual-earner families a positive experience is of paramount importance.

Gay and Lesbian Households

Another type of family, usually composed of two employed adults and included in the broader family definition, is headed by a gay or lesbian couple. One or both of the adults may have already been a parent or the couple may choose to adopt or give birth. With the increase in cases of donor insemination comes an increase in lesbian-headed families. In 2003, at least 250,000 U.S. children were being raised in two-parent, same-sex homes (Barrett, 2004).

What do we know about families of gays and lesbians? In the face of more prejudice, discrimination, and oppression when compared with those headed by heterosexuals, these families show positive adjustment in supportive environments (Patterson, 2000). Except for social stigma, no other significant differences in self-concept development, behavioral problems, intelligence, and psychiatric evaluations have been found. Children raised in homosexual households almost always develop a heterosexual orientation; typically, they do not have problems with gender, emotional, and social development nor in relationships with others. Researchers conclude that the children mature in a positive manner, and they do not consider the sexual orientation of their parents as a meaningful predictor of successful child development. Many children benefit from being taught increased empathy, tolerance, and respect for differences (Fitzgerald, 1999). A short story is told by two women who each gave birth to one boy (Wingert and Kantrowitz, 2000):

One of our sons, Jacob, told a little girl at preschool that he had two moms. Later she told one of the moms, "I have two granddads, so I guess that Jacob can have two moms."

In addition to unreasonable intolerance that can be directed against gays, lesbians, and their children, another major challenge has to do with lack of legal recognition and rights. Some progress has been made in terms of public acceptance. As compared with 1977 when 43 percent of respondents said that homosexual relations should be legal, 54 percent in 2001 said the same (Newport, 2001). Adoption by a same-sex partner is allowed in some states although only 39 percent of the general public is in favor of adoption rights for gay partners (Wingert and Kantrowitz, 2000). Perhaps, if those who are opposed come to understand that, as in all families, it is the quality of the relationships, not the structure, that makes a difference, the level of acceptance will rise (Fig. 13-12).

Adoptive Households

Compared to years ago when 80 percent of babies born out of wedlock in the United States were given up for adoption, in 2003 the rate was only 2 to 3 percent. Still there are at least 150,000 children adopted each year (Dunkin, 2000). Although having to deal with unique issues, such as explaining the adoption and the probable desire of a child to learn about biological parents, adoptive families compare quite favorably with biological units (Borders, Black, and Pasley, 1998). In one study, adoptive mothers reported spending more time with their children and having higher family cohesion than did mothers from other family types (Lansford et al., 2001).

Challenges include a societal assumption that biology equates to more love than is possible in an adoptive situation, emotional uncertainties, and, in many cases, an unknown genetic history. Yet, as Alison commented, "I have the best of two worlds—adoptive parents with whom I share a deep love and biological parents who made a very wise decision in my behalf."

Divorced Households

Divorce, a challenge for individuals as, discussed in Chapter 12, can be a process of family change if children are involved. A **binuclear family** is one in which marital separation has occurred (Ahrons, 1994). One reason for this term is to lessen the social stigma and deviant view. The phrase "child of a broken home," in contrast, is a negative label that conjures images of something that is faulty, unworkable, and unable to be fixed. The term *binuclear family* also shows that, even though a marriage ends, a family consisting of two biological parents continues.

Divorce occurs regularly in the United States. Since 1960, the divorce rate has more than doubled (Raymond, 2001). Obviously, millions of children are affected. No matter how positive the end results may be, the divorce of their parents is an extremely painful experience for children.

Perhaps no greater adjustment challenge exists than helping children cope with their parents' divorce. A positive beginning is to consider options to an

A Loving Family

The two parents took turns rocking 8-month-old Nicole, their precious daughter, during our informal interview. It was obvious that Dee and Shelly, a same-sex couple, share a stable, intimate love relationship and that their love for Nicole is unconditional and unlimited. "We have been together 6 years," they said. "We talked about having a child but wanted to wait until we were sure that our relationship was stable. When a couple chooses artificial insemination, it is a conscious decision. Putting the child first means that you will be sure of yourself and of the relationship."

When asked how they decided who would give birth, Dee with her quick wit, answered, "That was easy. I cannot handle pain!" Shelly added that age and family history were also important factors. Another decision had to do with the sperm donor. They considered a male friend but decided there were too many possible complications and opted for an anonymous donor from a highly reputable sperm bank. Seven attempts and thousands of dollars later, Shelly became pregnant.

In response to any negatives associated with the experience, they described a nonsupportive doctor and the muted feelings of joy related to pregnancy. "We felt a bit of shame at the first clinic. It was if we were doing something selfish so we went to another doctor and found support and acceptance. As to the pregnancy itself, our gay/lesbian friends did not relate to it, our families were still struggling to accept our relationship; we just did not feel as much validation as most parents do." An issue of concern is lack of legal recognition of their family because the state in which they reside does not allow civil unions. "I have no legal rights as a parent," Dee said, "and this is scary."

As for the positives, Shelly said, "There are so many." They then mentioned the ultimate joy of having a child, an enrichment of their lives, an emotional bonding, and a solidification of their relationship. "Our lives are child-centered right now, and we love it," they said.

Looking at Nicole who appeared so at peace in Dee's arms, I asked, "And what about her when she gets older?" Shelly said, "My worst nightmare is that she will be hurt by people who do not accept her." Dee quickly added, "Yet some of my best traits have come from being hurt. We will raise her in love and nurture her self-esteem and hope that these will shield her." The three of them represent all the finest in strong, healthy families. My wish, and I hope yours, is that Nicole will never experience hurt as a result of having two loving parents who just happen to be the same sex.

Figure 13-12

adversarial legal battle, such as mediation or a collaborative divorce (Thayer and Zimmerman, 2001), in order to focus on the children's best interests.

Divorce is a different experience for children than it is for adults. They feel rejected, angry, powerless, lonely, and guilty. They did not ask for divorce yet are forced into being part of a battle between two people they love, according to the authors of a recommended book, *The Co-Parenting Survival Guide* (Thayer and Zimmerman, 2001).

Loyalty conflicts, sometimes flipping from one parent to the other and back again, are common for children of divorce. Children often conceptualize divorce as a fight between two teams with the more powerful side winning the home turf, and will root for different teams at different times. (Wallerstein and Blakeslee, 1989, p. 13)

Adolescents have a different experience than younger children; more challenges exist because of their multiple developmental changes. Negative effects can be alleviated by a positive parent–adolescent relationship (Hines, 1997). Adult children are frequently shocked and may react in extreme ways. "I could not believe it when my parents who have been together for 36 years said they were divorcing. I wanted to blame one or the other and force them to stay together. I finally realized that I was thinking only of myself and not about their well-being," confided Diane. Hopefully, reading this section will motivate all children of divorce to make the effort to heal any old hurts.

How divorce affects children has been the source of numerous research studies (Fig. 13-13). More recent studies have focused on predivorce conditions as a factor in the outcome. Prior to their parents' divorce, male and female adolescents had more academic, psychological, and behavioral problems than did their peers whose parents stay married (Sun, 2001). Children's long-term welfare was linked to conditions both before and after their parents' divorce (Furstenberg and Kiernan, 2001). How divorce affects children is still unknown. An important consideration is how an unhappy living situation impacts child development.

Figure 13-13 Children feel a keen sense of loss when their parents divorce.

There is no evidence that children need two parents in order to grow into healthy adults. But there is a great deal of evidence that children raised in an environment of tension, conflict, and abuse either reenact these behaviors in adulthood or become withdrawn and depressed and take on the role of the victim. (Forward and Torres, 1986, p. 260)

Even if tension, conflict, and abuse do not exist, an environment lacking an intimate love relationship between two parents isn't an optimum one for children. They learn about relationships and marriages within a family, and those who witness an emotionally dead marriage are not gaining healthy messages about love.

The key to how well children do is in the hands of the divorcing parents. A challenge for all loving parents is to do everything possible to ensure that children do not suffer any more than necessary. Children are helped by realizing that self-esteem is not based on someone else's love for you; instead, it comes from within. Watching parents cope positively with divorce teaches valuable lessons.

Just as people are not trained to be married, they have little or no education in divorce.

Society is making some efforts to correct this deficit by requiring postdivorce counseling and offering classes and seminars for divorcing parents and their children. Should divorcing parents be required to learn how to help their children cope? Ideally, individuals would seek all available resources because a well-handled divorce alleviates much of a child's pain. Leftover hurt from divorce continues largely because of parental attitudes and behaviors. Children whose parents are committed to doing a better job with their divorce than they did with their marriage are fortunate. Following are some important guidelines.

Leveling.   Divorcing parents can make the crisis easier for their children by talking with them about the divorce. The child's age will influence the content of the discussion. Preferably, both parents will participate. Children then feel that both will continue to act as parents, and they are not as likely to take sides. At this time, and on a regular basis thereafter, children need reassurance that parental love continues and that the divorce, although painful to them, is the result of an adult relationship that did not work. Make sure that the message is clear that the children are not in any way at fault. The fulfillment of needs theory, discussed in Chapter 12, can be used with children old enough to understand. The marriage failed to meet individual needs, and neither parent is seen as the cause of the divorce.

Expressing.   Intense feelings surrounding divorce are best vented. No matter how much it hurts parents to experience a child's pain and anger, such disclosures are to be freely encouraged. Divorce leads to a feeling of loss, and grieving is in order. Parents may feel a need to suppress their own emotions in front of a child. Being out of control is not recommended; however, an honest "I am scared sometimes, too" or "I hurt, too" can be beneficial.

Normalizing.   It is best to keep life as normal as possible and avoid other major changes. Both parents can help by keeping children involved in activities and continuing to show an active interest. If a change is in order, you can make it easier by informing the children about it and listening to their input. You may need to be strong enough to hold fast against their objections.

Forming a positive parenting coalition.   When divorcing partners do not get along, fathers especially tend to distance themselves (Doherty, Kouneski, and Erickson, 1998). Thus, being able to co-parent in a positive way greatly benefits a child. Developing a "temporary alliance for the purpose of accomplishing a project" is how Emily and John Visher (1988) described a parenting coalition. The Vishers, authors, therapists, and stepfamily adults, founded Stepfamily Association of America, an organization dedicated to educating and supporting stepfamilies. A coalition involves both divorced parents cooperating and staying involved in raising the children; later, it can also include stepparents. Even though a coalition approach is challenging and often frustrating, loving parents who want to serve their children best find that it is a wise investment of their time, energy, and effort. In fact, it may be central to the welfare of a child.

Do you have to be a good friend with the other parent? The answer is no. An ideal situation is to have a high friendship and low preoccupation with that person.

If being friends isn't possible, maintaining a cordial, businesslike relationship is highly recommended. A connection with an "ex" will always be there because of a common bond to a child; yet, creating emotional distance is healthy. Children are the real winners when their parents get along. A basic step that divorced parents can take is to agree on a general "want" for the children, such as "We *want* the children to be spared as much pain as possible" or "We *want* to do what is best for the children." In developing a working relationship as co-parents, use the following steps from the book *Between Love and Hate: A Guide to Civilized Divorce* (Gold, 1996).

1. Be businesslike and relate to each other as people do in the workplace. Focus on solutions and use teamwork to reach objectives. Use businesslike communications throughout the process.
2. Separate how you feel about your ex-spouse from how you relate to the person as a parent.
3. Focus on what the children need.

Other recommendations are to use open communication, describe desired behavioral changes, and do not assume. One parent's interpretation is no more correct than is that of the other parent.

What not to do.   Parents can help children by eliminating all too common negative behaviors.

- *Do not* criticize the personhood of the other parent. Keep negative comments to yourself. Children perceive themselves as half of each parent, so berating your former spouse is hurtful and damaging to the child. "It feels like an arrow going right through me," said one child. If you are critical, direct your comment to the behavior of the person, as recommended for all criticism.
- *Do not* place a child in the middle of two warring camps. Children of divorce often speak of feeling torn. Parents add to the burden by setting up situations in which children are pulled in different directions: "Whom would you rather live with?" "Do you want to spend the holidays here or with your dad?" You may wish to offer a child alternatives, but be aware that having to make such decisions is difficult.
- *Do not* pump a child for information: "Who is your mom dating?" "How much money did your dad spend on you?" Putting a child on the spot is cruel.
- *Do not* use a child as a messenger. Closely related to pumping for information is to ask a youngster to relay a message: "Tell your dad that the child support check is late." "Ask your mom if she wants you to come this summer." The adults can communicate for themselves in an "adult" manner. If this seems impossible, communicate through the mail or through another person, not through the child.
- *Do not* add to a child's already weakened emotional state. "I am so unhappy. If only you lived with me, I would be much better" will only burden a child more. Or, if a child is angry at the other parent, do not increase the pain level. Instead, encourage the child to talk the problem

over with the person. If the other parent hurts the child by not being in contact or forgetting special days, listen to the pain and confine your comments to "I do not understand why this happens. Someday he or she is likely to regret not being a part of your life." You may inwardly feel justified by a child's resentment; however, do not feed the unpleasant emotional fire. Children do not benefit from feeling unloved and unwanted by either parent.

- *Do not* create more stress for the child. If finances are worrisome, for example, find a friend in whom to confide. Not recommended is to use child support and visitation as weapons in a struggle with the other parent. Paying support on time is in the best interests of a child. The reality is that only 48 percent of mothers receive the full amount that is due; the rest receive some, and others get nothing (Doherty, Koueski, and Erickson, 1998). Even though fathers typically pay support, noncustodial mothers bear equal responsibility. Spending quality time in a safe environment with a parent is in a child's best interests; to deny this to get back at the other person is childish and selfish. Both custodial and noncustodial parents can deprive and damage children. Loving parents do neither.

Parents who work together to set up custody arrangements and a reasonable, flexible schedule of visits are helping a child. A key guideline is to do what is in the best interests of the child. A father asked me once, "What do you think of this idea? My wife and I have joint custody, and we are thinking of having our 3-year-old live with her for a year in Montana and then a year with me in Nebraska and just keep trading off." My negative reaction was honest. Designed to make parents happy, it would likely make the child miserable.

Children typically appreciate being consulted about moving back and forth between households. The best course of action is to provide them with a number of choices that are acceptable to both parents and that do not indicate a preference for one or the other. The child's input should be neither judged nor criticized. Because parental conflict and distress can impair a child's adjustment, flexibility, congeniality, and cooperation are key elements in doing the best you can.

Ideally, both parents will remain actively involved in a child's life. Consistency and dependability about spending quality time with a youngster are essential to well-being. If one parent has custody and the child spends the most time there, that person can keep the other parent informed about the child's school progress, activities, health, and so on. If parents have difficulty in this area, a third party is the answer, and mediation is highly recommended.

Mediation is a form of Alternative Dispute Resolution (ADR) that is offered in many states to parents who are divorcing or involved in other child custody issues as an alternative to the traditional investigative or litigation process. Mediation is an informal process in which a neutral third party facilitates discussion between parties to reach a voluntary, negotiated resolution. The decision to mediate is completely voluntary in some states, although mandated by the courts in others. A mediator does not resolve the issues or impose a decision on the parties. Instead, the mediator helps the parties to agree on a mutually acceptable resolution.

Parties have an equal say in the process and decide settlement terms, not the mediator. Benefits of mediation follow.

- *Is confidential:* All parties sign a confidentiality agreement.
- *Avoids litigation:* Lengthy litigation *can* be avoided. Mediation may assist the parties in avoiding the uncertainty of judicial outcome.
- *Fosters cooperation:* Mediation fosters a problem-solving approach. Parents are often more willing to follow parenting plans they have developed together.
- *Improves communication:* Mediation provides a neutral and confidential setting where both parties can openly discuss their views on the underlying dispute. Enhanced communication can lead to mutually satisfactory resolutions. A neutral third party assists the parties in reaching a voluntary, mutually beneficial resolution. Mediation can resolve all issues important to the parties, not just the underlying legal dispute.

There is a movement in family law whereby divorcing couples can sign agreements with lawyers to not go to court. More specifically, the process is known as Collaborative Family Law (CFL) and the agreement to not go to court is binding on the lawyers, not the couple. If one or both clients are unsatisfied, either may still march the dispute to court. They will, however, have to find new lawyers.

At heart, the CFL process seeks to develop consensus between the parties for a mutually acceptable settlement. The settlement can include the division of assets, spousal or child support, and/or the ongoing care of children (Direnfeld, 2006).

Single-Parent Households

Even though a family endures as long as its members are alive, its structure may be changed by circumstances. Any serious examination of families today includes the alterations brought about by death of a parent, desertion of a parent, or parental divorce. According to the U.S. Census Bureau, 31 percent of U.S. households are single-parent households with children (U.S. Census Bureau, 2004). Even though a larger percentage of these families is headed by women (26%), the number of single-father families is five times greater than it was in 1970 (Fields and Casper, 2000).

An expectation is that more than half of the children born in the 1990s will spend time in a single-parent home (Kantrowitz and Wingert, 2001). In fact, about 35 percent of Hispanic, 66 percent of black, and 20 percent of white children now live with one parent (Demo, 2000). The most common type of **single-parent family** is one in which a divorced parent has the children in his or her care. This type is also known as a *binuclear* family. Terms such as *custodial* and *noncustodial parents* are used to identify physical and, typically, legal custody. Joint custody is becoming more prevalent. In the United States, in at least 40 states shared custody is written into law (Gillenkirk, 2000). More fathers today are seeking their full parental rights. Research finds few differences between children living in either a single-mother or single-father family (Downey, Ainsworth-Darnell, and Dufur, 1998).

Individuals who do not live with their children are considered noncustodial parents. A study indicates that both sexes appear to have difficulty staying
actively involved in their children's lives (Stewart, 1999). Still uncommon is the
mother in a noncustodial role. Negative societal attitudes make the role difficult.
Karen led a workshop for mothers without custody. Her objective was to encourage people to accept and empathize with women in this difficult role. "I
have suffered because of others' opinions of me," she admits, "and I have some
regrets. I do know that my relationship with my sons is loving and close, and I
honestly do not think it could have worked out as well if all this had not happened the way it did." The acceptance of mothers as loving noncustodial parents will be a step forward. Perhaps a simple statement made by Irene will put
this in perspective: "I did not give up my child. She just lives with her father
more than with me."

Regardless of whether the custodial parent is female or male, single parenting is a challenge. "It is the hardest job in the world, no doubt about it" and "I feel
I have to be all things to all people" are typical thoughts. Deciding to be the custodial parent requires objectivity and a great deal of thought. Too often, mothers assume custody just because society expects them to do so. An individual is wise to
assess honestly what is in the best interests of the children. Of course, in cases of
desertion or death, a parent has no choice.

Difficulties include the inordinate stress of trying to assume multiple roles
and attempting to handle all the children's pain; one's own feelings of guilt, anger,
and depression; time management; and finances. For women the latter is usually
quite challenging.

A common concern of single parents has to do with the welfare of children
without a same-sex parent in the household. In a comprehensive evaluation of research on this subject, no evidence was found for a benefit of living with a same-
sex parent (Powell and Downey, 1997). An interesting study of African American
children found that at lower socioeconomic levels, students in single-parent families actually scored significantly higher on academic tests than did those from
dual-parent families (Battle, 1998). Having another caring adult to share the load
is helpful; however, democratic discipline and other positive parenting strategies
can be used effectively by one as well as by two parents. Support groups are major
sources of help. Classes and seminars can offer practical advice and encouragement to parents floundering in their new (or old) role.

The benefits and rewards of single parenting can diminish the impact of the
problems. Most parents without partners proudly acknowledge:

- Heightened self-esteem and feelings of pride in all the accomplishments
  of single parenting
- Close, meaningful relationships based on shared coping, emotional ex-
  pression, and deep communication
- Self-respect and the pride of being self-sufficient
- Freedom to make solitary decisions on child raising

A study by Morrison (1995) showed many strengths of single parents, including flexibility and adaptability to change, less adult conflict and tension; and
more warmth, cooperation, and cohesiveness.

Contrary to what is implied by the stigma of single-parent families, children can do extremely well. Ryan was described by a high school counselor as an outstanding scholar, athlete, and all-around student—one of the best-liked kids in his large California high school. He said, "I know of no other student, past or present, whom I would most like to have as my own child than Ryan." This remarkable young man earned athletic and academic scholarships and graduated from Stanford University. In a letter of recommendation, his college baseball coach wrote:

> I have never had a student athlete that I have been more impressed with than Ryan Turner. He has an enthusiasm for everything he does that is contagious. He proved to be one of the most, if not the most, exceptional young men I have ever been associated with in my 21 years of collegiate coaching. Ryan is first class in every respect!

Ryan, now in his thirties, added to his laurels by being the first player signed by the Colorado Rockies and then earned an M.B.A. from Harvard Business School. This fine young man, who could be described as the "product of a broken home," was raised since age 5 by his single-parent mother Connie. Both son and mother deserve a great deal of credit (Fig. 13-14).

Parents without custody play a significant role in a child's life. As indicated earlier, children want and profit from a positive relationship with both parents. Successful noncustodial parents make parenting a high priority. Showing your love and concern, while resisting a temptation to spoil a child, is highly recommended. The ones who do an excellent job get to know their children even better and often develop a closer relationship than they had before. They do not cause problems for the other parent; instead, they are cooperative and flexible and attempt to make the most of their special role.

Noncustodial parenting can be frustrating. "I want to be involved, but she will not allow it," said one father in reference to his former spouse. "I have no idea what is going on with my two children except what they tell me every other weekend. I cannot get information from their father or their school," said a frustrated mother. The parent with custody can do a great deal to encourage positive participation of a child's other parent. Even without that positive involvement, children can do quite well. "Every child needs to feel that at least one adult is crazy about him or her" (Spezzano, 1992, p. 72). The love of both biological parents is even better. With all of its challenges and frustrations, single parenting is special and rewarding. Growing up in a binuclear family or with one surviving parent has its difficulties, yet the benefits can outweigh the costs. As with all of life's challenges, individuals create their own realities.

Figure 13-14 Proud single-parent mom Connie and son Ryan after the College World Series game victory.

Stepfamily Households

What is a stepfamily? Definitions vary even among the families themselves. The broadest concept of a **stepfamily** is a couple with one or both having at least one child from a previous relationship. The child or children may or may not live in the household with the couple. One or both of the partners may have been married before. About 75 percent of those who divorce marry again (U.S. Census Bureau, 2003). Divorce is the typical reason for the end of the former relationship, although stepfamilies also form after the death of a parent. A stepfamily also forms when a previously unmarried person with a child marries.

Stepfamilies come in many varieties, and the situation can be complicated. Both adults may have custody of children; one parent can have custody and the other can be a noncustodial parent; both can be noncustodial parents; or a stepparent may not have any biological children. The couple may add their own biological child to the existing family. As one who is familiar with the configurations, explanations are still difficult! If you are not yet married, you could join the increasing numbers of people who become stepparents in their first marriages. "Instant parent" is what they are sometimes called. Glen, a former student, wrote me a note: "Would you believe that I'm marrying a woman with two children? After hearing you talk about stepfamilies, now I am going to be in one!"

Men and women form stepfamilies for the same reasons they marry. They love each other, and they want to commit to a lasting relationship. For anyone considering stepfamily living, what is important is to take the time to "stop, look, listen, and learn." Preparing for a first marriage is important, and if you are going into a stepfamily, prepare, prepare, and prepare. Even though stepfamilies have existed throughout history, the 1990s produced more research than in the previous 90 years (Coleman, Ganong, and Fine, 2000). The studies unveiled the challenges, the strengths, and the ways to succeed.

For stepfamilies, a major challenge lies in overcoming society's image that spills over into how individuals perceive their family. What do you think when you hear the word stepmother? Most think of Cinderella or the wicked stepmother in the story of Sleeping Beauty. The image is powerful, and stepfamily stereotypes form early. A 3-year-old who had an excellent relationship with her soon-to-be stepmother asked on the day of the wedding, "As soon as you get to be my stepmother, will you beat me?" People presume that the stepfather will be cruel, the stepmother wicked, and the stepchildren poor maligned waifs. "To interact in the middle of such a dark cloud is crippling to many stepfamilies" (Visher and Visher, 1979, p. 6).

In one of the first studies of remarriage, **attitudinal environment,** or perceived support from the general society as well as specific people, was identified as a contributing factor to the success or failure of stepfamilies (Bernard, 1956). A favorable environment was found to be significantly related to family strength (Knaub, Hanna, and Stinnett, 1984). Greg pinpointed it well in a video program: "If you feel accepted from the outside, it helps you to accept yourself and the stepfamily from the inside." Support and involvement are needed from the extended family, including grandparents. "Grandparents are in an excellent position to build bridges or to build walls between stepfamily members" (Visher and Visher, 1982, p. 120). The educational system can play a major part in imparting accurate information about families and in encouraging an acceptance of the merits of all types of families (Pasley and Ihinger-Tallman, 1997) (Fig. 13-15).

Images of Stepfamilies

- A stepfamily is somewhat like a Cecil B. DeMille production—a cast of thousands (Westoff, 1977).
- The numbers of people involved and the subsequent myriad of relationships that are created contribute to the complexity of a stepfamily (Knaub, Hanna, and Stinnett, 1984).
- Being in a stepfamily ends one's fear of living a dull life. Stepfamilies that are born in pain can grow into joy (Adams, 1987).

Figure 13-15

Attitudes today are more accepting, and many adults and children perceive their stepfamilies as positive. Researchers are paying more attention to strengths. In 1989, only 4 of more than 50 self-help books contained a mention of the potential strengths of stepfamilies and (Coleman and Ganong, 1989); most research emphasized only the problems (Ganong and Coleman, 1996). Knaub, Hanna, and Stinnett (1984) were among the first to concentrate on the positives of remarriage and stepfamilies. Stepfamilies are strengthened in the same ways as other families are: communicating, showing appreciation, doing things together, handling conflict effectively, and perceived support (Knaub, Hanna, and Stinnett, 1984).

> The stepfamily is a courageous and positive new family unit. It is not second-class. We are a different kind of family and we face different kinds of problems than other families. But we will survive and provide a second chance of happiness for millions of adults and children. (Getzoff and McClenahan, 1984, p. 142)

Because of stepfamily uniqueness, special challenges are best handled before they lead to insurmountable problems. Following are solid recommendations from the Stepfamily Association of America (2004), an organization that has educated and supported stepfamilies for over 20 years. Elaborations of the recommendations follow the list.

- Nurture and enrich the couple relationship.
- Have realistic expectations.
- Develop new roles.
- Express and understand emotions.
- Seek support and see the positive.

Expectations must be closely examined. People entering into stepfamilies may have unrealistic ideas, representing opposite ends of a continuum. Some adults believe that because they love each other, the stepfamily will automatically succeed. "I love you, and you love me, and I know the children and we will love each other, too." Realistically, love, if it develops at all between stepparent and stepchild, takes time and effort. Both may have to settle for a feeling of care and concern.

The belief that parents should love all their children equally and that children should love both parents equally is not a reasonable expectation for stepfamilies. In fact, such injunctions can produce guilt and may inhibit the development of a caring relationship. (Kelley, 1992, p. 585)

Stepparents are advised to stop worrying about whether or not they love their stepchild and focus on establishing caring, openly communicative relationships. In this environment, love can grow (Bloomfield, 1993).

The opposite expectation is a sour idea that stepfamily life will be the pits. Some parents begin by thinking, "I just know it is going to be a terrible struggle," and it is not unusual for children to say, "I know I will hate my stepparent." Neither is realistic. Stepfamily success is clearly possible but not guaranteed. A common mistake is expecting a stepfamily to be like a biological one. A stepfamily is different, and "different" does not mean deficient. In a workshop the question was asked, "How are stepfamilies different?" A loud male voice boomed, "Blood!" He meant that the biological basis is missing for the stepparent and stepchild. When this is acknowledged and not considered as negative, a positive relationship can develop. Other expectations include what "should" happen. For example, "Mike, you should love the kids; after all, they are mine," or "Mary, you should be like a real mother to my kids," and "Son, you should respect Mike because he is my husband and your stepfather." As with all forcing words, the reaction is usually negative. Expressing a realistic expectation as a "want" is healthier.

It is realistic to realize that stepparenting is not like being a biological parent; nor is it equivalent to adopting a child. The stepparent is likely to be resented at first, be somewhat feared, and be compared, usually unfavorably, to the biological parent. Stepchildren are apt to be jealous of a stepparent's place of affection in their parent's life. A former spouse can magnify these feelings and make the situation even more uncomfortable. A stepparent can expect to hear, "You are not my parent, and I do not have to love you." A suggested reply is, "I know I am not your biological parent, and you do not have to love me. I am your stepmom (or stepdad), and I would like to have a positive relationship with you." It is best to contain negative reactions and continue to let the child know that you are concerned and that you care (Fig. 13-16).

Figure 13-16

Within a stepfamily, each person assumes new **roles,** or behaviors within a status. The **status,** or position, of stepparent is considered to be an achieved one because it is earned by individual effort. Lack of training for biological parents is the norm, and only recently have the roles of stepfather, stepmother, stepchild, and stepsibling been examined. This lack of role definition is positive in a sense, because it allows the development of a role that fits the particular situation. If you are the stepparent of a 2-year-old whose biological father is dead, you will play a different part in the child's life than you would if you were the stepparent of a child whose biological parents are divorced. In the former case, your role will be similar to that of the typical father. In the latter, your role would be as an additional significant adult in the child's life. Trying to replace the other biological parent is not recommended. Children do better if they are encouraged to have a tie with a biological parent that is different from their relationship with the stepparent.

The stepparent's role will vary depending on the living arrangements. Noncustodial stepparents can act more like just a friend, whereas a stepparent in the home will assume a parental role. Roles also differ depending on the age of the stepchild, his or her personality, and individual preferences. For example, a 6-year-old who is somewhat insecure may want a strong parental figure, whereas a strong-willed 16-year-old will prefer one who is flexible and friendly. A recommendation is to move slowly into a certain role. Stepparents who "come on like gangbusters" are usually resented. Shared or egalitarian marital roles work best. Resentment is likely when individuals feel that inequities exist. Research indicates that women in second relationships do a smaller proportion of housework than others because the man contributes more in this area (Sullivan, 1997).

Emotions are generally more intense, and often confusing, in a stepfamily. A full range of feelings is probable as people progress through stages of stepfamily life. People in stepfamilies are likely to have their share of hurt, disappointment, jealousy, fear, and anger. Freedom in expression and open communication are especially helpful. Empathy is sorely needed. Of utmost importance is for a stepparent to demonstrate warm and nurturing behavior as much as possible.

For a biological parent outside the stepfamily, acceptance of a new significant adult in your child's life is difficult. "When I heard my sons talking about their stepmother," one divorced parent said, "I wanted to scream that she is not any kind of mother to you. She is just the one who married your dad!" Stepparents may have jealous or resentful feelings toward the children's other parent. Keeping in mind what is best for the children is critical. Additional love and caring adults in their lives are bonuses. "No healthy stepcouple blocks a child from loving a natural parent" (Adams, 1987, p. 46). Additionally, no healthy parent blocks a child from loving a stepparent.

Jealousy and resentment related to a spouse's former mate are common. "I wish she would just go away," one stepparent said of her husband's ex-wife. "She calls and monopolizes his time, and what is so maddening is that he allows it!" Positive communication skills can enable partners to express these feelings in noncombative ways. And learning effective, businesslike ways of parenting with a former spouse, as discussed in a previous section, could alleviate these problems.

In a number of stepfamilies, as noted before, it is one person's first, not second, marriage. In a workshop, a young woman raised her hand and said, "I would like a different term instead of remarriage. This is my first marriage." Because of increased numbers of unmarried births, a high divorce rate, and marriages occurring at later ages, she has a lot of company. More than ever, first marriages today mean becoming an immediate parent. First-married partners in the stepfamily face some different challenges from those that confront remarried persons. Their emotional concerns may be acute as they deal with the role of stepparenting someone else's children when they have never parented before. Education and support are strongly advised.

A number of potentially stressful issues confront stepfamilies. Discipline and finances topped the list of identified problems for 80 stepfamilies (Knaub, Hanna, and Stinnett, 1984). Strongly recommended is to begin a new family system based on positive parenting principles and the style of democratic discipline described earlier. The use of the authoritative style, which is quite similar to the democratic style discussed earlier, is supported by research (Fine, Ganong, and Coleman, 1997). The authoritarian style is not healthy in biological families, and in stepfamilies it becomes a time bomb. Stepchildren do not usually accept a stepparent as an enforcer of limits, at least not initially. Having the biological parent take the lead at first is wise. Both adults working together and being supportive of each other is highly desirable.

If children move back and forth between households, binuclear family issues, identified in a previous section, need attention. A positive finding is that the proportion of children who report good relationships with their noncustodial fathers is higher in stepfamilies than in those where the mother does not have a partner (White and Gilbreth, 2001). The extended family becomes even more extended in that stepfamilies may have additional sets of grandparents and other relatives involved. How and where a stepfamily will spend holidays is an issue. Flexibility and compromise are necessary. In stepfamilies, people learn that holidays are not dates; instead, they are special times when family members can be together, regardless of the date. Other issues include who pays for what and for whom and in what ways are resources such as child support used; estate planning is of utmost importance. Developing a parenting coalition that includes stepparents is a wise investment of time and energy. Advantages are having more resources and people to deal with issues and events, less tension, more information about the children, less manipulation, and positive feelings for all concerned (Bloomfield, 1993).

A major challenge for stepfamilies is the higher divorce rate of 60 percent for remarriages (Marano, 2000). Various reasons have been suggested. "Dealing with stepchildren and ex-spouses, complex finances, the demands of two careers, and the need to meld two distinctive ways of doing things can create stresses that challenge the best of relationships" (Stuart and Jacobson, 1985, p. 230). Because of all the challenges, the interpersonal relations suggestions in this book are highly recommended.

One reason for lack of success is at the heart of all the others. When people in stepfamilies are neither educated nor prepared to meet the challenges, they find themselves hopelessly frustrated. "Stepfamilies must be built with more than good intentions, dreams, and hopes. Awareness, skills, and realistic expectations can provide a stable structure that permits the stepfamily to achieve its potential" (Einstein, 1982, p. 2).

In order to succeed, learning about this unique family type takes center stage. First, because stepfamily adjustment and integration take time, patience is encouraged. Books, workshops, classes, and programs about remarriage and stepfamilies are valuable educational resources. The Stepfamily Association of America, mentioned earlier, has local chapters throughout the United States. A step-by-step program manual for stepfamilies titled *Stepfamilies Stepping Ahead* (Burt, 1989) is an invaluable help, as are numerous other books and tapes available through the organization (see Resources at the end of this chapter).

Are the benefits worth the challenges? Thousands of stepfamily members would say they are. The "pluses" can include the following:

- Additional caring relationships within the stepfamily and the extended family
- Opportunities for learning and growing derived from other role models and from challenging situations
- Diversity of people and interesting situations
- Emphasis on deep communication and problem solving
- Focus on give-and-take, compromise, and sharing
- Living within intimate love relationships and happy marriages
- Satisfaction from succeeding in spite of challenges
- Joy from being cared for (and maybe even loved) by people who are not biologically related

Many stepfamilies do quite well. Family strength, marital satisfaction, and positive perceptions of family adjustment were found in an early study of 80 stepfamilies (Knaub, Hanna, and Stinnett, 1984). Within two or three years after stepfamily formation, most children adapt quite well (Demo, 2000). With no biological buffer of love, individuals can learn to care. Susie, a student, wrote that she had a stepfather and then added, "He's several *steps* above what I had." She described their relationship as very loving.

The absolute joy of being affirmed and loved by children who were not born to you is worth all the stressors along the way. Successful stepfamilies prove that human beings are capable of reaching out and developing long-term nurturing and loving family relationships that are not based on biology.

In tracing family diversity, a painful loss and ending can herald the beginning of a new and diverse type of family. The first is usually a single-parent or binuclear family. Life can be stressful and challenging, yet full of potential rewards. A stepfamily is possibly the next family type. Complexities and challenges are hallmarks of stepfamily life. Education and support can be of great help. Or a family can be diverse from its inception such as an adoptive family or one headed by same-sex parents. Asking the question of whether family structure matters, researchers found that processes—the relationships and what actually happens within families—are much more important than the type of family (Lansford et al., 2001). Perhaps, an author in a celebration of family diversity expressed it best:

> More important for children's development are close, involved relationships with a rich variety of family members and kin-support networks. Children are not disadvantaged by living in nontraditional family structures; rather, they are victimized by cultural intolerance and a reluctance to accept, embrace, and celebrate family diversity. (Demo, 2000, pp. 16–20)

If you know and value yourself, you are well equipped to meet the multiple challenges involved in parenting and developing strong families. The rewards are bountiful. Unique types of families that succeed illustrate excellent interpersonal relations. Such nourishing relationships are among the finest expressions of love (Reflect and Apply).

REFLECT AND APPLY

Reflect

♦ *Of the positive parenting behaviors, which did your parents use? If you are a parent, which are you using?*

♦ *What do you think or know would be painful for a child when parents divorce?*

♦ *Think of both the possible challenges and benefits of being in a stepfamily.*

Apply

♦ *Watch a current television program or a movie with special attention to how families are portrayed.*

♦ *Write three tips for divorcing parents in regard to their children.*

♦ *Ask someone who has had stepfamily experience about both the positives and the negatives.*

LOOKING BACK

- A family is a primary social group and has tremendous influence on the lives of its members.
- A family can be defined as a relatively small domestic group (related by biology, marriage, or adoption) that functions as a cooperative unit.
- Today's society includes several types of families. Identified high-quality family characteristics describe loving, successful relationships.
- Parenting is a major responsibility for which no formal training is mandated. Even though educational resources are available, adults do not typically take advantage of them. Ideally, adults will become educated and make thoughtful decisions about becoming parents.
- Parental responsibilities are numerous. Love and trust are basic to a child's healthy development.
- Fathers are becoming more involved in caregiving; their role is considered as significant as the mother's role.
- Discipline, defined broadly as the entire process of guiding and teaching a child from infancy to adulthood, has many dimensions. Two styles, authoritarian and permissive, are not recommended. Families can benefit by using democratic discipline.
- Positive parenting behaviors include admitting mistakes, spending quality time with children, demonstrating warmth and affection, showing appreciation, emphasizing uniqueness and freeing children from the restrictions of stereotypes, allowing choices, and managing conflict successfully.
- The role of a grandparent is usually extremely enjoyable and satisfying, and relationships between grandchildren and grandparents are typically loving.
- Today's typical family is no longer the "Father Knows Best" variety. Dual careers characterize the majority of families. Diversity in families is represented by gay and lesbian households, adoptive households,

divorced households, single-parent households, and stepfamily households. Research has demonstrated that the quality of family relationships rather than the type is critical in the positive adjustment of its members. Children can flourish in any type of loving environment.

- A major challenge faced by many parents is helping their children cope with divorce. Recommendations, if followed, can make divorce easier on children. If two biological parents are alive, children are best served by positive experiences with both. Developing a positive parenting coalition with a former spouse is often difficult yet definitely in the children's best interests.

- A binuclear family is one in which children have biological parents in different households. Regardless of custody arrangement, both parents have responsibilities. Children who are single-parented can adjust positively, and adults can enjoy many rewards.

- A stepfamily consists of a couple and at least one child from a prior relationship. Stepfamilies are rapidly increasing in numbers. Usually formed as a result of death or divorce, they can be complex and challenging.

- Education and support provide invaluable help for stepfamilies. Overcoming a negative societal image, having realistic expectations, developing new roles and relationships, handling all kinds of emotions, and dealing with unique issues are major tasks of stepfamily members. The high divorce rate for stepfamily couples would likely be lower if education about and preparation for stepfamily life were the norm.

- Successful stepfamily relationships develop through application of personal and interactive skills and exemplify what this book emphasizes: positive interpersonal relations.

The family has a special place in thinking about close relationships. Family relationships are central to human existence, health, and happiness.

—Elaine Berscheid and Letitia Anne Peplau

RESOURCES

Family Service America (local agencies in most communities). (800) 221–2681. http://www.fsanet.org.
Parenting classes and help available through:
American Red Cross
Community colleges/university continuing education programs
Cooperative Extension

Parent Effectiveness Training (PET)
Systematic Training for Effective Parenting (STEP)
YWCA
Divorce help for children and teens:
http://www.childrenanddivorce.com
http://www.teencentral.net
http://www.kidspeace.org

Parents Without Partners (local chapters in many communities). http://www.parentswithoutpartners.org
Stepfamily Association of America, Inc. (provides education and support with local chapters in many communities and has books and resources for sale). (800) 735–0329 or (402) 477–7837.
http://www.stepfam.org

Reflections and Applications

This section of the book is intended to involve you in looking at yourself and your relationships. We gain more by thinking and writing than just by reading. Be honest and strive for a deeper understanding of your life—and enjoy the process!

SELF-APPRAISAL

Before you read the book and complete the other activities in this section, use the following scale and rate yourself honestly in these areas. Each reflects the potential benefits of learning from this book and continuing to improve your interpersonal skills.

5 = Perfect (could not improve)
4 = Very good (almost to the desired level)
3 = Average (could be improved)
2 = Below average (could be much better)
1 = Poor (needs a great deal of improvement)

1. _____ How well do I really know and understand myself?
2. _____ How much regard do I have for myself?
3. _____ What do I think about my ability to change?
4. _____ How effectively do I manage stress?
5. _____ How well do I cope with crises?
6. _____ How do I rate my personal relationships (friendships, significant other)?
7. _____ How do I rate my family relationships?
8. _____ How do I rate my work or school relationships?
9. _____ How well do I handle my emotions?
10. _____ How happy am I?

Total your scores and divide by 10 to get an average score. If you have less than a 5.0 average, this book will help you. If you scored a 5.0 (perfect), you can benefit from learning what this book has to teach about perfectionism.

Honestly reflect on what you hope to gain from this book and then write your ideas below and on the back of this sheet. Be specific. After you have read the book, come back to what you wrote and see what you have accomplished.

Chapter 1

SELF-CONCEPT INVENTORY

Complete the inventory about yourself (two sides) and have at least two other people (preferably a male and a female) fill out similar inventories *about you*. One two-sided inventory for another person is provided from which you can make copies.

Descriptors: Describe yourself in the following four areas of self using at least four different descriptors for each (specific words, phrases, or sentences).

Physical (appearance, condition of body, health):

Mental (abilities, preferred ways of learning, attitude or mental outlook):

Emotional (usual feelings or typical ones in certain situations, mood):

Social (statuses, behaviors around others, preferences of social activities and interactions):

If I were to achieve my ideal self, would these descriptors be different and, if so, in what ways? Use other paper, if needed.

Physical:

Mental:

Emotional:

Social:

Complete the following sentences.

Some relationships that are important to me are

Two of my skills or talents are

Two characteristics or behaviors I appreciate in myself are

One thing I would like to improve about myself is

I am proud of myself for

A goal I have for myself is

What do I value? Name at least four.

For the next three questions, use other paper to answer each completely.

During an average weekday, specifically how do I spend my time?

What would I do with one million tax-free dollars?

If I were told that I had only 1 to 3 months to live, what would I do during that time?

The X on the continuum below shows how I assess my attitude.

Very negative	Negative	Average	Positive	Very positive

How do I rate my current level of self-esteem?

1 = very low 2 = low 3 = average 4 = high 5 = very high

What am I doing or what will I do to build or strengthen a positive attitude and self-esteem?

Identify one belief or thought about self that "comes true" in my behavior (a self-fulfilling prophecy).

Behavior(s) that demonstrate(s) this belief:

If this self-fulfilling prophecy is negative, how can I change it?

I have self-efficacy expectations about (list three):

SELF-CONCEPT INVENTORY

Please answer the following questions about _____.

My relationship to this person is as a(an) _____.

Descriptors: Describe this person in the following four areas of self using at least four descriptors for each (specific words, phrases, or sentences).

Physical (appearance, condition of body, and health):

Mental (abilities, preferred ways of learning, attitude or mental outlook):

Emotional (usual feelings or typical ones in certain situations, mood):

Social (behaviors around others, preferences for types of social activities, interactions):

If this person were to achieve his or her ideal self, would these descriptors be different and, if so, in what ways?

Physical:

Mental:

Emotional:

Social:

Complete the following sentences.

Some relationships that are important to this person are

Two of this person's skills or talents are

Two characteristics or behaviors this person appreciates about himself or herself are

One thing about himself or herself this person would like to improve is

One thing about himself or herself this person is proud of is

One of this person's goals is

What does this person value? Name at least four values.

For the next three questions, use other paper if you want.

During an average weekday, specifically how does this person spend her or his time?

What would this person do with one million tax-free dollars?

If this person had only 1 to 3 months to live, what would he or she do during that time?

Thinking of attitude as a broad outlook on life, place an X on the continuum to describe this person.

Very negative	Negative	Average	Positive	Very positive

Thinking of self-esteem as a value placed on the self or genuine regard for whom one is, what is this person's current level of self-esteem?

1 = very low 2 = low 3 = average 4 = high 5 = very high

THANK YOU VERY MUCH FOR YOUR HELP!

Chapter 2

PERSONALITY: THE CORE OF SELF

Drawing from mental, emotional, and social descriptors of the self as well as common behaviors, describe your personality using five or more words or phrases.

In what ways, if any, is your personality similar to the personality of other family members? Identify the person and the characteristics. If your personality is not at all like that of anyone in your family, speculate or explain why it isn't. Use other paper if necessary.

Disregarding chronological age, in which of Erikson's psychosocial stages do you think you are? Why?

What challenges or difficulties have you encountered or are you encountering in any of the stages?

Give an example of when you behaved from these ego states. Describe what you did or said.

(1) "parent"

(2) "child"

(3) "adult"

Monitor both positive and negative strokes given and received for a few days. Give examples of any or all types. Describe briefly what you learned from doing this.

Circle what you think (or know) your four MBTI preferences to be. For each preference describe some of your behaviors that support it. If you have none that do, explain why you think you tend to be more the opposite preference.

Extraversion	Introversion
Sensing	Intuition
Thinking	Feeling
Judgment	Perception

Identify a personality trait about yourself you especially like and one that is related to one of the MBTI preferences. Identify the preference. Describe how it helps you and for what reason(s) you like it.

Do the same with a personality trait about yourself you would like to change. Be sure to identify the MBTI preference.

CAREER CHOICES BASED ON MYERS-BRIGGS TYPE INDICATOR

Knowing your personality type can help you with career planning at every stage from your choosing your subjects and majors to choosing your first career. Students often have difficulty defining what kind of career they want and defining specific areas of a profession or the work environment they are most comfortable with. Personality type is a practical tool for investigating what satisfies your preference. Even when circumstances make it necessary for you to do work that you have not chosen or that you must do as part of your overall job description, knowledge and understanding of your personality type can help you discover and use your strengths to accomplish the work.

The following activity may assist you further in making career choices!!

Go to: http://www.geocities.com/lifeexplore/mbcareer.htm.

Find your Myers-Briggs type and review the career list that best matches your type and answer the following questions.

1. Do the careers listed match what you want to do for your career?

2. How does the Myers-Briggs assessment help you decide a course of study in school?

3. What additional information do you need to decide on a career choice?

Chapter 3

VALUES AND CHOICES

Use the same four values you identified in the Chapter 1 activity and describe as follows:

Value   *Received by Which Method(s)*   *Influence*

My 10-year decade was _____.

What significant event(s) occurred at that time and how were you influenced?

What significant event has influenced you in the past 5 years? How were your values affected?

Give any examples of values being transmitted to you by:

Moralizing

Laissez-faire or hands-off

Identify any of the recommended ways your values were developed.

As a parent, what are you doing or will you do to transmit values?

HOW WELL DO YOU MANAGE YOUR TIME?

Respond to the following statements and see how well you manage your time.

		YES	NO
1.	I think making lists and using planning guides are a waste of time.	____	____
2.	I have clear academic goals.	____	____
3.	I often complete assignments at the last minute.	____	____
4.	I am good at organizing my time.	____	____
5.	I need to be more motivated.	____	____
6.	When people stop by when I am studying it is easy for me to keep the visit short.	____	____
7.	I enjoy unannounced visitors.	____	____
8.	I am able to focus on important activities and not spend time on unimportant ones.	____	____

9. I try to be a perfectionist. — —

10. I have time to pursue leisure activities of my choosing. — —

Scoring: Even-numbered statements: 1 point for each NO
Odd-numbered statements: 1 point for each YES

If your score is:

8–10 You have good time management skills.

8–11 You are treading water—struggling daily to manage time.

8–12 Managing your time well is a problem and causes you daily stress.

8–13 You are on the verge of chaos—take steps to manage your time better NOW!

MAKING CHANGES. . . IT'S UP TO YOU!!

Pick any area of your life in which you might benefit from making a change. See how these steps can help you make a desired change.

STEP 1: COMMIT YOURSELF!!

Define the desired change—the goal to achieve. Be specific.

_____

_____

STEP 2: CHANGE HABITS!!

Identify a current HABIT that may hinder you from making the desired change or achieving your goal.

_____

_____

What change will you make? _____

_____

STEP 3:   ACTION. . . one step at a time!!

Identify steps you will take—create a timeline for these steps.

1. _____

2. _____

3. _____

STEP 4:   NEVER give up. . . focus on the positives of the GOAL. . . now it is time to EVALUATE.

1. Steps completed: _____

_____

2.   Steps not completed: _____

_____

3. Reevaluate—What are the barriers preventing me from achieving this step?

_____

4. Reward yourself for what you have accomplished!!

_____

Chapter 4

HAPPINESS—IT IS UP TO ME!

Finish these statements.

On a scale of 1 to 5 (1 = very unhappy, 2 = unhappy, 3 = moderately happy, 4 = happy, 5 = very happy), currently I rate myself _____.

In order to be satisfied, I need

An example of a time when life seemed especially wonderful was

An example of a time when life seemed extremely difficult was

From the rest of your life (80 percent for most readers of this text), describe a time when you created your own reality by making the situation happier or unhappier.

Decide to create your own happiness by:

Initiating Pleasure and "Smelling Roses"

In the first column, write a pleasurable activity and/or ways of "smelling roses" in your life. Then fill in the other columns. Continue on a sheet of paper, as this can be quite an eye-opening exercise.

     PLEASURE   HOW OFTEN DO I DO?   WHEN DID I LAST DO?

An example of the last time I enjoyed the "present" or "now" was

Use yourself, someone you know, or make up an example of:

"futurizing"

"pasteurizing"

Giving to Others

One way I "give to life" is

A nourishing, rewarding relationship I have is with

The last time I let her or him know how much I value this relationship was when I

Thinking and Acting Positively

Write an excuse you have made or one you could have made. Then reword it to reflect the truth.

Catch yourself using "cannot/could not" when not literally true. Write how you used it and what is actually true. Do the same for "should/should not" (or "have to," "must," "need to" or "ought").

Decrease the number of "bummer" words you use and increase the positives. Fill in the following blanks:

Instead of saying _____, I did (or can) say _____.

Briefly describe a situation or event in your past or present life. Show that you can consider alternatives by listing several choices you had or have. Do not evaluate a choice at this time and don't think "I cannot do that."

Briefly describe a problem or bothersome situation from your past. List any positive action steps you took in an effort to solve or change it. If you took no action, what *could* you have done?

The last time I procrastinated was

This example of procrastination was (positive or negative) because

Chapter 5

EMOTIONAL MONITORING AND LEARNING

Over a period of a week, keep an emotional diary. Whenever you become aware of a particular feeling, list the emotion, the reason for it, your physiological arousal (if apparent), and the way you expressed the emotion (verbally, nonverbally, or both).

List two emotions you commonly experience and then describe how you express them.

With whom do you feel most comfortable expressing these emotions? If you experience discomfort expressing them, with whom does this occur?

Finish these statements.

When I am slightly annoyed, I usually

When I am angry, I usually

I show my affection to _____ by

When I am happy, others know it because I

When I am proud, I usually

I am afraid of

I show fear by

When I am sad, I usually

I get sad when

I don't show affection to _____ because

As a result of your gender role, what idea did you receive regarding emotional expression?

From the following sources, list one message (verbal or nonverbal) you received concerning emotional expression.

Family

Peers

Ethnic group and/or religion

RATIONAL EMOTIVE BEHAVIOR THERAPY

Fill in the A, B, C boxes regarding an event in your life.

The Way It Was

Activating Event	*Belief*	*Consequences* *(emotions and behaviors)*

The Way It Could Have Been Using Thought-Changing

Activating Event	*Belief*	*Consequences* *(emotions and behaviors)*

Practice using REBT at least once a day and enjoy the results.

BEHAVIOR CHANGES

Describe a situation in which you could have or you did change your behavior, which resulted in a change in emotion or mood.

As silly as it might seem, try changing your facial expression and see if your emotion or mood changes. Especially try smiling when you aren't particularly happy or in a good mood. Don't give up too soon!

List ways in which you can usually elevate your mood. Check the ones that work the best and then don't forget to use them!

DEATH ANXIETY

Take the Death Anxiety Questionnaire (DAQ). Add up your score. (Your score will be between 0 and 30.) According to Conte, Weiner, and Plutchik, the average score for most people, regardless of age, is 8.5. What was your score? Was it higher or lower than the average score these researchers found? Why do you think this is so?

The DAQ identifies four specific aspects of death anxiety: fear of the unknown (items 1, 2, 12, 14, and 15), fear of suffering (items 3, 4, and 5), fear of loneliness (items 6 and 7); and fear of personal extinction (items 10, 11, and 13). Items 8 and 9 stand alone as other aspects of death anxiety.

How did you score on each of the four aspects? Reflect on what you learned from this exercise.

DEATH ANXIETY QUESTIONNAIRE

For each of the following items, indicate your response according to the following scale.

0	1	2
not at all	somewhat	very much

_____ 1. Do you worry about dying?

_____ 2. Does it bother you that you may die before you have done everything you wanted to do?

_____ 3. Do you worry that you may be very ill for a long time before you die?

_____ 4. Does it upset you to think others may see you suffering before you die?

_____ 5. Do you worry that dying may be very painful?

_____ 6. Do you worry that the persons closest to you won't be with you when you are dying?

_____ 7. Do you worry that you may be alone when you are dying?

_____ 8. Does the thought bother you that you might lose control of your mind before death?

_____ 9. Do you worry that expenses connected with your death will be burden to other people?

_____ 10. Does it worry you that your instructions or will about your belongings may not be carried out after you die?

_____ 11. Are you afraid that you may be buried before you are really dead?

_____ 12. Does the thought of leaving loved ones behind when you die disturb you?

_____ 13. Do you worry that those you care about may not remember you after your death?

_____ 14. Does the thought worry you that with death you may be gone forever?

_____ 15. Are you worried about not knowing what to expect after death?

Conte, H. R., Weiner, M. B., and Plutchik, R. (1982). Measuring death anxiety: Conceptual, psychometric, and factor-analytic aspects. *Journal of Personality and Social Psychology, 43,* 775–785.

Chapter 6

CALCULATING YOUR LONGEVITY

Respond to each item honestly and sum the various positive and negative factors to arrive at the appropriate number of years more (or less) than average you are likely to live.

PUT YOUR BEGINNING LIFE EXPECTANCY HERE (FROM HANDOUT 17-4)

For each grandparent who lived past 80, add 1 year.   _____

For each grandparent who lived to 70 but not 80 add 1/2 year.   _____

If your mother lived past 80, add 4 years.   _____

If your father lived past 80, add 2 years.   _____

For each grandparent, parent, or sibling who died of any type of heart disease before age 50, subtract 4 years.   _____

For each such relative dying of heart disease between age 50 and 60, subtract 2 years.   _____

For each such relative who died of diabetes or ulcers before age 60, subtract 3 years.   _____

Women: for each sister or mother who died of breast cancer before age 60, subtract 1 year.   _____

If your intelligence is *superior*, add two years.   _____

HEALTH HISTORY

If your mother was younger than 18 or older than 35 at your birth, subtract 1 year.   _____

If you are the first born in your family, add 1 year.   _____

Women: if you have had no children (or plan no children) subtract 1/2 year.   _____

If you have an annual physical exam, add 2 years.   _____

CURRENT HEALTH

If your weight is 10 to 30 percent above ideal weight shown in standard tables, the amount you must subtract depends on your age and gender.

For women, subtract 5 years if you are between 20 and 30; 4 years if you are between 30 and 50, and 2 years if you are over 50. For men, subtract 10 years if you are between 20 and 30, 4 years if you are between 30 and 45, and 2 years for any age over that. _____

If your weight is more than 30 percent above standard tables: Women, subtract 6 1/2 years if you are between 20 and 30, 5 years if you are between 30 and 50, and 4 years thereafter. Men, subtract 13 if you are between 20 and 30, 6 if you are between 30 and 40, and 4 years thereafter. _____

If your diet is genuinely low in fat and sugar, and you never eat past the feeling of fullness, add 1 year. _____

If you smoke 2 or more packs a day, subtract 12 years; if you smoke 1 to 2 packs a day, subtract 7 years; if you smokeless than 1 pack a day, subtract 2 years. _____

If you never drink, neither add nor subtract; if you are a heavy drinker, subtract 8 years; if you are a moderate drinker add 3 years, if you are a light drinker, add 1 1/2 years. _____

If you do some aerobic exercise at least 3 times a week, add 3 years. _____

If you sleep more than 10 or less than 6 hours per night, subtract 2 years. _____

If you have intimate sexual relations once a week or twice a week, add 2 years. _____

If you have a chronic health condition (e.g., high blood pressure, diabetes, ulcer, cancer) or are frequently ill, subtract 5 years. _____

YOUR CURRENT LIFE

If you have 4 or more years of college, add 3; if you have 1 to 3 years of college, add 2; if you have completed high school and gone no further, add 1; if you have less than an eighth-grade education, subtract 2. _____

if your occupation is at a professional, technical, or managerial level, add 1 year; if you work at unskilled work, subtract 4. _____

If your family income is above average for your education and occupation, add 1 year; if it is below average, subtract 1. _____

If your job is a physically active one, add 2; if it is sedentary, subtract 2. _____

If you now live in an urban area and have lived in urban areas most of your life, subtract 1; if you have spent most of your life in a rural area, add 1. _____

If you are married and living with your spouse, add 1. _____

If you are separated or divorced, subtract 9 if you are a man, 4 if you are a woman. _____

If you are widowed, subtract 7 if you are a man, 4 if you are a woman. _____

If you are a never-married woman, subtract 1 year for each decade unmarried past age 25. _____

If you are a never-married man and living with family, subtract 1 year for each decade unmarried past 25; if you live alone, subtract 2 years for each decade unmarried past 25. _____

If you have at least two close friends in whom you can confide, add 1. _____

If your personality is noticeably aggressive and hostile and you feel regularly under time pressure, subtract 2 to 5 depending on how much the description fits _____

If you are a calm, relaxed, easygoing person who adapts well to whatever happens, add 1 to 3 depending on how well the description fits. _____

If you are a basically happy person and have a lot of fun, add 2. _____

If you have had an episode of being depressed or very tense, guilty, or worried that lasted as long as a year or more, subtract 1 to 3 depending on how severe the depression was. _____

If you take a lot of risks, subtract 2; if you generally avoid risks, add 1. _____

Life Expectancy Table

Your Age in 1999	White		Black	
	Male	Female	Male	Female
10	74	80.2	67.1	75.3
12	74.1	80.3	67.3	75.4
14	74.3	80.3	67.6	75.5
16	74.4	80.4	67.5	75.6
18	74.6	80.4	68.2	75.7
20	74.7	80.5	68.5	75.5
22	74.9	80.6	68.8	76
24	75	80.6	69.1	76.2
26	75.2	80.7	69.5	76.4
28	75.4	80.8	70	76.6
30	75.6	80.9	70.4	76.8
32	75.8	81	70.9	77
34	76	81.1	71.4	77.3
36	76.2	81.2	71.9	77.5
38	76.4	81.4	72.4	77.8
40	76.7	81.5	73	78.2
42	77	81.7	73.6	78.5
44	77.3	82	74.3	78.9
46	77.7	82.2	74.9	79.4
48	78.2	82.6	75.7	79.8
50	78.7	82.9	76.4	80.4

Source: Statistical Abstract of the United States, 1992, U.S. Department of Commerce, p. 77.

Additional Website Activity

The following website can be used to calculate your longevity.

http://www.icmarc.org/xp/rc/planning/tools/retirement/longevity.html

Chapter 7

HOW WELL DO YOU LISTEN?

Using the scale, answer the following questions:
5 = almost always   4 = usually   3 = about half the time   2 = sometimes
1 = hardly ever

1. _____ I am interested in other people.
2. _____ I ask questions about other people's interests.
3. _____ The opinions of others are of interest to me.
4. _____ I am able to focus my attention on what someone is saying.
5. _____ I put aside my thoughts and feelings and concentrate on what is being said.
6. _____ I try to create a positive listening environment by getting rid of distractions and other obstacles.
7. _____ I realize I have a psychological filter and check it periodically so that it does not interfere with my listening.
8. _____ I approach others with the idea that they have something of value to contribute to a conversation.
9. _____ When listening, I face the person who is talking.
10. _____ I keep an open body position.
11. _____ When listening, my body is relaxed yet attentive.
12. _____ I maintain eye contact at least three-quarters of the time. When I look away, I quickly bring my eyes back to the speaker's face.
13. _____ When listening, my facial expression registers what I am thinking and feeling.
14. _____ My facial expression changes during a typical conversation.
15. _____ When listening, I nod my head affirmatively an appropriate number of times.
16. _____ During conversation I am comfortable with appropriate touching.
17. _____ When listening, I use brief verbal responses that show interest.
18. _____ I ask encouraging questions of the speaker.
19. _____ When listening, I try to find ways to clarify the speaker's point.
20. _____ I avoid negative listening behaviors.

Total your score. Give yourself a grade as follows:

95–100 = A+   90–94 = A   85–89 = B+   80–84 = B   75–79 = C+   70–74 = C
    65–69 = D+   60–64 = D   59 or below = Unsatisfactory

Most importantly, what can you do to improve your listening?

Observe two other people who are in a listening role. Briefly describe and evaluate their listening behaviors.

Listen for and then describe these types of listening.

Empathic:

Receptive:

Directive:

Chapter 8

IDENTIFYING CLOSED COMMUNICATION

Use the following letters to identify closed communication types. If the statement has more than one type, use more than one letter.

D = dogmatic   C = commando   G = grandiose

1. _____ That man has an obnoxious personality.
2. _____ He needs to listen more to other people's opinions.
3. _____ Jane always thinks of other's feelings.
4. _____ I think you should quit that job.
5. _____ It seems to me that he will never learn good money management skills unless he has his own income.
6. _____ Nobody appreciates what I do.

USING OPEN COMMUNICATION

Rewrite each of the statements above in the open style.

1. _____
2. _____
3. _____
4. _____
5. _____
6. _____

Listen for any example of closed communication, write it, and then reword it in the open style.

Ask someone to listen to you for any uses of fillers.

UNDERSTANDING PARALANGUAGE AND BODY LANGUAGE

While listening to a conversation, be aware of examples of paralanguage and body language. Describe some of these. Disregarding what was actually being said as much as possible, briefly explain what could be interpreted from the paralanguage and body language examples.

Pretend you are writing a script for a play. Write a short scene between two or more characters. Write the lines to be said and after each describe briefly the paralanguage and body language you want the characters to demonstrate.

Carry on a conversation with someone and try not to vary your body language during the time (same posture, facial expression, etc.). Hopefully, you will see how this creates a negative communication environment.

Chapter 9

SELF-DISCLOSURE

Using the following, identify each self-disclosing statement.

BD = basic data   P = preference   B = belief   F = feeling

_____ I was concerned when he was late coming home.

_____ I thought he might have had an accident.

_____ My opinion on that candidate is a positive one.

_____ I graduated from high school last year.

_____ I voted in the last election.

_____ I enjoyed the concert.

_____ I am disappointed because you don't want to go with me.

_____ I don't think that was a wise choice.

_____ I didn't like that restaurant.

_____ I was quite proud of my grade.

Now write one statement disclosing about yourself on each level.

BD _____

P _____

B _____

F _____

Fill in the blanks about your self-disclosure.

I enjoy sharing preference statements with _____ because

_____.

I am comfortable disclosing my beliefs with _____.

One person who shares beliefs with me is _____,

whereas _____ seems reluctant to do so.

My feelings in most situations are easy to disclose to _____

because _____.

One person who discloses feelings to me is _____.

A person who does not reveal feelings to me is _____.

SENSING, INTERPRETING, OR FEELING?

Tell which is provided in the statements using the following code.

S = sensing   I = interpretation   F = feeling

_____ It seems to me that she is upset.

_____ I am happy.

_____ I think that taking time to visit her was good for me.

_____ I heard what he said.

_____ I noticed that she didn't talk to him.

PERCEPTION CHECKING

Write what to say using perception checking. Because each scenario contains only sensing *or* interpretative information, you are to make up what is missing.

Your friend Jack tells you that he has seen your roommate and another person looking at apartments. Use perception checking in talking to your roommate about this.

1.

2.

3.

You think that your supervisor at work is unhappy with your performance. Use perception checking to speak to him or her about this.

1.

2.

3.

FEELING STATEMENT

Write a feeling statement about the supervisor situation described above. Remember that your feeling is related to your interpretation.

GIVING CRITICISM

A family member disturbs you by telling very negative, derogatory stories about a minority group. Write what you would say using recommendations for delivering criticism.

POSITIVE RESPONSES TO CRITICISM

Your employer has said to you, "You don't seem to care about your job." First, write the two-step response if you *understand the reason* for the criticism.

1.

2.

Then write the two-step response if you *do not understand the reason* for the criticism.

1.

2.

DIMENSIONS OF AWARENESS

Read the scenario regarding Terri and Matt in the Fair Fighting activity in this section of Reflections and Applications for Chapter 11. Pretend you are Matt before the fight begins. Write statements of awareness that he could have used in discussing the situation with Terri.

Sensing

Thinking

Feeling

Wanting

Acting

You might also try doing the same for Terri's dimensions of awareness. Use a separate sheet of paper.

Indicate several ways you can improve in the area of content (what you say) related to this chapter.

Chapter 10

FRIEND TO FRIEND

With a friend, talk about the following and then write a short summary of your discussion in each category.

SOCIAL EXCHANGE

What does each of us receive from our friendship? What more, if anything, would we like to receive from this friendship?

ATTRACTION FACTORS

Describe briefly how any of the following are involved in your friendship.

Proximity

Similarities

Complementarity

Reciprocity

CHARACTERISTICS AND BEHAVIORS

How would each of us describe a best friend? Which of the behaviors and characteristics do we possess? What do we like about each other?

EXPECTATIONS

What do we expect of each other in this friendship?

IMPROVING RELATIONSHIPS

Identify any situation in which you have or could have demonstrated the following positive characteristics.

Tolerance, acceptance, or appreciation of diversity

Empathy

Sensitivity

Cooperation

Assertiveness

Negotiation skills

COMPLETE THE FOLLOWING SENTENCES.

To me, a person is being difficult when he or she

I usually deal with this by

An effective way to deal with it might be to

I probably am "difficult" to others when I

UNLOAD YOUR GUNNYSACK

Using "I" statements, describe a resentment and then tell how you feel and what you want.

Resentment	*Feeling*	*Want*
(I resent it when you)	*(When this happens, I feel)*	*(I want you to)*

CONFLICT RESOLUTION

Think of a conflict that you have had with another person in the past 6 months. Use the eight-step approach to conflict resolution to evaluate how you managed the conflict and what you could have done differently to resolve the conflict. For example, Step One: Deal Effectively with Anger. Was there anger in the conflict? How did you deal with the anger (either yours or the person you were in conflict with)? What could you have done differently to help come to a resolution?

Step One: Deal Effectively with Anger:

Step Two: Do Your Homework (think before you approach):

Step Three: Set a Positive Tone:

Step Four: Use Ground Rules:

Step Five: Discuss and Define the Problem:

Step Six: Brainstorm Possible Solutions:

Step Seven: Evaluate and Choose Solutions:

Step Eight: Follow Up:

Chapter 11

ASSETS AND LIABILITIES

Your assets are what you have to offer a potential employer. These are strong points that will help you get and keep a job. Your liabilities are drawbacks or limitations that could hinder you from getting or keeping a job. Consider the following categories.

Interests	Education	Work Experience	Personality
Skills	Goals	Volunteer Work	Work Habits

In each of the areas, list assets and then liabilities. Use other paper and make long lists. Consider ideas from Chapter 10 (i.e., the table of positive personal qualities and work habits and the characteristics employers have identified as positive).

Now select what you consider to be your top six assets and your top three liabilities. Practice discussing your assets so that you can use them to answer interview questions, such as "Why should we hire you?" or "What do you have to offer?" Think about your liabilities and decide how you could discuss them if that is ever required. If you have any liabilities that can be changed before your job search, set a goal to do so.

JOB SATISFACTION

List as many as possible under the following columns.

What I Like to   Do What I Do Well

Circle any that you either *do* at your present job or those that you believe you *will be doing* at a future job.

The more you like to do and do well that you can actually *do* at work adds up to job satisfaction!

Chapter 12

NEEDS FULFILLMENT

Think of any relationship you have or want to have. In the left column, write five needs you would like to have fulfilled in the relationship and then describe them in behavioral terms. In the right column corresponding with each need, describe what the other person must be like and/or do in order to satisfy that need. Use the following example as a guide.

Need	Person
Companionship and enjoyable experiences. Both of us will have fun together on a regular basis because we enjoy each other's company and have several mutually enjoyable activities.	She (or he) will have many of the same interests as I do and enjoy several of the same activities. She (or he) will have a personality I like, and we will be able to have fun together by ourselves and in the company of others.

Need	Person
1.	1.
2.	2.
3.	3.
4.	4.
5.	5.

Now looking back, write about any of your needs that were not fulfilled in a past relationship. Or do so for a present relationship. Use your own paper.

FAIR FIGHTING

Read the following scenario. Then using the fair fighting criteria described in Chapter 11, identify all the ways in which this was an unfair fight. Jot these down in the margin.

Matt and Terri, who are engaged to be married, attended a wedding and reception together. At the reception Terri spent a great deal of time talking with friends of hers from high school whom Matt did not know and then she danced a few times with a former boyfriend. After the reception, they had the following conversation.

Terri: You are mad, I can tell.

Matt: No, I am not.

Terri: Come on, Matt. You have been quiet since we left the reception. I know you are.

Matt: I am surprised you even noticed.

Terri: What is that supposed to mean?

Matt: You were so busy having a great time.

Terri: What else are you supposed to do at a reception . . . sit alone and not talk to anyone like you do?

Matt: Like I do, huh? You were not exactly the friendliest person in the world when we went to my class reunion last summer!

Terri: No wonder. They were all so boring. At least my high school friends are fun.

Matt: You looked like you were having *a lot* of fun dancing with Paul.

Terri: So that's it! You are so insecure sometimes. I can't believe you would be jealous just because I danced with him. Remember when you danced with several old girlfriends at your reunion? Did I get jealous? No!

Matt: You would not ever get jealous because you think you are so much better than anyone else. Besides that, you do not show me enough affection. I give and give and do not get a lot in return unless you happen to be in the mood to really pay attention to me. You talk to your other friends more than you do to me and seem to enjoy their company more. You do not act like you're ready to get married; in fact, you do not even seem to really be in love with me. And every time we fight, you want to have the last word.

Terri: You sure seem to have a lot of complaints! And of course there's *nothing* wrong with you. Why don't you just find someone else?

Matt: Maybe I will! I hope you're satisfied that you have won another one.

Could you rewrite this scenario using positive, open communication and fair fighting suggestions?

Chapter 13

FAMILY PICTURE

Using any figures you want (human-like, stick figures, circles, squares, etc.), draw a diagram of your family. Label each figure with the person's name and relationship to you.

If possible, compare your diagram to others and think about how your concept of family is similar or different.

PARENTING BEHAVIORS

What do you want or would you like your child to be like when he or she is a young adult? First list or describe the characteristic in the left-hand column and then describe what would be advisable for you to do or not do in terms of parenting behaviors. Use other paper if necessary. **Use this as a guide now or in the future.**

Description of Young Adult   Parenting Behaviors

Write a brief summary of how applying the concepts, techniques, and skills from this book can make someone a better parent.

Glossary

Addiction: a physiological dependence.

Affection: a feeling of warmth and closeness based on the way another person relates to you personally.

Affirmation: a positive assertion

Anorexia nervosa: a life-threatening disorder that includes a distorted body image, refusal to maintain a healthy weight, and an intense fear of being overweight.

Approachability: a combination of circumstances in which the initiation of contact is likely to be positively received.

Attachment: the desire for the physical presence and emotional support of the other person as well as a preference for each other's company.

Attitude: a state of mind that is reflected in how a person approaches life.

Attitudinal environment: perceived support from the general society as well as specific people; a contributing factor to the success or failure of stepfamilies.

Attraction: a force that draws people together or a positive attitude toward another; the focus of psychological research.

Battered woman syndrome: a type of posttraumatic stress disorder.

Binge drinking: four consecutive drinks for a female and five for a male.

Biofeedback training: a series of steps by which a person learns to regulate physiological responses such as muscle tension, skin temperature, and heart rate.

Body image: a perception of one's appearance.

Caring: feelings of concern and responsibility for another's welfare; tenderness, which includes awareness of the other's needs and desires.

Chronic procrastination: the habit of postponing; it blocks happiness.

Codependency: often the result of an enabler focusing too much on the needs and behaviors of the other and both suffer as a result.

Cognitive restructuring: the process of changing your way of thinking.

Compliments: comments of admiration and praise.

Confidant: a significantly close personal friend with whom you can safely share your deepest concerns and joys.

Conflict: disagreement or a difference in thinking.

Content: the words and sentences uttered during the communication process.

Cooperation: working with others in a positive way toward a common goal.

Corporal punishment: the use of physical force with the intention of causing pain but not injury for purposes of coercion or control.

Creative thinking: thinking about ideas in different ways and generating a variety of solutions to problems.

Critical thinking: thinking differently about an issue, challenging assumptions, and examining the logic of differing points.

Deep relaxation: a profoundly restful condition in which you feel physically relaxed, somewhat detached from the immediate environment, and usually to some extent even from body sensations.

Dialect: a variety of a language that differs from other varieties of the same language, including distinct pronunciations, unique meanings, and different words altogether.

Dictator parent: a parent who has the same motive as the martyr parent: to control the child's life even after the child is an adult.

Ego states: facets of personality and related patterns of behavior.

Emotion: a feeling state that involves certain components.

Emotion-packed phrases: groups of words usually said as lead-ins to statements that carry an emotional punch.

Empathic listening: becoming aware of the speaker's experiences and feelings.

Empathy: being able to put yourself in another's place and see and hear from that person's perspective; a quality to be treasured.

Enabling: occurs when someone's actions directly, yet unintentionally, allow irresponsible, dysfunctional, or destructive actions of another person to continue.

Eustress: stress that is good for you.

Experiential learning: individual experiences and actual hands-on work.

Expressive behavior: the observable verbal or nonverbal actions.

External locus of control: a perception that outside-self factors control your life.

External stressors: demands from outside of self.

Extravert: outgoing person; showing an outward orientation and a preference to operate in the outer world of people and things.

Feedback: responding-with response of what you, as the listener, think, feel, or sense.

Gestures: movements of the hands and arms.

Health: a general feeling of physical and mental well-being.

Hearing: using the auditory sense to take in a message.

Heterosexism: the belief that anything other than a heterosexual orientation is wrong.

Humanism: often combined with existentialism; a major personality perspective.

Intelligence: an intellectual capacity or potential.

Internal locus of control: the belief that a person is in control of his or her own life.

Internal stressors: those stressors we create or magnify.

Interpersonal communication: a complex process of mutually exchanging messages between two or more individuals.

Interpersonal relations: an ongoing interactive process that includes initiating, building, and enriching relationships with different people in a variety of situations.

Interpersonal trust: the expectancy that another's word or promise can be relied upon.

Intimacy: a desire for confidential, close communication.

Intimate love: a deep, total experience composed of positive thoughts, feelings, and behaviors.

Introversion: an inner orientation and having an interest in the inner world of concepts and ideas.

Irrational beliefs: unreasonable and exaggerated thoughts.

Jealousy: a feeling related to the threat of or actual experience of loss.

Learning disabilities: a group of related and often overlapping conditions that lead to low achievement.

Listening: an active process of paying attention.

Living together loneliness (LTL): the result of a perceived discrepancy between expected and achieved contact.

Loneliness: a feeling of being alone and disconnected or alienated from positive persons, places, or things.

Love schema: a mental model consisting of expectations and attitudes about love.

Marriage: a socially approved and legally sanctioned mating arrangement, usually involving sexual activity and economic cooperation.

Meditation: a physical act of remaining quiet and focusing on one's breath, a word, or a phrase.

Minority: a disadvantaged group that lacks power within a society.

Minority groups: categories of people who lack power and who are disadvantaged in a society.

Multiculturalism: a movement that recognizes cultural diversity.

Multiple intelligences: a theory that eight different intelligences account for a broader range of human potential.

Optimal identity: a sense of psychosocial well-being.

Optimists: people with positive thoughts.

Paraphrasing: restating in your own words what you think the speaker said.

Passion: physiological arousal and an intense desire to be united with the loved one.

Passive behaviors: behaviors that allow others to be in control.

Patriarchal: (male-dominated) marital history.

Peak experiences: brief moments of extreme pleasure.

Perception: a mental process of creating meaning from sensory data that we receive through stimulation of our senses.

Perfectionism: belief that mistakes must never be made and that the highest standards of performance must always be achieved.

Pessimists: people with negative thoughts.

Physiological arousal: biological reactions and activities of the nervous system, various glands, and organs within the body.

Positive parenting: doing everything possible to learn about and raise a child with a goal of optimum development.

Positive reinforcement: a positive stimulus presented in an attempt to increase or strengthen behavior.

Prejudice: an attitude that others are inferior or less than you in some way.

Procrastination: the act of putting off activities.

Proximity: physical occupation of the same geographic area.

Receptive listening: a specific type with certain restrictions placed on responses.

Reciprocity: a tendency to like people who like you.

Respect: liking based on the person's admirable characteristics or actions and is cooler and more than affection.

Script analysis: a way of becoming aware of how your script developed.

Self-concept: the totality of your thoughts and feelings with reference to yourself; the foundation on which almost all your actions are based.

Self-disclosure: the act of making the self known by revealing personal information. In doing so, people and know and understand each other.

Self-efficacy: advocating for yourself.

Self-enhancement: the process of finding and interpreting situations that result in a positive view of self.

Self-esteem: the value that we place on ourselves.

Self-fulfilling prophecy: a thought or expectation that helps bring about a predicted event or behavior that then strengthens the original thought.

Self-handicapping: taking actions to sabotage your performance and increase the opportunity to excuse failure.

Self-verification: an intriguing theory that maintains that individuals have a strong desire to preserve their self-concept even if it is a negative one.

Sensitivity: an awareness or sense about the perceptions and perspectives of others.

Shyness: timidity and a feeling of unease in a social situation.

Slang: terms that are popular at a given time.

Social penetration theory: theory that explains that close relationships develop in terms of increasing self-disclosure.

Socialization: the process by which individuals learn their culture.

Statuses: a set of stages that an issue goes through to reach a final of one or one of the final stages.

Stonewalling: removing oneself from an interaction and employing a stony silence that conveys disapproval, icy distance, and smugness.

Subjective cognitive state: the cognitive state of awareness and appraisal.

Thinking: the ability to activate and then pursue mental activity.

Tolerance: putting up with something one does not like and not acting against people about whom one feels negatively.

Trait anger: a state of general hostility.

Transferable assets: desirable traits and skills valuable in all career fields and useful in almost every job.

Unconditional positive regard: a warm acceptance of each other's personhood.

Verbal aggression: verbal or nonverbal communication intended to cause psychological pain to another person or perceived as having that intent.

References

*ADAMS, T. (1987). *Living from the inside out.* Self-published. 1331 Philip St., New Orleans, LA 70130.

ADLER, J., and RAYMOND, J. (2001, Fall/Winter). Fighting back with sweat. *Newsweek,* 35–41.

AGARWALL, S., and VENKETESHWER RAO, A. (2000). Tomato lycopene and its role in human health and chronic diseases. *Canadian Medical Association Journal, 163*(6), 6.

AHMAD, K. (2000). Anger and hostility linked to coronary heart disease. *Lancer, 355* (9215), 1621.

*AHRONS, C. (1994). *The good divorce: Keeping your family together when your marriage comes apart.* New York: HarperCollins.

ALBRECHT, K. (1979). *Stress and the manager.* Englewood Cliffs, NJ: Prentice Hall.

ALCOHOL RESEARCH and HEALTH. (2000). Prenatal exposure to alcohol, *24*(1), 32–41.

ALLSOP, S., SAUNDERS, B., and PHILLIPS, M. (2000, January). The process of relapse in severely dependent male problem drinkers. *Addiction, 95* (1), 95–106.

ALTMAN, L., and TAYLOR, D. A. (1973). *Social penetration theory: The development of interpersonal relationships.* New York: Holt, Rinchart & Winston.

ALTSHUL, S. (2001, September). Protect yourself against HIV. *Prevention,* 53(9), 178–81.

ALZHEIMER'S ASSOCIATION. (2001). Frequently asked questions. Retrieved September 15, 2001 from http://www.alz.org.

AMATO, P. R., and ROGERS, S. J. (1997). A longitudinal study of marital problems and subsequent divorce. *Journal of Marriage and the Family,* 59 (3), 612–24.

AMERICAN CANCER SOCIETY (2001). *American Cancer Society predicts US cancer burden for 2001.* Retrieved July 15, 2001 from EBSCOhost database.

*AMES, L. B. (1992). *Raising good kids: A developmental approach to discipline.* Rosemont, NJ: Modern Learning Press.

ANDERSON, D. A., and WADDEN, T. A. (1999). Treating the obese patient. *The Journal of the American Medical Association, 8,* 156–67. Retrieved June 13, 2001 from http://www.ama-assn.org.

ANDERSON, K. E., CARMELLA, S. G., YE, M., BUSS, R. L. CHAP, L. MURPHY, L., and HECHT, S. S. (2001). Metabolites of a tobacco-specific lung carcinogen in nonsmoking women exposed to environmental tobacco smoke. *Journal of the National Cancer Institute, 93,* 378–81.

ANYANWU, E, and WATSON, N. (1997). Alcohol dependence: A critical look at the effects of alcohol metabolism. *Review of Environmental Health, 12*(3), 201–13.

ARDELT, M. (2000). Still stable after all these years? Personality stability theory. *Social Psychology Quarterly, 63*(4), 392–405.

ARMAS, G. C. (2002, February 8). Second marriage up, census says. Associated Press. Retrieved February 15, 2002 from Electric Library database.

ARNOLD, K. (1995). *Lives of promise.* San Francisco: Jossey-Bass.

ASCHWANDEN, C., and CEDERBORG, L. (1999, October). Run from your nasty habit. *Prevention,* 22.

AUCHINCLOSS, K. (2001, September 24). We shall overcome. *Newsweek,* 18–25.

AVERILL, J. R. (1997). The emotions: An integrative approach. In R. Hogan, J. Johnson, and S. Briggs (Eds.), *Handbook of personality psychology* (pp. 513–37). San Diego: Academic Press.

AVERSA, S. L., and KIMBERLIN, C. (1996). Psychosocial aspects of antiretroviral medication use among HIV patients. *Patient Education and Counseling.* 29(2), 207–19.

AVERY, C. S. (1989, May). How do you build intimacy in an age of divorce? *Psychology Today,* 27–31.

AXTELL, R. E., BRIGGS, T., CORCORAN, M., and LAMB, M. B. (1997). *Do's and taboos around the world for women in business.* New York: John Wiley & Sons.

AZERRAD, J., and CHANCE, P. (2001, September/October). Why our kids are out of control. *Psychology Today,* 43–48.

BACH, D. (2001). *Smart couples finish rich: 9 steps to creating a rich future for you and your partner.* New York: Broadway Books.

*BACH, G., and WYDEN, P. (1968). *The intimate enemy: How to fight fair in love and marriage.* New York: Avon.

BAILEY, J. M., BOBROW, D., WOLFE, M., and MIKACH, S. (1995). Sexual orientation of adult sons of gay fathers. *Developmental Psychology, 31,* 124–29.

BAKER, B. (2001, April). Grandparents speak out. *AARP Bulletin,* 31–32.

BAKER, K., BEER, J., and BEER, J. (1991). Self-esteem, alcoholism, sensation seeking, GPA, and differential aptitude test scores of high school students in an honor society. *Psychological Reports, 69,* 1147–50.

BANDURA, A. (1977). *Social learning theory.* Englewood Cliffs, NJ: Prentice Hall.

———. (1986). *Social foundations of thought and action: A social-cognitive theory.* Englewood Cliffs, NJ: Prentice Hall.

BARBACH, L., and GEISINGER, D. L. (1991). *Going the distance: Secrets to lifelong love.* New York: Doubleday.

BARBOR, C. (2001). The science of meditation. *Psychology Today, 34*(3), 54–58.

BARON, R. A. (1990). *Understanding human relations: A practical guide to people at work.* Boston: Allyn & Bacon.

—. (1998). *Psychology.* Boston: Allyn & Bacon.

BARTOLOMBO, J. (2000, March). Sweat away the stress. *Women's Sports and Fitness,* 108–09.

BATSON, C. D., POLYCARPOU, M. P., HARMON-JONES, E., IMHOFF, H. J., MITCHENER, C., BEDNR, L. L., KLEIN, T. R., and HIGHBERGER, L. (1997). Empathy and attitudes: Can feeling for a member of a stigmatized group improve feelings toward the group? *Journal of Personality and Social Psychology, 72*(1), 105–18.

BATTLE, J. J. (1998, July). What beats having two parents? *Journal of Black Studies, 28*(6), 783–801.

BATTY, D. (2000, December). Does physical activity prevent cancer? *British Medical Journal, 321*(7274), 1424–25.

BAUMEISTER, R. F. (1997). Identity, self-concept, and self-esteem: The self lost and found. In R. Hogan, J. Johnson, and S. Briggs (Eds.), *Handbook of personality psychology* (pp.681–703). San Diego: Academic Press.

*BAUMEL, S. (1995). *Dealing with depression naturally.* New Canaan, CT: Keats.

BEAUCHAMP, T. (2004). *The ethics of assisted suicide and euthanasia.* Baltimore: Johns Hopkins Press.

*BEATTIE, M. (1987). *Codependent no more.* New York: Harper/Hazelden.

———. (1989). *Beyond codependency and getting better all the time.* San Francisco: Harper & Row.

———. (1991). *A reason to live.* Whenton, IL: Tyndale House.

*BECK, A. (1988). *Love is never enough.* New York: Harper & Row.

BELSIE, L. (2002, February 8). America's on/off relationship with wedlock. *Christian Science Monitor,* 3.

BELSKY, J. K. (1988). *Here tomorrow: Making the most of life after fifty.* Baltimore: Johns Hopkins University Press.

BEM, S. L. (1974). The measurement of psychological androgyny. *Journal of Consulting and Clinical Psychology, 42*(2), 155–62.

———. (1975). Sex role adaptability: One consequence of psychological adaptability. *Journal of Personality and Social Psychology, 31,* 634–43.

———. (1993). *The lenses of gender.* New Haven, CT: Yale University Press.

BENET-MARTINEZ, V., and John, O. P. (1998). *Los Cinco Grandes* across cultures and ethnic groups: Multitrait multimethod analyses of the Big Five in Spanish and English. *Journal of Personality and Social Psychology, 75,* 729–50.

*BENSON, H. (1975). *The relaxation response.* New York: Avon.

———. (1987). *Your maximum mind.* New York: Random House.

———. (2001). Mind-body pioneer. *Psychology Today, 34*(3), 56–59.

BERGLAS, S., and JONES, E. E. (1978). Drug choice as a self-handicapping strategy in response to noncontingent success. *Journal of Personality and Social Psychology, 36,* 405–17.

BERK, L. S. (1996). The laughter-immune connection: New discoveries. *Humor and Health Journal, 5*(5). Retrieved July 15, 2001 from http://www.drleeberk.com.

BERK, L. S., FELTEN, D. L., TAN, S. A., BITTMAN, B. B., and

WESTENGARD, J. (2001, March). Modulations of neuroimmune parameters during the custress of humor-associated mirthful laughter. *Alternative Therapies, 7*(2), 62–66.

BERNARD, J. (1956). *Remarriage: A study in marriage.* New York: Russell and Russell.

BERNE, E. (1962). Classification of positions. *Transactional Analysis Bulletin, 1,* 23.

———. (1972). *What do you say after you say hello?* New York: Bantam.

BERRY, D. S. PENNEBARKER, J. W., MUELLER, J. S., and HILLER, W. S. (1997). Linguistic bases of social perception. *Personality and Social Psychology Bulletin, 23*(5), 526–37.

*BETTLELHEIM, B. (1987). *A good enough parent.* New York: Random House.

BIANCHI, S. M., MILKIE, M. A., SAYER, L. C., and ROBINSON, J. P. (2000, September). Is anyone doing the housework? Trends in the gender division of household labor. *Social Forces, 79*(1), 191–228.

BIANCHI, S. M., and ROBINSON, J. (1997). What did you do today? Children's use of time, family composition, and the acquisition of social capital. *Journal of Marriage and the Family, 59*(2), 332–44.

BILYEAU, N. (1998, April). Walk 45 minutes a day. *Health,* 73–75.

BLACK, S. (2000, December). A wake-up call on high-school starting times. *Education Digest, 66*(4), 33–37.

*BLOOMFIELD, H. H. (WITH FELDER, L.). (1996a). *Making peace with yourself.* New York: Ballantine.

*———. (1996b). *Making peace with your parents.* New York: Ballantine.

BLOOMFIELD, H., and GOLDBERG, P. (2000). *Making peace with your past.* New York: HarperCollins.

*BLOOMFIELD, H. H. (WITH KORY, R). (1978). *The holistic way to health and happiness.* New York: Simon & Schuster.

*———. (1980). *Inner joy: New strategies for adding (more) pleasure to your life.* New York: Wyden.

*———. (1993). *Making peace in your stepfamily.* New York: Hyperion.

BLUM, D. (1998, April). What makes Troy gay? *Health,* 82–87.

*BLUMENFIELD, W. J. (1992). *Homophobia: How we all pay the price.* Boston: Beacon Press.

BOGENSCHNEIDER, K. (1997). Parental involvement in adolescent schooling: A proximal process with transcontextual validity. *Journal of Marriage and the Family, 9*(3), 731–33.

*BOLLES, R. N. (2001). *What color is your parachute?* Berkeley, CA: Ten Speed Press.

*BOOHER, D. (2001). *E-writing: 21st century tools for effective communication.* New York: Pocket Books.

BOON, S. D., and BRUSSONI, M. J. (1998). Popular images of grandparents: Examining young adults' views of their closest grandparents. *Personal Relationships, 5,* 105–19.

BORDERS, L. D. BLACK, L. K., and PASLEY, B. K. (1998). Are adopted children and their parents at greater risk for negative outcomes? *Family Relations, 47,* 237–41.

*BORTZ, W. M. (1991). *We live too short and die too long.* New York: Bantam.

BOTHWELL, R., and SCOTT, J. (1997). The influence of cognitive variables on recovery in depressed inpatients. *Journal of Affective Disorders, 43*(3), 207–12.

BOWER, B. (2001). Healthy aging may depend on past habits. *Science News, 159*(24), 373.

BOWLIN, S. J., LESKE, M. C., VARMA, A., NASCA, P., WEINSTEIN, A., and CAPLAN, L. (1997). Breast cancer risk and alcohol consumption: Results from a large case-control study. *International Journal of Epidemiology, 26*(5), 915–23.

BRADSHAW, J. E. (1998). *Healing the shame that binds you.* Deerfield Beach, FL: Health Communications, Inc.

BRAMLETT, M. D., and MOSHER, W. D. (2001, May 31). First marriage dissolution, divorce, and remarriage: United States. Retrieved August 25, 2001 from http://www.cdc.gov/nchs.

*BRAMSON, R. M. (1988). *Coping with difficult people.* Garden City, NY: Anchor/Doubleday.

*———. (1992). *Coping with difficult bosses.* New York: Carol.

*BRANDEN, N. (1983). *Honoring the self.* Los Angeles: Tarcher.

*———. (1992). *The power of self-esteem.* Deerfield Beach, FL: Health Communications.

*BRANDEN, N., and BRANDEN, E. D. (1982). *The romantic love question and answer book.* Los Angeles: Tarcher.

*BRAVO, E., and CASSEDY, E. (1992). *The 9 to 5 guide to combating sexual harassment.* New York: Wiley.

*BRIGGS, D. C. (1970). *Your child's self-esteem.* Garden City, NY: Doubleday.

———. (1977). *Celebrate yourself: Enhancing your own self-esteem.* New York: Doubleday.

BRINK, S. (2000, January 17). Weighing alcohol's benefits. *U.S. News & World Report, 128*(2), 62.

———. (2001, May 7). Your brain on alcohol. *U.S. News & World Report, 130*(18), 50–57.

BRODY, G. H., MOORE, K., and GLEI, D. (1994). Family processes during adolescence as predictors of parent–young adult attitude similarity: A six-year longitudinal analysis. *Family Relations, 43,* 369–73.

BROOKS, G. R. (2001). Masculinity and men's mental health. *Journal of American College Health 49*(6), 285–87.

BUNTAINE, R. L., and COSTENBADER, V. K. (1997). Self-reported differences in the experience and expression of anger between girls and boys. *Sex Roles, 36*(9–10), 625–37.

*BURKA, J. B., and YUEN, L. M. (1983). *Procrastination: Why you do it, what to do about it.* Reading. MA: Addison-Wesley.

BURKE, E. (1999). Test-anxious learners. *Adults Learning, 10*(6), 23–24.

*BURNS, D. D. (1980). *Feeling good: The new mood therapy.* New York: New American Library.

*———. (1985). *Intimate connections.* New York: Morrow.

———. (1989). *The feeling good handbook.* New York: Morrow.

*BURT, M. (1989). *Stepfamilies stepping ahead: An eight-step program for successful stepfamily living.* Available from Stepfamily Association of America, Inc., 650 J St., Suite 205, Lincoln, NE 68508. Toll free: 800-735-0329.

*BUSCAGLIA, L. (1982). *Living, loving, and learning.* New York: Ballantine.

*———. (1984). *Loving each other.* Thorofare, NJ: Slack.

*———. (1992). *Born for love: Reflections on loving.* Thorofare, NJ: Slack.

BUSINESS WEEK. (1999, April 12). Who's stressed out at work? 26.

BUSS, D. M. (2000, May/June). Prescription. *Psychology Today,* 54–61.

BUTCHER, J. (2000). Sleep deprivation. *Lancet, 356*(9245), 1907.

*BUTLER, P. E. (1992). *Self-assertion for women.* New York: HarperCollins.

BUTLER, R. N. (2001, Fall/Winter). The myth of old age. *Newsweek,* 33.

BUTTON, E. J., LOAN, P., and DAVIES, J. (1997). Self-esteem, eating problems, and psychological well-being in a cohort of schoolgirls aged 15–16: A questionnaire and interview study. *International Journal of Eating Disorders, 21,* 39–47.

BUUNK, B. P., and PRINS, K. S. (1998). Loneliness, exchange orientation and reciprocity in friendships. *Personal Relationships, 5,* 1–14.

BYBEE, J., LUTHAR, S., ZIGLER, E., and MERISCA, R. (1997). The fantasy, ideal, and ought selves: Content, relationships to mental health, and functions. *Social Cognition, 15*(1), 37–53.

BYERS, E. S., and DEMMONS, S. (1999, May). Sexual satisfaction and sexual self-disclosure within dating relationships. *Journal of Sex Research, 36*(2), 180–89.

BYRNE, D. (1971). *The attraction paradigm.* New York: Academic Press.

CALABRESE, K. R. (2000, November). Interpersonal conflict and sarcasm in the workplace. *Genetic, Social and General Psychology Monographs, 126*(4), 459–95.

CANADIAN MANAGER. (1999, Summer). Meeting the people challenge, 20–24.

*CANFIELD, J., and SUCCONE, F. (1993). *101 ways to develop student self-esteem and responsibility.* Boston: Allyn & Bacon.

CARDUCCI, B. J. (WITH GOLANT, S. K.) (1999). *Shyness: A bold new approach.* New York: HarperCollins.

CARI, H. (1980, December). Nonverbal communication during the employment interview. *ABCA Bulletin,* 14–18.

*CARLSON, B., and SEIDEN, O. J. (1988). *Healthwalk.* Golden, CO: Fulcrum.

CARLSON, R. (1999). *You can be happy no matter what: Five principles for keeping life in perspective.* Novata, CA: New World Library.

CARMAN, M. B. (1997). The psychology of normal aging. *Psychiatric Clinics of North America, 20*(1), 15–24.

CARPER, J. (2000). *Your miracle brain.* New York: Harper Collins.

CARRIG, M. (1999). Interpersonal skills are key in office of the future. *TMA Journal, 19*(4), 53.

CARTER-SCOTT, C. (1989). Negaholism: How to recover from your addiction to negativity and turn your life around. New York: Villard.

CASTLEMAN, M. (1989). Sexual solutions. New York: Simon & Schuster.

CEJKA, M. A., and EAGLY, A. H. (1999). Gender-stereotypic images of occupations correspond to the sex segregation of employment. *PSPB, 25*(4), 413–23.

CENTER ON ADDICTION AND SUBSTANCE ABUSE. (2002). Retrieved January 2, 2006 from http://www.alcoholfacts.org/CASAAlcoholStatisticsAbuse.html.

CENTERS FOR DISEASE CONTROL AND PREVENTION. (1999). Youth risk behavior surveillance—United States, 1999. Retrieved August 20, 2001 from http://www.cdc.gov.

———. (2000). HIV/AIDS Update. Retrieved September 15, 2001 from http://www.cdc.gov.

———. (2001a). Tobacco information and prevention source. Retrieved September 15, 2001 from http://www.cdc.gov/tobacco.

———. (2001b). Teen pregnancy. Retrieved August 20, 2001 from http://www.cdc.gov/needphp/teen. (2005)

CERVONE, D. (2000). Thinking about self-efficacy. *Behavior Modification, 24*(1), 30–57.

CHANCE, P. (1988, February). The trouble with love. *Psychology Today,* 22–23.

CHANDLER, M. (2001, August 11). Gen Xer's saving habits vary. *Lincoln Journal Star,* p. 4A.

CHAPMAN, E. N. (1993). Your attitude is showing. Chicago: Science Research Associates.

CHIU, L. H. (1997). Development and validation of the school achievement motivation rating scale. *Educational and Psychological Measurement, 57*(2), 292–305.

CHOI, C. (2001, January 30). Women with high-profile jobs, ratings but still hold few top positions. Retrieved January 31, 2001 from http://www.DiversityInc. com.

CLARKSON, P. (1992). *Transactional analysis psychotherapy: An integrated approach.* London: Tavistock/Routledge.

CLASSEN, C., KOOPMAN, C., ANGELL, K., and SPIEGEL, D. (1996). Coping styles associated with psychological adjustment to advanced breast cancer. *Health Psychology, 15*(6), 434–37.

COHEN, D. A., and GELFAND, R. M. (2000). *Just get me through this!* New York: Kensington Books.

COLEMAN, M., and GANONG, L. H. (1985). Love and sex role stereotypes: Do macho men and feminine women make better lovers? *Journal of Personality and Social Psychology, 49*(1), 170–76.

———. (1989). Stepfamily self-help books: Brief annotations and ratings. *Family Relations, 38,* 91–96.

COLEMAN, M., GANONG, L., and FINE, M. (2000, November). Reinvestigating remarriage: Another decade of progress. *Journal of Marriage & the Family, 62*(4), 1288–1307.

COLGROVE, M., BLOOMFIELD, H. H., and MCWILLIAMS, P. (1991).How to survive the loss of a love. Los Angeles: Prelude.

CONGER, J. J., and PETERSON, A. C. (1984). *Adolescence and youth: Psychological development in a changing world.* New York: Harper & Row.

CONSUMER REPORTS ON HEALTH. (2001, February). Check your anger. *13*(2), 7.

COOKSEY, E. C., and FONDELL, M. M. (1996). Spending time with his kids: Effects of family structure on fathers' and children's lives. *Journal of Marriage and the Family, 58*(3), 693–707.

COOPERSMITH, S. (1967). *The antecedents of self-esteem.* San Francisco: Freeman.

COSTA, P. T., and MCCRAE, R. R. (1997). Longitudinal stability of adult personality. In R. Hogan, J. Johnson, and S. Briggs (Eds.), *Handbook of personality psychology* (pp. 269–85). San Diego: Academic Press.

COUSINS, N. (1979). Anatomy of an illness. New York: Bantam.

———. (1983). The healing heart. New York: Avon.

———. (1989). Head first. New York: Penguin.

———. (1991). The celebration of life. New York: Bantam.

COVEY, STEPHEN R. (2004). *The 8th habit: From effectiveness to greatness.* New York Free Press.

COWAN, C., and KINDER, M. (1987). Women men love, women men leave. New York: Clarkson N. Potter.

COWLEY, G. (2001, January 29). The skin-cancer scare. *Newsweek,* 58.

CREMER, B., and HAREL, Z., (2000). Adolescents: At increased risk for osteoporosis? *Clinical Pediatrics, 39,* 565–74.

CROSE, R. (1997). Why women live longer than men and what

men can learn from them. San Francisco: Jossey-Bass.

CROWDER, K. D., and TOLNAY, S. E. (2000). A new marriage squeeze for black women: The role of racial intermarriage by black men. *Journal of Marriage & the Family, 62*(3), 792–807.

CROWTHER, C. E. (1986). *Intimacy: Strategies for successful relationships.* Santa Barbara, CA: Capra.

CUMMINGS, E. M., and O'REILLY, A. W. (1997). Fathers in family context: Effects of marital quality on child adjustment. In M. E. Lamb (Ed.), *The role of the father in child development* (pp. 49–65). New York: Wiley.

CUNNINGHAM, M. (2001, February). The influence of parental attitudes and behaviors on children's attitudes toward gender and household labor in early adulthood. *Journal of Marriage and Family, 63,* 111–22.

CURRENT HEALTH 2. (2000, February). *If you don't snooze, you lose, 26*(6), 2. Retrieved June 18, 2001, from EBSCOhost database.

CULTER, B. (1989, September). Are you an average person? *Reader's Digest,* 189–95.

DAINTON, M. (1998, Summer). Everyday interaction in marital relationships: Variations in relative importance and event duration. *Communication Reports, 11*(2), 101–09.

DANIEL, A. G. F. (1998, October 26). Success secret: A high emotional IQ. *Fortune,* 293.

DANNER, D. D., SNOWDON, D. A., and FRIESEN, W. V. (2001). Positive emotions in early life and longevity: Findings from the nun study. *Journal of Personality and Social Psychology, 80*(5), 804–14.

*DAVIS, D. L. (1991). *Empty cradle, broken heart.* Golden, CO: Fulcrum.

DAVIS-PACKARD, K. (2000, August 15). Why the number of teen mothers is falling. *Christian Science Monitor, 92*(185), 1.

DAWSON-THREAT, J., and HUBA, M. E. (1996). Choice of major and clarity of purpose among college seniors as a function of gender, type of major, and sex-role identification. *Journal of College Student Development, 37*(3), 297–308.

DAY, R. D., PETERSON, G. W., and McCRACKEN, C. (1998). Predicting spanking of younger and older children by mothers and fathers. *Journal of Marriage and the Family, 60*(1), 79–94.

DEGAETANO, G., and SIMINI, B. (2001). Drink in moderation, says consensus panel. *Lancet, 357*(9267), 1511.

DEINER, E., and SELIGMAN, M. (2002). Very happy people. *Psychological Science, 13,* 80–83.

DEMARIS, A. (2001). The influence of intimate violence on transitions out of cohabitation. *Journal of Marriage and the Family, 63*(1), 235–46.

DEMO, D. H. (2000). Children's experience of family diversity. *National Forum, 80*(3), 16–20.

DERR, C. B. (1986). *Managing the new careerists: The diverse career success orientations of today's workers.* San Francisco: Jossey-Bass.

DEVLIN, B., DANIELS, M., and ROEDER, K. (1997, July). The heritability of IQ. *Nature, 388*(31), 468–71.

DEVRIES, B., DAVIS, C. G., WORTMAN, C. B., and LEHMAN, D. R. (1997). Long-term psychological and somatic consequences of later life parental bereavement. *Omega: Journal of Death and Dying, 35*(1), 97–117.

DIEGO, M. A., and FIELD, T. (2001). HIV adolescents show improved immune function following massage therapy. *International Journal of Neuroscience, 106*(1–2), 35–45.

*DINKMEYER, D., and McKAY, G. D. (1996). *Raising a responsible child.* New York: Simon & Schuster.

DOHERTY, W. J., KOUNESKI, E. F., and ERICKSON, M. F. (1998). Responsible fathering: An overview and conceptual framework. *Journal of Marriage and the Family, 60*(2), 277–92.

DOLGIN, K. L. (2001). Men's friendships: Mismeasured, demeaned, and misunderstood? In T. F. Cohen (Ed.), *Men and masculinity.* New York: Wadsworth.

DONALDSON, L., and SCANNELL, E. E. (1986). *Human resource development: The new trainer's guide.* Reading, MA: Addison-Wesley.

*DONNELLEY, N. H. (1987). *I never know what to say.* New York: Ballantine.

*DONNELLY, K. F. (2000). *Recovering from the loss of a parent.* New York: Berkley.

*———. (2001). *Recovering from the loss of a child.* New York: Berkley.

*DOWLING, C. (1991). *You mean I don't have to feel this*

way? New York: Charles Scribner's Sons.

DOWNEY, D. B., AINSWORTH-DARNELL, J. W., and DUFUR, M. J. (1998). Sex of parent and children's well-being in single-parent households. *Journal of Marriage & the Family, 60*(4), 878–93.

DOYLE, J. A., and PALUDI, M. A. (1998). *Sex and gender: The human experience.* Boston: McGraw-Hill.

DUNNING, D. (2001). *What's your type of career?* Palo Alto, CA: Davies-Black Publishing.

*DYER, W. (1976). *Your erroneous zones.* New York: Funk & Wagnalls.

*———. (1990). *The sky's the limit.* New York: Pocket Books.

*———. (1992). *Real magic.* New York: HarperCollins.

EDER, R. A., and MANGELESDORF, S. C. (1997). The emotional basis of early personality development: Implications for the emergent self-concept. In R. Hogan, J. Johnson, and S. Briggs (Eds.), *Handbook of personality psychology* (pp. 209–324). San Diego, CA: Academic Press.

*EDWARDS, D. (1989). *Grieving: The pain and the promise.* Salt Lake City: Covenant.

EHRENBERG, M. F., GEARING-SMALL, M., HUNTER, M. A., and SMALL, B. J. (2001). Childcare task division and shared parenting attitudes in dual-earner families with young children. *Family Relations, 50*(2), 143–53.

*EINSTEIN, E. (1982). *The stepfamily: Living, loving, and learning.* Boston: Shambhala.

EKMAN, P. (1994). Strong evidence for universals in facial expressions: A reply to

Russell's mistaken critique. *Psychological Bulletin, 115,* 268–87.

EKMAN, P., DAVIDSON, R. J., and FRIESEN, W. V. (1990). The Duchenne smile: Emotional expression and brain physiology. *Journal of Personality and Social Psychology, 58,* 342–53.

ELIOT, R. S., and BREO, D. L. (1984). *Is it worth dying for?* New York: Bantam.

ELLIS, A. (1977). The basic clinical theory of rational-emotive therapy. In A. Ellis and R. Grieger (Eds.), *Handbook of rational-emotive therapy* (pp. 3–34). New York: Springer.

———. (1984). The essence of RET. *Journal of Rational-Emotive Therapy, 2,* 19–25.

———. (1993). Reflections on rational-emotive therapy. *Journal of Consulting and Clinical Psychology 61*(2), 199–201.

———. (1996). The treatment of morbid jealousy: A rational-emotive behavior therapy approach. *Journal of Cognitive Psychotherapy, 10*(1), 23–33.

ELLSWORTH, B. A. (1988). *Living in love with yourself.* Salt Lake City: Breakthrough.

EMERSON, J. (2000). The sandwich generation. *DollarSense,* 8–10.

ENRIGHT, R. D. (2001). *Forgiveness is a choice.* Washington, DC: American Psychological Association.

ERIKSON, E. (1963). *The challenge of youth.* New York: Norton.

———. (1968). *Identity: Youth and crisis.* New York: Norton.

ERNST, F. H. (1973). *Who's listening?* Vallejo, CA: Addresso' set.

ETTER, J. F., BERGMAN, M. M., HUMAIR, J. P., and PERNEGERI, T. V. (2000). Development and validation of a scale measuring self-efficacy of current and former smokers. *Addiction, 95*(6), 901–14.

EVANS, K. (2000, April). Is stress wrecking your mood? *Health,* 118–29.

*EVANS, P. (1996). *The verbally abusive relationship: How to recognize it and how to respond.* Holbrook, MA: Bob Adams.

EYRE, L., and EYRE, R. (1993). *Teaching your children values.* New York: Simon & Schuster.

EYSENCK, H. J. (1988, December). Health's character. *Psychology Today,* 23–35.

FARLEY, C. J. (1997, November 24). Kids and race. *Time,* 88–91.

*FARRELL, W. (1986). *Why men are the way they are: The male-female dynamic.* New York: McGraw-Hill.

*FAST, J. (1970). *Body language.* New York: M. Evans.

FAVA, G. A., RAFANELLI, C., GRANDI, S., CONTI, S., and BELLUARDO, P. (1998, September). Prevention of recurrent depression with cognitive behavioral therapy. *Arch Gen Psychiatry, 55,* 816–20.

FERRENCE, R., and ASHLEY, M. J. (2000). Protecting children from passive smoking. *British Medical Journal, 321*(7257), 310–11.

FIELD, T. M. (1996). Touch therapies for pain management and stress reduction. In R. J. RESNICK and R. H. Rozensky (Eds.), *Health psychology through the life span: Practice and research opportunities* (pp. 313–21). Washington, DC: American Psychological Association.

FIELDS, J., and CASPER, L. M. (2000). America's families and living arrangements. Retrieved August 23, 2001 from http://www.census.gov.

FINE, M. A., GANONG, L. H., and COLEMAN, M. (1997). The relation between role constructions and adjustments among stepfathers. *Journal of Family Issues, 18,* 503–25.

FISHER, C. S., JACKSON, R. M., STUEVE, C. A., GERSON, K., JONES, L. M., and BALDASSARE, M. (1977). *Networks and places: Social relations in the urban setting.* New York: Free Press.

FITZGERALD, B. (1999). Children of lesbian and gay parents: A review of the literature. *Marriage & Family Review, 29*(1), 57–75.

*FLANIGAN, B. (1992). *Forgiving the unforgivable.* New York: Macmillan.

*————. (1996). *Forgiving yourself: A step-by-step guide to making peace with your mistakes and getting on with your life.* New York: Simon & Schuster.

FLETT, G. L., HEWITT, P. L., and DEROSA, T. (1996). Dimensions of perfectionism, psychosocial adjustment, and social skills. *Personality and Individual Differences, 20*(2), 143–50.

FOLSOM, A. R., and KUSHIT, L. H. (2000, January). Physical activity and incident diabetes mellitus in postmenopausal women. *American Journal of Public Health, 90*(1), 134–39.

FONOW, M. M. (1998). Difference and inequality.

In M. M. Fonow (Ed.), *Reading women's lives* (pp. 101–06). Needham Heights, MA: Simon & Schuster Custom Publishing.

*FORWARD, S. (WITH BUCK, C.). (1989). *Toxic parents: Overcoming their hurtful legacy and reclaiming your life.* New York: Bantam.

*————. (1991). *Obsessive love.* New York: Bantam.

*FORWARD, S., and TORRES, J. (1986). *Men who hate women and the women who love them.* Toronto: Bantam.

FOZARD, J. L. (1999). Epidemiologists try many ways to show that physical activity is good for seniors' health and longevity. Review of special issue of journal of aging and physical activity: The evergreen project. *Physical Fitness, 25*(2), 175–83.

FRANZ, C. E., MCCLELLAND, D. C., and WEINBERGER, J. (1991). Childhood antecedents of conventional social accomplishment in midlife adults: A 36-year prospective study. *Journal of Personality and Social Psychology, 60,* 586–95.

*FRIEDAN, B. (1993). *The fountain of age.* New York: Simon & Schuster.

FRIEDLAND, R. P. (1998). Exercise throughout life may provide protection against Alzheimer's. *Modern Medicine, 66*(6), 56.

*FROMM, E. (1956). *The art of loving.* New York: Harper & Row.

FUMENTO, M. (1998, May June). Weight after 50: Is there too much on our plate? *Modern Maturity,* 34–41.

FURSTENBERG, F. F., and KIERNAN, K. E. (2001). Delayed parental divorce:

How much do children benefit? *Journal of Marriage and the Family, 63*(2), 446–57.

THE FUTURIST. (1999). The dangers of passive smoking, *33*(1), 7.

GAGER, C. T., COONEY, T. M., and CALL, K. T. (1999). The effects of family characteristics and time use on teenagers' household labor. *Journal of Marriage and the Family, 61*(4), 982–94.

GALLANT, M. P., and CONNELL, C. M. (1997). Predictors of mammography use in the past year among elderly women. *Journal of Aging and Health, 9*(3), 373–95.

GANONG, L. H., and COLEMAN, M. (1996). A comparison of clinical and empirical literature on children in stepfamilies. *Journal of Marriage and the Family, 48,* 309–18.

GARDNER, H. (1983). *Frames of mind: The story of multiple intelligences.* New York: Basic Books.

GARDNER, H. (2002). Howard Gardner and Multiple Intelligences, The Encyclopedia of Informal Education, Retrieved from http://www.infed.org/thinkers/gardner.htm.

GARDYN, R., and LACH, J. (2000). Love is colorblind . . . or is it? *American Demographics, 22*(6), 11–13.

————. (1999). *Intelligence reframed: Multiple intelligences for the 21st century.* New York: Basic Books.

GERIATRICS. (2000). Alzheimer's: It's more than normal forgetfulness. *55*(2), 22.

*GETZOFF, A., and MCCLENAHAN, M. (1984). *Stepkids: A survival guide for* teenagers, in stepfamilies. New York: Walker.

GIBBS, N. R. (1993, May). How should we teach our children about sex? *Time,* 64–71.

———. (1995, October 2). The EQ factor. *Time,* 61–68.

GILLENKIRK, J. (2000, November 4). A revolution in American fathering. *America, 183*(14), 18–21.

GILLIGAN, C. (1982). *In a different voice.* Cambridge, MA: Harvard University Press.

GINOTT, H. (1965). *Between parent and child.* New York: Macmillan.

*———. (1969). *Between parent and teenager.* Toronto: Macmillan.

*GINSBURG, G. D. (1987). *To live again: Rebuilding your life after you've become a widow.* Los Angeles: Tarcher.

GINSBURG, K. R., FEIN, J. A., and JOHNSON, C. D. (1998). Violence prevention in the early years. *Contemporary Pediatrics, 15*(4), 97–110.

GLASER, S. (1986). *Toward communication competency.* New York: Holt, Rinchart & Winston.

GLASSER, W. (1965). *Reality therapy: A new approach to psychiatry.* New York: Harper & Row.

*———. (1984). *Control theory: A new explanation of how we control our lives.* New York: Harper & Row.

GLENN, H. S., and NELSEN, J. (1989). *Raising self-reliant children in a self-indulgent world.* Rocklin, CA: Prima.

GOFFMAN, E. (1959). *Presentation of self in everyday life.* New York: Anchor.

*GOLD, L. (1996). *Between love and hate: A guide to civilized divorce.* New York: NAL Dutton.

GOLDBERG, H. (1979). *The new male.* New York: Signet.

GOLDBERG, K. (1993). *How men can live as long as women: Seven steps to a longer and better life.* Fort Worth, TX: The Summit Group.

GOLEMAN, D. (1991, November 26). New way to battle bias: Fight acts, not feelings. *New York Times,* pp. C1, C8.

*———. (1995). *Emotional intelligence.* New York: Bantam Books.

———. (1997). Affective and nourishing emotions: Impacts on health. In D. Goleman (Ed.), *Healing emotions* (pp. 33–46). Boston: Shambhala.

———. (1998). *Working with emotional intelligence.* New York: Bantam Books.

GOODMAN, E. (2001, July 30). Women slighted by Bush plan. *Lincoln Journal Star,* p. 4B.

GORDON, S. (1996). *Why love is not enough.* Boston: Bob Adams.

GORRELL, C. (2000, November/ December). Live-in and learn. *Psychology Today,* 16.

———. (2001, September/ October). Finding fault. *Psychology Today,* 24.

GOTTMAN, J. M. (1991). Predicting the longitudinal course of marriages. *Journal of Marital and Family Therapy, 17,* 3–7.

*———. (1994a). Why marriages succeed or fail . . . and how you can make yours last. New York: Simon & Schuster.

*———. (1994b). What predicts divorce? The relationship between marital processes and marital outcomes. Hillsdale, NJ: Lawrence Eribaum Associates.

GOTTMAN, J. M., COAN, J., CARRERE, S., and SWANSON, C. (1988). Predicting marital happiness and stability from newlywed interactions. *Journal of Marriage and the Family, 60*(1), 5–22.

*GOULDING, M. M., and GOULDING, R. L. (1989). *Not to worry.* New York: Morrow.

GREENBERG, M. (1997). Highrise public housing, optimism, and personal and environment health behaviors. *American Journal of Health Behavior, 21*(5), 38–98.

GREENE, R. (1998, January 12). Political interest among freshmen hits new low, survey finds. *Lincoln Journal Star,* p. 3A.

GREENFIELD, S., and THELEN, M. (1997). Validation of the fear of intimacy scale with a lesbian and gay male population. *Journal of Social and Personal Relationships, 14*(5), 707–16.

GROSSMAN, A. H., and KERNER, M. S. (1998). Self-esteem and supportiveness as predictors of emotional distress in gay male and lesbian youth. *Journal of Homosexuality, 35*(2), 26–39.

GUILBERT, D. E., VACC, N. A., and PASLEY, K. (2000). The relationship of gender role beliefs, negativity, distancing, and marital instability. *Family Journal, 8*(2), 124–32.

*GULLO, S., and Church, C. (1988). *Loveshock: How to recover from a broken heart and love again.* New York: Simon & Schuster.

GUNNOE, M. L., and MARINER, C. L. (1997). Toward a developmental-contextual model of the effects of parental spanking on children's aggression. *Archives of Pediatrics & Adolescent Medicine, 151*(8), 768–75.

HALL, E. T. (1969). *The hidden dimension.* New York: Anchor/Doubleday.

———. (1973). *The silent language.* New York: Doubleday.

HALL, P. D. (1999). The effect of meditation on the academic performance of African American college students. *Meditation, 29*(3), 408–16.

*HALLOWELL, E. M. (1997). *Worry: Controlling and using it wisely.* New York: Pantheon.

HALPERN, D. F., and CROTHERS, M. (1997). Sex, sexual orientation, and cognition. In L. Ellis and L. Ebertz (Eds.), *Sexual orientation: Toward biological understanding* (pp. 181–97). Westport, CT: Praeger.

HAN, W. J., WALDFOGEL, J., and BROOKS-GUNN, J. (2001). The effects of early maternal employment on later cognitive and behavioral outcomes. *Journal of Marriage and the Family, 63*(2), 336–54.

HANNA, S. L. (1980). The strengths within families of remarriage: A descriptive study. Master's thesis, University of Nebraska, Lincoln.

———. (2002). *Career by design: Communicating your way to success.* Upper Saddle River, NJ: Prentice Hall.

———. (2003). *Person to person: Positive relationships don't just happen.* Upper Saddle River, NJ: Prentice Hall.

HANNA, S. L., and KNAUS, P. K. (1981). Cohabitation before remarriage: Its relationship to family strengths. *Alternative Lifestyles, 4*(4), 507–22.

HARJU, B. L., and BOLEN, L. M. (1998). The effects of optimism on coping and perceived quality of life of college students. *Journal of Social Behavior and Personality, 13*(2), 185–201.

HARRIS, S. (1982, April 3). When your leading role models are entertainers, what kind of a society will you have? *Lincoln Journal Star*, p. 6.

*HARRIS, T. (1969). *I'm ok, you're ok.* New York: Harper & Row.

*HARRIS, T. A., and HARRIS, A. B. (1985). *Staying ok.* New York: Harper & Row.

HARTSTEIN, N. B. (1996). Suicide risk in lesbian, gay, and bisexual youth. In R. P. Cabaj and T. S. Stein (Eds.), *Textbook of homosexuality and mental health* (pp. 819–33). Washington, DC: American Psychiatric Press.

HARVARD HEALTH LETTER. (1999, April). Moderate activity keeps heat, waistline in shape, 24(6), 4–6.

———. (2000, September). Five new treatments, 25(11), 2–3.

HARVEY, E. (1999). Short-term and long-term effects of parental employment on children of the National Longitudinal Survey of Youth. *Developmental Psychology, 35,* 445–59.

HASTINGS, S. O. (2000). Asian Indian "self-suppression" and self-disclosure. *Journal of Language and Social Psychology, 19*(1), 85–109.

HATFIELD, E., and RAPSON, R. L. (1996). *Love and sex: Cross-cultural perspectives.* Boston: Allyn & Bacon.

HAWKINS, A. J., and DOLLANITE, D. C. (1997). *Generative fathering: Beyond deficit perspectives.* Thousand Oaks, CA: Sage.

HAWKINS, A. J., and ROBERTS, T. (1992). Designing a primary intervention to help dual-earner couples share housework and child care. *Family Relations, 41,* 169–77.

*HAY, L. L. (1991). *The power is within you.* Carson, CA: Hay House.

HEALTH. (1997, July/August). No wonder health officials are down on Joe Camel, 48.

———. (1998, July/August). A strong vote for B vitamins, 15.

———. (2000, June). Vital statistics, 24.

HEIDER, F. (1958). *The psychology of interpersonal relations.* New York: Wiley.

*HELMSTETTER, S. (1989). *Predictive parenting: What to say when you talk to your kids.* New York: Pocket Books.

HENDERSON, C. W. (2000, May 20). Depression associated with increased risk for heart disease in men and women. *Women's Health Weekly, 11.*

*HENDLIN, S. J. (1992). *When good enough is never enough.* New York: Putnam's.

HENRY, D. B. (2000). Peer groups, families, and school failure among urban children: Elements of risk and successful interventions. *Preventing School Failure, 44*(3), 97–103.

HENSRUD, D. D. (2001, March 30). How to live longer. *Fortune, 143*(9), 210.

HEREK, G. M. (1996). Heterosexism and homophobia. In R. P. Cabaj and T. S. Stein (Eds.), *Textbook of homosexuality and mental health* (pp. 101–11). Washington, DC: American Psychiatric Press.

HICKLING, L. (2000, November 17). Study: Hearty laughter may be good for the heart. *Health News*. Retrieved July 15, 2001 from http://drkoop.com/news/stories/2000/nov/17_laughter.html.

HILL, L. A. (1994). Managing your career (Note 9-494-082). Boston: Harvard Business School Publishing.

HINES, A. M. (1997). Divorce-related transitions, adolescent development, and the role of the parent–child relationship: A review of the literature. *Journal of Marriage and the Family, 59*(2), 375–88.

HOFFMAN, R. M., and BORDER, L. D. (2001). Twenty-five years after the Bem Sex-role Inventory: A reassessment and new issues regarding classification variability. *Measurement & Evaluation in Counseling & Development, 34*(1), 39–55.

HOLMES, T. H., and RAHE, R. R. (1967). The social readjustment rating scale. *Journal of Psychosomatic Research, 11*, 213–18.

HORN, T. S., LOX, C., and LABRADOR, F. (1998). The self-fulfilling prophecy theory: When coaches' expectations become reality. In J. M. Williams (Ed.), *Applied sport psychology: Personal growth to peak performance* (pp. 74–91). Mountain View, CA: Mayfield.

HOSSAIN, Z. (2001). Division of household labor and family functioning in off-reservation Navajo Indian families. *Family Relations, 50*(3), 255–61.

HOWARD, G., WAGENNECHT, L. E., BURKE, G. L., DIEZ, R. A., EVANS, G. W., McGOVERN, P., NIETO, F. J., and TELI, G. S. (1998). Cigarette smoking and progression of atherosclerosis: The atherosclerosis risk in communities (ARIC) study. *Journal of the American Medical Association, 279*(2), 119–24.

HUPPE, M., and CYR, M. (1997). Division of household labor and marital satisfaction of dual income couples according to family life cycle. *Canadian Journal of Counselling 31*(2), 145–62.

HURDLE, D. E. (2001). Social support: A critical factor in women's health and health promotion. *Health and Social Work, 26*(2), 72–79.

HUSTON, M., and SCHWARTZ, P. (1996). Gendered dynamics in the romantic relationships of lesbians and gays. In J. T. Wood (Ed.), *Gendered relationships* (pp. 163–76). Mountain View, CA: Mayfield.

*HUTCHINSON, E. O. (1992). *Black fatherhood: The guide to male parenting*. Los Angeles: Impact.

HUTCHINSON, K., and COONEY, T. M. (1998). Patterns of, parent–teen sexual risk communications: Implications for intervention. *Family Relations, 47*(2), 185–94.

HUWIG, P. (2001, March). A look at lesbian domestic violence. *Lesbian News, 26*(8), 52.

HYATT, R. (1991, March). Self-esteem: The key to happiness. *USA Today*, 86–87.

ISHII-KUNTZ, M., and COLTRANE, S. (1992). Remarriage, stepparenting, and household labor. *Journal of Family Issues, 13*, 215–33.

JACKSON, C., HENRIKSEN, L., DICKINSON, D., and LEVINE, D. W. (1997). The early use of alcohol and tobacco: Its relation to children's competence and parents' behavior. *American Journal of Public Health, 8*(3), 359–64.

JACKSON, M. (1998, May 7). Working moms frustrated with trying to do it all. *Lincoln Journal Star*, p. 1.

*JACOBSON, N. S., and GOTTMAN, J. M. (1998a). *When men batter women: New insights into ending abusive relationships*. New York: Simon & Schuster.

———. (1998b, March/April). Anatomy of a violent relationship. *Psychology Today*, 60–64, 82.

*JAMES, J. W., and CHERRY, F. (1988). *The grief recovery handbook*. New York: Harper & Row.

JAMPOLSKY, G. G. (1979). *Love is letting go of fear*. Millbrae, CA: Celestial Arts.

JAMPOLSKY, G. G., and CIRINCIONE, D. V. (1979). *One person can make a difference*. New York: Bantam.

———. (1990). *Love is the answer*. New York: Bantam.

JARET, P. (1998, May/June). Only 5 a day. *Health*, 78–85.

———. (1999, January/February). Move the body, heal the mind. *Health*, 48–50.

*JASPER, J. (1999). *Take back your time*. New York: St. Martin's Griffin.

*JEFFERS, S. (1987). *Feel the fear and do it anyway*. New York: Fawcett Columbine.

*JEFFRIES, W. C. (1991). *True to type*. Norfolk, VA: Hampton Roads.

JEMMOTT, J. B., and JEMMOTT, L. S. (1996). Strategies to reduce the risk of HIV infection, sexually transmitted diseases, and pregnancy among African American adolescents. In R. J. Resnick and R. H. Rozensky (Eds.), *Health psychology through the life span: Practice and re-search opportunities* (pp. 395–422). Washington, DC: American Psychological Association.

JEVNE, R. (2000). *Hoping, coping, and moping.* Los Angeles: Health Information Press.

JINKS, J., and MORGAN, V. (1999). Children's perceived academic self-efficacy: An inventory scale. *Clearing House, 72*(4), 224–31.

JOHNSON, D. R., and SCHEUBLE, L. K. (1995). Women's marital naming in two generations: A national study. *Journal of Marriage and the Family, 57*(3), 724–32.

*JOHNSON, H. M. (1986). *How do I love thee?* Salem, WI: Sheffield.

JOHNSON, L. G., SCHWARTZ, R. A., and BOWER, B. L. (2000). Managing stress among adult women students in community colleges. *Community College Journal of Research and Practice, 24*(4), 289–301.

JOLLEY, R. P., ZHI, Z., and THOMAS, G. (1998). The development of understanding moods metaphorically expressed in pictures: A cross-cultural comparison. *Journal of Cross-Cultural Psychology , 29*(2), 358–76.

JONES, N. A., FIELD, T., FOX, N. A., DAVALOS, M., MALPHURS, J., CARAWAY, K., SCHANBERG, S., and KUHN, C. (1997). Infants of intrusive and withdrawn mothers. *Infant Behavior and Development, 20*(2), 175–86.

JORDAN, K. M., and DELUTY, R. H. (1998). Coming out for lesbian women: Its rela-

tion to anxiety, positive affectivity, self-esteem, and social support. *Journal of Homosexuality, 35*(2), 41–63.

JOSSELSON, R. (1992). *The space between us.* San Francisco: Jossey-Bass.

JOURARD, S. M. (1971). *The transparent self.* New York: Van Nostrand Reinhold.

JUNG, C. G. (1921). *Psychological types.* Princeton, NJ: Princeton University Press.

———. (1968). *Analytical psychology, its theory and practice.* New York: Vintage.

KAMO, Y., and COHEN, E. L. (1998). Division of household work between partners: A comparison of black and white couples. *Journal of Comparative Family Studies, 29,* 131–45.

KANTROWITZ, B. (2001, May 21). Parents today make more time for quality time. *Newsweek,* 53.

KANTROWITZ, B., and WINGERT, P. (2001, May 28). Unmarried with children. *Newsweek,* 46–55.

*KASL, C. S. (1997). *A home for the heart: Creating intimacy and community with loved ones and friends.* New York: HarperCollins.

KAUFMAN, G. (2000). Do gender role attitudes matter? *Journal of Family Issues, 21*(1), 128–44.

*KEATING, C. J. (1984). *Dealing with difficult people.* Ramsey, NJ: Paulist Press.

*KEEN, S. (1991). *Fire in the belly: On being a man.* New York: Bantam.

*KEIRSEY, D., and BATES, M. (1978). *Please understand me.* Del Mar, CA: Prometheus Nemesis.

KELLER, M. B., McCULLOUGH, J. P., KLEIN, D. N., ARNOW, B.,

DUNNER, D. L., GELENBERG, A. L., MARKOWITZ, J. C., NEMEROFF, C. B., RUSSELL, J. M., THASE, M. E., TRIVEDI, M. H., and ZAJBCKA, J. (2000). A comparison of nefazodone, the cognitive behavioral-analysis system of psychotherapy, and their combination for the treatment of chronic depression. *The New England Journal of Medicine, 342*(20), 1462–69.

KELLEY, H. H. (1950). The warm-cold variable in first impressions of persons. *Journal of Personality, 18,* 431–39.

KELLEY, P. (1992). Healthy stepfamily functioning. *Families in Society, 73,* 579–87.

KELLEY, R. M., SYNOVITZ, L., CARLSON, G., and SCHUSTER, A. L. (2001). Sexual behaviors of college students attending four universities in a southern state. *Research Quarterly for Exercise and Sport, 72*(1), A-31.

KELLY, W. E., and MILLER, M. J. (1999). A discussion of worry with suggestions for counselors. *Counseling and Values, 44*(1), 55–67.

*KENNEDY, A. (1991). *Losing a parent: Passage to a new way of living.* New York: HarperCollins.

*KENNEDY, E. (1975). *If you really knew me, would you still like me?* Niles, IL: Argus.

KESSLER, D. A. (1995). Nicotine addiction in young people. *New England Journal of Medicine, 333,* 186–89.

KEYES, K. (1975). *Handbook to higher consciousness.* Coos Bay, OR: Living Love.

KHAW, K., BINGHAM, S., WELCH, A., LUBEN, R., WAREHAM, N., OAKES, S., and DAY, N. (2001). Relation between plasma ascorbic acid and mortality in men and women in Epic-Norfolk Prospective study: A prospective population study. *Lancet, 357*(9257), 657–63.

KILBOURNE, J. (1995). Beauty and the beast of advertising. In P. S. Rothenberg (Ed.), *Race, class, and gender in the United States: An integrated study.* New York: St. Martin's.

*KILEY, D. (1989). *Living together feeling alone.* New York: Prentice Hall.

KNAUB, P. K., and HANNA, S. L. (1984). Children of remarriage: Perceptions of family strength. *Journal of Divorce, 7*(4), 73–90.

KNAUB, P. K., HANNA, S. L., and STINNETT, N. (1984). Strengths of remarried families. *Journal of Divorce, 7*(3), 41–55.

*KNAUS, W. J. (1998). *Do it now! Break the procrastination habit.* New York: Wiley.

KNOX, D., DANIELS, V., STURDIVANT, L., and ZUSMAN, M. E. (2001). College student use of the Internet for mate selection. *College Student Journal, 35*(1), 158–57.

KOBASA, S. C. (1979). Stressful life events, personality, and health: An inquiry into hardiness. *Journal of Personality and Social Psychology, 37*(1), 1–11.

KOHLBERG, L. (1963). The development of children's orientations toward a moral order 1: Sequence in the development of moral thought. *Vita Humana, 6,* 11–35.

KOWALKSI, K. M. (2001, April/May). Debunking myths about alcohol. *Current Health 2, 27*(8), 6–11.

*KROBGER, O., and THUESEN, J. M. (1993). *Type talk at work.* New York: Delacorte.

KUBANY, E. S., RICHARD, D. C., BAUER, G. B., and MURAOKA, M. Y. (1992). Verbalized anger and accusatory "you" messages as cues for anger and antagonism among adolescents. *Adolescence, 27,* 505–16.

*KUBLER-ROSS, E. (1969). *On death and dying.* New York: Macmillan.

KUMMEROW, J. M., BARGER, J. J., and DIRBY, L. K. (1997). *Work types.* New York: Time Warner Books.

KUNKEL, A. W., and BURLESON, B. R. (1999). Assessing explanations for sex differences in emotional support. *Human Communication Research, 25*(3), 307–40.

KURDEK, L. A. (1998). Relationships outcomes and their predictors: Longitudinal evidence from heterosexual married, gay cohabiting, and lesbian cohabiting couples. *Journal of Marriage and the Family, 60*(3), 553–68.

*KUSHNER, H. (1986). *When all you've ever wanted isn't enough.* New York: Pocket Books.

LACH, J. (2000). Asset analysis. *American Demographics, 22*(6), 15–17. Retrieved August 7, 2000 from EBSCOhost database.

LADANY, N., WALKER, J. A., and MELINCOFF, D. S. (2001). Supervisory style: Its relation to the supervisory working alliance and supervisor self-disclosure. *Counselor Education and Supervision, 40*(4), 263–76.

LANG, D. (1990). *Family harmony.* New York: Prentice Hall.

LANSFORD, J. E., CEBALLO, R., ABBEY, A., and STEWART, A. J. (2001). Does family structure matter? A comparison of adoptive two-parent biological, single-mother, stepfather, and stepmother households. *Journal of Marriage & the Family, 63*(3), 840–51.

LARKINS, M. (1999). Walking sharpens some cognitive skills in elderly. *Lancet, 354*(9176), 401.

LAUER, J., and LAUER, R. (1985, June). Marriages made to last. *Psychology Today,* 22–26.

LAUERMAN, C. (2001, August 7). Saving your skin. *Lincoln Journal Star,* p. 1D.

———. (1981, July). Little hassles can be hazardous to your health. *Psychology Today,* 58–62.

*LEBOEUF, M. (1979). *Working smart: How to accomplish more in half the time.* New York: McGraw-Hill.

LEE, I. M., PAFFENBAARGER, JR., R. S., and HENNEKENS, C. H. (1997). Physical activity, physical fitness and longevity. *Aging Milano, 9*(1–2), 2–11.

———. (2001). Physical activity and coronary heart disease in women: Is "no pain, no gain" passé? *The Journal of the American Medical Association, 285*(11), 1447.

LEE, I. M., REXRODE, K. M., COOK, N. R., MANSON, J. E., and BURING, J. E. (2001). Physical activity and coronary heart disease in women: Is "no pain, no gain" passé? *Journal of the American Medical Association, 285,* (11), 1447.

LEE, J. (1985, May 20). One less for the road. *Time,* 76–78.

*LESHAN, E. (1997). *It's better to be over the hill than under it.* New York: Newmarket.

Lev, E. L. (1997). Bandura's theory of self-efficacy: Applications to oncology. *Scholarly Inquiry for Nursing Practice, 11*(2), 21–37.

Levant, R. F., and Brooks, G. R. (1997). *Men and sex: New psychological perspectives.* New York: Wiley.

Levine, M. (1988). *Effective problem solving.* Englewood Cliffs, NJ: Prentice Hall.

Levoy, G. (1988, July/August). Tears that speak. *Psychology Today,* 8–10.

Lincoln Journal Star. (1998a, May 5). Survey shows steroid use even among 10-year-olds, p. 4A.

———. (1998b, May 21). Wasted time, p. 1C.

———. (2006a, January 2). Finding adulthood on the run, p. 1A.

———. (2006b, July 4). You really can't buy happiness, p. 2A.

Liu, C. (2000, May). A theory of marital sexual life. *Journal of Marriage and the Family, 62*(2), 363–73.

Long, V. O., and Martinez, E. A. (1997). Masculinity, femininity, and Hispanic professional men's self-esteem and self-acceptance. *Journal of Psychology, 131*(5), 481–88.

Lorenz, F. O., Simons, R. L., Conger, R. D., Elder, G. H., Johnson, C., and Chao, W. (1997). Married and recently divorced mothers' stressful events and distress: Tracing change across time. *Journal of Marriage and the Family, 59*(1), 219–32.

*Lukas, C., and Seiden, H. M. (1997). *Silent grief: Living in the wake of suicide.* New York: Bantam Books.

Lynch, J. J. (2000). *A cry unheard: New insights into the medical consequences of loneliness.* Baltimore, MD: Bancroft Press.

Lyubomirsky, S., King, L., and Diener, E. (2005). The benefits of frequent positive affect: Does happiness lead to success? *Psychological Bulletin, 131*(6), 803–55.

Maccoby, E., and Jacklin, C. (1974). *The psychology of sex differences.* Stanford, CA: Stanford University Press.

MacMillan, H. L. (1999). Slapping and spanking in childhood and its association with lifetime prevalence of psychiatric disorders in general population sample. *The Journal of the American Medical Association, 282*(21), 1990.

*Malone, T. P., and Malone, P. T. (1987). *The art of intimacy.* New York: Prentice Hall.

Maltz, M. (1960). *Psychocybernetics.* New York: Pocket Books.

Mangum, A. (2000, July). Walk your way to great health! *Prevention, 52*(7), 122–32.

Marano, H. E. (2000). Divorced? *Psychology Today, 33*(2), 56–61.

Markert, J. (1999). Sexual harassment and the communication conundrum. *Gender Issues, 17*(3), 18–21.

Markus, H. R., and Kitayama, S. (1998). The cultural psychology of personality. *Journal of Cross-Cultural Psychology, 29*(1), 63–87.

Marsh, P. (1988). Making eye contact. In P. Marsh (Ed.), *Eye to eye: How people interact.* Topsfield, MA: Salem House.

Marston, P. J., Hecht, M. L., Manke, M. L., McDaniel, S., and Reeder, H. (1998). The subjective experience of intimacy, passion, and commitment in heterosexual loving relationships. *Personal Relationships, 5,* 15–30.

Martin, M. M., Anderson, C. M., and Mottet, T. P. (1999). Perceived understanding and self-disclosure in the stepparent–stepchild relationship. *Journal of Psychology, 133*(3), 281–90.

Maslow, A. (1968). *Toward a psychology of being.* New York: D. Van Nostrand.

May, R. (1953). *Man's search for himself.* New York: Dell.

———. (1969). *Love and will.* New York: Norton.

Mayer, J. D., Caruso, D. R., and Salovey, P. (1999). Emotional intelligence meets traditional standards for an intelligence. *Intelligence, 27*(4), 267+.

McCarthy, B. (1988). Friends and acquaintances. In P. Marsh (Ed.), *Eye to eye: How people interact* (pp. 169–73). Topsfield, MA: Salem House.

McCarthy, K. (2001, March/April). Getting healthy in bed. *Psychology Today, 34*(2), 16.

McCormack, A. S. (1997). Revisiting college student knowledge and attitudes about HIV/AIDS: 1987, 1991 and 1995. *College Student Journal, 31*(3), 356–63.

McKay, J. R., Alterman, A. I., Cacciola, J. S., Rutherford, M. J., O'Brien, C. P., and Koppenhaver, J. (1997). Group counseling versus individualized relapse prevention aftercare following intensive outpatient treatment for cocaine dependence: Initial results.

Journal of Consulting and Clinical Psychology, 65(5), 778–88.

*McKay, M., Davis, M., and Fanning, P. (1983). *Messages: The communication book.* Oakland, CA: New Harbinger.

*McKay, M., and Fanning, P. (2000). *Self-esteem.* Oakland, CA: New Harbinger.

*McKay, M., Fanning, P., and Paleg, K. (1994). *Couple skills: Making your relationship work.* Oakland, CA: New Harbinger.

Mead, G. H. (1934). *Mind, self, and society.* Chicago: University of Chicago Press.

Meeks, B. S., Hendrick, S. S., and Hendrick, C. (1988). Communication, love and relationship satisfaction. *Journal of Personal Relationships, 15,* 775–73.

Megargee, E. I. (1997). Internal inhibitions and controls. In R. Hogan, J. Johnson, and S. Briggs (Eds.), *Handbook of personality psychology* (pp. 251–611). San Diego: Academic Press.

Mehrabian, A. (1968, September). Communication without words. *Psychology Today,* 53–55.

———. (1981). *Silent messages.* Belmont, CA: Wadsworth.

Merton, R. K. (1948). The self-fulfilling prophecy. *Antioch Review, 8,* 193–210.

Meschike, L. L., Bartholomae, S., and Zentall, S. R. (2000). Adolescent sexuality and parent–adolescent processes: Promoting healthy teen choices. *Family Relations, 49*(2), 143–54.

Michaud, E. (2000, February). When worrying becomes deadly. *Prevention, 52*(2), 134–42.

Mikula, G., Freudenthaler, H. H., and Brennacher-Kroell, S. (1997). Division of labor in student households: Gender inequality, perceived justice, and satisfaction. *Basic and Applied Social Psychology, 19*(3), 275–89.

*Miller, E. E. (1978). *Feeling good: How to stay healthy.* Englewood Cliffs, NJ: Prentice Hall.

*Miller, S., Nunnally, E. W., and Wackman, D. B. (1979). *Talking together.* Littleton, CO: Interpersonal Communication Programs.

*Miller, S., Wackman, D. B., Nunnally, E. W., and Miller, P. A. (1988). *Connecting with self and others.* Littleton, CO: Interpersonal Communication Programs.

Minton, L. (1993, March 7). Gay sensitivity sessions: Readers speak out. *Parade,* p. 12.

Misra, R., and McKean, M. (2000). College students' academic stress and its relation to their anxiety, time management, and leisure satisfaction. *American Journal of Health Studies, 16*(1), 41–51.

*Mitchell, W. (with Lemley, B.) (1997). *It's not what happens to you, it's what you do about it: Taking responsibility for change.* Denver, CO: Phoenix Press.

Mocharnuk, R. S. (2001). Lung cancer screening and prevention: Quit smoking! Retrieved August 12, 2001 from http://oncology.medscape.com/Meds.

Montgomery, B. M., and Trower, P. (1988). Friends and acquaintances. In P. Marsh (Ed.), *Eye to eye: How people interact* (pp. 164–69).

Topsfield, MA: Salem House.

Moore, A. (1999). This time the news is good: TT helps case arthritis pain. *RN, 62*(1), 16.

Moore, K., Babyak, M. A., Wood, C. E., Napolitano, M. A., Khatri, P., Craighead, E., Herman, S., Krishnan, R., and Blumenthal, J. A. (1999). The association between physical activity and depression. *Journal of Aging and Physical Activity, 7*(1), 55–61.

Moore, R. M. (1999). Interracial dating as an indicator of integration. *Black issues in Higher Education, 15*(26), 120.

Morrison, N. C. (1995). Successful single-parent families. *Journal of Divorce and Remarriage, 22,* 205–19.

Motte, P. (2000, May). Medical news: Easing pain with an embrace. *Health,* 98.

*Moyers, B. (1993). *Healing and the mind.* New York: Doubleday.

Murray, H. A. (1938). *Explorations in personality.* New York: Oxford University Press.

*Myers, D. G. (1992) *Pursuit of happiness.* Dresden, TN: Avon.

*Myers, D. G., and Diener, E. (1995). Who is happy? *Psychological Science,* 10–19.

Myers, I. B. (1980). *Introduction to type.* Palo Alto, CA: Consulting Psychologists Press.

*Myers, I. B., and Myers, P. B. (1995). *Gifts differing.* Palo Alto, CA: Consulting Psychologists Press.

Nahom, D., Wells, E., Gillmore, M. R., Hoppe, M., Morrison, D. M., Archibald, M., Murowchick, E.,

WILSDON, A., and GRAHAM, L. (2001). Differences by gender and sexual experience in adolescent sexual behavior: Implications for education and HIV prevention. *Journal of School Health, 71*(4), 153–58.

NAJEM, G. R., BATUMAN, F., SMITH, A. M., and FEUERMAN, M. (1997). Patterns of smoking among inner-city teenagers: Smoking has a pediatric age of onset. *Journal of Adolescent Health, 20*(3), 226–31.

NAMEROW, P. B., KALMUSS, D., and CUSHMAN, L. F. (1997). The consequences of placing versus parenting among young unmarried women. *Marriage and Family Review, 25*(304), 175–97.

NAMER, K. M. (1998, July). Lose pounds for good. *Prevention,* 98–104.

NATIONAL CENTER FOR CHRONIC DISEASE PREVENTION AND HEALTH PROMOTION. (2006). Healthy Youth. Retrieved November 5, 2006 http://www.cdc.gov/ healthyyouth/skincancer/ guidelines/summary/htm.

NATIONAL CENTER FOR HEALTH STATISTICS. (2001). Life expectancy. Retrieved August 16, 2001 from EBSCOhost database.

NATIONAL COUNCIL ON THE AGING. (1998). Sex and aging. *Patient Care, 32*(20), 14.

NATIONAL DEPRESSIVE AND MANIC-DEPRESSIVE ASSOCIATION. (2001). Diagnosis, treatment and support. Retrieved July 28, 2001 from http://www.ndmda.org.

NATIONAL HIGHWAY TRAFFIC SAFETY ADMINISTRATION. (2003). Fatalities. Retrieved January 2, 2006 from www-nrd.nhtsa.dot.gov/departments/nrd-30/ncsa.

NATIONAL INSTITUTE OF DRUG ABUSE. (2006a). Retrieved March 13, 2006 from http://www.drugabuse.gov.

NATIONAL INSTITUTE OF DRUG ABUSE. (2006b). *Anabolic steroid abuse.* Retrieved November 5, 2006 from http://www.nida.nih.gov/ drugpages/steroids.html.

NATIONAL INSTITUTE OF MENTAL HEALTH (2001). The numbers count. Retrieved July 23, 2001 from http:// www.nimb.nih.gov.

———. (2001). Depression. Retrieved July 28, 2001 from http://www.nimh.nih.gov.

NATIONAL STRATEGY FOR SUICIDE PREVENTION. (2001). Retrieved May 22, 2001 from http://www.mentalhealth. org/suicideprevention.

*NELSEN, J. (1996). *Positive discipline.* New York: Ballantine.

*NEWMAN, M., and BERKOWITZ, B. (1974). *How to be your own best friend.* New York: Ballantine.

*NEWPORT, F. (2001, February 5). Morality, education, crime, dissatisfaction with government head list of most important problems facing country today. *Gallup Poll Analyses.* Retrieved August 13, 2001 from http://www.gallup.com/ poll/releases/pr010205.asp.

NEWPORT, F. (2001, June 4). American attitudes toward homosexuality continue to become more tolerant. *Gallup Poll Analyses.* Retrieved August 14, 2001 from http://www.gallup.com/ poll/releases/pr010604.asp.

NICHOLAS, D. R. (2000). Men, masculinity, and cancer: Risk-factor behaviors, early detection, and psychosocial adaptation. *Journal of American College Health, 49*(1), 27–33.

*NORRIS, P. A., and PORTER, G. (1987). *I choose life.* Walpole, NH: Stillpoint.

*NORWOOD, R. (1985). *Women who love too much.* Los Angeles: Tarcher.

OBISESAN, T. O., HIRSCH, R., KOSOKO, O., CARLSON, L., and PARROTT, M. (1998). Moderate wine consumption is associated with decreased odds of developing age-related macular degeneration in NHANES-1. *Journal of American Geriatric Society, 46*(1), 1–7.

*O'CONNOR, D. (1985). *How to make love to the same person for the rest of your life and still love it!* Toronto: Bantam.

O'KOON, J. (1997). Attachment to parents and peers in late adolescence and their relationship with self-image. *Adolescence, 32*(126), 471–82.

OLDS, R. S., and THOMBS, D. L. (2001). The relationship of adolescent perceptions of peer norms and parent involvement to cigarette and alcohol use. *Journal of School Health, 71*(6), 223–28.

OLSON, D. H., DEFRAIN, J., and OLSON, A. K. (1999). *Developing skills for life.* Minneapolis, MN: Life Innovations, Inc.

OMAHA WORLD HERALD. (2001, June 26). Divorced women surpass widows in number, poverty risk, p. 2.

ORNISH, D. (1998). *Love and survival: The scientific basis for the healing power of intimacy.* New York: HarperCollins.

OSOFSKY, J. D. (1995). The effects of exposure to violence

on young children. *American Psychologist, 50*(9), 782–88.

OTHMER, S., PHILLIPS, J., and ROOST, A. (2001). The promise of neurofeedback. *San Diego Psychologist, 10*(4), 1–5.

PACKARD, M. (1992). *An investigation of family relations courses taught in high schools in the United States.* Unpublished master's thesis, University of Nebraska, Lincoln.

PARK, S. Y., BELSKY, J., PUTNAM, S., and CRNIC, K. (1997). Infant emotionality, parenting, and 3-year inhibition: Exploring stability and lawful discontinuity in a male sample. *Developmental Psychology, 33*(2), 218–27.

PASLEY, K., and IHINGER-TALLMAN, M. (1997). Stepfamilies: Continuing challenges for the school. In T. W. Fairchild (Ed.), *Crisis intervention strategies for school-based helpers* (pp. 60–100). New York: Scribner.

PATIENT EDUCATION MANAGEMENT. (2001). Get patients to tune into their brain: Monitor physical signals to teach stress reduction, *8*(4), 43–44. Retrieved June 19, 2001 from EBSCOhost database.

PATTERSON, C. J. (2000). Family relationships of lesbians and gay men. *Journal of Marriage and the Family, 62*(4), 1052–69.

PATTERSON, C. J., and CHAN, R. W. (1997). Gay fathers. In M. E. Lamb (Ed.), *The role of the father in child development* (pp. 245–60). New York: Wiley.

PAUL, E. L., and BRIER, S. (2001). Friendsickness in the transition to college: Precollege predictors and college adjustment correlates. *Journal of Counseling and Development, 79*(1), 77–89.

*PEARSALL, P. (1988). *Super Joy.* New York: Doubleday.

*PECK, M. S. (1978). *The road less traveled.* New York: Simon & Schuster.

PEDEN, A. R., RAYENS, M. K., HALL, L. A., and BEEBE, L. H. (2001). Preventing depression in high-risk college women: A report of an 18-month follow-up. *Journal of American College Health, 49*(6), 299–306.

PEDERSEN, B. K., RHODE, T., and ZACHO, M. (1996). Immunity in athletes. *Journal of Sports Medicine and Physical Fitness, 36*(4), 236–45.

PEDIATRICS. (2001). Tobacco's toll: Implications for the pediatrician. *107*(4), 794–98. Retrieived September 15, 2001, from EBSCOhost database.

*PENNEBAKER, J. W. (1997). *Opening up: The healing power of expressing emotions.* New York: Guilford.

PENNEBAKER, J. W., MAYNE, T. J., and FRANCIS, M. E. (1997). Linguistic predictors of adaptive bereavement. *Journal of Personality and Social Psychology, 72*(4), 863–71.

PENNEBAKER, R. (1992, June). Go ahead, say it! *Parents,* 71–77.

PENNINX, B., GURAINIK, J. M., PAHOR, M., FERRUCCI, L., CERHAN, J. R., WALLACE, R. B., and HAVLIK, R. J. (1998). Chronically depressed mood and cancer risk in older persons. *Journal of the National Cancer Institute, 90*(24), 1888–93.

PEPLAU, L. A., COCHRAN, S. D., and MAYS, V. M. (1997). A national survey of the intimate relationships of African American lesbians and gay men: A look at commitment, satisfaction, sexual behavior, and HIV disease. In B. Greene (Ed.), *Ethnic and cultural diversity among lesbians and gay men* (pp. 11–38). Thousand Oaks, CA: Sage.

PEPLAU, L. A., and SPALDING, L. R. (2000). The close relationships of lesbians, gay men and bisexuals. In C. Hendrick and S. Hendrick (Eds.), *Close relationships: A sourcebook.* Thousand Oaks, CA: Sage.

PETH-PIERCE, R. (1998). *The NICHD study of early child care.* Washington, DC: National Institute of Child Health and Human Development.

PETRESS, K. (1999). Listening: A vital skill. *Journal of Instructional Psychology, 26*(4), 261–62.

PHELPS, S., and AUSTIN, N. (2000). *The assertive woman.* Atascadero, CA: California: Impact Publishers.

PHINNEY, J. S., FERGUSON, D. L., and TATE, J. D. (1997). Intergroup attitudes among ethnic minority adolescents: A causal model. *Child Development, 68*(5), 955–69.

PIAGET, J., and INHELDER, B. (1969). *The psychology of the child.* New York: Basic Books.

*PIPHER, M. (1994). *Reviving Ophelia: Saving the selves of adolescent girls.* New York: Putnam

*PITTMAN, F. (1998). *How taking responsibility can make you grow up.* New York: Golden Books.

PLUTCHIK, R. (1980). *Emotion: A psychoevolutionary synthesis.* New York: Harper & Row.

PODELL, R. M. (1992). *Contagious emotions: Staying well when your loved one is depressed*. New York: Pocket Books.

*PORAT, F. (1988). *Self-esteem: The key to success in work and love*. Saratoga, CA: R & E.

*POTTER, L. L. (1979). *When someone you love dies: A book to share feelings*. Self-published. Available from Tom Potter, 1800 Memorial Drive, Lincoln, NE 68502.

POULSON, R. L., EPPLER, M. A., SATTERWHITE, T. N., WUENSCH, K. L., and BASS, L. A. (1998). Alcohol consumption, strength of religious beliefs, and risky sexual behavior in college students. *Journal of American College Health*, 46(5), 227–32.

POWELL, B., and DOWNEY, D. B. (1997). Living in single-parent households: An investigation of the same-sex hypothesis. *American Sociological Review, 62*, 521–39.

*POWELL, J. (1969). *Why am I afraid to tell you who I am?* Niles, IL: Argus.

*———. (1976). *Fully human, fully alive*. Valencia, CA: Tabor.

POWERS, D. A., and ELLISON, C. G. (1995). Interracial contact and black racial attitudes: The contact hypothesis and selectivity bias. *Social Forces, 74*, 205–26.

PRAGER, K. J., and BUHR MESTER, D. (1998). Intimacy of social and personal relationships. *Journal of Social and Personal Relationships, 15*(4), 435–69.

PREBOTH, M. (2000). Clinical review of recent findings on the awareness, diagnosis and treatment of depression.

American Family Physician, 61(10), 3158–61.

PRENTICE-DUNN, S., JONES, J. L., and FLOYD, D. L. (1997). Persuasive appeals and the reduction of skin cancer risk: The roles of appearance concern, perceived benefits of a tan, and efficacy information. *Journal of Applied Social Psychology, 27*(12), 1041–47.

PROVINI, C., and EVERETT, J. R. (2000). Adults mourning suicide. *Death Studies, 24*(1), 1–19.

PSYCHOLOGY TODAY. (2000, November). Behind closed doors. 6–15.

*QUINN, P. O. (2001). *ADD and the college student: A guide for high school and college students with attention deficit disorder*. Washington, DC: Magination Press.

RADECKI, C. M., and JACCARD, J. (1996). Gender-role differences in decision-making orientations and decision-making skills. *Journal of Applied Social Psychology, 26*(1), 76–94.

RADKOWSKY, M., and SIEGEL, L. J. (1997). The gay adolescent: Stressors, adaptations, and psychosocial interventions. *Clinical Psychology Review, 17*(2), 191–216.

RALOFF, J. (2000, April 22). Boning up on calcium shouldn't be sporadic. *Science News, 260*–61.

RANGE, L. M., WALSTON, A. S., and POLLARD, P. M. (1992). Helpful and unhelpful comments after suicide, homicide, accident, or natural death. *Omega, 25*(1), 25–31.

RATHUS, S. A. (1999). *Psychology*. Fort Worth, TX: Harcourt Brace Jovanovich.

RAUSCHER, F. H., KRAUSS R. M.,

and CHEN, Y. (1996). Gesture, speech, and lexical access: The role of lexical movements in speech production. *Psychological Science, 7*(4), 226–31.

RAYMOND, J. (2001, February). The ex-files. *American Demographics, 60*–64.

*REAL, T. (1997). *I don't want to talk about it: Overcoming the secret legacy of male depression*. New York: Scribner.

RICHARDS, J. M., and GROSS, J. J. (2000). Emotion regulation and memory: The cognitive costs of keeping one's cool. *Journal of Personality and Social Psychology, 79*(3), 410–24.

RIOS, D. M. (1993, August 23). Now the blame falls squarely on men. *Lincoln Journal Star*, p. 6.

*ROGERS, C. (1961). *On becoming a person*. Boston: Houghton Mifflin.

*———. (1972). *On becoming partners: Marriage and its alternatives*. New York: Delacorte.

*———. (1978). The necessary and sufficient conditions of therapeutic personality change. In E. A. Southwell and M. Merbaum (Eds.), *Personality readings in theory and research*. Monterey, CA: Brooks/Cole.

*———. (1980). *A way of being*. Boston: Houghton Mifflin.

ROGERS, S. J., and WHITE, L. K. (1998). Satisfaction with parenting: The role of marital happiness, family structure, and parents' gender. *Journal of Marriage and the Family, 60*(2), 293–308.

ROKACH, A. (1990). Surviving and coping with loneliness. *Journal of Psychology, 124*, 39–54.

————. (2000). Perceived causes of loneliness in adulthood. *Journal of Social Behavior and Personality, 15*(1), 67–84.

ROSENBAUM, M. E. (1986). The repulsion hypothesis: On the nondevelopment of relationships. *Journal of Personality and Social Psychology, 51,* 1156–66.

*ROSENBERG, E. (1983). *Growing up feeling good.* New York: Beaufort Books.

ROSENBERG, M. (1979). *Conceiving the self.* New York: Basic Books.

ROSENTHAL, R., and JACOBSON, L. (1968). *Pygmalion in the classroom: Teacher expectations and student intellectual development.* New York: Holt, Rinehart & Winston.

ROSS, L. (1977). The intuitive psychologist and his shortcomings: Distortions in the attribution process. In L. Berkowitz (Ed.), *Advances in experimental social psychology,* 10. New York: Academic Press.

ROSS, S. E., NIEBLING, B. C., and HECKERT, T. M. (1999). Sources of stress among college students. *College Student Journal, 33*(2), 312–18.

ROTENBERG, K. J. (1997). Loneliness and the perception of the exchange of disclosures. *Journal of Social and Clinical Psychology, 16*(3), 259–76.

ROTHS, L., HARMIN, M., and SIMON, S. B. (1966). *Values and teaching.* Columbus, OH: Merill.

ROTTER, J. B. (1972). *Applications of a social learning theory of personality.* New York: Holt, Rinehart & Winston.

————. (1975). Some problems and misconceptions related to the construct of internal versus external control of reinforcement. *Journal of Consulting and Clinical Psychology, 43*(1), 56–57.

————. (1990). Internal versus external control of reinforcement. A case history of a variable. *American Psychologist, 45*(4), 489–93.

ROTTER, J. B., CHANCE, J. E., and PHARES, E. J. (1972). *Application of a social learning theory of personality.* New York: Holt, Rinehart & Winston.

ROUILLARD, L. (1993). *Goals and goal setting.* Menlo Park, CA: Crisp.

RUBIN, L. B. (1985). *Just friends: The role of friendship in our lives.* New York: Harper & Row.

————. (1975). *Compassion and self-hate: An alternative to despair.* New York: Ballantine.

————. (1983). *One to one: Understanding personal relationships.* New York: Pinnacle.

*RUBIN, T. I. (1988). *The angry book.* New York: Macmillan.

RUBIN, Z. (1970). Measurement of romantic love. *Journal of Personality and Social Psychology, 16,* 265–73.

————. (1973). *Liking and loving.* New York: Holt, Rinehart & Winston.

SAAD, L. (1999, September 3). American workers generally satisfied, but indicate their jobs leave much to be desired. *Gallup Poll Analyses.* Retrieved August 14, 2001 from http://www.gallup.com/poll/releases/pr990903.asp.

————. (2001, May 24). Majority considers sex before marriage morally okay. *Gallup Poll Analyses.* Retrieved August 16, 2001 from http://www.gallup.com/poll/releases/pr010524.asp.

SALMELA-ARO, K., and NURMI, J. E. (1996). Uncertainty and confidence in interpersonal projects. Consequences for social relationships and well-being. *Journal of Social and Personal Relationships, 13*(1), 109–22.

SALT, R. E. (1991). Affectionate touch between fathers and preadolescent sons. *Journal of Marriage and the Family, 53*(3), 545–54.

SALZBERG, S., and KABAT-ZINN, J. (1997). Mindfulness as medicine. In D. Goleman (Ed.), *Healing emotions* (pp. 107–44). Boston: Shambhala.

*SANDERS, C. M. (1992). *Surviving grief and learning to live again.* New York: Wiley.

SATCHER, D. (2001). Why we need an international agreement on tobacco control. *American Journal of Public Health, 91*(2), 191–93.

*SATIR, V. (1972). *Peoplemaking.* Palo Alto, CA: Science and Behavior Books.

*————. (1976). *Making contact.* Millbrae, CA: Celestial Arts.

*————. (1978). *Your many faces.* Millbrae, CA: Celestial Arts.

*————. (1983). *Conjoint family therapy.* Palo Alto, CA: Science and Behavior Books.

*————. (1988). *The new peoplemaking.* Mountain View, CA: Science and Behavior Books.

SAVIN-WILLIAMS, R. C. (2001). *Mom, dad, I'm gay: How families negotiate coming out.* Washington, DC: American Psychological Association.

SCHACHTER, S., and SINGER, J. E. (1962). Cognitive, social, and physiological determinants of emotional state. *Psychological Review, 69,* 379–99.

SCHEFLEN, A. E. (1972). *Body language and social order.* Englewood Cliffs, NJ: Prentice Hall.

*SCHMIDT, J. A. (1976). *Help Yourself: A guide to self-change,* Champaign, IL: Research Press.

SCHULZ, B. (1988, March/April). Finding time. The World pp. 2–3.

SCHULZ, R., BOOKWALA, J., KNAPP, J. E., SCHEIER, M., and WILLIAMSON, G. M. (1996). Pessimism, age, and cancer mortality. *Psychology and Aging, 11*(2), 304–09.

SCREENING FOR MENTAL HEALTH, INC. (2001). National depression screening day. Retrieved July 28, 2001 from http://www.nmisp.org/depression.htm.

SEGALL, R. (2001). Sleep on it. *Psychology Today, 34*(2), 18.

*SELIGMAN, M. E. P. (1995). *The optimistic child.* Boston: Houghton Mifflin.

*———. (1998). *Learned optimism.* New York: Pocket Books.

SELYE, H. (1974). *Stress without distress.* Philadelphia: Lippincott.

———. (1976). *The stress of life.* New York: McGraw-Hill.

SENIOR, K. (2001). Should stress carry a health warning? *Lancet, 357*(9250), 126.

SEVERE, S. (1997). *How to behave so your children will too!* New York: Viking.

SHAKOOR, A. T. (2000). Career success in the new millennium. *Black Collegian, 30*(2), 60.

SHAVER, P., SCHWARTZ, J., KIRSON, D., and O'CONNOR, C. (1987). Emotion Knowledge: Further exploration of a prototype approach. *Journal of Personality and Social Psychology, 52*(6), 1061–86.

SHENK, D. (1998). Data smog: Surviving the information glut. Retrieved, Abacus.

SHENK, D. (2004). Information overload. Retrieved March 2006 from www.challies.com/archives/0748.php.

SHERMIS, M. D., and LOMBARD, D. (1998). Effects of computer-based test administrations on test anxiety and performance. *Computers in Human Behavior, 14*(1), 111–23.

SHIKANY, J. M., and WHITE JR., G. L. (2000). Dietary guidelines for chronic disease prevention. *Southern Medical Journal, 93*(12), 1138–52.

SIMMONS, W. W. (2000, December 26). When it comes to having children, Americans still prefer boys. *Gallup Poll Analyses.* Retrieved August 16, 2001 from http://www.gallup.com/poll/release/pr001226.asp.

SIMON, S. B., HOWE, L. W., and KIRSCHENBAUM, H. (1991). *Values clarification: A handbook of practical strategies for teachers and students.* New York: Warner.

*SIMONTON, O. C., MATTHEWS-SIMONTON, S., and CREIGHTON, J. (1978). *Getting well again.* New York: Bantam.

*SIMONTON, S. M. (1984). *The healing family.* New York: Bantam.

SIMS, D. (1985). The grief process. *The Compassionate Friends Newsletter, 8*(2), 1, 6.

SINATRA, S. T. (1999). *Heartbreak and heart disease: A mind/body prescription for healing the heart.* New Canaan, CT: Keats Publishing, Inc.

SINGH, B. R. (1996). The genetic environmental influences on individual cognitive function or IQ. *Educational Studies, 22*(1), 41–56.

SKAALVIK, E. M. (1997). Self-enhancing and self-defeating ego orientation: Relations with task and avoidance orientation, achievement, self-perceptions, and anxiety. *Journal of Educational Psychology, 89*(1), 71–81.

SKINNER, B. F. (1953). *Science and human behavior.* New York: Macmillan.

———. (1987). *Upon further reflection.* Englewood Cliffs, NJ: Prentice Hall.

SMITH, M. K. (2000). Howard Gardner and multiple intelligenees. *The encyclopedia of informal education.* Retrieved November 5, 2006 from http://www.infed.org/thinkers/gardner.htm.

SMITH, D. M., and GATES, G. J. (2001, August 22). Gay and lesbian families in the United States: Same-sex unmarried partner households, 1–4. Retrieved September 1, 2001 from http://www.hrc.org.

*SMITH, S. (1993). *Succeeding against the odds.* Los Angeles: Tarcher.

SMITH-WARNER, S. A., SPIEGELMAN, D., YAUN, S. S., VANDENBRANDT, P. A., FOLSOM, A. R., GOLDBOHM, R. A., GRAHAM, S., HOLMBERG, L., HOWE, G. R., MARSHALL, J. R., MILLER, A. B., POTTER, J. D., SPEIZER, F. E., WILLETT, W. C., WOLK, A., and HUNTER, D. J. (1998). Alcohol and breast cancer in women:

A pooled analysis of cohort studies. *Journal of the American Medical Association, 279*(7), 535–40.

*SMOLIN, A., and GUINAN, J. (1993). *Healing after the suicide of a loved one.* New York: Simon & Schuster.

SMYTH, J. M. (1998). Written emotional expressions: Effect sizes, outcome types, and moderation variables. *Journal of Consulting and Clinical Psychology, 66*(1), 174–84.

*SOLOMON, R. C. (1988). *Love: Reinventing romance for our times.* New York: Simon & Schuster.

SOLOMON, S. M. (2000). Childhood loneliness: Implications and intervention considerations for family therapists. *Family Journal, 8*(2), 161–64.

*SPEZZANO, C. (1992). *What to do between birth and death: The art of growing up.* New York: Morrow.

SPIEGEL, D. (1993). *Living beyond limits: New hope and help for facing life-threatening illness.* New York: Times Books.

———. (1996). Cancer and depression. *British Journal of Psychiatry, 168*(30), 109–16.

———. (1999). Healing words: Emotional expression and disease outcome. *The Journal of the American Medical Association, 281*(14), 1328.

STACK, S., and ESHLEMAN, J. R. (1998). Marital status and happiness: A 17-nation study. *Journal of Marriage and the Family, 60*(2), 527–36.

STAKE, J. E. (2000). When situations call for instrumentality and expressiveness: Resource appraisal, coping strategy choice, and adjustment. *Sex Roles: A Journal of Research.*

STANARD, R. P. (2000). Assessment and treatment of adolescent depression and suicidality. *Journal of Mental Health Counseling, 22*(3), 204–17.

STANLEY, S. M., MARKMAN, H. J., PRADO, L. M., OLMOS-GALLO, P. A., TONELLI, L., ST. PETERS, M., LEBER, B. D., BOBULINSKI, M., CORDOVA, A., and WHITTON, S. W. (2001, January). Community-based premarital prevention: Clergy and lay leaders on the front lines. *Family Relations, 50*(1), 67–76.

*STEARNS, A. K. (1984). *Living through personal crisis.* Chicago: Thomas More Press.

*STEINBERG, L., and LEVINE, A. (1997). *You and your adolescent.* New York: HarperCollins.

*STEINEM, G. (1992). *Revolution from within: A book of self-esteem.* Boston: Little Brown.

STEINER, C. (1974). *Scripts people live.* New York: Bantam.

STEPFAMILY ASSOCIATION OF AMERICA. (2001). Facts & FAQ—Stepfamily. Retrieved September 9, 2001 from http://www.saafamlies.org.

STEPHEN, A. (1999, April 2). Bigger and better here: Road rage. *New Statesman, 129*(4430), 1.

STERNBERG, R. J. (1986). A triangular theory of love. *Psychological Review, 93,* 119–35.

———. (1987). *The triangle of love: Intimacy, passion, commitment.* New York: Basic Books.

———. (1998). *Love is: A new theory of relationships.* New York: Oxford University Press.

*STERNBERG, R., and WHITNEY, C. (1991). *Love the way you want it.* New York: Bantam.

STEVENS, D., KIGER, G., and RILEY, P. J. (2001). Working hard and hardly working: Domestic labor and marital satisfaction among dual-earner couples. *Journal of Marriage and the Family, 63*(2), 514–26.

STEWART, S. D. (1999, November). Nonresident mothers' and fathers' social contact with children. *Journal of Marriage and the Family, 61*(4), 894–907.

STODGHILL, R. (1998, June 15). Where'd you learn that? *Time,* 52–59.

STONE, A., SMYTH, J. M., KAELL, A., and HUREWITZ, A. (2000). Structured writing about stressful events: Exploring potential psychological mediators of positive health effects. *Health Psychology, 19*(6), 619–24.

STONEY, C. M., and ENGEBRETSON, T. O. (2000). Plasma homocysteine concentrations are positively associated with hostility and anger. *Life Sciences, 66*(23), 2267–75.

STOWERS, D. A., and DURM, M. W. (1996). Does self-concept depend on body image? A gender analysis. *Psychological Reports, 78*(2), 643–46.

STRAUS, M. A., and YODANIS, C. L. (1996). Corporal punishment in adolescence and physical assaults on spouses in later life: What accounts for the link? *Journal of Marriage and the Family, 58*(4), 825–41.

STRONG, B., DEVAULT, C., and SAYAD, B. W. (1998). *The marriage and family experience:*

Intimate relationships in a changing society. Belmont, CA: Wadsworth.

STUART, R., and JACOBSON, B. (1985). *Second marriage.* New York: Norton.

STURM, W. (2000, February). Does obesity contribute as much to morbidity as poverty or smoking? *Healthcare for Communities.* Retrieved June 13, 2001 from http://www.hsrcenter.ucia.edu/hcc/viewallhccp.html.

SUEDFELD, R., and PENNEBAKER, J. W. (1997). Health outcomes and cognitive aspects of recalled negative life events. *Psychosomatic Medicine, 59*(2), 172–77.

SUITOR, J. J., and CARTER, R. S. (1999). Jocks, nerds, babes and thugs: A research note on regional differences in adolescent gender norms. *Gender Issues, 17*(3), 87–101.

SULLIVAN, M. (1996). Rozzie and Harriet? Gender and family patterns of lesbian coparents. *Gender and Society, 10*(6), 747–67.

SULLIVAN, O. (1997). The division of housework among "remarried" couples. *Journal of Family Issues, 18,* 205–23.

SULLUM, J., and CLARK, M. M. (2000). Predictors of exercise relapse in a college population. *Journal of American College Health, 48*(4), 175–81.

SUN, Y. (2001). Family environment and adolescents' well-being before and after parents' marital disruption: A longitudinal analysis. *Journal of Marriage and the Family, 63*(3), 697–713.

TANNEN, D. (1990). *You just don't understand: Women and men in conversation.* New York: Ballantine.

———. (2001). *I only say this because I love you: How the way we talk can make or break family relationships throughout our lives.* New York: Random House.

TAYLOR, E., and OLSWANG, S. G. (1997). Crossing the color line: African Americans and predominantly white universities. *College Student Journal, 31*(1), 11–18.

TERRY, S. (2000, April 10). The unexpected consequences of living together. *Christian Science Monitor, 1.*

THARINGER, D., and WELLS, G. (2000). An attachment perspective on the developmental challenges of gay and lesbian adolescents: The need for continuity of caregiving from family and schools. *School Psychology Review, 29*(2), 158–72.

THAYER, S. (1988, March). Close encounters. *Psychology Today,* 30–36.

THAYER, E. S., and ZIMMERMAN, J. (2001). *The co-parenting survival guide.* Oakland, CA: New Harbinger Publications.

THOMAS, B. S. (1997). Direct and indirect effects of selected risk factors in producing adverse consequences of drug use. *Substance Use & Misuse, 32*(4), 377–98.

THORTON, J. (2000, July). Cheat and run. *USA Weekend,* 6–7.

THUN, M. J., PETO, R., LOPEZ, A. D., MONACO, J. H., HENLEY, S. J., HEATH, C. W., and DOLI, R. (1997). Alcohol consumption and mortality among middle-aged and elderly U.S. adults. *New England Journal of Medicine, 337* (24), 1705–14.

TICE, D. M., and BAUMEISTER, R. F. (1997). Longitudinal study of procrastination, performance, stress, and health: The costs and benefits of dawdling. *Psychological Science, 8*(6), 454–58.

*TIEGER, P. D., and BARRON-TIEGER, B. (1995). *Do what you are: Discover the perfect career for you through the secrets of personality type.* Boston: Little, Brown.

*———. (1997). *Nurture by nature: Understand your child's personality type—and become a better parent.* Boston: Little, Brown.

TIGGEMANN, M. (2001). The impact of adolescent girls' life concerns and leisure activities on body dissatisfaction, disordered eating, and self-esteem. *Journal of Genetic Psychology, 162*(2), 133–42.

TIME. (1982, January 15). We're going down, Larry, 21.

*TRICKETT, S. (1997). *Anxiety and depression: A natural approach.* Berkeley, CA: Ulysses Press.

TROCKEL, M. T., BARNES, M. D., and EGGET, D. L. (2000). Health-related variables and academic performance among first-year college students: Implications for sleep and other behaviors. *Journal of American College Health, 49*(3), 125–31.

TUBESING, D. A. (1981). *Kicking your stress habits: A do-it-yourself guide for coping with stress.* New York: New American Library.

UMBERSON, D., ANDERSON, K., GLICK, J., and SHAPIRO, A. (1998). Domestic violence, personal control, and gender. *Journal of Marriage and the Family, 60*(2), 442–52.

UNIVERSITY OF COLORADO. (2005), Glossary, Social Science Department.

U.S. Census Bureau. (2000). Working, single and teen moms. Retrieved May 7, 2001 from http://www.census.gov.

———. (2000, March). Current population survey. Retrieved July 8, 2001 from http://www.census.gov.

U.S. Department of Agriculture. (2001). Expenditures on children by families. Retrieved September 4, 2001 from http://www.usda.gov/cnpp/Crc/Crc2000.pdf.

U.S. Department of Health and Human Services. (2001). Retrieved March 13, 2005 from http://www.hhs.gov/safety/index.shtml.

*Vail, E. (1982). *A personal guide to living with loss.* New York: Wiley.

Vandervoort, D. (2000). Social isolation and gender. *Current Psychology, 19*(3), 229–336.

Vella, M. L., Persic, S., and Lester, D. (1996). Does self-esteem predict suicidality after controls for depression? *Psychological Reports, 79*(3, Pt. 2), 1178.

Veniegas, R. C., and Peplau, L. A. (1997). Power and the quality of same-sex friendships. *Psychology of Women Quarterly, 21*(2), 279–97.

Verloop, J., Rookus, M. A., VanderKooy, K., and VanLeeuwen, F. E. (2000). Physical activity and breast cancer risk in women aged 20–54 years. *Journal of the National Cancer Institute, 92*(2), 128–36.

Vernarbc, E., and Phillips, K. (2001). How to cope with job stress. *RN, 64*(3), 44–49.

Verschueren, K., Marcoen, A., and Schoefs, V. (1996). The internal working model of the self, attachment, and competence in five-year-olds. *Child Development, 67* (5), 2493–511.

*Vinton, E. C. (1998). *How to set limits: Defining appropriate boundaries of behavior for your children—from infants to teens.* Lincolnwood, IL: Contemporary Books.

Viorst, J. (1986). *Necessary losses.* New York: Ballantine.

*Visher, E., and Visher, J. (1979). *Stepfamilies: Myths and realities.* Secaucus, NJ: Citadel.

———. (1982). *How to win as a stepfamily.* Chicago: Contemporary Books.

*———. (1988). *Old loyalties, new ties.* New York: Brunner Mazel.

*Vogt, W. P. (1997). *Tolerance and education: Learning to live with diversity and differences.* Thousand Oaks, CA: Sage.

*Von Oech, R. (1983). *A whack on the side of the head: How to unleash your mind for innovation.* New York: Warner.

Wade, C., and Tavris, C. (2002). *Invitation to psychology.* Upper Saddle River, NJ: Prentice Hall.

———. (2005). *Invitation to psychology.* Upper Saddle River, NJ: Prentice Hall.

Wade, T. J. (1996). The relationships between skin color and self-perceived global, physical, and sexual attractiveness, and self-esteem for African Americans. *Journal of Black Psychology, 22*(3), 358–73.

Waite, L. J. (2000). The negative effects of cohabitation. *The Responsive Community, 10*(1). Retrieved from http://www.gwu.edu/?ccps/rcq.

Walker, V., and Brokaw, L. (1998). *Becoming aware.* Dubuque, IA: Kendall/Hunt.

Wallerstein, J. S., and Blakeslee, S. (1989). *Second chances: Men, women and children a decade after divorce.* New York: Ticknor & Fields.

Ward, C. A. (2000, October). Models and measurements of psychological androgyny: A cross-cultural extension of theory and research. *Sex Roles: A Journal of Research,* 529.

*Wegscheider-Cruse, S. (1988). *Coupleship: How to have a relationship.* Deerfield Beach, FL: Health Communications.

Weidner, G. (2000, May). Why do men get more heart disease than women?: An international perspective. *Journal of American College Health, 48*(6), 291–94.

*Weil, A. (1995a). *Health and healing.* Boston: Houghton Mifflin.

———. (1995b). *Spontaneous healing.* New York: Fawcett Columbine.

*Weiner-Davis, M. (1992). *Divorce busting: A revolutionary and rapid program for staying together.* New York: Simon & Schuster.

Wells, A. J. (1998). Heart disease from passive smoking in the workplace. *Journal of American College of Cardiology, 31*(1), 1–9.

Wheeler, P. (2001). The Myers-Briggs Type Indicator and applications to accounting education research. *Issues in Accounting Education, 16*(1), 125–50.

White, H. R. (1997). Alcohol, illicit drugs, and violence. In D. M. Stoff and J. Breiling (Eds), *Handbook of antisocial behavior* (pp. 511–23). New York: Wiley.

WHITE, J. W., and BONDURANT, B. (1996). Gendered violence in intimate relationships. In J. Wood (Ed.), *Gendered relationships* (pp. 197–210). Mountain View, CA: Mayfield.

WHITE, L., and GILBRETH, J. G. (2001). When children have two fathers: Effects of relationships with stepfathers and noncustodial fathers on adolescent outcomes. *Journal of Marriage and Family, 63*(1), 155–67.

WHITEHEAD, B. D., and POPENOE, D. (2001, June 27). Singles sock soul mates for marriage. *Gallup Poll Analyses.* Retrieved August 23, 2001 from http://www.gallup.com/poll/releases/pr010627basp.

*WHITFIELD, C. L. (1987). *Healing the child within.* Deerfield Beach, FL: Health Communications.

*WHITLOCK, K. (1989). *Bridges of respect: Creating support for lesbian and gay youth.* Philadelphia: American Friends Service Committee.

Why am I crying? (2001, October). *British Medical Journal, 323,* 1010.

WILLIAMS, J. M., and HARRIS, D. V. (1998). Relaxation and energizing techniques for regulation of arousal. In J. M. Williams (Ed.), *Applied sport psychology: Personal growth to peak performance* (pp. 219–36). Mountain View, CA: Mayfield.

WILLIAMS, R. L., and LONG, J. D. (1983). *Toward a self-managed life style.* Boston: Houghton Mifflin.

*WILLIAMS, W. (1988). *Rekindling desire: Bringing your sexual relationship back to life.* Oakland, CA: New Harbinger.

WILLIAMSON, A. M., and FEYER, A. M. (2001). Moderate sleep deprivation produces impairments in cognitive and motor performance equivalent to legally prescribed levels of alcohol intoxication. *Professional Safety, 46*(1), 17.

WINGERT, P. (2000, June 12). Young and overweight. *Newsweek,* 52.

———. (2001, May 21). Parents today make more time for quality time. *Newsweek,* 53.

WINGERT, P., and KANTROWITZ, B. (2000, March 20). Gay today: The family. *Newsweek,* 50–53.

WITT, S. D. (1997). Parental influence on children's socialization to gender roles. *Adolescence, 32*(126), 253–59.

WOLVIN, A., and COAKLEY, C. G. (1988). *Listening.* Dubuque, IA: Wm. C. Brown.

WOMEN IN BUSINESS. (2000, July–August). Money wise: Saving for retirement vital for women, 42. Retrieved August 7, 2000 from EBSCOhost database.

WOO, T. O., and MIX, P. (1997). Self-enhancing reactions to performance feedback in an academic setting. *Journal of Social Behavior and Personality, 12*(2), 481–500.

WOOD, J. T. (2001). *Gendered lives: Communication, gender, and culture.* Belmont, CA: Wadsworth.

*WOODWARD, J. C. (1988). *The solitude of loneliness.* Lexington, MA: Heath.

WOOLLAMS, S., and Brown, M. (1979). *TA: The total handbook of transactional analysis.* Englewood Cliffs, NJ: Prentice Hall.

WORCHEL, S., and SHEBILSKE, W. (1989). *Psychology: Principles and application.* Englewood Cliffs, NJ: Prentice Hall.

WORLD HEALTH ORGANIZATION. (1998). Passive smoking does cause lung cancer, do not let them fool you. Retrieved from http://www.who.ch.

WORTMAN, C. B., BATTLE, E. S., and LEMKAU, J. P. (1997). Coming to terms with the sudden, traumatic death of a spouse or child. In R. C. Davis, A. J. Lurigio, and W. G. Skogan (Eds.), *Victims of crime* (pp. 108–33). Thousand Oaks, CA: Sage.

*WUH, H. C. K., and FOX, M. (2001). *Sexual fitness.* New York: G. P. Putnam's Sons.

XIE, X., and LIN, S. (1997). Gender differences in perceptions of family roles by Chinese university students. *Perceptual and Motor Skills, 84*(1), 127–30.

YEUNG, W. J., SANDERG, J. F., DAVIS-KEAN, P. E., and HOFFERTH, S. L. (2001, February). Children's time with fathers in intact families. *Journal of Marriage and the Family, 63,* 136–54.

YIP, P. (2001, September 15). Divorce will also bring financial repercussions. *Lincoln Journal Star,* p. 6A.

YOUTH RISK BEHAVIOR SURVEILLANCE—UNITED STATES. (2003). Retrieved August 20, 2001 from http://www.cdc.gov.

*ZIMBARDO, P. G. (1977). *Shyness: What it is, what to do about it.* New York: Jove/HBJ.

*An asterisk indicates recommended reading.

Index

Note: Locators in italics indicate figures and tables.

439